Process Think: Winning Perspectives for Business Change in the Information Age

Varun Grover
University of South Carolina, USA

William J. Kettinger
University of South Carolina, USA

IDEA GROUP PUBLISHING
Hershey USA • London UK

Senior Editor:	Mehdi Khosrowpour
Managing Editor:	Jan Travers
Copy Editor:	John Syphrit
Printed at:	BookCrafters

Published in the United States of America by
Idea Group Publishing
1331 E. Chocolate Avenue
Hershey PA 17033-1117
Tel: 717-533-8845
Fax: 717-533-8661
E-mail: jtravers@idea-group.com
Website: http://www.idea-group.com

and in the United Kingdom by
Idea Group Publishing
3 Henrietta Street
Covent Garden
London WC2E 8LU
Tel: 171-240 0856
Fax: 171-379 0609

Library of Congress Cataloging-in-Publication Data

Grover, Varun, 1950-
    Process think: winning perspectives for business change in the
    information age/Varun Grover, William J. Kettinger.
        p. cm.
    Includes index.
    ISBN 1-87828-968-3 (cloth)
        1. Organizational change--Management. 2. Information technol-
ogy--Management. I. Title. II. Kettinger, William J.

HD58.8 .G773 1999
658.4' 06 21--dc21   99-044627

British Cataloguing in Publication Data
A Cataloguing in Publication record for this book is available from the
British Library.

Process Think: Winning Perspectives for Business Change in the Information Age

Table of Contents

INTRODUCTION i

PART I: CHANGE STRATEGIES THAT WORK 1

Chapter 1: Conducting Business Process Change: 2
Recommendations from Studies of 25 Leading Approaches
      William J. Kettinger and James T. C. Teng
      University of South Carolina, USA

Chapter 2: Strategies for Business Process Reengineering: 23
Evidence from the Field
      Michael J. Earl, Jeffrey L. Sampler and James E. Short
      London Business School, UK

Chapter 3: Tactics for Managing Radical Change 47
      Donna B. Stoddard, Harvard Business School, USA
      Sirkka L. Jarvenpaa, University of Texas at Austin, USA

Chapter 4: Initiating and Implementing Business Process Change: 73
Lessons from Ten Years of Inquiry
      James T.C. Teng, Varun Grover, Kirk D. Fiedler
      University of South Carolina, USA
      Seung Jeong, Kook Min University, Korea

Chapter 5: Business Process Change and Organizational Performance 115
      Subo Guha, NCR Corporation, USA
      Varun Grover, William J. Kettinger and
      James T.C. Teng, University of South Carolina, USA

PART II: PROCESS MANAGEMENT NUTS & BOLTS 148

Chapter 6: Methods for Business Process Reengineering 149
      Richard J. Mayer, Texas A&M University, USA
      Perakath C. Benjamin, Paula S. deWitte, Bruce E. Caraway
      and Michael K. Painter, Knowledge Based Systems Inc., USA

Chapter 7: Closing the Business Process Reengineering Gap: 190
Using the REAL Framework to Identify, Define, and Understand
Business Processes
      'Jon Jasperson, University of Oklahoma, USA
      Eric L. Denna and Lee Tom Perry, Brigham Young Univ. USA

Chapter 8: Basing an IS Strategy on the Organization's 209
Process Architecture

        Martyn Ould
        Venice Consulting Ltd., UK

PART III: THE MULTIDIMENSIONAL EVOLUTION OF 227
PROCESS MANAGEMENT

Business Change and Information Management
Chapter 9: Managing Information about Processes 228
        Thomas H. Davenport, University of Texas, Austin USA
        Michael C. Beers, Ernst & Young Center for Business
                Innovation, USA

Business Change and Supply Chain Management
Chapter 10: The New Waves of Business Process Redesign and 250
IT in Demand/Supply Chain Management: Hard Choices for
Senior Managers
        Donald A. Marchand
        International Institute for Management Development, Switzerland

Business Change and Management of Innovation
Chapter 11: Enterprise Process Innovation: Strategies and Issues 272
        Arun Rai, Georgia State University, USA
        Jesus A. Ponce de Leon, Southern Illinois Univ., Carbondale, USA
        Arlyn J. Melcher, Southern Illinois University, Carbondale, USA

Business Change and Management Control
Chapter 12: Reengineering Effectiveness and the Redesign of 292
Organizational Control: A Case Study of the Inland Revenue
Authority of Singapore
        Siew Kien Sia, Nanyang Technical University, Singapore
        Boon Siong Neo, Nanyang Technical University, Singapore

Business Change and Partnership Management
Chapter 13: The Impact of IOS-Enabled Business Process Change 315
on Business Outcomes: Transformation of the Value Chain of
Japan Airlines
        Akemi Chatfield, Australian Graduate School of Management
        Niels Bjorn-Andersen, Copenhagen Business School, Denmark

PART IV: A WINDOW INTO THE 21ST CENTURY 341

Chapter 14: IT: The Next 110010_2 Years 342
        Varun Grover, University of South Carolina, USA
        Albert H. Segars, University of No. Carolina, Chapel Hill, USA

Chapter 15: Information Futures: Producer and Consumer Views...........357
      James E. Short
      London Business School, UK

Chapter 16: Service: The Future 366
      Richard T. Watson, University of Georgia, USA
      Leyland F. Pitt, University of Wales, Cardiff, UK
      Pierre R. Berthon, University of Wales, Cardiff, UK

Chapter 17: The Futures of IT Management.................................378
      M. Lynne Markus
      Claremont Graduate University, USA

INDEX 396

INTRODUCTION

When we put together our first book on Business Process Change back in the early 1990s, it was during a time of tumultuous organizational uncertainty. The pendulum of change was being pulled to the extreme right —Process over people was the call of the day.

Forces converged to make reengineering happen:
* the recessionary climate triggered the need to get quick solutions - often to cut costs;
* the IT productivity paradox placed pressure on executives to leverage their massive investments in information technology;
* the total quality movement, while emphasizing the importance of business processes, was losing momentum as executives looked for more radical means to achieve performance gains;
* prominent consultants gave legitimacy to it by writing popular books on the topic; and,
* the imminent bandwagon effect occurred!

These forces engulfed the corporate world in a mentality of "breakdown" and "reconstruct." Radical reengineering demanded that nothing be held sacred in the push toward process efficiencies and performance payoffs. Many dramatic success stories appeared repeatedly in the popular press... "Ford cuts accounts payable headcount by 75%"; "Mutual Benefit Life improves insurance underwriting efficiency by 40%"; "Xerox redesigns its order fulfillment process and improves service levels by 97% and cycle times by 70%, savings $500 million." People hyped this phenomenon under the rubric of business process redesign, business process reengineering and business process innovation. Consultants repackaged old methodologies, created glossy brochures and charged thousands for their claimed proprietary solutions. Surveys of senior executives placed reengineering as the top management initiative being undertaken by companies to achieve strategic goals. Academics, both cynics and proponents (ourselves included), wrote scholarly prose on why they had seen this all before, or why they thought such a radical change was new and necessary!

After some pause in the extreme, the pendulum began to swing in the opposite direction — People over process became the new mantra. Talk of reengineering failures began to pervade the press. The headlines screamed about the "human cost of reengineering." With recessionary pressures alleviated, the need to sacrifice people in the painful course of layoffs did not seem as urgent. Cynics questioned - is it necessary to be so radical? Can we ignore organizational culture in imposing change? Are we losing vital organizational learning when we eliminate middle managers? Can we accomplish unidimensional change through only information technology, without considering jobs, roles, rewards, skills, and structures? Are cost objectives that important? Isn't there a better way to accomplish process change?

Having traversed through a decade that first glorified reengineering and then assailed it as a failure, we are now entering a more contemplative phase where we recognize that neither extreme view is correct.

Perhaps only some of the early 1990s reengineering concepts will be sustained in the next millenium. For example, such reengineering requirements as "radical change", "IT-centric solutions", "top-down initiation", and "breakthrough performance" are giving way to the reality that there is more than one way to conduct business change. Incremental and continuous approaches that are more humanistic, employ bottom-up involvement, and that are focused within functions have proven successful in some companies. Even Hammer admits that he erred in his assertion that reengineering must be radical. While, the "automate or obliterate" theme incited tremendous initial enthusiasm, Hammer now asserts that "radicalness" is not as vital to successful process change as is solid "process-based" analysis.

It is our belief, that the greatest contribution of the past decade's experience with reengineering has been to bring business process thinking to the forefront of management practice. "Process Think" is a managerial orientation to act proactively in identification of process opportunities, a capability to apply process concepts in problem solving, and a demonstrated willingness to transfer process thinking to fellow employees, customers and partners. Process thinking managers have the capability to intuitively see the implications of their actions across the company and project themselves into the situations of their customers. Based on a ten-year study of process based improvement at the Bose Corporation involving one of the editors of this book, process thinking occurs when pervasive enterprise-wide process awareness perpetuates internal improvement efforts and, eventually, influences improvements in external value-chain relationships with customers and suppliers. Today companies are less likely to actively promote radical reengineering as the answer to their performance woes. Instead, success of business process change is dependent on how well process thinking is accepted, internalized and institutionalized.

Institutionalization of process thinking is manifested in a "process management" program which involves formalizing the planning, structuring, and evaluation of business processes. Firms that engage in process management apply a multitude of methods to gather information, redesign (perhaps radically, followed by incremental improvements) and assess their processes. This portfolio of business change could include some higher risk/reward projects and some lower risk/reward ones. One thing is certain, reengineering is fundamentally a "change" initiative and, as such, requires an inter-disciplinary approach that transcends functional boundaries and specialties. Coordination across the enterprise is necessary, while parochial perspectives will only encourage organizational resistance. Fostering process thinking and properly employing proven change management techniques play a key role in the optimization of processes that satisfy organizational and, in many cases, inter-organizational needs.

Ironically (unlike the early 1990s), it has been the evolution to wide spread intuitive process thinking that now allows companies to more effectively make use of the rapidly advancing information technologies. Gone are the days when IT alone was viewed as a silver bullet capable of immediately correcting ingrained process inadequacies. Today's process thinking managers know to approach a business problem from a process perspective first before rushing to the latest and greatest technology. In practice, process thinkers are constantly scanning their environment, examining process activities, attempting to make sense of the fundamental business models at work, factoring in competitive issues, and, in their mind, designing business process solutions that leverage the capabilities of the latest technology. Where once IT was segmented in the minds of general managers as a function discreet from their own problem solving domain, they are now growing comfortable fashioning process improvements that make use of the latest IT advances. In this way, business process change has proven to be a very important and sustainable management concept that facilitates a manager's understanding of how to appropriately position IT applications within business situations.

Pervasive process thinking will prove to be a critical development in management practice in the 21st century. This is particularly important because we have reached a point in the information age where workers must be capable of flexibly exploiting IT within their unique work context on a continual basis to meet changing needs. Managers recognize that we have embarked on an information revolution, the outcome of which is far from clear. The Internet and electronic commerce is giving them new ways to think about processes as they exist within virtual organizations, across supply chains, and marketing practices. As these technical trends continue to accelerate, we can only anticipate that companies and industries will be forced to face more dramatic changes as a consequence of the merciless pace and immense possibilities availed in more powerful networked technologies.

So as we enter the new millenium, business process change is at an important crossroad. Gone is the unbridled enthusiasm for easy process reengineering projects with huge pay-offs. This has been replaced with a more contingent view of process change. Business process change today must be more personal, dynamic and seamlessly supported by new IT. The growing ubiquity of process thinking is helping to see that this condition will be satisfied. Interestingly, the pervasiveness of new and far more sophisticated IT will test a company's ability to quickly modify business models, and corresponding processes, and in doing so, place renewed importance on process thinking and successful business process change methods and techniques.

So now is the time to contemplate, reflect and renew. What have we learned from these pendulum swings? What aspects of "Business Process Change" will be sustainable in the next century? How has "Process Think" better enabled flexible and dynamic rethinking of process based solutions? What lessons from the past assure success in the information age? Beginning to address these questions is aim of this book. Ultimately, we are all faced with the truth that "Business Change" is one of the only certainties we have about what lies ahead in the in the 21st century. Hopefully, by better understanding how to build, maintain and evaluate business processes we prepare ourselves, in no small way, for facing our future challenges.

The chapters of this book reflect a diversity of perspectives. Some derive these perspectives through examination of the past and what seems to work. Others provide tools to cope with change in the future, including a few clairvoyant attempts to use foresight and wit to "predict" future trends.

We are indeed fortunate enough to have been involved in much of this work, either directly through our own research or through editorships of special sections of highly regarded journals. Collectively we believe this compilation of work reflects a rich repertoire of key elements of Process Think in the Information Age.

Figure 1

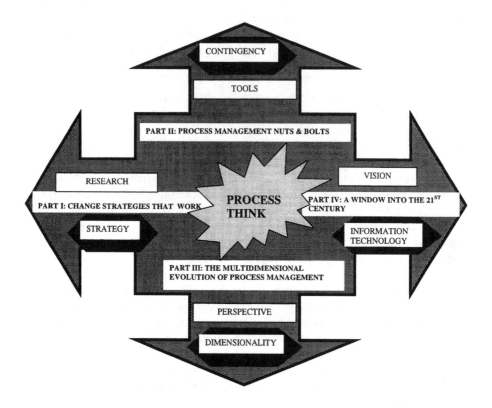

Five themes are reflected in the 17 chapters of the book:
* Change management strategies
* The methods for change
* The multidimensionality of change
* The contingent nature of change
* The information age and the future

As Figure 1 suggests, the chapters are organized in four sections (see Figure 1) that offer important insights concerning Business Process Change. Part I provides empirical research that draws from numerous companies that have engaged in business process change. The five chapters present these results and derive key strategies and lessons for companies embarking on process change in the future. Part II delves into the nuts and bolts of process change by summarizing tools and methods for analyzing processes in a manner consistent with organizational orientation and strategy. Part III explores process change from a number of diverse perspectives: information management, supply chain management, management of innovation, management control, and partnership management. This section emphasizes the multidimensional nature of process change as well as the contingencies reflected in the different ways it can be used in different contexts. Finally, Part IV brings the information age and information context to the forefront, by speculating in a lighter, yet intelligent, vein on the newer environment for business process change.

In preparing this work we are particularly appreciative to the Journal of Management Information Systems and The DATABASE for Advances in Information Systems (The publication of the ACM Special Interest Group on Management Information Systems - SIGMIS), for permitting us to reprint selective copies of articles that appeared in special sections we edited in each journal. In particular, we would like to thank Mr. Peter Covey, Executive Editor of M. E. Sharpe Publishing Inc. for granting us permission to reprint articles that appeared in two different issues of JMIS. We would also like to thank Dr. Vladimir Zwass, Editor-in-Chief of JMIS, for providing us with the opportunity to produce two well received special issues on this topic. In addition, we would like to thank Dr. Ephraim R. McLean, Editor of DATABASE, for his support and approval to reproduce selective articles from a special section of DATABASE that Varun Grover edited. Of course we want to convey our thanks to all the authors for their hard work in making this project a success. We wish you all pleasant process thought in the Information Age!

Varun Grover
William J. Kettinger

Part I

Change Strategies
That Work

CHAPTER 1

Conducting Business Process Change: Recommendations from a Study of 25 Leading Approaches

William J. Kettinger and James T. C. Teng
University of South Carolina, USA

Business process change is maturing. Gone are the days of unbridled enthusiasm and easy targets for radical overhaul. Ten years of business process reengineering has taught us that failure is a frequent outcome. Surprisingly, even given setbacks, firms are moving ahead with business process change projects. However, unlike their early predecessors, today's process change projects are more likely to focus on enterprise wide mega-processes such as new product development, integrated supply chain, web-portal based order fulfillment, and financial management processes, including treasury and risk management. Today, BPR projects are more likely to include the use of enterprise resource planing software (e.g., SAP) or entail the development of new marketing or supply channels supported by electronic commerce.

Senior executives undertaking these process projects typically do not refer to these efforts as "reengineering" and instead call them "e-Commerce initiatives", "ERP/supply-chain projects" or "process improvement efforts." Regardless of the name, executives learned from the results surfacing from early business process change cases. They realize that all projects are not alike. Efforts range in depth and strategic impact and these differences affect project success. Projects aimed at improvements along multiple "strategic" dimensions such as time, cost, quality, satisfaction and product innovation are perceived to have higher payoffs than unidimensional projects focusing only on cost reduction (Grover, Jeung, Kettinger and Teng, 1995)

Over the past ten years, we have learned that when a process view is restrained to only the boundaries of a traditional functional area and has the primary objective of cutting costs, reengineering projects tend to merely simplify and automate narrowly defined internal processes to "make them more efficient." It is this perception of reengineering, as being "narrowly focused" and "nonstrategic," that has received the brunt of criticism equating it to little more than downsizing (Hamel and Prahalad, 1994). However, as determined by the authors in a study of reengineering methods practiced by 25 leading BPR consultants (See Appendix A), the contemporary view of business process change holds that it involves a fundamental and strategic analysis of the firm. New projects focus on mega business processes that span across logically related functions (and organizations) to achieve broad, strategically defined outcome. This mature type of strategy driven business process change begins with "generation" and "cultivation" of innovative strategies—it has more to do with integrating a business process view into strategic development, than it does with "engineering." We term this more mature understanding of process change "Business Process Regeneration" (BPR) rather than reengineering. By significantly improving a firm's operating capabilities, Business Process Regeneration allows the implementation of new strategies and, even more importantly, leads to envisioning of entirely new strategic options.

For example, Progressive Corporation, a large car insurance company in the U.S.A., has been successful using BPR to target the market of high-risk drivers. Studiously avoided by other insurers, these customers are (profitably) welcomed by Progressive. For years Progressive's secret was a regenerated underwriting process that was more detailed and precise than those of their competitors and that led to very precise pricing decisions. Eventually, Progressive's larger competitors began copying its underwriting process and invading its niche. Progressive's response was more BPR, this time of its claims process. By exploiting a technique called "immediate response," Progressive can now dispatch an adjuster to examine a claimant's car on the day of the accident-in many cases, going to the accident site itself. Having protected its competitive turf, Progressive then realized that its regenerated processes allowed it to enter new markets (those of standard and low risk drivers). Progressive business strategy is now based on first-class business processes that provide high degrees of customer service. Progressive has also regenerated its pricing process to provide more detailed customer information increasing satisfaction. BPR helped Progressive to poach on new territory, identifying unexploited strategic opportunities for unanticipated customer needs and types.

Maturity in Business Process Change Methods

In response to senior managers' pleas for better methods and measures, the authors undertook a study to help derive a generic planning and implementation guide incorporating leading BPR practice. Based on a survey of BPR consultants, the proposed Business Process Regeneration Method incorporates those project activities and tasks that have been most successfully employed by many of the leading consulting houses in conducting business process change. In deriving and validating the Process Regeneration Approach (See Table 1) the authors undertook case and field research as outlined in Appendix A. In sum, the authors conducted a series of semi-structured interviews with BPR consultants and market research firms to gain a systematic understanding of BPR methodology. Interview notes were compiled to develop descriptions for each methodology's phases, activities and tasks.

Survey results indicate that the BPR consulting firms are evolving their methods to be more strategy driven with greater consideration of competitive factors in project planning. Reportedly, successful methods recognize resistance to change and attempt to minimize this through an assessment of cultural readiness and activities to establish project buy-in. Leading methodologies permit focus on mega business processes that span logically related functions and are often inter-organizational in scope. Where advantageous, surveyed methods attempt to

Table 1: Revitalizing Business Processes

Phase 1: Strategy Linkage
This phase emphasizes the securing of management commitment and the discovery of re-generation opportunities, including the matching of corporate strategy with emerging information technology (IT) levers. This phase requires the selection of a business process to be re-engineered and the definition of the project scope and approach.

Phase 2: Change Planning
This phase ensures the careful preparation and launching of the re-generation project which encompasses the assignment of a re-generation team, the setting of performance goals, project planning and stakeholder/employee notification.

Phase 3: Process Pathology
This phase involves the documentation and critical analysis of the pathologies of the existing process.

Phase 4: Social Re-Design
Social Re-design is the phase in which a new process is designed. The focus of this phase is directed at selection between alternative process designs that meet strategic objectives as well as integrate new human resource and organizational architectures.

Phase 5: Technical Re-Design
The focus of this phase is directed at selection between alternative process designs that meet strategic objectives as well as integrate new IT architectures. This phase entails prototyping of process alternatives and development of the selected IT platform.

Phase 6: Process Re-Generation
In accordance to the human resource architecture specified and IT platform developed, this phase uses change management techniques to implement the new process.

Phase 7: Continuous Improvement
In this phase the performance of the redesigned process is measured and linked to the firm's quality improvement plans.

leverage information technologies (IT) capabilities for coordinating cross-functional activities, but unlike earlier reengineering efforts, the methods surveyed are becoming less IT driven. As opposed to being cost or efficiency focused, the study indicates that methods accommodate measurement of performance gains that are more broadly and strategically defined.

Based on descriptions and analysis of 25 BPR methodologies surveyed, a composite Process Regeneration Method Framework was derived using an inductive process of pattern identification, incorporating those common activities and tasks reported important towards BPR project success (See Step 5 of Appendix A for more detail). A further validation check was conducted through interviews with BPR project managers at a number of actual corporate reengineering field sites (See Step

Table 2. The Process Re-generation Method

Phase 1: The Link with Strategy

Activities	Tasks
Secure Management Commitment	Identify Champion and/or Expert
	Conduct Re-generation Overview
	Assign Top Management Task Force
Discover Re-generation Opportunities	Review Strategy *and* Business Performance
	Identify Business Processes
	Conduct High-Level *Evaluation* of Business Processes
	Identify Candidate Processes
Identify IT Levers	Review IT Plan
	Target IT Levers
Align with Corporate Strategy	Link IT/Process/Strategy
Select Process	Conduct Preliminary Analysis of Candidate Processes
	Prioritize and Select Process
	Determine Project Scope

Phase 2: Planning the Change

Activities	Tasks
Inform Stakeholders	Identify Stakeholders
	Initiate Communications Campaign
Organize Re-generation Team	Identify Process Owner
	Determine Re-generation Team Skill Requirements
	Select Re-generation Team Members
Conduct Project Planning	Conduct Re-generation Team Training
	Set Project Schedule
	Allocate Resources
Set Performance Goals of a "Re-designed" Process	Determine External Process Customer Requirements
	Develop "Stretch Targets" and Process Attributes
	Review Current Process Performance
	Determine Feasible Performance Range
	Set Improvement Objectives

Phase 3: Analyzing Problems in the Process

Activities	Tasks
Document Existing Process	Capture Process
	Capture Communications
	Determine Process Costs
	Document Job and IT Roles
Uncover Pathologies	Detail Internal Customers Process Requirements
	Identify Non-Value Adding Activities
	Analyze Problem Causes
	Assess Conformance to Detailed Customer Requirements
	Summarize and Rank Process Pathologies

Table 2. The Process Re-generation Method

Phase 1: The Link with Strategy

Activities	Tasks
Secure Management Commitment	Identify Champion and/or Expert
	Conduct Re-generation Overview
	Assign Top Management Task Force
Discover Re-generation Opportunities	Review Strategy *and* Business Performance
	Identify Business Processes
	Conduct High-Level *Evaluation* of Business Processes
	Identify Candidate Processes
Identify IT Levers	Review IT Plan
	Target IT Levers
Align with Corporate Strategy	Link IT/Process/Strategy
Select Process	Conduct Preliminary Analysis of Candidate Processes
	Prioritize and Select Process
	Determine Project Scope

Phase 2: Planning the Change

Activities	Tasks
Inform Stakeholders	Identify Stakeholders
	Initiate Communications Campaign
Organize Re-generation Team	Identify Process Owner
	Determine Re-generation Team Skill Requirements
	Select Re-generation Team Members
Conduct Project Planning	Conduct Re-generation Team Training
	Set Project Schedule
	Allocate Resources
Set Performance Goals of a "Re-designed" Process	Determine External Process Customer Requirements
	Develop "Stretch Targets" and Process Attributes
	Review Current Process Performance
	Determine Feasible Performance Range
	Set Improvement Objectives

Phase 3: Analyzing Problems in the Process

Activities	Tasks
Document Existing Process	Capture Process
	Capture Communications
	Determine Process Costs
	Document Job and IT Roles
Uncover Pathologies	Detail Internal Customers Process Requirements
	Identify Non-Value Adding Activities
	Analyze Problem Causes
	Assess Conformance to Detailed Customer Requirements
	Summarize and Rank Process Pathologies

6 of Appendix A for more detail).

The derived Process Regeneration Method moves through seven phases (See Table 2). The first phase, Strategy Linkage, involves a rethinking of the strategic direction of the business and laying a vision for the future. It requires a high level understanding of the business processes and their performance. The output of this phase leads to the selection of the processes for regeneration. The second phase, Change Planning, includes project planning and the setting of the climate for change. The Process Pathology phase involves the capture of existing process activities and the determination of existing problems. Social Redesign and Technical Redesign involve recursive phases of creatively designing new process types that best link to strategic objectives. The Process Regeneration Phase requires critical socio-technical design to properly integrate the new process into the organization and entails people and technology process synthesis. Finally the Continuous Improvement Phase recognizes that even rejuvenated processes must be continually maintained and improved.

To assist strategic planners in designing a BPR project plan, Table 2 presents the detailed Process Regeneration Method including phases, activities and tasks. With tasks defined as steps that need to be accomplished for a particular activity in process regeneration. It is clear that the inclusion and sequence of phases, activities and tasks of a project will vary in actual practice. Surveyed techniques borrowed from many management disciplines are also suggested.

Phase 1: Strategy Linkage

The strategy linkage phase kicks off with up-front project planning and might be viewed as a "meta model" of regeneration where both the need for change and feasibility for change are examined. It emphasizes securing management commitment and the discovery of regeneration opportunities. This phase also includes the selection of a business process to be reworked and the definition of project scope. Due to the strategic nature of BPR and the extent of risk involved, much championship from the top is necessary.

Securing Management Commitment

It is a corporate leader who provides the legitimacy to initiate BPR and to ensure that it is implemented. To spearhead the effort, a "regeneration champion" typically emerges or is identified. The champion tends to be a high-ranking manager with significant authority and influence to mobilize resources and stimulate enthusiasm for BPR. For example, Aetna's President, Ron Compton, felt that the company had become a large self-satisfied behemoth, out of touch with its environment and customers. Organized as a traditional functional hierarchy with 16 business units and 42,000 employees, Aetna was slow to respond to market and regulations. To reverse the trend, Mr. Compton challenged the business unit heads to break the cycle of mediocre performance and reinvent the way they did business through regeneration.

A consultant can also serve as a regeneration catalyst and present the potential benefits and costs to senior management. A prototypical executive orientation includes: introduction to regeneration and its techniques; past cases successes and failures; a discussion of the company's problems; how regeneration would enhance the company's strategic objectives; organizational implications; and, a consideration of a plan-of-action. Based on a preliminary decision to move ahead, members of senior management, along with consultants (if used), form a high level regeneration task force responsible for conducting the remaining activities and tasks of the STRATEGY LINKAGE and CHANGE PLANNING phases until a project team is formally assigned.

An effective technique for securing broad-based support for regeneration is the Search Conference, which brings all stakeholders related to a process, including customers, shareholders and suppliers, into the same room to help define both the need for change and how changes should be achieved (Pasmore, 1994). All participants are encouraged to freely communicate their beliefs concerning environmental, social and technical issues related to a proposed regeneration project in a situation of consequence. The effectiveness of search conference is enhanced by the real time dialogue where understanding is reached by "seeing the big picture" and commitment to change is nurtured by active participation.

Discovering Process Opportunities

Prior to identifying candidate processes for regeneration, senior managers conduct a high-level evaluation of their overall corporate business conditions in the context of strategy. Using such techniques as Competitive Analysis, Value Chain Analysis and Critical Success Factors (CSF), a clear assessment of corporate goals, objectives and Key Performance Indicators (KPIs) are outlined. This task is followed by the identification of major corporate processes that support the business objectives and goals. This assessment quickly targets candidate processes.

Two approaches used for defining processes are the "comprehensive" and "targeted" methods. The targeted method defines processes most vital to the organization, as determined by discussions among top management or managerial interviews (Davenport and Short, 1990). The advantages of a targeted approach are fast payoff and timeliness of project completion. Targeted approaches typically identify those "core" processes that will result in the highest regeneration payoff. The Core Process Framework, as developed at McKinsey Co. Inc., views a company as being made up of 3-5 core processes each consisting of a set of interrelated subprocesses and activities, decisions, information and material flows, together determining competitive success (Ostroff and Smith, 1992). Core process identification requires executives to rethink the firm's value chains and organizational structure.

The comprehensive approach, on the other hand, attempts to identify all the processes within an organization and prioritize them. This comprehensive approach can be labor intensive and time consuming, however, it offers a well thought out rationale for regeneration with project prioritization that is consistent with corporate strategic goals. Planning tools such as Information Systems Planning (ISP), Business Systems Planning (BSP) and CSFs may be used in comprehensive identification of business processes (Kettinger, Teng and Guha, 1996). Methods for Information Architecture (IA) design may be utilized for identification of an organization's business processes. By using an established IA, processes are identified in relation to data classes, data entities, functional departments and application systems. Such a comprehensive approach was used by Rank Xerox U.K. employing ISP to uncover 18 "macro" business processes and 143 "micro" processes. The Charles Schwab

Corporation also used this approach to build a global business model encompassing 24 business processes.

Following process identification, the top management task force completes a preliminary analysis of the "health" of each business process to identify candidates for process regeneration. This preliminary effort need not be precision- or detail oriented. High-level criteria, both quantitative and qualitative, should be employed in this evaluation. The output of this activity is typically a "short" list of candidate processes for regeneration.

One technique helpful here is the "Process Selection Impact Statement," that offers a high level assessment of a broader set of organizational factors such as management and employee culture, availability of IT levers, level of difficulty and risk in regeneration, the process selection impact statement (Table 3). Similar to an

---

Table 3. Process Selection Impact Statement

To help determine the need for change of a particular candidate process, two questions for each alignment factor may be asked:

(1) Strategy
(a)   To what extent does the process need to be changed to support corporate strategy?
(b)   To what extent is it feasible to design a process to better support corporate strategy?

(2) Management
(a)   To what extent do current management systems, styles, values and measurements need to be changed to improve process efficiency and effectiveness?
(b)   To what extent is it feasible to change management systems, styles, values and measurements to improve process efficiency and effectiveness

(3) People
(a)   To what extent do jobs, skills, behaviors and culture of people need to be changed to improve process efficiency and effectiveness?
(b)   To what extent is it feasible to change jobs, skills, behaviors and culture of people to improve process efficiency and effectiveness?

(4) Structure
(a)   To what extent does organizational use of teams, co-ordination mechanisms and formal and informal structure, need to be changed to improve process efficiency and effectiveness?
(b)   To what extent is it feasible to change organizational use of teams, co-ordination mechanisms and formal and informal structures, to improve process efficiency and effectiveness?

(5) Information and Technology
(a)   To what extent does the current use of information and technology need to be changed to improve process efficiency and effectiveness?
(b)   To what extent is it feasible to change information and technology to improve process efficiency and effectiveness?

environmental impact statement, this prioritization exercise facilitates the comparison of candidate processes and brings to light hidden opportunities and problems involved in each process. Using such an assessment, Union Carbide made a strategic decision to emphasize commodity chemicals rather than specialty products, indicating the regeneration of its manufacturing process to achieve the lowest possible cost and provide added value in delivery and service. In addition, it is necessary to specify the level of effort required to conduct the selected regeneration project. This includes the evaluation of necessary resources and other high-level budgeting issues.

Identifying IT Enabling Opportunities

Information Technology is a catalyst, magnifying regeneration effects. Underlying BPR efforts are technologies such as Local Area Networks (LANs), object oriented systems, imaging, Electronic Data Interchange (EDI), Executive Information Systems (EIS), expert systems, client-server architecture, workgroup technologies and decision support systems. Coordination technologies, groupware and workflow are critical IT enablers that facilitate group cohesion, enterprise information sharing and process workflow automation. For example, Tupperware identified EIS and EDI as enablers of its global manufacturing operations.

Davenport and Short offer a practical framework for analyzing the matching of IT capabilities to a candidate process' requirements. As shown in Table 4, candidate processes can be classified into different types (see column of the table) based on dimensions of entities (interorganizational, interfunctional or interpersonal), objects

Table 4. Using IT to Enable the Process

Process Type	Typical BPR Requirements	Capabilities of the Enabling IT
Inter-organizational (e.g., ordering) from suppliers)	Transform unstructured processes into routinized transactions.	IT such as EDI and shared data bases lower transaction costs and eliminate intermediaries.
Interfunctional (e.g., new product development)	Transfer information rapidity across large distances.	IT such as CAD and WANs that support simultaneous work in different locations.
Interpersonal (e.g., approving a bank loan)	Remove intermediary and connect two parties within a process.	IT such as groupware and imaging that facilitate role and task integration.
Physical (e.g., manufacturing)	Reduce or replace human labor in a process.	IT such as CAM and robotics which increase outcome flexibility and process control.
Informational (e.g.,creating a WWW proposal)	Bring vast amounts of information into a process.	IT such as AI, multimedia and the WWW provide unstructured information and routinize decision logic.
Operational (e.g., order processing)	Change the sequence of tasks and allow some tasks to be done simultaneously.	IT such as electronic commerce, workflow sys. and shared data bases that reduce time and cost and increase output quality.
Managerial processes (e.g., budget preparation)	Bring complex analytical methods to bear on a process	IT such as expert systems and EIS that improve analysis and increase participation.

(physical or informational) and activities (operational or managerial). Requirements associated with each process type are briefly described in the second column (e.g. allowing detailed tracking of a purchase order's status). Capabilities of available IT that support these requirement are briefly described in the last column (e.g. workflow and imaging technologies that provide a detailed transaction trail).

Strategic vision to leverage structural differences or distinctive competencies with IT, relative to industry competitors, can be the basis for changing a firm's competitive position. Senior IS staff, along with the task force members, may review the corporate IT plan to determine the extent to which the firm's overall IT architecture meets identified strategic goals and objectives. The output of this activity is a "short" list of IT enablers for candidate BPR processes. In Table 5, several brief BPR case examples are provided to illustrate the enabling role of IT.

Table. 5. Company cases illustrating they used IT	
Type of Information Technology	Case Example
CAD/CAM and Telecommunication	At Texas Instruments (TI), new product developments are now conducted at locations in a number of different countries: India, Malaysia, Japan and the U.S. The company's CAD/CAM systems and its global computer network enables design teams in different countries to achieve a high level of collaboration, while permitting them to work on different parts of the design in a parallel fashion without the time-consuming flow of documents. As a result, the development cycle time for various products decreased substantially. The time needed to develop a calculator, for example, declined 20% soon after design drawings began to be sent electronically in 1989 and a further decrease of 17% has been achieved since then.
DataBase	In this well-publicized case at Ford Motor Corp., the old accounts payable process involved three functions: purchasing, inventory and account payable, which participated in the process serially with many intermediate steps and sequential flow of paper documents. With direct access to a shared database, the three functions now participate in the re-engineered process in a parallel fashion. The re-engineered process achieved a 75% reduction in the workforce required, from 500 to only 125.
Imaging	At Bank One, the serial flow of paper documents has been drastically changed through the use of imaging technology which enables many functions to perform different steps for the mortgage approval process on the same document in a parallel pattern. As one bank officer examines the document to verify the applicant's employment status, another can do credit scoring and yet another one can perform credit inquiry.

Table. 5 (continued). Company cases illustrating they used IT	
Type of Information Technology	**Case Example**
Expert Systems	At PHH Fleet America, a division of PHH, the Driver Service case manager can rely on the skills they have learned and an expert knowledge base for answering most of customers' questions on their leased vehicles. They refer the more difficult problems to expert maintenance mechanics who can not only solve the problems but add it to the case managers' knowledge base.
Federated DataBases	At Pacific Bell, the development of federated databases has been instrumental to the success of its attempt to re-engineer the Centrex customer service process. Prior to re-generation, providing a customer with a Centrex telephone service took eleven jobs and more than five business days. Service representatives had to update 9 or more computer systems, making frequent errors and rework and consulting customers several times. Now, Centrex service coordinators handle all interactions with customers. Using a computer workstation that interface with all nine systems, they can now provide the service usually in the same day.
Telecommunication and GroupWare	At Hewlett-Packard Co., the sales process underwent significant change as 135 sales representatives began to use laptop computers to retrieve up-to-date inventory information from corporate data base during customer meetings. In addition, they can now use the portable computers to communicate with their peers and superiors, enabling frequent exchange of sales intelligence among the salespersons as well as timely dissemination of corporate directives pertaining to promotion, pricing and discounting. The results showed that time spent in meetings decreased by 46% and travel time was cut by 13%. Meanwhile, time spent with customers increased 27% and sales rose by 10%.

Aligning with Corporate Strategy and Selecting a BPR Project

As a final activity of this planning phase, the top level management task force next makes a high-level assessment of the "short listed" candidate processes and their alignment to strategies, products and services provided by the firm. This analysis includes potential redesign impacts on the firm's performance measures. Factoring in the results of the two previous activities, an overall assessment should indicate the level of difficulty in regenerating each process.

The Process Prioritization Matrix technique can be used in making the final selection of a process for regeneration consistent with corporate strategy. Employing this technique, a matrix relates candidate processes to a firm's critical success factors (CSF) as determined by the top executive. A scoring method is used that results in row totals reflecting the overall strategic relevance of a process to the various critical success factors, with highest row totals receiving top priority in project selection. When used in conjunction with cost and risk factors, this analysis can pinpoint a final process selection (Kettinger et. al., 1996).

Phase 2: Change Planning

The CHANGE PLANNING Phase begins the actual conduct of a BPR project with the launching of the project and includes assignment of a BPR working team, the setting of performance goals, project planning and stakeholder/employee communication.

Informing Stakeholders and Organizing the Regeneration Team

Managing change and potential resistance to the regeneration requires an in-house public relations campaign that focuses on the project's "challenges as opposed to threats", the "risk" of not proceeding and clear definitions of project success and levels of involvement. This is accomplished by stimulating themes of pride, innovation, achievement and cooperation. A message from the CEO or president, addressing the need, scope, commitment and leadership of the project is often communicated to all stakeholders, with regular updates.

The next task of this activity is the naming of a "process owner", who is responsible for the project and accountable for its results. While the appointment of a project leader typically comes from internal ranks, many companies enlist the help of consultants as either co-leaders or facilitators. Team member selection criteria include strategic planning background, past TQM or industrial engineering expertise and finance, marketing and project management experience. A talent mix frequently includes those knowledgeable in the functional areas of the selected process and also those with creative talents for process design; human resource and change specialists to assist in organizational structural changes; operations researchers and IS professionals with process modeling and simulation skills.

In the Aetna Life and Casualty case cited earlier, an internal group was formed. Headed by Dan Hickey, the group consists of 15 members selected from various functional areas. After training together, the first task was to explain to 42,000 employees why regeneration was needed to revitalize the company's business. For each project, top level executive sponsorship was arranged first. The team then drew from an affected functional area. Since its formation, the group has successfully completed 10 projects and the sales and operating performance of Aetna's Property and Casualty unit has improved significantly, showing an average of $10 million payback for each project.

Preparing the Project Schedule and Setting Performance Goals

Setting lofty goals establishes the organizational momentum to achieve significant change. Based on the preliminary analysis, process performance targets should strive for very high, but achievable goals. Research indicates that projects focusing on multiple measure of performance that are directly linked to strategic objectives have the greatest overall performance impact (Grover, et. al., 1995). These "stretch goals" are typically based on "world-class" standards or "best practice" as set by industry leaders and determined through formal bench-marking techniques. At Aetna all business units were required to compare themselves to the top three performers in their industries and to strive to be 'number one." The customers for each business process were carefully identified and their requirements and expectations clarified. The benchmarking of performance measures on core processes were based on "best in class" competitors. In addition, these performance goals were derived from process customers' requirements.

Misalignment of process measures with the goals and missions of the firm can be costly. For example, at Sears Automotive Service, sales quotas were used as a performance measure, resulting in allegations that customers were systematically charged for needless repairs. This practice led to customer dissatisfaction and law suits against the company. Techniques used to assist in setting performance goals include: brainstorming, "Out-of-Box Thinking", "Visioning" and Affinity Diagramming. To understand customer needs better, BPR project teams often use such techniques as: Customer Interviews, Focus Groups, Quality Function Deployment, Transaction Analysis and Customer- Supplier Protocol Modeling (Kettinger and Hackbarth, 1998).

Phase 3: Process Pathology
Documenting the Existing Process

This activity typically involves the development of high-level diagrams of the selected process, with later decomposition into several levels representing relationships between activities, information and other relevant process characteristics. The participants in a process are usually interviewed to reveal the flow of information and linkages. Useful rules of thumb include:

1. Depict the process from its starting node to its end node, which may include several functional departments, internal and external customers and external linkages;
2. Identify components of the process such as information systems, human (jobs), controls, physical and other process resources;
3. Document performance of the existing process in terms of customer satisfaction, inventory turnover, cycle time, waiting queues, defect rates, activity times, transfer rates, priority rules and other relevant measures;
4. Indicate processing time, transport time and waiting costs and use these benchmarks to measure the improved process;
5. Decompose a large process into a set of subprocesses and assign team members to the appropriate subprocesses based on their expertise.

Many documentation techniques and tools are used to support process capture including: Data Flow Diagramming, Block Diagramming, Process Flowcharting and commercially available work flow design tools. IDEF, a process definition and design methodology developed by the U.S. Air Force is a popular structured technique for capturing the existing process (Mayer, Benjamin, Caraway and Painter, 1995). To develop a detailed measurement of the current process cost in both manpower and monetary terms, Activity Based Costing is often used. To document the process relative to jobs and IT, Job Analysis and Critical Incident Technique is frequently employed. To capture such dimensions as the frequency and purpose of formal and informal communication, such techniques as Communication Media Analysis and Speech Interaction Modeling, Customer-Supplier Modeling can be used (Kettinger and Hackbarth, 1998). The information from these analyses can provide a baseline to facilitate later socio-technical design.

Uncovering Process Pathologies

Process pathologies including authorization levels, business policies, work flow activities, manual tasks and job roles that hinder and fragment the overall effectiveness of a business process may be identified and targeted for change. For example, if the goal is to reduce time and cost, it may be beneficial to depict the elapsed time, bottleneck delays, labor requirements and incremental costs of each activity. At Bell Atlantic Corporation, for example, a customer order for hooking up to a long-distance carrier took 15-25 days and passed through 25 hands. Through the analysis of process pathologies, many "irrelevant" serial steps were eliminated and an order is now filled in just a few hours. The performance of the existing process may also be compared to the requirements determined earlier for both internal and external customers; deviations may then be analyzed and causes traced. Many commonly used TQM and industrial engineering techniques are particularly effective at determining the root causes of problems in the existing process, these include: Fishbone Analysis, Force Field Analysis, Statistical Process Control (SPQ) and Pareto Diagramming. Once identified, process pathologies may be rank ordered and prioritized in terms of criticality and their relative "contribution" to deviation from desired performance measures. This step makes it more likely that the new process ideas generated will indeed eliminate existing pathologies and meet performance goals.

Phases 4 & 5: Social and Technical Re-Design

The SOCIAL AND TECHNICAL Redesign phases involve iterative design through the exploration of process alternatives that meet strategic objectives and integrate new human resource and organizational change architectures. This redesign should strive to achieve a proper "fit" between people, work process, information management and technology in a newly configured socio-technical system.

Exploring Alternative Designs

Often referred to as "visioning", this task involves translating the outlined strategy and external and internal inputs into specific process attributes with measurable objectives. To achieve process breakthroughs, new process attributes should be defined based on what is necessary from a business standpoint, rather than what just seems "do-able". Such brainstorming techniques as word and thought variation, creativity barrier exploration, idea generation exercises and open-forum, noncritical discussion are frequently used here.

The Regeneration team next considers IT's enabling affect on various design alternatives. For example, an imaging system for credit transactions and authorizations using expert systems and workflow automation may provide a better means of handling forms processing, routing and approval. An alternative may be to consider a wide-area network application tied into the corporate database server to allow immediate approvals on-line by remote sales personnel. Each of these solutions entail different work flow activity, staffing and cross-functional support. Alternative process design "concepts" may also be subjected to high-level process prototyping using process simulation and "what if" analysis. This high level prototyping can include feedback from customers and employees used as role-playing and paper process testing. As a result of these analyses, a selection of a specific new process alternative may be made for subsequent detailed design.

Designing the New Process

One major focus in design is on leveraging time. Time can be saved by eliminating multiple approval levels and noncritical control checks, by integrating data processing into the work that produces the information, by eliminating wait buffers and by integrating multiple tasks. An important regeneration possibility involves the substitution of sequential activities for simultaneous ones. This reduces the waiting time and may be achieved by applying on-line databases and information networks across the process. Separate tasks within processes may be integrated into one job description to keep important information from being lost. For example, prior to regeneration, it took 700 writers, artists and designers at Hallmark to produce 40,000 cards. This consumed a considerable amount of time due to redundant activities and vast portages between departments. There was a recognized need to reduce work fragmentation by integrating tasks. The regenerated process now uses self managed teams that work together, focusing on particular holidays, producing cards in one-half the original cycle time.

Appropriate information, including immediate feedback on performance, should also be provided to the line workers to ensure that problems are resolved immediately. At Kodak, the 1500-employee black and-white film production process is extensive and complicated. After regeneration it was divided into "streams" and customer satisfaction was made the key performance measurements. For those streams not having direct customer contact, internal customers were identified and their satisfaction measured. This calibration of process performance measures helped to improve the performance dramatically, cutting response time in half. As the teams were given "ownership" of the processes, i.e. the team members could jointly decide what to do when unexpected situations occur without asking the superiors in the hierarchy, the "buck passing" syndrome may be alleviated.

Designing Human Resource Architecture

The probability of success of BPR projects is expected to be high if the people involved have cross-functional and multi-discipline backgrounds. Designing new human resource architectures to support a new process design entails redefinition of job titles and positions, application of team-based management techniques, performance evaluation with reward structures based on group performance and modification of control structures that require managers to be equals as well as team leaders. Such change occurred at Pacific Bell, where providing a customer with CENTREX service once required eleven different jobs and access to nine separate databases. After regeneration, these jobs were consolidated into "Case Manager" positions providing customers with a single contact with Pacific Bell. The skills and authority of case managers were significantly "empowered" to cover cross-functional knowledge and decision-making; in essence these individuals were allowed to "control the process."

The human resource implications of team-based structures require considerable deviation from conventional personnel management practice. At AT&T's Network Systems Division, for example, the traditional function-based performance standards are replaced by holistic external performance objectives. Employees are now awarded bonuses for higher customer satisfactions rather than higher sales, higher inventory turnover or lower cost. In addition, the division no longer assigns discreet budgets for each functional department. Budgets are now set by processes. At Modicon, Inc., a maker of automation-control equipment, product development is no longer the sole responsibility of the engineering function. In the past, manufacturing typically did not get involved in this process until the design was brought into the factory. At that late point design changes were very costly. Now, a team of 15 managers from engineering, manufacturing, marketing, sales and finance routinely work together on the design process. This cross-functional collaboration has eliminated many unnecessary delays and costly change and brought six products to market in one-third of the time.

The regeneration team begins redesigning human resource architecture with brainstorming sessions. These sessions concentrate on job assignments, organizational structures, layers of management and authorizations, extent of team-based structures, reward structures and performance metrics. Using such techniques from job design, socio-technical systems design, and team-based management, the new team structures may call for some existing jobs to be eliminated and others altered in terms of skill requirements (Taylor and Felten, 1993). In some cases, completely new jobs may be established. Using the new human resource architecture, associated communication channels are designed to enhance role-based communication and message routing. Finally, a comprehensive training and education is organized to help employees to develop skills and knowledge required in their new job assignments.

Selecting an IT Platform

Often, the IT required for the regenerated process must support communication between decentralized systems and tie suppliers and vendors using wide-area networks. Therefore, the required IT platform should be compatible with the enterprise-wide IT architecture in terms of migration and interoperability. The contribution of the IT architecture can be seen in the case of Continental Bank. The bank's CIO was in charge of strategic planning for the regeneration. Under her leadership, a comprehensive IT architecture was developed to support the bank's new business strategy. This was accomplished through examination of overall strategies and the functions delivering products and services critical for each strategy. Interactions between functions and data necessary to be shared was next examined. Using this model, a strategy was developed which included a new data base design and application development plan supporting multiple regenerated processes.

Prototyping the Holistic Process

Prototyping the entire process design (tasks, people and technology) is next undertaken to provide top management with a more detailed understanding of the new process characteristics, process flow, job assignments, IT infrastructure and system requirements before it "goes live". This is similar to the idea of prototyping in the traditional information systems sense, where the system behavior can be "tried out" to solicit users' feedback. Here, the entire process may be "rehearsed" (possibly with a selected group of real customers) using such techniques as role playing, paper process tests and workflow designs to identify further opportunities for refinements.

If the decision is to move ahead, the determination of the best phasing strategy should be made including phasing for human resource reorganization, IS development and implementation and process procedure/policy cut over. Some forms of piloting may also be conducted to help determine the best overall conversion strategy.

Phase 6: Process Re-Generation

The actual implementation of a regenerated process demands considerable attention to change management. The Process Regeneration phase involves the implementation of human resource changes and development and deployment of IT support. Throughout this phase, a number of proven techniques may be applied to assess the resistant forces that prevent the desired change. For example a popular technique, force field analysis, provides stimuli for generating solutions to implementation problems. Through its pictorial representation of a "tug of war", analysts identify forces that are "tugging" to the left of center in the direction of "catastrophe," and forces currently "tugging" to the right, toward the ideal situation."

Developing and Deploying IT

The primary task of the IT professional(s) on the regeneration team during the Process Regeneration phase is the development and deployment of new information systems and technology to support the new process. Detailed systems analysis specifications are developed. This task may have already taken place at a higher-level prior to final design selection, but must be completed in a detailed fashion before coding, testing and other steps for actually implementing the information systems can be undertaken. In some cases, existing systems and technology may be replaced entirely with new hardware platforms and application programs. The IT staff assigned to the BPR Team should oversee systems integration, testing and walk-through procedures. Next, application databases and client interfaces are typically implemented and coordination with existing systems operation is tested.

Reorganizing

This activity focuses on the smooth transition to a new organization including reorganization and staff reductions, team and employee selection, job rotation and employee training. Based on the new process design, new organizational structures and job assignments must be conveyed to the affected employees outlining their future roles and performance expectations. A plan for developing knowledge and skills for the employees is prepared. In addition to specific job and systems training, education may also be given in terms of the new cultural philosophy. Incentives and reward structures must be implemented.

Dramatic changes during this step will cause anxiety that must be addressed by continual communication between top management, the regeneration team and employees. A number of communication-based "persuasion" techniques have proven effective. Based on the "elaboration likelihood model" and "appropriateness-consistency-effectiveness model" from organizational behavior, these techniques articulate strategies of influence which can be used in situations where individuals publicly or privately resist BPR implementation. Successful Persuasion techniques shown to be successful in easing anxiety and resistance to change include "rejection-then-retreat", "the commitment and consistency rule", "social proof", "liking" and "artificial scarcity" (Melone, 1995).

Implementing redesigned processes involves significant changes in appraisal and compensation. At GE's lighting business and the Government Electronics group in Motorola, peers evaluate the performance of an individual. Sometimes as many as 20 people are involved in reviewing a single employee with rewards based on team performance in addition to individual performance. Employees are now also paid on the basis of the skill they develop rather than merely the individual work they perform. At Chesebrough-Pond Inc., factory line workers now routinely scan on-line information on sales and stock availability and make adjustments to the production schedules. The term "employee empowerment" is no longer an abstract concept but a reality.

Phase 7: Continuous Improvement

Post implementation measurement is the final phase to determine whether performance goals have been met.

Measuring Performance

Evaluation includes the monitoring of qualitative and quantitative performance measures set in the CHANGE PLANNING Phase. A comparative analysis of customer requirements to process performance goals should be conducted to identify unmet expectations that demand further design improvement. Due to BPR's greater reliance on self-managed team structures and the use of generalists, a detailed audit of the redesigned process may be prudent to ensure process integrity. Individual and team satisfaction measures should be analyzed as well as the communications flows between jobs, activities and subprocesses. The results of this evaluation may require immediate modifications to the new process or feed into a firm's total quality management activity. Such a feedback loop provides an audit of the performance of the redesigned process.

Linking to Quality Improvement

While the BPR goals differ from quality programs that aim at incremental gains, the CONTINUOUS IMPROVEMENT phase provides a fundamental link between the more radical focus of BPR and the continuous incremental improvements of TQM. It may be necessary to continually fine tune certain aspects of the new process until acceptable performance gains are achieved. By using traditional TQM techniques such as Statistical Process Control, the defined process performance measurements can be monitored continuously to ensure that additional process improvements are made over a period of time. This link between BPR and quality improvement can be seen at Deere & Company, the giant farm equipment manufacturer. The company had engaged in TQM prior to its attempt at regeneration. After two decades of experience with product improvement techniques, Deere has learned that 50% of the cost saving opportunities are usually in product and process design, 30% in streamlining inventory flow and 20% in automating manufacturing and applying new computer technology. In regenerating the new product development process, for example, Deere adopted such techniques as the quality function deployment (QFD) from TQM to translate customer needs into specific product requirements. After many years of regeneration efforts, new product development now involves a number of functions that collaborate in every phase of the process.

This BPR/TQM link is not unusual, such companies as DuPont, Ford, American Express and Eastman Chemical have merged their quality and reengineering support groups. Many firms are now beginning to better integrate these various process change methods with other approaches of process management. In fact, some firms have constructed a "process management portfolio" that may include several high risk, high payoff radical regeneration projects and more incrementally oriented process improvement and quality projects. Increasingly senior managers will be called upon to posses the sophistication needed to understand alternative process change methods in order to manage the firm's process management portfolio strategically.

Concluding Remarks: Further Validation and Use of the Method

Based on a study of 25 leading process change methods, this article provides a synthesized and strategically-oriented method to assist strategic planners in understanding the relationships between phases, activities and tasks of a Process Regeneration project. As indicated in Step 6 of the study's research steps (Appendix A), the researchers have attempted to ascertain additional validity of the composite phase activity-task sequence of the Regeneration method through field verification at three actual BPR case sites. The three firms: AT&T GBCS, Comdisco Inc. and Bowater Inc., each had completed a comprehensive BPR project. In-depth field interviews were conducted in these companies. Results of these interviews indicated that the sequence of phases, activities and tasks at the three sites were closely aligned with those of the composite Process Regeneration Method as outlined in this article. In fact, the mapping between the method and AT&T's BPR project had an almost 100% fit. Comdisco Inc. and Bowater Inc. were particularly interesting as both firms had undertaken an initial unsuccessful BPR projects with a preconceived solution centered around information technology (IT) applications. They initially conducted the Technical Redesign and Regeneration phases first, but soon realized that the "solution" did not serve their business needs. To avoid failure, in both cases, the project teams reverted back to the Strategy Linkage and Change Planning phases, as outlined in the Regeneration method, to develop a business vision and justification first. The fact that the project teams reverted back to the sequence of phases as laid out by the Process Regeneration Method's phase-activity-task sequence demonstrates additional validity of the framework.

While the Regeneration method includes common traits among the 25 surveyed methods, it was also found that some BPR methodologies have less fully developed activities and techniques for preparing an organization for the change and for "institutionalizing" the change over the long run. For example, our findings indicate that several methods surveyed do not link BPR projects to continuous improvement programs and methodologies that do not clearly include activities for determining human communication patterns, or the development of a human resource architecture. Thus, while no process change method can guarantee success, the proposed Regeneration method is generally more complete and potentially more effective, than many of the methods currently being practiced.

While the Regeneration methodology should be more effective than many of the surveyed approaches, this does not mean that each and every task included in the method should always be attempted. In practice, phases, activities, tasks and techniques may be added, adjusted, or deleted to meet specific project requirements. For example, a high risk player, looking for large returns, may bypass detailed examination of the current process and focus immediately on new and innovative process designs.

Clearly, we are now well underway on our journey to understand business process change. A learning curve effect indicates that the longer a company deals with these issues, the more efficient it becomes in latter projects. Competitive pressures, coupled with advances in technologies, will continue to demand an overhaul of business processes. However, the days of unbridled "Greenfield" reengineering have drawn to an end. Future benefits in process change will have to be gained through careful strategic regeneration planning and through the use of more sophisticated methods.

Appendix A. The Research Method

Research Steps and Descriptions

Step 1   Literature review on state-of-the-art in BPR planning and implementation methodologies.
These research sources included scholarly and trade literature, on-line market intelligence services and market research reports. This investigation led to a list of information sources for further data collection.

Step 2   Collect service and product information from BPR consultants and vendors.
BPR practice information was requested from these sources and systematically filed.

Step 3   Conduct semi-structured on-site and telephone interviews of selected BPR consultants and vendors.
Where additional information was deemed necessary, a request was made to conduct an interview. Semi-structured interview began with open ended questions regarding their BPR planning and implementation approach. The interview progressed into details concerning methodologies practiced and use of advanced techniques.

Step 4   Establish research databases of BPR methods.
A research data base was established containing the description of 25 methodologies for conducting BPR. The consultants surveyed included A.T Kearney, AT&T GBSC, Booz Allen & Hamilton, CSC Index, D. Appleton, Ernst & Young, EDS, Gateway, Hammer & Co., ISS, KBS Inc., McKinsey Co., Meritus, Nolan & Norton, Oxford Associates, Price Waterhouse, SRI, TI and Wang.

Step 5   Analyze compiled methodologies and derive a composite BPR Framework
Using the descriptions of 25 methodologies, an inductive discovery process was followed by the researchers to produce a composite Phase-Activity-Task Framework for business process regeneration. See Table 1 and Table 2.

Step 6   Examine validity of the BPR Framework in three case sites.
The researchers next attempted to ascertain additional validity of the composite Phase-Activity-Task Framework for BPR through field verification at three sites. The three

firms had each completed a comprehensive BPR project prior to the interview. In-depth interviews were conducted in these companies with the BPR project directors. Results of these interviews indicated that the sequence of phases, activities and tasks at the three sites were closely aligned with those of the framework.

References

Davenport, T. H. and Nohria, N., Case management and the integration of labor. *Sloan Management Review*, 11-23 (1994).

Davenport, T. H. and Short, J. E., The new industrial engineering: information technology and business process redesign. *Sloan Management Review*, Summer, 11-27 (1990).

Grover, V., Jeung, S., Kettinger, W.J., and Teng, J., The implementation of business process re-engineering. *Journal of Management Information Systems*, 12 (1), 109-145(1995).

Hamel G. and Prahalad, C. K., *Competing for the Future*. Harvard Business School Press (1994).

Kettinger, W. J., Teng, J. and Guha, S., Informational architectural design in business process re-engineering. *Journal of Information Technology*, 11 (4), 27-40 (1996).

Kettinger, W.J., and Hackbarth, G., "Selling in the Era of the 'Net': Integration of Electronic Commerce in Small Firms, " *Proceedings of the Eighteenth International Conference on Information Systems*, Atlanta GA, December 15-17, 120-140, (1997).

Mayer, R. J., Benjamin, P. C., Caraway, B. E. and Painter, M. K., A framework and a suite of methods for business process re-engineering. In V. Grover and W.J. Kettinger (eds), *Business Process Change: Re-engineering Concepts, Methods and Technologies*, Idea Publishing, Harrisburg, PA, 245-290 (1995).

Melone, N. P., When people work scared: understanding attitudes and gaining compliance in business process re-engineering. In V. Grover and W. J. Kettinger, (eds), *Business Process Change: Concepts, Methods an Technologies*, Idea Publishing, Harrisburg, PA, pp. 475-492 (1995).

Ostroff, F. and Smith, D., Redesigning the organization the horizontal organization. *The McKinsey Quarterly*, 1, 148-169 (1992).

Pasmore, W. *Creating Strategic Change: Designing the Flexible High -Performance Organization*, John Wiley, N.Y. (1994).

Taylor, J. C. and Felten, D. F., *Performance by Design: Sociotechnical Systems in North America*. Prentice Hall, Englewood Cliff, NJ (1993).

CHAPTER 2

Strategies for Business Process Reengineering: Evidence from Field Studies

Michael J. Earl, Jeffrey L. Sampler and James E. Short
London Business School, UK

It is not unusual for management research to lag behind management practice; in some ways it is inevitable. Business process reengineering (BPR), it is claimed, was pioneered in a few large corporations in the 1980s (Hammer and Champy, 1993). It was first described and explained at the turn of the decade (Davenport and Short, 1990; Hammer, 1990) and since then an evolving stream of research has been reported (Caron, Jarvenpaa and Stoddard, 1994; Davenport and Stoddard, 1994; Grover, Fiedler and Teng, 1994; Short and Venkatraman, 1992). This paper reports results from case study research on relationships between business process reengineering (BPR), business strategy planning, and information systems (IS) planning. These questions are particularly relevant due to the rapid escalation in the size and scope of reengineering projects.

Our work has been guarded by the following questions:

- How have business process reengineering initiatives evolved in organizations?
- How has planning for BPR been integrated with strategic business planning? With IS planning?
- Is there evidence that the character, scope, and size of BPR projects depends on the degree of integration between BPR, strategic business planning, and IS planning?
- To what extent has the degree of planning integration between BPR, strategic business, and IS affected change management policies and practices in firms undergoing BPR?

In approaching these questions we have surfaced a number of definitions of business process reengineering. Reengineering has been defined by consultants practicing it in the field as an approach to planning and controlling "radical" organizational change. BPR has meant redesigning existing business processes and implementing new ones. "Business processes" have been defined as "logically related tasks performed to achieve a defined business outcome" (Davenport and

Short, 1990) where processes are "any activity or group of activities that take an input. Add value to it, and provide an output to an internal or external customer" [28]. We will refer to business process reengineering in its current practice usage as approaches for initiating and managing "radical" changes in existing business processes. However, we note also the importance of organizational change theories and their implications for intervention techniques, such as reengineering, that disrupt established work routines, resource dependencies, and human resource policies (Gersick, 1991; Pfeffer and Salancik, 1978; Tushman and Romanelli, 1985).

Framework for Analysis

Although a relatively new field of inquiry, there are theory-based perspectives through which we can study emerging practice in BPR. Below we review four perspectives—organizational processes, strategy, IS, and change management and control—that provide grounding for our investigation into planning integration.

Process

Processes are intrinsic to organization design. Academicians and practitioners alike have long used process concepts to distil and to elaborate characteristics of organization structure, work role behavior, and resource interdependence (Pettigrew, 1992; Van de Ven and Poole, 1990; Victor and Blackburn, 1987). In organizational process research, for example, Weick (1979) has argued that organizations construct processes from a set of "cycles" using "assembly rules"-in short, organizations build routines based on goal-directed rules and procedures, where rules are seen as constraints on action (Drazin and Sandelands, 1992). Other researchers have defined processes as coordination systems for managing resource dependencies in firms, using ideas from computer science and coordination theory to map process hierarchies and resource coordination (Malone and Crowston, 1994).

Definitions of business processes have looked chiefly at the structure and specific ordering of work, using ideas from industrial engineering and, in some circumstances, from systems dynamics where the process focus crosses firm boundaries (Forrester, 1961) . Thus, Davenport (1992) defines business processes as "the specific ordering of work activities across time and place, with a beginning, an end, and clearly identified inputs and outputs." The process objective is customer value added: processes are the structure by which organizations do what is necessary to produce value for customers. Such definitions generally have implied process hierarchies. Davenport (1992) separates "operational" from "management" processes: others define "core" and supporting processes using ideas borrowed from value chain analysis (Kaplan and Murdock, 1991).

Reengineering practitioners have expanded the key ideas in business process redesign to include concepts of incremental and radical change in organization structure, work role behavior, task interdependence, human resource policies, and rewards (Hammer and Champy, 1993). This evolution of practice-based ideas, grounded in the "organizational experiments' underway, has led organization theorists to call for increased academic research into business processes and their relationships to organization form (Daft and Lewin, 1993). Whether one regards this as a case of theory leading practice, or practice leading theory (Barley, Meyer and

Gash, 1988), the interest in process-based work seem clearly to call for greater understanding of this domain.

Strategy

Strategy researchers have continued to debate both the sources of competitive advantage and firm performances (the "content" of strategy) and models of the strategic planning process (the "process" view). In firm performance, two contrasting perspectives are dominant: one looks to the importance of external market factors in predicting firm performance, the other looks to factors internal to the organization. The external "industry forces" view derived much force from the work of Porter (1980) who applied principles of industrial economics to strategy. The dominant principle is that (industry) structure determines the conduct (strategy) of firms, and the collective conduct of firms then determines the overall performance of firms in the industry (Bain, 1968). Under these assumptions, strategy was concerned mainly with the placement of products in desirable market niches and defending those niches (Porter, 1980). A second perspective has been the resource-based view of the firm, which emphasizes unique combinations of resources that firms employ to obtain above-average rates of returns (Barney, 1986; Rumelt, 1974; Wernerfelt, 1984) . Extensions of the resource view have shifted the focus from unique tangible resources as competitively advantageous, to a focus on intangible assets, such as knowledge (Winter, 1987) , core competencies (Prahalad and Hamel, 1990) , or learning (Senge, 1990) as the primary source of advantage.

Whether internally or externally derived, these models of firm performance give little emphasis to shifts in information technology that devalue existing resources or market positions (Sampler and Short, 1994), or radical change approaches, such as reengineering, which disrupt established resource dependencies and/or processes of resource allocation.

At the heart of the second debate is whether strategy formulation and strategy implementation are distinct, separable activities. Many models of strategic planning assume this distinction and posit that strategy formulation initiates strategy development (Mineberg, 1990). Strategy is then implemented through a "series of subactivities which are primarily administrative" (Andrews, 1982).

Alternatively, other researchers hold that strategy formulation and implementation are not separable, that is, "'thinking cannot be separated from doing" (Mineberg, 1990). Here the argument is that strategies emerge incrementally over time (Mintzberg and Waters, 1985). The IS planning literature has also been influenced by the incremental view (Earl, 1994).

The two views have obvious implications for BPR. For example, is process reengineering a means of achieving resource-based competitive advantage? When implemented, can it help create or sustain advantageous product-market positions? Moreover, if these are the goals of BPR projects, how might BPR planning methodologies relate to contrasting models of the strategy-making process?

Information Systems

As the scope and importance of IS have increased within firms, IS planning agendas have evolved to broader strategy and organizational concerns (Venkatraman, 1991). Interrelationships between IS and other organizational functions have led to various approaches and methodologies for planning integration (Cash, McFarlan and McKinney, 1983; Earl, 1987; Henderson and Sifonis, 1988; King, 1978; King and Zmud, 1983; Lederer and Mendelow, 1989; Pyburn, 1983; Ward, 1987).

Henderson and Venkatraman (Henderson and Venkatraman, 1993) recast much of the earlier planning work in developing their proposed business—19 strategic alignment model (SAM). The SAM model is more comprehensive in that it extends the concept of alignment from the firm's business and IS strategy domain to the decisions undertaken by managers to design organizational units and the internal work processes and information flows necessary to execute strategy. However, the SAM framework was developed before attention to reengineering and process redesign rekindled interest in the enabling role of IT in process innovation and change (Davenport, 1992). The question thus presents itself: what are the implications of BPR for the strategic alignment model?

Managing Change and Control

BPR projects imply organizational change. Indeed, their goal may be strategic change. At present, however, there is no coherent theory of change within BPR research (Earl and Khan, 1994). The debate centers around whether radical or incremental change is most effective and how such shifts occur within organizations.

Much research has argued that the introduction of innovations or radical shifts must be paced with a gradual, persistent introduction into the organization. The logic is to allow for a period of adjustment to, and understanding of, the capabilities and implications of the innovation and/or radical change (Age and Aileen, 1970; Hughes, 1971; Rogers, 1983). In contrast, others have argued that following the introduction of an innovation, the period of adaptive behavior and change is relatively short (Tyre and Orlikowski, 1994). This suggests that radical shifts may have to be executed quickly, rather than gradually.

The decision of how to introduce an innovation is further complicated by the behavioral implications for those affected by the change. The typical radical change approach associated with BPR is to determine the new optimal procedures through various techniques and then to implement optimized procedures quickly (Hammer, 1990; Hammer and Champy, 1993). Such sweeping structural changes are intended to change behavior rapidly, but they also create uncertainty and insecurity (Tsunami, Newman and Romanelli, 1986). The contrary view is that people or team-building interventions, which are slower than structural interventions, will result in greater building of commitment (Beer, 1980).

The reengineering practitioners (Davenport, 1992; Hammer and Champy, 1993) also argue that performance measurement and management controls can help motivate and reinforce desired process-oriented behaviors. Research is tentative on this front, but the balanced scorecard systems of Kaplan and Norton (Kaplan and Norton, 1993), which stress internal metrics of excellence and learning as well as external measures, may provide a way forward. An alternative perspective is to recognize that controls and performance measures can be used to drive strategic renewal (Simons, 1994) including, presumably, BPR.

As described in Figure 1, these four perspectives ground our framework for analysis. In our preceding discussion we acknowledge that we may have implicitly suggested that effective integration of BPR, strategic business and IS planning requires an alignment between the four domains. In this sense, business process reengineering does prompt an added dimension for strategic alignment models such as that of Henderson and Venkatraman (1993). Thus, Figure 1 suggests a tentative "process alignment model." Its conceptual value may be either a revised alignment framework or an argument for adding a pro-

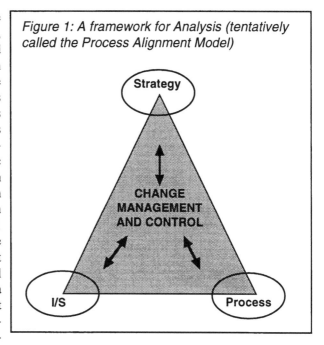

Figure 1: A framework for Analysis (tentatively called the Process Alignment Model)

cess dimension to existing alignment models. We address this question again at the end of the paper.

We turn now to assess qualitatively the interrelationships of the four domains in our case studies. We first outline our case methodology and case selection criteria. We then discuss the cases themselves, after which we derive and present a taxonomy of BPR strategies suggested by our analysis.

Methodology

We conducted four in-depth case studies over the last two years to help us understand how firms define and manage the relationship between business strategic planning, process reengineering projects, and IS strategic planning. Three of the four firms are large, diversified companies with significant market shares in their respective industries. The fourth is a mid-sized firm, ranked in the second half of the twenty largest building societies (savings and loan institutions) in the United Kingdom.

The unit of analysis in our company case studies was reengineering projects, defined as projects of at least six months' duration, incorporating dedicated personnel with the objective of using process-based concepts and tools to analyze, make recommendations upon, and change an existing business process. We conducted lengthy, semi-structured interviews in each company with three to ten interviewees, the number depending on the size and complexity of the reengineering project or projects under study. All interviewees were senior executives and/or line business managers with responsibility for strategic business planning, IS planning, and/or process reengineering. Where applicable, the entire reengineering team, composed generally of five to nine individuals, was interviewed at least once.

Interviews were supplemented by archival studies of reports, memoranda, and presentation materials in each firm. We gathered case-level data consistent with the logic and steps outlined in case study methodologies as described by Campbell (1975), Eisenhardt (1989) and Lee (1989), although work reported at this stage must be considered preliminary. In two companies, large-scale reengineering initiatives had been broken down into defined projects, and here we were able to look specifically at project work through its full cycle of planning and implementation. However, in the two other case studies reported, the reengineering initiatives were in different stages of execution. In the pharmaceutical company, for example, the firm (described later) had just completed the planning phase and was moving into project implementation. We describe our case selection procedures in greater detail below, after briefly outlining questions asked. As discussed earlier, we were interested in the evolution of BPR initiatives suggested by each of the four perspectives in our conceptual framework. Our main questions were as follows:

- What is the relationship between business strategy planning, IS planning, and process reengineering projects in the firm?
- To what extent are there defined planning roles and/or specified sequences of planning activities linking business strategy planning, IS planning, and BPR?
- How often are defined planning roles and/or activity sequences violated in the normal course of events?
- What are the key mechanisms for planning integration (e.g., teams, task forces, planning routines, planning behaviors, etc.)?
- What other factors influence planning roles and planning integration (e.g., political considerations, competitor actions, partner and/or alliance initiatives, etc.)?

For these questions, we interviewed the line business manager with responsibility for setting and implementing strategy in their respective strategic business units (SBUs). In all but one case, corporate strategic planning was not involved directly at the level of the process reengineering project. In one firm, however, reengineering projects were tied directly to the business strategic planning process. In the case of the U.K. building society, the reengineering sponsor was the firm's chief executive officer (CEO), and here we interviewed the senior management team and viewed reports responsible for specific implementation projects.

We selected the four case studies from a larger research effort underway studying sixteen reengineering projects in twelve firms. In each project, a minimum of four stakeholders were interviewed: project (reengineering) sponsor, project manager (operational), major customer, and business planner. On projects involving a clearly defined IS support role, the IS project manager or systems development manager was interviewed. Our survey instrument includes items in five areas: actors (roles) involved; project tasks (activities, tasks sequences); time (synchronization of activities, event criticality); resources (process-based methods and tools, IT support); and planning integration (relationship of project planning to business strategic and IS planning). Examples of questions in each of the five sections are given in the appendix.

Our four "archetypal" cases were selected on both analytical and practical grounds. Following Eisenhardt's (1989) discussion of theoretical sampling, we chose cases to help illustrate four "polar types" of planning integration observed in the larger sample. As Pettigrew (1992) and others have argued, given the limited number of cases that can be studied in many areas, and particularly here in the BPR-planning integration area, it makes sense to choose extreme cases where the focus of inquiry is "transparently observable." Moreover, practically speaking, the sixteen projects under study in the larger research effort were not all completed (many are multiyear efforts). We have elected in this paper to report on work in progress and on our observation of polar types with the view that this analysis will contribute to our emerging understanding of BPR planning integration.

To provide readers with a view of the full sample of sixteen reengineering projects, Table 1 illustrates each project by firm, industry, business objective, key process(es), and project status. We note that projects 1-4 in firms 1-4 were those selected as archetypes.

Case Study Results

We turn now to describing our four cases in two parts. The next section presents each case and detailed observations on planning integration. The section after that presents an aggregate analysis of all cases, organized by key factors emerging from the interviews and our analysis.

Organization 1: Semiconductor Manufacturing

Organization 1 is a large semiconductor manufacturing firm. Radical shifts in semiconductor product and process technologies have fundamentally changed the industry in recent years. Increasing demand for specialized (custom) chips has dramatically shortened product life-cycles for mainstay commodity products, accelerating time-based competition across the industry.

By the late 1980s, senior business unit executives at Organization 1 recognized that the company would have to derive the majority of its future revenues from custom manufactured products. The problem was "how to get there from here." A long string of process improvement and quality programs throughout the 1980s had been initiated with mixed results. Few interviewees disputed the importance of these efforts, but likewise, fewer still felt the efforts had been entirely successful.

A broad business unit reengineering program was begun in early 1990, supported by a new, internal process engineering competency group. Composed of functional managers, business analysts, and software developers experienced in manufacturing operations, systems analysis, and the then growing interest in specialized reengineering practices, the group was responsible for developing internal competencies in process concepts, methodologies and tools necessary for reengineering practice. By late 1990, the group had grown to twenty-three full-time professionals.

Working with-group-level and key functional managers, the internal process engineering team defined six core semiconductor business processes. These processes included strategy development, product development, customer design support, manufacturing development, and customer communications. A sixth process, order fulfillment, was selected as the first core process for reengineering. Three characteristics contributed to its selection: first, the large number of customer-facing interfaces and handoffs in the process; second, the implications for time compression, cost efficiencies, and improved customer interaction in simplifying the interfaces; third, the view that the benefit/risk of tackling OF was more easily calculated than for the other core processes, OF was defined broadly as starting with a customer need for a specific product and ending with the receipt of the product at the customer's site. To document the OF process, and the effect of interventions on the order flows of semiconductor products, the team used process decomposition and analysis techniques suggested by industry research and developed internally by the process engineering team. Following three months of intensive work, the team recommended to senior management that process improvement activities already underway were insufficient: OF required redesign.

Group management's decision to completely reengineer OF was formalized in late 1992. The reengineering team continued work on disaggregating and defining key workflows and documenting "best in class" performance in each process category. For example, for the order entry process, the team used airline reservations agents as the benchmark process. Team members visited several travel reservations systems (TRS) to evaluate reservations procedures and agent workflows. An early comparison showed that while a typical reservations agent could book a complex travel agenda in under twenty minutes, the semiconductor firm's "reservations activities" involved many individuals and could take as long as two weeks to schedule an order.

The team completed its analysis by mid-1993, recommending a two-phase implementation plan including process education for employees and "showcase" pilot projects to provide "proof of concepts" to build support for reengineering change initiatives. Interviewees reported that several problem areas have arisen as the business unit moved further into reengineering implementation: first, the high-level process mapping exercises are moving quickly to more granular subprocesses, where negotiations on resource utilization, workflows, and management responsibilities are more operationally complex. Resistance among functional managers is increasing as tradeoff decisions on component lot sizes, line speeds, and inventory holding become more complex to negotiate. Second, dependence on better information technology in areas including information access, software development, and communications is escalating rapidly, partly driven by the increased need for functional managers to negotiate tradeoff decisions.

Third, new metrics for process improvement have invariably been added to existing functional metrics, thereby increasing complexity in measurement and control. As one senior manufacturing manager told us, "increasingly our jobs will be to simplify the measures of performance as we move to the next level of redesign. We've tended to do the reverse—to add metrics while keeping the old ones around for comfort. In many cases, the two tell you to do different things. It's not always clear how to sort them out."

The decisions taken at Organization 1 emphasize the importance of manufacturing operations and supply chain logistics in reengineering. Strategy formation was seen classically as product-market-customer segmentation, and the implications of changing product technologies in customer use. Reengineering was defined chiefly as functional integration and metrics to measure end-to-end cycle time improve-

Table 1: Case Data, Field Study of Process Reengineering Projects 1991-94

Firm	Project	Industry	Business objective	Key processes	Project status
1	1	Semiconductor manufacturing	Reduced cycle time Customer integration	Order fulfillment	3
2	2	Insurance	Restructure cost base Reduced cycle time	Underwriting Claims	3
3	3	Pharmaceutical	New product development Reduced cycle time	Design (R&D) Development Launch	2
4	4	Financial services	Improved management communications, decision making	Direction Management Implementation Management Understanding	2
5	5	Manufacturing	Restructure cost base Reduced cycle time Customer integration	Integrated supply chain	3
6	6	Manufacturing	Business and systems integration Improved marketing	Integrated planning, logistics, and financial management	4
7	7	Communications	Customer integration (corporate customers)	Network provisioning	3
7	8	Communications	Residential customer quality	Billing Revenue assurance	4
8	9	Construction	Forward integration (Independent agents)	Job identification (project specification)	4
8	10	Construction	Backward integration (functional integration)	Sell (sales) Mill (manufacturing information) Roll (order scheduling) Bill (billing, credit information)	4
9	11	Financial services	Customer Integration (corporate customers)	New product development	4
9	12	Financial services	Functional integration Lower costs Improve quality	Accounts reconciliation Cash management	4
10	13	Health care services	Customer integration Lower order costs	Customer communications Order management	4
10	14	Health care services	Cost reduction Improved decision making	Financial accounting Accounts payable Accounts receivable	2
11	15	Petroleum	Cost reduction Improved decision making	Financial control Inventory control Fixed assets	4
12	16	Health care services	New business development	Provider networks Financial planning Financial control Service quality	2

Key: Project status: 1 = approved; 2 = in progress; 3 = nearing completion, 4 = completed.

ment. The role of IS was largely to contribute skills in systems analysis as part of the broader reengineering methodology developed by the process engineering group.

We have selected the label "engineering strategy" to describe the activities undertaken by Organization 1. This strategy is related to industrial engineering and process engineering projects where the goal is optimization of work flows and the precise scheduling and coordination of interdependent work tasks and related activities. The BPR projects evolved independently of formal business or strategic IS planning, yet the project strategy could achieve strategic change. The engineering strategy appears to be the generally implied approach to BPR in the majority of cases and literature to date.

Organization 2: Property and Casualty Insurance

Organization 2 is a large, multi-line property and casualty insurance company. This industry has been hit by a variety of competitive threats in the last decade, ranging from severe earthquakes, storms, and other environmental hazards, to declining profitability in traditional product and service lines in many customer segments. Some insurers have aggressively targeted niche market segments in mature product areas with favorable results. But many of the older, traditional carriers have faced steadily eroding market share and losses.

Organization 2 has lost money in the property and casualty (P&C) market since the late 1980s, with subsequent downgrading of the firm's Standard and Poor's bond rating. Interviewees reported that numerous reorganizations, most focused on realigning headquarters and field staff ratios and responsibilities, had failed to take the required effect.

In the early 1990s, the decision was made to reorganize the P&C division into multiple business areas and to restructure field operations to change customer and agent (distributor) relationships. In this decision, the initial planning sequence began classically with business strategy and structure. Product service market areas, and their respective field operations implementation, were refocused and reorganized. This was led by senior management-the sponsor was the P&C division president.

The second initiative focused on reengineering division-level "macro" business processes (planning phase). This effort, led jointly by IS systems personnel and line business managers, defined upwards of fifteen different processes using structured process decomposition techniques developed by the team and taken from various industry sources. The project team itself, which ranged from six to ten individuals over the course of the initiative, followed a participate design strategy to maximize employee ownership of the results. The team gathered data from a large percentage of the total number of employees in the business unit (almost 20 percent), through surveys, interviews, customer workshops, "brown paper process modeling sessions," and other meeting and data input formats. The methodology and process analysis approach emphasized workflows and their associated information flows within the business unit.

Following the process design and reengineering phase, the team turned to implementation activities, focusing on several cross-functional "streams" keyed to expected impact on revenue performance. For example, streams focused on underwriting, claims, and producer (new business) processes, supported by IS. The implementation plans for the various projects were timed between twelve and twenty-four months.

The emphasis and procedures taken at Organization 2 emphasize a classic top-down strategy, bottom-up implementation approach. Reengineering was initiated after decisions regarding business strategy and structure were taken. The participative approach to generating process designs and reengineering alternatives across the division emphasized both senior management and team concerns with implementation effectiveness. The IS roles in this effort were judged by interviewees as contributing process analysis (systems analysis) skills, as providing adequate communications and information access to support redesigned business processes, as "broker" between multiple business functions coming together in the new process design. With the exception of greater emphasis on process as opposed to purely systems design, these IS roles are well-understood responsibilities in any large cross-functional systems project.

We denote Organization 2's activities as "systems strategy." IS planning has largely driven BPR initiatives and systems analysis is a central activity. Providing information access and communications is a goal of business and systems (architectural) design. The success of such a strategy is heavily dependent on the state of partnership between business and IS professionals in the firm. Surveys, interviews, "brown paper bag modeling sessions" and the like organized by company 2 can be seen as necessary prerequisites to build and sustain the required partnership.

Organization 3: Pharmaceuticals

Organization 3 is a large, diversified pharmaceuticals firm. In response to the many changes in health care policy and administration taking place in the United States and Europe over the last decade, this firm, like its primary competitors, has acquired several related health care businesses and focused on improving internal operations. Company profitability has remained strong even given the state of industry flux, but there is widespread concern that the industry at large is entering a period of reduced profitability amid increased regulatory unrest.

In early 1992, the company's CEO announced a broad corporate initiative focused on the company's core values, its leadership practices, and the linkages of these values and practices to daily work. The initiative followed top executive visits to manufacturing and service firms in Japan, Europe, and the United States. While not formally a benchmarking exercise, the trips served to heighten senior management attention to innovative practices implemented in selected 'best in class" firms.

A decision was made soon thereafter to rethink the firm's strategy and operating plans, with emphasis on strategic planning, process integration, and "breakthrough projects" targeted at new product development (discussed below). Interviewees noted that the clear emphasis of management was on "reenergizing" the link between planning and action. "The problem," one interviewee noted, "was that too often plans were thrown over the wall for implementation without clear guidelines for action and follow-up. This was recognized as an old problem that had to be solved."

A dedicated cross-functional team, composed of nine business and IS managers, was put together in mid- 1992. The team made an early commitment to new group-oriented software products then coming on market. The software served two key purposes: as the team's own internal workflow analysis system and as the team's project archive. The team's immediate activity over the next ten months was to develop a high-level planning methodology with the stated emphasis on explicitly linking planning activities to "measurable outcomes."

The team devised an "integral 10:3:1 planning cycle," composed of a ten-year planning forecast, three-year requirements for capabilities development, and one-year "breakthrough" reengineering projects. The ten-year planning forecast developed both business (customer, product, market) and process strategies, where processes were defined as major operational activities supported by sustaining processes. For example, operational processes included drug discovery, drug development, and drug launch, supported by sustaining processes including human resources, finance, and information technology.

The ten-year plan included requirements for three-year "core capabilities" development, these capabilities serving as platforms for breakthrough process improvement projects. "Breakthrough" projects were in turn implemented through multiple one-year reengineering projects. For example, as part of the ten-year forecast, the team defined three core business processes for new product development: product creation, demand creation, and order fulfillment. Within these three core business processes, three-year requirements for five breakthrough projects were defined: for product creation, drug discovery and drug development; for demand creation, new product launch and life-cycle management; and for order fulfillment, supply chain management. For each breakthrough project, processes were identified for one year reengineering projects. For example, within drug development, reengineering projects were defined for clinical trial supplies, clinical study processes, and regulatory dossier preparation. In all cases, the process analysts' approach emphasized workflows and their associated information flows across functional units.

The strategy planning—process integration approach was piloted in 1993. Two pilots were run sequentially to allow refinements to be transferred from pilot one to pilot two. Interviewees report that the 10: 3:1 planning framework (1) legitimizes investment in process capabilities as an important element of competitive strategy at the business unit level; (2) provides a defined sequence of activities integrating strategy and process planning objectives; (3) tends to locate the selection criteria for breakthrough projects away from political or other considerations; and (4) "more rationally" drives reengineering project selection. Adopting the framework, interviewees noted, was widely understood by most line business managers to have elevated the process concept into the strategy domain.

Regarding the role of IS, again, as we saw in Organizations 1 and 2, a major activity was to contribute systems analysis and project management skills to the team planning effort. An added role was to influence and facilitate the team's investment in group support software for internal workflow coordination and project data archiving.

We denote Organization 3's planning approach "bureaucratic strategy" because it relies on formal planning procedures and coordination of interdependent subtasks reminiscent of rule-based approaches falling under a mechanistic model of organization (Emery, 1969; Galbraith, 1973) . Such models have been shown to be robust in hierarchically coordinating large numbers of interdependent subtasks, but have limited capacity to reexamine and/or remake decisions. Organization 3's efforts to "informate" the planning process with group-oriented software can be seen to address part of the problem of effective lateral decision processes (Galbraith, 1973). However, the team's charter did not include reexamining managerial decision making, even if adoption of the group-oriented software could be viewed as a precursor to exactly this issue.

Organization 4: Building Society

Organization 4 is a mid-sized building society in the United Kingdom, providing mortgage loans to home buyers and financing these mortgages through savings accounts with different terms, rates, and tax benefits. Industry deregulation in the late 1980s found larger, nationwide building societies entering banking and insurance markets. While several of the mid-sized building societies intended to follow suit, a downturn in the economy and uncertain profitability in several larger firms forestalled many of these efforts, Organization 4 among them.

In mid-1990, Organization 4 began a series of internal changes to prepare for the expected, though postponed, entry into new financial markets. The traditional centralized head office, working through a region and branch structure, was reorganized into product divisions better able to specialize in different product markets and absorb newly acquired businesses (much of the growth in this industry in the late 1980s had come through acquisitions and mergers). This added cost in the short run and increased fragmentation in a company unused to the idea of differentiated, and at times competing, product market strategies. There was also concern over profitability. The company had survived in the economic downturn, but turnover was below projections.

Market shifts and structural change in the organization set the stage for what senior management described as "an organizational experiment" built around the radical reshaping of management processes. The top dozen senior managers in the company were called together for a week-long retreat and asked to bring their problems and solutions with them. The mission and goals were still to drive the organization, but management processes—the ways in which managers around the company came together to set business strategy, develop implementation plans, allocate people and resources, and measure progress—were to change. The company's leadership wanted to do more than designate teams and other cross-functional, coordination mechanisms; the intent was to reshape the processes by which managers worked on a day-to-day basis in the firm.

The first step was to design a new set of management processes that emphasized decision making and communications flows across managers in the company. This necessitated two major changes across the organization (the "organizational experiment"): a new way of describing how work was done, and a complete replacement of old definitions of what was done. In brief, all job titles were thrown out, and a new language for organizational roles, meetings, and teamwork was introduced. For example, all "'jobs" were redefined as "roles"; "meetings" were recast as "events"; "'team members" became "team players." The intent was to reinforce a new way of working by introducing a new "corporate language" for describing work.

At the senior management level, the executive team defined three "macro" management processes: the Direction Management Process (DMP), which included business development and customer relationships; the Implementation Management

Process (IMP), which defined the required capabilities to implement decisions taken by the DMP; and the Understanding Process (UP), discussed in more detail below. Examples of the IMP process included process architecture (somewhat analogous to the process engineering function in a manufacturing organization), customer engagement processes, process quality measurements, customer satisfaction processes, and risk management.

The direction management and implementation processes were themselves defined within a company-wide Understanding Process (UP). The Understanding Process involved a substantial commitment by managers, supervisors, and employees to continuously appraise and solicit interaction and comments from all personnel in the firm. The goal was to continuously surface issues and problem areas across the entire company every two weeks. The output to the cycle was "understanding events," typically large meetings (often company-wide) involving all levels of management held when an internal "issueometer" reached a pre-specified level (the "issueometer" was a "problem metric" devised to assess the frequency and severity of issues raised in the biweekly cycle). Of course, company-wide or otherwise very large "understanding events" were not required at every two-week cycle, but the intent of the system was to allow different groupings of "team players" to call for events as circumstances dictated. The frequency of events varied widely according to need, but in one IMP project, seven understanding events were held in the first two weeks to clarify direction and allocations of team resources.

The image created by these process definitions and cycles of management participation in direction, implementation, and understanding processes is one of continuously appraising what (DMP) and how (IMP) work was done. This echoes Deming's (1987) Plan-Do-Check-Act (PDCA) sequence—indeed, many of the pictures produced by Organization 4 describing the cycling of managerial work in the DMP, IMP, and UP processes are reminiscent of Deming's point that PDCA cycles represent work on processes, not on specific tasks or problems (the assertion is that processes can never be "solved," only worked on, and in this cycle problems get solved) (Walton, 1987).

The new process design was rolled out in 1993. As noted, implementation required new role definitions for all employees, new forms of personnel assessment and development, new payment systems-in short, a different culture of managerial operations. Resistance to these changes had been tempered by skepticism that the new design would actually take hold, but as implementation rolled out, a number of managers and employees left, uncomfortable with the changes. A relatively small percentage of employees was asked to leave (under 5 percent). A year after the "experiment, " work force retention has been surprisingly high (over 80 percent), although much of this can perhaps be explained by regional employment patterns in the United Kingdom and the depressed state of financial services employment generally.

Interviewees reported that one or two problems were the most difficult: the changes required in personal attitudes about how work was completed and evaluated (for example, how individuals worked with each other became an explicit determinant of pay), and the uncertainty created in focusing first on how things were done, not on what was done. Managers and employees long accustomed to working on specific problems, tasks, and/or processes found the emphasis on events, communications, and direction setting difficult and time-consuming. The perception among many who left was that "little work was getting done." The belief among those making the changes was that attention to "how" (e.g., processes) meant that the "right work was getting done."

The role of IS in the changes to organization design was minimal in terms of technology. Few projects concentrated on systems *per se*—those that did focused on customer information (the Customer Requirements Implementation Process was one example). However, interviewees believed that IS personnel brought important systems thinking to the process design, although this expertise was often poorly communicated.

More important than the role of IS in supporting the process change was the role of the process change on IS. The IT function was reorganized around processes, including systems development, information design, and customer systems. The systems development process team developed and used a rule-based system development methodology incorporating object-oriented design. When the company producing the object-oriented software went into liquidation, Organization 4 acquired the intellectual rights to the product.

In the first year of the new organization, costs fell and profits rose by over 60 percent in a flat mortgage market. The result quelled many a skeptic, although top management at Organization 4 believe that the "experiment" is still very much in its early stages.

We denote the strategy undertaken at Organization 4 "ecological" as the scale and pattern of attempted change are reminiscent of Hannan and Freeman's (1989) work on organizational ecology (in particular, their contention that organizations are structured systems of routines). Much of Organization 4's efforts to redefine roles, processes, and communications presupposes the view that structural inertia (conditions that impede change) must be overcome by changes of state in structured routines. This is much the sense of Organization's 4's "experiment" in evolutionary change.

Four Strategies for BPR

The four cases selected can be seen, we argue, as archetypes of different BPR strategies. Using the four domains outlined in the conceptual framework illustrated in Figure 1, these strategies are presented as "polar types" in Table 2.

The "engineering strategy" typified by Organization 1 has the characteristics of an improvement project driven by identification of an operational problem where process reengineering is one part of the required business change. We have seen similar characteristics in a BPR program in a major photocopier company. In both cases it was clear that the firms were no longer competitive in order fulfillment. Benchmarking of best in class lead times and inventory management influenced reengineering goals and helped make the case for radical performance improvement. Cross-functional teams of line managers were assembled to design new and integrated cross-functional and cross-entity production, logistics, and inventory processes. Workflow analysts identified redundant stops and time buffers, plus activities that were performed well from a local perspective, but not from a global process level. In each case, one particular IT application was required in the

Table 2: BPR Strategies

BPR strategies	Process Perspective		Strategy perspective		IS perspective		Change management perspective	
	Process paradigm	Process attributes	Strategic motive	Strategic scope	Dominant IS contribution	IS expertise	Change initiation	Change sponsor
Ecological	Process as management design	Decision responsibilities and decision flows	Dynamic adaptation	Enterprise	Process consciousness	Systems modeling	Vision	CEO
Bureaucratic	Process as corecapability	Value chains & workflows	Resource capability	SBU	Process construction	Systems awareness	Strategic planning	SBU Management team
Systems	Process as systems opportunity	Information systems opportunities & information workflows	Information leverage	Cross-functional information-intensive activities	Process coordination	Systems analysis	IS planning	Process owner
Engineering	Process as workflow optimization	Work roles activities & workflows	Benchmarking & efficiency	Cross-functional operations-intensive activities	Process integration	Systems design	Operational problem	Line management

reengineered process. In the semiconductor company it was a worldwide "reservation system" for order taking and scheduling. In the photocopier company, it was a supply chain decision support system to inform all managers in the nodes between functional organizations and supply chain processes of time and resource interdependencies across the chain.

The "systems strategy" typified by Organization 2 identifies reengineering opportunities through IS planning, where often investment priorities are positively weighted in favor of BPR projects. For a period in Organization 2 when information systems proposals were made, those with apparent BPR potential were subjected to short "fly-by" feasibility studies involving benchmarking, rough benefits assessment, and evaluation of management willingness to change. If the outcome was promising, a fuller review of strategic needs, operational performance, and systems requirements was commissioned. In a food and drink company, the corporate IS group had authority to review all business unit IS plans. If an opportunity was found to initiate a BPR study, a corporately funded consulting team was sent in to do much the same sort of business systems analysis as in Organization 2.

As described earlier, the project work in Organization 2 then took on the character of what one observer has called "doing information systems work properly." We see in the systems strategy the application of systems analysis skills at the process level, and an emphasis on both work flows and information flows using traditional and more modern flowcharting techniques. Providing information access and communications for coordination becomes the goal of systems design, Projects, however, are most probably led by managers who have performance responsibility for the process, but work in close partnership with the IS function.

The "bureaucratic strategy" uses formal strategic planning to promote and legitimize the idea of formulating and investing in process capabilities as one element of competitive strategy at the SBU level. As epitomized by Organization 3, business strategy-making comprises both product-market-customer decisions and process decisions, the latter concerned with the building of core capabilities to support the former. Typically the focus of a BPR project becomes a breakthrough activity in the primary value chain, thereby having potentially high customer impact.

In our archetypal case, IS expertise raised BPR awareness by arranging management team seminars and workshops, typically employing both external consultants and in-house BPR expertise. Where breakthrough reengineering projects were identified, the IS function was involved in building new or replacement process infrastructures including IT applications, operational procedures, and performance metrics. Momentum, however, depends on continued commitment of the management team, and, critically, sponsorship and championship by one of its members. Otherwise token or ephemeral BPR initiatives can result in compliance with the formal strategic planning regime.

The "ecological strategy" of Organization 4 is much more of an holistic, cultural approach intended to raise process consciousness and establish a new routine of managerial decision making. The espoused logic is that if management decision-making processes are redesigned to engage all levels of the organization, BPR initiatives and related continuous process improvements implemented through specific implementation projects—will result. In Organization 4, the CEO and top management team began this by creating three "macro" processes: the Direction

Management Process, the Implementation Management Process, and the Understanding Process.

New language and roles were defined to achieve culture change and to raise process consciousness. In two large FMCG (fast-moving consumer goods) companies, we have found CEOs who changed the performance measurement systems to emphasize customer service, product development time, quality and brand share. In both cases, line managers then turned to BPR as a means of initiating performance improvement on these metrics.

In our archetypal case, the CEO believed that he and the management team were engaged in an "organizational experiment" to achieve a vision of continuous, dynamic adaptation. The IS function had a limited and relatively late role in this endeavor. Systems were to be adapted to report on, and render more visible, process performance. As BPR initiatives were identified, CASE-based modeling software was used to reconceptualize core processes. We select the label "ecological" because of the emphasis on creating deep-seated process thinking throughout the organization in the pursuit of organizational adaptation.

These four strategies suggest that a richer and wider set of BPR practices is being deployed in organizations than has been documented hitherto. Implications arise for both research and practice.

Implications and Conclusions

The research underpinning this paper was done in the spirit of grounded theory (Glaser and Strauss, 1961), exploring reengineering initiatives in the field to examine interactions or integration of planning processes and BPR. Following the advice of Eisenhardt (1989), we selected four distinctive case studies from our sample that demonstrated substantial and interesting variation across the four domains of the framework for analysis shown in Figure 1. The cases suggest four strategies for BPR that we have structured as a taxonomy of polar typos or clusterings (Table 2) that can be identified in cases other than those presented here.

Inevitably, a taxonomy based on such inductive and interpretive enquiry is tentative. Nevertheless we suggest that there are several implications for reengineering practice and some potentially promising directions for further research.

Implications for Practice

First, the taxonomy reinforces the view that there is more than one way of initiating and implementing BPR. We do not at this stage offer any contingency theories to propose the contexts in which each of the BPR strategies may work. Indeed, there may be an element of choice here, particularly as demonstrated by our examples of the ecological strategy, where the CEOs pursued very personal campaigns to change their organizations. Nor can we claim that any strategy is more effective than others. However, our data suggest that the engineering and systems strategies may result in more definitive and enduring BPR projects. In contrast, the bureaucratic and ecological strategies may have created more widespread process and BPR awareness in the organizations in question.

Indeed, each strategy does appear to favor, produce, or imply a different concept of process. The levels of analysis and the motivations, labeled in Table 2 process attributes and process paradigm in use, are substantially different. We do not make any value judgments about each, but we do suggest that the taxonomy is useful in extending whatever process thinking managers and reengineers initially adopt. For example, the more conventional view of BPR, represented by the engineering strategy as cross-functional workflow optimization, has instant, practical appeal. Considering information systems developments as vehicles for BPR or BPR as a means of implementing more viable system—is potentially a further valuable political insight implied by the systems strategy. Seeing BPR as a means of building requisite core capabilities, as depicted in the bureaucratic strategy, is both a way of identifying and selecting reengineering projects and a vehicle for reminding management that business strategy comprises more than just product-market analysis and positioning. Seeing BPR as an opportunity to rethink management processes and improve decision making, as embodied by the ecological strategy, again widens the reengineering opportunity set as well as suggesting the creation of an organizational context in which BPR projects may be propagated.

The different strategic perspectives also serve to remind practitioners that there may be alternative sources of competitive advantage to that of best-in-class operational performance implied by the engineering strategy. Indeed, the systems, administrative, and ecological strategies may create in turn more sustainable sources of competitive advantage. The systems strategy may do so by leveraging firm-specific information assets, the bureaucratic strategy by aligning process investment with product-market positioning, and the ecological strategy by achieving deeper-seated changes in managers' mindsets, ultimately manifesting itself in higher-quality decisions.

The enabling role of information technology is seen to vary within each strategy, implying that not all BPR projects require substantial investment in IT. An important but not necessarily dominant investment in IT applications is likely under the engineering and systems strategies, respectively. The idea of process architectures seems to fit the bureaucratic strategy, especially where core operational capabilities are being laid down. Under the ecological strategy, information systems are required for quite different purposes, either for modeling new ways of thinking or to direct attention to process metrics in performance measurement.

For IS managers in particular, we also can suggest that the requisite skill set will vary. Creative systems designers may propose sophisticated solutions for process integration within engineering strategies. The skills of systems analysis, including the rediscovered techniques of operations research, industrial engineering, and organization and methods, can help convert IS projects into more radical BPR exercises under the systems strategy. Besides building architectures, we have seen IS personnel very much acting as reengineering educators and consultants under bureaucratic strategies. The expertise—technical and behavioral—of modelers may be required in the ecological strategy.

Finally, practitioners probably will recognize the importance of sponsorship in business process reengineering, but our taxonomy proposes that the level and character of sponsorship vary widely. In our cases, where CEO sponsorship really mattered was in the ecological strategy. Other line and staff managers become candidates for sponsorship under the other three remaining strategies.

Directions for Research

Several of the implications for practice also prompt questions for further research. However, the overriding need is to test the taxonomy further for completeness, robustness, and content. Completeness may be addressed by replicating our investigation on a larger sample of BPR initiatives. Testing for robustness of the four (or more) polar type strategies requires more classical research methods, starting with operationalization of our four domains into measurable constructs. Then tighter cluster analysis can be done and tests of association carried out between the BPR strategies and the suggested components.

There also may be a prior or complementary need to test our conceptual framework for analysis—that is, to refine further our "process alignment model." This implies the need for integration between the domains of process, strategy, information systems, and change management and control. Certainly by using this framework for analysis, a degree of alignment is suggested in each of our four strategies. The operationalized constructs discussed above could be employed in tests of alignment.

Both academics and practitioners are likely to be interested in more evaluative research. It would be interesting to examine whether any particular BPR strategy outperforms others. Tests of success are notoriously difficult in the planning arena; a variety of quantitative and qualitative assessments would be required of both the process and outcomes of the strategies.

Finally, some obvious contingency tests are possible. For example, are certain BPR strategies associated with differences in planning and control style, organization size, external environment, industry sector, or information-processing contexts? Indeed, are they mutually exclusive?

Conclusion

These directions for further research could be important in advancing business process reengineering from the status of a contemporary phenomenon to a more robust management practice with stronger theoretical foundations . We submit that understanding of linkages between business process reengineering and strategic planning is likely to rest in the four domains that made up our initial framework for analysis: process, strategy, information systems, and change management and control. Our taxonomy could provide a useful platform for researchers interested in carrying out more field studies of BPR and strategy. In the meantime, it also offers some managerial implications for those actually engaged in business process reengineering.

Appendix: Interview Questionnaire: Selected Questions

A. Respondent Background Information

"Please give us some background information on your current role and previous experience."

A1. Describe your current role and responsibilities.
A2. How long have you been in your current role?
A3. Whom do you report to?
A4. How long have you been with the company?

A5. What was your last position?

B. Project History

"A very important part of our work is develop a picture of the (reengineering) project's history. First we'll ask you to describe the project, and then we'll move to questions about the project's developmental history."

B1. What was the project? (respondent's definition)

B2. What was the composition of the project team and/or major stakeholders? (e.g., what were the key project roles?)

B3. What were the major goals and objectives of the project as you see them? (three or four most important only)

B4. What was the rough timeline for completion? (if the project is nearing completion, please give anticipated completion date).

B5. Was the project completed on schedule? (if no, where were the delays? What were the sources of the delays?)

B6. How did the company come to inmate the project?
B6.1 Was there a triggering event?
B6.2 Who proposed the project?
B6.3 Did anyone oppose it? Who? Why?
B6.4 How was the opposition conveyed?

B7. Once the decision for action was made:
B7.1 What were the main project activities and implementation plan?
B7.2 How did those favoring the project support it during the major phases?
B7.3 What did those opposing the project do?
B7.4 Did sponsorship change over the course of the project?

C. Functional Integration, Organizational Change

C1. Which functional organizations were involved?

C2. At what stages of the project did they become involved?

C3. Did the number of functional organizations involved remain the same over the life of the project? If not, please explain.

C4. What role(s) did IT play on this project?
C4.1 What is your evaluation of IT's contribution?

C5. What types of organizational changes have occurred?
C5.1 Were these changes anticipated?
C5.2 How were anticipated changes communicated to those affected?

C6. Were any change management programs or techniques used?
C6.1 If so, what and how did they work?
C6.2 Who was involved?

D. Planning Integration

D1. Please describe the firm's general business planning process.

D2. What formal procedures are in place to link different planning agendas in the firm? (e.g.. strategy, IS, process reengineering, change management and HRM)

D3. Are there informal mechanisms? If yes, what are they?

E. Use of Process Methods and Tools

E1. Did the (business unit) (reengineering team) evaluate process-oriented methodologies and tools for its own use?

E1.1 Which ones?

E1.2 What was decided? (e.g., what action was taken?)

E2. Did the (business unit) (reengineering team) evaluate process-oriented methodologies and tools for informing and/or educating customers?

E2.1 Which ones?

E2.2 What was decided?

E3. If yes to E1 and/or E2, what is your evaluation of the effectiveness of the methodologies and/or tools used?

F. Project Results

"We'd like now to ask you about the results of the project."

F1. What were the key performance results?

F2. Were there different short-term and long-term performance impacts?

F3. What were the key lessons learned?

References

Andrews, K.R. (1982). *The Concept of Corporate Strategy.* Homewood, IL: Irwin.

Bain, J.S. (1968). *Industrial Organization,* 2d ed. New York: Wiley.

Barley, S.R.; Meyer, G.W.; and Gash, DC. (1988). Cultures of culture: academics, practitioners, and the pragmatics of normative control. *Administrative Science Quarterly, 33,* 24-60.

Barney. J.B. (1986). Strategic factor markets: expectations, luck and business strategy. *Management Science,* 32, 1231-1241.

Beer, M. (1980). *Organization Change and Development.* Santa Monica, CA: Goodyear.

Campbell, D.T III (1975). "Degrees of freedom" and the case study. *Comparative Political Studies,* 8.2, 178-193.

Caron, J.R.; Jarvenpaa, S.L.; and Stoddard, D.B. (1994). Business reengineering at CIGNA Corporation: experiences and lessons from the first five years. *MIS Quarterly,* 18.3,233-250.

Cash, J.I.; McFarlan, F W.; and McKinney, J. L. (1983) *Corporate Information Systems Management: Text and Cases.* Homewood, IL: Irwin.

Daft, R.L., and Lewin, A.Y. (1993). Where are the theories for the "new" organizational forms? an editorial essay. *Organization Science* 4,4, i-vi.

Davenport, T H. (1992). *Process Innovation.* Boston: Harvard Business School press.

Davenport, T.H. and Short. J E. (1990) The new Industrial engineering: information technology and business process redesign. *Slogan Management Review* 31(4), 11-2 1.

Davenport, T.H. , and Stoddard, D.B. (1994). Reengineering: business change of mythic proportions? *MIS Quarterly.* 18(2), 121-127.

Drazin. R , and Sandelands (1992). L Autogenesis: a perspective on the process of organizing *Organization Science,* 3(2), 230-249.

Earl, M.J. (1987). Information systems strategy formulation. In R J. Boland. Jr, and R.A. Hirscheim (eds), *Critical Issues in Information Systems Research* Chichester, UK: Wiley.

Earl, M.J. (1994). The new and the old of business process redesign. *Journal of Strategic Information Systems,* 3(1), 5-22.

Earl, M J , and Khan, B. How new is business process redesign? *European Management Journal,* 12, I (1994). 20-30.

Eisenhardt K.M. (1989). Budding theories from case study research. *Academy of Management Journal,* 35(4), 699-138.

Emery, J.C.(1969). *Organizational Planning and Control Systems.* New York: Macmillan.

Forrester, J.W.(1961). *Industrial Dynamics.* Cambridge, MA: MIT Press.

Galbraith, J.R. (1973). *Designing Complex Organizations.* Reading, MA: Addison-Wesley.

Gersick, C.J G. (1991). Revolutionary change theories: a multilevel exploration of the punctuated equilibrium paradigm. *Academy of Management Renew, 16(1),* 10-36.

Glaser, B G , and Strauss, A.L. (1961). *The Discovery of Grounded Theory. Strategies for Qualitative Research.* New York: Aldine.

Grover, V.; Fiedler, K.D.; and Teng, J.T.C. (1994). Exploring the success of information technology enabled business process reengineering. *IEEE Transactions OR Information Management,* 4(3), 276-283.

Age, J., and Aileen, M.(1970). *Social Change in Complex Organizations.* New York: Random House.

Hammer. M. (1990). Reengineering work: don't automate, obliterate. *Harvard Business Review,* 90(4), 104-112.

Hammer, M., and Champy, J. (1993). *Reengineering the Corporation A Manifesto for Business Revolution.* New York: Harper Business, 1993.

Hannan, M.T., and Freeman. J. (1989). *Organizational Ecology.* Cambridge, MA: Harvard University Press.

Harrington, H.J.(1991). *Business Process Improvement.* New York: McGraw Hill.

Henderson, J.C., and Sifonis, J.G. (1988). The value of strategic planning: understanding consistency, validity and IS markets. *MIS Quarterly,* 12(2), 187-200.

Henderson, J.C., and Venkatraman, N. (1993). Strategic alignment: leveraging information technology for transforming organizations. *IBM Systems Journal,* 32(1), 4-1 6.

Hughes, W.R. (1971). Scale frontiers in electric power. In W.M. Capron (ed.), *Technological Change in Regulated Industries.* Washington, DC: Brookings Institute.

Kaplan, R.B.. and Murdock. L (1991). Core process renewal. *McKinsey Quarterly,* 2, 15-26.

Kaplan, R., and Norton, D. (1992). The balanced scorecard: measures that drive performance. *Harvard Business Review* (January-February).

King, W.R. (1978). Strategic planning for management information systems. *MIS Quarterly,* 2, 27-37.

King, W R., and Zmud, R.W. (1983). Managing information systems policy planning, strategic planning and operational planning. *Proceedings of the Second ICIS,* December.

Lederer, A.L., and Mendelow, A.L.(1989). Coordination of information systems plans with business plans. *Journal of Management Information System, 6(2),* 5-19.

Lee, A. S. (1989). A scientific methodology for MIS case studies. *MIS Quarterly,* 13(1), 33-50.

Malone, T.W., and Crowston, K. (1994). The interdisciplinary study of coordination. *ACM Computing Surveys,* 26(1), 87-119.

Mintzberg, H., and Waters, J.A. (1985). Of strategies. deliberate and emergent. *Strategic Management Journal,* 6, 257-272.

Mineberg, H. (1990). The design school. reconsidering the basic premises of strategic management. *Strategic Management Journal. 11,* 171-195.

Mohr, L.B. (1982). Explaining Organizational *Behaviour. San* Francisco. CA: Jossey-Bass.

Pettigrew, A M. (1992). The character and significance of strategy process research. *Strategic Management Journal,* special issue (Winter), 5-16.

Pfeffer, J , and Salancik. G. (1978). *The External Control of Organizations. New* York. Harper and Row.

Porter, M.E.(1980). *Competitive Strategy Techniques for Analyzing Industries and Competitors.* New York: Free Press.

Prahalad,C.K ,and Hamel, G. (1990). The core competence of the corporation. *Harvard Business Review* (May-June), 79-91.

Pyburn, P . (1983). Linking the MIS plan and corporate strategy: an exploratory study *MIS Quarterly,* 7(2), 1-14.

Rogers, E.M.(1983). *Diffusion of Innovations.* New York : Free Press.

Rumelt, R.P. (1974). *Strategy Structure and Economic Performance.* Cambridge. MA. Harvard University Press.

Sampler. J.L., and Short, J.E.(1994). An examination of information technology's impact on the value of information and expertise: implications for organizational change. *Journal of Management Information Systems,* II, 2 (Fall), 59-73.

Senge, P.M. (1990). *The Fifth Discipline.* New York : Doubleday.

Short, J.E., and Venkatraman, N. (1992). Beyond business process redesign: redefining Baxter's network. *Sloan Management Review,* 34(1), 1-21.

Simons, R.(1994). *Levers of Control How Managers Use Innovative Control Systems to Drive Strategic Renewal.* Boston: Harvard Business School Press.

Tsunami, M ; Newman, W.; and Romanelli, E.(1986). Managing the unsteady pace of organizational revolution. *California Management Review* (Fall), 29-44.

Tushman, M., and Romanelli, E. (1985). Organizational evolution: a metamorphosis model of convergence and reorientation. In L.L. Cummings and B.M. Staw (eds.), *Research in Organizational Behaviour, vol. 7* . Greenwich, CT: JAI Press, 171-222.

Tyre, M.J., and Orlikowski, W.J. (1994). Windows of opportunity: temporal patterns of technological adaptation in organizations. *Organization Science,* 5(1), 98-118.

Van de Ven, A H., and Poole, M.S.(1990). Methods for study innovation development in the Minnesota Innovation Research Programme. *Organization Science,* 1, 313-335.

Venkatraman, N.(1991), Information technology-induced business reconfiguration: the new strategic management challenge. In M.S. Scott-Morton (ed.), The *Corporation of the 1990s.* Oxford. Oxford University Press.

Victor, B., and Blackburn, R.S. (1987).Interdependence: an alternative conceptualization. *Academy of Management Review* 12(3), 486-498.

Walton, M.(1990). *Deming Management at Work.* New York: G P. Putnam & Sons.

Ward, J M. (1987). Integrating information systems into business strategies. Long Range Planning, 20(3), 19-29.

Weick, K.E.(1979). *The Social Psychology of Organizing,* 2d ed. New York Random House.

Wernerfelt, B. (1984). A resource based view of the firm. *Strategic Management Journal,* 5(12), 171-180.

Winter, S.G. (1987). Knowledge and competence as strategic assets. In D. Teece (ed.), *The Competitive Challenge.* Cambridge, MA: Ballinger, 159-184.

Source: Reprinted by special permission of the *Journal of Management Information Systems*, Vol. 12, No. 1, 1995, pg. 31-56.

CHAPTER 3

Business Process Redesign: Tactics for Managing Radical Change

Donna B. Stoddard
Harvard Business School, USA

Sirkka L. Jarvenpaa
University of Texas at Austin, USA

Many organizations are in the midst of *planned* revolutions to respond to the turbulent business environment. Organizations that prospered in the 1980s as contractors to the U.S. military are a good case in point. Many of these firms are transforming themselves into commercial competitors. They are redefining their products, people, structures, systems, and culture to compete in the commercial sector. For example, over 50 percent of the revenue of Rockwell International came from the defense sector in the late 1980s, in 1993 only some 20 percent came from that sector. The organization has undertaken massive conversion of not only its assets, but also its culture, work processes, thought patterns, and so on, to become a major player in telecommunications, automobile parts manufacturing, factory automation, and commercial electronics. Rockwell is accomplishing so-called organizational transformation—"Profound fundamental changes in thought and actions, which create an irreversible discontinuity in the experience of a system" [Adams, 1986, p.278].

Business process redesign (BPR), also known as reengineering (Hammer and Champy, 1993) or process innovation (Davenport, 1993), is offered as an enabler of organizational transformation (Davidson, 1993;Tushman and Romanelli, 1986). Organizations embrace a BPR approach when they believe that a radical improvement can be achieved by marrying business process, organization structure, and IT change. Former defense contractors and traditional commercial sector companies, such as IBM Credit Corporation and Ford (Hammer and Champy, 1993), alike have embraced BPR to speed up slow or "broken" business processes. Others, such as Taco Bell (Harvard Business School, 1992), have embraced BPR to enable the redefinition of their business.

Information technology is usually a necessary but insufficient factor in achieving business process redesign. IT has been described as both a strategic catalyst and an enabler of BPR (Davenport, 1993; Hammer and Champy, 1993). Yet, the absence of needed IT capabilities can be a major inhibitor to BPR. For example, a manager described how the data architecture that a company's London office had established in the late 1980s made it relatively easy to develop new applications to support a process that had been redesigned. The lack of such a well-defined data architecture in the firm's U.S. operation meant that significantly more resources had to be committed to accomplish applications of similar scope.

A systems planning or data-modeling project may provide the genesis for BPR as the organization wakes up to the fact that a planning process that focuses on technology may not deliver the business solutions it needs. For example, when asked why BPR had become a major agenda item, the chief information officer (CIO) of a major insurance company noted:

> In the late 1980s, I began to look at how technology was linked to our overall corporate strategy. I tried to assess how new applications impacted the enterprise—my intuition was that we were investing a lot but not getting the desired productivity. As I began to focus on what we were doing, it was clear that, generally, we did not change the processes that were being automated. Rather, we took sophisticated applications and layered them onto an old organization. I began to envision a need to reengineer. Further, in all of our years of focus on the technology, it was as if we had been looking through the wrong end of the telescope.

Reengineering is reportedly *radical change.* "Process innovation involves stepping back from a process to inquire as to its overall business objective, and then effecting creative and radical change to realize orders-of—magnitude improvements in the way that objective is accomplished" (Davenport, 1993, p. 10). In their book, *Reengineering The Corporation,* Hammer and Champy (1993) note:

> Reengineering can't be carried out in small and cautious steps. It is an all-or-nothing proposition that produces dramatically impressive results. Most companies have no choice but to muster the courage to do it. For many, reengineering is the only hope for breaking away from the ineffective antiquated ways of conducting business that will otherwise destroy them.

One manager explained, "BPR is about changing the engines of a *flying* airplane." BPR is one approach to organizational transformation.

Is BPR radical change? What are the necessary tactics to accomplish radical change? In this paper, we contrast change tactics that promote radical change with tactics that promote incremental change. We then analyze three BPR efforts to understand whether, how, and why revolutionary tactics were used or not used. We conclude with implications to practice and research.

Overall, the three initiatives differed in terms of the scope and planned depth of change. The use of revolutionary tactics varied across the initiatives, but also by the phases of the initiatives. The three cases suggest that BPR may be a revolutionary approach to design. The realization of the design might take a long time and involve an evolutionary approach.

Change Outcomes: Determining the Degree of Planned Change

The planned outcomes of change can be described in terms of scope and depth.

Scope includes the breadth of change. Depth involves the nature of change. Radical change is high on both scope and depth.

Scope of Change

The scope of change denotes the organizational reach of change—for example, whether the impact of change will be contained within one function, one organization, or will cut across organizational boundaries (Benjamin and Levinson, 1993). Although BPR by definition (Hammer and Champy, 1993; Short and Venkatraman, 1991; Venkatraman, 1994) spans functional boundaries, there seems to be a wide disparity in how narrowly or broadly a process is viewed from one BPR initiative to another —this results in differing degrees of cross-functional scope. The much-celebrated Ford Motor Company accounts payable BPR project was largely limited to one functional area—accounting (Hammer, 1990). By contrast, IBM Credit Corporation collapsed a number of functional areas with its BPR initiative (Hammer and Champy, 1993). Singapore Tradenet illustrates the transformation of relationships across a number of trade-related coordinating bodies (King and Konsynski, 1990).

Planned Depth of Change

The nature of change is dependent on the strategic intentions as well as the context of change (Orlikowski, 1993). BPR efforts often start with the following intentions: to dramatically reduce cost, to dramatically improve customer service or employee quality of life, or to reinvent the basic rules of business. For example, IBM Credit Corporation sought to reduce the turnaround time for quotations to customers. The focus of its initiative was efficiency, attempting to cut costs by cutting time per quotation and by improving the number of deals handled with the existing staff (Hammer and Champy, 1993). At Procter and Gamble, management hoped to increase customer service effectiveness when it worked with Wal-Mart to reengineer the order-management/inventory process for Pampers diapers (Hammer and Champy, 1993). When Taco Bell management recognized that they were in the fast-food business, not in the Mexican-food business, BPR was used to transform the organization into the newly redefined business (Harvard Business School, 1992).

To transform an organization, a deep change must occur in the key behavior levers of the organization: jobs, skills, structures, shared values, measurement systems, and information technology (Hall, Rosenthal and Wade, 1993). The greater the extent of planned change to the change levers, the deeper the planned change. For example, Otis Elevator (Stoddard and McFarlin, 1986) changed its work procedures for managing service requests, employee roles, culture, IT, and measurement and control systems in an effort to improve customer service.

BPR is commonly facilitated by information technology (Davenport, 1993; Hammer and Champy, 1993). IT-enabled outcomes, in turn, have been described in terms of organizational efficiency, effectiveness, or whether the application transforms the organization (Gibson and Jackson, 1987):

> Applications in the *efficiency* category allow users to work faster and often at measurably lower cost. Applications in the *effectiveness* category allow users to work better and often to produce higher quality work. Applications in the *transformation* category change the basic ways that people and

departments work and may even change the very nature of the business enterprise itself.

This classification of change is consistent with the depth of change. When the only change lever used is IT (i.e., IT-enabled change), mere automation of manual tasks occurs, resulting in efficiency gains. Effectiveness, in turn, requires changes not only in technology, but also in skills, job roles, and work flow. Transformation in turn assumes a major change in most of the change levers of the organization, including structure, culture, and compensation schemes. Automation is the least deep; the transformation is the deepest form of change.

In addition to BPR accomplishing cross-functional and transformational changes, it is also expected to change the organization fast. For example, Hammer and Champy (1993, p.212) note that "Twelve months should be long enough for a company to move from articulation of a case for action to the first release of a reengineered process."

Change Process: Determining the Tactics of Change

The pace of change is dependent on the process— that is, tactics, or tech-niques—used to encourage an organization's members to accept and to enact a proposed change (Nutt, 1986). A change process that complies with current organi-zational values and norms, skills, structures, and incentive systems is inherently evolutionary. By contrast, change that challenges or undermines the status quo, creates a new vision, and accomplishes fundamental change in values and norms, work practices, and structures is revolutionary change (Orlikowski, 1993). Our basic supposition for managing change in BPR is simple: different initiatives require different change management tactics depending on the type of change. Radical change (a transformational change in a short period of time) usually necessitates revolutionary change tactics; likewise, incremental change suggests evolutionary change tactics.

Evolutionary Change

Evolutionary change models assume that change is adapted to the pace and capabilities of people and widespread, frequent, and open communication is a key tactic to enable incremental change (Eldredge and Gould, 1972; Kilmann and Covin, 1988; Leonard-Barton, 1988). Evolutionary models also assume that change cannot be fully planned at the outset and those who will be affected by the change must lead and participate in the change process (Leonard-Barton, 1988). Broad participation from various levels usually means that the pace of change is adapted to the capabilities of the least changeable element or group in the organization.

As such, evolutionary change models suggest a gradual, staged sociotechnical change approach. The change tactics derived from this view reflect two basic assumptions about change: (1) change takes time and is best accomplished in small increments at a time, and (2) change is a recursive adaptation process between the technology and the user environment. Although this incremental, cumulative view of change has a long tradition in various facets of science (for example, biology

(Eldredge and Gould, 1972) and social science (Loye and Eisler, 1987)), new theories challenge these underlying assumptions of change.

Revolutionary Change

According to radical change theorists (e.g., Gibson and Jackson, 1987; Tushman, Newman and Romanelli, 1986; Tushman and Romanelli, 1985), a fundamental organization change cannot be accomplished piecemeal, gradually, or comfortably. Rather, the change must unfold rapidly. The creation of new forms and processes requires difficult compact revolutions. Although revolutionary change theories acknowledge the existence of incremental changes during periods of stability (i.e., equilibrium), they argue that any major change can only come as a result of revolutionary upheaval (i.e., "big bang").

In the vocabulary of radical change theorists, fundamental change requires a *deep structure or paradigm shift* change (Gersick, 1991), that is, the basic assumptions, business practices, culture, and organizational structure change. The existing deep structure persists and limits change during stable periods but must be dismantled and reconfigured in periods of revolutionary change. Unless the deep structure is changed, the behaviors migrate back toward the status quo once the formal change program is declared to be over. Some level of identity crisis, disorder, and ambiguity usually precedes a deep structure change (Orlikowski, 1993).

Radical change *outcomes* (i.e., broad and deep changes) require revolutionary change *processes,* particularly when the time frame is short (see figure 1). The reverse is not, however, true. A process can be revolutionary without the outcomes of change being radical (Gersick, 1991).

Radical change theorists have proposed a number of revolutionary tactics to accomplish radical change (Gibson and Jackson, 1987; Nadler, 1988; Tushman et al., 1986; Tushman and Romanelli, 1985). A new vision is needed to free existing members of the legacies of the past, allow them to see alternatives, and build confidence and capabilities for the future. New managers are needed to accomplish "frame-breaking" change. Current employees should be excluded because of cognitive, motivational, and obligational barriers to change. Existing managers and employees, many of whom are comfortable with the status quo, may have difficulty

---

Figure 1: Process and Outcome of Change

		Process	
		Evolutionary	Revolutionary
Outcome	Incremental	*Incremental improvement*	*Little benefit for risk and pain*
	Radical	*Continuous incremental improvement over a long period of time*	*Radical change in a short period of time*

performing "out-of-the-box thinking." Also, existing employees may fear losing control, opportunities, or power, and that they cannot accomplish the new tasks. Existing employees might be further constrained because of legions to stakeholders inside and outside the organization who prefer the status quo. Tushman et al. (1986) found that "externally recruited executives are three times more likely to initiate frame-breaking change than existing executive teams. Frame-breaking change was coupled with CEO succession in more than 80 percent of the cases." Hall et al. (1993, p.124) reported that in four of the five successful BPR initiatives, "new chief executives were brought in before or during the projects."

Moreover, revolutionary change must start in populations that are small and isolated before the change is spread further (Gersick, 1991). Isolation helps the group avoid having its focus and energies diluted by the surrounding inertia. Some existing organizational members might also have to be removed in order to communicate that resistance will not be tolerated. An organization that holds onto its promise of no layoffs violates the basic tenet of revolutionary change: people must qualify for change rather than have change adapted to people.

Proponents of revolutionary models argue that a failure, or a crisis, is required to set the stage for revolutionary changes. Gersick (1991) similarly argues that people appear most capable of creating and accepting new solutions when they face insurmountable problems that cannot be solved with the current deep structure. Crises help provide decisive breaks in systems' inertia and can tap major sources of energy for creating the new rules for the workplace. A crisis is particularly necessary to generate receptivity to changes in a wider population.

Communication about the change should be first targeted to a small group of gatekeepers and spread only after the change has taken a hold in that group. Kanter et al. note, "Too often, communication translates into a unilateral directive. Real communication requires a dialogue among the different change makers" (Kanter, Stein and Jick, 1992).

Radical theorists do not refute that an anticipated crisis might be a sufficient motivator for radical change. That is, management can "create a crisis" and a sense of urgency to motivate organizational members to get on board with a change program (Kanter, Stein and Jick, 1992). They do, however, caution that "only a farsighted minority of firms initiate upheaval prior to incurring performance declines" (Tushman, Newman and Romanelli, (1985). In addition, the "old" organization might have to be dismantled and left disorganized for some periods of time before fundamental changes take hold.

Gersick (1991) believes that successful radical change requires the creation of temporal milestones. Temporal milestones occur when people become acutely aware that the time is finite and they have to move on. She maintains that if organization members begin to realize that a particular era has ended, then they may accept that the approaches that they had previously chosen might no longer be appropriate. Temporal milestones help to create the sense of urgency, and make people reevaluate past choices and take new steps.

Evolutionary and Revolutionary Change Tactics

A comparison of the evolutionary and revolutionary change models suggests some similarities and some major differences. Both evolutionary and revolutionary models advocate having senior executive support or sponsorship of any large-scale change initiative. Both argue for clear objectives and vision. However, the revolutionary models call for leadership from outside the organization, and the evolutionary models for leadership from the existing senior management. The evolutionary tactics call for broad participation of the current process owners and contributors in the design and implementation. The revolutionary tactics call for the exclusion of the current process owners and users. While the evolutionary models advocate broad, organization-wide communication, the revolutionary models suggest more selected and focused, face-to-face, one-on-one communication. The evolutionary model advocates flexible milestones; the revolutionary model advocates rigid milestones. The evolutionary model proposes that change can be driven by a desire for self-improvement; radical change proposes that people must believe cognitively and sometimes experience emotionally the crisis state of the organization. In summary, to accomplish deep structural change, the radical models suggest that people cannot be assumed to be capable of change; rather, they have to be qualified for change. The evolutionary models argue for adapting change to people.

IT and Models of Change

The revolutionary and evolutionary perspectives also prescribe different sequencing of technology changes. Under evolutionary change, a gradually staged sociotechnical change occurs. Either a social-system-, or a technical-system-first strategy is followed. Revolutionary change assumes simultaneous change of both technical and social systems (i.e., the all-at-once strategy).

Liker et al. suggest four alternative approaches to managing technology paced change based on the pace and scope of sociotechnical change: all-at-once, technical-system-first, social-system-first, or gradually staged sociotechnical change (Liker, Roitman and Roskies, 1987). The all-at-once strategy assumes that an organization would attempt to make rapid, radical change in its technical and social systems concurrently. The technical-system-first approach suggests a more gradual change; IT changes are expected to induce social changes. The social-system-first approach calls for "getting your house in order" before making major technological changes. It assumed unfreezing and changing (Lewin, 1957) the social system before installing a new technology.

Studies on the implementation of production technologies underscore an interactive, staged approach to change (Leonard-Barton, 1988). Highly successful technology transfers has been found to require the mutual adaptation of the organization and technology. Change emerged slowly and gradually as large and small recursive cycles bridged the gaps and misalignments between technology and the rest of the organization. Much of this change process could not have been planned in the beginning.

Several others describe technology-based change as an emergent process: the users and consequences of information technology emerge unpredictably from complex social interactions (Markus and Robey, 1988). For example a study on the introduction of CT scanners in radiology describes how changes to the structure of the radiologists' work emerged unplanned over time from their interactions with the technology (Barley, 1986). In a study of eighty-five public libraries, the highest-

Table 1: Evolutionary and Revolutionary Change Theories: A Comparison of Tactics

	Evolutionary	Revolutionary
Leadership	Use insiders	Use outsiders
Employee involvement	Use current managers and employees who are representative of the population of employees	Exclude current managers and employees where possible. Involve only "best of the breed" and those who are dissatisfied with the status quo. Employ employees full-time. Isolate the reengineering team
Communication	Broadly communicated plans	One-on-one communication to key stakeholders only
Motivation	Self-improvement	Crisis or failure
Milestones	Flexible	Firm
Culture/structure change	Adapt to existing employees	Qualify employees for change who fit with new culture and organizational structure
IT change	Process or social system first. Alternatively, gradual, staged implementation of technology and social systems	Simultaneous change of technology and social systems

performing libraries implemented a balanced level of both technological and organizational changes rather than one or the other (Damanpour and Evan, 1984). However, the sequencing of these innovations also affected performance. Libraries that adopted organizational innovations first were ultimately the best performers.

Table 1 contrasts the change tactics for the evolutionary and revolutionary change models in seven areas: leadership, employee involvement, the strategy for communication, the motivation for BPR, milestones, organization structure/culture and IT. We next analyze the use and more importantly the context of use of the revolutionary and evolutionary change tactics in three BPR initiatives. We start by outlining the research approach.

Research Approach

A case study method was deployed to explore how and why different change management tactics were used. A multiple-case design involved three BPR initiatives in three different companies. The three cases varied in terms of the expected change outcomes. The BPR initiative was the unit of analysis. A BPR initiative could be one project or a set of interrelated projects.

The first author's organization had an established relationship with the three companies resulting from previous research and educational activities. At the time of the study, one of the BPR initiatives had been completed and hence represented a retrospective case study. The other two initiatives were in the phases of pilot and initial field implementation. Hence, the design phases represented retrospective research; the pilot and implementation phases represented concurrent data collection involving contact between the researcher and the organization every three to five months over an eighteen-month study period. Both researchers (or a researcher and a research assistant) were present in all key interviews, allowing crosschecking of facts and impressions.

In each case study, retrospective data were collected on what practices and organizational interventions triggered the organization to initiate the efforts. The data collection involved primarily semistructured interviews with open-ended questions. Site visits were supplemented with telephone interviews. An interview guide was used in most of the interviews (see appendix). The number of people interviewed per case study varied from eight to twenty-five; most were managers and employees involved in the BPR initiative. In all cases, the business process owner, the IT director, and members of the BPR team were interviewed. The company executive management was interviewed in two companies. The interviewees were supplemented with the reviews of memos and project reports and observations of new technology and work procedures.

Background on Three Reengineering Initiatives

Table 2 outlines the organizational context of the initiatives and describes the planned changes in tasks, structure, systems, and culture at the three organizations: FinanceCo, DefenseCo, and FoodCo.

FinanceCo is a large financial services company. One of the main divisions of the firm began BPR in late 1980s with an attempt to transform the company from a mass marketer to a personalized services company. The division had experienced declining margins because of problems with persistence and higher costs to acquire customers. The BPR initiative was aimed to result in significant improvements in overall profitability and growth.

DefenseCo was a large manufacturer of industrial equipment. The BPR initiative occurred in the largest business that primarily sold military equipment to the U. S. government. Because of the restructuring and the downsizing of the U.S. defense industry, the company faced the challenge of maintaining a profitable division with a significant reduction in demand. Cost cutting and downsizing had become the order of the day. The new competitive environment had already resulted in major cycle-time reduction in submitting proposals to the government from six to twelve months to three months. Further, the time between the award of the manufacturing contract to the delivery of the equipment was cut from twenty-four months to twelve. All this put pressure on purchasing to reduce its cycle time and hand-offs.

FoodCo was a large food retailer and manufacturer. The BPR effort was undertaken in the manufacturing unit of the firm that had nearly forty manufacturing plants all across the United States. The head of the unit had previously implemented an integrated manual manufacturing system in one of the plants in the 1960s and now envisioned implementing a standard computer-based MRPII system in all of the

Table 2: Overview of Re engineering Initiatives

	FinanceCo 1993	DefenseCo 1993	FoodCo 1993
Company context	Mail order insurance. Revenue in excess of $600 million, employs 2,000 people	Industrial equipment manufacturer whose defense segment had revenue of approximately $1.3 billion	Food manufacturer with revenue in excess of $1.5 billion and 3,500 employees
Reengineering initiative description	Sought to transform company. Eight to ten reengineering initiatives underway. Three initiatives were testing new ways of doing busi ness The others were reengineering work flow in opera tions areas.	Refined work in the purchasing area in one of the companies in the defense systems segment.	Implementation of an MRPII system in forty plants ranging from bakeries and milk-processing plants to nonfood plants.
Changes to tasks	Jobs to be completely redefined. A process-based vision and a new strategic business model were developed for the company.	Jobs were completely redefined as buyer and planner position was combined into a com-modity administrator role.	Jobs, processes, and information flow to be redefined and standardized across the plants.
Structural changes	Moving toward a management through team structure and a flatter organization.	Eliminated a number of middle-manager positions.	Headquarters functions redefined to enable implementation.
Information systems changes	Moving from main-frame systems and toward a client-server/Windows environment.	Installed Macintosh computers in an environment that had traditionally been only IBM. Also, introduced prototyping with users in an environment em-bracing traditional sy-stems development life-cycle approach to development.	To replace three PC-based manufacturing control systems plants had imple-mented in nonstandard ways. Installing MRPII and IBM AS4OO computers, new technologies for the company.
Cultural changes	Cultural audit sug-gested need to significantly change the culture.	A more participative culture was introduced as employees were involved in the design and development of the new system.	Many plant employees would have to interface with computers for the first time. Interdependence between plant departments would increase dramatically.

plants in order to enhance each individual plant's effectiveness, enhance overall control, and allow the unit to leverage its size with customers and suppliers.

Scope of BPR Initiatives

The scope of BPR varied across the three initiatives. At FinanceCo, the scope

Figure 2: Planned Outcomes: A Comparison of Cases

		Scope of Change		
		Functional	Cross-functional	Organization-wide
Planned Depth of Change	Efficiency	DefenseCo		
	Effectiveness		FoodCo	
	Transformation			FinanceCo

included the entire organization of more than 2,000 people. The initiative was expected to take seven to ten years. In 1992, FinanceCo had over twenty BPR implementation teams in progress. In early 1993, they had eight teams in progress and in the summer of 1993, six teams. At FoodCo, most of the manufacturing unit's 3,500 employees would be affected. The initiative was estimated to cost $40 million, with savings of $200 million over ten years. The initiative was expected to take 6.5 years to complete. At Defense-Co, the scope was limited to the purchasing department of 165 people; the initiative was completed in three years from its inception (see Figure 2).

Planned Depth of BPR Initiatives

The most radical outcomes were sought after at FinanceCo, followed by FoodCo. At FinanceCo, the BPR was initiated as a result of redefining the company's strategy; management sought to transform the organization, which was losing market share and experiencing declining profitability. The functional work processes, structures, and values cemented with information technology would have to be changed to enable a new business strategy. FinanceCo expected both to offer new and innovative products and to be able to support its customers in new and innovative ways. For example, the customer would be served by a dedicated crossfunctional team that handled both sales and service transactions for the company's varied products.

At DefenseCo, the BPR initiative was to improve the flow of work while doing more with less. The redesigned process was also expected to provide management with better metrics to measure how well the department was doing. Customers (e.g., manufacturing) had traditionally viewed the service level of the purchasing department as poor. The department was inundated with paper, and it was not unusual for purchase orders to be misplaced or to get lost in someone's in-basket. The BPR effort was to move away from a functional view to a process view. Two job categories would be collapsed to one and one-third of the department's staff would be eliminated.

At FoodCo, the expectations were more of effectiveness, followed by efficiency. The senior vice president for manufacturing explained,

Table 3: Hammer's Reengineering Principles: Mapping of Three Cases

	FinanceCo	DefenseCo	FoodCo
Organize around outcomes not tasks	Yes	Yes	No
Have those who use the output of the process perform the process	Yes	Somewhat	Somewhat
Subsume information-processing work into the real work that produces the information	Yes	Yes	Yes
Treat geographically dispersed resources as though they were centralized	NA	NA	Yes
Capture work once and at the source	Yes	NA	Yes
Link parallel activities instead of integrating their results	Yes	Yes	Phase 3
Put the decision point where the work is performed and build control into the process	Yes	Yes	Yes

Adapted from Hammer (1990) and Hammer and Champy (1993).

For a number of years I have envisioned implementing a standard computer-based system in all of our facilities, that would not only enhance our
ability to manage individual plants but would provide the information we
need to leverage our size when we deal with suppliers and customers. The
challenge that we face as we try to accomplish this is that there are vast
differences in the characteristics and life cycles of the products produced
in our 40 plants. Yet, if we are successful at implementing a standard
process and system, the opportunity is enormous.

In the late 1980s the head of the business unit had established a team to compare
the unit's manufacturing systems with those of competitors. The team found that
FoodCo's systems and processes were highly inadequate. Hence, the need for BPR
was developed based on senior management's vision and the knowledge of what
other organizations had been able to accomplish as a result of redefining their
processes. Management expected the BPR to yield major savings from reduced plant
losses, reduced per-unit purchasing costs, inventory value reduction, potential
increases in public sales, and overall improvements in productivity. Other benefits
were expected from better-organized information, improved customer service,
improved performance visibility, availability of instant standard-based productivity
variances, improved costing/pricing, and full integration of product and business
functions.

In all three initiatives, the firm's management believed that they had undertaken
BPR. Table 3 maps the three initiatives to Hammer's (Hammer, 1990; Hammer and
Champy, 1993) principles of BPR. In two of the organizations, management called
the initiatives business process reengineering; in the third case, the organization
referred to the initiative as business process optimization. In the next section, we

analyze the use of the evolutionary and revolutionary change tactics in the three initiatives.

Change Tactics Observed in BPR Initiatives

No initiative solely used either revolutionary or evolutionary tactics.
Rather, the initiatives sampled both types of tactics although to a varying extent by the phase of the initiatives. The more frequent use of revolutionary change tactics occurred during design than during implementation at FinanceCo and FoodCo. FinanceCo and FoodCo exhibited a revolutionary approach to design, but an evolutionary approach to change during implementation. DefenseCo deployed both revolutionary and evolutionary tactics during design and implementation.

Hence, the more radical the planned change, the more the organizations employed revolutionary change tactics during design, but not necessarily during implementation. This finding is somewhat paradoxical given that the majority of actual change occurs during implementation. Table 4 compares the change tactics used for each BPR initiative. Table 5 summarizes whether the use of *revolutionary tactics* decreased or increased during the initiatives' pilot and implementation phase from that of the design phase.

Leadership

The leadership change tactics used at FinanceCo and FoodCo were revolutionary during design, but evolutionary during implementation. At DefenseCo, the approach to leadership was a mix of evolutionary and revolutionary during design and implementation.

All three initiatives used new management talent in the beginning. This inflow did not, however, continue over time. FinanceCo made the most use of outside managers in the beginning. A new president and a new senior vice president of operations/customer marketing were hired, and BPR emerged as a way to prototype and implement the ideas that surfaced from the new strategic planning process. The new president of the organization regularly endorsed the reengineering initiatives and was actively participating in the communication to the broader organization. The senior vice president was seen as the owner and champion of the reengineering effort.

At DefenseCo and FoodCo, the momentum for BPR was established by managers who had been part of the organization for a number of years. However, in both cases, new managers were brought in to provide day-to-day project leadership after the initiatives had been funded. At DefenseCo, a manager came from another part of the company. The new manager scrutinized the proposal and was initially quite skeptical about the need for the initiative:

> Since I had been a customer of the purchasing area, I knew there was an opportunity to make changes that would result in better service to customers and reductions in head count. I was initially skeptical of the BPR initiative and, quite frankly, almost pulled the plug on the initiative. When the BPR initiative proposal crossed my desk, we were in a downsizing phase. I knew that I could eliminate people from the purchasing area and I didn't need a computer system to do that. From November until January, the initiative was essentially on hold until I warily agreed to move forward. Even so, I

Table 4: Change Tactics: A Comparison of Cases

Use of tactics	FinanceCo		DefenseCo		FoodCo	
	Design phase	Pilot/ implementation phase	Design phase	Pilot/ implementation phase	Design phase	Pilot/ implementation phase
Leadership/ management	Revolutionary	Evolutionary	Evolutionary/ revolutionary	Evolutionary/ revolutionary	Revolutionary	Evolutionary
Employee involvement	Revolutionary	Evolutionary	Evolutionary/ revolutionary	Revolutionary/ Evolutionary	Revolutionary	Evolutionary
Communication	Evolutionary	Evolutionary	Evolutionary	Evolutionary	Evolutionary	Evolutionary
Motivation for BPR	Revolutionary	Evolutionary	Revolutionary	Revolutionary	Evolutionary	Evolutionary
Milestones	Evolutionary	Evolutionary	Revolutionary	Revolutionary	Revolutionary	Evolutionary
Change of structure and culture	Revolutionary	Evolutionary	Revolutionary	Revolutionary	Revolutionary	Evolutionary
IT change	Revolutionary	Evolutionary	Evolutionary	Evolutionary	Revolutionary	Evolutionary

Table 5: Increase or Decrease of Revolutionary Tactics in Pilot/Implementation Phase *Compared to Design Phase*

	FinanceCo	DefenseCo	FoodCo
Leadership/management			
- New managers and leaders	↓	↓	↓
- Full-time dedicated managers	↓	No change	↓
- Outside consultants	↓	No change	↓
Employee involvement			
- Quality members (best of breed type)	↓	↑	No change
- Full-time team members	↓	↑	↑
- Isolated teams from rest of operations	↓	No change	↓
Communication			
- Limited (need to know only)	No change	No change	No change
Motivation for BPR			
- Crisis	↓	No change	No change
Milestones			
- Rigid	No change	No change	↓
Culture and structure change			
- Layoffs of employees	No change	↑	No change
- New structures (departments,teams)	↓	↑	↑
- New roles	↓	↑	↓
- New compensation schemes	↓	↑	↓
IT change			
- Simultaneity of technology and social system changes	↓	No change	↓

agreed to move forward with the stipulation that the initiative would have to generate head count savings that were not volume generated. Further, we would have to be able to cut cycle times and throughput.

FoodCo hired a manager specifically to manage the BPR initiative who had implemented an MRPII system at a smaller manufacturer. The manager was promoted three times during his first eighteen months with the company, reflecting the need to ensure that he had sufficient resources to carry out the BPR and legitimize the business changes he was attempting. A full-time management team was also initially dedicated to manage the business conversion and training associated with the system.

During the pilots and initial implementation, fewer full-time management resources were dedicated to the efforts at FinanceCo and FoodCo. At FinanceCo, an officer of the company who coordinated the reengineering initiatives on a full-time basis during design was assigned additional responsibilities during pilots and implementation. At FoodCo, a dedicated management team decreased over time. For example, a training manager initially working full-time on the initiative also began to perform additional activities.

All three companies utilized outside consultants, although the use decreased during implementation except at DefenseCo. At FinanceCo and FoodCo, their roles also changed. Their activities were more strategic in the early phases than in the later phases. At FoodCo, they helped to define the project and validate the business case before funding was approved. At FinanceCo, the consultants helped to develop the new business strategy and provided the tools and methods for BPR. During implementation, the consultants' role was limited to one of performing audits of the initiatives and assisting in software development.

By contrast, at DefenseCo, the consultant played a major role through design and implementation. The consultant's package inspired a vision for BPR and new roles. The consultant assisted with modifications to the package that was purchased. The consultant managed the implementation to new processes including the training of employees.

Employee Involvement

Employee involvement tactics were revolutionary at FinanceCo and FoodCo during design, but evolutionary during implementation. At DefenseCo, the employee involvement was somewhat more revolutionary in implementation than in design.

At FinanceCo and FoodCo, employees selected to work on the design of the new processes were considered to be "best of breed." At FoodCo, the design team included two management-level people from each plant type. At FinanceCo, a crossfunctional, multilevel team of six employees worked with outside consultants to develop a new strategy that guided the work of the specific implementation initiatives.

In both FinanceCo and FoodCo, employees assigned to design and test the new processes were dedicated full-time to the effort and were physically separated from those who were using traditional work approaches. They were also constantly reminded by management that they were embracing the new business strategy, whereas others were in the old business." At FoodCo, plant employees were relocated to headquarters to work on the BPR initiative.

At both FinanceCo and FoodCo, the number of full-time people declined as the projects approached the pilot stage. Similarly, more "representative" people from the work force were involved. The pilots also occurred in the normal work areas.

DefenseCo's approach to employee involvement can be characterized as a somewhat evolutionary change tactic in design with a revolutionary flavor in implementation. In design, the employees were expected to continue to perform their work as it had been traditionally defined. The employees participated part-time in the design activities. The opportunity to participate in the design and testing of the new processes was a public acknowledgment that the person was a "high performer." Because of the drastic reduction of departmental staff during implementation, proportionately more people were excluded from new work processes at DefenseCo than in the other two initiatives. Also, during implementation, all employees switched to the new work approaches rather than the organization maintaining both the new and the old ways of doing business.

Communication

None of the initiatives followed a revolutionary tactic in communicating about the initiative. Rather, all initiatives emphasized broad communication, an evolutionary tactic, from the start.

At FinanceCo, early in the initiative, the senior leadership met with employees at all levels to explain the new business vision, strategy, and how the BPR would affect employees. A videotape simulating new work processes was shown in small interactive round-table discussions. The reengineering teams also prepared numerous articles for the parent company's newspaper and for the organization's own newsletter, and set up a kiosk in a lobby to inform employees and customers of the reengineering initiative. A course that covered the basics of the new strategy was added to the organization's training curriculum.

At FoodCo, the plant representatives in the BPR team were expected to keep their plants up to date with the initiative's progress. In addition, the BPR team held weekly meetings, published widely distributed newsletters every two to three months, and offered conceptual and hands-on training on MRPII. The corporate staff was being informed about the initiative primarily through the sponsor of the initiative until his retirement in the fall of 1992.

DefenseCo held weekly 6:30 A.M. breakfast meetings open to people from all departments. During those meetings, employees involved in the BPR provided status reports, and both team members and senior management were available to answer questions. But only the same 40 or so employees of the department's 160 employees tended to come regularly to the meetings.

In all three initiatives, broad communication continued during the pilot and early-implementation phases; the impact of communication, however, decreased over time. When some of the employees first heard of the initiative (usually in the design phase), they believed that the changes were imminent or already happening. Since nothing was implemented for some time, employees began to question whether change was forthcoming and tended to pay less attention to what was being communicated.

Motivation for BPR

During design, FinanceCo exhibited a revolutionary tactic to motivating the company for the change; during implementation, the tactic was evolutionary. At FoodCo, the motivation was evolutionary in nature in both design and implementation. At DefenseCo, the motivation was characterized as revolutionary during design and implementation.

At the time of approval, management at FinanceCo and at DefenseCo communicated the BPR effort in crisis terminology. FinanceCo's employees were told that financial results were poor and, if they were to stay in business, the company had to change. However, perhaps because of the length of the initiative, the need somewhat changed in the eyes of those conducting pilots. They saw themselves as helping to implement the organization's new customer-focused service and sales strategies rather than trying to turn around the firm's financial performance.

At DefenseCo, the declining defense budgets demanded that either DefenseCo employees and managers figure out how to do more with less to compete for the declining defense dollar or, as one manager noted, "None of us will have jobs." The crisis mentality was sustained in implementation, largely because of continuing personnel layoffs.

At FoodCo, the BPR was presented as an opportunity for the division to generate more wealth for the company. The BPR's financial implications represented significant cost reductions, 80 percent of which would be due to material cost reductions. Employees were also informed of the benchmark study, that the organization had conducted showing that its information systems capabilities lagged behind those at other food manufacturers. During implementation, the initiative was associated with, as well as suffered from, the need to cut operating costs drastically. The organization had experienced an unexpected "down" year followed by some plant closings, consolidations, and organizational downsizing. The financial situation resulted in the initiative becoming under more financial scrutiny. The project experienced a reduction in its resources.

Milestones

At FoodCo and at DefenseCo, a revolutionary approach was deployed for managing milestones during design. The revolutionary tactic was maintained at DefenseCo during implementation, but not at FoodCo. FinanceCo exhibited an evolutionary approach to milestones during design and implementation.

Rigid milestones were established at FoodCo and DefenseCo for schedule and benefits. DefenseCo adhered to those deadlines. The same applied to FoodCo in the design and pilot phases. In implementation, some slippage occurred because of resources diverted from the initiative.

Flexible milestones were used at FinanceCo. The BPR involved experimenting with new ways of doing business, and an overall timeframe was developed for the companywide reengineering initiative. Where prior organizational experiments suggested a project would yield positive results, milestones were set. For those projects initiated to test "new" approaches, the milestones were flexible.

Change of Current Structure and Culture

The three BPR projects planned revolutionary changes to the structure and culture. The changes can be characterized as evolutionary at FinanceCo and FoodCo (particularly in view of the planned changes). The changes were most profound at DefenseCo, although contained to one department.

Since the beginning of design, FoodCo and FinanceCo spent resources on employee training and education for the new required behaviors and values. Maintaining the necessary level of funding for education became a challenge over time. The pace of behavior and value changes slowed down with the decreased educational budgets during pilots and implementation.

At FinanceCo, major organizational changes were piloted, but few were seen to be implementable organization-wide because of cost and risk. During the pilot phases, some key managers began to manage across functions and products (i.e., by processes). Crossfunctional teams were piloted. For example, personal customer-service teams provided a single point of contact for a customer. The organization also experimented with team-based and skill-based compensation. A senior manager elaborated:

Compensation will be based on jobs skills, willingness to continue to learn and develop, and the ability to function in a team environment. Our new job evaluation system will motivate people to develop a wider array of skills. Goal-sharing will tie individual rewards to the performance of the team and the corporation as a whole.

The proposal for the skill-based compensation was shelved, however, because management was unable to develop a cost-effective and fair transition plan to the new scheme. Most other structural/cultural changes were scaled down or put on hold.

At FoodCo, relatively little was accomplished in terms of cultural change because of plant resistance, project delays, the reduction of resources devoted to the change, and the focus on systems rather than on overall processes. For example, the initial planned called for hiring outside consultants not only to design but also to manage the education and training programs. This was ruled out later because of cost. Instead, representatives from plants were groomed to be coaches. Because of their limited time and resources, the training was mostly on PC skills and on the mechanics of the system ("keyboarding"). Little time was spent on conceptual training for the new processes. Also, the design was revised during the pilot stage because of plant resistance to the new ways of working. According to a BPR team member,

[P]eople felt we were intruding on their "turf" They insisted on replicating their old work patterns. We lacked the power to offset this resistance. Our progress was dependent on cross functional agreements that were very time consuming to negotiate.

At DefenseCo, the structure and culture of the purchasing organization was significantly changed. Yet, the fact that the initiative was restricted to one function made the organizational changes relatively easier than at FinanceCo and FoodCo. Financial reward structures were revamped to reflect the new expanded jobs and responsibilities. Most supervisory-level jobs were eliminated as many controls were automated, and employees were empowered to make decisions that previously had to be approved by a superior.

IT Change

At FinanceCo and FoodCo, the approach to IT was revolutionary in design and evolutionary in implementation. DefenseCo's approach was evolutionary in both design and implementation.

At FinanceCo and FoodCo, IT helped to envision new ways of working. At FinanceCo, there were a number of host systems that the customer management teams had to access in order to respond to customer requests and to prepare sales proposals. These legacy systems were product-based, not customer-based. The new PC-based front-end systems would allow a team member simultaneously to access a number of host systems and build an integrated view of a customer's relationships. Over time, additional distributed customer databases and application systems were to be rolled out. For example, a new order-entry system would allow a nonexpert (such as a member of a customer management team) to take information from the customer. The system would automatically process simple orders.

At FoodCo, the BPR initiative was to implement a standard information system across a heterogeneous set of plants. The system was to push information and decision making down to the plants as well as to allow better integration of plant information at headquarters. To materialize the cost savings from IT investments, business processes would have to be streamlined and standardized.

Similarly, at DefenseCo, the knowledge of available technology had inspired the BPR initiative. A manager elaborated:

> The purchasing manager saw an article which described a purchasing system that had been developed and installed by a consultant at another company. The manager contacted the consultant and become further convinced that the system would improve the flow of work within the department. The solution would also equip the department with Macintosh computers that could be used as front-ends to host based systems.

None of the initiatives, however, adopted the IT revolutionary change tactic, the "all-at-once" strategy in implementation. At FinanceCo, the pilot teams first learned their new roles; the new IT platform and applications were introduced over a three-year period. The delay reflected the lead time to develop the new systems. At FoodCo, a technical system preceded the social-system changes.

At DefenseCo, the process resembled one of gradual adaptation of the system and the new organizational roles. The design and implementation of the technology were iterative. In stage one, the consultant came up with a conceptual design to which DefenseCo's management agreed. In stage two, the consultant worked with frontline employees from the purchasing area to design the final roles and system. In the first release, the jobs/roles remained unchanged; however, buyers and planners were asked to train one another on their respective jobs. The new roles and enhanced IT capabilities were introduced in multiple stages.

All BPR efforts experienced problems scaling up from prototyping to pilots and full-scale implementation. The IT departments were fundamentally challenged in supporting the initiatives. At both FinanceCo and FoodCo, the IT department's competency was in host-based systems. The new computer-based system was a distributed system on a platform unfamiliar to the IT organization. FinanceCo hired new IT personnel as well as training many of its existing staff in new development tools and methods. At FoodCo, a group comprised of plant managers, not IT personnel, was charged with implementing the new system, roles, and processes. Yet, the implementation required close cooperation and coordination (i.e., partnership) between the plants and the division's centralized IT group.

Similarly, at DefenseCo, the system chosen by the purchasing department was based on a platform the IT group had no experience with. The iterative development approach was also unfamiliar to them. The IT department's skills and knowledge were focused on on-line mainframe transaction-based applications and on traditional systems development methodologies. Their limited personal-computer knowledge was on the IBM type of equipment, not on Macintosh. An information technology manager noted:

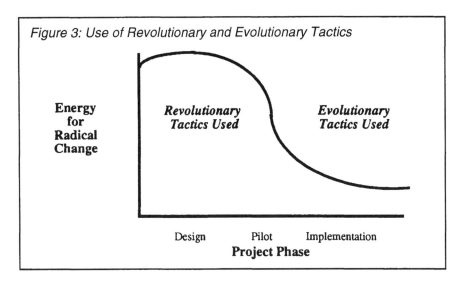

Figure 3: Use of Revolutionary and Evolutionary Tactics

The consultant's proposal threatened our fortitude. The iterative development process was not in sync with what our staff had been told. People kept asking me, "How could it be OK for the user to see the application before it was done?"

Status of Initiatives

At the end of 1993, the three initiatives were at the following stages: DefenseCo's initiative was successfully completed in 1992; the FoodCo and FinanceCo efforts were in the midst of pilot and field implementation phases. At FoodCo and FinanceCo, the pace of implementation had slowed down considerably. At FoodCo, the second release of the system initially scheduled for Fall 1993 was rescheduled to Spring 1994. The third release was put temporarily on hold until the operational benefits accrued from the second release were known.

Discussion of Findings

Our proposition was that accomplishing radical change requires revolutionary change tactics: the more radical the change outcomes (see Figure 3), the more revolutionary the tactics. We discussed three reengineering initiatives and described whether and how they used revolutionary change tactics. None of the cases subscribed religiously to revolutionary tactics.

The revolutionary tactics were used more in design than in implementation in the two projects with the most radical planned outcomes. The projects exercised an evolutionary approach to the pilot and implementation phases. For example, at FoodCo, the plant manager was given discretion as to when the new process and system would be implemented in a particular plant. The implementation teams at both FoodCo and FinanceCo included increasing numbers of part-timers and fewer consultants than in the design teams. One manager at FoodCo remarked on the pace,

> This is really nothing new. Long initiatives always tend to lose momentum the longer they are around. Scarce corporate dollars tend to go for newer, 'better" initiatives.

They are many reasons why FinanceCo and FoodCo did not exercise revolutionary tactics in implementation, whereas DefenseCo did. Here we speculate on a few reasons, including the size of the initiatives, motivation, senior management involvement, and lead times for IT development. Another set of reasons relate to the benefits that accrue from the use of evolutionary tactics.

The narrow scope of the DefenseCo initiative appeared to facilitate its use of revolutionary tactics. In large efforts, the financial and human costs and risks of the revolutionary tactics appear to be unpalatable. For example, the larger the initiative, the more dedicated full-time labor power is needed. However, it is difficult to sustain large teams of full-time members. Several managers remarked on how restructuring and reorganizations easily undermined teams' efforts. Noted one:

> The toughest thing is to leave the team alone. In a changing environment, you are constantly restructuring and regrouping. It is tempting to regroup the team as well. This sets the team back.

The use of revolutionary tactics appeared to require a true crisis in an organization. It was not sufficient to communicate an anticipated crisis. FoodCo and FinanceCo experienced declining profitability, but neither was in a true financial crisis. By contrast, DefenseCo's survival was a daily topic in management and employee discussions.

The use of revolutionary tactics also required active top-management involvement. The champion had to be personally involved in the design and implementation team activities, and had to serve as cheerleader, coach, and referee. Keeping the sponsor and champion intact appeared to be more challenging the greater the scope and planned depth of change. For example, at FoodCo, the sponsor retired. Later, the initiative's champion was promoted and stepped further away from the day-to-day activities of the initiative. The team began to feel detached from the organization's leadership. Without strong and visible management support, the team migrated toward more comfortable evolutionary tactics.

Although IT was a critical enabler of new visions and designs in all three initiatives, the absence of needed IT capabilities and skills set the initiatives back, particularly in the case of FinanceCo. Poor infrastructure and poorly defined data architectures meant that significant resources had to be committed to accomplish applications that supported a process perspective. This meant that a simultaneous change of technology and social systems could not occur. At FoodCo, a package was purchased that allowed the "technical-system-first" approach. However, this approach lost the synergistic benefits of implementing the social and technical changes together.

There were also many benefits that accrued from the use of evolutionary tactics. None of the projects used a revolutionary tactic to communication. All projects practiced open communication. Some managers felt that secrecy around initiatives early on would have led to even more resistance and reduced potential "buy-in" in implementation.

In addition, broad communication resulted in some positive unanticipated consequences. One manager remarked: "People begin to implement the changes on their own, without being part of the formal change effort." Broad communication also helped to get new champions and sponsors to step in when the original reengineering leaders began to redirect their attention.

Yet, the three initiatives we studied suggest that effectively communicating to a broad audience was a major challenge. All three reengineering initiatives received feedback that much more communication was necessary than had been done to keep the rest of the organization sufficiently abreast of the progress. One leader commented:

> You always underestimate the amount of communication you have to do. Always triple what you think it takes. Most communication is needed at the management level, particularly the middle management. The front line group is much quicker to seize the opportunity.

Flexible milestones appeared to increase creativity and "out-of-the-box" thinking. They were also seen to decrease senior management's tendency to micromanage the team, to focus the team on strategic rather than tactical objectives. The lack of rigid milestones also helped the teams to spend more time communicating to those not directly involved what had been accomplished so far.

In none of the BPR initiatives did the organization take advantage of new business opportunities, new facilities, or newly opened locations. So-called "greenfield" implementation means engaging in "engineering" a new business rather than "reengineering" or "renovating" an existing business. None of the firms had the option to divest their current business wholesale and invest in a new one. One executive remarked:

> To use the clean slate approach to reengineering means new business and new entrepreneurs; yet most corporate boards are intolerant of new entrepreneurial ventures.

Conclusion

Our analysis of three reengineering initiatives suggests that BPR does not always result in radical change in a short period of time. Although the FoodCo and FinanceCo initiatives had radical objectives, the progress slowed down in implementation as evolutionary tactics were used. None of the projects used a "clean slate," or greenfield, type of implementation. The findings of the current study go counter to Hammer's definition of reengineering:

> When someone asks us for a quick definition of business process reengineering, we say that it means "starting over." It doesn't mean tinkering with what already exists or making incremental changes that leave basic structures intact. It isn't about making patchwork fixes—jury-rigging existing systems so that they work better. It does mean abandoning long-established procedures and looking afresh at the work required to create a company's product or service and deliver value to the customer.

In other words, our analysis suggests that although reengineering can deliver radical designs, it does not necessarily promise a *revolutionary approach to change*. Moreover, a revolutionary change process might not be feasible given the risk and cost of revolutionary tactics. Sustainable incremental improvement via an evolutionary change process might be what companies should sometimes expect as success from BPR. Companies need to tailor the expectations and change management tactics of BPR to the initiative's scope, depth, and available implementation time.

The current findings are, of course, highly preliminary. They are based on three case studies. The findings may not be generalizable to initiatives with different motivations and contexts. We invite other researchers to replicate and expand on the current findings. We also call for more research attention to managing change in BPR. BPR is not just about envisioning new ways of working. It is about implementing those new ways. Work is particularly needed on the contingency factors for the successful management of BPR change. Such work should take multiple viewpoints, including the organization, work group, and individual. One might assess the risk propensity of BPR champions who are willing to use revolutionary tactics in implementation and compare their attitudes to change with an organization's overall climate toward change. Similarly, much work remains on developing measures to assess the magnitude of change accomplished in processes, behaviors, values, and so on. The role of information technology in BPR needs clarification. IT researchers might address the transformation that internal IT groups must undergo to support BPR initiatives.

APPENDIX A: Interview Guide

1. What were the responsibilities of the person being interviewed in general and in terms of the current reengineering initiative?
2. How did reengineering get started? Why was it started?
3. How were consultants used on the initiative?
4. What did the organization do to get ready for reengineering?
5. When did the initiative get formally launched? When was the team formed?
6. What have been the major events and milestones of the initiative?
7. What events and milestones are forthcoming?
8. What were the objectives of the initiative at the beginning, at the end of design, at the end of pilot? How were the objectives established and communicated?
9. Who was involved in the initiative? Were they full-time/part-time? Who was excluded?
10. Who was the sponsor of the initiative? What was the sponsor's background? What did they do for the initiative?
11. Who was the champion of the initiative? What was the champion's background? What did they do for the initiative?
12. How was the initiative communicated to those not involved? When did the communication take place? What was the form and medium?
13. What type of milestones did the initiative have? Were they flexible or rigid?
14. What type of training was provided?
15. What was done to prepare the organization for behavior and attitude changes?
16. How has the organization changed to accommodate the new processes?

17. What was the role of IS function and information systems applications?
18. How else has the change been managed on the initiative?
19. What were the main lessons from the initiative?

References

Adams, J.D. (1984). *Transforming Work.* Alexandria, VA: Miles River Press,.

Barley, S.R. (1986). Technology as an occasion for structure: evidence from observations of CT scanners and the social order of radiology departments. *Administrative Science Quarterly, 31,* 78-108.

Benjamin, R.I., and Levinson, E. (1993). A framework for managing IT-enabled change. *Sloan Management Review* (Summer), 23-33.

Damanpour, F., and Evan, W. (1984). Organizational innovation and performance: the problem of organizational lag. *Administrative Science Quarterly, 29,* 329-409.

Davenport, T. (1993). *Process Innovation.* Boston: Harvard Business School Press.

Davidson, W.H. (1993). Beyond re-engineering: the three phases of business transformation. *IBMSystems Journal, 32(1),* 65-79.

Eldredge, N., and Gould, S.J. (1972). Punctuated equilibria: an alternative to phyletic gradualism. In *Models in Paleo biology.* San Francisco: Freeman, Cooper.

Gersick, C.I. G. (1991). Revolutionary change theories: a multi level exploration of the punctuated equilibrium paradigm. *Academy of Management Review, 16(1),* 10-36.

Gibson, C.F., and Jackson, B.B.(1987). *The Information Imperative.* Lexington MA: Lexington Books.

Hall, G.; Rosenthal, I.; and Wade, I.(1993). How to make reengineering really work. *Harvard Business Review* (November-December), 119-131.

Hammer. M. (1990). Reengineering work: don't automate, obliterate. *Harvard Business Review* (July-August), 104-112.

Hammer, M., and Champy, I. (1993). *Reengineering the Corporation.* New York: Harper Collins.

Harvard Business School. (1992). Taco Bell. Case study No.6924/58, Boston,.

Kanter, R.M.; Stein, B.A.; and Jick, T.(1992). *The Challenge of Organizational Change.* New York: The Free Press.

Kilmann, R.H., and Covin, T.J.(1988). *Corporate Transformation: Revitalizing Organizations for a Competitive World.* San Franscisco: Jossey-Bass.

King, J., and Konsynski, B.(1990). Singapore TradeNet: a tale of one city. Harvard Business School, 9-191-009.

Leonard-Barton, D. (1988). Implementation as mutual adaptation of technology and organization. *Research Policy, 17,* 251-267.

Lewin, K. (1957). Frontiers in group dynamics: concept, method, and reality in social science. *Human Relations,* 5-42.

Liker, J.; Roitman, D.B.; and Roskies, E. (1987) Changing everything all at once: work life and technological change. *Sloan Management Review* (Summer), 29-47.

Loye, D., and Eisler, R.(1987). Chaos and transformation: implications of nonequilibrium theory for social science and society. *Behavioral Science, 32,* 53-65.

Markus, M.L., and Robey, D. (1988). Information technology and organizational change: causal structure in theory and research. *Management Science,* 34, 5 (May), 583-598.

Nadler, D.A. (1988). Organizational frame bending: types of change in the complex organization. In R.H. Kilmann and T.J. Covin (eds.), *Corporate Transformation: Revitalizing Organizations for a Competitive World.* San Francisco: Jossey-Bass.

Nutt, P.C. (1986). Tactics of implementation. *Academy of Management Journal, 29(2),* 230-261.

Orlikowski, W.I. (1993). CASE tools as organizational change: investigating incremental and radical changes in systems development. *MIS Quarterly, 17(3)*, 309-340.

Short, I.E., and Venkatraman, N. (19991). Beyond business process redesign: refining Baxter's business network. *Sloan Management Review* (Fall), 7-21.

Stoddard, D., and McFarlan, W. (1986). Otisline (A). Harvard Business School, 9-186-304.

Tushman, M.L.; Newman, W.H.; and Romanelli, E. (1986). Convergence and upheaval: managing the unsteady pace oforganizational evolution. *California Management Review, 29(1)*, 29-44.

Tushman, M., and Romanelli, E.(1985). Organizational evolution: a metamorphosis model of convergence and reorientation. In L. Cummins and B. Staw (eds.), *Research in Organizational Behavior,* vol.7. Greenwich, CT: JAI Press, 171-222.

Venkatraman, N. (1994). IT-enabled business transformation from automation to business scope redefinition. *Sloan Management Review* (Winter), 73-88.

Source: Reprinted by special permission of the Journal of Management Information Systems, Vol. 12, No. 1, 1995, pg. 81-107.

CHAPTER 4

Initiating and Implementing Business Process Change: Lessons Learned from Ten Years of Inquiry

James T. C. Teng, Varun Grover, and Kirk D. Fiedler
University of South Carolina, USA

Seung R. Jeong
Kook Min University, Korea

Over the past decade, a convergent set of communications and computing technologies are being recognized as facilitators of fundamental business change (Davenport and Short, 1990; Teng, Grover, Fiedler 1994a). Facilitated by these ITs, traditional "industrial age" structures based on functional hierarchy are changing into "information age" structures that are oriented toward collaboration across functions and a focus on business processes. Under the banner of business process reengineering (BPR), alternatively known as business process redesign, many organizations have undertaken critical analysis and redesigned existing processes to achieve breakthrough performance gains through IT (Stewart, 1992; Teng, Grover and Fiedler, 1994a). However, with increased acceptance and several years of field experience, there is growing realization that IT is a critical enabler, but reengineering involves complex socio-technical change in the organization (Mumford, 1994; Smith and Willcocks, 1995). Davenport and Stoddard (1994), for example, have questioned the clean-slate approach, IS leadership, top-down design and other commonly accepted "myths" of reengineering based on their field observations. Case studies conducted by Stoddard and Jarvenpaa (1995) indicated that organizations often attempt "revolutionary" process design but take an "evolutionary" approach in implementing the design due to political, organizational and resource constraints. The set of BPR cases examined by Hall, Rosethall and Wade (1993) revealed the complex multi-dimentional change in the organization engendered by a reengineering project which includes roles and responsibilities, performance measures and incentives, organizational structure, IT applications, shared values (culture), and skill requirements. Factors found to be related to BPR failures, according to the research conducted by Bashein, Markus and Riley (1994), include

Funding for the research was provided by a grant from the United States Dept of Education

the wrong sponsor, a cost-cutting focus, a narrow technical focus, and a number of other organizational conditions. Among leading BPR practitioners, issues in managing the complex organizational change have also become the focus of attention. Champy (1995) has recommended a number of steps to improve "reengineering management" including securing top management support and communicating the rationale for reengineering to employees.

Given the organizational complexity of reengineering, it is important that we develop a high-level strategic perspective on this multi-faceted organizational phenomenon associated with initiating and implementing complex business process change. To help develop this strategic perspective, a framework of organizational change for process reengineering is presented in this chapter[1]. The framework identifies the various sources of organizational impetus leading to reengineering, strategies for change initiation, enablers of process changes, elements of change implementation, and the directions of organizational change stemming from BPR. To explore the validity of the framework, we have embarked on a program of research. The results of three studies from this research program are reported in the second half of the paper which provide strong and convincing empirical support to many key elements of the framework

A Framework of Organizational Change for Process Reengineering

Process reengineering takes place in the context of people and organization, and any attempt at BPR without appropriate plans for organizational change would greatly increase the risk of failure (Bashein et al., 1994). A rich literature base exists within the broad areas of organizational change (Lewin, 1951), innovation (Damanpour, 1991), organizational development (French and Bell, 1978; Pasmore, 1994) and socio-technical design (Mumford, and Weir, 1979) that generally deal with planned change. In addition, since BPR is typically enabled by information technology (Teng, Grover and Fiedler, 1994b), research in MIS planning and implementation can also be brought to bear on the planning and implementation of reengineering projects (Lucas, 1978; Ginzberg, 1981). Drawing on these diverse literature, various elements of organizational change associated with BPR were identified and presented in Figure 1. In this framework, elements of five broad phases of organizational change are depicted: sources of organizational impetus leading to BPR, initiating process change, selecting change enablers, managing change implementation, and directions of organizational change stemming from redesigned processes. While the middle three phases correspond to specific actions in managing the process change, the first and the last phase represent the interface between the process change effort and the rest of the organization in terms of input/causes (impetus of change) and output/influence (directions of organizational change). These phases of organizational change will be discussed in the following sections.

Organizational Impetus for BPR

To reengineer business processes, an organization must give up the peace and comfort associated with the status quo and embark on a potentially chaotic change process. Several sources of impetus facilitating the drive toward BPR are identified in Figure 1 and discussed below.

Innovative Environment and BPR Initiatives.

Process reengineering may be conceptualized as a form of organizational innovations, an important and well-researched area in management (Lewin, 1951). While no empirical studies have been reported on patterns of BPR innovation, many reported reengineering cases corroborate central notions of organizational innovation such as those discussed below: championship, management support, cross-functional collaboration, and the facilitating role of "structural overlay." (Grover, Teng, and Fiedler, 1993).

The importance of championship has been demonstrated in general innovation adoption (Damanpour, 1991) and in IT innovation (Beath and Ives, 1989). The role of a 'BPR champion' in reengineering efforts has also been identified in many organizations in mobilizing resources necessary to launch the BPR initiative. The decisive influence of a BPR champion, for example, provided the initial impetus toward reengineering at Aetna Insurance. In 1990 Aetna's president Ron Compton felt that the company had become a large self-satisfied behemoth, and too slow to respond to market and regulations. To reverse the trend, Ron Compton challenged the business unit heads to break the cycle of mediocre performance and get involved in process reengineering (Davis, 1993).

As revealed by a field study based on 20 reengineering projects (Hall et al., 1993), top management involvement and participation are critical to the success of BPR initiatives. Process reengineerings often involves radical changes. People are wary of change and will resist it unless top management is committed to change. One

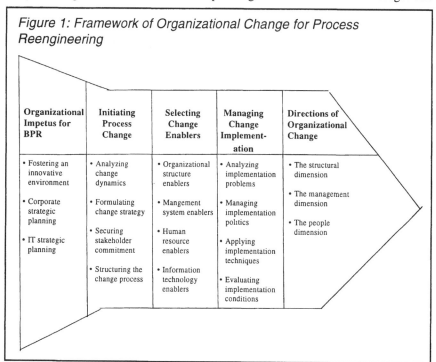

Figure 1: Framework of Organizational Change for Process Reengineering

Organizational Impetus for BPR	Initiating Process Change	Selecting Change Enablers	Managing Change Implement-ation	Directions of Organizational Change
• Fostering an innovative environment • Corporate strategic planning • IT strategic planning	• Analyzing change dynamics • Formulating change strategy • Securing stakeholder commitment • Structuring the change process	• Organizational structure enablers • Mangement system enablers • Human resource enablers • Information technology enablers	• Analyzing implementation problems • Managing implementation politics • Applying implementation techniques • Evaluating implementation conditions	• The structural dimension • The management dimension • The people dimension

way to secure this support, for example, is through an executive orientation (Bashien et al. 1994) on topics such as BPR introduction, how BPR enhances a firm's strategic objectives, IT and organizational enablers of BPR, and reengineering techniques/ methodologies.

Research has shown that organic organizations have higher capacity to innovate. In contrast to mechanistic organizations, organic organizations can be expected to foster a higher level of individual initiatives and innovative behaviors, as these organizations have more flexible work rules and higher organizational integration which refers to the extent of interdepartmental interaction such as the free exchange of ideas and participation in common projects (Burns and Stalker, 1961). Besides having more innovative potential, firms with higher level of inter-department integration can be expected to welcome (or at least offer less resistance) to reengineering initiatives which often involve business processes that cross functional boundaries. Thus, if integration is lacking in an organization planning to launch BPR, steps should be taken to encourage cross-functional interaction and cultivate a more collaborative culture.

The idea of "structural overlay" refers to the imposition of an "organic overlay" such as venture teams on top of a "mechanistic" organization, which typically relies on centralized decision making and formalized rules, to improve its innovative potential (Pierce and Delbecq, 1977). The depth and magnitude of organizational changes associated with reengineering often warrant the dedicated efforts of a "venture group" in order to create and sustain an environment that is conducive to innovative changes. At Federal Express, for instance, a "Strategic Integrated Systems Group" was established with responsibilities for designing and implementing IT-enabled process changes (Davenport and Short, 1990). At Hallmark, a formal senior position was established for reengineering which has since dramatically shortened new product development cycle time (Stewart, 1992).

Corporate Strategic Planning and BPR Initiatives.

Before launching a process reengineering project capable of achieving breakthrough performance, it is important to recognize that it is a strategic endeavor, and the processes selected for reengineering should be critical to the firm's strategic objectives (Fiedler, Grover and Teng, 1995). In addition, the planning for organizational changes associated with BPR is difficult to conduct without strategic direction from the top. Thus, BPR initiatives receive impetus from corporate strategic planning while attempting to identify and prioritize processes for BPR, to set reengineering performance goals consistent with strategic objectives, and to plan for organizational changes emanating from BPR.

While it is possible to identify candidate processes for reengineering intuitively and quickly, many organizations prefer a more systematic approach to ensure linkage between BPR and corporate strategy (Grover, Fiedler and Teng, 1994; Kettinger and Teng, 1998). In a number of reported cases, this is facilitated by an "enterprise model" involving the identification of all business processes in the organization to establish the basis for a long-term BPR program. At Charles Schwab Corp., for example, this model consists of 24 interrelated business processes representing every activity of the brokerage firm (Bartholomew, 1991). This strategic approach to BPR was also reported at Marion Merrel Dow, Inc. where a steering committee identified eight enterprise-wide mega-processes that are critical to the pharmaceutical company's success: customer processes, delivery fulfillment, revenue cycle, manufacturing cycle, operations, planning, demand creation, product development, and executive processes. These mega-processes are then subdivided into 30 subprocesses (Davis, 1993). Once a set of business processes for the firm are identified, techniques such as the Critical Success Factors method can then be applied to identify a set of candidate processes for reengineering that are critical to the firm's strategic performance. Union Carbide, for example, made a strategic decision to emphasize commodity chemicals rather than specialty products, which dictated the reengineering of its manufacturing process to achieve lowest possible cost and provide added value in delivery and service (Stewart, 1993).

In setting strategic direction to reengineering, performance measures for redesigned processes should be consistent with the firm's long-term strategic goals, not just short-term results such as sales volume. These goals are typically related to service quality and customer satisfaction. Methods developed within the Total Quality Management (TQM) discipline such as QFD (quality function deployment) may be applied for this purpose (Akao, 1990). Empirical studies conducted by Hall et al. (1993) indicate that greater performance improvements can be achieved by setting multiple performance measures that are linked to strategic objectives of the firm. At Aetna, for example, the claim processing for its property and casualty business took two days to get through to an agent, and over a week to fill a claim. In reengineering this process, performance goals were determined through benchmarking with the 'best in class' competitors. After a thorough study of customer needs, the redesigned process not only improved customer satisfaction but also cut costs. This was achieved through the closure of 120 local offices and providing 24-hours a day 800-number service through 22 full service centers (Davis, 1993).

IT Strategic Planning and BPR Initiatives.

While the deployment of IT is not always required for reengineering, it is a powerful enabler (Teng, Grover and Fiedler, 1994b). In most cases, BPR initiatives would be difficult to implement without IT applications such as imaging, data base and client-server architecture. Through aligning IT strategies with overall corporate strategies, IT strategic planning efforts can generate impetus for BPR by attempting to identifying IT enablers of reengineering, and developing an information resource architecture that facilitates BPR (Grover, Fiedler and Teng, 1994). At PHH Corp., for example, this IT-corporate strategy alignment led the $4 billion company to rethink its strategy in relation to IT, freeze investment in traditional automation of existing procedures and redeploy the resources to redesigning age-old processes (Betts, 1992).

Many forms of IT that are important to reengineering are of recent origin. Because these technologies are rapidly evolving, advice on their applicability to BPR should be sought from IT professionals. Thus, participation of senior IT executives is important in efforts to identify IT enablers of BPR. Further, careful evaluation is needed to determine the 'fit' between the desired IT enabler and the existing information resource architecture. This architecture reflects data and other information resources such as telecommunication and applications required by the various business processes. A particularly important element of this architecture is data, since properly designed data bases can support cross-functional applications, and the data base structure can remain stable while applications undergo changes (Teng and Kettinger, 1995). At Continental Bank, for example,. a comprehensive information resource architecture was developed through examination of the overall strategies and the various functions delivering products and services critical to the strategies. The interactions between these functions and their shared data were also examined, leading to the design of an enterprise model which provided the base for their technology strategy that included an IT platform, data base design, and application development plan (Alter, 1990). If integrated data bases can not be developed within a reasonable time frame, "composite" systems that pull data from various functional data bases (or smaller extracts of those databases) may be developed. Pacific Bell adopted this approach to support the case managers of its Centrex system operation (Davenport and Nohria, 1994).

Initiating Process Change

The conceptual and theoretical root of BPR may be traced to the socio-technical systems approach which views a work system as an open system consisting of two interacting subsystems — the technical and the social (Mumford, 1994). With this approach, we optimize the entire work system, not just the technical subsystems (Bostrom and Heinen, 1977), emphasizing changes to human resources in light of altered tasks or processes. Bostrom and Heinen (1977) found that exclusive focus on the technical subsystems concerning task and technology variables in MIS systems design and implementation may have contributed to many MIS problems and failures due to neglect of the social subsystems. Building upon theories of systems change, socio-technical design and other related research, several critical elements for change planning and management are identified for *initiating process change* in a BPR project. These include analyzing change dynamics, formulating change strategy, securing stakeholders commitment, and structuring the change process. A number of change management techniques and methods are selected from the field of organizational development and socio-technical design theories to illustrate their applicability in process reengineering. More comprehensive treatments of these methods may be found in the works of French and Bell (1978), and Pasmore (1994).

Analyzing Change Dynamics.

As BPR often involves radical change, level of resistance may be strong. In initiating major change programs, according to Kotter and Schlesinger (1979), we should pay attention to the four most common reasons people resist change: a desire not to lose something of value, a misunderstanding of the change and its implication, a belief that the change does not make sense for the organization, and a low tolerance for change. In analyzing resistance to change, Markus (1983) suggests that a political perspective is appropriate when (1) organizational participants disagree about the nature of the problem that the proposed system is supposed to solve, (2) it is uncertain whether the system will solve the problem, and (3) the power bases involved are highly valued and in short supply. Thus, it is not surprising that political game playing is common in MIS implementation (Grover, Lederer, and Sabherwal, 1988). As process reengineering often involves complex socio-technical changes with impacts on many stakeholders' power base in the organization, analysis of the causes of resistance and political power dynamics are necessary in order to formulate specific change strategy and secure management commitment, which are discussed next.

Formulating Change Strategy.

Jarvanpaa and Stoddard (1995) discuss the distinction between evolutionary and revolutionary change strategy in process reengineering in terms of the socio-technical perspective. Revolutionary change strategy calls for simultaneous change of both technical and social systems, while evolutionary change may involve the choice of technical system first, social system first, or gradual staged socio-technical change (Liker, Roitman, and Roskies, 1987). If the forces of resistance is strong, risk of revolutionary change strategy would increase. When an evolutionary strategy is adopted, change is adapted to the pace and capabilities of people, and frequent and open communication are considered essential (Jarpenpaa and Stoddard, 1995). Revolutionary strategy, on the other hand, requires a paradigm shift (Gersick, 1991), and the existing structure must be dismantled and reconfigured to prevent the tendency for behaviors to migrate back toward the status quo once the change program is over. Generally speaking, radical outcomes involving broad and deep organizational changes warrant the consideration of radical change strategy. However, results from the change dynamics analysis as discussed above should be taken into serious consideration in selecting a change strategy.

In his large-scale field study of implementing planned change, Nutt (1986) identified four types of tactics used by managers: intervention, participation, persuasion, and edict. His research results indicate that intervention was generally the most effective among the four tactics. In intervention, change agents would create rationales for action, compare the organization's performance with comparable organizations, establish new standards to judge performance, and develop descriptions of how current operations could be improved (Nutt, 1986). In reengineering terms, these correspond to benchmark analysis, setting process performance goals, and new process design. The participation tactics was the second most successful category of tactics. In this approach, a task force for change implementation was formed to include important stakeholders to help develop solutions to change problems. This is similar to forming a BPR project team with members drawn from the affected functional areas. If important stakeholders are included in the team, this should enhance the likelihood of project success. The third category of implementation tactics is persuasion, where experts or consultants are allowed to control the project with little or no management review. These experts would attempt to "sell" the changes to the various stakeholders. As Nutt's (1986) empirical results indicate this approach, along with the edict tactics, are much less effective than intervention and participation, the use of these two tactics in BPR project implementation are not advisable. However, change agents should take advantage of the persuasion technique. Instead of letting consultants do all the convincing, project team members can "win over" employees who resist the change process by following various strategies of influence (Melone, 1995) in communicating the rationale and benefits of reengineering to them.

Securing Stakeholders Commitment.

A stakeholder is anyone with a vested interest in the business process. This includes employees involved in the process activities, suppliers and customers (Davenport, 1993). To succeed in the change program, commitment to change from these stakeholders must be secured. A number of approaches to securing commitment have been discussed in the literature. Prototyping the change process so the various stakeholders can better appreciate how the new process works, is effective in facilitating communication and building commitment. Davenport (1993) emphasized the importance of open and honest communication at all levels and throughout the initiative. Another way to build commitment is the search conference (SC) technique (Pasmore, 1994) which brings all stakeholders into the same room to discuss the need for change and how to best achieve it. All stakeholders are encouraged to speak their beliefs freely, and commitment to change may be nurtured through active participation and efforts to recognize the overall context of change.

Kotter and Schleinger (1979) identified five methods for dealing with resistance to change: education and communication, participation and involvement, facilitation and support (e.g., training), negotiation and agreement, manipulation and co-optation (e.g., assigning resisters to key roles in the change process), and explicit and implicit coercion. Although some extreme conditions may call for possible use of methods such as manipulation and coercion, likelihood of poor morale and even sabotage increases. For long-term effectiveness, the first three methods are recommended.

Structuring the Change Process.

To help organize the BPR project, we need to bring some degree of control and structure to the otherwise chaotic process by recognizing certain critical roles and tasks for the change endeavor (Davenport, 1993). The roles of BPR project sponsor, process owner and change agents are especially significant. The sponsor of reengineering projects plays a pivotal role in legitimizing and driving the change process. Senior functional or IS executives with transformational leadership abilities are good candidates for this role. A senior manager among employees affected by the project is to be selected and appointed to the role of process owner by the project sponsor. The process owner should possess leadership skill as well as operational competence to achieve the process performance goals.

Change agents consist of project team members who must actually carry out the detailed redesign work and implement the change. Typically, members are drawn from multiple functional areas and provided training in teamwork and group dynamics. To ensure timely attention to change management, a smaller, separate team dedicated to organizational change management may also be needed (Davenport 1993).

Selecting Change Enablers

Enablers of process change are not restricted to IT. Successful BPR implementation can be facilitated by enablers related to organizational structure, management systems and human resource development. These aspects of change were often neglected in IT-enabled change programs, severely limiting their prospect of success (Scott Morton, 1991).

Organizational Structure Enablers.

Research has shown that better performance may be attained through cross-functional reengineering efforts than projects confined within a traditional function (Hall et al., 1993). To facilitate cross-functional cooperation, functional structure can be modified through structural enablers such as cross-functional teams, case managers and process generalists.

The use of cross-functional teams has played a central role in many reengineering efforts. At Modicon, Inc, a maker of automation-control equipment, product development is no longer the sole responsibility of the engineering function. In the past, manufacturing wouldn't get involved in this process until the design was brought into the factory when their suggestions on the design changes become very costly. Now, a team of 15 managers from engineering, manufacturing, marketing, sales and finance routinely work together on the process. This cross-functional collaboration has eliminated many unnecessary delays and costly changes, helping to bring products to market in one-third of the time it would normally take (Byrne, 1993).

Another structural enabler for reengineering is the establishment of a case manager who has access to the latest status information on a given transaction and serves as the single contact point for customers. At Pacific Bell, for example, providing a customer with a Centrex telephone service used to take eleven jobs and more than five business days. Service representatives had to update 9 or more computer systems, causing frequent errors and rework, and required several consultations with the customer. After reengineering, a Centrex case manager can handle all contact with customers. Using a computer workstation that interfaces with all nine systems, he can usually provide the service in the same day (Davenport and Nohria, 1994).

While case managers coordinate work performed by many functional specialists, a process generalist can perform all their work and eliminate the need for the specialists altogether. Given proper safeguards against frauds, this may result in totally efficient 'cross-functional' coordination, as there are no longer separate functions to coordinate. At IBM Credit, the financing service division within IBM, a single generalist is now performing credit checking, pricing and other activities previously done by four different specialists in processing loan requests. This arrangement has reduced the application turnaround time from six days to just four hours. With no additional workforce, the redesigned process is able to handle 100 times as many applications as before (Hammer and Champy 1993).

Management Systems Enablers.

Structural changes in an organization such as those discussed above can help to ease the burden of ponderous hierarchies. These changes alone, however, will not be sufficient. In redesigning a process, it is often necessary to change the basis of employees' work evaluation. In the context of functional specialization, employees are evaluated on narrow, internally oriented performance objectives, i.e., the small pieces of the work assigned to his or her department rather than the quality of the entire output. Successful BPR efforts, however, are based on external performance objectives such as customer satisfaction and overall product/service quality. For example, at AT&T's Network Systems Div. the traditional function-based performance standards are replaced by holistic external performance objectives. Employees are now awarded bonuses for higher customer satisfactions, rather than higher sales, higher inventory turnover or lower cost. In addition, the division no longer assigns discreet budgets for each functional department. Budgets are now set by processes (Byrne, 1993).

With the spread of work teams and the realignment of performance objectives, it becomes necessary to return decision making power to the point where problems occur. This means employee empowerment without waiting for 'vertical' layers of approvals, which were the basis of the old functional structure and internal performance objectives. At Chesebrough-Pond's Inc., for example, factory line workers can now routinely scan on-line information on sales and stock availability to adjust the production schedules. Previously, these scheduling decisions were made by their managers (Treece, 1994).

Human Resource Enablers.

In a traditional functional hierarchy, employees often rely on just one specialty for their entire career. To make a meaningful contribution to a cross-functional team, however, it is necessary to have at least some rudimentary knowledge of other functions in order to communicate effectively with personnel from other departments. This need for multiple skill and knowledge, of course, is even more evident if the organization plans to install case managers and process generalists. Important human resource enablers for process reengineering include multiple skill development and rewarding team performance.

These changes in training, appraisal and compensation have been implemented in many firms when implementing BPR. At GE's lighting business and the Government Electronics group in Motorola, for instance, peers and others above and below the employee evaluate the performance of an individual in a process. Reward is now based on team performance in addition to individual performance. Furthermore, these companies also altered the basis of work compensation. Employees are now paid on the basis of the skill they develop rather than merely the individual work they perform (Byrne, 1993).

Information Technology Enablers.

Conceptually, an organization should be able to redesign business processes without modern IT. However, most successful BPR efforts would be difficult to consummate without the enabling IT (Teng, Grover and Fiedler, 1994b). One important impetus for the reengineering initiative, as discussed earlier, is the effort of information systems strategic planners to identify IT enabling opportunities. This identification effort depends on a proper understanding of the role of IT in facilitating process reconfiguration through BPR. Many firms have successfully capitalized on the enabling role of IT and reconfigured their business processes from a highly serial pattern with many intermediate steps to a parallel pattern permitting several functions to proceed independently (Teng, Grover and Fiedler, 1994a). In the well-publicized case at Ford Motor Corp. for example, the old accounts payable process involved three functions: purchasing, inventory and account payable, which participated in the process serially with many intermediate steps and sequential flow of paper documents. With direct access to a shared data base, the three functions now participate in the reengineered process in a parallel fashion, achieving a 75% reduction in the workforce required (Hammer, 1990). In addition to shared data bases, the application of imaging and the new web technology may also help to break the serial pattern of work flow, as different functional personnel access the same digitized document simultaneously.

Cross-functional collaboration is greatly facilitated by the application of tele-communication technologies such as local area network and a variety of office systems products under the rubric of "groupware." At Hewlett-Packard Co., for example, the sales process underwent significant change as 135 sales representatives began to use laptop computers to retrieve up-to-date inventory information from corporate data base during customer meetings (Berger, Angiolillo, and Mason, 1987). In addition, they can now use the portable computers to communicate with their peers and superiors, enabling frequent exchange of sales intelligence among the salespersons as well as timely dissemination of corporate directives pertaining to promotion, pricing, and discounting. The results showed that time spent in meetings decreased by 46%, and travel time was cut by 13%. Meanwhile, time spent with customers increased 27% and sales rose by 10%.

Increasingly, by combining both telecommunication and shared computing resources, a shared environment for team work may be developed. Currently, a number of emerging technologies, including workflow software, intranet and the popular CAD/CAM systems, hold great promise in providing this shared environ-ment for effective team work (Ellis, ,Gibbs, and Rein, 1991). At Texas Instrument, the company's global network and advanced computing resources enable design teams for new product development in different countries to sustain a high level of collaboration, while permitting them to work on different parts of the design directly without sequential flow of documents. As a result, the development cycle time decreased substantially. The time needed to develop a calculator, for example, declined 20% soon after design drawings began to be sent electronically in 1989, and further decrease of 17% has been achieved since then (Magnet, 1992).

Managing Change Implementation

The selection of proper change enablers should help to lay a solid foundation for the successful implementation of process change. However, to actually establish these enablers and carry forward other process design features requires careful management of the change implementation process itself. As amply demonstrated by the case studies conducted by Smith and Willcocks (1995), change implementa-tion requires flexibility and a multidisciplinary perspective, paying attention to a myriad of human, social, cultural and political issues, while not allowing a rigid BPR methodology and technical issues to subvert human and organization consider-ations. Several critical aspects of managing change implementation associated with BPR will be discussed here, including approaches to analyzing implementation problems, managing implementation politics, and applying implementation tactics.

Analyzing Implementation Problems.

During the course of change implementation, the dynamics of change may itself change from time to time. New sources of resistance not anticipated in the beginning may emerge later. It is necessary to periodically assess and analyze the forces that are favorable as well as unfavorable to the change efforts. To facilitate this assessment, the force field analysis technique developed by Miller (1987) may be applied. Aided by a pictorial representation of a "tug of war," analysts using this technique would identify forces that are currently "tugging" to the left of the center line in the direction of "catastrophe," and forces currently "tugging" to the right toward the ideal situation. Based on the "tug of war" metaphor, the technique provides stimuli for generating solutions to implementation problems in three ways: 1) strengthen a currently present positive force, 2) weaken an already present negative force, and 3) add a new positive force.

Managing Implementation Politics.

The force field analysis as described above involves mostly political forces. To strengthen, weaken or add forces requires active management of implementation politics through subtle actions on people's perceptions and motivations. To strengthen a positive force, for example, the BPR team may attempt to communicate clear images of the future to organizational members, and to increase the level and extent of participation. Weakening a negative force, on the other hand, may require directing people's attention to the consequences of not carrying out change and giving them time and "excuse" to disengage from the present position (Smith and Willcocks, 1995). Adding a new positive force normally involves the mobilization of power in support of the planned change through negotiation and coalition building (Keen, 1981).

Applying Implementation Techniques.

The field of organization development (OD) is concerned with planning and implementing change in organizations. A number of OD techniques may be applied in BPR implementation, especially as tools for the management of implementation politics. For example, the organization mirror technique developed by French and Bell (1978) can be used to ease the conflict between individuals and groups. The technique prescribes a set of activities in which one group gets feedback from a number of other groups about how it is perceived. These feedback would help to identify sources of the conflicts and develop possible solutions.

Directions of Organizational Change

Is process reengineering just a management fad of the 90's? Are we beginning to alter the very structure of organizations based on business processes rather than functional specialization? To help answer these questions, three dimensions of the possible organizational changes stemming from process reengineering are identified: the structural dimension, the management dimension, and the people dimension. Several salient attributes of this change are identified in Figure 2 in relation to each of the three dimensions. There are undoubtedly other important aspects to this complex organizational change process (Lambert and Peppard, 1993), but the intent here is to highlight the most significant trends. It should also be noted that the discussion focuses on changes within individual organizations, radical IT-induced changes to relationships between organizations, which have profound ramifications for corporate strategies, are not included.

The Structural Dimension of Organizational Change.

Advanced IT applications, according to research conducted by Malone and

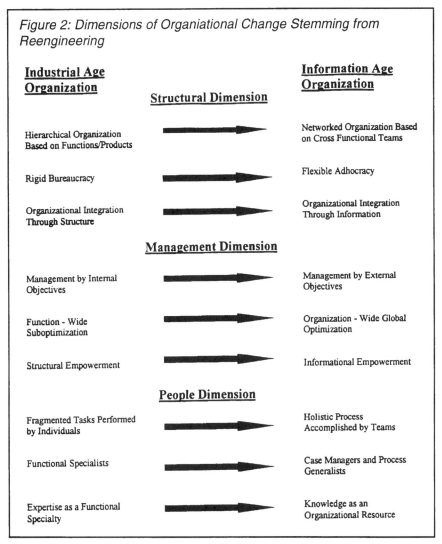

Figure 2: Dimensions of Organiational Change Stemming from Reengineering

Rockart (1991), would initially allow organizations to increase the amount and effectiveness of coordination with existing structures. Innovative use of advanced IT, however, would inevitably lead many firms to develop new, coordination-intensive structures. This can best be illustrated by the Frito-Lay case. With a sales force of 10,000, keeping the traditional hierarchical structure would lead to many layers of middle management in order to absorb the colossal amount of communication and coordination. At Frito-Lay, however, a coordination-intensive structure was developed to replace the traditional hierarchy with the aid of IT. A hand-held computer is given to each of the 10,000 salespersons to record sales data on 200 grocery products. Each night, the data is transmitted to a central computer which will send instructions back to the hand-held computers on changes in pricing and product promotions the next morning. In addition, weekly summaries and analysis are available to senior executives through an Executive Information Systems (EIS),

Malone and Rockart, 1991).

Will the success in process reengineering create momentum toward coordination-intensive structures centered around basic business process? How do organizations based on business processes differ from traditional hierarchies? While a full treatment on this complex issue is beyond the scope of this paper (Scott Morton, 1991), a few significant contrasts are identified in Figure 2. Networked organizations, according to Rockart and Short, "are usually conceived of as communication-rich environments, with information flows blurring traditional intracompany boundaries," which can be thought of more as interrelationships within or between firms to accomplish work than as 'formal' organizational design per se (Rockart and Short (1991). Thus, as an organization reengineers and improves its cross-functional processes, it will take on certain characteristics of a networked organization. For example, Chrysler Corp. has instigated a series of reforms since the late 80's to improve collaboration between functional departments. The product design function is now working closely with the engineering function and thus no longer fight turf wars with each other (McWhirter, 1992). A number of prominent firms, including IBM, Xerox and Hallmark, have adopted a reorganization approach centered around core business processes. At Hallmark, the traditional functional structure is undergoing an interesting transformation. Before the process reengineering efforts, the development of a new greeting card took two years because of a long list of serial steps in sketches, approvals, cost estimates, and proofs, which traverse many different departments. After reengineering, specialists such as writers, artists, and designers from various departments work side by side in teams. As a result, the cycle time for new card development was cut by half. The company still has functional departments, but the departmental headquarters now serve mainly as "centers of excellence" to which workers can return for training between projects, like the 'homerooms' in high schools (Stewart, 1992).

In general, functional hierarchies depend heavily on rules, procedures and upward referral which invariably increase the tendency for them to become rigid bureaucracies. This tendency may be avoided when functional specialists participate in a variety of teams attempting to accomplish different business processes at different times. These teams are given the "ownership" of the process and do not need to await several levels of approvals before making important decisions. This inherent flexibility is one of the most striking characteristics of an organizational form called "ad hocracy" which has the ability to readily create and disband ad hoc teams on an on-demand basis. If the reengineering movement continues to gather momentum, many organizations would take on characteristics of ad hocracies.

Since most traditional hierarchies are organized around specialized functional departments, it is almost against their nature to conduct "cross-functional" endeavors. With most information flowing vertically to facilitate task assignments, lateral sharing and exchange of information related to common processes between functions is difficult in a hierarchy, and territorial battles are often waged between functions to the detriment of the overall organization. Such familiar patterns of organizational life can be expected to subside in a networked organization where cross-functional teams determine their own responsibilities, and proceed to execute these duties with full access to necessary information.

With all these expected advantages, how does one decide whether it is right to begin the transformation toward a networked organization? The most important questions to ask in this regard is the organization's size and its capacity to effectively cope with the ever increasing level of uncertainty. If the firm is over sized, i.e., the revenue per employee figure is much lower than a comparable competitor's, or it is slower than the competitors in developing new products, and in drawing up new pricing and marketing strategies, then serious consideration should be given to reengineering and even restructuring.

The Management Dimension of Organizational Change.

What does the future hold for management if more and more organizations gravitate toward reengineering and networked organization? There is little doubt that reengineering is not a panacea for all the ills of the functional hierarchy, but there are strong possibilities that some of the age old organizational maladies will finally respond to treatments. One of the most persistent problems in a hierarchy, for example, is "suboptimization" which results from the decomposition of overall organizational goals into subgoals for individual departments. Another age old problem of hierarchical bureaucracy is the tendency to "pass the buck" to higher levels when exceptional situations occur. Many organizations struggle to "decentralize" decision making in order to make the firm more responsive. Many of these dysfunctional may be alleviated with process reengineering. One of the central principles of reengineering is careful calibration of process performance goals, linking to external objectives such as delivery time and customer satisfaction. At Kodak, for example, the 1,500-employee black-and-white film operation was reengineered, and the performance evaluation is now based on customer satisfaction (Stewart, 1992). Since the process is extensive and complicated, it is divided into "streams." For those streams not having direct customer contact, internal customers were identified and their satisfaction measured. This calibration of process performance measures helped to improve the performance of the process dramatically, cutting response time in half. As the teams were given "ownership" of the processes, i.e., the team members could jointly decide what to do when unexpected situations occur without asking the superiors in the hierarchy, the "buck passing" syndrome may be alleviated.

Why networked organizations, with all the potential benefits discussed above, have waited a few centuries before descending upon us? One reason is limited access to information in the traditional hierarchies which may be intentional or due to primitive information technologies, or both. With the rapid diffusion of information technologies, access to corporate data bases and freedom to communication more widely with e-mail, employees can increasingly make more informed decisions with less reliance on formal vertical information flow (Brousell, Appleton, and Moad, 1992). Such "informational empowerment" is in contrast to the position-based power in traditional hierarchies. At North American Aircraft Division of Rockwell International Corp., for example, the introduction of an executive information systems (EIS) gave rise to additional reporting structures which were not included in the formal organizational chart (Armstrong, 1990). The implications of this development for the conduct of management in the future is far reaching. One may view this development as a form of "creeping" reengineering of managerial processes: the process of management may change as a result of informational empowerment without blessing from top management.

The People Dimension of Organizational Change.

When the world entered the industrial age, the "economy" of the assembly-line production forced millions of workers to repetitively perform extremely specialized tasks. What effects will reengineering have on individual workers? Will the movement help to emancipate the workers from rigid rules and put meaning back into their work? While these questions will probably remain unanswered for decades, there are reasons to believe that the overall pattern of change may eventually lead to more 'people-friendly' organizations. With the spread of parallel operations and close collaboration with other functions, there will be a need for workers to broaden their portfolio of skills. At Bank One, for example, reengineering was achieved through cross training of employees in several related functions. At PHH, a $4 billion firm specializing in employee relocation and other business services, functional areas have shrunk in size as they have given up operational duties to case-management oriented processes (Davenport and Nohria, 1994).

With the division of labor being the modus operandi for Taylorian management in the industrial age, a departure from this principle can be expected as we enter the information age with the emergence of cross-functional teams to replace functional departments as the basic vehicle for accomplishing work in the organization. This requires making teams, not individual specialists, the focus of organization performance and design (Ostroff and Smith, 1992),. To achieve effective team work, each worker should develop several competencies. The reward system in the team-based organization must be designed to reinforce not just individual skill development and performance, but also team performance.

As engineers, financial analysts, planners, and other knowledge workers in the organization participate in a variety of teams, an enormous organizational consequence will quietly emerge: their knowledge and expertise become a shared resource to be tapped by the entire organization on an on-demand basis. The use of expert systems and e-mail (to communicate with remote experts) further amplifies the efficient and effective use of expertise throughout the organization. At PHH Fleet America, a division of PHH, the Driver Service case manager can rely on the skill they have learned and an expert knowledge base for answering most of customers' questions on their leased vehicles. They refer the more difficult problems to expert maintenance mechanics who not only can solve the problems but add it to the case managers' knowledge base (Davenport and Nohria, 1994). Therefore, as the organizational change progresses, knowledge and expertise will be released from the 'functional cages' and synergistically utilized as an organizational resource. The networked firm will thus progress toward a "learning organization" and become more intelligent and adaptive than its previous bureaucratic incarnation (Hodgetts, Luthans, and Lee, 1994)

In summary, the people dimension of the coming organizational transformation involves a transition from individuals performing fragmented tasks to team members working together for a process, a shift from exclusive reliance on specialists to the development of generalists, and utilizing expertise as an organizational-wide resource rather than a functional specialty. It is important to realize that the performance gains from reengineering and organizational change stem not only from a more "rational" process with fewer steps, but also from motivated employees who attach more meaning to their work.

Empirical Evidence from The Field

We have developed a framework of organizational change for process reengineering. While recognizing the importance of BPR methodologies in success-ful process change efforts (Kettinger, Teng and Guha, 1997), we treat the current process redesign movement as an organizational innovation and change phenom-enon and focus our attention on the macro level strategic factors that are of fundamental significance to the long term viability of the initiative in organizations. If the framework is valid, we may develop many strategic guidelines for successfully implementing process change in organizations. As researchers, however, we hesitate to offer these guidelines without first collecting empirical evidence from the field that support key precepts of the framework. To accomplish this, we have conducted a program of research to examine the validity of the framework. In this paper, we will report results of three field studies from this research program that address these aspects of the framework:

1) *Organizational impetus for BPR* — In the first study, we focus on the beginning phase of our change framework to examine the impact of innovative environ-ment and corporate and IT strategic planning on BPR initiatives and success.

2) *BPR implementation problems and success*— How critical is the management of organizational change to BPR success? What is the extent of difficulty of change management and other BPR implementation problems? These are the types of questions probed in the second study to examine the severity of various BPR implementation problems and how they are related to success.

3) *Profiling successful BPR projects* — Does more radical change lead to greater BPR project success? Do successful projects place more emphasis on social design and process transformation than technical design? These are some of the questions examined in the third study to probe how change management is manifested in actual conduct of BPR projects in terms of project strategy, stages and activities.

As complete and detailed reporting of all three studies would be impossible within the space of one paper, results of each study will be presented below in summary forms. Interested readers may refer to more detailed coverage of the study results published separately — Teng, Fiedler and Grover (1998) for Study One, Grover, Jeong, Kettinger, & Teng (1995) for Study Two, and Teng, Jeong & Grover (1998) for Study Three.

Summary of Study One: Organizational Impetus for BPR

In this study, we seek to gather empirical evidence from the field to demonstrate the organizational impetus for BPR discussed in the first phase of our change framework. For example, will organic organizations with more decentralized decision making and greater collaboration across departments more likely to initiate reengineering projects? Will better IT strategic planning through greater integration with corporate strategic planning generate greater impetus to process reengineering? In this study, we seek to answer these questions empirically to provide support to the key contentions presented in the conceptual framework.

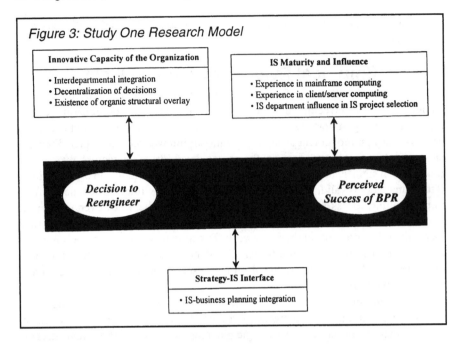

Figure 3: Study One Research Model

Research Model.

Specifically, we attempt to examine three sources of influence on BPR initiatives: 1) the innovative capacity of the organization, 2) IS maturity and influence and 3) strategy-IS interface. We will study how these factors are related to: 1) the decision to reengineer and 2) perceived success of BPR projects. These independent and dependent variables for the study are depicted in the research model shown in Figure 3.

As can be seen in Figure 3, the three variables included to gauge the innovative capacity of the organization were discussed previously (see the section "Innovative environment and BPR initiatives"). Integration and decentralization of decisions are related to the idea of organic organization. In contrast to mechanistic organizations, organic organizations can be expected to foster a higher level of individual initiatives and innovative behaviors. As BPR often require collaboration between different departments participating in the same business process, interdepartmental integration may provide a more receptive environment for not only launching a reengineering project, but facilitating its implementation also. However, the very success of BPR may require more decentralized structure as reengineering typically calls for the empowering of on-site personnel in the field (O'Hara and Watson, 1995). To compensate for the possible loss of innovative capacity in mechanistic organizations, a structural "organic overlay" may be superimposed on top of these organizations (Pierce and Deldecq, 1977). Unencumbered by the regular bureaucracies, such structural overlays typically take the form of a "venture group" dedicated to searching and introducing innovative ideas (Zmud, 1982).

In developing our conceptual framework, while discussing IT strategic planning and BPR initiatives, we pointed out that, though the application of IT is not absolutely necessary for reengineering, it is an important and often essential enabler of BPR. Three measures of IS maturity and influence are thus included in this study to assess the impact of IT competence on process change initiatives. Experience with mainframe computing would generally be indicative of IS maturity in terms of technical competence accumulated. It has been pointed out that client-server systems represent a revolutionary departure from the traditional environment through its enabling role in facilitating the emerging management and organizational forms based on empowering on-site personnel and lateral collaborations, which are consistent with the principles of reengineering (O'Hara and Watson, 1995). Several researchers have studied the power and influence of the IS function in the organization (Lucas, 1984; Saunders and Scamell, 1986). In this study, we choose one decision area that is integral to IS responsibility — the selection of IS projects, and attempt to explore how the influence of IS in this decision may be related to reengineering project initiatives.

In our conceptual framework presented earlier, while discussing IT strategic planning and BPR initiatives, we stressed the alignment of IT strategies with overall corporate strategies as a main source of impetus for process reengineering. In this study, the variable representing strategy-IS interface is IS-business planning integration which refers to the extent to which IS planning activities are aligned with and influence overall strategic planning of the business (Premkumar and King, 1992).

Research Methods and Results.

An empirical field study was conducted by gathering data from practicing IS executives. A survey instrument was developed and iteratively refined through a multistage process to enhance its content validity (Nunnally, 1967). The final questionnaire was administered to a sample of 900 executives drawn from a database of 5,000 IS executives provided by an information service firm. The sample was selected on the basis of revenue (greater than $50 million). Of the 900 initial mailings, 45 were returned as undeliverable. A total of 313 completed responses were received yielding an effective response of 36.6%.

Previously validated instruments were used either directly or modified, and others were developed from a review of the literature. Information on the *BPR decision* was obtained with a simple yes/no question: have you attempted business process redesign in your organization? The approach for measuring reengineering success used in this study is the "perceived level of success." (DeLone and McLean, 1992), and the respondents were asked to answer one seven-point scaled question about the *perceived success* level of their reengineering projects (1: unsuccessful, 7: successful). The measure for interdepartmental integration was adopted from Grover (1993). Centralization of decision making was assessed via a measure developed and validated by Ramamurthy (1990) based on the work of Miller and Friesen (1982). Measurement of the existence of organic structural overlay is objectively accessed. All variables for IS maturity and influence are assessed objectively. The scale for IS-business planning integration was based on the work of Premkumar and King (1992). Of the 313 firms, 219 (70%) indicated that reengineering has been attempted in their companies. Seven relationships were examined and the results are presented in Table 1.

The first relationship is strong as the data showed higher degree of interdepartmental integration for reengineering firms than non-reengineering firms ($p < .001$).

Table 1: Study One Results — Organizational Impetus for BPR

Independent Variables	Mean (Overall) (N = 313)	Mean (BPR) (N=219)	Mean (Non-BPR) (N = 94)	T-Test for BPR Decisions	Correlation with BPR Success
Innovative Capacity of the Organization					
1) Interdepartmental integration	4.94	5.11	4.55	***	.2400 ***
2) Centralization of decisions	5.07	4.95	5.34	**	.0252
3) Existence of organic structural overlay				***	n.s.
IS Maturity and Influence					
4) Experience in mainframe computing (years)	21.47	22.72	18.20	**	.0918
5) Experience in client/server computing (years)	3.16	3.43	2.16	***	.0547
6) IS department influence in IS project selection	3.89	3.73	4.27	**	- .1598 *
Strategy-IS Interface					
7) IS-Business Planning Integration	5.12	5.32	4.67	***	.2203 ***

⁺ Maximum sample size (N) are indicated in the table. Actual N for the various cells vary slightly.   * $p < .05$ ** $p < .01$ *** $p < .001$

Among reengineering firms, the extent of interdepartmental integration is significantly correlated to perceived level of success ($r = .24$, $p < .001$). The second relationship is moderate as reengineering companies showed less tendency to centralize decisions than non-reengineering firms ($p < .01$), but no relationship was detected for success. The result for relationship 3 is based on a chi-square table (not shown) which indicates that, with the organic structural overlay, organizations are more likely to attempt BPR than without the overlay ($p < 0.01$). Among BPR firms, however, no difference was found between the two groups in perceived success. For IS maturity and influence, we found that reengineering firms have more experience in mainframe and client/server computing than non-reengineering firms. Interestingly, for relationship 6 the data suggests that the extent of IS influence in IS project selection is higher among non-reengineering firms than reengineering firms. This means that user influence, rather than IS influence is higher among reengineering firms than non-reengineering firms. Further, this user influence is also significantly associated with perceived reengineering success ($r = .1598$, $p < .05$). Finally, for the last relationship in Table 1, we found that IS-business planning integration is significantly greater for reengineering firms than for non-reengineering firms ($p < .001$), and that it is significantly related to perceived success ($r = .2203$, $p < .001$).

Discussion of Findings.

The results for the first two relationships suggest that the expanded capacity for innovation in organic organizations may be particularly helpful in reengineering projects initiatives. While decentralized decision making may facilitate the adoption of the reengineering concept, interdepartmental integration is important to both the decision and success. Thus, the likelihood of succeeding in reengineering, which typically involves the institutionalization of inter-functional cooperation and free flow of ideas, would increase for those organizations that have already been predisposed to this type of practice and culture. On the other hand, decentralized organizations that are low in inter-functional collaboration may have better chance in undertaking the BPR initiative, but extra efforts may be needed in breaking down the walls between functional departments in order to succeed.

The study results indicate that these six factors have facilitating influence on companies' decision to initiate reengineering efforts:

- Decentralization of decisions
- Existence of organic structural overlay
- Experience in mainframe computing
- Experience in client/server computing
- IS-business planning integration
- Use influence in IS project selection

The following three factors, however, may facilitate both the reengineering decision as well as the eventual success:

- Inter-departmental integration
- Use influence in IS project selection
- IS-business planning integration

As can be seen, all 7 factors are potential sources of facilitating influence on the reengineering decision. While factors related to IT competence such as experience in mainframe and client/server computing may facilitate the decision to reengineer, they are not critical to the eventual success. On the other hand, factors having significant relationships beyond the initial decision include variables pertaining to innovative capacity of the organization and Strategy-IS interface. The only IS factor in this group: user influence in IS project selection, also relates to the organizational context of BPR. These findings strongly suggest that technical IT competence as a critical enabler is necessary but never sufficient for reengineering success. Organization contextual conditions such as interdepartmental integration, user influence in IS decisions and IS-business planning integration potentially have influence on reengineering implementation beyond the initial decisions. The pattern of results from Study One, therefore, have provided very strong overall empirical support to the propositions we made earlier in the conceptual framework on the organizational impetus for process and organizational change.

Summary of Study Two: BPR Implementation Problems and Success

The overarching theme of this study revolves around "implementation success," an issue of central concern to both the academics and practitioners. As discussed in the conceptual framework earlier, changes stemming from process reengineering is complex and not easily accomplished, involving the manipulation of interactive relationships among such organizational subcomponents as management, people, structure, technology and rewards. Understanding impediments to process change and the use of appropriate tactics to minimize these impediments should increase the chances of reengineering implementation success. Drawing from the large body of literature on implementation within innovation, socio-technical design, planning and the management information systems fields, this study is focused on the following questions:

1) What are the problems related to implementation of business process reengineering?
2) What is the relative severity of these problems?
3) How do these problems relate to the success of business process reengineering?

Research Method.

Following a review of past research of innovation and implementation, a grouping of recognized implementation problems were categorized within each of four themes: management support, technological competence, change management and project preparation. Given the lack of theoretical or empirical evidence on BPR, a careful review of the popular literature was undertaken to identify specific problems experienced in actual BPR implementations. A combined problem set of past cited and BPR-specific implementation problems formed our derived implementation problem set. Further validation of the problems and their categorization was achieved through face to face interviews with three managers who had participated in reengineering projects in four organizations. Interviewees were given the initial version of the categorized problem list and problems were added, deleted or modified during the interviews. Based on these field interviews, individual implementation problems were modified and new problems were added based on their experience. These interviews alerted the researchers to an additional category for project management problems (Kettinger, Guha and Teng, 1995). Next, a Q-sort procedure was conducted to further validate the problem categorizations. This resulted in the Project Preparedness category being divided into "Project Planning" and "Process Delineation." The final set of 64 problems used for field data collection are grouped into these six categories:

- *Management Support* problems consist of potential problems related to management's active understanding and support for reengineering.
- *Technological Competence* problems relate to the technical infrastructure and expertise within the organization.
- *Process Delineation* problems are potential problems with identification of appropriate parameters for the process involved.
- *Project Planning* problems include potential problems with planning, setting up the team and other preparation for the reengineering project.
- *Change Management* problems focus on potential problems due to failure to manage change from the old process to the new process.
- *Project Management* problems deal with the actual conduct of the project.

The unit of analysis for this research is a single reengineering project. The survey instrument was used to solicit the significance of each item in the problem set to the project identified. Respondents were asked to rate the extent to which they encountered each problem on a five point scale where 1 = not a problem to 5 = an extreme problem. Reengineering success was measured multi-dimensionally using two different perspectives: perceived level of success (Delone and McLean, 1992) and goal fulfillment (Hamilton and Chervany, 1981; Schriven, 1972).

For perceived level of success, respondents were asked to answer one five-point scaled question about the perceived success level of their reengineering project. The goal fulfillment perspective measure is characterized as objective compared to the subjective nature of perceived success. A typical question in this perspective would be: to what extent is the goal(s) of reengineering fulfilled? Such comparison is particularly meaningful as a success measure since reengineering has been conceptualized as a deliberate change initiative aimed at 'breakthrough' performance gains, and the setting of performance improvement goals is central to the reengineering concept. Thus, all of the possible goals of process performance must be considered. The present study used five commonly emphasized goals. These were (1) cost reduction, (2) cycle-time reduction, (3) customer satisfaction level increase, (4) worker productivity increase, and (5) defects reduction (Davenport, 1993; Morris and Brandon, 1993). In the questionnaire, for each of the above performance goals, respondents indicated the planned level of performance improvement (before reengineering) and the actual level of improvement achieved (after reengineering implementation). They were also guided to leave the spaces blank if the presented goal was not applicable to their reengineering projects. For the performance indicator, we compared the actual level of improvement to the planned level, via the ratio.

To help ensure validity, respondents must have actively participated in at least one reengineering project (Huber and Power, 1985). A total of 853 questionnaires were sent to members of the Planning Forum, which is the international business organization focusing on strategic management and planning. Respondents were still asked to complete a part of the questionnaire and return it, even if no reengineering project had been completed by an organization. A total of 239 usable responses were returned resulting in a final response rate of 29.2 percent. Of the 239 respondents, 105 (44%) had concluded at least one reengineering project and were able to respond to the entire instrument. These firms vary in sizes and belong to a variety of industries.

The six categories of implementation problems were developed prior to data collection via conceptual analysis as well as field work. Before attempting rigorous data analysis, however, it was necessary to ensure homogeneity for each grouping and there is no 'hidden' grouping of problems within a category. For each of the six categories, principal component analysis was performed on the items, applying the scree test and the "eigenvalue greater than one" rule. In addition, loadings greater than .40 (in absolute value) were used in deciding whether an item was considered part of a factor, to enhance the chances of cleanly separating items into conceptually sound factors (Churchill, 1979). Results of this analysis leads to the dropping of some items. For three of the six categories, the one-factor structure is confirmed, and each of the remaining three categories is split into two factors. The final classification thus consists of nine categories of implementation problems.

Severity of Implementation Problems.

To assess the relative severity of the various BPR implementation problems, each potential problem receive a 'severity score', i.e., the percentage of respondents who rated them as either a major problem or an extreme problem (i.e., 4 or 5 on a 5-point scale). The average severity score for each of the final nine problem categories are indicated below:

- Change management (mean score = 21.9)
- Technological competence (mean score = 18.2)

- Strategic planning (mean score = 17.2)
- Time frame (mean score = 16.4)
- Management support (mean score = 15.6)
- Human resource (mean score = 14.5)
- Process delineation (mean score = 14.0)
- Project management (mean score = 11.7)
- Tactical planning (mean score = 10.3)

The results clearly indicate that change management problems are perceived as most severe in implementing process change. Problems such as communicating reengineering rationale to employees, politics of reengineering efforts, and commitment to new values, which have been suggested by reengineering experts and researchers (Caron, Jarvenpaa, and Stoddard, 1994; CSC Index (1994)) as significant BPR issues, were among the change management problems identified in this study. This finding reveals and reaffirms the fundamental nature of reengineering which typically entails multi-dimensional organizational changes involving roles/responsibilities, performance measures/incentives, shared values (culture), organizational structure, skill requirements, in addition to information technology applications. According to Hall et al. (1993), these changes constitute the 'depth' dimension of change required for process reengineering. The difficulty in managing these changes is further compounded by the 'breadth' of reengineering projects which often involve processes that span across different functional boundaries.

The socio-technical nature of reengineering is vividly and 'literally' demonstrated by the two most severe types of implementation problems: change management and technology competence. However, the order is of utmost significance here: social first and technology second. Information technology is an important enabler, but the reengineering project itself involves significant changes in areas such as roles and responsibilities, organizational structure, and shared values, and none of these changes can take place in an orderly fashion without careful planning and conscientious efforts to communicate with, educate and motivate the affected employees.

Relating Reengineering Problem Severity and Project Success.

To assess the relationship between various sources of implementation difficulties and reengineering success, the average score for each of the nine categories is correlated to the success measures. For overall success, the 5-point scale as described earlier was used. For the other five specific success measures, such as cost, cycle time and defects reduction, we seek to capture the extent to which planned performance goals have been realized. This was represented by the ratio between the actual performance gain and planned performance gain. The results of the correlation analysis are shown in Table 2. As expected, all correlation coefficients are negative, as more success should be associated with less problems. The nine problem categories are listed in descending order of the magnitude of their correlation with overall success. For specific performance goals, rankings of correlations are assigned only to those that are statistically significant. In an attempt to explore patterns, the correlations for each column in the table were split at the median, and the top five classified as H (high) as opposed to the bottom four which were designated L (low).

As can be seen, coefficients in the overall success column are all significant. In fact, all but one are highly significant at $p < 0.01$. In addition, the magnitude of the

Table 2: Correlations between Problem Categories and Reengineering Success+

Problem Category	Overall Success (N = 95)	Cost Reduction (N = 49)	Cycle-Time Reduction (N = 55)	Customer Satisfaction Increase (N = 38)	Productivity Increase (N = 46)	Defects Reduction (N = 25)
Human Resource	-0.51*** (1) (H)	-0.47*** (1) (H)	-0.30** (3) (H)	-0.40** (1) (H)	-0.43*** (2) (H)	-0.49** (2) (H)
Project Management	-0.42*** (2) (H)	-0.35** (5) (H)	-0.33** (2) (H)	-0.36** (3) (H)	-0.33** (4) (H)	-0.48** (3) (H)
Management Support	-0.36*** (3) (H)	-0.29** (8) (L)	-0.10 (L)	-0.25 (L)	-0.25* (7) (L)	-0.34* (9) (L)
Change Management	-0.35*** (4) (H)	-0.43*** (3) (H)	-0.34** (1) (H)	-0.35** (4) (H)	-0.49*** (1) (H)	-0.39* (8) (L)
Tactical Planning	-0.33*** (5) (H)	-0.37*** (4) (H)	-0.25* (5) (H)	-0.38** (2) (H)	-0.33** (4) (H)	-0.43* (7) (L)
Process Delineation	-0.30*** (6) (L)	-0.44*** (2) (H)	-0.29** (4) (H)	-0.34** (5) (H)	-0.43*** (2) (H)	-0.45* (5) (H)
Strategic Planning	-0.28*** (7) (L)	-0.32** (6) (L)	-0.18 (L)	-0.31* (6) (L)	-0.33** (4) (H)	-0.45** (5) (H)
Time Frame	-0.27*** (8) (L)	-0.27* (9) (L)	-0.19 (L)	-0.20 (L)	-0.21 (L)	-0.47** (4) (H)
Technological Competence	-0.19* (9) (L)	-0.30** (7) (L)	-0.12 (L)	-0.30* (7) (L)	-0.22 (L)	-0.51*** (1) (H)
Average Correlation	-0.33	-0.36	-0.23	-0.32	-0.34	-0.45

+ Overall success is based on a 5-point scale. All other success measures are achieved/planned performance level ratios.
Numbers in parentheses following the coefficients are rankings for significant correlations based on magnitude.
For each column, the five highest correlations are classified H (high), the rest L (low). There are six H's for the last two columns due to identical correlations.

* Significant at the 0.10 level;
** Significant at the 0.05 level;
*** Significant at the 0.01 level.

correlations is large with six of the nine exceeding 0.30. While this is somewhat expected, the ranking pattern contains some interesting results and offers fresh insights. Human resource problems, which were originally categorized as part of the change management category, are very highly negatively correlated ($r = -0.51$) with perceived BPR success. While change management concerns the organizational context for change such as politics, communication, commitment and resistance to change at the policy level, human resource problems focus on specific *tasks* pertaining to people within the project domain itself. These tasks include training personnel affected by the redesigned process, developing new skills needed by the new process and setting up management systems to cultivate required values. This result suggests that to the extent that these critical human resource arrangements are not made in the actual conduct of the project, the success of the project may be in jeopardy. This finding once again demonstrates the overwhelming importance of managing organizational change and the social dimension of BPR initiatives. Failure to prepare the affected employees for the new 'world order' of BPR and cultivate new values which sustain the new order can lead to detrimental outcome for the project.

The ranking of correlations for overall success contains some surprises. Technology competence, while being regarded as the second most severe type of problems, correlated the least with overall success. Note that the magnitude of the correlation ($r = -0.19$) is substantially lower than that for human resource problems ($r = -0.51$). Thus, reengineering project members may experience a great deal of difficulty in obtaining IT related skills and infrastructure, but the lack of such problems will by no means guarantee project success. Apparently, taking good care of the required technology may be necessary but not at all sufficient for the eventual success of reengineering.

Patterns of Findings.

To gain more insight into the study findings, we will attempt to take a broad examination of the overall patterns of results. To explore these patterns, both severity and its relationship to success are included in Table 3. As the research objective is to explore general patterns rather than striving for precision in analysis, statistical measures are designated as either H (for the top five scores) or L (for the bottom four scores). This classifications scheme should help us to develop an overall portrayal of the various problem categories, as indicated in the last column of the table.

Change management stands out as the most severe source of difficulty in reengineering. It also has relatively high correlation (negative) with most success measures. The overall pattern is designated "HS-HC" (high severity-high correlation). This pattern clearly indicates that change management occupies the center stage in business process reengineering implementation. The daunting tasks in breaking the organizational status quo and introducing new practices, new values and new structures must have been overwhelming for most reengineering team members, and our study results confirm this. The good news is that efforts devoted to solving these difficult change management problems should 'pay off' in terms of reengineering project success. The warning message is, however, equally striking — inability to manage organizational change in reengineering will most likely lead to project failure!

For the other eight categories of implementation problems, we found either a

Table 3: Ranking Patterns of Severity and Problem – Success Correlations

| Ranking of problem severity+ | | Correlation between problems and reengineering success++ | | | | | | |
Problem Category	Average Severity Score	Overall Success	Cost Reduction	Cycle Time Reduction	Customer Satisfaction Increase	Productivity Increase	Defects Reduction	Pattern of Severity vs. Correlation+++
Change Management	H (21.9)	H	H	H	H	H	L	HS – HC
Technological Competence	H (18.2)	L	L	L	L	L	H	HS – LC
Strategic Planning	H (17.2)	L	L	L	L	H	H	HS – LC
Time Frame	H (16.4)	L	L	L	L	L	H	HS – LC
Management Support	H (15.6)	H	H	L	L	L	L	HS – LC
Human Resource	L (14.8)	H	H	H	H	H	H	LS – HC
Process Delineation	L (14.0)	L	H	H	H	H	H	LS – HC
Project Management	L (11.7)	H	H	H	H	H	H	LS – HC
Tactical Planning	L (10.3)	H	H	H	H	H	L	LS – HC

+ A problem category with average severity score greater than 15 percent is classified H (high); otherwise it is classified L (low).

++ For each success measure the five highest correlations with problem categories are classified H (high); the rest are classified L (low). For productivity and defects, identical correlations result in six H's.

+++ HS = high severity; HC = high correlation; LS = low severity; LC = low correlation.

"HS-LC" pattern or a "LS-HC" pattern. In fact, with only a few exceptions, all four categories having higher severity (HS) are weakly correlated with the various success measures (LC). This "HS-LC" pattern suggests that implementation problems related to technological competence, strategic planning (of reengineering), project time frame and management support are quite difficult to manage, but reducing these problems does not necessarily pave the way to success. In other words, addressing these vital problems is a necessary but not sufficient condition for reengineering success.

Interestingly, the opposite pattern (LS-HC) was found for the four categories having less severity (LS). These categories include human resource, process delineation, project management and tactical project planning. These problems may not be major sources of difficulty during reengineering, but tendency to neglect them will prove detrimental to project success. This is particularly evident in mitigating human resource problems through training of personnel affected by the new process, developing new skills, and instituting new management systems to cultivate required values. Given other implementation problems, especially change management problems, reengineering team members may not always focus their attention on these problems. However, the redesigned process primarily depends on people, not machines to operate. Poorly trained and under-motivated employees will inhibit success!

With the exception of change management, the overall 'macro' patterns as discussed above indicate the existence of two groups of implementation problems — one with the HS-LC pattern and one with the LS-HC pattern. The four categories included in the HS-LC group seem to relate more to the general project context and environment, whereas the second group (LS-HC) more directly involves the reengineering project itself. Problem categories in the first group include technological competence, strategic planning, time frame, and management support problems. These types of problems are often discussed in the context of MIS implementation and are not unique to reengineering (e.g., Ginzberg, 1981; Lucas, 1978). However, due to the breadth and depth of change required for reengineering, these problems will be potentially more difficult to manage and solve than in traditional MIS project context.

On the other hand, reengineering team members may have unintentionally treated 'lower-level' details of reengineering work lightly, perhaps a natural response after having handled the difficult organizational change and strategic planning problems. However, human resource, process delineation, project management and tactical project planning efforts correspond directly to the core tasks of reengineering, and the consequence of neglecting these vital tasks will increase the likelihood of project failure. An inappropriately scoped process (process delineation) (Hall et al., 1993) and an inadequate BPR methodology (project management) (Kettinger, Teng, and Guha, 1997) can seriously jeopardize the project. Human resource problems also correspond to the tactical dimension. While change management concerns the general *organizational context* for change at the *policy* level, human resource problems focus on the *specific tasks* pertaining to people such as training and skill development within the project domain itself. When these tasks are done poorly, the new process will be staffed by unskilled and under-motivated employees. This would certainly lead to project failure even if the overall environment has been favorable with respect to management support, commitment to change and required technological competence.

Implications.

The study clearly demonstrated the central importance of change management in reengineering implementation, as discussed in the conceptual framework presented earlier. Not only was change management regarded as most challenging to undertake, but also it showed a critical relationship to project success. On the other hand, technological competence was viewed as difficult, but had the least potential influence on project success. Thus, both social and technical components of reengineering initiatives have been recognized by the respondents as difficult, but the social elements are truly critical to reengineering success. While much conceptual discussion and numerous anecdotal accounts have been reported emphasizing the people and organizational aspects of reengineering, this is the first piece of empirical evidence based on a large sample showing a direct reflection of the socio-technical characteristics of reengineering projects in the minds of those who have attempted it. This is a critical step in the development of the reengineering field, as the confirmation of reengineering as essentially managing process and organizational change in a complex socio-technical setting, has profound implications for both researchers and practitioners. Change management is a complex multi-faceted process, and the steps and guidelines outlined in our framework for process and organizational change should help to lay the groundwork for further development in the field.

The study results have important implications for MIS professionals. Our findings suggest that technological competence is necessary but never sufficient for reengineering success. To succeed in reengineering, it is critical to master change management which demands sophisticated people and business skills. MIS professionals, being accustomed to more 'structured' projects aimed at automation of existing procedures, may need reorientation and additional training for the 'unstructured' project environment in reengineering (Markus and Robey, 1995).

Summary of Study Three: Profiling Successful BPR Projects

We have presented a framework of organizational change for process reengineering. One question that is difficult to answer conceptually, however, concerns the optimal extent of change. Analyzing the existing business procedure has been the modus operandi for a generation of IS professionals who are accustomed to the Systems Development Life Cycle (SDLC) framework which typically entails the computerization of existing processes (or modest changes to these processes). When they are called upon to participate in BPR projects, to what extent should they adhere to the "clean slate" approach in process redesign (Hammer and Champy, 1993) and pay less attention to the analysis of existing business procedures? If fundamental redesign is called for, should they implement the new design through radical changes to the organization (Hammer and Champy, 1993)? Or perhaps it is better to attempt more incremental adjustments that may be easier to manage (Stoddard and Jarvenpaa, 1995).

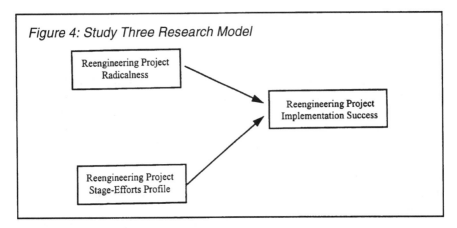

Figure 4: Study Three Research Model

Research Model.

In this study, we seek to provide substantive answers to these questions based on empirical evidence collected from more than one hundred BPR project partici-pants. This is accomplished by examining the relationships between characteristics of the reengineering project (refered to as "project profile") and implementation success. Specifically, two aspects of the project profile will be examined: radicalness of the project and the strength of effort spent on the various stages of the project (referred to as "stage-efforts"). As shown in Figure 4, the proposed research model relates the two independent variables regarding project profile to reengineering implementation success in order to answer these important questions:

1) Are reengineering projects aimed at more radical change leading to higher implementation success?
2) If limited attention and resources must be allocated among the different stages of a reengineering project, which stage (or stages) should receive more empha-sis in order to achieve higher implementation success?

This study is based on a set of survey questions directed at respondents who also participated in Study Two: 239 members of Planning Forum, a professional associa-tion focusing on strategic management and planning. Of the 239 respondents, 105 (44%) had completed at least one BPR project (refered to as "reengineering firms") and were able to respond to the entire questionnaire.

Measurement of Research Variables

To measure the degree of radicalness of a reengineering project, we adopt the multi-dimensional view commonly ascribed to by BPR practitioners and research-ers. The set of field case studies reported by Hall, et al. (1993) has demonstrated that, to achieve performance breakthrough, the redesign should fundamentally change a spectrum of related organizational elements: 1) roles and responsibilities, 2) mea-surements and incentives, 3) organizational structure, 4) information technology, 5) shared values, and 6) skills. Based on this work, we measure the degree of BPR project radicalness along seven dimensions — six of these were drawn from Hall, et al. (1993) as listed above, and the seventh dimension pertains to change to the patterns of process work flow. Respondents were asked to "assess the <u>extent of change</u> your team has attempted in redesigning the process in terms of the following

Table 4:   Reengineering Project Stages and Tasks

Stage 1. Identification of BR Opportunities

- Establish a steering committee for overall BR planning
- Secure management commitment
- Align with corporate and IT strategies
- Identify major business processes with a "business model"
- Understand customers' requirements
- Prioritize processes and select one for implementation

Stage 2. Project Preparation

- Plan for organizational change (e.g., inform stakeholders)
- Organize a BR team for the selected process
- Train the BR team members
- Conduct project planning

Stage 3. Analysis of the Existing Process

- Analyze existing process structure and flows
- Identify value-adding activities
- Identify opportunities for process improvement

Stage 4. Development of a Process Vision

- Understand process customers' requirements
- Identify process performance measures
- Set process performance goals
- Identify IT which enables process redesign
- Develop a vision (preliminary sketch) for the redesigned process

Stage 5a. Solution: Technical Design

- Develop and evaluate alternative process designs
- Detailed process modeling (entities, relationships, etc.)
- Design controls for process integrity
- IS analysis and design for the new process
- Prototype and refine the process design

Stage 5b. Solution: Social Design

- Empower customer contact personnel
- Define jobs and incentives
- Develop and foster shared values
- Define skill requirements and career paths
- Design new organizational structure
- Design employee performance measurement schemes
- Design change management program

Stage 6. Process Transformation

- Develop test and rollout plans
- Implement the social and technical design
- Train staff and pilot new process

Stage 7. Process Evaluation

- Monitor performance
- Continuous improvement

7 dimensions (1 = moderate change, 3 = substantial change, 5 = radical change)."

Although not all responding companies are expected to use formal methodologies, both formal and informal approaches to BPR project have several generic stages, and certain tasks are typically performed within each stage (Kettinger, Guha and Teng, 1993). To evaluate the strength of efforts spent in various stages of the project (i.e., stage-efforts), an eight-stage framework was adopted based on a number of published reengineering methodologies (Kettinger, Teng and Guha, 1997). The respondents were presented with the outline of the eight-stage framework with a set of specific tasks within each stage, as shown in Table 4. The instruction was "for each stage, please enter a number between 1 and 5 to indicate the strength of the effort that your project team has attempted to complete those tasks (1 = very weak, 2 = weak, 3 = median, 4 = strong, 5 = very strong)." Further, they were instructed to leave the box blank "if the stage was not attempted."

As in Study Two, reengineering project success was measured multi-dimensionally based on two different perspectives: perceived level of success (DeLone and McLean, 1992) and goal fulfillment (Hamilton and Chervany, 1981; Schriven, 1972). In this study, respondents were asked to answer one five-point scaled question about the perceived success level of their project. Five commonly emphasized BPR goals were presented to the respondents: 1) cost reduction, 2) cycle-time reduction, 3) customer satisfaction level increase, 4) worker productivity increase, and 5) defects reduction (Davenport and Short, 1990; Morris and Brandon, 1993). For each goal, respondents indicated the planned level of performance improvement (before reengineering) and the actual level of improvement achieved (after project implementation). They were also directed to leave the spaces blank if the presented goal was not applicable to their projects. For each performance indicator, we compute a "ratio of fulfillment" which is the actual level of improvement divided by the planned level.

Stage-Efforts Profile.

The average strength of effort (on a scale of 1 to 5) showed the following stage-effort pattern:

- Stage 3 (analysis of the existing process) — 3.94
- Stage 1 (identification of reengineering opportunities)— 3.80
- Stage 4 (development of a process vision) — 3.63
- Stage 2 (project preparation) — 3.46
- Stage 6 (process transformation) — 3.39
- Stage 5a (solution: technical design) — 3.37
- Stage 7 (process evaluation) — 3.21
- Stage 5b (solution: social design) — 3.09,

The results show that the stage that received the most emphasis is the "analysis of the existing process" stage, indicating that the "clean slate" approach to BPR is rarely found in practice. This is not unexpected given the tangible nature of the existing process and the need to identify redundant tasks in the current procedure. It appears that most reengineering practitioners believe it is prudent to thoroughly comprehend the existing process before developing visions for a new one. Surprisingly, the sample firms focused least on the social design stage while the literature emphasized the importance of designing change management programs, incentives,

Table 5: Correlation Analysis for Radicalness and Success

Project Success	Patterns of process work flows	Roles and responsibilities	Performance measurements & incentives	Organizational structure	Information technology applications	Shared value (culture)	Skill requirements	Overall extent of change
Overall success level	.427 ***	.324 ***	.351 ***	.102	.280 ***	.173 *	.166	.409 ***
Cost reduction #	.269 * / .092	.159 / .194	.231 / .093	.260 * / .030	.165 / -.000	.139 / .058	.129 / .022	.291 ** / .110
Cycle time reduction #	.191 / .127	.134 / .050	.198 / .194	.033 / -.157	.033 / -.021	.111 / .029	.098 / .008	.171 / .052
Customer satisfaction increase #	.258 / .242	.187 / .129	.282 * / .366 **	.180 / -.242	-.022 / .039	-.019 / .024	-.112 / -.168	.182 / .098
Worker productivity increase #	.122 / .061	.107 / .197	.159 / .431 ***	.131 / .069	.011 / -.187	.047 / .053	-.043 / -.132	.125 / .134
Defects reduction #	-.124 / -.073	-.041 / .109	.151 / .044	.113 / .011	-.091 / -.380 *	.058 / -.133	-.218 / -.272	-.015 / -.173

*   Significance at $p < .10$ ** Significance at $p < .05$ *** Significance at $p < .01$
#   The first figure is the correlation with actual level of improvement, the second figure, the ratio of fulfillment.

measurement systems, developing values, and defining skill requirements (Hall, et al., 1993; Stoddard and Jarvenpaa, 1995). It should also be noted that the first four stages were ranked as one to four, indicating firms usually put more emphasis on early rather than later stages of reengineering projects.

Project Radicalness and Success.

The results of correlation analysis between radicalness and reengineering success are presented in Table 5. For perceived level of success, we found strong positive relationships between radicalness and success. Of the seven change dimensions, four — work flow patterns, roles and responsibilities, performance measurements and incentives, and IT applications — were significant at the .01 level and one — shared values (culture) — was significant at the .10 level. Although both skill requirements and structure dimensions failed to have significant associations, overall radicalness (the average of the 7 dimensions) was highly correlated with success ($r = .409$, $p < .01$). Thus, the findings generally support the contention that *likelihood of reengineering success increases with more thorough and substantial change to the key elements of the organization* (Hall, et al., 1993).

For the goal-fulfillment indicators, the study found only a few significant associations. However, it is revealing to note and interpret how certain improvement goals are associated with specific changes. First, some support was found for the relationship between cost reduction and changes in work patterns and organizational structure. Current patterns of work flow and organizational structure, often in the form of redundant processing steps and personnel, may have caused many cost-related problems, and become targets for radical changes, especially when cost reduction is a primary goal. While these relationships were found for actual cost reductions, they did not hold for ratio of fulfillment possibly due to overly ambitious goals. Second, radical change in performance measurements and incentive systems were related with worker productivity and the level of customer satisfaction. These findings suggest that by fundamentally altering measurement and incentive systems, companies can more accurately measure employees' performance and reward them on the basis of the value they add in serving the ultimate customer, thus increasing productivity and customer satisfaction. A somewhat surprising finding is the lack of relationship between cycle time reduction and any change dimensions. The data suggests that cycle time improvement tends to reach a certain plateau and stays there regardless of the magnitude of the change effort. One possible interpretation is the physical limitation to how fast a process can be completed. Even with drastic changes to a process, there is always a minimum of time needed to accomplish the tasks required. Finally, there was also a lack of relationship between defect reduction and the various change dimensions. In fact, possibility exists that a negative relationship may develop, as in the case between changes in IT application and the ratio of fulfillment in defect reduction. It seems likely that modest change is optimal for defect reduction, and too much changes may lead to chaos and more possibilities for mistakes. Future research should carefully investigate these curious findings further.

Relating Stage-Efforts Profile and Success.

As can be seen in Table 6, most stages (seven out of eight) were significantly associated with perceived overall success. While we found moderate effects in

Table 6: Correlation Analysis for Project Stage-Efforts and Implementation Success

Project Success	Identification of BPR opportunities	Project preparation	Analysis of the existing process	Development of a process vision	Solution: technical design	Solution: social design	Process transformation	Process evaluation
Overall success level	.247 **	.244 **	.139	.242 **	.199 *	.390 ***	.432 ***	.547 ***
Cost reduction #	.134	.103	.013	.095	.165	.314 **	.220	.386 ***
	-.116	.205	.269 *	.188	-.000	.203	.339 **	.577 ***
Cycle time reduction #	.039	.042	.072	.219	.033	.274 **	.267 *	.342 **
	-.126	.122	.196	.225	-.021	.108	.222	.455 ***
Customer satisfaction increase #	.248	-.064	.156	.232	-.022	.354 **	.211	.374 **
	.122	.147	.280 *	.392 **	.039	.360 **	.310 **	.404 **
Worker productivity increase #	.092	.080	.038	.214	.011	.294 **	.213	.314 **
	.000	.115	.261 *	.193	-.187	.470 ***	.299 *	.619 ***
Defects reduction #	.184	-.171	.020	.172	-.091	.399 **	.257	.351 *
	-.025	.154	.285	-.064	-.380 *	.071	.275	.551 ***

* Significance at p < .10   ** Significance at p < .05   *** Significance at p < .01
\# The first figure is the correlation with actual level of improvement, the second figure, the ratio of fulfillment

identification, preparation, and vision stages, the strongest effects were observed in the social design, process transformation, and process evaluation stages. This confirms the importance of change management and human resource management programs in BPR. Also, the findings highlight the significance of later stages of reengineering, particularly continuous monitoring and evaluation for BPR success.

Interestingly, we found that the effort directed at analyzing existing processes did not affect the overall success of implementation. Fundamentally, BPR seeks to *change* existing processes to improve efficiency and effectiveness, and the lack of impact of effort spent on analyzing the existing process is certainly logically consistent with the very concept of reengineering. However, this is the first piece of empirical evidence that demonstrates this important point. The results, however, do not suggest that this project stage should be eliminated. The findings do indicate that too much emphasis on the analysis of existing business processes are not likely to make BPR implementation more successful.

The potential impact of technical design effort on success, although significant, is the weakest. This lends further support to recent realization among IS practitioners and researchers that process reengineering is, first and foremost structural and organizational change (Davenport and Stoddard 1994). Information technologies are important and often essential enablers, but the implementation involves multi-dimensional organizational change. Technical design effort appears to offer very moderate relief to these change problems and make limited contribution to project success.

The table also showed several significant associations with goal-fulfillment measures. The most impressive finding is the strong effects of the last three stages (social design, process transformation, and evaluation) on the various goal-fulfillment indicators. Other stages had only a few associations, and they were weaker than those for the last three stages. These results imply that programs for change management, human resource management, and continuous improvement are critical for success with respect to any goal-fulfillment criterion. Findings from the study have significant implications for both research and practice. The strong positive relationships between radicalness and implementation success suggests that likelihood of reengineering success increases with more thorough and substantial change of the key elements of the organization. It is important, however, not to equate "radical" process change, as described in this study, with the reckless overhaul of a process without considering its human and organizational ramifications. In fact, the study shows that in addition to changes in work flow patterns and the application of IT, organizational elements such as the roles and responsibility as well as performance measurement and incentives are also highly related to perceived success. IS and BPR professionals can enhance prospect of project success through thorough and substantial changes to both the technical and the social components of the process.

Patterns of Findings.

Further insights into the importance of social and organizational elements in process change can be gained by examining both the average stage-efforts and the impact of these efforts on perceived project success (Table 6). By juxtaposing these two results, as can be seen in Table 7, an interesting pattern emerges: extent of effort

Table 7:   Stage-efforts Vs. Impact on Perceived Project Success

Stage	Average effort [#]	Correlation with perceived success [#]
Stage 3: Analysis of the Existing Process	3.94 (1)	.139 (8)
Stage 1: Identification of BPR Opportunities	3.80 (2)	.247 ** (4)
Stage 4: Development of a Process Vision	3.63 (3)	.242 ** (6)
Stage 2: Project Preparation	3.46 (4)	.244 ** (5)
Stage 6: Process Transformation	3.39 (5)	.432 *** (2)
Stage 5a: Solution: Technical Design	3.37 (6)	.199 * (7)
Stage 7: Process Evaluation	3.21 (7)	.547 *** (1)
Stage 5b: Solution: Social Design	3.09 (8)	.390 *** (3)

[#] Numbers in the parentheses indicate ranking

devoted to a stage appears to be inversely related to its potential impact on perceived project success. For example, stage 3 (analysis of the existing process) received the most effort on average, but it has no significant correlation with perceived success. On the other hand, stage 7 and 5b (process evaluation and social design) received the least effort, but ranked on the top in terms of potential impact on both perceived success as well as specific goals. These results strongly suggest that:

1) IS and BPR professionals have not paid sufficient attention to the later stages of reengineering projects such as social design, process transformation and evaluation;

2) Additional effort directed at these later stages will likely be more effective than at other stages in improving the odds of project success.

As the number of reengineering failures increases, these results provide specific guidelines to reengineering project implementation for IS and BPR professionals that are based on solid empirical research rather than consultants' subjective opinions.

Conclusion and Future Studies

Recent developments in process reengineering have taken many organizations down the path of unprecedented organizational change. To prepare for these changes, a conceptual framework is developed to depict elements of organizational change associated with process reengineering: sources of organizational impetus leading to reengineering initiatives, change initiation, selecting process change enablers, change implementation, and the various dimensions of possible organizational change resulting from redesigned business processes. In discussing these elements, we stress that process reengineering is much more than applying IT to streamline complicated procedures. It is first and foremost a multi-faceted process of change involving organizational structure, management systems, human resource architecture and many other aspects of organizational life.

The prescriptive guidelines derived from the conceptual framework have received substantial and convincing support in the three empirical studies summarized above. Results of the first study confirmed that organic organizations with greater interdepartmental integration, more decentralized decision making and higher strategy-IS integration exhibit greater impetus toward process change initiatives. The true nature of business process reengineering projects — social-technical design — was vividly demonstrated in both the second and the third study. Results of the second study indicate that, among a number of reengineering implementation problems, change management was regarded as the most severe by project participants. In addition, we also found that, while both change management and technological competence problems were regarded as very difficult by project participants, the former was related much more strongly to reengineering success than the latter. In a similar vein, the third study reveals that social design received the least attention from project participants, and yet is very strongly related to success. Thus, the evidence suggest that in implementing process change, social design is first and technical matters are second.

With empirical support based on large field sample, the organizational change framework for process reengineering presented in this paper should prove helpful in providing a high-level perspective for guiding the planning and implementation of BPR initiatives. Indeed, recent trends in research and practice have shifted from a narrow "one-shot" redesign effort to an on-going "process management" orientation which emphasizes the critical importance of human and organizational factors in not only the initial but the continuing sustainable success of BPR (Davenport, 1995).

Reengineering initiatives involve multi-faceted socio-technical change, and efforts to understand this complex phenomenon is only beginning. The conceptual framework and empirical evidence presented in this paper need to be refined and extended with further theoretical and empirical work. Future studies may systematically examine factors underlying success as well as failures[2]. Secondly, the frameworks and perspectives presented here represent general trends which need to be refined through contingency-based research approaches. The directions of organizational changes stemming from BPR, for example, may be extended through examining how these patterns of change vary in speed and scope for various types of organizations, and how different industries may involve different facilitating and inhibiting factors. Further, future studies may also consider the role of organizational learning (Magnet, 1992) and quality of work life issues (Cranny, Smith, and Stone, 1992) which are closely related to the organizational change process and its ultimate success.

Endnotes

1 For a more detailed treatment of this framework, refer to Teng, Grover and Fiedler (1996)
2 One study we conducted recently involves a set of reengineering cases having a range of outcomes — from highly successful to miserable failures (Guha, Grover, Kettinger and Teng, 1997).

References

Akao, Y. (1990) *Quality Function Deployment: Integrating Customer Requirements into Product Design.* Cambridge: Productivity Press.

Alter, A. (1990-December) The Corporate Make-over. *CIO*, 32-42.

Armstrong, D. A. (1990-April) The People Factor in EIS Success. *Datamation*, 73-79.

Bartholomew, D. (1991 July) Charles Schwab Bullish on Reengineering. *Information Week*, 12-13.

Bashien, B. J., Markus, M. L. and Riley, P. (1994) Preconditions for BPR Success. *Journal of Information Systems Management,* 1, 7- 13.

Beath, C. and Ives, B. (1989) The Information Technology Champion: Aiding and Abetting Care and Feeling. *Journal of Management Information Systems,* 6(2), 104-115.

Berger, J. Angiolillo, P., and Mason, T. (1987-October) Office Automation: Making it Pay Off. *Business Week,* 134-146.

Betts, M. (1992-March) Mature Firms Plan an IS-Driven Overhaul.. *CIO,* 97.

Bostrom, R.P. and Heinen, J.S. (1977) MIS problems and failure: a socio-technical perspective (part I). *MIS Quarterly,* 1(3), 17-32.

Brousell, D. Appleton, E. and Moad, J. (1992-June) Levi Strauss's CIO on the Technology of Empowerment. *Datamation,* 121-124.

Burns T., and Stalker G. (1961). *The Management of Innovation.* London.: Tavistock Publications.

Byrne, J. A. (1993- October 20) The Horizontal Corporation: it's About Managing Across, not Up and Down. *Business Week,* 76-81.

Caron, J.R. Jarvenpaa, S.L. and Stoddard, D.B. (1994) Business Reengineering at CIGNA Corporation: Experiences and Lessons Learned From the First Five Years. *MIS Quarterly,* 18(3) 233-250.

Champy, J.A. (1995) *Reengineering Management: The Mandate for New Leadership.* Harper Collins Publishers, Inc.

Churchill, G.A., Jr. (1979) A paradigm for developing better measures of marketing constructs. *Journal of Marketing Research,* 16(1) 64-73.

Cranny, C.J., Smith, P.C. and Stone, E.F. (1992) *Job Satisfaction: How People feel About their Jobs and How it Affects Their Performance.* New York: Lexington Books.

CSC Index. (1994) *State of Reengineering Report.* CSC Index..

Damanpour, F. (1991) Organizational innovation: a meta-analysis of effects of determinants and moderators. *Academy of Management Journal.*

Davenport, T. H. (1993) *Process Innovation: Reengineering Work through Information Technology,* Harvard Business School Press.

Davenport, T. H. and Nohria, N. (1994) Case Management and the Integration of Labor. *Sloan Management Review.* 4, 11-23.

Davenport, T.and Short, J. (1990) The new industrial engineering: information technology and business process redesign. *Sloan Management Review,* 2, 11-27.

Davenport, T.H. (1995) Business process reengineering: where it's been, where it's going. In *Business Process Change: Concepts, Methods & Technologies.* (Edited by V.Grover and W.J. Kettinger). Idea Publishing. Harrisburg, PA.

Davenport, T.H. and Stoddard, D.B. (1994-June) Reengineering business change of mythic proportions? *MIS Quarterly,* 121-127.

Davis, T. R. V. (1993-July/August) Reengineering in action. *Planning Review,* 49-54.

DeLone, W. and McLean, E.R. (1992) Information systems success: The quest for the dependent variable. *Information Systems Research* 3(1), 60-95.

Ellis, C. A.,Gibbs, S. J. and Rein, G. L. (1991) Groupware: some issues and experiences. *Communications of the ACM.* 34(1), 38-58.

Fiedler, K.D., Grover, V. and Teng J.T.C., (1995) Empirical Study of Information Technology Enabled Business Process Redesign and Corporate Competitive Strategy, *European Journal of Information Systems,* 4, 17-30.

French, W.L. and Bell, C.H. (1978) Organization Development. Englewood Cliffs, NJ: Prentice Hall.

Gersick, C.J.G. (1991) Revolutionary change theories: a multilevel exploration of the punctuated equilibrium paradigm.. *Academy of Management Review,* 16 (1), 10-36.

Ginzberg, M.J. (1981) Early diagnosis of MIS implementation failure: promising results and unanswered questions. *Management Science*, 27(4), 459-478.

Grover, V. (1993) "An Empirically Derived Model for the Adoption of Customer-based Interorganizational Systems," *Decision Sciences,* 24(3), 603-640.

Grover, V. Fiedler, K.D. and Teng, J.T.C. (1994) Exploring the Success of Information Technology Enabled Business Process Reengineering. *IEEE Transactions on Engineering Management,* 41(3), 1-8.

Grover, V., Jeong, S.Y., Kettinger, W.J., and Teng, J.T.C. (1995) The implementation of business process reengineering. *Journal of Management Information Systems,* 12(1), 109-144.

Grover, V., Lederer, A.L., and Sabherwal, R. (1988) Recognizing the politics of MIS. *Information and Management.,* 14, 145-156.

Grover, V., Teng, J.T.C., and Fiedler, K.D. (1993) "Information Technology Enabled Business Process Redesign: An Integrated Planning Framework," *Omega: the International Journal of Management Science,* 21(4), 433-447.

Guha, S, Grover, V., Kettinger W.J. and Teng, J.T.C. (1997) "Business Process Change and Organizational Performance: Exploring an Antecedent Model," *Journal of Management Information Systems,* 14(1), 119-154.

Hall, G., Rosenthal J. and Wade, J. (1993) How reengineering really work. *Harvard Business Review,* 71(6), 119-131.

Hamilton, S. and Chervany, N.L. (1981) Evaluating information system effectiveness - part I: Comparing evaluation approaches. *MIS Quarterly,* 5(3), 55-69.

Hammer, M. (1990, July-August) Reengineering Works: Don't Automate, Obliterate. *Harvard Business Rev*iew 68(4), 104-112.

Hammer, M. and Champy, J.(1993) *Reengineering the Corporation: A Manifesto for Business Revolution.* Harper Collins Publishers, Inc.

Hodgetts, R. M., Luthans, F. and Lee, S. M. (1994) New paradigm organizations: from total quality to learning to world-class. *Organizational Dynamics* 5-19

Huber, G.P. and Power, D.J. (1985) Research notes and communications retrospective reports of strategic-level managers: Guidelines for increasing their accuracy. *Strategic Management Journal,* 6, 171-180.

Keen, P.G.W. (1981) Information systems and organizational change. *Communications of the ACM.* 24(1), 24-33.

Kettinger, W.J and Teng, J.T.C., (1998) "Aligning BPR to Strategy: a Framework for Analysis," *Long Range Planning,* 31(1), 93-107.

Kettinger, W.J., Teng J.T.C., and Guha S.,(1997) "Business Process Change: A Study of Methodologies, Techniques and Tools," MIS Quarterly, 21(1), 55-80.

Kettinger, W.J., Guha, S. and Teng, J.T.C. (1995) The process reengineering life cycle methodology: a case study. In Grover, V. and Kettinger, W.J. (Eds) *Business Process Change: Reengineering Concepts, Methods and Technologies*, Harrisburg, PA: Idea Publishing Inc., 210-244.

Kettinger, W.J., Guha, S. and Teng, J.T.C. (1993) Business process reengineering: Building the foundation for a comprehensive methodology, *Journal of Information Systems Management* Summer, 13-22.

Kotter, J.P., and Schlesinger, L.A. (1979-Mar/Apr) Choosing strategies for change. *Harvard Business Review.,* 106-113.

Lambert, R.and Peppard, J. (1993) Information technology and new organizational forms: destination but no road map?. *Journal of Strategic Information Systems*, 2(3), 180-205.

Lewin, K. (1951) *Field Theory in Social Science.* New York: Harper and Row.

Liker, J. Roitman, D.B., and Roskies, E. (1987-Summer) Changing everything all at once: work life and technological change. *Sloan Management Review.,* 29-47.

Lucas Jr., H.C. (1984-Jan) Organizational Power and the Information Services Department. *Communications of the ACM,* 27(1), 58-65.

Lucas, H.C. (1978) Empirical evidence for a descriptive model of implementation. *MIS Quarterly*, 2(2), 27-41.

Magnet, M. (1992-November) Who is winning the information revolution?. *Fortune*, 110-117.

Malone, T. W. and Rockart, J. F. (1991-September) Computers, networks and the corporation. *Scientific American*, 128-136.

Markus, M.L. (1983) Power, politics and MIS implementation. *Communications of the ACM*. 26(6), 583-598.

Markus, M.L. and Robey, D. (1995) Business process reengineering and the role of information systems professionals. In Grover, V. and Kettinger, W.J. (Eds) *Business Process Change: Concepts, Methods and Technologies* Harrisburg, P.A.: Idea Publishing Inc.

McWhirter, W. (1992-November 9) Chrysler's second amazing comeback. *Business Week*, 51.

Melone, N.P. (1995) When people work scared: understanding attitudes and gaining compliance in business process re-engineering. In *Business Process Change: Concepts, Methods, & Technologies.* (Edited by V.B. Grover and W.J. Kettinger). Idea Publishing. Harrisburg, PA.

Miller, D. and Friesen, P.H. (1982) "Innovation in Conservative and Entrepreneurial Firms: the Third Link," *Strategic Management Journal* 3, 1-25.

Miller, W. (1987) *The Creative Edge.* Reading, MA: Addison-Wesley.

Morris, D. and Brandon, J. (1993) Re-engineering your business. New York: McGraw-Hill, Inc.

Mumford, E. (1994) New Treatment or Old Remedies: Is BPR Really Socio-technical Design? *Journal of Strategic Information Systems*, 3(4), 313-326.

Mumford, E. and Weir, M. (1979) Computer Systems in Work Designs: The ETHICS Method. New York : Wiley.

Nunnally, J. (1967) *Psychometric Theory,* New York, NY : McGraw-Hill Book Company.

Nutt, P.C., (1986-June) Tactics of implementation. *Academy of Management Journal.*, 230-261.

O'Hara, M.T. and Watson, R.T. (1995) "Automation, Business Process Reengineering and Client Server Computing," In V. Grover and W.J. Kettinger (eds.), *Business Process Change: Reengineering Concepts, Methods and Technology*, Idea Publishing, Harrisburg, PA, 143-164.

Ostroff, F., and D. Smith, (1992) The horizontal organization. redesigning the corporation. *McKinsey Quarterly.* 1, 148-167.

Pasmore, W. (1994) *Creating Strategic Change: Designing the Flexible High-Performance Organization.* New York : Wiley.

Pierce J. L. and Delbeeq A. L. (1977) Organizational Structure, Individual Attributes and Innovation. *Academy of Management Review.* 2, 27-37.

Premkumar, G. and King, W.R. (1992) "An Empirical Assessment of Information Systems Planning and the Role of Information Systems in Organizations," *Journal of Management Information Sysems.*, (2), 94-125.

Ramamurthy, K. (1990) *Role of Environmental, Organizational and Technological Factors in Information Technology Implementation in Advanced Manufacturing: an Innovation-Adoption-Diffusion Perspective*, Unpublished Doctoral Dissertation, University of Pittsburgh.

Rockart, J. F. and Short, J. E. (1991) The networked organization and the management of interdependence. In M. S. Scott Morton (Editor), *The Corporation of the 1990s: Information Technology and Organizational Transformation*, Oxford University Press, 191-192.

Saunders, C.S. and Scamell, R.W. (1986) Organizational Power and the Information Services Department: A Reexamination. *Communications of the ACM* 29(2), 142-147.

Schriven, M. (1972) The methodology of evaluation: Formative and summative evaluation. In C.H. Weiss (Eds.), *Evaluating Action Programs*. Allyn and Bacon, Boston, MA.

Scott Morton, M. S. (Editor), (1991) *The Corporation of the 1990s: Information Technology and Organizational Transformation*, Oxford University Press.

Smith, G. and Willcocks, L., (1995) Business process reengineering, politics management: from methodologies to processes. In V. Grover and W.J. Kettinger (Eds), *Business Process Change: Reengineering Concepts. Methods and Technologies.* Idea Publishing. Harrisburg, PA.

Stewart, T. A. (1992) The search for the organization of tomorrow. *Fortune*, May, 92-98.

Stewart, T. A. (1993) Reengineering; the hot new managing tool. *Fortune*, August, 41-48.

Stoddard, D. and Jarvenpaa, S. (1995) Business process reengineering: Tactics for managing radical change," *Journal of Management Information Systems* 12(1), 81-108.

Teng, J.T.C. and Kettinger, W.J., (1995) "Business Process Redesign and Information Architecture: Exploring the Relationships", Data Base, 26(1), 30-42.

Teng, J.T.C., Grover, V., and Fiedler, K. (1994a), Business process reengineering: Charting a strategic path for the information age. *California Management Review* 36(3),9-31.

Teng, J.T.C. Grover, V. and Fiedler, K.D. (1994b) Re-engineering Business processes Using Information Technology. *Long Range Planning*, 27(1), 95-106.

Teng, J.T.C., Fiedler K.D. and Grover V., (1998) An Exploratory Study of the Influence of the IS Function and Organizational Context on Business Process Reengineering Project Initiatives. *OMEGA*, 26(6), 679-698.

Teng, J.T.C., Grover, V. and Fiedler, K.D., (1996) Developing Strategic Perspectives on Business Process Reengineering: from Process Reconfiguration to Organizational Change. *OMEGA*, 24(3), 271-294.

Teng, J.T.C., Jeong S. R and Grover V., (1998, June) Profiling Successful reengineering projects. *Communications of the ACM*, 41(6), 96-102.

Treece, J. B. (1994-Bonus Issue) Breaking the chains of command. *Business Week*, 112-114.

Zmud R. (1982) Diffusion of Modern Software Practices: Impact of Centralization and Formalization. *Management. Science,*. 28(12), 420-430.

CHAPTER 5

Business Process Change and Organizational Performance: Exploring an Antecedent Model

Subo Guha
NCR Corporation, USA

Varun Grover, William J. Kettinger and James T.C. Teng
University of South Carolina, USA

In recent years, both academics and practitioners have challenged the ways in which organizations structure themselves. Traditional models of hierarchy and control have been described as pathological, appropriate for an erstwhile era of stability but inappropriate for today's dynamic business world. Organizational change has been advocated over the past decade under banners of downsizing, restructuring, and business process reengineering. These projects often engender themes of empowerment, teamwork, and customer orientation. While billions of dollars have been committed to redesign of organizational business processes, including investment in technology infrastructure, consulting, and people, the results are ambivalent at best. Some reports indicate that as many as 70 percent of reengineering projects fail. The question is: Why? Clearly, with a critical mass of business process change (BPC) projects behind us, the time is rife for leveraging their collective experience and isolating key attributes of successes and failures.

While a number of recent studies have attempted to investigate BPC and organizational change endeavors, they are mostly limited in scope. Three attributes characterize recent work on BPC. First, they are often atheoretical. This would suggest that the diverse research streams in strategic management, innovation, organizational behavior, implementation, and the like provide only limited guidance on change efforts. Second, these studies suffer from a limited repertoire of variables, often isolating their scope of investigation to information technology (IT), strategic orientation, or change management. While circumscribing the research domain of BPC in this manner is effective in channeling research resources, it precludes investigation of a phenomenon that has a wide variety of contingency factors. Third, many recent studies look at single organizations and single BPC projects. The advantages of indepth case studies notwithstanding, without variance or divergence in variables, it is difficult to interpret results in a manner that instills confidence in terms of external validity.

The research challenge, then, is one of leveraging existing theory and examining diverse attributes of BPC across multiple contexts. Such an approach, if accomplished through cross-case analysis, can complement theories that assume an invariant relationship between independent and dependent variables. While we make no pretensions of having eliminated the concerns outlined above, we attempt to examine antecedents to BPC outcomes by applying a theoretical framework that includes a wide variety of variables consistently across three case studies with diverse outcomes. Our central question is simple: *What factors facilitate and inhibit the success of large-scale BPC endeavors?*

Research Model

The concept of BPC has evolved over the past several years. The radical tone of earlier business reengineering has been somewhat tempered by a degree of contextual realism (Caron, Jarvenpaa and Stoddard, 1994; Earl, 1994). Further, earlier practices and writings espoused an IT-centric position, which is now being reconciled with a more holistic approach to BPC (Grover, Jeong, Kettinger and Teng, 1995), including consideration of IT, organizational structure, strategy, information, change management, evaluation methods, and more incremental process change methods such as total quality management (TQM) (Harkness, Kettinger and Segars, 1996).

BPC is defined here as an organizational initiative to design business processes to achieve significant (breakthrough) improvement in performance (e.g., quality, responsiveness, cost, flexibility, satisfaction, shareholder value, and other critical process measures) through changes in the relationships between management, information, technology, organizational structure, and people (Kettinger, Guha and Teng, 1995). These initiatives may differ in scope from process improvement to radical new process designs that are contingent upon the degree of change undertaken in each organizational subsystem and their interactions. Therefore, in any examination of BPC outcomes, consideration should be given to (a) the environmental conditions for change and (b) the ability of the organization to manage change in those conditions. Kettinger and Grover (1995) considered both of these aspects in the BPC management model shown in Figure 1 and described briefly below.[1] This model guides our study of facilitators and inhibitors of successful BPC.

The relationships presented in the framework are based on relevant work in organizational change, strategic management, innovation, and information systems (IS). The general thesis of this framework is that *any significant business process change requires a strategic initiative where top managers act as leaders in defining and communicating a vision of change. The organizational environment, with a ready culture, a willingness to share knowledge, balanced network relationships, and a capacity to learn, should facilitate the implementation of prescribed process management and change management practices. Process and change management practices, along with the change environment, contribute to better business processes and help in securing improved quality of work life, both of which are requisite for customer success and, ultimately, in achieving measurable and sustainable competitive performance gains.*

Each component of the framework is described below as it is applied to the subsequent case analysis. Following the description, salient dimensions of the component, referred to as "constructs," are identified. During the case study, each

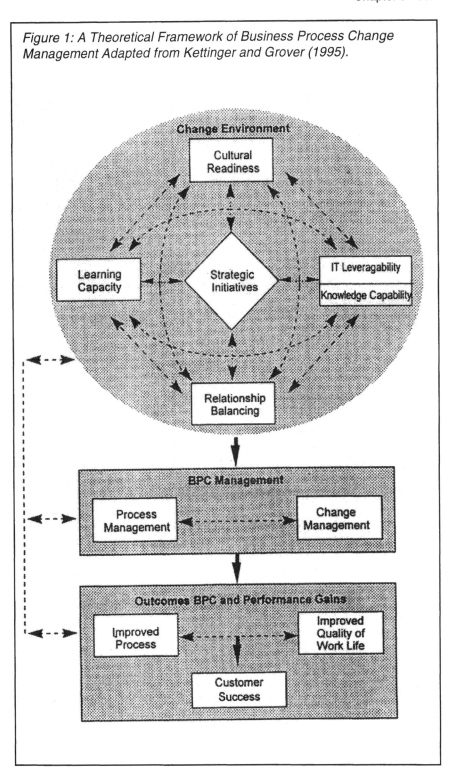

Figure 1: A Theoretical Framework of Business Process Change Management Adapted from Kettinger and Grover (1995).

construct is probed so that we can classify the organization into several categories. For example, one of the constructs for the "strategic initiatives" component is stimuli, and the resulting probe classifies an organization into one of two categories: proactive versus reactive.

Strategic Initiatives

Process change typically begins with strategic initiatives such as envisioning, commitment, and enabling from the senior management team (Kotter, 1995). These could be a reaction to a need (e.g., poor performance) or a proactive push to leverage potential opportunities (Earl, 1994). Evidence also exists that strategic change, and arguably process change, is often incremental, informal, emergent, and is based on learning through small gains (Harkness et al., 1996; Mintzberg and Waters, 1985). Top management is key in establishing innovative organizational cultures (Grover et al., 1995; Wiersema and Bantel, 1992). Transformational leaders create a vision for the organization that generates commitment using involvement-oriented management (Hambrick, 1994; Nadler and Tushman, 1990). This vision might establish a sense of urgency (Kotter, 1995), encourage the pursuit of change (Tushman and Romanelli, 1985), and be integrated at some point with corporate strategy (Earl, 1994; Grover et al., 1995). Initiatives could be forced on the organization through mandate (autocratic) or pushed through consensus within existing systems of the organization (bureaucratic) (Shrivastava, 1994). Alternatively, champions of change could emerge to seek out creative ideas and make them tangible (Tushman and Romanelli, 1985) through coalition building, knowledge sharing, and persuasion (Beath, 1991; Melone, 1995). In sum, the strategic initiatives involve delineation of a specific plan of action and then motivate the entire firm toward achievement of this goal.

Therefore, the key constructs that can be probed here are: *stimuli* (proactive versus reactive), *formulation scope* (incremental versus revolutionary), *decision making* (autocratic, bureaucratic, champion emergence), and whether the change process is *strategy led* (onset, eventually, none).

Learning Capacity

Organizational learning has been the subject of much study (Argyris and Schoen, 1978; March, 1991; Senge, 1990; Simon, 1991). Management, innovation, and organizational literature assume that learning is stimulated by the need for organizational adjustment in response to some ill-defined stimuli (Dodgson, 1994). This makes it particularly relevant to BPC, where the quest is to improve competitiveness and productivity in uncertain environments. The major goal of learning is to provide positive outcomes through effective adaptation to environmental changes and improved efficiency in the process of learning. Adaptation entails appropriate responses to technological changes and learning from other organizations that have achieved the best practices in the industry (Freeman and Perez, 1988). Increased efficiency in learning has been a primary focus of industrial economists who posit the notion of "learning by doing" (Arrow, 1962) and accumulation of knowledge through cross-functional interfaces (Adler, 1990). Declarative knowledge (i.e., bodies of organized information) facilitates learning in a collective fashion (Corsini, 1987). Such knowledge can be accumulated through the development of a knowledge base (Metcalf and Gibbons, 1989), a focus on core competencies (Hamel and Prahalad, 1994; Teece, Pisano and Schuen, 1990) that provide uniqueness to declarative knowledge, and technological/R&D development, which stimulates procedural knowledge (Corsini, 1987). Also, external information scanning can enhance the bounded rationality of individuals within the firm and provide key information on BPC. This may be carried out by technology gatekeepers (Allen, 1977), boundary spanners (Michael, 1973), or customers (Von Hipple, 1988). A qualitative description of learning may be based on Argyris and Schoen's (1978) three-tier typology. Single-loop learning maintains stable relationships and works within existing norms, policies, and procedures, while double-loop learning challenges existing systems and their assumptions (Lant and Mezias, 1992; March, 1981). Higher-level learning (deutero) occurs when members reflect on past learning experiences to learn and discover strategies for learning. Thus, higher-level learning affects the entire organization, develops understanding of causation and complex associations involving new actions, and is characterized by change in network relationships and decision making (Fiol and Lyles, 1985). In sum, learning organizations are characterized by the ability to adapt and improve, to build internal and external knowledge, and to achieve higher levels of learning that may be critical to successful BPC.

The key constructs that can be probed here are: *adaptation* (response to technology change, learning from others), *improved efficiency* (learning by doing), *declarative knowledge* (R &D) (resources and technology development, knowledge base, focus on core competencies), *external information use* (boundary spanners, technology gate- keepers, customers), *learning type* (double-loop, deutero).

Cultural Readiness

Organization culture facilitates (or inhibits) the integration of individual learning with organizational learning by influencing an organization's ability to learn, share information, and make decisions (Kilman, Saxton and Serpa, 1986). The importance of organization culture is best understood in terms of cultural beliefs, values, and norms (Kilman et al., 1986; Schein, 1984). Beliefs shape interpretations of information, while value systems relate behaviors across units and levels of the organization. Values often exhibit a propensity to resist change because of their shared nature (Fitzgerald, 1988). Norms are the unwritten and socially transmitted guides to behavior. Norms that promote change include risk taking, openness, shared vision, respect and trust, high expectation for action, and a focus on quality (O'Reilly, 1989). Norms that discourage change include risk avoidance, ambivalence, group think, and excessive competition (O'Reilly, 1989). Leadership or change agents that can diagnose and influence cultural readiness for change may be a prerequisite for BPC (Tushman and Nadler, 1986). Klempa (1995) distinguishes between heterogeneous and homogeneous culture, where the former is more risk seeking and aggressive and the latter more cautious. Also, the potential to promote a common culture and innovative behavior can be enabled by open communications and information sharing. In sum, cultural readiness can be enabled by leadership or change agents, can open communication, and can define the risk-taking propensity in the firm.

The key constructs that can be probed here are: *change agents and leadership, risk aversion* (cautious, aggressive), and *extent of open communications.*

IT Leveragability and Knowledge-Sharing Capability

The sensing, collection, organization, communication, and use of information are critical to the knowledge-based organization (Huber and McDaniel, 1986; Marchand and Stanford, 1995). IT is an organizational resource, providing the necessary means to accomplish required knowledge processing and, thereby, inducing organizational change (Grover, Teng and Fiedler, 1995; Hammer and Champy, 1993; Keen, 1981; Markus and Robey, 1988). Zuboff (1988) calls the process of change caused by IT "informating," with direct consequences on information flows, knowledge, culture, people, and tasks. Davenport (1993) explains IT's process impacts in terms of organization streamlining/simplification, capturing and distributing information, coordination, monitoring, analysis and decision making, and parallelism-enabling process change (Davenport, 1993; Ives and Vitale, 1988). The role of IT can be described in terms of the technological, organizational, and emergent imperatives depending on the extent to which IT is the dominant factor in BPC (Markus and Robey, 1988). The emergent perspective suggests a mutual, bidirectional relationship between IT and the organization, which is consistent with the sociotechnical change perspectives (Cherns, 1976; Mumford, 1994). However, communications technologies, particularly groupware, have received attention with respect to their direct effects on organizational structures and processes (Ellis, Gibbs and Rein, 1991; Huber, 1984; Huber, 1990; Keen, 1991; Keen, 1988; Teng, Grover and Fiedler, 1994). These technologies can facilitate learning and knowledge development through a process of coordinated interaction among individuals. The ability to share knowledge enhances an organization's proclivity to change (Charan, 1991; Nonaka, 1991) as transparent data access empowers individuals and knowledge workers reinforce one another's expertise. In sum, IT can play a varied role in business change; its communications infrastructure and the extent of knowledge sharing can create an environment facilitative of successful BPC.

The key constructs that can be probed here are: *IT role* (enabling, sociotechnical, dominant factor) and *use of communications technology.*

Network Relationships Balancing

Successful change processes often require the proactive leveraging of boundaries and relationships. This is typically the result of balancing internal and external networks in terms of the dialectic of cooperation and competition (Charan, 1991; Nonaka, 1991). The literature suggests that under most circumstances cooperative interpersonal and group behavior results in superior performance (Johnson and Johnson, 1989; Shaw, 1958). However, research also indicates that a manageable level of conflict can enhance individual and group performance. For example, it is possible that competitive controversy within generally cooperative groups (e.g., interfunctional) can result in greater openness, knowledge, and understanding (Tjosvold and Deemer, 1980). In terms of interorganizational processes, the literature indicates the benefits of "partnering" on a long-term cooperative basis with external suppliers (e.g., Crosby, 1994; Frey and Schlosser, 1993; Hahn, Kim and Kim, 1986). In sum, organizations that recognize the need to manage this competition and cooperation dialectic continuously have a greater propensity to benefit from employee incentives and controls as well as to instill change more effectively.

The key constructs that can be probed here are: *interorganizational linkages* and *crossfunctional cooperation* (cooperative, competitive).

Change Management Practice

Change management involves effectively balancing forces in favor of a change over forces of resistance (Stehel, 1992; Teng, Grove and Fiedler, 1996). Organizations, groups, or individuals will resist changes that are perceived as a threat to their frame of reference. Planned change can be conceptualized by Lewin's (1952) phased pattern of change involving unfreezing, moving, and refreezing. More recently, Beers (1987) suggests that corporate transformations require a general dissatisfaction with the status quo by employees who have to change (i.e., a readiness to change), a vision of the future, and a well-managed change process. However, the degree of change has been subject to debate. Strassman (1994), for instance, is a strong opponent of the visionary rhetoric and violent image of reengineering. He suggests that, to be effective, any way to improve the way people work must be evolutionary, not revolutionary. Revolutionary and evolutionary change theorists have proposed a number of contrasting tactics for accomplishing change (Stoddard and Jarvenpaa, 1995). These tactics vary in the type of employee involvement, scope of communication for change, and the nature of leadership (Harkness, Kettinger and Segars, 1996). In general, direct confrontation of forces of resistance will probably only increase resistance capacities (Melone, 1995; Stehel, 1992). In sum, change management involves countering resistance to change. It is often done in a phased manner, but the tactics used could vary depending on the scope of change required.

The key constructs that can be probed here are: *pattern of change, management's readiness to change* (committed, participative, resistant), *scope of change* (improvement, radical change), *managed change* (alleviation of dissatisfaction; a vision for change; and a well-managed process of change, evolutionary or revolutionary change tactics use).

Process Management Practice

Process management (PM) has been defined as a set of concepts and practices aimed at better stewardship of business processes (Davenport, 1995). PM combines methodological approaches with human resource management (Anderson, Rungtusanatham and Schroed, 1994; Grover et al., 1995; Kettinger et al., 1995) to improve the outcome of BPC. Various methods, typically adapted from industrial engineering, total quality, and IS practice, have been used in PM (Kettinger et al., 1995). Critical in PM is the notion of process measurement and going beyond typical financial indicators to effectively collecting process information and metrics (Davenport and Beers, 1995). Further, improved feedback and auditing of the process, by tying it back to corporate objectives, is critical to achieving organizational effectiveness (Teng, Grover and Fiedler, 1994). From the Japanese quality movement, PM has benefited from techniques (e.g., seven quality control tools (Ishikawa, 1986)) to better manage and control manufacturing (less equivocal) processes, as well as from techniques (e.g., seven management and planning tools (Mizuno, 1988)) to represent concepts and relationships (e.g., affinity and relationship diagrams) for less controllable processes. Adapted methods for more radical/BPR include process visioning and idea-generation/creativity techniques (Davenport, 1993; Hammer and Champy, 1993); strategic linkage and process delineation (Teng et al., 1992); process capture (e.g., IDEF0 (Mayer, Benjamin, Caraway and Painter, 1995)); customer requirements determination (e.g., Quality Function Deployment (Akao, 1990); process modeling (e.g., IDEF, (Mayer et al., 1995), Role Activity Diagramming (Hackvale and Ould, 1995), Event-Driven Modeling (Denna, Jasperson and Perry, 1995); process simulation (Van Med, Bots, and Sol, 1995); process rules specification and database design (Appleton, 1995); and process measurement (e.g., Customer Value Analysis (Kanesvsky and Housel, 1995)). Augmenting PM's methodological approaches are a set of employee practices regarding individual and team work, including how work is designed (Hackman and Oldham, 1979) and levels of participation in decisions (Cherns, 1976). PM can supplement traditional sociotechnical perspectives by including quantitative process goals such as output, productivity, costs, and profit measures.

The key constructs that can be probed here are: *process measurement* (use of process metrics, process information capture, improvement feedback loop, audit), *use of tools and techniques,* and *use of team-based structures.*

Outcomes of BPC and Performance Gains

Outcomes of BPC can be measured at various levels. At the process level, continuous improvement and radical BPR can be placed along a continuum of change. Davenport [1993, p.7] suggests that both approaches share the same unit of analysis, require rigorous measurement of process performance such as quality, cycle time, costs, and ultimately customer satisfaction (Hammer and Champy, 1993). These can be benchmarked against expectations and actual performance— ultimately leading to bottom-line indicators such as profitability and market share improvement. More recently, however, many leading firms that undertake BPC to meet strategic goals recognize that they can only accomplish their objectives through people and, therefore, are placing employee quality of work life (QWL) issues paramount in their BPC expected outcomes. If human needs have been considered and change effectively managed, employees should experience improved working conditions in redesigned process tasks; this should increase employee job satisfaction and pride in work and strengthen their commitment to the organization (Cranny, Smith and Stone, 1992). Ultimately, this should make employees more productive in their jobs and better able to serve their customers. Embedded in the QWL concept are "Theory Y" assumptions that people "like" to work, "enjoy" challenging work, and are willing to "take responsibility" for work outcomes (McGregor, 1960). In sum, successful BPC can be characterized by process outcomes that exceed expectations, including customer satisfaction, and improved QWL.

The key constructs that can be probed here are: *gaps between effectiveness expectations (goals) and actual performance improvements, and QWL* (employee satisfaction).

Methodology

We chose embedded multiple case-study analysis to investigate the research questions concerning the broad and complex phenomenon of BPC (Eisenhardt,

1989;Yin, 1989). Embedded implies the use of multiple units of analysis: (1) the firm (business processes and strategy), (2) the BPC team, and (3) the BPC project. Also, since the focus was on studying antecedents to organizational performance, care was taken to include relatively homogeneous BPC initiatives with variance across cases on the outcome measure. This would enable "theoretical" replication with contradictory results in order to allow us to examine any differences that might exist in antecedents (Yin, 1989).

The selection criteria used were:

- The project should have been completed.
- It should involve a major BPC project with organizational implications.
- At some point the project should have had breakthrough performance expectations.
- The project should focus on cross-functional processes.
- Initial assessment of outcomes should be unambiguous.

To identify the sites, a secondary literature search was conducted to identify major BPC efforts. This initial search of BPC efforts identified over eighty firms. The next stage was the soliciting of firms' interest in participating in the study. Of the ten firms that met the criteria, three made a commitment to participate in the study.

Data Gathering

Data-collection methods included a semistructured case protocol, a quantitative questionnaire, multiple documents and archival records, and telephone interviews. Such triangulation reduces bias and is recommended in case research (Yin, 1989). Literature regarding BPC projects, including data on company performance, was studied prior to and after each set of interviews. This approach provided richness and depth and enhanced the construct validity of the study. Interviews provided the major source for primary data. Several case respondents provided the investigators with reports and memoranda directly related to the BPC project. These included an overview of the project, any consultant presentations, systems or business plans, and notes compiled by the team. Other sources included company public information such as 10K, letters to shareholders, and annual reports for the current year as well as for the period during which the BPC projects were conducted. Online searches yielded several articles regarding the project or various issues, plans, or financial conditions that would provide additional insight into the case profile.

In all cases the focal point for contact was a senior-level manager in the company who was directly responsible or integrally involved with the project from beginning to end. To eliminate any bias by a single respondent, attempts were made to ensure triangulation of data from multiple sources in the organization. Respondents with the following profiles were sought out and interviewed:

1. Senior management, process champion, and BPC team leader (to discuss strategy and process implementation, corporate culture, learning and effectiveness);
2. Functional associates (to discuss culture and change process and expectation

gaps).

Most of the interviewees were either sponsors of the BPC or major team members who had a good, objective, and knowledgeable view of the project. Each interview was taped with the permission of the respondents. The nature and objective of the study were first explained to the respondent(s), who were also informed up front about expectations of involvement and the duration of the interview, as well as being reassured about issues of confidentiality. This was important since BPC tends to involve deviations from corporate strategy that firms are reluctant to release, especially to the competition. This provided a means to ensure integrity of the research and allowed the respondent to answer more openly and objectively.[2]

Each interview was conducted by using a standard case study protocol to ensure reliability (Yin, 1989). The resultant protocol was based on the BPC management model described earlier and contained major constructs and probes. "How" and "why" questions were raised in an open-ended fashion. Responses were solicited in a semistructured manner.

Given the exploratory nature of the research, explanation building and pattern matching were used to provide evidence of links between constructs. The qualitative data also provided content and discovery of elements that surround each construct to identify those facilitating and inhibiting factors that lead to ultimate BPC goals.

Brief Background

The three cases studied were Paper Co.,[3] Comdisco Inc., and AT&T GBCS. All of these projects were complete at the time of the study's data gathering, which allowed investigators to gauge the gap between initial expectations and actual results. Each company had objectives of major breakthrough performance. However, upon completion, the actual measured performance ranged from poorer results (Paper Co.) to a very successful turnaround in corporate-wide performances (AT&T). For example, the AT&T case involved a business mandate and an expectation to overcome serious financial problems. Comdisco and Paper Co. intended to radically overhaul their IT infrastructure. While both of these cases were initiated with similar intentions, they eventually took different paths. Comdisco's objectives and methods evolved during the course of its project from a radical posture to a more continuous improvement project. Interestingly, this continuous improvement effort was determined to be moderately successful. Paper Co., on the other hand, marched forward toward a goal of radical overhaul of its IT processes but failed to meet expectations for major performance breakthroughs.

Paper Co. is one of the largest producers of paper, focusing primarily on the computer printing market in the United States. It is a decentralized organization with numerous geographically separated divisions. The company had developed independent information systems optimized for each division; however, on a corporate-wide basis they were little more than "islands of automation." Corporate management in Connecticut was extremely frustrated by the poor information access capabilities and, in 1988, ventured into BPC to improve knowledge transfer across multiple divisions. The company initiated the effort proactively and had "revolutionary" expectations of results. The initial IT focus and leadership, however, proved inappropriate, and the project began to involve other functional management and to gravitate toward a business focus. The effort, however, continued to suffer from resistance from functional management, who opposed drastic alteration of their operations for process-wide optimization. Although the project had some success in improving information access, overall the extent of BPC success was considered low due to its inability to effect improvements in the bottom line of the firm.

Comdisco Inc. is a $2.21 billion computer leasing and asset management firm, well known for its disaster recovery services. In 1991, the company launched a BPC effort as a reaction against escalating costs, stagnant stock prices, flat revenues, excessive cycle time, and poor customer service. Initially, the project focused on IT but soon the BPC teams learned from their mistake and gravitated toward a business focus. Eventually, Comdisco underwent several continuous improvement BPC efforts to improve these operational metrics. The company did realize several benefits from the BPC effort while experiencing some setbacks in other areas. Overall, its effort can be classified a moderate success in BPC implementation.

AT&T GBCS, a division of AT&T Co. (now Lucent Corp.), is a major manufacturer of PBX switches. In 1988, GBCS faced grave financial conditions, dwindling market share, low customer and employee satisfaction, and lengthy cycle time. A top-down mandated BPC initiative mobilized the entire company to participate in a major process redesign effort that was facilitated by competent consultants and state-of-the- art BPC methodologies and techniques. This radical process redesign led to a successful $250 million turnaround with six consecutive profitable quarters (for the first time in GBCS history). GBCS boasts one of the best customer and employee satisfaction ratings in the industry, and payment collections within 90 days jumped from 25 percent to 70 percent.

Construct	Comdisco evidence	AT&T evidence	Paper Co. evidence
Table 1: Summary of Strategic Initiative Results			
Stimuli			
Proactive	Reactive	Reactive	Proactive
Reactive			
Formulation scope			
Incremental	**+ Eventually**	Revolutionary	**+/- Revolutionary**
Revolutionary	**became**		
	incremental		
Decision making			
Autocratic	Bureaucratic	Autocratic	Bureaucratic
Bureaucratic	Champion	Champion	Champion
Champion	emergence	emergence	emergence
emergence			
Strategy led			
Onset	Eventually	**+ Onset**	Onset
Eventually			
No			

Research Findings

This section covers each construct of the research model with summative findings for each case. Whenever appropriate, respondents' statements are quoted to illustrate the construct. Consistent with the research objectives, specific probes were made concerning each construct. The tables in each subsection summarize interpretation of the data gathered for each construct. In addition, any construct that had a positive or negative influence on conducting BPC, or on overall BPC effectiveness, was documented with either a plus (+) or a minus (—) sign. These positive or negative influences were identified and cross-validated either through direct statements by the respondents during the interview or from other data sources. Those with significant impact on the project success are in bold type. In some instances, a +/— is used to denote both positive and negative influences of the construct on project outcome.

Strategic Initiative (Table 1)

Stimuli

Two of the BPC projects were strategically very *reactive,* with AT&T in a "do or die" situation and Comdisco reacting to the price pressures and customer service problems. Paper Co., in contrast, wanted to maintain industry leadership with innovative IT solutions and started its BPC project as a strategically proactive initiative.

AT&T GBCS had the most severe financial condition prior to BPC, which was a primary stimulus to initiate major changes. As the respondent explained, "The climate was such that it was very difficult to maintain market share, GBCS had a lot of competition. Customer satisfaction ratings were not what we wanted them to be. And the profitability of our large PBX business was in worse shape than it had ever been. There was literally no profitability to be [had] in that market We were losing a tremendous amount of money." Operating costs had been steadily rising and margin steadily declining, but the biggest areas of concern was profitability and customer satisfaction.

Comdisco, also classified as "reactive," had several external stimuli to undertake BPC. These can be listed as: "competitive intensity—price pressure... cost escalation not in sync with revenue growth ... inordinate cycle time [for service delivery] ... inefficient staffing and too many hierarchical layers [and a] new transaction processing paradigm." Reacting to these problems, the company initiated the BPC effort in an attempt to radically improve performance.

Unlike the other two cases, Paper Co. was proactive in its BPC effort. As a market share leader and in strong financial condition, the company was looking for BPC opportunities to improve operational efficiencies and strengthen its market position even further. The BPC initiative began as an IT overhaul effort due to the frustration expressed by senior management in accessing information from its information systems. Paper Co. had different computers, operating systems, and programming languages at every location. Senior executives' frustration was evident. One IS executive indicated that "when they asked for something, it would have to be collected from many systems. If it was a onetime thing, we did not bother to write interfaces. We collected key data in one location."

An interesting finding is that, in Comdisco and Paper Co., the project was initiated by the IS group. However, there was not significant buy-in from the entire organization, and the resulting success was moderate and lower. AT&T, on the other hand, had significant stimuli from all functions and the project was led by the CEO. This "sense of urgency" stimulus resulted in corporate-wide buy-in and propelled the entire organization to change for success. As AT&T achieved the highest level of success among the three cases, this might suggest that, to be successful, a BPC project aimed at changing the performance of the firm cannot be led by IT alone and that IT innovations must be backed by a sense of urgency in other business functions in the organization.

Formulation Scope

AT&T formulated and maintained a strategy of *revolutionary* change from the start. Both Comdisco and Paper Co. started with a grand scheme to redesign their IT infrastructure to improve organizational performance, but, in the case of the former, because of risk aversion and cultural issues, Comdisco was unable to launch a major revolutionary effort. Instead, the firm achieved several smaller successes through process improvements. Respondents at Comdisco stated that adoption of the continuous improvement approach by the BPC team was a positive influence on their project. Paper Co., on the other hand, had a combination of positive and negative views on its revolutionary scope because it did appreciate the value of a business-

Table 2: Learning Capacity			
Construct	Comdisco evidence	AT&T evidence	Paper Co. evidence
Adaptation			
Response to technology change Learning from others	Response to technology change Learning from others	+ Learning from others	Response to technology change
Improved efficiency			
Learning by doing	Learning by doing	Learning by doing	- Insufficient learning by doing
Declarative knowledge			
R&D resources and technology development Knowledge base Focus on core competencies	Knowledge base Focus on core competencies	Knowledge base	Technology development Knowledge base
External information use			
Boundary spanners Technology gatekeepers Customers	+ Boundary spanners Technology gatekeepers Customers	+ Boundary spanners Technology gatekeepers Customers	Boundary spanners + Technology gatekeapers Customers
Learning Type			
Deutero Double-loop	Deutero	Deutero	— Insufficient deutero learning

focused linkage to IT change, but was unable to fulfill the potential of this revolutionary change due to a lack of change vision and cultural obstacles.

Decision Making

Of the three cases, AT&T was the only *autocratic* and mandated initiative. In contrast, a local functional team within Comdisco and Paper Co. started the BPC effort, elevated it to the corporate level, and eventually received a *bureaucratic* consensus to proceed as a corporate-level initiative. In all three cases, a BPC champion emerged or was appointed to spearhead the project. Although not mentioned as a positive influence by the interviewees, the emergence of a champion is considered critical to BPC success (Davenport, 1993; Hammer and Champy, 1993).

Strategy Led

Because of its focus on incremental improvements, Comdisco did not initially devise a corporate strategic plan that tied in with the BPC efforts. Over time, however, the considerable success from these improvement efforts caught senior executives' attention and they eventually included BPC as an integral part of the business and strategic plans. The BPC efforts at AT&T were led by strategy from the top down. The fact that AT&T made the BPC effort central to its strategic goals at the onset and measured organizational success throughout the change efforts was repeatedly cited by interviewees as a major facilitator of success. In the case of Paper Co., the effort was also strategy led at the onset, but the strategy had more to do with IT planning than with corporate-wide business planning.

Learning Capacity (Table 2)

The research model provides a framework in understanding an organization's capability to learn in its quest to successfully change business processes. Almost all cases showed some propensity to create a learning environment. Key patterns observed included:

- Learning from others (each firm had an understanding of best in class vendors);
- Learning by doing (learn from mistakes and successes);
- Use of external experts and "voice of the customer" to understand process requirements.

Adaptation

While "response to technology change" played a role in the initial IT-focused effort at Comdisco and Paper Co., the "learning from others" adaptation mechanism at AT&T pushed for best-in-class benchmarking practice. Other indicators of this probe include AT&T's adherence to its adapted PQMI process management methodology and its overall continuous learning philosophy. Respondents strongly endorsed benchmarking (learning from others) as a positive influence on BPC success, as it helped them set goals and measure their achievements continuously in the quest to becoming a world-class organization with respect to customer satisfaction, employee satisfaction, and cycle time.

Improved Efficiency

All but Paper Co. had a tendency to improve learning efficiency through "learning by doing." On the advice of consultants, Paper Co. executives eventually saw that their IT-driven approach was somewhat misguided, but the overall level of learning by doing remained insufficient and was regarded as a source of negative influence on their final project outcome. Their BPC team observed that this deficiency was a result of constant resistance from functional managers who refused to adopt major change recommendations. The consultants repeatedly recommended that senior officials coerce these managers into adopting major changes, but to no avail. In contrast, both AT&T and Comdisco showed the ability to learn through the process. The Comdisco team was able to convince various functional managers who were initially resistant to BPC to adopt the BPC philosophy once they saw successes in smaller projects. The company began to adopt a process-focused orientation based on this experience. Also, the immediate retreat from an IT-focused change effort was a clear indicator that Comdisco had been very efficient in its organizational learning process.

Declarative Knowledge

To stay competitive, all three firms understood the value of competing with superior expertise and of developing a cumulative knowledge base. Comdisco's effort in this area directly touches upon its core competencies—superior customer service and expertise in disaster recovery. The BPC efforts, aided by IT-enabled cross-functional information sharing, were specifically designed to keep improving and enhancing this core competency. We saw a clear pattern of efforts to enrich the knowledge base for the purpose of better understanding the customer. As a result, the knowledge worker in Comdisco was expected to become more of a generalist than a functional expert. This focus on core competency was not seen in the other two cases. Paper Co. means of improving declarative knowledge is to enhance operational efficiencies.

External Information Use

One clear pattern that emerged from the three cases was the value of external information use in enhancing learning capacity. All three companies had many technology gatekeepers who scanned the environment for new developments and opportunities. In the case of Paper Co., technology gatekeeping resulted in the significant introduction of systems that improved information access throughout several divisions of the company. All three companies also made good use of customer surveys to assess gaps in customer service. At Comdisco, for example, customer surveys helped the company measure the degree of success or satisfaction with current and new processes. These surveys also provided an audit trail of its improvement effort and a linkage to the firm's overall performance. The most beneficial source of external information in all three cases, however, came from consultants, who acted as "boundary spanners." A large consulting company was retained by AT&T to conduct in-depth case studies on twenty-four processes and identified problem areas. This proved to be a major facilitator to BPC success, as it set the stage for understanding the degree of problems with the current process and helping them to develop goals for improvement. These surveys and case studies were used to measure performance after completion of the project to show net realized benefits. These consultants were integral to the BPC teams and assisted in multiple functional areas such as systems development and strategic positioning. The company also recruited AT&T QUEST, the AT&T quality consulting organization, to make sure it followed the PQMI methodology. Paper Co.'s use of consultants was also important, as their recommendations led the firm (unfortunately too late and halfheartedly) to move away from an IT-centric endeavor toward a business-focused BPC effort.

Learning Type

Interestingly, the two more successful projects —Comdisco and AT&T—had a deutero-loop type of learning and were willing to adopt a strategy for learning based on past failures. Comdisco understood its multimillion-dollar mistake in attempting a grand-scale IT-led change initiative without a business focus, and it altered its course accordingly. The following quotation demonstrates this deutero pattern of learning: "We spent a lot of money on new technology and the people and consultants on the IT side and reengineer through technology.... we should have held off, until the business side had truly reengineered. And then we could have come in with IT to further reengineer. So that was what I consider a big lesson." For Paper Co., there were no major leaning-type indicators. The company had a very traditional management style and did not adapt and change strategies for learning based on lessons learned. This was in fact deemed a major inhibitor to success by the interviewees, as the firm failed to implement changes as it had envisioned.

Cultural Readiness (Table 3)

Each case differed in its cultural systems. Comdisco and Paper Co. had more traditional rigid functional hierarchies, and the BPC project encountered several pockets of resistance even though senior managers in both companies were enthusiastic and supportive of change.

Table 3: Summary of Cultural Readiness Results			
Construct	Comdisco evidence	AT&T evidence	PaperCo. evidence
Change agents and leadership	**+ Change agents** Sr. mgt. commitment	Change agents **+ Sr. mgt. commitment**	**+/— Sr. mgt commitment**
Risk aversion **— Aggressive**	Cautious Aggressor	**+ Cautious**	Aggressive
Open communications	**+ Medium**	**+ High**	**— Low**
Cross-training	Not assessed	Not assessed	**— Low**

Change Agents and Leadership

According to Mintzberg and Westley (1992), a "visionary leader" is a single leader who influences change. In the cases we studied, however, change did not come from a single visionary leader but may be the collective result from a team of change agents (e.g., a BPC team) or in many cases appointed BPC champions. This power of visionary leadership in the form of self-directed teams may be a manifestation of the organization's cultural potency (Saffold, 1978), which is a summative index of the power of the organization's cultural paradigm to initiate change. For both Comdisco and AT&T, there was a high level of cultural potency in the company to change beliefs, value systems, and norms. In the Comdisco case, the vision and influence to change culture came primarily from change agents, namely, from the BPC team, even though a senior management champion was appointed. AT&T had a true "top- down" vision of change from senior management, and the entire corporation responded. A facilitator in Paper Co. was also senior management's enthusiasm for change and the leadership they provided in setting the direction. But this was neutralized by a lack of change agents and leadership from middle management, which slowed down the momentum for change.

Risk Aversion

With respect to risk aversion, Comdisco was seen as more "cautious" than AT&T and Paper Co., which resulted in incremental but successful process improvements. The BPC effort at Comdisco followed a very pragmatic approach to rationalize the need for change. There was not a mandate from senior management and, in fact, emphasis was placed on participation and giving credit whenever such recognition is justified. The BPC team took a low profile and achieved consensus by involving senior management and educating the functional areas about why change is needed, as evident from the following dialogue: "We don't come out there and beat our chest and say 'we just reengineered this other process and saved the company $6 million,' absolutely no way. We take a very low profile, work with the senior management and it becomes management sponsored, it becomes their idea, because then they feel part of it when the savings come."

AT&T definitely took a more aggressive stance to change; this can be attributed to the grave financial situation under which it was operating. Responding to the mandate from the corporate office, the culture in AT&T was conducive to aggressive risk taking to maximize return. Paper Co. also adopted a proactive stance to change and boldly attempted to overhaul its IT infrastructure. This, however, turned out to be detrimental and was considered an inhibiting factor to its success, as the aggressive tactics blinded it to the overall business impact of the proposed changes.

Open Communications

In all cases, senior management participated in "town hall" type meetings soliciting input as well as providing clear directions and vision. AT&T in particular scored very highly in this dimension as the organization believed in full disclosure and open communications. The teams consisted of cross-functional members who openly discussed the process tasks (non-value-adding activities) and identified areas for improvement. They presented results to the executive council, who then communicated the decisions to all division vice presidents. The organization in general

Table 4: Summary of IT Leveragability and Knowledge-Sharing Capability Results

Construct	Comdisco evidence	AT&T evidence	Paper Co. evidence

IT role
  Enabling
  Sociotechnical
  Dominant factor
	— Enabling	+ Enabling	— Dominant factor

Use of communications technology	Low	Low	Medium

valued open communications, which eventually became one of the value statements of the organization called the "common bond." The common bond consists of organizational principles by which AT&T associates are expected to abide and live in the workplace. GBCS also measured associate satisfaction as a part of overall organizational performance and process success. The "common bond" and the use of AT&T PQMI continuous process improvement methodology provided an institutionalized process that fostered a culture for adapting to change.

In Comdisco and Paper Co., the CEO sat in on the brainstorming sessions and prompted the teams for major change ideas. However, the level of open communication was not seen in lower functional levels, primarily because of the more rigid organizational structures. Comdisco, however, did communicate that the BPC project should also benefit employees, and this engendered some sense of open informal communication. Paper Co., on the other hand, had a very traditional and hierarchical management structure and was not strong in "open communications," particularly in the earlier stages of the change effort. A related manifestation of this was the fact that top management was supportive of change but middle management was not. Open communication improved somewhat at Paper Co. after quality training was conducted in all divisions as a part of the BPC effort. This candid observation was provided by one Paper Co. respondent during an interview: "We are now putting everybody at this plant through training and trying to break down barriers, open things up, push decision making down as low as we can. We are starting to do all that now, but we were not doing that then." Overall, weak communication was cited as an inhibitor to success at Paper Co. A general pattern that clearly emerged from all three cases is the tremendous influence of open communication on BPC success. To succeed, senior management must continuously communicate the importance of the BPC effort and how it would affect the organization.

Cross-Training

A factor that may have limited Paper Co.'s success is the lack of cross-training and personnel movement within the organization. Paper Co. typically employed people in the same function for many years, which made it more difficult for the firm to adapt to a cross-functional form. The lack of cross-training was one reason why there was no upward movement of Paper Co. employees to top executive positions.

Construct	Comdisco evidence	AT&T evidence	Paper Co. evidence
Table 5: Summary of Network Relationship Results			
Interorganizational linkages	None	None	None
Cross-functional cooperation			
Cooperative		**+ Cooperative**	**+/- Cooperative**
Competitive	**-Competitive**		Competitive

Because this was a "new" construct identified during the Paper Co. case study, no information on this was gathered from earlier studies at AT&T and Comdisco.

IT Leveragability and Knowledge-Sharing Capacity (Table 4)

IT Role and Extent of Knowledge Sharing

Respondents in all three cases unanimously agreed that BPC needs to adopt a sociotechnical design approach. Comdisco and Paper Co. learned the hard way when they approached BPC with an IT-only view and reverted back to a more sociotechnical design orientation. However, each case demonstrated the value of IT in improving:

- Information and knowledge sharing across functions;
- Consistency of information and service across functions;
- Communications between functions that could lead to associate satisfaction and employee productivity improvements, especially with the use of communications technology.

One pattern that emerges from the Paper Co. and Comdisco cases is that IT-led projects, which often fail to capture the full business and human dimensions of processes, are less likely to succeed. This was demonstrated by Markus and Keil (1994) in their description of a large-scale change management project that failed for reasons unrelated to technical feasibility and reliability. Benjamin and Levinson's (1993) study also confirmed the importance of relying on appropriate implementation and change management techniques to ensure project success.

Use of Communications Technology

Communications technology was not seen as a major IT enabler in these cases but as more of an organizational efficiency enabler. In the Paper Co. case, the use of e-mail, which did not exist before, provided better cross-divisional communications. However, this was not considered a major technology enabler to achieve the breakthrough successes of BPC. This may be related to the nature of the projects where process automation was not a major focus in the BPC effort.

Table 6: Summary of Change Management Results

Construct	Comdisco evidence	AT&T evidence	Paper Co. evidence
Pattern of change			
No formal process			
Semiformal process	Semiformal	Formal phased	No formal process
Formal phased process	process	change	
Management's readiness to change			
Committed			
Participative	+/— **Participative**	**+ Committed**	**+/—Participative**
Resistant	Resistant		Resistant
Scope of change			
Improvement	Improvement	Radical change	Radical change
Radical change			
Managed change		**+/— Overall**	**— Overall**
Alleviate employee dissatisfaction	Yes	**Yes**	**No**
Vision for change	Yes	**Yes**	**No**
Well-managed process of change	Semiformal	**Formal**	**None**
Evolutionary or revolutionary change tactics used	Evolutionary	**Revolutionary**	**Revolutionary**

Network Relationships (Table 5)
Interorganizational Linkages

None of the cases had any evidence of interorganizational process linkages. However, Paper Co. did express an interest as an ultimate objective in tying customers into its process with common ordering systems.

Cross-Functional Cooperation

Respondents at Comdisco and Paper Co. indicated high levels of cooperation among the cross-functional members of the BPC team. Cooperation between functions was a different story. At Comdisco, a negative influence was the considerable competition between functions that showed up as these functions were being integrated into a single process. Both Comdisco and Paper Co. had several pockets of resistance by functional managers during the design phases. Paper Co. was a mixed bag: There was a lot of enthusiasm at the brainstorming sessions between functions but severe resistance by functional managers to the proposed radical change. Several line managers went so far as to comment: "What do these process teams know about our jobs? We have been doing this for ten years and now they want to change how we work!" This level of resistance can be very detrimental to the BPC success in that the resulting process redesign may become less innovative. For Paper Co., the "cooperative" construct received a +/— mark because the company did see increased communications volume and increased synergy between the functions once the process was implemented.

For the cross-functional cooperation construct, we saw nearly total cooperation at the AT&T site. It came as no surprise that it emphatically regarded this as greatly facilitative to project success. This may have been the result of the mandate placed on the entire corporation to change.

Change Management (Table 6)

Pattern of Change

While Paper Co. and Comdisco showed little or no formality in their process of change, AT&T followed a structured methodology, and we could see a pattern of changes in phases. In all three cases, however, there was no clear evidence for change phases as outlined by Lewin (1952). For Paper Co. and Comdisco, this is not at all surprising since both projects were initially led by the IS group and no formal methodology for process change was employed. This may be a major reason Paper Co. never saw the radical changes it expected. AT&T experienced less resistance, and we believe that disciplined approach to change management contributed to its success.

Management's Readiness to Change

In all three cases there was a clear pattern that senior management was supportive of the projects. AT&T had full commitment from all levels of management. At Comdisco there was participative support from senior management. However, at the middle- management level, where the impact of the proposed changes was to be felt, there was initial reluctance to adopt the changes. The team had to quantify the benefits to remove the emotional side of the resistance. This was indicated by the following comment from a respondent: "Because it was a measure of dollars and cents it was less of an emotional issue. People saw this map of all those [expletive] awful flows all over the place and bullet points which mean wait times; visually it looked ridiculous."

Paper Co.'s condition was similar to that of Comdisco, with high-level participation but significant resistance by middle-level management. This indicates that, for BPC efforts to succeed, senior management readiness for change is a necessary but not sufficient condition for success. In addition, it is important that all levels of the organization exhibit readiness for change. Lacking this, a BPC project would experience great difficulty in change management and results are likely to fall short of expectations.

Scope of Change

The scope of BPC projects at Paper Co. and AT&T created radical expectations for improved performance. At Paper Co., high performance payoffs were expected but significant organizational changes were not envisioned, and the project focused primarily on IT changes. AT&T, however, was prepared to make any organizational changes that were necessary to optimize performance. As for Comdisco, one saw a clear case of gradual improvement, as the company was not prepared to make any major radical changes to the organization and the team quickly found out that the best way to succeed was to recommend more incremental changes that management would support. Credibility established with these small successes eventually paved the way for larger-scale changes.

Managed Change

Management at AT&T made every effort to ensure that employee satisfaction was considered when making changes, and there was a clear commitment to initiate changes that could alleviate employee dissatisfaction. AT&T executives attempted to search all corners of the organization for change opportunities. One senior executive articulated a *"vision for change* that provided a high-level road map where we wanted the organization to go." The process of change, however, was well managed with the aid of a formal methodology. As apart of this managed process, for example, the BPC teams were to sit with all the functional associates affected by the changes, who were provided with an explanation of what the changes meant for their current roles and responsibilities. To succeed at revolutionary changes, AT&T also attempted revolutionary change tactics. For example, middle and lower management were forcefully instructed to carry out whatever steps were needed to achieve the radical high-level BPC goals laid out by senior management.

In addition to the many positive attributes, as described above, the managed change at AT&T was also seen as having some negative influence on success also. The respondents acknowledged one major problem in their change management process that they could improve. Because of the lack of a well-defined rollout program, certain functions in the newly designed process were being updated earlier than others. But, since the new process required cross-functional knowledge sharing, this lack of synchronized implementation caused considerable delays.

As at AT&T, the Comdisco BPC team also sought change opportunities that alleviate employee dissatisfaction. In fact, the CEO attended BPC brainstorming sessions dedicated to this purpose. An evolutionary sociotechnical change approach, which was not fully planned, was evident at Comdisco. As described by one respondent, "It takes three months of really hard work and three months of just hand holding. ... they appreciate the three months of hand holding."

Paper Co. showed no indication that it took steps to remove employee dissatisfaction. Senior management did provide a vision for change, but employees were generally excluded from participating in the process redesign. Overall, management of the change process was problematic, and many desired radical changes were never implemented because of the constant resistance from functional managers, who had been entrenched in the old processes for more than twenty or even thirty years. The consultants had recommended the use of an external party, called a "challenger," to

Construct	Comdisco evidence	AT&T evidence	PaperCo. evidence
Process measurement			
Use of process metrics	**+ Process metrics**	**+ Process metrics**	**— Audit of IS metrics**
Process information capture	Process information capture	Process information capture	
Improvement feedback loop		Improvement feedback loop	
Audit		Audit	
Tools and techniques	High	High	Low
Team based	Yes	Yes	Yes

Table 7: Summary of Process Management Results

constantly push the team for more radical changes. The company, however, did not deploy any such unbiased person to break the current frame of mind. Failure to do this was considered an inhibitor to success, as one respondent lamented: "Yeah, we all saw it could be done but we couldn't... and that's one of our weak points."

Process Management (Table 7)
Process Measurement and Tools and Techniques
AT&T was by far the most sophisticated of the three cases in process management. The company's long experience in the quality movement and the development of their own process management methodology (PQMI) helped place them in this leadership category. AT&T uses process mapping and diagnosis techniques to study the process as well as measurements of process performance using quality techniques. Process documentation was done through process flow chart analysis and quality techniques like fishbone and root cause analysis. A major facilitator of success at AT&T was its use of process metrics that quantified the process value and goal expectations.

Comdisco also used formal techniques successfully for process analysis and design. In fact, one of the cited success factors at Comdisco was the team's ability to measure changed processes and to articulate their value to management and functional groups. Comdisco used process metrics as a tool to convince functional managers who were reluctant to undergo BPC. "We started to measure cycle time. And then we communicated that... we broke the process down into dollars and cents to take the emotion away. And then, I think, people were more willing to sit down and .... the metrics allowed the team to objectively persuade the value of the initiative."

At Paper Co., techniques and methods such as DFD, CASE tools, and simulation were used for process analysis and design. These, however, are used mostly for

---

Table 8. Summary of Outcomes and Performance

Construct	Comdisco evidence	AT&T evidence	Paper Co. evidence
Process performance improvements	(A) Cycle time (87 days to 2) (B) Processing cost ($6,000 to $300-500; 8 layers to 2) (B) Quality (C) Customer satisfaction	(A) Cycle time (52 weeks to 5 days) (A) Customer satisfaction (25% to 70%) (B) Revenue/market share ($250m turnaround)	(B) Information access (C) Customer satisfaction (C) Reduce operations cost (D) Profitability/ market share
Quality of work life improvements	Medium employee satisfaction	High employee satisfaction	Low/medium employee satisfaction
Overall results	Moderate	Higher	Lower

Legend: A = exceeded goal; B = met goal; C = marginal improvements but did not meet goal; D = no success.
* Paper Co. referred to customer satisfaction as customer service.

information systems development and did not serve the purpose of BPC well. Further, quality tools were not utilized. As a result, there was a lack of process metrics and process information capture for the business process. The biased focus on IS processes did produce audit trails for IS metrics, but this was later viewed as misguided and an inhibitor to success.

Team Basis

All of the cases used teams extensively in the BPC project as well as in the organizational design of the new processes. At Comdisco, the BPC teams were cross-functional and the new processes also used team-based structures. When the BPC project began, AT&T had already begun to implement more horizontal organizational structures. One of the problems identified within AT&T was too many management layers, with vice presidents all over the organization. The BPC teams sought to tie different functions together and at the same time reduce the number of layers. The BPC teams at Paper Co. did not succeed in implementing major changes to the company's rigid organizational structure, but they did use teams during the redesign effort.

Outcomes of BPC and Performance Gains

BPC outcomes or performance gains were assessed to validate the research model claim that a successful BPC initiative should see improvements in "Process Performance" and "Quality of Work Life" (QWL) (Kettinger and Grover, 1995). Semistructured interviews were used to derive primary information on outcomes for each project. Respondents were asked to state their expectations of project achievements. To separate "stated goals" from "actual goals" (in an attempt to remove possible bias of only stating goals that were actually achieved), probes were used to reveal all goals. Actual performance gains were determined through multiple sources such as statements from the respondents with supporting quantified data, documented performance results, and external sources of information such as financial reports (10K, press releases, etc.). Project expectations were compared against actual results for all goals (e.g., cycle time, profitability, market share, quality, cost, QWL) to see if actual performance met expected goals as understood at the onset of the project (see Table 8).

In all the cases there was an expectation of improving operational efficiencies, whether cycle time reductions or processing/operational cost reductions. In addition, all companies expected to see gains in customer satisfaction. Comdisco had specific expectations for service quality increases, while AT&T and Paper Co. looked for drastic improvements in profitability and market share growth. In fact, at AT&T GBCS, the BPC project did result in dramatic performance benefits. AT&T continuously compared targeted with actual process performance and found that it was exceeding its expectations for cycle time (A) and customer satisfaction (A) improvements. For example, AT&T GBCS had a poor pre-BPC project customer satisfaction rating of 25 percent (meaning only 25 percent were fully satisfied with their product/service). However, their post-BPC customers satisfaction rating was 75 percent, exceeding its expected goal. In terms of financial performance, AT&T set high performance expectations that were met with six positive financial quarters. AT&T's BPC project was attributed with "bringing... a solid P&L statement" and determined by management as meeting (B) their lofty financial expectations "by turning the company to the black."

Comdisco met or exceeded performance improvements in the areas of cost reduction (B) and cycle time reduction (A). Their order-processing time went from eighty-seven days to two days, and significant reductions in time were seen in the accounts-receivable process. While Comdisco's processing costs were slashed from $6,000 per order to a range of $300-500 per order, pre-BPC project expectations that this could be accomplished were high, therefore, this only received a "meets" (B) expectation rating. Continuous process Improvements permitted a gradual reduction in qualify voids (B), allowing eventual attainment of this goal. Reports of perceived customer satisfaction improvements were mixed. Comdisco was unable to provide any measurable proof that customer satisfaction increased and, thus, was ranked as only marginally meeting this goal (C).

Paper Co. had high hopes that reengineering would add significantly to its bottom line, extending its relative competitive strength in its industry. In reality, the project's primary focus on IT changes alone saw only significant improvements in information access (B) among its divisions. While end users had better access to information, it was generally held that the high expectations for improvement in customer service (C) and cost reductions (C) went virtually unanswered. In terms of actual financial performance of Paper Co., there was no indication of any bottom-line improvements or market share growth. For example, during the period of the BPC project at Paper Co. (1988-91), net income dropped from $164 million to $45 million and revenue dropped from $1.33 billion to $1.19 billion. The project's inability to achieve unrealistically high expectations for substantial financial benefits was the principal reason the overall project was not seen as a success (D). Ironically, while Paper Co. initiated its project in a proactive manner (during a period when the company was in a fairly strong competitive position), by the end of the BPC project the company was experiencing unanticipated financial pressures.

While pre-project expectation levels for quality of work life improvements resulting from the BPC projects were not as explicitly stated as were process performance improvements, employee satisfaction metrics were monitored during the course of each project. In the case of AT&T, its concerted effort to achieve "associate satisfaction" through "the Common Bond" paid off with a post-project measure of employee satisfaction at one of the highest levels in its industry. Comdisco also made modest strives in QWL through team- and quality-based changes. Although not consciously intended, Paper Co. also experienced some minor gains in employee satisfaction within the divisions affected by the BPC project. These improvements may be partially explained by a limited "Hawthorne effect" that occurs as a result of conducting a BPC project. Specifically, increased attention placed on employees and the solicitation of their opinions may result in more of a sense of involvement in the organization and modestly increase their employee satisfaction.

Implications

Overall, the results from the three case studies demonstrated that constructs capturing dimensions of the BPC management model provide a framework for studying business process change. In addition, this research indicates that certain constructs in the model had more impact on the outcome of projects than others. These were primarily due to the change environment within which BPC is to occur. Table 9 offers, under each of the BPC framework's major concepts, a synopsis of significant constructs and the context in which they were viewed as either facilitators or inhibitors of each case's outcome.

While the granularity of this analysis does not allow us to "predict" success, based on a simple summation of facilitators and inhibitors in each case, the results seem to indicate that successful projects have more facilitators. Some may have a more local impact on a certain aspect or phase of BPC. However, we believe that the inference that a highly successful BPC effort should demonstrate numerous positive facilitators and minimize inhibitors is reasonable. As indicated in Table 9, AT&T was classified as the most successful project consistently showing positive facilitators in all of the BPC management framework's dimensions. At the other extreme, Paper Co., which had many more inhibitors, was the least successful project. Inhibitors show the greatest clustering in the areas of cultural readiness and change management. These, in fact, were the major issues that the respondent continuously pointed to during interviews as the major problems they foresaw in future BPC efforts. While this research found an important role for IT in support of BPC, the message from these case studies is that *IT should not drive a BPC project.*

While broad generalizations from these three case studies may be premature, the patterns in Table 9 indicate several important themes that could have implications for both research and practice:

- There tend to be strategic "stimuli" ranging from financial pressures, continued market leaderships, customer dissatisfaction and/or organization inefficiencies that trigger firms to undertake business process change. The stimulus itself is not necessarily a determinant of success.
- Organizations attempting to change performance radically seem to require some "sense of urgency" in their business situation, which translates in turn into a compelling vision that is espoused throughout the organization. Interestingly, at least according to these preliminary findings, BPC does not have to be proactive to be successful.
- Incremental process change can work but appears to be appropriate when risk aversion is lower and environmental conditions less dire.
- Successful BPC projects are enabled in organizations that: (1) have a propensity to learn from best practice and customer needs; (2) leverage external information and experts; and (3) exhibit deutero learning whereby employees individually and collectively reflect on their past experiences, modify their course when necessary, and discover new opportunities.
- Successful BPC projects establish an objective and unbiased team or individual that continues to push the organization and line functions to find new innovative processes. These "challengers" must be empowered to implement the changes without barriers from functional managers.
- An important ingredient in the right cultural mix for successful BPC is leadership from the top, together with an atmosphere of open communication, participation, and cross-training.

Table 9: Significant Facilitators and Inhibitors of Business Process Change Outcomes

Case	Strategic initiative	Learning capacity	Cultural readiness	IT& knowledge sharing	Network relationships balancing	Change management practice	Process management practice	Outcome
AT&T	+ top down, strategy led from onset	+ adaptation of best in class benchmarks. + heavy use of external information including consultants; exploited boundary spanning internal expertise and techniques, including PQMI methodology.	+ change agent leadership from top pushed cultural reform of corporate beliefs and values. + push for an extremely open environment -- town-hall meetings. Team, employees, and mgt. all in council to form "common bond."	+ design was attempted from the beginning as sociotechnical, IT played an important but supporting role.	+ complete cooperation across functions and management levels based on a vision statement that laid out a mandate.	+ management conveyed ready strenuous support and the seriousness of the situation and associates participated fully +/- poorly sequenced rollout causes some delays in implementation.	+ heavy use of process tools & evaluation metrics including measures of goal expectations and actual performance impacts.	High

+ indicates a positive influence on project success.

- indicates a negative influence on project success.

Com-disco	+ wanted dramatic change but recognized that risk aversion was high, made quick move to incrementalism	+ heavy use of external information including consultants, customer surveys and internal audit trials.	+ team-based change agents with senior mgt. champion, did not include middle mgt. + risk aversion pushes for incremental changes. + open mgt. and team brainstorming, but org. barriers still problematic.	- began project with concept that IT was principal driver of change, recognized this was not working and modified effort to a non IT-based redesign.	- pockets of cross-functional resistance and competition. This was not completely resolved in implementation.	+/- Management readiness to effect change but middle/functional mgt. drags feet.	+ process metrics used as a persuasion tool to remove emotion and motivate cooperation.	Moderate
Paper Co.	+/- charged ahead with a revolutionary project but unable to realize radical change. Had to fall back to whatever was doable when all else failed.	- refusal of functional mgt. to adapt major changes or lessons learned. + Technology scanners exploit IT's capabilities. - Not much deutero learning, rigid mgt. style slow to alter strategy. External consultants finally convinced a move away from IT centric approach, but too late.	+/- senior mgt. change agents set direction, middle mgt. resists. - over aggressiveness blinded attention to overall business impact. - limited communication outside function - lack of cross-training and no upward movement	- IT dominated approach with little integration of business case or sociotechnical issues, viewed as a limiting factor.	-/+ severe resistance by functional mgt. to radical designs, but some synergy after implemented	+/- management readiness to effect change but middle/functional mgt. counters with reactive position. - did not convey importance to employee satisfaction in redesign	- used limited process metrics and tools and instead relied on IS auditing techniques; this was later viewed as a negative.	Lower

+ indicates a positive influence on project success.

- indicates a negative influence on project success.

- Successful BPC involves the coalescence of "IT" and business best practice, whereby IT plays a supportive, but not always commanding role that is linked to the business case for BPC. Balanced consideration of the social, technical, and business value elements should be maintained throughout the project.
- To quell likely pockets of resistance, an organization's "vision" for change must be embraced throughout all levels of the organization, especially by those functional and middle-level managers affected by the process change. To achieve this requires continuous articulation and communication of the value of reporting results and how each individual contributing and accountable to the overall company's change effort. At this individual level, concern should be placed on how the BPC will improve employee satisfaction and the QWL.
- Measurement is key to success. A well-defined process management approach should include a documented methodology of change, use objective and quantified metrics showing the value of change, continuously communicate process metrics to senior management, and possess a well-documented rollout of the new process design.

The current findings are, of course, preliminary. They are based on only three case studies, and claims of external validity must await further examination with a wider sample of projects with different motivations and contexts. However, the BPC management framework provided a good structure for the case studies and we are encouraged that future research will continue to refine the framework. Further, while this study focused on a flat model — where all constructs were considered antecedents to success — more elaborate testing would involve interrelationships between components of the model. For instance, how does a conducive change environment facilitate change and process management practices? Is there symbiotic interaction between change and process management? We believe that similar studies, while limited in their ability to establish invariant relationships between variables in the positivist tradition, provide tremendous opportunity to provide rich contextual framing of firms undertaking BPC. Consistent application of frameworks that are flexible in their interpretation, as are the practices of the phenomenon being investigated, can then lead to significant theoretical insights. Such an effort can refine the research model's dimensions and provide more depth to its constructs. These efforts can also complement or lead to further external validation through large-scale survey-based empirical analysis. The ultimate goal, however, may not be deterministic but may be to provide managers with insight into which situational conditions best predict the strength that particular facilitators or inhibitors will have on BPC project success.

Conclusion

Responsive, global, networked, team-based, knowledge-based — are some of the watchwords for contemporary organizations. Their currency indicates the importance of change as organizations work to reinvent themselves along these untested dimensions. The three cases discussed in this paper epitomize the contrasts between and within firms that undertake major change. While many change management prescriptions are affirmed through these analyses, we would like to leave the reader with three simple but overarching observations, based on our experience with BPC.

First is the notion *of balance. As* the old adage goes, "Too much of anything is bad." We observed that being too technocentric, too bureaucratic, or too inflexible were *all* detrimental to success. Firms that carefully balance the social and the technical, leadership and participation, emergent and deliberate strategy, and technology and business, among others, have the greatest propensity for success. This leads to the second observation, *reevaluation.* Even balances have to be reevaluated periodically. Firms that plan still have to evaluate. Deviations from the course of the plan should not be interpreted as failure but as opportunity to reevaluate and learn. Organizations are complex and interactive, and outcomes of major changes cannot be planned with precision: we must "learn to learn" and continue to "learn by doing." And finally, consistent with this complexity, is the recognition of *interdependence.* One part of an organization that performs major change in isolation, without examining the impact or inputs from the broader context, will belie the essence of the organizational entity. Similarly, inhibitors in the change environment can have a multiplier effect on the conduct of change management. In contrast, effective change management, despite the context, can have a recursive impact on the nature of the context itself. In sum, BPC requires effective management of balance, reevaluation, and interdependence. The successful case in our sample demonstrated all three.

Endnotes

1. Interested readers are referred to a more comprehensive description of the model in Kettinger and Grover (1995).
2. In many instances the respondent provided sensitive information and the investigators were requested to use the content of that information with professional judgment and solely for academic exercise.
3. The name of this company was disguised to maintain confidentiality.

References

Adler, P. (1990). Shared learning. *Management Science, 36(*8), 938-957.

Akao, Y.(1990) *Quality Function Deployment: Integrating Customer Requirements into Product Design.* Cambridge, MA: Productivity Press,.

Allen, T.(1977). *Managing the Flow of Technology.* Cambridge, MA: MIT Press.

Anderson, J.C.; Rungtusanatham, M.; and Schroeder, R.G. (1994). Theory of quality management underlying the Deming management method. *Academy of Management Review, 19(3),* 472—509.

Appleton, D. (1995).Business reengineering with business rules. In V. Grover and W.J. Kettinger (eds.), *Business Process Change: Reengineering Concepts, Methods and Technologies.* Harrisburg, PA: Idea Group Publishing.

Argyris, C., and Schoen, D.A. (1978). *Organization Learning: A Theory of Action Research.* Reading, MA: Addison-Wesley.

Arrow, K.*(1962).* The implications of learning by doing. *Review of Economic Studies, 29,* 166:170.

Beath, C.M. (1991). Supporting the information technology champion. *MIS Quarterly, 15(3),* 355-372.

Beers, M. (1987). Revitalizing organizations: change process and emergent model. *Academy of Management EXECUTIVE* (February), 51—55.

Benjamin, R.I., and Levinson, E. (1993). A framework for managing IT-enabled change. *Sloan Management Review, 20(1)*, 2333.

Caron, J.R.; Jarvenpaa, S.L.; and Stoddard, D. (1994). Business reengineering at CIGNA corporation: experiences and lessons from the first five years. *MIS Quarterly, 18(3)*, 233-250.

Charan, R. (1991). How networks reshape organizations—for results. *Harvard Business Review*, 69, 104-115.

Cherns, A. (1976). The principles of sociotechnical design. *Human Relations, 29(8)*, 783-792.

Corsini, R. (1987). *Concise Encyclopedia of Psychology*. New York: Wiley.

Cranny, C.J.; Smith, P.C.; and Stone, E.F.(1992). *Job Satisfaction: How People Feel about Their Jobs and How It Affects Their Performance*. New York: Lexington Books.

Crosby, P.B. (1994). *Completeness: Quality for the 21st Centupy*. New York: Plume Books.

Davenport, T.H. (1993). *Process Innovation: Reengineering Work through Information Technology*. Boston: Harvard Business School Press.

Davenport, T.H.(1993). Need radical innovation and continuous improvement? -- integrate process reengineering and TQM. *Planning Review, 22(3)*, 6-12.

Davenport, T.H.(1995). Business process reengineering: where it's been, where it's going. In V. Grover and W.J. Kettinger (eds.), *Business Process Change: Reengineering Concepts, Methods and Technologies*. Harrisburg, PA: Idea Group Publishing.

Davenport T.H., and Beers, M.C.(1995). Managing information about processes. *Journal of Management Information Systems, 12(1)*, 57-60.

Denna, E.; Jasperson, J.; and Perry, L. (1995). Reengineering and REAL business process modeling -- event driven modeling. In V. Grover and W. J. Kettinger (eds.), *Business Process Change: Reengineering Concepts, Methods and Technologies*. Harrisburg, PA: Idea Group Publishing.

Dodgson, M. (1994). Organizational learning: a review of some literatures. *Organization Studies, 14(3)*, 375-394.

Earl, M.J. Viewpoint: new and old of business process redesign. *Journal of Strategic Information Systems, 3(1)*, 5-22

Eisenhardt, K. (1989). Building theories from case study research. *Academy of Management Review*, 14(4), 532-550.

Ellis, C.A.; Gibbs, S.J.; and Rein, G.L. (1991). Groupware, some issues and experience. *Communications of the ACM, 34(1)*, 38-57.

Fiol, C.M., and Lyles, M.A.(1985). Organizational learning. *Academy of Management Review, 10(4)*, 803-813.

Fitzgerald, T.H. (1988). Can change in organizational culture really be managed? *Organizational Dvnamics, 17*, 5-15.

Freeman, C., and Perez, C. (1988). Structural crisis of adjustruent: business cycles and investment behaviour. In G. Dosi et al. (eds.), *Technical Change and Economic Behavior*. London: Pinter, 38-66.

Frey, Jr., S.C., and Schlosser, M.M. (1993). ABB and Ford: creating value through cooperation. *Sloan Management Review, 34*(1), 65-72.

Grover, V.; Jeong, S.Y.; Kettinger, W.J.; and Teng, J.T.C. (1995). The implementation of business process reengineering. *Journal of Management Information Systems, 12(1)*, 109-144.

Grover, V.; Teng, J.T.C.; and Fiedler, K. (1993). Business process re-design: an integrated planning framework. *OMEGA: The International Journal of Management Science, 21(4)*, 433-447

Grover, V.; Teng, J.T.C.; and Fiedler, K. (1995). Technological and organizational enablers of business process reengineering. In V. Grover and W.J. Kettinger (eds.). *Business Process Change: Reengineering Concepts, Methods and Technologies.* Harrisburg, PA: Idea Group Publishing.

Hackman, J.R., and Oldham, G. (1979). *Work Redesign.* Reading, MA: Addison-Wesley.

Hahn, C.K.; Kim, KR.; and Kim, J.S. (1986). Costs of competition: implications for purchasing strategy. *Journal of Purchasing and Materials Management, 22(3),* 2-7.

Hambrick, D. (1994). Top management groups: a conceptual integration and reconsideration of the "team" label. *Research in Organizational Behavior,* 16), 171-213.

Hamel, O., and Prahalad, C.K.(1994). Competing for the future. *Harvard Business Review,* 72(4), 122-132.

Hammer, M., and Champy, J. *(1993). Reengineering the Corporation.* New York: Harper Collins.

Harkness, W.L.; Kettinger, W.J.; and Segars, A.H. (1996). Sustaining process improvement and innovation in the information services function: lessons learned at the Bose Corporation. *MIS Quarterly, 20(3),* 349-368.

Huber, G. P. (1984). The nature and design of post-industrial organizations. *Management Science, 30(8),* 928-951.

Huber, G.P. (1990). The impacts of advanced information technologies on organizational design, intelligence. *Academy Management Review* (1990).

Huber, G.P., and McDaniel, Jr., R.R. (1986). Exploiting information technologies to design more effective organizations. In M. Jarke (ed.), *Managers, Micros and Mainframes.* New York: John Wiley, 221-236.

Huckvale, T., and Ould, M. (1995). Process modeling—who, what and how— role activity diagramming. In V. Grover and W.J. Kettinger (eds.), *Business Process Change: Reengineering Concepts, Methods and Technologies.* Harrisburg, PA: Idea Publishing.

Ishikawa, K. (1986). *Guide to Quality Control,* 2d ed. Tokyo: Asian Productivity Organization.

Ives, B., and Vitale, M. R. (1988). After the sale: leveraging maintenance with information technology. *MIS Quarterly, 12,(1),* 7-22.

Johnson, D.W., and Johnson, R.T. *(1989).Cooperation and Competition: Theory and Research.* Edina, MN: Interaction.

Kanesvsky V., and Housel, T. J. (1995).Value based business process reengineering: an objective approach. In V. Grover and W.J. Kettinger (eds.), *Business Process Change: Reengineering Concepts, Methods and Technologies.* Harrisburg, PA: Idea Publishing.

Keen, P. (1991). *Shaping the Future: Business Design through Information Technology.* Boston: Harvard Business School Press.

Keen, P.G.W. (1981). Information systems and organizational change. *Communications of the ACM, 24(1),* 24-33.

Keen, P.G.W. (1988). *Competing in Time: Using Telecommunications for Competitive Advantage.* Cambridge, MA: Ballinger, 1988.

Kettinger, W.J., and Grover, V. (1995).Toward a theory of business process change management. *Journal of Management Information Systems, 12(1),* 1-30.

Kettinger, W.J.; Guha, S.; and Teng, J.T. (1995). The process reengineering life cycle methodology: a case study. In V. Grover and W.J. Kettinger (eds.), *Business Process Change: Reengineering Concepts, Methods and Technologies.* Harrisburg, PA: Idea Publishing, 210-244.

Kilman, R.; Saxton, M.; and Serpa, R. (1986). Issues in understanding and changing culture. *California Management Review, 28(2),* 87—94.

Klempa, M.J. (1995). Understanding business process reengineering: a sociocognitive contingency model. In V. Grover and W.I. Kettinger (eds.), *Business Process Change: Reengineering Concepts, Methods and Technologies.* Harrisburg, PA: Idea Publishing.

Kotter J. P. (1995). Leading change: why transformation efforts fail. *Harvard Business*

Review, 73(2), 59-67.

Lant, T.K., and Mezias, S.J. (1992). Managing discontinuous change: a simulation study of organizational learning and entrepreneurial strategies. *Strategic Management Journal, (July)*, 147—179.

Lewin, K. (1952). Group decision and social change. In G.E. Swanson, T.N. Newcomb, and E.L. Hartley (eds.), *Reading in Social Psychology.* New York: Holt.

March, J.G. (1981). Footnotes to organizational change. *Administrative Sciences Quarterly, 26*, 563-577.

March, J.G. Exploration and exploitation in organizational learning. *Organization Science, 2*, 1(1991), 71-87.

Marchand, D.A., and Stanford, M.J. (1995). Business process redesign: a framework for harmonizing people, information and technology. In V. Grover and W.J. Kettinger (eds.), *Business Process Change: Reengineering Concepts, Methods and Technologies.* Harrisburg, PA: Idea Group Publishing.

Markus M.L., and Keil, M.(1994). If we build it they will come: designing information systems that users want to use. *Sloan Management Review, 35* (Summer), 11-25.

Markus, M.L., and Robey, D. (1988). Information technology and organizational change: causal structural theory and research. *Management Science, 34(5)*, 583-598.

Mayer, R.J.; Benjamin, P.C.; Caraway, B.E.; and Painter, M.K. (1995).A framework and a suite of methods for business process reengineering. In V. Grover and W.J. Kettinger (eds.), *Business Process Change: Reengineering Concepts, Methods and Technologies.* Harrisburg, PA: Idea Group Publishing.

McGregor, D. (1960). *The Human Side of Enterprise.* New York: McGraw-Hill.

Melone, N.P. (1995). When people work scared: understanding attitudes and gaining compliance in business process re-engineering. In V. Grover and W.J. Kettinger (eds.), *Business Process Change: Reengineering Concepts, Methods and Technologies.* Harrisburg, PA: Idea Group Publishing.

Metcalf, S., and Gibbons, M. (1989). Technology, variety and organization. In R. Rosenbloom and R. Burgleman (eds.), *Research in Technology Innovation, Management and Policy.* New York: JAI Press.

Michael, D. (1973). *On Learning to Plan — And Planning to Learn.* San Francisco: Jossey-Bass.

Mintzherg, H., and Waters, J.A. (1985).Of strategies deliberate and emergent. *Strategic Management Journal, 6, 257—272.*

Mintzberg, H., and Westley, F. (1992). Cycles of organization change. *Strategic Management Journal, 13*, 39-59.

Mintzberg, H.; Brunet, J. P.; and Waters, J.A. (1986). Does planning impede strategic thinking? Tracking the strategies of Air Canada from 1937 to 1976. *Advances in Strategic Management, 4.* Greenwich, CT: JAI Press, 3-41.

Mizuno, S. (1988). *Management for Quality Improvement:* The *7 New QC Tools.* Cambridge, MA: Productivity Press.

Mumford, E. (1994). New treannent or old remedies: is business process reengineering really sociotechnical design? *Journal of Strategic Information Systems, 3(4)*, 313-326.

Nadler, D., and Tushman, M. (1990). Beyond the charismatic leader: leadership and organizational change. *Cahfornia Management Review, 32(2)*, 77-97.

Nonaka, I. (1991). The knowledge creating company. *Harvard Business Review, 69*, 96-104.

O'Reilly, C. (1993). Corporations, culture, and commitment: motivation and social control in organizations. *California Management Review, 31(3)* 9-25.

Saffold, G.S. (1988). Culture traits, strengths and organization performance: moving beyond strong culture. *Academy of Management Review, 13(4)*, 546-558.

Schein, E.H. (1984). Coming to a new awareness of organizational culture. *Sloan Management Review, 25* , 3-16.

Senge, P. *(1990). The Fifih Discipline.* New York: Doubleday.

Shaw, M.E. (1958). Some motivational factors in cooperation and competition. *Journal of Personality, 26,* 155-169.

Shrivastava, P. (1994). *Strategic Management: Concepts and Practices.* Cincinnati: South-Western Publishing.

Simon, H.A. (1991). Bounded rationality and organizational learning. *Organization Science, 2(1),* 125-134.

Stehel, P.(1992). *Breakpoints: How Managers Exploit Radical Change.* Boston: Harvard Business School Press.

Stoddard, D., and Jarvenpaa, S. (1995). Business process reengineering: tactics for managing radical change. *Journal of Management Information Systems, 12(1),* 81-108.

Strassman, P.A.(1994). The hocus pocus of reengineering. *Across the Board* (June), 35-38.

Teece, D.; Pisano, G.; and Schuen, A. (1990). Firm capabilities, resources, and the concept of strategy. CCC Working Paper No 90-8, University of California, Berkeley.

Teng, J.T.C.; Grover, V.; and Fiedler, K.D. (1994). Business process reengineering: charting a strategic path for the information age. *California Management Review, 36(3),* 9-31.

Teng, J.T.C.; Grover, V.; and Fiedler, K.D. (1996). Developing strategic perspectives on business process reengineering: from process reconfiguration to organizational change. *OMEGA, 24(3),* 271-294.

Teng, J.T.C.; Kettinger, W.J.; and Guha, S. (1992).Business process reengineering and information architecture: establishing the missing links. *Proceedings of 13th Annual, International Conference on Information Systems,* Dallas.

Tjosvold, D., and Deemer, D. (1980). Effects of controversy within a cooperative or competitive context on organizational decision making. *Journal of Applied Psychology, 65,* 590-595.

Tushman, M., and Nadler, D. (1986). Organizing for innovation. *Cahfornia Management Review, 28(3),* 74-92.

Tushman, M., and Romanelli, E. (1985). Organizational evolution: a metamorphosis model of convergence and reorientation. *Research in Organizational Behavior, 7,* 171—222.

Van Med, J.W.; Bots, P.W.G.; and Sol, H.G. (1995). Lessons learned from business engineering with the Amsterdam police force -- dynamic modeling. In V. Grover and W.J. Kettinger (eds.), *Business Process Change: Reengineering Concepts, Methods and Technologies.* Harrisburg, PA: Idea Group Publishing.

Von Hipple, E. (1988). *Sources of lnnovation.* New York: Oxford University Press.

Wiersema, M., and Bantel, K.(1992). Top management team demography and corporate strategic change. *Academy of Management Journal, 35(1),* 91-121.

Yin, R.K. (1989). *Case Study Research: Design and Methods,* 2d ed. Newbury Park, CA: Sage Publications, 1989.

Yin, R K. (1989). Research design issues in using the case study method to study management information systems. In *The Information Systems Research Challenge: Qualitative Research Methods,* no. I. Boston: Harvard Business School Press, 1-6.

Zuboff, S.(1988). *In the Age ofthe Smart Machine.* New York: Basic Books.

Source: Reprinted by special permission of the Journal of Management Information Systems, Summer 1997, Vol. 14, No. 1, pg. 119-154.

Part II
Process Management
Nuts & Bolts

CHAPTER 6

Methods For Business Process Reengineering

Richard J. Mayer
Texas A&M University, USA

Perakath C. Benjamin
Paula S. deWitte
Bruce E. Caraway
Michael K. Painter
Knowledge Based Systems, Inc., USA

As organizations seek to obtain strategic advantages by redesigning the way they do business, they are finding the process fraught with uncertainty. Put simply, change is difficult. In some instances, the prospect of change is so onerous that the only way to effect change is to liquidate the existing enterprise and start again. A consensus is emerging that successful organizations of the next millennium will be those that embrace *continuous change* as a business paradigm. Such organizations will be able both to adapt to changes in the marketplace and to lead the market in directions optimal to the organization's goals by continually adapting their products, processes, and internal structures to changes in the business environment.

The technique for Business Process Reengineering (BPR) has evolved as a powerful and practical tool enabling rapid enterprise restructuring and change management. The deluge of published literature on BPR and related techniques, such as Continuous Process Improvement (CPI), evidence the popularity of the reengineering paradigm in the industry and research community (for example, Hammer and Champy (1993) and Morris and Brandon (1993)). Conspicuous in their absence, (though not surprisingly, given the novelty of the technique), however, are scientific methods and theories focused on BPR. The purpose of this chapter is to describe a *framework and a suite of methods* for BPR, and the role of these methods in realizing the practical benefits of BPR. We foresee this framework establishing the conceptual foundations for a more comprehensive *BPR theory* that we are developing.

Business Process Reengineering

The term *Business Process Reengineering* has, over the past couple of years, gained increasing circulation. As a result, many find themselves faced with the prospect of having to learn, plan, implement, and successfully conduct a real Business Process Reengineering (BPR) endeavor, whatever that might entail, within their own business organization. Amid all the fervor over BPR, there has been an understandable amount of effort exerted in defining exactly what BPR is as well as how to best accomplish it. Although many definitions have been proposed, the majority provide only vague, high-level philosophical approaches. Even the term "reengineering" is something of a misnomer. It suggests that the business process was initially engineered at its inception (Morris and Brandon, 1993). We will now make our own attempt at clarifying the terminology relevant to BPR.

Hammer and Champy (1993) define [Business Process] Reengineering as "the fundamental rethinking and radical redesign of business processes to achieve dramatic improvements in critical, contemporary measures of performance, such as cost, quality, service, and speed." *Continuous Process Improvement* (CPI) is the collection of activities that are systematically and continuously performed to bring about enhancements in enterprise performance. The main difference between BPR and CPI is in the extent of improvements targeted by these two methodologies. BPR targets radical change while CPI is focused on incremental change. A related methodology, *Total Quality Management* (TQM) is "a means of operating a business that seeks to maximize a firm's value through maximizing customer satisfaction at the lowest possible cost" (Spitzer, 1993). Therefore, TQM is the systematic application of methods and tools to accomplish CPI.

One of the predominant distinguishing characteristics of *engineering* that separates it from other professions is the creation and use of models. Whether those be physical models, mathematical models, computer models, or structural models; engineers build and analyze models to predict the performance of designs or to understand the behavior of devices. In the context of BPR then, we use the term "engineering" in the broad sense to mean the creation of a process system with predictable behavior using some methodology that employs models as a basic tool. Whether that new system embodies an incremental refinement of an existing process or a paradigm shift, the engineering element must provide the modeling support required. Incremental improvement employs models that enable quantitative analysis of a proposed change to an element of a process. Continuous improvement using such models can achieve the lowest cost, highest performance implementation of a process. Breakthrough change of a process (paradigm shifts) generally is preceded by establishing a shared understanding of the fundamental nature of the situation at hand. This can be accomplished by teams building models that capture knowledge and experiences from which such an understanding evolves.

For this chapter, we define BPR as the use of scientific methods, models, and tools to bring about the radical restructuring of an enterprise that results in significant improvements in performance. The phrase "the use of scientific methods, models, and tools" reiterates the importance of using methods and tools when initiating a BPR effort. This is important, for there has been a surprising abundance of sophisticated software supporting BPR, but there has been a noticeable lack of standard, robust methods for successfully engaging in BPR.

In general, scientific methods and tools may include any of those available to assist in a BPR effort. For the purposes of this paper, we are specifically concerned with the use of the IDEF (Integration Definition) Methods, Systems Simulation, and Activity-Based Costing. The purpose of this paper is to present a framework for Business Process Reengineering that is centered around the use of *methods, models, and tools* that can provide the necessary guidance to successfully implement a BPR effort.

A Framework for BPR

Frameworks

The term *framework* has been defined in several different ways. In general a framework can be defined as a basic structure, arrangement or system. In this sense, it refers to a structure that serves to hold the parts of something together. From an information system development viewpoint, a framework is "an organization of characterized situation types that are known to occur commonly during a system life cycle" (Mayer, et al. 1992). In essence, a framework is an organizing structure for a system. Frameworks provide for expressions of the characteristics of the conceptual parts of a system and the interrelationship between these parts. We define a *BPR Framework* as a characterization of BPR in terms of 1) a set of guiding principles for BPR, 2) the BPR process (a set of BPR activities and their interrelationships), and 3) a set of methods and tools for BPR and the role of these methods and tools in supporting the BPR process.

We will now outline a framework for BPR. The focus of the paper will be on describing the role of the IDEF methods in supporting the BPR activities in the framework and will focus attention on the relationship between the BPR process and the BPR enabling methods.

It is important that a BPR framework be comprehensible and that the underlying methods be easy to understand and apply to any given application scenario. This is especially true for those who are interested in making BPR an organic function of their enterprise. In such a case, the enterprise's own personnel would perform and manage the BPR effort themselves without having to rely on some outside source of expertise to guarantee success.

Proposed BPR Framework

The proposed BPR Framework is shown in Figure 1.

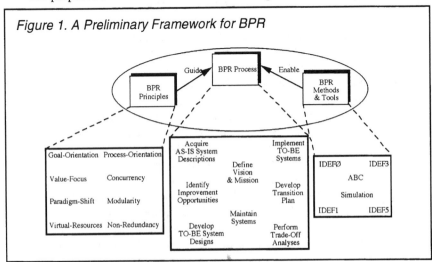

Figure 1. A Preliminary Framework for BPR

The top half of the figure (enclosed within an ellipse) illustrates the fundamental structure of our BPR Framework. The BPR *process* is at the heart of the framework. The BPR process is a collection of activities that are performed in typical BPR projects, along with the relationships between these activities. The activities are performed opportunistically; that is, there is no predefined temporal ordering that can be prescribed for the activities that are invoked as required by the BPR team members of the organization involved in the BPR effort. These activities and their interrelationships are described briefly in the section entitled "The BPR Process." The BPR *principles* provide the philosophical and conceptual underpinnings to structure and guide the BPR process. These guiding principles have been incorporated as part of our characterization of BPR in order to set the context for the BPR process description, and are briefly outlined in the section entitled "BPR Principles."

The focus of this chapter, however, is on a set of BPR *Methods and Tools*. The BPR Methods and Tools facilitate the BPR process by providing support for the knowledge acquisition, design, and analysis activities of BPR. This chapter describes a subset of the Air Force IDEF suite of methods (Painter, 1991b) and the role played by these methods in BPR projects. We also make reference to two other well known BPR-enabling techniques, Activity-Based Costing (ABC) (Kaplan, 1990) and Systems Simulation (Shannon, 1975).

BPR Principles

This section summarizes a few important principles of BPR. Some of these principles have been described in detail in (Hammer and Champy, 1993). This list is partial, and is presented here to both stimulate more work in the development of BPR theories and focus attention on the scientific aspects of BPR.

- **Institute-Leadership.** Among the principles of BPR, effective leadership is first on the list, and first in importance. Characteristics of an effective leader include competence, commitment, involvement, and genuine interest in people and their activities. A leader is found in front of his followers, *leading* the way. Leadership includes granting stewardship coupled with clear accountability. Good leaders encourage creativity, initiative, and trust.

- **Goal-Orientation.** The principle of goal-orientation states that the processes of an enterprise must be organized around goals (outcomes) and not tasks. This principle helps ensure that the activities of an organization are structured in a manner that emphasizes the accomplishment of business goals.

- **Responsiveness to customer needs.** BPR activities are ultimately devoted to increasing customer (the acquiring agent) and user (the actual operator of an end product) satisfaction. This devotion necessitates responsiveness to customer needs and priorities. Such responsiveness includes dedication to satisfying needs that are explicitly stated as well as those that are merely expected.

- **Process-Orientation.** The principle of process-orientation states that the users of process output must perform the process. A secondary process orientation principle is to create and empower process owners, and make them responsible for process outputs. Process-orientation leads to greater accountability for process performance.

- **Value-Focus.** The value-focus principle states that non-value added activities must be identified and targeted for elimination. This principle ensures that business activities are focused on keeping customers satisfied, because "value" is defined in terms of perceived benefits to the customer. Techniques such as ABC and Simulation facilitate the realization of the value-focus principle.

- **Virtual-Resource.** The virtual-resource principle states that geographically distributed resources and agents must be treated as if they were centralized. This principle ensures the best utilization of organization assets, promotes sharing of enterprise knowledge, and minimizes chances of local performance optimization (thereby ensuring global optimization).

- **Concurrency.** The principle of concurrency states that activities must be performed concurrently to the greatest extent possible within the budget constraints of an organization. This principle is motivated in part by the success of the science and by the practice of Concurrent Engineering over the past decade.

- **Non-Redundancy.** The principle of non-redundancy (with reference to information capture) states that information must be captured only once, and at the source. This principle will enhance the cost-effectiveness of the information systems that support the business process.

- **Modularity.** The modularity principle states that the decision making agents must be placed (to the extent practical) where the work is performed. A direct implication of this principle is that control will be engineered into the business process.

- **Paradigm-Shift.** The paradigm-shift principle states that business engineers must not limit their thinking: that is, encourage "thinking out-of-the-box." Such "paradigm-shift" thinking leads to radical and fundamental changes that are the target of reengineering initiatives.

- **Management Information and Knowledge Assets.** The basic principles represented here are that first, information and knowledge are resources (like manpower, materials, and machines) that can be leveraged to achieve competitive advantage, and second, that actual realization of the "Information Integrated Agile Enterprise" vision can only be accomplished by taking full advantage of those resources.

The BPR Process

This section provides a brief description of the BPR process. BPR is intrinsically complex and requires the concerted effort of personnel with many different kinds of skills and experience. Successful reengineering requires a close-knit team that is committed to the accomplishment of the project objectives. However, the human and organizational aspects of the BPR process are beyond the scope of this paper. We focus on the task aspects of activities that we believe are important for the success of BPR projects, and the interrelationships between these activities. Given the complexity of BPR, it is important to note that BPR activities do not fit cleanly into a "cookbook" procedure. Rather, it is useful to conceptualize the BPR activities described in this section as "modes of thought" that humans use in an opportunistic and iterative fashion. Business reengineering activities involve many different cognitive tasks such as conceptual design and analysis, detailed design and analysis, etc., as sketched in Figure 2. The description presented in this section is therefore a coarse-grained characterization of the BPR process that (hopefully) provides prac-

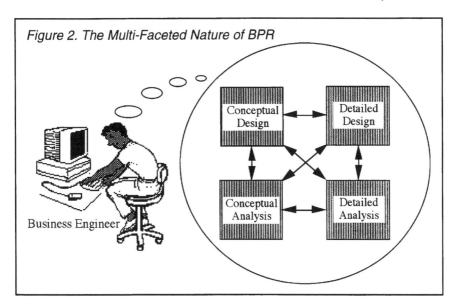

Figure 2. The Multi-Faceted Nature of BPR

titioners with insight into the nature of the underlying activities.

Define BPR Vision, Mission, and Goals

An essential, and early step in a BPR project is to clearly understand the mission of the organization implementing and define a vision for the reengineering effort that is consistent with this mission. An enterprise mission statement is a statement about an enterprise that summarizes the reasons for its very existence. For example, the mission statement of a Widget manufacturing company may be "To be worldwide market leaders in the Widget business." It is important to be cognizant of the enterprise mission while developing the vision of a BPR effort. A statement of the vision of a BPR effort may be "To reduce the profit margin of the XYZ Company by 100% over the next two years." Vision definitions typically cover long periods in time and are at a coarse level of granularity (that is, they are not very detailed). BPR envisionment is usually done by top-management executives, and lead to the definition of BPR goals and objectives. The goal(s) describe the desired outcome(s) of a BPR project. The objectives are a more detailed description of the goals.

Other preliminary BPR activities include:
- Selecting a BPR project leader and assembling a BPR team,
- Establishing the scope and the level of detail of the BPR effort, and
- Developing a time and resource schedule for the BPR project.

Acquire AS-IS System Descriptions

An important initial activity for BPR projects is to acquire descriptions of the business systems.[1] Knowledge Acquisition (KA) has been the subject of much research over the past two decades, particularly in the Artificial Intelligence (AI) community. The research results have benefited industry significantly. The main AI application of KA techniques has been in the field of Expert Systems (Waterman, 1986). The use of KA for traditional information system design has been through information analysis methods such as the Nijssen Information Analysis Methodology (NIAM) (Nijssen, 1978), the Entity-Relationship (ER) method (Chen, 1976), the Object Modeling Technique (OMT) (Rumbaugh, et al., 1991), and the IDEF suite of methods (Painter, 1991). Each of these methods has been used with varying degrees of success in several application areas.

KA methods facilitate the acquisition and design of both *descriptions* and *models*. The differences between descriptions and models are important, and are summarized in the following. Descriptions reflect the state of the world as known or believed to be true by an agent. Models built from structured, accurate descriptions are used by decision makers to reason logically from observations to conclusions (e.g., regarding cause and effect relations in our organization). Unfortunately, what we know about the world is often incomplete and, hence, descriptions are often partial. To fill in the gaps, we employ models based upon idealizations. Idealizations are typically precise concepts that can be used to build models. Models built from these idealizations can be validated against a set of observations, but are not true or false. Models can be used in a valid context to predict characteristics that we cannot directly observe or easily measure. For example, while the concepts of points and lines from our grade-school geometry don't actually occur in the real world, we use them every day to compute a variety of useful data, from the amount of cloth in a shirt to the structural characteristics of a space craft. The ability to acquire and represent descriptions and idealizations is important for BPR. Descriptions provide factual evidence of what the organization does and how it performs its activities. Models are useful in predicting data (particularly economic and performance data) that otherwise would be expensive or even impossible to acquire. Together, descriptions and models provide the business engineer with the information needed to determine 1) what to change, 2) how to change, and 3) what will be the result of the change. The IDEFØ method (as described in the section entitled "Overview of the IDEFØ Function Modeling Method") was designed to support the development of models, and the IDEF3 and IDEF5 methods (as described in the sections entitled "Overview of the IDEF3 Process Description Capture Method" and "Overview of the IDEF5 Ontology Description Capture Method," respectively) were designed to facilitate the capture and analysis of descriptions.

An important requirement of KA methods is the ability to acquire and represent knowledge at multiple levels of abstraction and from multiple points of view. The ability to represent information taken from multiple perspectives is essential to manage complexity and facilitate communication in BPR projects. This is to 1) account for the difference in the cognitive skills of humans and 2) enhance the synergy between different views. Managing knowledge at multiple levels of detail is vital to managing complexity through information hiding.

Once a raw system description has been acquired, it needs to be refined to produce a more structured, knowledge-rich description, through a *validation* process. Validation is the process of ensuring that the description is an adequate representation of the real system with reference to the analysis goals. Description refinement involves two major activities: 1) consistency checking (semantic validation) and 2) syntactic validation. Consistency checking is the process of ensuring that the facts in the description are consistent with each other. This can be done incrementally during the knowledge acquisition process, or after an initial set of facts has been gathered. Syntactic validation ensures that the description is structured according to the syntax rules of the knowledge representation methods.

The results of applying the KA process are 1) functional models, 2) process descriptions (process maps), and 3) ontology descriptions (object-based descriptions). The role of the IDEF methods in KA is described in the section entitled "Capturing the AS-IS System Description."

Identify Improvement Opportunities

The identification of business process improvement opportunities is a vital, though complex activity in the BPR process.[1] In simple terms, identifying improvements is an activity (rather than an end state) directed toward finding ways to work smarter, not harder. Working smarter starts with examination of the basic business goals and customer needs. From a review of these items, a new business design can be conceived. In BPR, this design activity is often referred to as "out-of-the-box" thinking. However, approaching large organizations with out-of-the-box thinking and no methodology is dangerous (Jones, 1994). In the following sections, we present a methodology that involves several interrelated activities including 1) analysis of AS-IS processes, 2) evaluation of reference models and benchmarks, 3) cause and effect analysis, 4) constraint discovery and analysis, and 5) envisionment of TO-BE processes and the quantitative/qualitative evaluation of those designs. An understanding of the philosophy of this methodology can be acquired by considering the following excerpt from (Jones, 1994).

In Jazz, there is a well established and accepted idea of "playing" outside. This means that an experienced Jazz musician will deviate from the original structure and the rest of the band will follow. The idea is to go outside enough to create tension and hence excitement. The problem here, however, is the same for out-of-the-box organizational thinkers. If you go too far outside and don't have a thorough understanding of the musical/organizational structure, you get chaos.

We need to use innovation (dynamic quality) to make major changes to the company and its products. But, this needs to be tempered with continuous improvement of existing process, products, and structures (static quality) if a company wants to be successful in a competitive world market. To improve productivity and innovation, we must define and measure what we mean by improvement. We need to measure and report on productivity and innovation as often as we measure and report on profit and growth if we intend to increase the real wealth of the company.

Many out-of-the-box and other "brilliant" ideas need to be verified before they are used to put companies out of business. The farther out-of-the-box, the more verification. This is not suggesting analysis to the point of paralysis. As is usual with thinking that is three-standard-deviations from the mean (systems jargon for "out-of-the-box"), it can be true wisdom or utter nonsense. A powerful systems view supported by business modeling (including cybernetic models) and simulation (with animation) with metrics for quality (Statistical Process Control and/or ISO 9000) and performance (Activity-Based Costing or Economic Value Added) is mandatory for reengineering any large organization.

AS-IS Process Analysis

Establish Analysis Goals

An important activity in the process analysis process is to identify and characterize system analysis goals. These analysis goals are often the same as, or are derivable from, the BPR goals and objectives (as described in the section entitled "Define BPR Vision, Mission, and Goals"). The BPR analysis goals are an important determinant of the analysis approach required. For example, the analysis goal "to estimate the approximate lead time for the procurement process" suggests a qualitative IDEFØ-based analysis approach (see the section entitled "The Role of IDEFØ in Activity Analysis"). On the other hand, the goal "to determine the effect of a 50% reduction in program budget on the system throughput" may require the use of a quantitative simulation-based analysis approach (see the section entitled "The Role of IDEF3 in Simulation-Based Process Analysis").

Classify Activities and Objects

This activity involves the selection of activities and objects in the model and classifying these based on the role they will play in the analysis. The nature of the classification performed, therefore, is influenced by the analysis goals. The analysis goals suggest the use of a particular analysis approach or technique(s). The selected analysis approach, in turn, determines the kinds of classification required to make the analysis meaningful. Note that the IDEFØ, IDEF3, and IDEF5 methods provide classification mechanisms that are useful for analysis. However, the techniques of Activity-Based Costing (ABC) (Kaplan, 1990) and Simulation Modeling (Shannon, 1975) suggest additional classification schemes that enrich the analysis process. To illustrate, for the purposes of ABC, it is useful to classify activities as follows (McDonald, 1993):

- Value-adding vs. Non Value-adding (often called "Value-added" and "Non Value-added" in the literature): activities that are perceived to generate valuable output(s) of value to the customer are value-adding and those that are not are non value-adding. Value, according to (McDonald, 1993) is anything ". . . that directly increases the profitability, capability, or mission-readiness of the organization."
- Primary vs. Secondary: activities that directly support the primary goals (or mission) of a system. A secondary activity is an activity that supports a primary activity.
- Discretionary vs. Required: discretionary activities are those that may or may not be performed, at the discretion of the system personnel. Required activities are those that must be performed as required by external or internal policy or mandate.

Perform Quantitative Analysis

Quantitative analysis methods play an important role in business process analysis. Many of the quantitative analysis methods were developed as part of the field of study called Operations Research (OR). Quantitative OR techniques that are relevant for process analysis are Queuing Theory, Systems Simulation, Linear Programming, Dynamic Programming, and Network Techniques (Phillips, et al., 1976). The cost accounting method, Activity-Based Costing (ABC) has gained popularity in recent years as an analysis tool for BPR (Kaplan, 1990). The main advantage of quantitative methods is that they facilitate the evaluation of performance in a quantitative way (with numbers). These methods have been successfully used for a number of applications over the past four decades. The main limitation of quantitative techniques, however, is that they often are constrained by restrictive assumptions.[2] The section entitled "The Role of IDEF3 in Simulation-Based Process Analysis" will show the utility of the IDEF3 method for performing simulation analysis.

Perform Causal Analysis

Causal Analysis is an important component of business system (and business process) analysis. The main goal of BPR causal analysis is to identify cause and effect chains that link aspects of the system (usually the "controllable" system factors) to the performance goals of the system. An important step in causal analysis is to identify causal associations between system factors.[3] These associations must be characterized in enough detail so that the effect of the factor change on the association can be accurately estimated. Influence diagrams (Richardson, 1981) and Ishikawa Diagrams (Gitlow, et al., 1989) have been shown to be useful helping identify qualitative causal relationships. An influence diagram showing the causal relationships between production rates and Work In Process (WIP) is shown in Figure 3. The '+' indicates direct proportionality and the '-' depicts inverse proportionality.

Discover and Analyze Constraints

The role of constraints in business analysis and reengineering has gained much attention in recent years through the work of the physicist, Eliyahu Goldratt (Goldratt, 1985). Goldratt's Theory of Constraints (TOC) is an approach to discovering the constraints that limit the accomplishment of the organizations' goals. The TOC philosophy seeks continuous improvement by systematically breaking the identified constraints. Goldratt defines a constraint as anything that limits a system from achieving higher performance versus its goal. We define a constraint as a relationship that is maintained as true in a given context. Analysis of constraints is key to understanding relationships between the different components of a system and the whole of which they are a part. Constraints encapsulate the assumptions, policies, and procedures of an organization. From a BPR perspective, three kinds of constraints are important 1) constraints that improve an organization's throughput, 2) constraints that limit an organization's throughput, and 3) constraints that should be enforced to improve an organization's throughput (KBSI, 1994b). The knowledge structuring

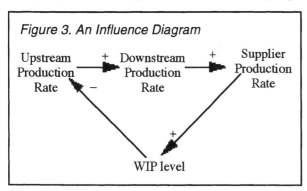

Figure 3. An Influence Diagram

and analysis mechanisms provided by the IDEF methods facilitate the discovery and analysis of constraints.

Locate Reference Technologies and Models

A careful study of existing "best in class" processes, systems, and success stories is useful for the success of a BPR project. This may be done through a survey of industry, assessing published reference models (for example, by using the electronic World-Wide Web on the Internet) or reviewing published BPR "success stories." The organization performing the BPR project must then try to leverage the existing knowledge and technology to make the effort more cost-effective.

Envision TO-BE Processes

The capacity to envision solutions to a problem is a critical, though difficult aspect of any problem solving endeavor. In BPR, it is important to envision promising TO-BE processes as part of the reengineering process. This envisionment of TO-BE processes is inductive and involves hypothesizing possible solutions to a given problem. Knowledge of state-of-the-art techniques and tools will facilitate this envisioning process. Ready access to reference technologies and models will also accelerate the identification of possible TO-BE process alternatives.

Develop TO-BE System Designs

System design is at the heart of BPR. Although it is often difficult to determine when analysis completes and when design begins (design and analysis are closely interlocked in many practical situations), this section is focused on describing salient aspects of the system design activities. We will focus attention on the design of the processes that the system will support.

Currently, process design is often thought of more as an art than as a science. For this reason, the actual task of designing a TO-BE process can prove to be quite difficult. In actuality, it may be better to think of process design as an iterative process of refinement. Rather than being a set of clearly defined, sequential steps, the design process may be better represented by a set of successive, though less-precise stages that eventually lead to an ideal process design for a given scenario. The process engineer who undertakes the process design challenge does not follow a list of sequential design steps, but, rather, relies on a set of acquired process design skills that will be employed in any one of a variety of process design scenarios that might be encountered.

Initially, the process engineer has some set of desired outputs from which to design a process. It is these outputs, often realized in the form of either a product, system, or service, which give the process engineer a purpose. Along with this set of desired outputs, the process engineer will (hopefully) have some idea of the inputs that will be necessary in generating those outputs. Depending on the process to be designed, the inputs might be the raw materials used in a manufacturing process or the information used in a business process. At this point, the link between the inputs and the outputs is called a "process" and could be thought of as just a "black box" which takes in a given set of inputs and produces a set of desired outputs. It is this black box, though, that the process engineer must be willing to open. Upon opening the box, he or she must design the inner workings—the process which actually "makes the box work."

At this point, the process engineer must start with a generalized process that will "fit in the box." In other words, the engineer must provide a starting point at which to begin designing the process. This generalized process may be based on a process that exists in a similar scenario with outputs similar to those desired of the TO-BE process. If no reference process is known to exist, the process engineer must identify some experience or knowledge base from which the generalized process can be (organically) developed.

Once a generalized process has been identified, the next step involves decomposing it into a set of more specific activities or tasks that can be performed by assignable resources. As the tasks are identified an "extended process" will become apparent. That is, one task will take in a given set of inputs and will result in some set, intermediate outputs which will then, in turn, be used as a set of inputs for the next task until the desired set of outputs results.

In the following section, eight principles of process design have been compiled. These represent a set of basic tenets that one should consider when designing a process as in a TO-BE system design.

Principles of Process Design

The **first** principle of process design is that it is a design endeavor. That is, it is primarily inductive in nature. When faced with a design situation, the designer will generally start with a design that is already familiar and try to modify that design to address the new situation.

The **second** principle of process design is that it is not a process. Rather, it is a set of skills that are employed in an opportunistic fashion.

The **third** principle of process design is that it is object design; processes produce some output object(s) and consume or are triggered by some input object(s). One mode of thought for a process designer is the design of the input and output objects. The design of the structure of the input/output objects, their roles relative to a process (supply versus control for inputs, measurement versus product for outputs), and their frequency/rate of arrival are all considered as part of the design process. One of the key aspects of process design is determining which of the input/output objects specified in the requirements for the process are modifiable and which are fixed, which are controllable and which are uncontrollable, and which are independent and which are dependent. An experienced process designer is always looking for ways to design the input or output objects to both streamline the resulting process and also to optimize the upstream and downstream interfacing processes.

The **fourth** principle of process design is that it is decomposition and allocation; processes must be specified to a level of sub processes that can be allocated to specific resources available in the execution environment. One of the reasons for process redesign is that the resources available and their capabilities change over time. Thus, a process that was once acceptable because there was a highly capable resource available, becomes no longer acceptable due to the loss of that resource, the unavailability of a replacement, and vice versa. Process design involves decomposition of sub processes until a level is reached in which the sub processes can be allocated to an available resource.

The **fifth** principle of process design is that it is input/output contiguity; during the decomposition process, the input/output of each sub process must be specified and matched with the input available and the output required at the position of the sub process in the process flow. When there is not a match, additional processes may have to be added to make the interface or the sub process must be modified to perform the interface function itself. When neither occurs, another decomposition must be considered.

The **sixth** principle of process design is that it is failure management; the possible failure modes, those considered expected or reasonable, of the resulting system must be identified. For each possible failure modes (and for possible combinations of failure modes) the effects of failure must be predicted. Then, a design decision must be made to determine whether the sub processes will be added to detect and manage the effects of each possible failure mode.

The **seventh** principle of process design is that it is by-product (waste or scrap) management. During the execution of a process, products will be produced that are not useful as input to downstream processes or considered a part of the desired output of the overall process. These types of objects must be identified and sub processes put in place to collect and dispose of them properly.

The **eighth** principle of process design is that it is execution resource management. During the execution of a process, there are normally multiple activations of the process being attempted simultaneously. In normal situations there are limited resources available to perform the sub process instances. This naturally results in resource contention situations for which resource management sub processes must be added by the process designer.

Practical Guidelines for Process Design

One approach to process design that implements the above-described principles focuses on the objects and their state changes. This approach helps to achieve a "change in view" of the domain experts. It is fairly clear that domain experts are most knowledgeable about the As-Is process and that knowledge and expertise is required to drive out symptoms and root causes. However, it can be an impediment to innovation to use the domain experts in the To-Be process design, especially if the domain experts are currently the owners of the As-Is processes. If individuals are too attached to an existing process, it is difficult for those same individuals to develop breakthrough ideas about a new process. More likely, such individuals will work toward small improvements rather than large improvements. For them, it is often simply too difficult to see how to make major improvements. By using an alternative approach in the To-Be design—specifically viewing the system from an object state in which one begins looking at the end of the process first—one can effectively shift the perspective of domain experts and allow them to think "out of the box." Another important element is to set the context of To-Be design in "green light mode." In other words, when the goal is to truly achieve massive improvement of business processes, one needs to be somewhat non-judgmental. A tone needs to be set for domain experts attempting process improvement—going for the gold means opening oneself to any idea that can in fact lead to substantial changes. This mindset is important to ensuring that the full creativity of the group can be explored, thereby maximizing the chances of achieving truly breakthrough results. This especially true since BPR efforts are complex and expensive.

Object centered process design intentionally starts with an attempt at a definition: what does success look like at the end of process? We form our definition in the context of an object—either real or virtual—produced by a process. We then work backward through the process and look at intermediate states of that object, and identify in those intermediate states the additional states and components that are collected about that object. In the end, we ask, "Have all objects and components been produced?" In the intermediate stages, some of information and components produced are included. In the beginning, an object is defined but there are no values for its attributes. For example, the designer's sketch of an automobile defines what needs to be there, but there are no components. Intermediate objects have subassemblies. By the end of the process, we have a complete and functional automobile object.

The next step involves filling in this map of transitions from one object state to another state, and identifying the process steps needed to go from one state to the next (see Figure 4). This now gives us a basic network that shows us the relationships between the objects producing and the processes needed to add the information—the fundamental architecture of the To-Be process. Now we need to begin to flesh this out with additional information. One major step is to examine the goals, the disconnects, and the root causes from As-Is analysis, and to compare the To-Be design with those. We want to ensure that we have identified some kind of process step or activity or some kind of piece of information that, in fact, satisfies those particular goals. Some of those goals may be performance goals such as desired cycle time (i.e., the time it will take each process step to be executed). Perhaps these goals will have types of information not easily captured in process models. For instance, if we have goals associated with costs, quality, etc. object state transition diagrams with associated processes need to have additional quantitative information identified that will show how those particular goals will be satisfied. For example, a quality goal to achieve certain yield might require adding a process step to address quality from the perspective of designing a procedure to assure quality control and that assurance steps and metrics are measured. Processes might include sampling, checking, or whatever is required to be most effective in achieving that quality performance goal.

We now have the definition of the object we're producing from its final state to the initial state (working backward). We have identified process steps to effect each transition. Even in an object-oriented design method process diagramming is used in order to ensure that the process steps, resulting from the object transition design,

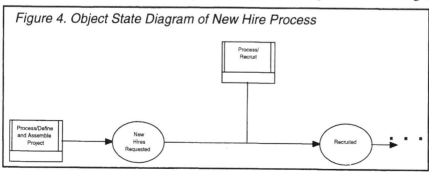

Figure 4. Object State Diagram of New Hire Process

fit together into a logical pattern. In addition to the process logic, this step also generally includes the allocation of each process step to an organization unit. Such resource allocations must be verified as consistent with those manageable by the existing or envisioned management organization.

Perform Trade-off Analysis

The purpose of trade-off analysis is to evaluate the relative merit of completing alternative process/system design alternatives. The system design will be carried forward up to a stage in which such analysis is possible. Often, trade-off analysis and system design are done incrementally, and iteratively; that is, trade-off analysis is performed initially with a partial system design, the analysis results are used to refine the design, the analysis is invoked again, and so on. Depending on the goals of the BPR effort, the nature of the analysis may vary from *Qualitative* (rough-cut, order of magnitude) to *Quantitative*. Trade-off analyses often focus on measures of system performance and include cost/benefit analysis. Trade-off analysis is difficult in practice because of the existence of multiple, competing criteria. Multiple-criteria decision support techniques may be applied to guide the analysis process. The IDEF methods can be used effectively in conjunction with analysis techniques such as ABC and simulation to perform trade-off analyses.

Of particular importance is the tradeoff between process streamlining and flexibility. Paradoxically, these two qualities are competing design goals. Greater efficiency, accomplished primarily through process streamlining, often results in less flexibility. Likewise, enhancement of flexibility levies constraints on attainable efficiency. The appropriate balance between these competing design goals is sought initially through accounting for known downstream concerns. For example, where demand for parallel products (e.g., automobile offerings with either standard or automatic transmissions) can be anticipated, manufacturing process flexibility becomes more important than it would be otherwise (Cook, 1990).

Develop Transition Plan

After the TO-BE process/system design has been determined, the next step is to develop a plan for transition to the redesigned process from the AS-IS process. The overall transition strategy must align the organizational structure, information systems, and business policies and procedures with the re-engineered processes/systems. The transition plan often includes 1) a system integration strategy, 2) a technology strategy, and 3) an information system strategy. The IDEF0 and IDEF3 methods have been shown to be effective tools for representing and communicating the transition plans.

BPR efforts will result in various forms of implementations depending on the nature of the change required. Some changes may involve only policy change, while others may require complete business and information system restructuring. Regardless of the extent of the implementation itself, success depends upon effective implementation planning. If done correctly, implementation planning will mitigate the two major risks of failure that inhibit implementations: 1) meeting initial expectations of time and expense, and 2) risk of change to an ongoing operation.

Transition Process Design

The foundation for a BPR implementation plan is laid by preparing a business case. The BPR method and software tools available today allow us to capture the evolution of those business case concepts through the As-Is and on into the To-Be. Along with the various function, process, object, and information descriptions at each stage we can also identify the various dependencies among the views. This allows us to take the next critical step, which is to design a process for moving the organization from the As-Is into the To-Be, as well as the resources required enabling that transition.

Further, we can use this functional modeling framework as our initial business case to create a detailed architecture or project view of the changes we wish to make. As we analyze the existing system and define and describe the To-Be system, we can add additional relevant activities and begin to assign the time and resource allocations needed to perform the implementation.

Integration of Information Infrastructure and Functional/Business Views

Many enterprises today undertake Business Process Reengineering (BPR) *and* Information Infrastructure (II)[1] modernization efforts to drastically reduce costs and improve performance. While these efforts would appear to be complementary, they are rarely conducted jointly. That is, although it might make sense to conduct BPR and information infrastructure modernization efforts in a highly coordinated fashion, there has been little success to date in making the attempt. The importance of coordinating such efforts in the BPR transition plan is obvious when one considers the implications of making changes to the business process and/or the supporting network hardware and communications infrastructure. Making changes to the logic and structure of a business process generally introduces new requirements on the supporting infrastructure. Likewise, making changes to the network hardware, communications, and application infrastructure can have dramatic impacts on the performance of business processes and the end user's ability to perform (Painter, 1996). Most successful BPR efforts involve the IT evolution as a part of the design process and all successful BPR efforts must involve IT in the implementation planning and execution.

Evolving the To-Do From the As-Is and To-Be

One of the most powerful and beneficial aspects of the methods and tools identified earlier in this chapter is that they make possible a systematic, traceable, and significantly automated transition planning process. The IDEF models that were created during the As-Is can be mapped to those created during the To-Be and an initial list of change requirements generated. Additional requirements for the construction of the To-Be components can be added and the result organized into a work breakdown structure (WBS).

Recent developments in BPR software technologies enable automatic migration of these WBS activity/relationships into a process modeling environment. The benefit here is that we can now define the causal and time sequential relationships between the activities that we have planned.

The process model view also permits us to identify the time duration aspects of the activities. In two steps, we have taken the activities and initiatives needed to solve the root cause problems and generated all of the key functional, sequential, resource

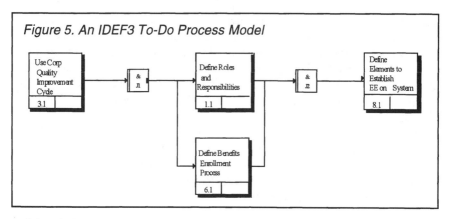

Figure 5. An IDEF3 To-Do Process Model

and time information to serve as the foundation of the To-Do Implementation Plan. Using the BPR methods and technologies plus the knowledge of the BPR team, an initial project plan is created automatically just as it was done early in the Project Definition. So the BPR team has available a "Strawman" transition plan that can evolve as the BPR implementation progresses. This permits the team to make, among other things, estimates of the implementation costs as the project progresses. Similarly, alternative strategies, which were identified during the Project Definition Phase, are easily incorporated into the To-Do Activity and Process models. Alternatives that were identified subsequent to the Project Definition Phase are also easily added. Alternatives are typically analyzed for impact on ROI and risk. Available BPR software technology permits the BPR analyst to evaluate the key performance measures (e.g., cycle time, cost, quality, utilization, revenue generation) through simulation and cost/benefit analysis. In addition, such factors as favorable customer impact and cultural impacts must be considered.

Implement TO-BE Systems

The purpose of this activity is to test, implement, and document the TO-BE

Figure 6. Transition Project Plan for a Reengineered Process

	Task Name	Duration	May 4, '97	May 11, '97	May 18, '97	
1	Critical Business Issue	1d				
3	Critical Process	10d				
4	New Hire Process	10d				
6	Use Corp Quality I	1d				
7	Define Roles and I	1d				
9	Define Benefits Er	1d				
11	Define Elements t	1d				
13	Establish Std. EE C	1d				
15	Establish and Mai	1d				
17	Measure Critical E	1d				
19	Partner with Busi	5d				
20	Establish Ade	1d				
22	Coordinate Be	1d				
24	Understand B	1d				

process/system. This will typically start with a test and tryout phase. The test results will be used to refine and harden the requirements of the TO-BE process/system. The test procedures must, in addition to evaluating nominal functionality, analyze boundary cases and failure modes. The final implementation is often done in an incremental/phased manner. It will often involve purchase of technology, hiring of workers, training (of new and existing workers), restructuring the organization, and reallocation of resources.

Maintain Systems

This activity refers to the continuous maintenance of the system over extended periods of time. Because the requirements of a system change over time, it is important that a system respond appropriately to these changes. Mechanisms must be in place to incorporate incremental changes in the system descriptions over extended periods of time.

A Suite of Methods for BPR
Overview of Methods

The use of methods is critical to the success of the framework for Business Process Reengineering. Informally, a method is a procedure for doing something (i.e., an attempt to capture the "best practice" or experience). Moreover, the method may have a representational notation to communicate this procedure more effectively. More formally, a method consists of three components, as illustrated in Figure 7: definition, discipline, and use. The definition contains the concepts, motivation, and theory supporting the method. The discipline includes the syntax of the method, a computer-interpretable format (e.g., ISyCL (Mayer, 1991)), and the procedure governing its use. Many methods have multiple syntaxes that have either evolved or are used for aspects that are different from their original use. Perhaps the most visible component of a method is the language associated with the discipline. Many system analysis and engineering methods use a graphical syntax to display collected data so that key information is unambiguously displayed. The third component, the use, refers to the context-specific application of the method.

Formal methods provide the structure and guidelines for successfully defining the boundaries of reliable application. The graphical languages of methods highlight key information so that it may be easily identified and extracted. In other words, methods provide the practitioner with tools useful in dissecting the world into more manageable pieces while bringing the more important facts into focus (Painter, 1991a). As a result, the non-pertinent information is discarded while the useful pieces of information remain.

It is this capacity–assisting and motivating the intellectual activities of the human mind–that makes the use of methods so attractive. But, it is important to

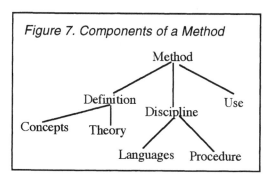

Figure 7. Components of a Method

remember that methods neither make the decisions, create the insights, nor discover the problems. Just as shovels themselves do not dig holes but rather provide leverage for a human to dig, methods provide leverage for the human mind to more effectively accomplish a job.

As one might expect, multiple methods exist for various applications. Similarly, for the purposes of the BPR framework, several different methods are required to perform certain tasks in successfully employing the framework. Rather than attempting to analyze a given organization with a single "super method," an attempt which would undoubtedly result in an overly complex and burdensome model, the use of the IDEF methods serves as a more useful, efficient, and effective means. A set of methods originally designed to be used in quick and efficient analysis, the IDEF methods represent a set of independent, self-standing methods that are still highly useful when employed in an integrated fashion; hence the meaning of their name, Integrated DEFinition (IDEF).

In summary, methods facilitate BPR by enhancing:
- the speed and accuracy with which you extract knowledge/ information from the members in the organization, and
- the effectiveness of presenting that information to other members for validation and consensus building.

Overview of the IDEFØ Function Modeling Method
Basic Concepts of IDEFØ

The IDEFØ Function Modeling method is designed to model the decisions, actions, and activities of an organization or system. IDEFØ was derived from a well-established graphical language known as the Structured Analysis and Design Technique (SADT). The Air Force commissioned SADT developers to develop a function modeling method for analyzing and communicating the functional perspective of a system. Effective IDEFØ models assist in organizing system analysis and promoting effective communication between the analyst and the customer. Furthermore, the IDEFØ modeling method establishes the scope of analysis either for a particular functional analysis or for future analyses from another system perspective. As a communication tool, IDEFØ enhances domain expert involvement and consensus decision-making through simplified graphical devices. As an analysis tool, IDEFØ assists the modeler in identifying the functions performed and what is needed to perform them. Thus, IDEFØ models are often created as one of the first tasks of a system development effort.

The IDEFØ model diagram displayed in Figure 8 is based on a simple syntax. Each activity is described by a verb based label placed in a box. Inputs are shown as arrows entering the left side of the activity box while the outputs are shown as exiting arrows on the right side of the box. Controls are displayed as arrows entering the top of the box and mechanisms are displayed as arrows entering from the bottom of the box. Inputs, Controls, Outputs, and Mechanisms (ICOMs) are all referred to as concepts.

An IDEFØ model diagram is then composed of several activity boxes and related concepts to capture the overall activity. IDEFØ not only captures the individual activities but also reveals the relationships between and among activities through the activities' related concepts. For example, the output of one activity may

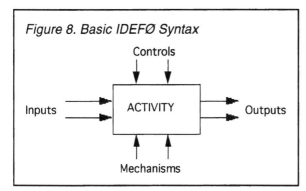

Figure 8. Basic IDEFØ Syntax

in turn become the input, control, or even a mechanism of another activity within the same model (Figure 9).

Modeling From an IDEFØ Perspective

IDEFØ includes both a procedure and a language for constructing a

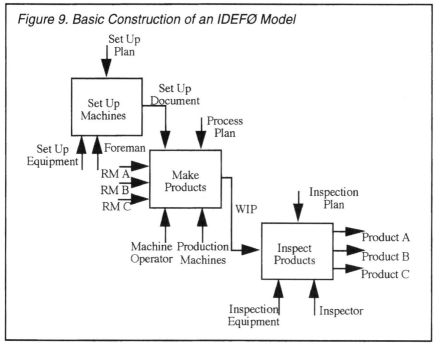

Figure 9. Basic Construction of an IDEFØ Model

model of the decisions, actions, and activities in an organization. Applying the IDEFØ method results in an organized representation in a non-temporal, non-departmentalized fashion of the activities and important relations between them. IDEFØ is designed to allow the user to "tell the story" of what an organization does; it does not support the specification of a recipe or process. Such detailed descriptions of the specific logic or the timing associated with the activities requires the IDEF3 Process Description Capture Method.

A strategy for organizing the development of IDEFØ models is the notion of *hierarchical decomposition* of activities. A *box* in an IDEFØ model, after all, represents the boundaries drawn around some activity. Inside that box is the breakdown of that activity into smaller activities, which together comprise the box at the higher level. This hierarchical structure helps the practitioner keep the scope of the model within the boundaries represented by the decomposition of the activity.

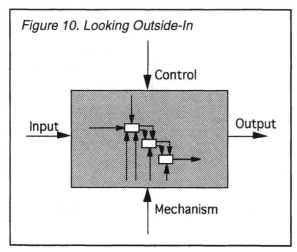

Figure 10. Looking Outside-In

Control

Input

Output

Mechanism

This organization strategy is also useful for hiding unnecessary complexity from view until a more in-depth understanding is required (Figure 10).

IDEFØ captures "what" the organization does and thus, more specifically, is very effective in identifying the core activities and secondary functions of the organization. The actual act of identifying what the organization does will often result in answering the more important question of "why" the organization does what it does. This represents the first step of many BPR efforts focused on identifying candidate organizational areas for BPR. An activity for which one cannot answer the question of "why do we perform this activity?" is a definite target for BPR.

Overview of the IDEF3 Process Description Capture Method
Basic Concepts of IDEF3

One of the most common communication mechanisms to describe a situation or process is a story told as an ordered sequence of events or activities. IDEF3 is a scenario-driven process flow modeling method created specifically for these types of descriptive activities. IDEF3 is based on the direct capture of descriptions, of the precedence and causality relations between situations and events, in a form that is natural to domain experts in an environment. The goal of IDEF3 is to provide a structured method for expressing the domain expert's knowledge about how a particular system or organization works.

An IDEF3 Process Flow Description captures a network of relations between actions within the context of a specific scenario. The intent of this description is to show "how" things work in a particular organization in the context of a particular problem-solving (or recurring) situation. IDEF3 uses the "scenario" as the basic organizing structure for establishing the focus and boundary conditions for the process description. This feature is motivated by the tendency of humans to describe what they know in terms of an ordered sequence of observed activities experienced within the context of a given scenario or situation. The natural tendency toward organizing thoughts and expressions within the context of a process description has motivated widespread use of the scenario as an informal framework for proposing alternative "external views" of possible system designs, the roles of which will be to support the activities of the organization within the established context. Such development approaches have been referred to as "External Constraint-Driven Design" approaches, and have been repeatedly demonstrated in practice as an effective mechanism for the design of new systems. Figure 11 shows an IDEF3 Process Flow Diagram.

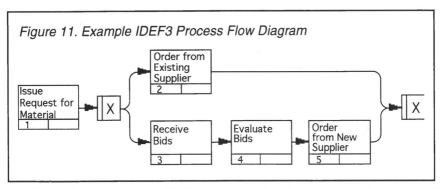

Figure 11. Example IDEF3 Process Flow Diagram

The basic syntactic unit of IDEF3 graphical descriptions within the context of a given scenario is the Unit of Behavior (UOB) represented by a box. The UOB may further be classified as a function, activity, action, act, process, operation, event, scenario, decision, or procedure, depending on its surrounding structure. Each UOB represents a specific view of the world in terms of a perceived state of affairs or state of change relative to the given scenario. Each UOB can have associated with it both "descriptions in terms of other UOBs," otherwise called decompositions, and a "description in terms of a set of participating objects and their relations," called elaborations (Figure 12).

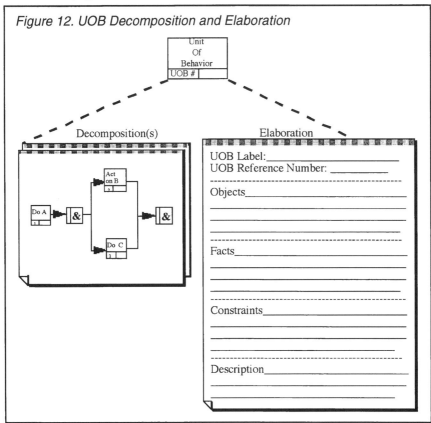

Figure 12. UOB Decomposition and Elaboration

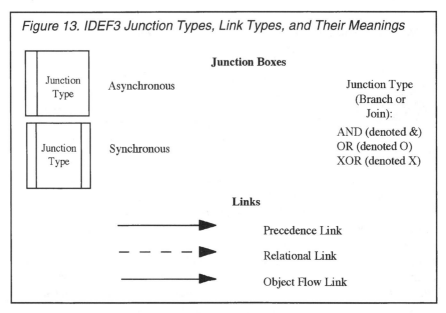

Figure 13. IDEF3 Junction Types, Link Types, and Their Meanings

UOBs are connected to one another via junctions and links (Figure 13). Junctions provide the semantic facilities for expressing synchronous and asynchronous behavior among a network of UOBs. Links are 1) temporal precedence, 2) object flow, or 3) relational. Relational links are provided to permit constraint capture not accommodated by the default semantics of the precedence and object flow links.

The IDEF3 Process Description Capture Method is used by system developers to capture domain-expert knowledge about the "behavioral" aspects of an existing or proposed system. Process knowledge that has been captured using IDEF3 is structured within the context of a scenario, making IDEF3 an intuitive knowledge acquisition device for describing a system. Unlike IDEFØ models that adopt a single perspective of the system and explicitly remove all temporal logic to promote generality and simplification, IDEF3 serves to structure different user descriptions of the temporal precedence and causality relationships associated with enterprise processes. The resulting IDEF3 descriptions provide a structured knowledge base from which analysis and design models can be constructed.

Description Capture From an IDEF3 Perspective

Two modeling modes exist within IDEF3: process flow description and object state transition description. Process flow descriptions are intended to capture knowledge of "how things work" in an organization. The object state transition description summarizes the allowable transitions an object may undergo throughout a particular process. Both the Process Flow Description and Object State Transition Description contain units of information that make up the description. These models form the basic units of an IDEF3 description.

An IDEF3 Process Flow Description captures a network of relations between actions within the context of a specific scenario. The intent of this description is to show how things work in a particular organization in the context of a particular problem-solving (or recurring) situation. IDEF3 uses the "scenario" as the basic organizing structure for establishing the focus and boundary conditions for the process description. This feature is motivated by the tendency of humans to describe what they know in terms of an ordered sequence of activities which they have experienced or observed within the context of a given scenario or situation. The natural tendency toward organizing thoughts and expressions within the context of a process description has motivated widespread use of the scenario as an informal framework for proposing alternative "external views" of possible system designs, the roles of which will be to support the activities of the organization within the established context. Such development approaches have been referred to as "External Constraint-Driven Design" approaches, and have been repeatedly demonstrated in practice as an effective mechanism for the design of new systems.

Overview of the IDEF1 Information Modeling Method
Basic Concepts of IDEF1

IDEF1 was designed as a method for both analysis and communication in the establishment of requirements. IDEF1 is generally used to 1) identify what information is currently managed in the organization, 2) identify which of the problems identified during the needs analysis are caused by lack of management of appropriate information, and 3) specify what information will be managed in the TO-BE implementation.

IDEF1 captures what information exists or should be managed about objects within the scope of an enterprise. The IDEF1 perspective of an information system includes not only the automated system components, but also non-automated objects such as people, filing cabinets, telephones, etc. IDEF1 was designed as a method for organizations to analyze and clearly state their information resource management needs and requirements. Rather than a database design method, IDEF1 is an analysis method used to identify the following:

1. The information collected, stored, and managed by the enterprise,
2. The rules governing the management of information,
3. Logical relationships within the enterprise reflected in the information, and
4. Problems resulting from the lack of good information management.

The results of information analysis can be used by strategic and tactical planners within the enterprise to leverage their information assets and achieve competitive advantage. Their plans may include the design and implementation of automated systems which can more efficiently take advantage of the information available to the enterprise. IDEF1 models provide the basis for those design decisions, furnishing managers with the insight and knowledge required to establish good information management policy.

IDEF1 uses simple graphical conventions to express a powerful set of rules that help the modeler distinguish between 1) real-world objects, 2) physical or abstract associations maintained between real-world objects, 3) the information managed about a real-world object, and 4) the data structure used to represent that information for acquiring, applying, and managing that information. IDEF1 provides a set of rules and procedures for guiding the development of information models. One IDEF1 goal is to provide a structured and disciplined process for analyzing information managed by an organization. This goal is accomplished by the evolutionary process defined in the method and by the measurable results and specific products required by the method. IDEF1 enforces a modularity that eliminates the incompleteness, imprecision, inconsistencies, and inaccuracies found in the modeling process.

There are two important realms for modelers to consider in determining information requirements. The first realm is the real world as perceived by people in an organization. It is comprised of the physical and conceptual objects (e.g., people, places, things, ideas, etc.), the properties of those objects, and the relations associated with those objects. The second realm is the information realm. It includes information images of those objects found in the real-world. An information image is not the real-world object, but the information collected, stored, and managed about real-world objects. IDEF1 is designed to assist in discovering, organizing, and documenting this information image, and thus is restricted to the information realm.

An IDEF1 *entity* represents the information maintained in a specific organization about physical or conceptual objects. An IDEF1 *entity class* refers to a collection of entities or the class of information kept about objects in the real-world. There are two basic concepts that distinguish entities:

1. They are persistent. The organization expends resources to observe, encode, record, organize, and store the existence of individual entities.
2. They can be individuated. They can be identified uniquely from other entities.

Entities have characteristic *attributes* associated with them. Attributes record values of properties of the real-world objects. The term *attribute class* refers to the set of attribute-value pairs formed by grouping the name of the attribute and the values of that attribute for individual entity class members (entities). A collection of one or more attribute classes which distinguishes one member of an entity class from another is called a *key class*.

A *relation* in IDEF1 is an association between two individual information images. The existence of a relation is discovered or verified by noting that the attribute classes of one entity class contain the attribute classes of the key class of the referenced entity class member. A *relation class* can be thought of as the template for associations that exist between entity classes. An example of a relation in IDEF1 is the label "works for" on the link between the information entity called "Employee" and the information entity called "Department." If no information is kept about an association between two or more objects in the real-world, then, from an IDEF1 point of view, no relation exists. Relation classes are represented by links between the entity class boxes on an IDEF1 diagram. The diamonds on the end of the links and the half diamonds in the middle of the links encode additional information about the relation class (i.e., cardinality and dependency). Figure 14 illustrates the manner in which IDEF1 diagrams are drawn.

Overview of the IDEF5 Ontology Description Capture Method
Ontologies

Historically, ontology has chiefly been thought of as an attempt to "divide the world at its joints:" to discover those categories, or *kinds*, into which the world's denizens naturally fall. Natural science can be viewed as an example of ontology *par excellence*. Perhaps the chief goal of subatomic physics, for example, is to develop

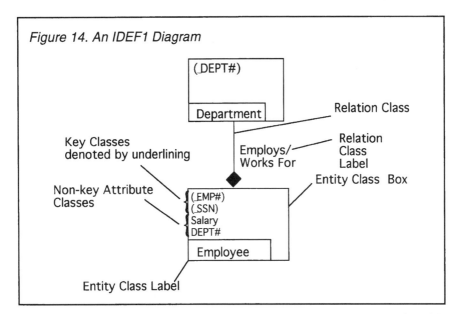

Figure 14. An IDEF1 Diagram

a taxonomy of the most basic kinds of objects that exist within the physical world–electrons, protons, muons, etc. This sort of inquiry is not limited to the natural sciences, however. The abstract sciences as well—mathematics, in particular—can be thought in part at least as an attempt to discover and categorize the domain of abstract objects such as prime numbers, abelian groups, and topological spaces.

The natural and abstract worlds, however, do not exhaust the applicable domains of ontology. For there are vast, human designed and engineered systems—manufacturing plants, businesses, military bases, etc.—in which the task is just as relevant, and just as pressing. Here, though, the ontological enterprise is motivated not so much by the search for knowledge for its own sake, as, ideally, in the natural and abstract sciences, but by the need to understand, design, engineer, and manage such systems effectively. This being the case, it is useful to adapt the traditional methods and tools of ontology to these domains as well.

IDEF5 Concepts

The notion of "kind" (as distinct from class or type) is a central concept of IDEF5. It is important to recognize the distinction between the usual meaning of "kind" and what it represents in IDEF5. In naturally occurring systems, all objects of the same kind often have a distinguishing set of properties which must be maintained to remain a member of that kind. That is, the properties for membership are essential properties of the member. Thus, the usual notion of a kind is a collection of objects, all of which share a common nature (i.e., a set of properties that belong essentially to all and only the members of the kind). However, in the manufacturing systems, objects frequently must have a certain set of properties to become part of a kind but are not required to keep those properties to remain part of the kind. Consider the semiconductor manufacturing domain.

A chemical has certain properties that identify it as an etchant, and all etchants have those properties. This is the traditional idea of a natural kind. Contrast this with the kind of object a manufacturing "rework" item represents. A rework item might be any wafer that has more than three defects. Therefore, a wafer with four defects becomes a rework item. However, after one or more of the defects on a wafer is repaired, it is still a rework item. In fact, it remains so until it is reclassified by an inspector as an acceptable wafer or it is discarded. This is an example of the "kinds" that typically arise in human-designed systems. IDEF5 supports the identification of both notions of kinds.

In other words, when an ontology is built for a certain human-designed system, the broader notion of a kind allows the objects within a system to be divided and categorized in useful and informative ways. An ontology categorization scheme is justified only insofar as it is useful for organizing, managing, and representing knowledge or information in the system so categorized. If objects of a certain kind, K, play a useful role in the system, that is all the justification necessary to admit them into the system ontology, irrespective of whether the defining properties of K are essential to its members.

There is more to characterizing objects in a system than merely listing their properties. In the context of a given system, it is equally important to detail the associations that objects in the system can and do bear to one another. Just as with properties, system-essential associations must be distinguished from system-accidental associations partially because associations occur that way and also because the association may be a defining property of a kind (e.g., the marriage association and the kind "married"). A system-essential association relative to two (or more) kinds, K_1 and K_2 is an association that must hold whenever there are instances of K_1 and K_2. A system-accidental association relative to K_1 and K_2, by contrast, is one that need not hold between *any* instance of those kinds. In addition, system-essential relations don't need to hold between *all* possible instances of the participating kinds.

The IDEF5 method has three main components:
1. A graphical language to support conceptual ontology analysis,
2. A structured text language for detailed ontology characterization, and
3. A systematic procedure that provides guidelines for effective ontology capture.

The IDEF5 Language

IDEF5 provides several schematic (diagram) types for the visualization of an ontology. These schematics are useful conceptual aids for both the construction and the validation of the ontology. *Classification Schematics* are used in IDEF5 to show "subkind-of" relations between kinds in an IDEF5 model. The classification relations selected for use in IDEF5 incorporates prominent AI research results (Brachman, 1983; Gruber, 1992). IDEF5 supports three types of classification mechanisms: 1) generalization/specialization, 2) AKO (a kind of), and 3) description subsumption (see Figure 15).

Generalization/specialization relations (also called superset/subset links) represent the specialization of a kind by another kind. For example, a **hex-headed bolt** kind is a specialization of a **fastener** kind for bolts with hex heads. AKO relations are useful for classifying natural kinds. For example, a **dog** kind is a kind of a **mammal** kind. Description subsumption relations are useful for classifying abstract kinds. The fact *a square is a rectangle with four equal sides* would be captured in a

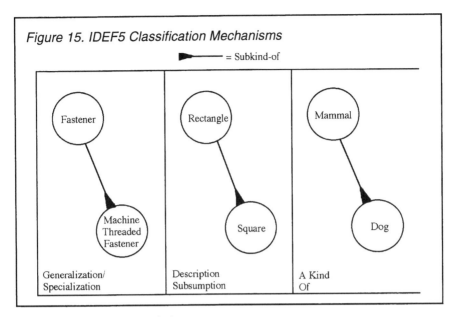

Figure 15. IDEF5 Classification Mechanisms

▶—— = Subkind-of

Generalization/
Specialization

Description
Subsumption

A Kind
Of

description subsumption relation.

Composition Schematics are provided in IDEF5 to discover and characterize different uses of the part-whole relation. The part-whole, or meronymic relation (derived from the Greek *meros* = part) is very important in several application areas including the manufacturing, engineering, and business domains. For this reason, IDEF5 provides the structures needed to express several different interpretations of this relation.

A composition schematic is a special type of *Relation Schematic* in IDEF5. Relation schematics are used to represent the relations between kinds in an ontology. The capture of knowledge about relations is critical to knowledge acquisition, because relations specify the behavior governing interactions between the components of a complex system. For example, the relations between the electrical (distribution) system and the power system will determine how the engine starts. Figure 16 illustrates the use of a relation schematic used to describe a semiconductor manufacturing facility.

Figure 16 asserts the relation between a wafer and a conveyer. It also shows the relation between an instance of a kind (My-Wafer) and the kind (Wafer).

The IDEF5 Elaboration Language provides a structured text format for capturing complex relation

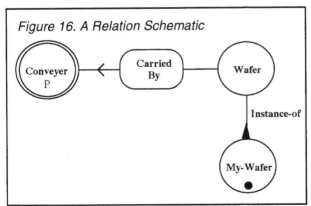

Figure 16. A Relation Schematic

knowledge at any level of complexity. The Elaboration Language can express everything that can be recorded using the Schematic Language; it can also express knowledge that is beyond the scope of the Schematic Language. For example, the five-place relation $z = a + b + c + d$, where z, a, b, c, and d are integers, can only be expressed in the Elaboration Language.

The IDEF5 Procedure

The IDEF5 procedure is an important component of the ontology description method and consists of the following five activities:
1. Organize and Scope the Project: this activity will establish the purpose, viewpoint, and context for the ontology development project and assign roles to the team members.
2. Collect Data: this activity will acquire the raw data needed for ontology development.
3. Analyze Data: this activity will analyze the data to facilitate ontology extraction.
4. Develop Initial Ontology: this activity will develop a preliminary ontology from the acquired data.
5. Refine and Validate Ontology: this activity will refine and validate the ontology to complete the development process.

Although the above activities are listed sequentially, there is a significant amount of overlap and iteration between the activities. Thus, for instance, the initial ontology development (Activity # 4) often requires the capture of additional data (Activity #2) and further analysis (Activity #3). Each of the five activities will involve other activities and tasks. A more detailed description of the IDEF5 method is found in (KBSI, 1994a).

The Role of IDEF Methods in BPR

Initial Activity Modeling

As discussed in the section entitled "The BPR Process," the first step of the BPR process is to define the vision, mission, and goals of the BPR effort. It is at this point that the initial IDEFØ modeling is to begin. Revisiting the enterprise mission statement during this step of the BPR process lends itself to using IDEFØ to capture the top-level activities of the enterprise which begin to become apparent at this stage.

Capturing the AS-IS System Descriptions

The IDEFØ models initiated in the first step will be further developed in capturing the AS-IS System Description. These models will be employed to identify those areas of the enterprise that are candidates for BPR. Again, the resulting activity model(s) will provide insight into "what" and "why" certain activities are performed. If the actual existence of a given activity is difficult to legitimize as a result of IDEFØ modeling, this is a definite signal that the activity in question may be unnecessary and would be a legitimate candidate for BPR.

As the activity models become more detailed through decomposition, the practitioner may find the description moving away from the what and why toward a description that conveys "how" an activity is performed. This phenomena is often indicated when the practitioner starts capturing information about the activities in terms of timing and sequence as well as the decision logic information required to describe activities that may need to be performed in parallel.

IDEFØ and IDEF3 complement each other well and it is often the case that the practitioner will find that switching from IDEFØ to IDEF3 and vice versa is highly useful in capturing the AS-IS system descriptions. Each method provides a unique perspective through which to view the organization and the functions it performs. The knowledge organization and structuring mechanisms provided by IDEFØ and IDEF3 enhance the productivity of this process. Conceptually, the difference in the ability of the two methods to support analysis stems from inherent differences in the level of representation abstraction that these methods were designed to support. Thus, for example, an arrow between two activity boxes in IDEFØ carries no temporal semantics. In IDEF3, an arrow between two UOB boxes is used to represent a precedence relationship. The sophisticated detailing capabilities of IDEF3 therefore make it a suitable vehicle for launching quantitative analysis efforts such as discrete-event simulation. The more abstract representational apparatus provided in IDEFØ makes it a powerful tool for qualitative/conceptual design and analysis activities.

The main advantages of IDEFØ and IDEF3 for acquiring business process descriptions are summarized as follows:

- Ability to express function and process knowledge: facilitates representation of "what" a system does (IDEFØ) and "how" a system works (IDEF3). IDEFØ is designed to capture and organize information about the functions performed by an organization and their interrelationships in terms of their inputs, outputs, controls, and mechanisms. IDEF3 facilitates the capture of process knowledge: the temporal and logical relationships between activities and the roles played by objects that participate in these activities.
- Ability to model at multiple levels of abstraction: the decomposition mechanisms in IDEFØ and IDEF3 are useful for both selective information hiding and for focusing attention on specific areas of concern. IDEF3 also supports the representation of alternative viewpoints through the use of multiple decompositions.
- Ability to capture and represent object knowledge: this capability is useful to show the role of objects in accomplishing system goals. Object roles are restricted to inputs, outputs, controls, and mechanisms in IDEFØ. IDEF3 objects are categorized as agents, participants, affected, created, and destroyed.
- Ability to represent multiple perspectives: IDEF3 supports the representation of alternative viewpoints through the use of multiple decompositions. This capability is particularly useful for large systems analysis projects involving multi-disciplinary teams.

Identify Improvement Opportunities

The Role of IDEFØ in Activity Analysis

IDEFØ has been shown to be a valuable aid in process analysis studies (KBSI, 1993b). The following example illustrates the role of IDEFØ in supporting *Activity Analysis* (Activity Analysis is an important part of ABC[4]).

Consider a generic purchasing department that supports the various departments of the company by processing and, subsequently, filling any purchase request that is generated by those departments. Suppose that the purchasing department

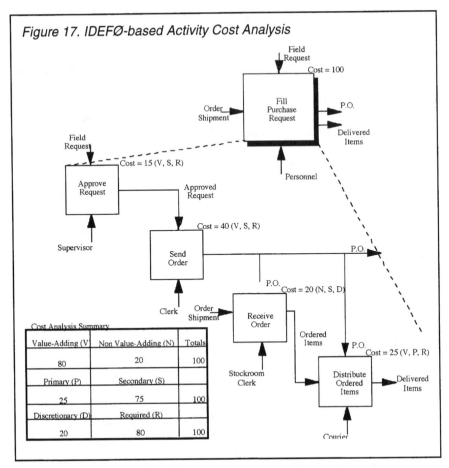

Figure 17. IDEFØ-based Activity Cost Analysis

manager initiates a BPR effort. The manager uses the IDEFØ method to help identify process improvement opportunities relevant to the "Fill Purchase Request" function. An IDEFØ-based representation of this function is shown in Figure 17.

The Fill Purchase Request function results in "Delivered Items" as shown in Figure 17. The decomposition of Fill Purchase Request has four activities: 1) Approve Request, 2) Send Order, 3) Receive Order, and 4) Distribute Ordered Items, as shown. We have deliberately simplified the activity descriptions to illustrate the main concepts of activity analysis and qualitative cost analysis. The main objects in the model are the IDEFØ ICOMs. The Approved Request is produced and is used in the activity "Send Order." The resulting Purchase Order (P.O.) is then used to check that the correct items have been received in the "Receive Order" function. The Ordered Items are then distributed to the person(s) from whom the purchase request originated. The items are distributed using the P.O. as a guide in identifying and locating the order originators in the field.

An important activity to support ABC is to classify activities under the three ABC-based schemes as described in the section entitled "AS-IS Process Analysis." The categories selected are shown in parentheses next to the activity costs. (The coding scheme for the activity categories is given in the table shown in the lower left

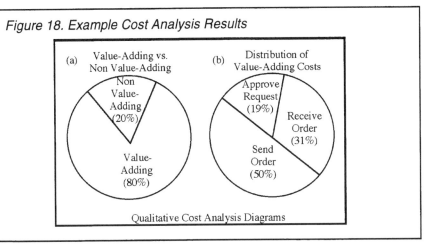

Figure 18. Example Cost Analysis Results

(a) Value-Adding vs. Non Value-Adding

Non Value-Adding (20%)

Value-Adding (80%)

(b) Distribution of Value-Adding Costs

Approve Request (19%)

Receive Order (31%)

Send Order (50%)

Qualitative Cost Analysis Diagrams

of Figure 17.) Notice that the only Value-Adding activity (coded 'V') is Distribute Ordered Items. It is interesting to note that some of these activity categorizations are viewpoint-dependent. For example, the Approve Request, Send Order, and Distribute Ordered Items activities are categorized as *Required*. That is, these activities are "Required" from the point of view of the purchasing department manager. Suppose that the activity Send Order is a requirement from the viewpoint of the purchasing department manager, but from the CEO's viewpoint, this activity is not always required because there is also the option of manufacturing the required item in house. Therefore, from the CEO's perspective, the Send Order activity is categorized as *Discretionary*. This illustrates the fact that the same activity can (conceivably) be categorized differently, when viewed from different perspectives.

After the activities have been categorized and the cost information specified, the next step is to summarize the cost information. Such "cost roll-up" computations provide valuable information for decision support. Example cost summaries that may be generated for this example are shown in Figure 18.

The advantages/benefits of IDEFØ-based activity analysis (illustrated through this example) are:
1. Helps focus attention on problem areas: for example, high cost non value-adding activities could be candidates for reorganization or elimination under the BPR initiative.
2. Suggests areas for more detailed analysis: by focusing attention on high cost activities, the analysis may lead to more detailed analysis efforts such as discrete-event simulation studies.

The Role of IDEF3 in Simulation-Based Process Analysis

Simulation analysis[5] has been shown to be useful for three important reasons: 1) to evaluate the effect of randomness, 2) to measure the effect of shared resources, and 3) to estimate the impact of alternative organization policies on system performance (KBSI, 1994a). We now describe a simple example to demonstrate the utility of IDEF3 in supporting simulation-based process analysis. Consider our previous IDEFØ model of Fill Purchase Request. This model captured the four basic sub-activities that are required to fill a purchase request independent of the sequence and

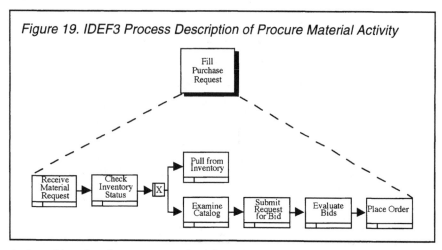

Figure 19. IDEF3 Process Description of Procure Material Activity

timing of the related process steps. In order to describe the details of this activity, we have created an IDEF3 description of the process of Fill Purchase Request (Figure 19). Initially, a request for material is received, at which time the inventory is checked to see if the material is currently available. If the material is available, it is pulled from stock. If the material is not available, the stockroom personnel check the material catalog and submit a request for bid. Incoming bids are evaluated and a subsequent order is placed to the appropriate vendor. We will show the utility of IDEF3-based simulation analysis technique for reengineering this process.

- **Effect of Randomness.** Suppose that in this example, the originating department of the incoming material requests is a major determinant of the proportion of requests that are filled by pulling from inventory. Suppose further that the distribution of this proportion is a random variable that varies from department to department. Therefore, we need to build a separate simulation model (for modeling this request for each department) that uses a different input proportion probability distribution. Because of the randomness in arrivals and the random decision logic that consequently results at the fan-out junction (see Figure 7), the cost of the scenario will also vary randomly. The need for a dynamic analysis method that accounts for random behavior is apparent from this example. Dynamic design and analysis software tools can be used to evaluate the effect of randomness on the cost of a system over time (for example, queuing analysis tools, simulation tools). These tools will generate data for analyzing the time varying behavior of costs.

- **Effect of Shared Resources.** Suppose that in this example, the Pull from Inventory process and the Evaluate Bid and subsequent processes process are performed by the same individual, say Storeroom Clerk. Storeroom Clerk is an example of a "shared resource:" that is, a resource that is shared by two different processes. When such shared resources are also scarce resources (that is, they have a finite capacity), their impact on the cost of a process can be significant. The IDEF3 method by itself does not provide sufficient information to accurately quantify the impact of shared resources on organization performance metrics such as cost. However, IDEF3 models can be used to rapidly generate discrete-event simulation model specifications (see Benjamin, et al. (1993)).

The analysis of simulation output data will help evaluate the impact of shared resources on the process cost.

- **Sensitivity Analysis.** Suppose that in this example, the material requests that are waiting for processing by Storeroom personnel wait in a "stack" inside the "in-box" located at the storeroom office. Suppose further that the Storeroom personnel pick up the waiting requests from the box on a "first-come-first-serve (fcfs)" basis. Now, suppose that the manager of the company decides that all waiting requests must be processed using a "priority rule" rather than the fcfs policy. That is, requests are given a priority according to originating department: claims with a higher priority number must be processed before claims with a lower priority number. Before implementing this new policy, the manager would like to evaluate the impact of this policy change on 1) resource utilization, 2) average request process time, and 3) average request process cost. A simulation-based sensitivity analysis can be used to quantitatively evaluate the policy change. As described earlier, the IDEF3 knowledge structures make the transition to a simulation model relatively straightforward.

This simple example illustrates the utility of IDEF3 for dynamic process analysis that leads to the identification of process improvement opportunities. We will now summarize the role of IDEF∅ and IDEF3 in BPR.

IDEF∅ and IDEF3 as BPR Enablers: A Summary

The role of IDEF∅ as a BPR enabler can be summarized as follows:

1. Helps focus attention on *what* happens in an organization: although IDEF∅ also allows for the modeling of *how* things are done in an organization to a limited degree, this is more naturally accomplished by the IDEF3 method. Focusing on what happens (rather than how) is very valuable for BPR projects that emphasize fundamental and radical improvement opportunities, rather than incremental gains.

2. Facilitates modeling at multiple levels of abstraction: IDEF∅ promotes a hierarchical or top-down analysis approach to model development. This is a powerful and valuable feature that manages complexity and facilitates communication.

3. Focuses functional relationships: the IDEF∅ ICOMs (Inputs, Outputs, Controls, and Mechanisms) provide a structured framework for performing functional analysis. The IDEF∅ diagramming mechanisms present an activity-centered view of the organization, and help establish how activities consume resources to deliver value to customers.

The role of IDEF3 as a BPR enabler can be summarized as follows:

1. Helps focus attention on *how things work* in an organization: descriptive and prescriptive knowledge of how organizations perform their work are important for BPR projects. Descriptions of how things work help acquire the AS-IS business scenarios. Prescriptions of how things should work are the subject of the TO-BE business scenarios.

2. Facilitates modeling from multiple perspectives and at multiple levels of abstraction: modeling at multiple levels of abstraction helps manage complexity. Allowing for multiple perspectives facilitates bottom-up modeling. Often the same function or activity can be detailed from different perspectives. IDEF3

allows for the recording of these multiple perspectives.

3. Facilitates both Top-Down and Bottom-Up modeling: this provides flexibility to the personnel performing the BPR work.

4. Facilitates both Process-Centered and Object-Centered Analysis: two modes of description exist within IDEF3: process flow description (PFD) and object state transition network (OSTN) description. The PFDs focus attention on the processes to describe how things work in an organization. The OSTNs provide an object-centered view of the organization by studying the allowable states of an object, and the rules governing the transitions between these states. Our experience indicates these two viewpoints can be used synergistically in BPR projects.

5. Facilitates modeling of temporal and logical relationships: IDEF3 mechanisms, such as temporal relation links and junctions, enable the modeling of complex, real world behavior. This gives domain experts the facility of describing in considerable detail how things work in their organizations. This feature is particularly useful in situations in which the IDEF3 models are used as the basis to quantitatively assess the performance of a business process. For example, IDEF3 models have been used to rapidly prototype quantitative simulation models (KBSI, 1992).

The Role of IDEF5 in BPR Constraint Analysis

The role of IDEF5 in BPR will be illustrated through a simple example. Consider the XYZ manufacturing company that makes widgets. Consider a hypothetical AS-IS scenario: widgets are assembled from manufactured component types A and B (Figure 20). Suppose that the analysis of the AS-IS process results in a redesign of the widget. The change in the design specification is that component type B is replaced by component type C (the TO-BE scenario). This denotes a structural change in the product specification of the widget. An ontology model of widget (Figure 20) may represent the two components B and C as *variants* of a more abstract part type, say X. Variants are varieties of a component or product that have similar overall functionality but have significantly different design specifications. For example, the automatic transmission and the manual transmission are variants of the transmission system. The IDEF5 Elaboration Language (see the section entitled "The IDEF5 Languages") can be used to record important characteristics of the Variant-of relation. For instance, the Elaboration Language may be used to make assertions such as "Different variants necessarily require different manufacturing processes." The nature of the manufacturing processes actually needed will need to be derived from the process planning knowledge base.

Knowledge of the ontological difference between the widget structures in the AS-IS and TO-BE situations facilitates the flow of information that is necessary for change impact prediction. Specifically, the impacts of the change in the product structure of the widget must be effectively propagated to all relevant decision-making units of the enterprise. For instance, the impact of the structural change in the widget may have a dramatic impact on the manufacturing process as shown in Figure 21. The XYZ company does not have the technology to make components of type C. Thus, it needs to out-source this item and assemble the purchased components with the type A components made in house, as shown in Figure 3. The

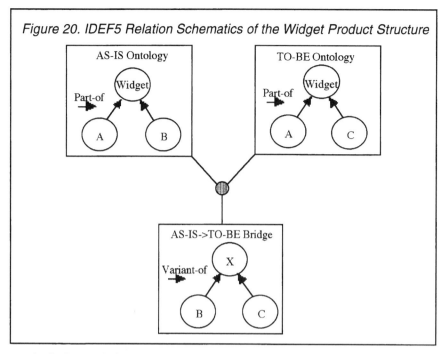

Figure 20. IDEF5 Relation Schematics of the Widget Product Structure

ontological knowledge about the Widget (stored in the IDEF5 models) provides useful information needed to generate the TO-BE process model from the AS-IS process model. More specifically, a detailed characterization of the Variant-of relation provides clues that a fundamental change in the manufacturing process will be required; this ontological knowledge, along with knowledge about the techno-logical constraints relevant to the XYZ company, are needed to design the new (or redesigned) manufacturing process shown in Figure 21. In the example XYZ company, ontological knowledge helped "discover" the *constraining relationship* between the structure of the AS-IS manufacturing process model and the structure of the TO-BE process model. Ontologies have been found to be useful in identifying underlying relationships (and constraints) between different domain areas and between different functional units of an enterprise. The discovery and analysis of constraints is an important BPR activity (see the section entitled "Discover and Analyze Constraints").

Develop TO-BE System Designs

After performing the AS-IS Process Analysis, evaluating just how the current system performs, discovering constraints, and identifying reference technologies and models, the next step involves conceptualizing the TO-BE system. The use of IDEF0 and IDEF3 will continue during the planning and design of the newly reengineered activities and processes of the system. Once these are established, IDEF1 will provide the medium for modeling the information necessary to support the reengineered system and will provide the road map for designing the necessary information systems. (For example, document management systems or enterprise information delivery systems.)

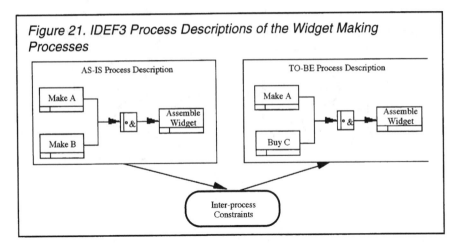

Figure 21. IDEF3 Process Descriptions of the Widget Making Processes

The Role of IDEF1 in BPR Information Requirements Analysis

The IDEF1 Information Modeling Method facilitates the identification and analysis information requirements. It is useful for the analysis of both AS-IS and TO-BE systems. Our experience indicates that IDEF1 is particularly useful in the AS-IS->TO-BE transition phase. Specifically, AS-IS information analysis is often performed toward the end of the AS-IS analysis step just prior to initiation of the TO-BE phase. The TO-BE information model will be used to identify and structure that information which is crucial to establishing and successfully performing the TO-BE activities and functions.

It is expected that the TO-BE information model will be much more streamlined and precise than the AS-IS model because noncritical, redundant, and often useless information will no longer need to be managed. At the same time, the TO-BE model will also capture newly discovered information that was not used in the AS-IS, but is now deemed to be critical to the success of the system organization. In other words, the core information that is vital to keeping the organization's competitive advantage, as well as transaction-based information and office automation-based information, needs to be managed. This information, therefore, must be identified and analyzed.

To illustrate the utility of the IDEF1 method, consider the Widget example described in the section entitled "The Role of IDEF5 in BPR Constraint Analysis." The change from the AS-IS to the TO-BE production system had the following implications for the information systems:

1. New Information: the XYZ company requires a new information system to manage the procurement process from procured item "C." For example, a system to track and monitor the performance of the suppliers of "C" may need to be developed. IDEF1 will help analyze the information requirements leading to the design and implementation of the system.

2. Unnecessary Information: because item "B" is no longer required, the information relevant to this item (production reports, quality reports, inventory reports, etc.) will no longer need to be generated. XYZ's production information systems will need to be redesigned to service the modified

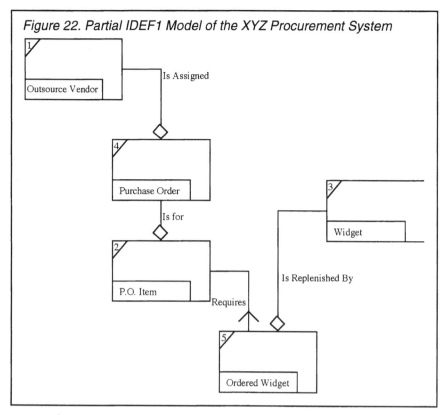

Figure 22. Partial IDEF1 Model of the XYZ Procurement System

requirements.

Figure 22 shows a partial IDEF1 diagram that portrays the information managed by XYZ's procurement system.

Summary and Conclusions

This paper described a framework for BPR. An important component of this framework is a suite of methods and tools for BPR. Attention is focused on a subset of the IDEF suite of methods (Painter, 1991b). The role of the IDEF methods in facilitating the BPR process was illustrated using a simple example. The paper also shows how the IDEF methods can be combined with analysis methods such as simulation and ABC. The methods presented in this paper will likely benefit two groups of people:

1. BPR methodologists and scientists: by providing a framework that integrates the different components of BPR and clarifies the basic BPR concepts.
2. BPR Practitioners: by providing a set of well-researched and widely-used methods and demonstrating the utility of these methods for BPR projects.

Endnotes

[1] We use the term *system* in this paper to refer to " . . a group or set of objects united by some form of regular interaction or interdependence to perform a specified function"

(Shannon, 1975). This (generic) definition allows us to talk about the activities that an organization performs, the objects (such as agents and resources) that participate in these activities, and the constraints maintained by an organization performing these activities.

[2]   Systems Simulation is a notable exception, though being fairly robust for analysis assumptions.

[3]   System factors are relevant objects or properties of the system that are necessary to characterize the system and that have some influence on the structure or behavior of the system.

[4]   ABC is a powerful cost accounting technique that has been the subject of intense interest in recent years. The technique is well documented in Cooper (1988), Kaplan (1988), Brimson (1991), and O'Guin (1991).

[5]   Systems simulation is a powerful and well-established tool for the design and analysis of complex systems (Forrestor, 1961; Shannon, 1975; Pritsker, 1979; Pegden, et al., 1989). The authors have successfully used simulation for process analysis and design in a variety of applications (Mayer, 1989; Benjamin, 1991; Benjamin, et al., 1993).

References

Benjamin, P. C. (1991). Towards a New Method for the Design of Robust Systems using Computer Simulation Experiments. *Ph.D Dissertation, Texas A&M University*, College Station, TX.

Benjamin, P. C., Fillion, F., Mayer, R. J., and Blinn, T. M. (1993). Intelligent support for simulation modeling: a description-driven approach. *Proceedings of the 1993 Summer Simulation Conference*, Boston, MA.

Booch, G. (1991). *Object-Oriented Design with Application*, Redwood City, CA: Benjamin Cummings.

Brachman, R. J. (1983). What IS-A Is and Isn't: An Analysis of Taxonomic Links in Semantic Networks. *IEEE Computer, 1, 6, 10*, 30-36.

Brimson, J. (1991). *Activity Accounting*, New York, NY: John Wiley.

Chen, P. P. S. (1976). The Entity-Relationship Model–Toward a Unified View of Data. *ACM Transactions on Database Systems*, 1, 9-36.

Cook, W. J. (1990, October 22). Ringing in Saturn: GM's New Factory Heralds an American Manufacturing Revolution. *U.S. News & World Report*, 51-54.

Cooper, R. (1988). Elements of activity-based costing. *Journal of Cost Management*, 3-23.

Forrester, J. W. (1961). *Industrial Dynamics*, Cambridge, MA: MIT Press.

Gitlow, H., Gitlow, S., Oppenheim. A., and Oppenheim, R. (1989). *Tools and Methods for the Improvement of Quality*, Homewood, IL: Irwin.

Goldratt, E. (1985). *Theory of Constraints*, New York, NY: North River Press.

Gruber, T. R. (1992). Ontolingua: A Mechanism to Support Portable Ontologies, *Knowledge Systems Laboratory Technical Report KSL 91-66*, Final Version, Stanford University.

Hammer, M. and Champy, J. (1993). *Reengineering the Corporation: A Manifesto for Business Evolution*, New York, NY: HarperCollins Publishers.

Interleaf, Inc. (1994). *The Document Management Guide*, Waltham, MA: Interleaf.

Jones, J. I. (1994). *Organizational Metaphysics or Tavern Topics for Out-Of-The-Box Thinkers*, Informal Working Paper, Priority Process Associates, Inc. Rochester Hills, MI.

Kaplan, R. S. (1988). One cost system isn't enough. *Harvard Business Review*, 61-66.

Kaplan, R. S. (1990, February). The Four-Stage Model of Cost Systems Design. *Management Accounting*, 22-26.

Knowledge Based Systems Inc. (1992). *Knowledge-Based Assistant for Simulation Model Generation from IDEF3 Descriptions*. National Science Foundation Phase II SBIR Grant No. III-9123380.

Knowledge Based Systems, Inc. (1993). *Cost Benefit Analysis Support Environment (CBASE) for C4 Applications*, Final Report. Air Force Phase I SBIR Contract No. F19628-93-C-

0154.

Knowledge Based Systems, Inc. (KBSI). (1994a). *Ontology Description Capture Method.* KBSI Technical Report Number KBSI-IICE-94-TR-01-09-93-02. College Station, TX.

Knowledge Based Systems, Inc. (KBSI). (1994b). *A Method for Constraint Discovery.* KBSI Internal Report. College Station, TX.

Mayer, R. J. (1988). Cognitive Skills in Modeling and Simulation. *Ph.D Dissertation, Texas A&M University*, College Station, TX.

Mayer, R. J. and Decker, L. (1991). *ISyCL Technical Report.* KBSL Technical Report Number KBSL-89-1002. Knowledge Based Systems Laboratory — Texas A&M University, College Station, TX. Air Force Human Resources Laboratory, Wright-Patterson Air Force Base, OH.

Mayer, R. J., deWitte, P. S., and Blinn, T. M. (1992). *Framework of Frameworks.* Knowledge Based Systems, Inc. Internal Report. College Station, TX.

McDonald, K. K. (1993). The Use of IDEFØ in Activity-Based Costing: Evaluating the Costs of Doing Business in a Service Industry. *Proceedings of the May 1993 IDEF Users Group Conference.* College Park, MD.

Morris, D. and Brandon, J. (1993). *Re-engineering Your Business*, New York, NY: McGraw-Hill.

Nijssen, G. M. (1978). On conceptual schemata, databases, and information systems. Paper presented at: *Data Bases — Improving Usability and Responsiveness Conference.* Haifa, Israel.

O' Guin, M. (1991). *The Complete Guide to Activity-Based Costing*, Engelwood Cliffs, NJ: Prentice Hall.

Painter, M. P. (1991a). *Integrating Methods: Aftermath to the Tower of Babel Knowledge Based Systems, Inc., Internal Technical Report.* College Station, TX.

Painter, M. P. (1991b, May). Information Integration for Concurrent Engineering (IICE): Program Foundations and Philosophy. *Proceedings of the May 1993 IDEF Users Group Conference.* College Park, MD.

Painter, M., Mayer, R., and Menzel, C. (1992). Integrating Methods: Aftermath to the Tower of Babel, *Proceedings of the October 1992 IDEF Users' Group Conference.* Washington, D.C.

Pegden, C. D., Shannon R. E., and Sadowski R. P. (1991). *Introduction to Simulation Using SIMAN*, New York, NY: McGraw-Hill.

Phillips, D. T., Ravindran, A., and Solberg, J. (1976). *Operations Research: Principles and Practice*, New York, NY: Wiley.

Pritsker, A. B. and Pegden, C. D. (1979). *Introduction to Simulation and SLAM*, New York, NY: Halsted Press.

Richardson, G. P. and Pugh, A. L. (1981). *Introduction to Systems Dynamics Modeling With DYNAMO*, Cambridge, MA: MIT Press.

Rumbaugh, J., Blaha, M., Premerlani, W., Eddy, F., and Lorenson, W. (1991), *Object-Oriented Modeling and Design*, Englewood Cliffs, NJ: Prentice-Hall.

Shannon, R. E. (1975). *Systems Simulation*, Englewood Cliffs, NJ: Prentice-Hall.

SofTech. (1981, June). *Integrated Computer-Aided Manufacturing (CAM) Function Modeling Manual (IDEF$_0$)*, Technical Report UM 110231100.

Spitzer, R. E. (1993, June). TQM: The Only Source of Sustainable Competitive Advantage. *Quality Progress*, 59-64.

Waterman, D. A. (1986). *A Guide to Expert Systems*, Reading, MA: Addison Wesley.

CHAPTER 7

Closing the Business Process Reengineering Gap: Using the REAL Framework to Identify, Define, and Understand Business Processes

'Jon (Sean) Jasperson
University of Oklahoma, USA

Eric L. Denna and Lee Tom Perry
Brigham Young University, USA

In a *Harvard Business Review* article, Michael Hammer shouted: "Don't automate, obliterate!" (Hammer, 1990). Later he added: "Forget everything you have known about how business should work - most of it is wrong" (Hammer and Champy, 1993). In the early 1990s many management consultants were using these two charges to challenge organizations to rethink and to redesign their organizational work processes. However, by the mid 1990s, reports of the low success rate of business process reengineering (BPR) began to appear and the new founded BPR movement began to lose some of its luster (see King, 1994; Moad, 1993; Stewart, 1993; McPartlin, 1993).

In our experience, the primary reason reengineering projects fail is the lack of alignment among an organization's business processes, structures and stewardships, strategy, measurements, and information technology (IT) application architecture. We call these five factors business solution components. We believe the reason for the lack of solution component alignment is the lack of a theory about the nature of business processes and their relationship with the other solution components. In this chapter, we discuss the essential nature of business processes by describing how to model business processes using the REAL Business Process Modeling framework (McCarthy, 1982; Denna, Cherrington, Andros, and Sawyer-Hollander, 1993; and Denna, Jasperson, Fong, and Middleman, 1994). This chapter describes a conceptual foundation for defining business processes and doing reengineering that significantly increases the likelihood of reengineering success.

The chapter first discusses BPR's lack of a definition for a business process. We then introduce the notion of an event-driven theory of business processes by making a distinction among business processes, information views, business artifacts, information processes, and decision processes. We introduce a modeling tool called REAL Business Process Modeling that uses entity-relationship (E-R) diagram notation to model the essential nature of business processes. We conclude the chapter by showing how a precise definition of business processes provides a way for organizations to define, to clarify, and to align stewardships and structures, strategy, measurements, and IT application architecture.

The Business Process Reengineering Gap

When introducing his reengineering principles, Hammer (1990) observed: "Creating new rules tailored to the modern environment ultimately requires a new conceptualization of the business process - which comes down to someone having a great idea (p. 108)." This raises an interesting question: Possibly, BPR projects frequently fail, not because of what BPR is, but because of what it is not? When individuals and teams are equipped only with principles and prescriptions, perhaps great ideas are harder to come by than they were led to believe. Moreover, are great ideas really enough? For successful implementation, don't organizations also need to think about how each BPR initiative fits into a larger whole?

While principles and prescriptions are enormously helpful, there is an incredibly huge gap between them and BPR. While reengineering advocates advise starting with a blank piece of paper, the important question is: How do we fill that blank piece of paper? Neither principles nor prescriptions really answer this question. Although principles and prescriptions are necessary, they are not sufficient. If BPR's failure rate is ever going to be significantly reduced, it needs a methodology and tools. A BPR methodology not only assists professionals in understanding how to fill the blank sheet of paper, a side-benefit of a well-defined BPR methodology, is that it also enhances and refines both principles and prescription.

Building a BPR methodology, first requires a giant step backward. Methodologies are not simply pulled out of a hat. A primary benefit associated with building a BPR methodology is the discipline it brings to our thinking about business processes. Before we can build a BPR methodology, we must refine our definition of business processes.

So What is a Business Process?

To understand the nature of business processes let's take a look from a couple of different perspectives. First, we will examine the "organization as a system" perspective and second the "events" perspective of business processes.

The "Organization as a System" Perspective of Business Processes

Looking at the organization as a system (see Figure 1) suggests that there are three basic types of business processes:

The *acquisition/maintenance/payment process* consists of a series of business activities that result in the acquisition of goods and services needed by the organization (e.g. supplies, inventories, human skills and availability, or financing). This process also includes maintaining and paying for goods and services acquired so the resources are available when needed by the organization. The acquisition/maintenance/payment process is rather generic across organizations in that there are only a few different ways to acquire, maintain, and pay for resources. Any differences are driven primarily by characteristics of the process (e.g. the type of resource being acquired, the means of communication between the buyer and supplier, and the means of payment).

The *conversion process* can actually involve a variety of processes that transform the goods and services acquired into goods and services for sale to customers. The nature of the conversion process varies widely across industries ranging from assembling and manufacturing enterprises to distribution and professional service firms. First, and foremost, the nature of conversion processes is largely a function of the variety of extant methods and technologies for transforming goods and services acquired into goods and services for customers (e.g. assembly, excavation, education and training, distribution). The nature of the conversion process is also shaped by other factors such as customer preferences, societal and regulatory requirements, and management policy.

The *sales/collection process* involves attracting customers to acquire an organization's goods and services, delivering goods and services to customers, and collecting payment for the goods and services delivered. As with the acquisition/maintenance/payment process, the sales/collection process has a fairly predictable nature across organizations. Therefore, any differences are driven primarily by the type of resource being sold and the type of payment method utilized by the customer.

The "organization as a system" perspective simply provides a framework for classifying any business process and understanding how the processes are interrelated. Furthermore, this perspective helps ensure completeness in identifying an organization's processes.

Figure 1: The Organization as a System

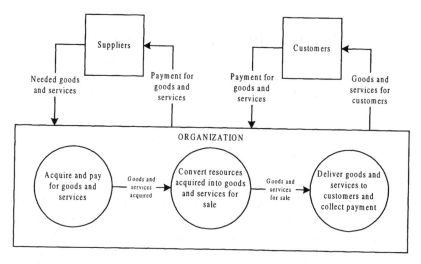

The "Events" Perspective of Business Processes

The building block of business processes is an individual business event. In a nutshell, business events are *any strategically significant business activity management wants to plan, control, and/or evaluate.* Why the "and/or"? It is because some events management can, and should, plan, control, and evaluate. Examples include Salesperson Calls on Customer, to Order Goods/Services From Vendor, to Ship Goods to Customer, to Receive Customer Payment. Other events, however, management can only plan for or evaluate. These events are typically outside the scope of an organization's business processes, and thereby, outside its control. Examples include Change Prime Interest Rate, Competitor Changes Prices, or Competitor Introduces New Product.

Although the concept of a business event is rather straightforward, identifying business events can be a bit challenging. The difficulty lies in seeing through that which can obscure our vision of business events. Instead of standing out in plain view, many times business events lie under a thick cover of views, business artifacts, and information and decision processes.

Distinguishing Business Events From Views of Events

Imagine that a salesperson for a large computer manufacturer sells 2,000 computers to a wealthy retail magnate. How many different views are there of this one simple business event? That depends on who wants to know about new customer orders. Let's list just a few of the possibilities:

- Production personnel want to know about the order to plan production processes.
- Marketing wants to know about the order to possibly adjust prices, plan advertising, and target future sales efforts.
- Personnel want to know about the order to pay sales commissions.
- Executive managements wants to know about the order to plan, control, and evaluate its impact on the organization.
- Investors and creditors want to know about orders to assess the profitability of their investments and the likelihood of returns on their investment.

Not only are there a variety of different information customers interested in knowing about the order, each view of the order is different. Each class of information customer wants to know something a bit different from the others. Traditionally, we have addressed this diversity by building a different system for each view. Each system captures slightly different data about the same business event, each selecting its own subset of available data about the events and recording it in its own classification scheme. As Drucker (1992) points out, the variety of systems (both financial and nonfinancial):

> ... increasingly overlap. They also increasingly come up with what look like conflicting, or at least incompatible, data about the same event; for the two look at the same event quite differently. Till now this has created little confusion (p. C1).

Anyone who has tried to reconcile the data that support the alternative views across an organization understands what we mean by conflicting views. Reconciling differences among the conflicting views is difficult at best, and occasionally impossible. Any reconciliation achieved is destroyed whenever one or more of the views change. The important point here is that these seemingly irreconcilable and diverse classification schemes (views) are simply alternative ways of looking at the same phenomena "business events". Unfortunately, the morass of views make identification of the events somewhat challenging.

Distinguishing Business Events From Business Artifacts

Business events are often confused with business artifacts. Business artifacts include multi-copy forms, checklists, or reports. Business artifacts are used to drive many traditional business processes. As a result, we see overly complex and burdensome processes characterized by large numbers of multi-copy forms routed to different functions, where each functional area believes it requires it's own copy of each form. As the size of the organization grows, so do the number of people handling all the different forms. Eventually, forms management takes on a life of its own, replacing concern for the underlying business events with turf battles over who gets what copy of which form. In these situations, what must be uncovered is what the artifacts represent. As a general rule, forms are inevitably linked to business events. For example, invoices are inevitably linked to business events such as Purchase Goods From Vendor; Checks to Cash Disbursement, Bills to Customer Buys Goods, and so forth. Unless an organization is careful, it may soon confuse business events with information and decision processes leaving the former largely unmanaged.

Distinguishing Business Events From Information Processes

A common error is confusing information processes with business events. The relationship between the two is fairly simple - business events trigger information processes. Information processes come in three flavors: record business event data, maintain reference data, and report useful information. Recording business event data is triggered by the occurrence of events within organizations' business processes like Deliver Goods to Customer, Receive Customer Payment, Call on Customer. Maintaining reference data is triggered by the occurrence of other events that trigger the need to change data about an organization's resources, actors, or locations. For example, Customer Moves triggers the need to update a customer's address; Employee Gets Married triggers the need to update an employee's marital status; or Vendor Changes Product Price triggers the need to update the current cost of something purchased from a vendor.

Distinguishing Business Events From Decision Processes

Decision processes either trigger information processes or business events. Decision processes break down into three managerial responsibilities: plan, control, and evaluate business processes. Plans are formulated around business processes, business events, and the rules surrounding them. The purpose of control decisions is to trigger business events. For example, the decision to buy a new truck triggers the business event Buy Truck. When decision-makers want to evaluate business processes and events they trigger the reporting information process, then receive useful information. Typically, evaluation decisions lead to subsequent planning and control decisions. For example, a manager evaluates information about machine failures on an assembly line then decides to trigger the Buy Machine event (a control decision). While there is an implicit logic to these decisions, unless the relationship between business, information, and decision processes is kept clear, significant confusion can result. With practice, one can quickly begin to cut through the fog and identify the business events that management wants to plan, control, and/or evaluate. Once the underlying events are identifies, then we can begin to build business process models.

REAL Business Process Modeling

REAL Business Process Modeling (BPM) is a formal method of representing the essential characteristics of business processes and events. The title REAL is an acronym for Resources, Events, Agents, and Locations which, as we will discuss in this section, collectively describe the essential characteristics of business processes and events. REAL BPM builds upon the concepts first proposed by McCarthy (1982) to model event-driven accounting database structures.

This approach is more concerned about what is modeled than how. By this we mean the REAL BPM concepts are independent of diagraming techniques. REAL BPM is more a philosophy of what is modeled than another modeling technique. It is a way to use familiar modeling tools (e.g. E-R and object-oriented (OO) diagrams) to model business processes with an emphasis on identifying and describing the essence of a business process and communicating this essence to business and technical people. In this chapter, we will use the basic constructs of E-R diagraming (less the cardinality notation) to illustrate the modeling concepts. However, we must emphasize again that other diagraming techniques can also be used to develop REAL business process models. The REAL BPM methodology proposed here is indepen-dent of any particular modeling technique.

Some may suggest that workflow diagrams already model business processes. As we have analyzed workflow diagrams we have found them to provide a tangled picture of business, information, and decision processes. Because they lack a theory of what a business process is, they do not provide a precise definition of a business process. Furthermore, this confusion about the essence of the business process provides little guidance for defining the nature of the supporting information and decision processes. Without a clear differentiation among business, information, and decision processes, reengineering teams struggle to know what workflow activities are critical and how they interrelate. REAL BPM simply formalizes the process of identifying and defining business processes and provides a basis for determining the remaining elements of a business solution.

The heart of REAL BPM focuses on answering the following five questions about each business event. We combine the first two questions for ease of discussion:

What happened and when? The "what" refers to which business event occurred. The "when" describes the order of the events, what time the event started, and sometimes even the time it ended. This is because often it is important to know how long it took to complete an event. For example, when cleaning a carpet, performing an audit, performing open heart surgery, turning a part on a lathe, or a myriad of other business events, we must know the length of time for the individual events in order to effectively plan, control, and evaluate them.

What roles were played and who/what performed the roles? We must know what roles were performed and who/what performed them. Roles can range from internal responsibilities (e.g., salesperson, cleaning person, supervisor, or inspector) to external roles (e.g., customer or supplier). These roles can be performed by individuals, organizations, or programmable machines (such as robots or computers). Those performing roles are referred to as agents. Events involving the exchange of resources between organizations always involve both internal and external agents, each performing a different role during the execution of the event. For example, the internal role of a salesperson may be performed by a person or a computer terminal that interacts with someone or something playing the external role (customer). Whether the event involves the exchange of resources or not, we must capture data about the roles played and the agents involved. This information is critical to support those individuals who plan, control, and evaluate business events.

What kinds of resources were involved and how much was used? All business events involve the use of one or more resources. We must also know the type and quantity of resources involved in each event. Identifying and measuring some resources is fairly straightforward, while with others it is not. For example, a sale of groceries (the resource) is easily measured. However, we could also argue that several other resources are involved (e.g., the cash register, bags to package the groceries, and electricity to power the cash register) which are much more difficult to measure. At what point do you stop identifying the type and quantity of resources? It depends on the preferences of those planning, controlling, and evaluating the business events. Regardless of the level of detail, we must have information about the type and quantity of resources involved in each event.

Where did the event occur? Lastly, we must know where events occur. With today's organizations and information technology spread all over the globe, events can occur anywhere and the customer need not be physically present. To the extent that it is important, we should make sure data about the location of an event are captured. Sometimes the location of the event is provided by the location of the agents or resources involved. However, when the event location cannot be derived from association with the resources or agents, we must explicitly specify the event location.

The important point to emphasize is the impact of recording the essential characteristics of business events, then making them available to information customers across the organization. Once the essential data about the event are recorded, we can support an infinite number of information customer views.

Business Processes and Business Events

Although the definition of a business event is rather straightforward, starting the process of identifying business events may seem a bit nebulous. The process becomes easier when you divide the business into distinct processes. As we mentioned earlier, in the most generic sense, every organization, regardless of its purpose, goods and services, location, or ownership, has three basic business

processes:
- Acquisition/payment process
- Conversion process
- Sales/collections process

Lets's take a look at each one in turn.

Acquisition/Payment Process

The acquisition/payment process includes the business events involved in acquiring, paying for, and maintaining the goods and services needed by the organization. The focus is on purchasing only what is needed and can be paid for, receiving only what is ordered, paying for only that which is received, and making sure the resources acquired are available when needed. Organizations acquire a wide variety of goods and services including:

- Human resources (e.g., people's time and skills)
- Financial resources
- Supplies
- Inventories
- Property, plant, and equipment
- New ideas (e.g., research and development)
- Miscellaneous services (e.g., legal, power, telephone, protection, medical, financial, and custodial)

Regardless of the type of goods and services, each causes only minor alterations in the nature of the generic acquisition/payment process. The more common types of acquisition/payment processes are those for human resources (personnel/payroll processing), financial resources, inventories, and fixed assets. The basic nature of the process, regardless of the type of resource being acquired, has the following types of events:

- Request the good or service
- Select a supplier
- Order the good or service
- Receive the good or service
- Inspect the good or service
- Pay for the good or service

If we think through the events in the process carefully, we will notice some organizations may sequence the events differently, may use a subset of the events, or may add more detailed events. Nonetheless, the basic nature of the process is fairly stable across organizations and resources.

Conversion Process

The conversion process focuses on developing and executing the most efficient and effective processes for converting goods and services acquired into goods and resources for sale. Conversion processes across, or even within, organizations are very diverse and depend on the type of good or service being produced; the technology and resources utilized; the restrictions of regulators, governments, society, or customers; and the preferences of management. When conversion processes are unique, valuable, and difficult to imitate they create distinctive competence for an organization. Some of the more general types of conversion processes include:

- Assembling
- Growing
- Excavating
- Harvesting
- Basic manufacturing (e.g., metals, woods, and chemicals)
- Finished manufacturing (e.g., tools, instruments, and components)
- Cleaning
- Transporting
- Distribution
- Providing (e.g., power, water, protection, and communication)
- Educating
- Discovering (e.g., research and development)

The diversity of conversion processes makes it difficult to propose a single generalized conversion process. Assembling a toy car is vastly different from defending a client in court or discovering a cure for a crippling disease. Furthermore, any one organization may utilize more than one type of conversion process to generate goods and services for customers. Nonetheless, at the heart of any conversion process is a sequence of business events that serves to convert goods and services acquired into goods and services for customers.

Sales/Collection Process

The sales/collection process includes the sequence of events involved in exchanging goods and services with customers for payment. Essentially, the sales/collection process is the mirror image of the acquisition/payment process. Whenever one organization or individual acquires and pays for goods and services someone else is selling the good or service and receiving payment. Although there is some diversity across the types of goods and services sold, the basic process typically involves the following events:

- Receive an order for goods or services
- Select the good or service to be delivered
- Inspect the good or service to be delivered
- Prepare the good or service for delivery
- Deliver the good or service
- Receive payment for the good or service

As with the acquisition/payment process, some organizations may sequence the events differently, may use a subset of the events, or may add more detailed events. Regardless, the basic nature of the process remains intact.

Business events and business processes are related because a business process is a sequence of business events. Once a business process has been identified, we can begin decomposing the process into a sequence of discrete business events that management wants to plan, control, and evaluate. One frequently asked question is: How far do you go when decomposing business processes into business events?

Decomposing Business Processes

The extent to which business processes should be decomposed into business events is fairly simple to determine. Decompose the processes to the level that management wants to plan, control, and evaluate. The appropriate level is one in which a more generalized model would overlook critical events while a more detailed model would include minutiae. Each business process is composed of a series of discrete business events. For example, selling mail-order merchandise might involve the following business events: Accept customer order; Select, inspect, and package merchandise; Ship merchandise; and Receive customer payment. However, someone may rationally argue that the process really involves just two events: Ship merchandise and Receive payment.

So which is right? The answer depends on the level of detail at which management wants to plan, control, and evaluate the business process. Because of the diversity of management styles, resource availability, and employee talent, differences will exist across enterprises regarding the level at which organizations manage business processes. Instances will exist in which the sequence of events within the same process in two different organizations is reversed. For example, some organizations may insist on the following sequence: Receive payment and then Ship merchandise.

The sequence of events may be a function of the technique for achieving an objective. For example, constructing a building begins with excavation work and laying the foundation. Then the building can be framed, siding put in place, plumbing and electrical systems installed, drywall hung, and so forth until the building is completed. In this, case construction techniques and laws of nature determine the event sequence.

Sometimes the sequence of events is dictated by customer preference. Suppose a car dealership operates in four different cities several miles apart. Customers visit the lots and order cars which may be on other lots. Initially, customers are told to drive to the other lot to pick up the car. However, because many customers might be unwilling to drive to the other lot, they cancel their orders. Astute business people will realize something needs to change to stop losing customers. Rather than make the customer pick up the car at another lot, dealers instigate a new business event called "Transport Car" and then have an employee drive the ordered car to the lot nearest the customer or even to the customer's house. Adding a Transport Car event represents management's attempts to meet the customer needs and to have the information they want to plan, control, and evaluate the event.

Because of the nature of these three basic business processes (acquisition/ payment, conversion, and sales/collection) and their interrelationships, an organization can be accurately characterized as a system that acquires inputs, process the inputs into outputs, and sells the outputs to customers. This is a helpful characterization because we can begin to model the entire organization, its processes and events, using some rather simple modeling techniques. These models enhance communications among those responsible for solving business problems.

REAL Business Process Modeling Methodology

As with any modeling effort, developing the model requires significant practice. Because of the managerial focus of this book and chapter we intend to provide an overview for managers rather than a detailed tutorial for developers. Those interested in a detailed description of REAL BPM should refer to Denna, et al. (1993).

We hope by introducing the steps in developing a model that you see that developing REAL business process models is fairly straightforward. Becoming an expert at REAL BPM is far more dependent on business expertise than modeling experience. Unlike other modeling philosophies, the sophistication of REAL BPM is demonstrated by the simplicity, not complexity, of a specific process model. The REAL BPM methodology can be summarized in the following three steps.

Step 1. Identify business events and represent each with a box. The first task in REAL business process modeling is to become familiar with the business process and its underlying events. One must focus on identifying the activities management wants to plan, control, and evaluate, while making sure not to confuse business events with information processes. Figure 2 shows the first step in modeling the business events for a mail-order company's sales/collection process. At the heart of identifying business events is differentiating them from information and decision processes. For example, when a Customer Places An Order (a strategically significant business activity management wants to plan, control, and evaluate) it triggers an information process (Record Customer Order) which collects data about the business event to generate useful information (another information process) to support a variety of decision processes (selecting merchandise to purchase, choosing how many people to have answering telephones at various times of the day, or deciding on discounts to give to various customers). Again, the focus is on the business event, leaving the information and decision process modeling to be defined by the resulting REAL business process model. Continuing the analysis of the mail-order process subsequent events such as Ship Merchandise and Receive Payment would each be identified separate from their related information and decision processes.

Step 2. Identify the general business rules surrounding each event by specifying relationships between each event and its related agents, resources, and locations that serve to complete the description of what happens, when, who is involved, what

Figure 2: First Stage REAL Business Model

```
┌─────────────────────┐
│   Customer Places   │
│       Order         │
└─────────────────────┘


┌─────────────────────┐
│                     │
│  Ship Merchandise   │
│                     │
└─────────────────────┘


┌─────────────────────┐
│                     │
│  Receive Payment    │
│                     │
└─────────────────────┘
```

Figure 3: Complete REAL Business Process Model

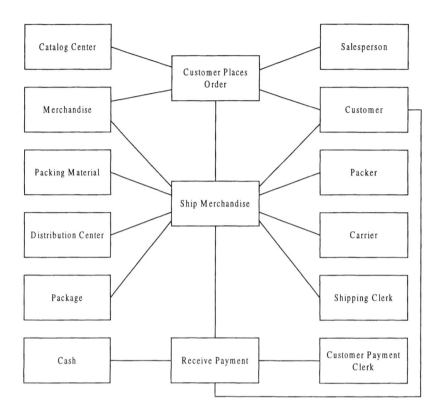

is involved, and where the event occurs. Again, our theory of business processes suggests that such information models the essential characteristics of the business process. In the mail-order example, completing the description of the Customer Places Order event involves identifying who is involved (Salesperson and Customer), what is involved (Merchandise), and where it occurs (Catalog Center). Ship Merchandise involves Customer, Packer, Carrier, and Shipping Clerk (who is involved?), Packing Material, Merchandise, and Package (what is involved?), and the Distribution Center (where it occurs?). The same analysis could be applied to the Receive Payment and any other event management wants to plan, control, and evaluate. In Figure 3 we represent the results of our analysis of the mail-order sales/collection process by connecting the agent, resource, and location boxes to the event boxes with a line. For ease of analysis and validation, the resources and locations are placed on the left side of events and the agents are on the right side.

Step 3. Validate the REAL business process model with the business person. Once an initial draft of the REAL BPM is completed, the next step is to validate the model's accuracy with business people. The validation should be performed by those who understand the details and objectives of the business process and events being modeled and management's objectives concerning planning, controlling, and evaluating the business process. Validation sessions should result in either the confirma-

Figure 4: Lower Level REAL Business Process Model

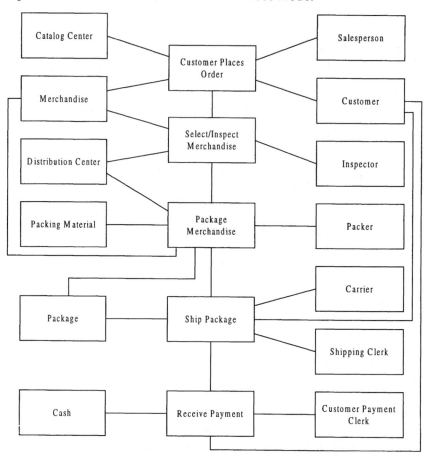

tion of the model's accuracy or modification of the model.

Modifications that might result from validation sessions typically involve decomposing one or more business events into more detailed business events. For example, in the mail-order sales/collection example, management may decide the Ship Merchandise event needs to be decomposed into three events (Inspect Merchandise, Package Merchandise, and Ship Package) as shown in Figure 4. The choice to decompose to a lower level of detail is determined by management. The justification for additional decomposition is management's preference about the level of detail it needs to plan, control, and evaluate the business process. Regardless of the level of abstraction, however, the same modeling concepts are applied.

Only a few simple concepts are required to begin developing fairly precise models of business processes and events. The event-driven theory, which supports REAL BPM, serves as a template or pattern for identifying business events and facilitates conceptualization and definition of business processes. Furthermore, as we will see later, it facilitates communicating a businessperson's definition of a business process to others to help coordinate the development of an organization's strategy, structures, measurements, and IT application architecture. Lastly, as is explained in detail in Denna, et al. (1993), REAL BPM provides a basis for developing a data model to support event-driven IT applications.

The complexity of REAL BPM is largely dependent upon the scope of the business process being modeled. The scope can range from a single business event to processes involving dozens of events. However, the essence of the model, no matter how large, rests on identifying and relating an organization's resources, events, agents, and locations. In fact, REAL BPM provides a conceptual basis for developing extended enterprise models that span traditional organization boundaries. Such models are becoming more and more common as organizations develop closer ties with vendors and customers and begin sharing both information and processes common to the organizations.

Regardless of the scope, the fundamental unit of analysis is the business event, because everything revolves around accurately identifying and describing business events. Identifying business events rests upon what management needs to plan, control, and evaluate their business.

REAL BPM: The Foundation for Defining Business Solutions

If BPR is intended to begin with a blank piece of paper, it is important to orchestrate change from a whole systems mind set. Critical to BPR's success is the ability to anticipate ripple effects across systems. When we rethink business processes at the start of a BPR project it is much like dropping a pebble into a placid pond. The ripples quickly begin to spread, disturbing the entire body of water.

Given this, another contributor to the high failure rate of BPR projects is the lack of alignment among business solution components. The five solutions components, as depicted in Figure 5, are business processes, structures and stewardships, strategy, measurements, and IT applications architecture. Having defined the nature of business processes and how to model them, it is time to discuss how models of business processes can help align the other business solution components.

Figure 5: Event-Driven Solution Perspective

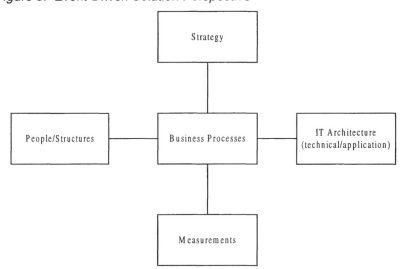

Business Processes and Organization Structures and Stewardships

Traditional organization structures are delineated by functional boundaries (e.g. production, accounting, information, systems, marketing, or finance). One of the problems arising from functional boundaries is the business processes to be managed are arbitrarily divided among the various functions creating gaps and overlaps of responsibilities. The alternative is to have a process driven organization structure. Defining the nature of business processes and their specific events automatically defines the stewardships of participants. For example, the REAL business process model of the mail-order process defined several different stewardships that would typically be scattered across at least three different functions (e.g. Sales/Marketing, Logistics, and Finance). Our experience has shown that if you want to manage a process and make sure it is properly planned, controlled, and evaluated, the process events and all their stewardships must be contained within one organizational structure. Otherwise, the process and it supporting systems will eventually become arbitrarily divided among separate functional units with their attendant gaps, overlaps, and hand-offs.

Business Processes and Strategy

Defining business processes benefits strategic thinking by providing a precise way to think about what a business does and what it should do in the future. The lack of a clear definition of business processes has been the principal cause of a long-standing disconnect between strategy formulation and implementation. Strategists have been consistently inept at translating strategic objectives into concrete business processes. REAL modeling provides the needed know-how for finally making this important connection. It is possible to reengineer business processes to accomplish strategic objectives.

Strategic thinking provides reciprocal benefit to BPR by furnishing a frame for prioritizing business processes and events. An experience at a large aerospace company shows why this contribution is critical. The company hired consultants to help it reengineer one of its plants. The effort created a great deal of enthusiasm among managers and workers, and was considered an unmitigated success. When another consulting firm was hired to help the company with its strategy, it was discovered that much of the reengineered work was strategically unimportant.

One approach to strategic thinking, strategic improvising (Perry, Stott, Smallwood, 1993), identifies four categories of business processes:

- Unit of Competitive Advantage (UCA) Processes - the processes and capabilities that create distinctiveness for the business in the marketplace.
- Value-added support processes - processes that facilitates the accomplishment of UCA processes.
- Essential support processes - processes that neither create advantage nor facilitate the processes that create advantage, but must be done if businesses are to continue to operate.
- Nonessential support processes - processes that have lost their usefulness but continue to be done because of tradition.

These four categories of business processes can be used to scope BPR initiatives. They suggest what business processes to reengineer first and interdependently,

Figure 6: Traditional IT Business Application Architecture

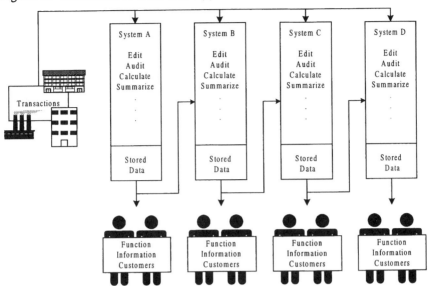

what processes to reengineer separately, and what processes to eliminate, not reengineer.

Business Processes and IT Architecture

Defining the business process also serves as a foundation for developing an IT application architecture that overcomes the weaknesses of the traditional IT architecture. Traditional IT architectures (see Figure 6) are driven by functional boundaries that define various views of the business (e.g. production view, accounting view, or marketing view). Because these views have overlaps and gaps, so do the systems supporting the functions. The resulting IT application architecture can quickly resemble a bowl of spaghetti, replete with redundancies in data and process and with multiple reconciliation points that keep information systems and accounting personnel trapped in low value-added work.

A business event-driven IT application architecture, on the other hand, allows an organization to support any business events and processes with the three technical components illustrated in Figure 7. The Business Event Processor applies business rules while the business event occurs and captures data about the business event at the same time. The data captured by the Business Event Processor is stored in the Business Data Repository. The repository allows all business data to be integrated so that the Reporting Facility can be used by any information customer to generate any type of useful information within the scope of the data stored in the repository. The views of the business can range from financial statements to production schedules to customer analyses and profiles to employee productivity reports. The breadth of information available to information customers is dependent on the number and scope of the business processes included in the repository. Applications in an event-driven architecture are simply collections of recording and reporting rules that govern the capturing and reporting of business data and information. There

Figure 7: Event-Driven IT business Application Architecture

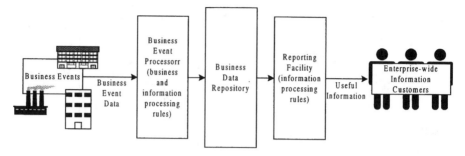

is no need for any other IT components regardless of the number or type of business processes included in the scope of the business solution domain.

Business Processes and Measurements

Traditional business measurements are typically aligned to functional boundaries, except for accounting information which is typically considered either useless or confusing. Therefore, since each function has only a portion of a business process, the functional systems can only provide partial views of the business processes. Furthermore, because the functionally driven systems have significant gaps and overlaps in terms of stored data and processing, an organization can only get partial, overlapping, or even competing views or measurements. Furthermore, traditional views often do not provide information that enables an organization to manage its business processes.

Focusing on business processes can result in a fundamental shift in the types of measurements an organization uses to plan, control, and evaluate its business processes. For example, rather than look at cost variances, organizations can look at the actual costs of business events over time and recognize trends. The focus on business processes suggests the need for looking at process or cycle times, resource utilization, employee productivity, or resource availability and needs. The event-driven IT application architecture makes such measurements both possible and affordable.

Conclusion: An Agenda for Next-Generation BPR

Cypress (1994) created a distinction between first-generation and second-generation business process reengineering. His point was that BPR had reached a plateau. In order to move to a higher level and attack broader and tougher business processes, BPR needed to incorporate more MS/OR (management science/operations research) thinking. Beyond, the suspiciously self-serving nature of his argument, there are two points to make. First, the link between BPR and MS/OR is a natural one. They are both business solutions that focus on business processes. Second, the author was making exactly the wrong argument for creating the next generation of BPR. Progress is not served by returning to business solution philosophies that failed in the past.

While BPR experienced a recent fall from grace, the hope created by BPR remains alive and well. Variations on the original theme are appearing with great rapidity in business periodicals, trade books, and the programs of professional and academic conferences. The agenda for next-generation BPR has become more substantive and less evangelical. As we stated at the beginning of this chapter, our focus has been on introducing a theory of business processes and their relationship with an organization's structures and stewardships, strategy, measurements, and IT (information technology) application architecture. We also introduce a tool for modeling the essential nature of business processes called REAL Business Process Modeling. Our hope is that as the agenda for next-generation BPR continues to be shaped by the three core ideas presented in this chapter.

- First, next-generation BPR must be based on a clearer definition of business processes. Focusing on defining business processes involves separating business processes from information and decision processes. It also involves the recognition that business processes can be reduced to a series of business events.
- Second, the principles and procedures of BPR must enable communication across organization stakeholders by creating a common understanding of the essence of business processes and events.
- Third, successful BPR must provide a foundation for integrated business solutions.

For the last 30 years managers have been spectators watching a parade of proposed business solutions affecting processes, strategy, structures and stewardships, information systems, and measurements. Each solution has provided valuable and important contributions, but their contribution to business success has been consistently unspectacular. Why have these solutions fallen short? Because there has been no way to think about them together. However, when we adjust our view and see business processes and events as integrative mechanisms, something profound happens. Suddenly, we have a precise way of understanding organizational behavior. Information system architectures can be build to reflect the nature of business processes and events. Reengineering and strategy implementation are one and the same process because strategies are used to scope BPR projects around the strategically more important business processes and events. Organizational structures can be designed around stewardships over specific business processes and events. Finally, measurements make more sense to businesspeople because they are directly linked to the performance of specific business processes and events.

Chaos theorists discuss the sensitive dependence of systems on initial condition (Gleick, 1987). Similar principals affect the world of ideas. A small, but fundamental oversight can wreak havoc over the life-cycle of an idea. The premise of this chapter is that the BPR movement made an early, critical error by not insisting on greater precision about the basic nature of business processes and events. The contribution we make, while subtle, is unquestionably significant. REAL BPM provides tremendous leverage because it corrects this early oversight in BPR's history.

A editorial which was highly critical of BPR appeared in *The Economist* (see Editorial, 1994). It concluded: "It is clearly time to reengineer the reengineers." Our remedy is less radical precisely because it is more focused. All that reengineers really need is a conceptual foundation for reengineering. REAL BPM provides this foundation because it offers a more precise definition of business processes and events, which from our point-of-view is exactly what the doctor ordered.

References

Cypress, H.A. (February 1994). "Re-engineering," *ORMS Today.*

Denna, E.L., J.O. Cherrington, D.P. Andros, and A. Sawyer-Hollander (1993). *Event-Driven Business Solutions.* Homewood, IL: Business-One Irwin.

Denna, E.L., J. Jasperson, K. Fong, and D. Middleman (Spring 1994). "Modeling Conversion Process Events." *Journal of Information Systems*, pp. 43-54.

Drucker, P. (1 December 1992). "Be Data Literate–Know What to Know." *The Wall Street Journal.*

Farmer, J.R. (March 1993). "Reengineering: Achieving Productivity Success." *APICS - The Performance Advantage.*

Gleick, J. (1987). *Chaos: Making a New Science.* New York: Penguin Books.

Hall, G.J. Rosenthal, and J. Wade (November-December 1993). "How to Make Reengineering Really Work." *Harvard Business Review.*

Hammer, M. (1990). "Reengineering Work: Don't Automate, Obliterate." *Harvard Business Review*, pp. 104-112.

Hammer, M. and J. Champy. (1993) *Reengineering the Corporation: A Manifesto For Business Revolution.* New York, NY: HarperCollins Publishers.

King, J. (13 June 1994). "Rengineering Slammed." *Computerworld*, pp. 1, 14.

Ligus, R.C. (January 1993). "Methods to help Re-engineer Your Company for Improved Agility." *Industrial Engineering.*

McCarthy, W.E. (July 1982). "The REA Accounting Model: A Generalized Framework for Accounting Systems in a Shared Data Environment." *The Accounting Review.*

McPartin, J.P. (1 February 1993). "Just Chasing Rainbows? Critics Brand Much of The Reengineering Clamor as Sheer Marketing Hype." *Information Week.*

Moad, J. (1 August 1993). "Does Reengineering Really Work?" *Datamation.*

Parker, J. (May 1993). "An ABC Guide to Business Process Reengineering." *Industrial Engineering.*

Perry, L.T., R.G. Scott, and W.N. Smallwood (1993). *Real-Time Strategy: Improvising Team-Based Planning for a Fast-Changing World.* New York, NY: Wiley.

Stewart, T.A. (23 August 1993). "Reengineering: The Hot New Managing Tool." *Fortune.*

CHAPTER 8

Basing an IS Strategy on the Organization's Process Architecture

Martyn A Ould
Venice Consulting Ltd, UK

Information systems (IS) should support and enable an organization's processes. The IS strategy should therefore be based on the process architecture of the organization. This chapter answers two questions: how can we build a process architecture that is truly rooted in the business itself, and how can we use that architecture to inform the development of the IS strategy? Recent experience with STRIM® has led to its extension to the *Riva* method which, inter alia, provides a tool that helps senior management and IS providers to bridge the gap between business drivers and IS drivers. The key lies in recognizing that for every *essential business entity* which the business deals with there are (or should be) three 'natural' processes – the *case*, *case management*, and *case strategy processes* – and that each of these can be seen as both provider and user of information in the business, and hence as potential beneficiaries of the IS strategy.

This chapter outlines the use of the *Riva* approach in this area and illustrates it with examples adapted from studies.

Forensic Process Modelling

In the early days of the process modelling method STRIM, our interest was primarily in the modelling of existing processes, in particular for simple understanding of what was going on, for diagnosis of process-related problems, and for the specification of information systems that would support the existing process. STRIM uses the *Role Activity Diagram* (RAD) as its principal notation and underlying the RAD are two main concepts: the *role* and the *interaction*. A very simple example adapted from an actual case study appears in figure 1. The book *Business Processes* (Ould, 1995) provides the full background to the interpretation of a RAD; here it will be sufficient to point out the following features:

- The process shown is the process for handling the lifetime of a single product.
- It is 'triggered' (activated) by the approval of development of the product (see the arrowhead at the top of the *Product Development Team* box).
- There are two possible outcomes: the product is withdrawn and its life is ended, or the product is cancelled.

- The process involves the collaboration of four roles, each shown as a grey box.
- The roles interact (horizontal lines connecting white boxes in roles).
- Roles carry out activities (black boxes), start concurrent threads of activity (with pyramids at the top), and take different paths at certain points (with inverted pyramids at the top).
- Many roles can be active at one moment and any role may have many threads of activity active at any one moment.

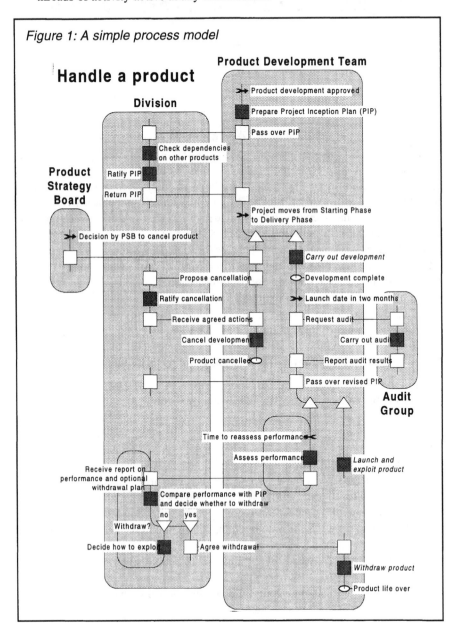

Figure 1: A simple process model

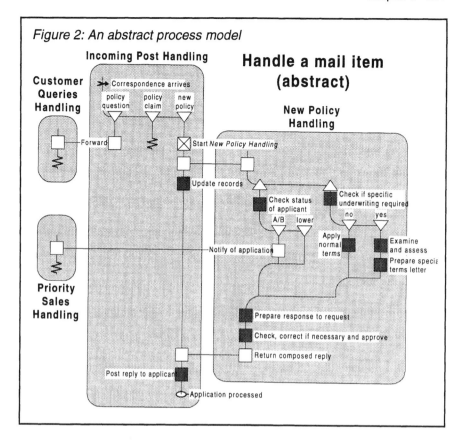

Figure 2: An abstract process model

When our concern is simply for modelling as-is processes, roles generally correspond to 'concrete' objects in the real world, in the organization as it operates: job titles, posts, departments or functional groups. Figure 1 is an example of such a 'concrete' process model. In many cases we find it useful to work with the more abstract notion of a role as an area of responsibility. A role taking the form of such a 'gathering' of activity and decision-making might be coherent for a variety of reasons. It might require a particular set of skills, and hence would be unlikely to be spread over different concrete roles. Or it might need to be separated from other roles for reasons of policy, often to do with oversight or regulation: certain types of decision must be approved by a role that is separate from the role making the decision, there must be independence of approval; equally, in regulated industries and services there must be independently exercised oversight of the operation of the process and this again speaks for a separate oversight 'area of responsibility', or role. This opportunity to think in concrete or abstract terms gives us the ability to use a RAD as a tool for examining the way in which the process is divided across a number of players, an examination that might lead us to question whether it is really necessary to split the work in this way.

Whenever we take a coherent set of related activities and decisions and split them across a number of different roles we create the need for the roles to interact in order to pass things around, to keep each other informed, to instruct, to report, etc.

It is as if we had taken the neat, ideal, circular pizza and cut it up to give to people around the table, with threads of melted cheese tying them together as the parts are separated. An as-is RAD would show concrete roles corresponding to identifiable posts etc. in the organization; they would be interacting in concrete ways: exchanging information, meeting, making joint decisions, giving orders, delivering results, and so on. An abstract RAD would stand back from the concrete and present the essence of the process, what remained after the organizational structure had been removed and the 'real' process distilled out.

In summary, the RAD becomes a way of challenging both the culture, and the separation of roles and responsibilities between different roles in the organization.

Figure 2 gives an example of such an abstract model. Note how, in particular, role names express areas of responsibility, and interactions are expressed in terms of their intent rather than a particular mechanism.

RADs offer reengineering opportunities at the level of identifying where organizational structures might be simplified or absent or inappropriate. This modelling and diagnosis aspect of process modelling is covered in *Business Processes* (Ould, 1995).

The Dissection Lesson – Cutting up the Organization

A RAD is very much a network. It shows how a group of roles interact to achieve a goal. In particular it allows the full concurrency of the process to be captured, perhaps with some roles existing in many instances all operating concurrently, perhaps with concurrent threads of activity within the role instances, all interacting at appropriate moments in their activity, for decision-making or receiving instructions or whatever. The roles and their interactions form a network (statically and dynamically).

In the early days of STRIM we were often asked how one could draw a hierarchical decomposition of the activities of an organization using RADs. Could RADs have 'sub-RADs'? Such a question begged the question of whether a model of a process could (or indeed should) be hierarchical. Our response was another question: 'is that hierarchical structure present in the real world that you are modelling, or do you simply want to represent the process hierarchically because you feel comfortable with a hierarchy?'. If that hierarchy is not in the real world, what sense is there in modelling our process as if it were? And, in such a hierarchy, what would it actually mean to say that processes *A1* and *A2* are 'below' process *A*? Presumably it could only mean that if process *A* was done then at some point processes *A1* and *A2* might be done – *A1* and *A2* were 'encapsulated' in *A*. But this simply does not feel like the real world. Our obsession with hierarchies has got the better of us. And we have probably been encouraged by the developers of process diagramming tools who find hierarchies easy to implement.

With this mindset, the entire organizational activity becomes a monolith that we chop up into smaller pieces, which are in turn chopped up into smaller pieces. And the only relationship we have defined between these pieces – which we still call processes – is that of encapsulation. But what about situations where one process starts another, such as when the process that manages our product portfolio decides that we need to start development of a new product? And what of situations where two processes communicate, such as when all of the product development process instances communicate their progress and forecasts to the process looking after the product portfolio? How will our hierarchy exhibit those two crucial *dynamic relationships* – process activation and process interaction? The answer is of course that it won't. The hierarchy has in fact hidden the actual, dynamic relationships between concurrent processes and shows only invented relationships.

What we *do* see in the real world is another network – a network of processes operating largely independently but with certain dynamic relationships. And it is these dynamic relationships – which of course operate across the dreadful hierarchy – that are truly interesting, rather than the static relationship of encapsulation which, at best, can only be regarded as an attempt to make a model more 'readable'. Unfortunately, in making the model more readable, the ploy has also made it wrong – the major structural feature of the model has no counterpart in the real-world. The hierarchy has no dynamics – we have thrown the most important feature of the real world away. All models are wrong but some are useful, except that hierarchical models are both wrong and not useful!

It is all rather as if we had been invited into the dissecting room for an anatomy lesson. The anatomist approaches the body with a large axe and swiftly chops it into seven (plus or minus two) pieces of roughly the same size and labels them *Body Part 1* through *Body Part 7*. They then take *Body Part 1* and render it down into seven (plus or minus two) smaller parts which are labelled *Body Part 1a* through *Body Part 1g*. This is dissection as some process modelling would have us go about it. What guides the division into these parts? The seven plus or minus two rule plays a major role, but beyond that little guidance is available. Sometimes a spurious sequence is invoked: analyze market, design product, manufacture product, sell product – with lists of activities strung beneath these lumps on the kebab stick, all notion of concurrency lost.

However, in the real world of dissection, the anatomist looks for the real

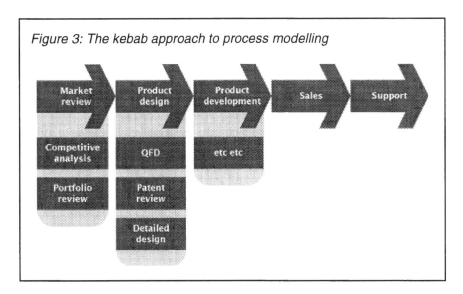

Figure 3: The kebab approach to process modelling

'subsystems' and separates out for us the nervous system, the digestive system, the musculature, and so on, preserving the dynamic connections between them: the points where the nerves activate the muscles, the point where the muscles operate the digestive system, the point where the digestive system relays messages to the nervous system. We see the dynamics between the concurrent systems – in particular their interactions.

It is now as if we had taken a rough diamond and produced cut gemstones by seeking the natural cleavage planes, where the axe-anatomist would produce more rough diamonds by simply smashing the larger piece into smaller pieces.

How do we find these natural cleavage planes in the organizational activity? Put more particularly, how do we find the *real* processes in the organization, the processes that arise from the business that the organization is in? The processes that are of the essence of the business? The processes that the organization must have if it is in this business? And how do we then establish the dynamic relationships that exist between those processes? In short how do we draw up a business-driven *process architecture* for the organization?

This was the question that I addressed in a paper *Designing a reengineering-proof process architecture* (Ould, 1997) and which I shall outline next.

Process Architectures – Starting in the Right Place

Suppose we are faced with a service company, or a support group in a larger organization, or an R&D company. How do we deduce its process architecture? How do we decide what processes it has and what their relationships are? To answer this would be useful in itself, but I want to strengthen the question: how can we produce a process architecture that is *neutral*, one that is independent of the structures within the organization and independent of the organization's culture, one that would be 'true' no matter how the organization chose to run itself? If I could come up with such an architecture, it would surely be a sound basis on which to design new processes, to invent new structures, to change a culture, or to build an IS strategy. By being neutral, the process architecture would allow me to question everything that is at my disposal: how I choose to run my business. Do I want to have a command and control organization, or one with a high degree of empowerment? Do I want a strong hierarchy of control or a flat structure where consensus operates? The only statements our neutral process architecture would make would be 'invariant' statements, statements that are true simply because we are in this business.

Our starting place for such a neutral process architecture can only be the business that the organization is in, and we start by characterizing that business by listing the *essential business entities* (EBEs). An EBE is something which the organization must deal with if it is in this business, and without which it would not be in this business. EBEs are the things which are the *essence* of the organization's business.

I said we are interested in 'the business that the organization is in'. If we had a characterization of that, we could immediately challenge just what business the organization really *is* in, or thinks it is in, or wants to be in. When we list the EBEs, we are making precisely that decision. Water utility company would most likely include *customer, customer contact, asset, supplier,* and *annual return to the regulator* in its list of EBEs, for instance. If it does not have customers it can't sell anything. If it has customers they will contact it – perhaps through a call centre, or by post, or through their web site – and such contact cannot be engineered away. If it does not have assets (reservoirs, pumping stations, etc.) it has nothing to sell. Of course, it could buy the water it sells to its customers from the owners of such assets and pay them for the use of their pipework. But then it would not be in the same business – that is a decision it could make. If it wants to operate in the water supply market – a regulated market in the UK – then its annual return to the regulator cannot be avoided. And so on.

The list of EBEs will sometimes be far from obvious. In some work for pharmaceutical company *P*, we looked at the processes for supplying formulated drugs to clinical trials. For the organization concerned – the Pharmacy within *P* – the most obvious EBE was the initial request from the clinician for certain supplies ('2,000 packs of twenty 5mg tablets each, to be supplied to clinic *X* by 1st August'); this was what they were in 'business' to deal with. Such a request triggered a whole process of acquisition of the raw drug compound, its formulation into tablets, its packing and transportation, with all the necessary quality control and record keeping for traceability. Another EBE was the individual 'patient pack' – it is clearly the subject matter of their 'business' – a Pharmacy supplying clinical trials must deal with such things. A patient pack (as far as the Pharmacy was concerned) had a lifetime that started from the moment it acquired some unique identity, and 'finished' when it arrived at the clinic. (There were other EBEs that were well understood and visible to the group in the Pharmacy but we need not go into them here.)

But there was one EBE that had not been recognized as such. It was 'the change of mind of the clinician about the supplies for a trial'. There was no way in which the Pharmacy could ignore such things, no way they could reengineer such things away. If they were running a Pharmacy they would have clinicians changing their minds – it is in the nature of clinical trials that the structure and protocols of a trial can change as development proceeds. The group concerned had tended to treat these entities (changes of mind) as disruptions to the normal flow of things and they did their best to accommodate them in a more or less ad hoc fashion. They were invariably successful in accommodating these 'disruptions' but at considerable cost. They had no clear process for dealing with them, no roles allocated to the negotiation and closure of the change across all the supplies currently going through or planned for the Pharmacy in the next twelve months.

The moment we recognize such changes of mind as EBEs – entities that are part of our business, that we have to deal with – we immediately recognize the need for a process to handle them, and the need to manage the flow of such changes of mind that will come in (and which are of course more numerous than the original requests).

This gives us the clue for the next stage in the construction of the process architecture in **Riva**. (I shall elide some steps – see (Ould, 1997) for fuller details.)

For each EBE we hypothesize that there is a *case process* and a *case management process*. The case process is the process that handles a single instance of the EBE. So, given the EBE *Request for supplies for clinical trial*, we hypothesize there is a process called *Handle a request for supplies for clinical trial*, a process that is triggered by acceptance of the request and has as its goal the receipt of the correct supplies at the designated clinic by the date required. The case management process is the process that manages the flow of instances of the case process. So, given the EBE *Request for supplies for clinical trial*, we hypothesize there is a process called *Handle the flow of requests for supplies for clinical trial*. This process is the one that receives the requests from the customer (clinicians), perhaps negotiates on dates (looking across the future workload), allocates slots in the production schedule, negotiates with the department that manufactures the raw material, timetables the work required, and finally 'kicks off' the case process. During the lifetime of a request for clinical trial supplies, the case management process will be monitoring the progress of the instance of the case process – remember that the Pharmacy is preparing many supplies for many different trials at any one time – and it will be doing all the management things one might expect: allocating resources, scheduling and rescheduling, monitoring, urging, and so on. When it achieves its goal, the case process delivers to the end customer, the clinician.

Figure 4 summarizes the situation for the case and case management processes, the first concentrating on a single instance of the EBE, the second on the set of EBE instances in hand at any one moment.

If we think of the EBE list as a searchlight we can see it illuminating that part of the organizational activity that interests us: so far we have clinical trial supplies requests and changes to them. If we increase the intensity we will see 'smaller' EBEs, such as the individual patient pack. Within the supplies for one clinical trial will be a pack of tablets for each patient. The very nature of clinical trials means that these exist – they are an EBE for the Pharmacy. Moreover, we can recognize that one request for supplies *generates* many patient packs – this is a dynamic relationship between the EBEs. When we have listed our EBEs we can identify these *generates*

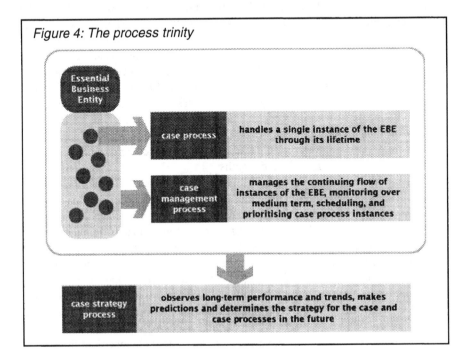

Figure 4: The process trinity

Essential Business Entity

case process — handles a single instance of the EBE through its lifetime

case management process — manages the continuing flow of instances of the EBE, monitoring over medium term, scheduling, and prioritising case process instances

case strategy process — observes long-term performance and trends, makes predictions and determines the strategy for the case and case processes in the future relationships between them, yielding a diagram such as that in figure 5. Here, we have provided some context by showing the requests for trials supplies and the changes to the requests both being generated by a 'larger' EBE, the clinical trial itself.

Let's return to the water utility *W*. Examination of their IS group's corporate data model yielded an EBE relationship diagram in under a day, part of which is shown in figure 6.

The next step in *Riva* is almost mechanical. We take the EBE relationship diagram and transform it into a process architecture using a handful of simple rules. (Again, I have simplified the approach for brevity's sake.) For each EBE we

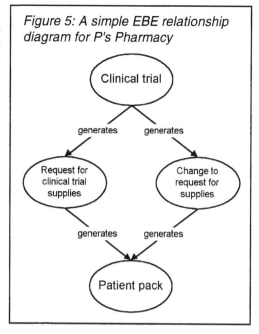

Figure 5: A simple EBE relationship diagram for P's Pharmacy

place a corresponding case process and case management process in the process architecture. For each relationship between two EBEs in the EBE relationship diagram we place corresponding relationships between their case and case manage-

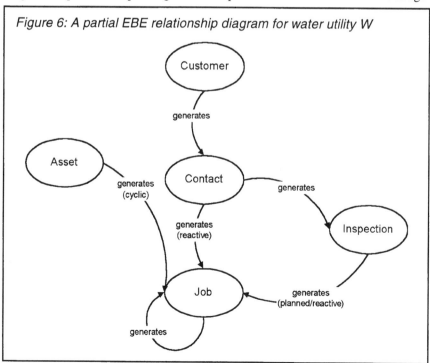

Figure 6: A partial EBE relationship diagram for water utility W

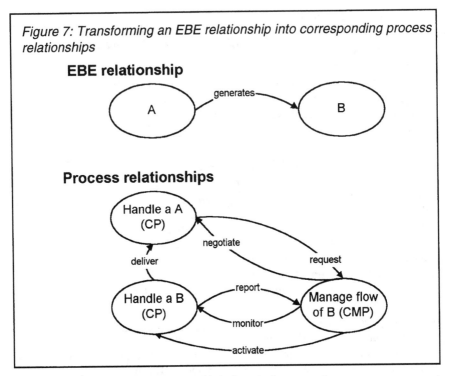

Figure 7: Transforming an EBE relationship into corresponding process relationships

EBE relationship

Process relationships

ment processes. Figure 7 shows how this is done in the general case; arrows represent dynamic relationships of different sorts between the processes. (CP = case process, CMP = case management process)

If we apply this simple rule to the EBE relationship diagram in figure 6 we obtain the process architecture in figure 8, after a little simplification.

Note how this process architecture is totally derived solely from an analysis of the business that the organization is in or wants to be in. We have not been concerned at all with the structures that the organization has or with its culture. Those will only become apparent when we start opening the boxes on the process architecture. Only then will we start to look at the roles and their interactions and hence at the way the organization chooses to do its business. Our process architecture is a true representation of what must be happening somewhere, somehow in the business, but it is a *neutral* representation that does not prejudge structure or culture.

In *Riva* we go a step further and make one more hypothesis: for each EBE there is a *case strategy process*. This is the process that is concerned with trends to do with the EBE and strategic decisions about the future handling of that EBE. Take company *W* and its *Customer contact* EBE.

When I ring the company's call centre I start the case process *Handle a customer contact*. This process will continue until my call is closed to my satisfaction. At the call centre, the case management process *Handle the flow of customer contacts* will be in progress constantly, monitoring load, allocating resources etc. And within the organization there will be the case strategy process *Handle the strategy for customer contacts*. This process will look at the rates of calls over the recent past, the way they are distributed through the day, how long it takes for them to be cleared, how many

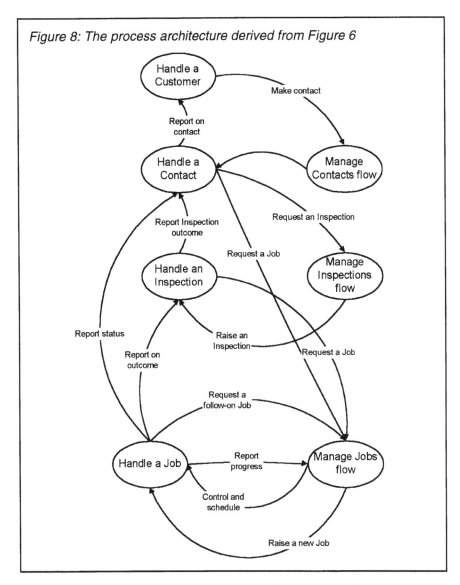

Figure 8: The process architecture derived from Figure 6

get escalated to management, and the trends in all these things. The organization's performance in dealing with this EBE is monitored and analyzed, and the analysis is input to formulation of the strategy for the future: just how much will the planned increase in the use of water metering change the profile and nature of calls? what extra skills will be needed at the call centre to manage the new profile? will the current case process and case management process still be appropriate? what extra loads will be placed on the supporting technologies? what new capability should we be looking for in the technology we deploy? do we need to make a step improvement in the service to customers? The other key input to the process is of course the current business drivers and changes in the business environment. The output of the case strategy process will be new strategy and policy which might in turn be translated into changes to the case and case management processes and the way they are organized. Those latter two processes are in fact the subject matter of the case strategy process.

Let's look at what a *Riva* process architecture now offers us in the following three situations: modelling an as-is organization, designing a new set of processes for an organization, or developing an IS strategy to support the organization.

If we are modelling the way an organization works today, this neutral process architecture tells us that, if the organization thinks it is in the business characterized by the EBEs, then it will have these processes with these relationships. They might not be recognized by the organization, but we have in front of us the most 'natural' possible division of the organizational activity into processes, one made along the natural cleavage planes of the organizational activity. When we start to put what we observe actually happening in the real world into the boxes representing the case and case management processes we shall be teasing apart the tangle of activity in the most natural way possible. The roles that we draw on our RADs will be concrete roles: posts, job titles, departments, etc. And their interactions will be concrete interactions: the passage of documents, the holding of meetings, approval signatures, requests, etc. The process architecture is a powerful place to start, far more so than an as-good-as-random 'dissection'. And if our model starts to look a tangle it is giving us a clear message about the organization's processes: they are in a tangle. We would do ourselves no service by finding another way of drawing the model that did not look so tangled. An as-is model is useless if it is not revealing. Figure 9

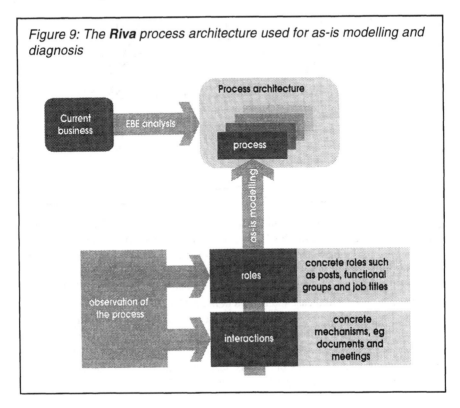

*Figure 9: The **Riva** process architecture used for as-is modelling and diagnosis*

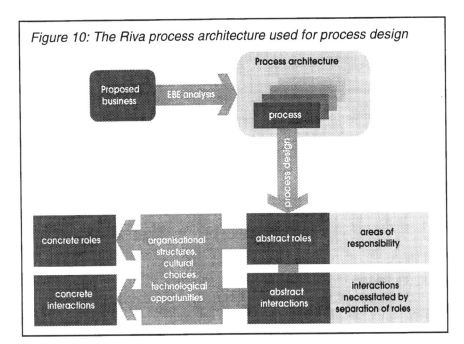

Figure 10: The Riva process architecture used for process design

summarizes the situation.

If we are designing a new set of processes, perhaps for a new organization, our neutral process architecture is again an ideal starting point: if we are in this business we must have these processes with these dynamic relationships. We can now start designing the processes individually knowing precisely how their interactions will appear. As we set about designing each in turn we can start to make decisions about what sort of culture we want to carry forward into the processes, what sort of structures we want to support the process, what sorts of technologies we will use to provide the plumbing necessary for information flow – all the organization-specific decisions. And we can make those decisions for *our* organization against a neutral process architecture. Figure 10 summarizes the situation.

Finally, if we are concerned with the IS support for the organization, the process architecture tells us what processes we have and therefore what processes need supporting to a greater or lesser degree. The precise degree will of course be determined by the business drivers that are at the top of the organization's list, today, in today's climate. They may be to do with cost competitiveness, customer satisfaction, the exploitation of corporate knowledge, or a host of other things. The next section picks up this theme in more detail.

IS Provision Requirements – some Experiences

Within the *Riva* method, we can now see that for every *essential business entity* which the business is concerned with there are (or should be) three natural processes – the case, case management, and case strategy processes (see figure 4). Each of these can be expected to be both a provider and a user of information, and hence a potential beneficiary of the IS strategy.

We can characterize those expectations briefly as follows.

IS support for the case process will be about the capture, storage, presentation and processing of information about individual cases. When I call my water company, my name and account number (or perhaps the number of the telephone I am calling from) will allow the information systems to bring up my details and a summary of recent contacts on a screen in front of the person taking my call. The time frame of IS support for the 'lifetimes' of contacts with customers will be short- to medium-term: some contacts will be cleared during the call, some will need action that will continue for perhaps weeks as visits to the customer's premises are arranged, take place and get closed off. The time frame of IS support for the 'lifetimes' of the customer will be medium-term to long-term, since an instance of the case process for an individual customer will last as long as the customer is a customer.

IS support for the case management process will be about the flow of cases at any one time – typically rates and levels – and about exceptions that are raised by the case process instances. As call centre manager I expect to see on a screen in front of me who is doing what, what the waiting queue of callers looks like, and how it is building or falling. The actual allocation of calls to call centre staff is being dealt with automatically by my smart telephony system, leaving me to manage the staffing levels and deal with exception conditions. The time frame for such IS support will typically be short-term allowing minute-to-minute management of the centre.

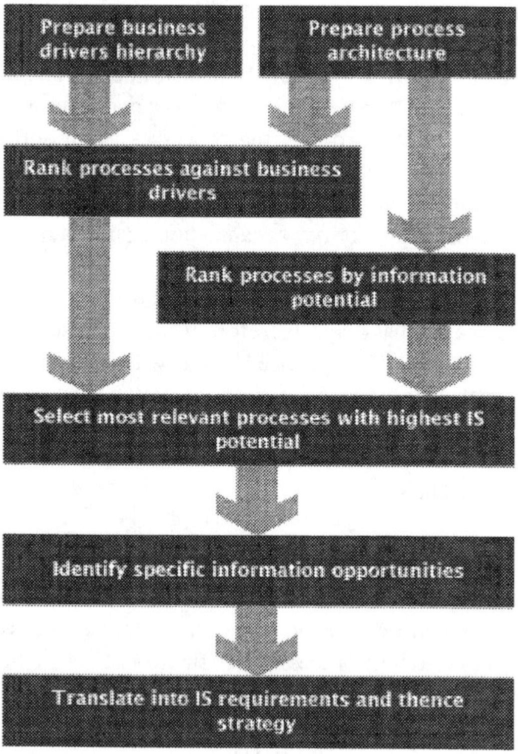

IS support for the case strategy process is about the longer term capture, storage, analysis and presentation of past cases. We will think in terms of data warehousing and data marts, the ability to slice and dice the case data, computer simulation of the business and its flows, experimentation with different future scenarios, and modelling of new structures and processes. The time frame for such IS support will be medium and possibly long term depending on the time horizon of the business.

Riva allows the process architecture to be used from either of two directions: from the business or from the IS group. In the first case we start with the business

Figure 11: Steps from the business drivers to an IS strategy in **Riva** managers, and, from their business perspective, lead them to a vision of the IS provision that would best serve their business. In the second case we start with the IS group and their strategists, and, from a clear understanding of the current IS provision, lead them to a vision of how the IS could be better aligned with the business's goals and operation. Let's look at these two in turn, using some examples adapted from real projects.

Utility company *R* sought a business-driven IS strategy, one founded in the needs of the business rather than the capabilities of technology. For any business, the issues that drive management action vary in time as priorities change. Those business drivers will have different time horizons and the role of IS is to support them accordingly. But the jump from business drivers to information technology strategy is a big one: we needed to break it into a number of smaller steps that could be taken individually in, say, a single workshop of senior managers.

The *Riva* approach in this area is summarized in figure 11. The first step involves the brainstorming of those business drivers: ignoring information systems, what's driving the business and changes in the business today and in the foreseeable future? Following Gilb's *System Attribute Specification* method (Gilb, 1987) we develop a hierarchy of drivers with lower levels making the 'woolly' upper levels more specific and finally, if appropriate, measurable. At the highest level in our case study the drivers include safety, expanding the customer base and satisfying the regulator. Each of these can then be decomposed in turn to bring the area into finer focus. If the driver is 'we must expand the customer base', the next level down might be 'we must have more flexible pricing', 'we must package our offerings better', 'we must improve the quality of our *A* service', 'we must understand better who is buying what'. If we develop the driver that 'we must have more flexible pricing', we shall come to drivers such as 'we must know which of our assets are being used and how much', and 'we must be able to construct more flexible contracts'. This analysis might already have been done by the organization and we can pick it up directly; otherwise a traditional facilitated workshop will yield the information.

While this work is progressing, a process architecture can be constructed for the organization. If someone can be found within the organization who knows its business, such an architecture can be constructed to a useful level of accuracy and depth within two days. In a simplified form it can then be used in a further workshop of senior management at which two steps can be taken. Firstly the list of processes is examined to see which have potentially the most to gain from having accessible information. Secondly, the processes are examined to assess how far each will help the organization meet the demands of each of the 'leaf-node' drivers.

At transport utility *T* we worked with senior managers responsible for large chunks of the company. Simple round-the-table scoring allowed us to rank the processes according to their 'information content' – clearly, processes with the most to gain from strong IS provision would be of greatest interest to us in developing the IS strategy. Similarly, a traditional matrix of drivers against processes was used to score each process according to its contribution to each driver and thence to derive a further ranking. With a simple combination of rankings we were able to quickly prepare a shortlist of the processes that were most important to the business *and* had most to gain from strong IS provision. In a final bout of workshops we worked with the same managers to draw out improvements in information quality or accessibility for each of those processes, knowing now that we were addressing the big hitters. These requirements could then be translated into requirements on the IS provision.

At this stage we are of course simply characterizing the IS provision in terms of what it would *achieve* as opposed to what it would look like – 'timely analysis of the usage that each asset component had and of its costs, available at the desk of group D', 'timely costing of alternatives packages, available at the desk of group E', and the like. The remaining step is that to the technologies that could be used – data warehousing, client-server architectures, web-based information gathering etc. This remains a technical step to be made by those familiar with the technologies concerned, but the senior managers now have a clear vision of why those technologies are relevant to their business – one of the hardest steps to make – and we have made the bridge for them using the process architecture. If a three-tier client-server IS architecture is proposed to satisfy the information needs of the asset case strategy process, managers can trace them back to the business drivers concerned with their need for pricing flexibility, and the proposal becomes meaningful.

Coming at the question from the other direction, the IS group at water utility company W wanted to develop an IS strategy that was not just aligned to the business, but was aligned in a way that was accessible by senior management. The strategy would need to map a path from the existing provision to the new world. Again the process architecture provided the bridge.

Figure 12 summarizes the overall process.

For an IS group the preparation of a process architecture can be kick-started by using the corporate data model as a checklist of EBEs. (There will be many things that an organization collects data about that do not represent the 'work items' that we look for in EBEs, but it would be unusual for there to be an EBE about which no data is kept.) The standard approach summarized above is used to prepare the process architecture. The important outcome is the shortlist of case, case management, and case strategy processes. While this work was going on at W, a parallel team were preparing an inventory of existing systems and their users. Those systems were then mapped onto the process architecture – knowing the users of

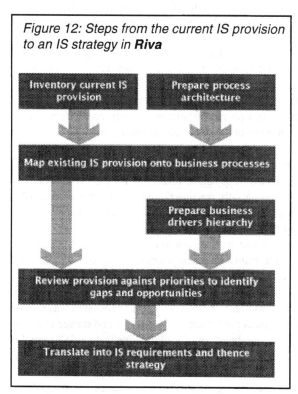

Figure 12: Steps from the current IS provision to an IS strategy in **Riva**

the system allowed us to determine what processes they were involved in when they made use of the system.

The result was a gap analysis (Figure 13) – certain processes were well supported by the current IS provision. But an analysis of the business drivers of W pointed to process areas of the business that would become important before long and which would need increased support from IS. It was now possible to prepare a 'shopping list' of systems and architectural changes necessary to make them possible. The business case to management could now be aligned to the business's processes and drivers, offering the opportunity of a much richer form of justification than a cost-benefit comparison – IS could be painted much more easily as an enabler for the business, a case that has traditionally been difficult for any IS group.

Conclusions and Summary

The *Riva* method takes the process modelling approach of STRIM using Role Activity Diagrams with their concentration on roles and interactions and adds the concept of the process architecture. By being based on the essential business entities of the organization concerned, a *Riva* process architecture is rooted in the real business. By being based solely on the subject matter of the organization it is also neutral, that is independent of how the organization chooses to do its business, in particular its organizational structures and culture.

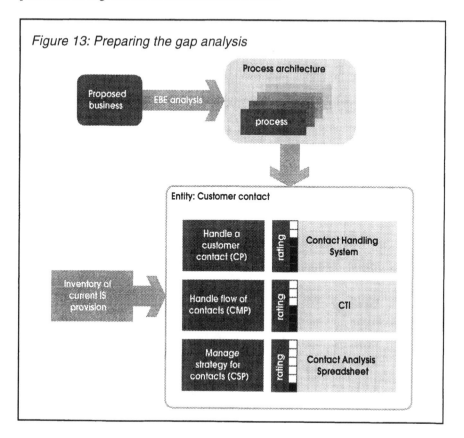

Figure 13: Preparing the gap analysis

If a new organization is being conceived, each process in the architecture can then be designed, and structural and cultural policies taken into account in the choice of roles and their interactions. If, on the other hand, processes are being modelled as-is (perhaps for improvement, training, or just simple understanding), the process architecture gives the most natural division of the organizational activity into coherent processes. The process architecture defines the essential dynamic relationships between the processes, relationships that will be seen in detail at the Role Activity Diagram level.

Because it is deduced from the business of the organization, a **Riva** process architecture provides a business-focussed bridge between the concerns of senior management and the organization's information systems strategy. This bridge can be used by management to reach towards the IS requirements, or by the IS group to push the IS strategy towards the business's goals and drivers.

Acknowledgments

My thanks go to colleagues who have contributed to the ideas in this chapter, in particular Tim Huckvale, Steve Summers and Richard Erskine.

References

Gilb, Tom. 1987. *Design by Objectives*. North-Holland.

Ould, Martyn A. 1995. *Business Processes – modelling and analysis for re-engineering and improvement*, John Wiley, Chichester.

Ould, Martyn A. 1997. Designing a reengineering-proof process architecture. *Business Process Management Journal*, Vol 3, 3, pp 232-247.

Part III
The Multidimensional
Evolution of Process
Management

CHAPTER 9

Managing Information about Processes

Thomas H. Davenport
University of Texas, Austin

Michael C. Beers
Ernst & Young Center for Business Innovation, Boston

One of the most important recent directions in organizations is the adoption of process-oriented approaches to organizational change. Processes are structured sets of work activity that lead to specified business outcomes for customers. The earliest process thinking might be attributed to pioneers of industrial engineering such as Taylor (1911) and Gilbreth (1931); in the middle of this century processes were also adopted as the primary work unit for such pioneers of quality management as Shewhart (1931), Deming (1986), and Juran (1974). In the 1990s, broad, cross-functional business processes were made the focus of corporate reengineering efforts in the work of Davenport and Short (1990), Hammer (1990), and others. Processes also gained increased importance in organization-wide incremental improvement programs (Harrington, 1991; Huber and Power, 1985).

Most of the process change initiatives occurring in organizations today can be described by two broad (and sometimes overlapping) categories. *Quality management* often referred to as total quality management (TQM) or continuous improvement, refers to programs and initiatives that emphasize incremental improvement in work processes and outputs over an open-ended period of time. *Reengineering,* also known as business process redesign or process innovation, refers to discrete initiatives that are intended to achieve radically redesigned and improved work processes in a bounded time frame. Programs of these types, and various combinations or permutations of them, have become pervasive in large organizations. In one broad survey of U.S. and European firms, 69 percent of U.S. companies and 73 percent of European companies surveyed had adopted reengineering programs (Davenport, 1993); in a 1989 study of 149 U.S. firms, 75 percent had quality management programs in place, and an additional 9 percent planned to initiate one (Walsh, 1989).

As these programs become common in firms, managers are beginning to address the means by which processes can become institutionalized in day-to-day management. These means include process-oriented organizational structures, human resource management approaches, and information systems architectures (Davenport, 1994). Interestingly, while information technology was recognized early in the life of reengineering as a critical enabler of new process designs (Davenport, 1990), the role of information itself in process management has rarely been addressed, and then only in the context of quality management (Garvin, 1987; Goldralt, 1990).

In the past, firms have generally measured and monitored their performance through the use of financial information, usually accounting-based (Johnson and Kaplan, 1987). As Eccles (1991) and Kaplan and Norton (1992) have argued, financial indicators alone are usually insufficient for the effective management of organizational performance. Firms also need to manage operational performance— that is, the efficiency and effectiveness with which the day-to-day activities of the organization are carried out. While there are other operational units (e.g., functions or divisions) in which operational performance can be measured, cross-functional processes are preferable because they do not let internal organizational boundaries stand in the way of improved customer performance (Schonberger, 1990). Processes can also be leading indicators of future financial performance (Soin, 1992).

It is perhaps obvious that information about process characteristics, performance, and outputs is critical for process management. Information suggests both the need for and the direction of potential process improvements, and aids in predicting and diagnosing problems with processes. Because customers are typically the recipients of process outputs, information about customer satisfaction with processes can also help an organization to react to changes in the marketplace.

But if these benefits are obvious, they have not yet been translated into concerted action. Even some of the most process-oriented firms in the United States have not fully developed infrastructures for providing process performance information to managers and workers. One survey of quality practices found that "techniques for measuring the overall results of quality programs are not yet well developed" (Walsh, 1989). Another survey of firms that had applied for the Malcolm Baldrige National Quality Award found that, among other problems, quality measures emphasized downstream and financial phenomena (rather than broad process information), and were generally poorly organized (Easton, 1993). As a result of these problems, most firms find it very difficult to know if their operational performance is improving or not, and in what areas of the business they face performance problems.

The role of process information is better understood in quality management programs than in process reengineering programs. Some previous research has identified the management of information as an important component of an effective quality program; Garvin (1987) compared Japanese and U.S. firms in the air conditioner industry on quality management practices, and found that firms with high-quality products had better approaches to the management of quality information. The Malcolm Baldrige Quality Award (National Institute of Standards and Technology, 1993) cites "Information and Analysis" as one of the seven factors on which firms are evaluated. Fifty-five of the seventy-five points awarded in this category are for the scope, management, and use of internally oriented information; the other twenty points are assessed on the basis of competitive comparisons and benchmarking. The director of the Baldrige Award program stated that "Information systems is a major theme of the Baldrige Award. Quality-conscious companies are more data rich [than other companies]" (Kiley, 1991).

Yet even in quality programs, the role of information may not be well understood. Little prescriptive literature exists to assist firms in managing information about business processes. Indeed, though Information and Analysis is a category of the Baldrige, it is the second lowest in weight, comprising only 8 percent of the total score. Three Baldrige winners told us that the information category was the weakest in their applications, and Baldrige examiners have noted in conversation with us that firms interpreted the category in a wide variety of ways— more so than for other factors.

For example, among the firms that win Baldrige awards, some emphasize their customer information systems as the key to their quality performance, which is not necessarily evidence of an orientation to process information. At the Ritz-Carlton hotels, it is clear that points on this category were scored not for process information, but for having a customer information system that was shared across some hotels. Granite Rock, another I 992 Baldrige Award winner, was cited in winning the award not for its process information but for its use of an automated teller-like machine enabling customers to purchase rock or cement at any hour (Caldwell, 1992). Eastman Chemical's distinctive competence in the "Information and Analysis" category primarily involved its chemical process control systems. In short, a wide variety of information-oriented capabilities can help firms to win the Baldrige.

Firms undertaking reengineering programs have also not fully realized the importance of process information. Though many firms have reengineering initiatives underway, few are yet at the stage where their reengineered processes are fully implemented and operational. As a result, only a few firms have given serious attention to ongoing process management, and hence to the information they would use for this purpose. Furthermore, the rhetoric of reengineering sometimes emphasizes the creative side of process change over the virtues of measurement and analysis (Davenport and Stoddard, 1994). However, as firms move further through the life-cycle of these radical change programs, they will need to begin measuring processes and their outputs, and to continually refine their designs.

Our purpose in the research was to explore how leading firms use information about processes for the purpose of managing and improving those processes. Among the issues addressed are the following:

- Why should process-oriented information be managed?
- What kind of process information should be collected?
- By what means can its collection and distribution be made routine?
- How should the process information be used?
- How does process information lead to business change?
- What are some examples of firms that do a good job of this?

The next section describes our research approach. We then develop a context and conceptual framework for understanding process information, its types, and challenges for management. Following this, we suggest an approach to process information management for the practitioner, with examples of leading practices we have come across in our research. We conclude with a summary and put forth some implications for subsequent research.

Table 1: List of Organizations Surveyed	
American Airlines	GM Hughes Electronics
Analog Devices	Hewlett- Packard
AT&T Network Systems Transmission*	IBM*
AT&T Universal Card*	PHH Corporation
Computer firm (anonymous)	Pacific Bell
Dell Computer	Public Service Electric & Gas
Eastman Chemical*	Process industry firm (anonymous)*
Engineering and construction firm	Ritz-Carlton Hotels*
Federal Express*	Union Pacific Railroad
General Motors (Cadillac division)*	Xerox*
	* Baldrige Award winners.

Methodology

The research approach we followed involved structured interviews with twenty firms, each of which had strong, successful programs in process improvement, process innovation, or both (Table 1). Nine of the twenty organizations had won Malcolm Baldrige Quality Awards, and are thus externally certified leaders in the management and improvement of processes (one of these nine requested that it not be identified). As the 1993 award criteria note, "Pursuit of quality and operational performance goals of the company requires that process management be based on reliable information, data, and analysis" [National Institute of Standards and Technology, 1993, p. 3].

With each firm we conducted a structured interview (see the appendix for interview questions) assessing various aspects of process information management. The interviews were conducted in most cases either with quality managers or information managers who had quality or reengineering responsibilities. In each case they appeared to be the most informed representative available on process information issues (Housel, Bell and Kanevsky, 1994). Because our respondents did not always view their activities in the terms of our questions, and because many firms we interviewed had only limited process information management activities, we felt that quantitative analysis of the survey results was not appropriate. We therefore primarily employed the interviews to gather what we considered leading practices and well-defined tactics and strategies. During the period of our research, we also came across several firms that suffer from poor management of process information, and they are mentioned anonymously on occasion below.

We also explored in greater detail the approaches to process information management at one company, AT&T Universal Card, for which a brief case study is provided below. We found that this organization had one of the most sophisticated and advanced approaches to managing process information, and that a more detailed look at its practices would be useful to researchers and practitioners. Both the semistructured interviewing and the case study method are consistent with the exploratory analysis appropriate to any area of emergent management practice such as this (Eisenhart, 1989).

Conceptual Background
Two Types of Process Information -- Measures and Ideas

Defining process information is a difficult undertaking, whether in the context of improving or innovating processes. Process quality is an ambiguous objective that can be measured in multiple ways. Some researchers have attempted to define specific measures of quality. Garvin (1987) cites eight dimensions of quality: performance, features, reliability, conformance, durability, serviceability, aesthetics, and perceived quality. In examining service quality, one study (Zeithaml, Parasurman and Berry, 1990) identified five attributes of quality service: reliability, responsiveness, assurance, empathy, and tangibles. Most customer transactions today, even in manufacturing organizations, include both product and service components: in such environments, both types of measures should be collected.

Quality information, then, is partly a set of measures about the performance of products or services, which are the outputs of processes. It is also possible, indeed important, to measure some processes, such as the time and cost consumed by their execution. How long it takes and how much it costs to fill a customer order may be just as important as whether the order was filled correctly or not, and whether the shipped product arrived in one piece. Customers will not be satisfied unless performance is good on all of these dimensions.

Customer satisfaction is another key measurement of process performance, and while clearly correlated with output quality, should be independently measured. Low customer satisfaction when internal process measures are high may indicate that the wrong internal factors are being measured. Reengineering practitioners at Pacific Bell (Housel, Bell and Kanevsky, 1994) have observed that there may also be other desirable measures of a process, including its variability (a key measure in continuous improvement programs), its flexibility, the job satisfaction of those who carry it out, and the value added by it. Table 2 lists some of the many possible measures of processes.

It should also be noted that some measures of process performance are easier to identify than they are to create. Measures are often tied to organizational structures, definitions of terms, institutionalized systems, and politics. Process cost is a particularly good example. Over the past several years, many firms have tried— with substantial difficulty—to create activity-based cost systems. While these might be aggregated to yield process—based cost measures, the aggregation will also not be without complications. It will take substantial investment in change before many firms can easily compile cost information across a process.

The example of process cost also raises the issue of whether some measures should not be collected because they divert management attention from the real issues of performance and customer satisfaction. Johnson (1992) has argued that activity-based cost measures have not helped to increase competitiveness in the U.S. firms that adopted them: "These activity-based cost management tools did not generate process maps, had no customer focus, and did not lead to bottom-up ideas for generating continuous process improvement." In business environments where managers are overly oriented to cost, perhaps process cost information should be deemphasized or should not be employed as a performance measure.

In addition to measures, there are other, less structured characteristics of

Table 2: Alternative Process Measures				
Cost	Time	Product quality	Service quality	Customer satisfaction
Product/output	Elapsed	Performance	Reliability	Levels
Activity-based	Active	Features	Responsiveness	Complaints
Against targets	Against	Reliability	Assurance	Suggestions
or budgets	customer	Conformance	Empathy	
Waste or cost	request	Durability	Tangibles	
of quality		Serviceability		
		Aesthetics		
		Perceived quality		

processes that are also useful to identify and collect. These might be collectively referred to as "ideas." These include current and best practices, improvement possibilities, and potential or actual applications of technology, human resource innovations, and so on. The goal of identifying and gathering these process attributes is to leverage them—that is, to spread them around the organization so that they can be applied to other similar processes.

Of course, ideas are notoriously difficult to structure and maintain in a systematic approach (whether computerized or not) (Walsh and Ungson, 1991). Perhaps someday there will be automated systems that can determine a structure for, categorize, automatically identify, and selectively prune databases of ideas. As of now, this is a very labor-intensive activity.

To maintain a database of process best practices, for example, requires a high level of ongoing attention, and most firms are unwilling to pay for this type of role. Firms also need to collect not just the idea itself but also the name and means of accessing a person who can interpret the idea and elaborate further on its context and relevance.

Two Learning Loops for Process Information

The two types of process information described—measures and ideas—are often associated with different types of learning. Argyris and Schön (1978) coined the term "double-loop learning" to distinguish between two different but related types of learning. One loop can be described as feedback between a narrowly defined task and its outcome; the commonly used analogy is a thermostat reacting to temperature. For a human example, a line worker in a manufacturing facility who refines his work procedures to become more efficient in fabricating a subassembly is employing single-loop learning. He is focusing on the effects of his behavior on the process and its output. For process information, this loop can be thought of as *performance* loop, describing process and/or process output performance (see Figure 1).

The other loop of double-loop learning requires an evaluation and judgment of the broader goals of the task or process. If that same worker stepped back to question whether or not his or her particular subprocess was necessary or appropriate or might be best employed at another stage of the assembly process, he or she would be practicing double-loop learning. The second loop might be termed a *relevance* loop, generating information that describes the relevance of the process to the environment. Double-loop learning requires not only focus on task efficiency, but also on

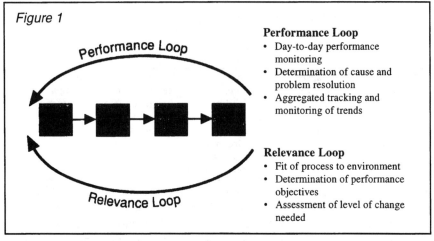

Figure 1

Performance Loop
- Day-to-day performance monitoring
- Determination of cause and problem resolution
- Aggregated tracking and monitoring of trends

Relevance Loop
- Fit of process to environment
- Determination of performance objectives
- Assessment of level of change needed

evaluation of the nature of the task itself and how it fits into a more broadly defined process.

Relevance loop information for business processes is most commonly found in firms approaching broad, cross-functional processes from an innovation or reengineering standpoint. They ask such questions as:

- What is the real purpose for this process?
- How does it support our strategy?
- To what degree does it meet the real needs of our customers?
- What performance objectives should it achieve?
- In an ideal world, how should this process he performed?
- What aspects of the process could be completely eliminated?

The learning from this sort of analysis is typically used in the design of a new process in a process innovation initiative, and the information is gathered in an ad hoc fashion through benchmarking, customer interviews, and brainstorming. It may be motivated by a particular change objective, such as cost reduction or increased production efficiency (McKinnon and Bruns, 1992). However, even in reengineering initiatives, few firms have institutionalized relevance loop learning for a process. This is an important step toward "continuous innovation," a concept that has been discussed with respect to products, but not for processes (Nonaka, 1991).

One reason why relevance loop information about processes is not more widely used is because it is difficult to manage such information. It tends to come from a wide variety of sources; in widely different forms, levels of accuracy, and degrees of structure. Synthesis and creativity, as well as some degree of rigor, are required to interpret such information. Making use of relevance loop information demands an understanding of both the process and the broader context within which it fits; this may include the organization's strategy, competitor approaches, and benchmarks or analogs in other firms. Only senior managers are likely to have access to all of this knowledge (Kotter, 1982), and many of them do not seek it.

Toward A Process for Managing Process Information

In analyzing our interview and case study materials, we found many useful leading practices that both practitioners and researchers may want to explore further. These practices took place at various points in an overall life-cycle of information management and use. Therefore, consistent with the conceptual focus of the paper, we employ the concept of an information management process as the structure for describing leading practices. Such a structure has been previously employed by Taylor (1986) in analyzing the value added to information. Such a process view of information management breaks down the overall task into its key activities, with recommended management tactics for each one. Four discrete steps in managing process information are discussed below: identification, collection, distribution, and use (Figure 2). As discussed below, the steps do not always take place in this sequence. The roles of performance and relevance loop information also vary by the stage of the process, as discussed below.

Identification of Process Information

Identification of the right sort of information—what is needed, and no more— on process performance is the first task an organization faces in managing process information. If this task is done poorly, the overall system for managing process information cannot be effective. More often than not, managers and process workers are confronted by too much information to be thoughtfully considered in a decision-making process. The challenge is to extrude the slender filament of germane information from the piles of the trivial and irrelevant (Goldralt, 1990).

It is often not a straightforward task to identify the right measures for a process and the products or services it produces. Not only are the potential measures numerous (see Table 2), some of them are difficult to operationalize. If empathy with the customer is a critical aspect of service quality, as research cited above has demonstrated, how should this be measured and reported? Do numbers of customer complaints tell us something about our overall service, or are they just a few bad examples (or a few vocal customers)? Substantial thought must be given to measure selection and development, and firms should expect that their process information will change as they learn.

Clearly, with all the potential measures available, a key task of defining process performance information is to filter or "boil down" the number of measures for a process, or at least to channel the right measures to the right individuals. No single

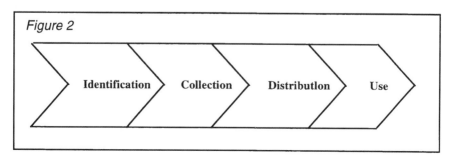

Figure 2

Identification > Collection > Distribution > Use

manager could fully comprehend all of the measures described above for a process. Furthermore, there are multiple processes to manage, the Ritz-Carlton hotel chain, for example, collects daily measures on 720 different processes. The number of measures multiplied by the number of processes would equal many thousands of items. In dealing with proliferation of measures, some sort of aggregation technique might be employed, at Pacific Bell, for example, eighty measures of customer service process performance were mathematically aggregated into four. While this aggregation approach lowers the number of measures, the resulting measures may not be easily comprehended by the managers who must use them. Another approach is to select those particular performance measures that best reflect the strategic objectives for the process.

Our interviews indicate that leading quality-oriented firms are relatively skilled at identifying information in the performance loop. These companies measure process performance across dimensions of time, cost, and quality, and are committed to the continuous improvement of their processes and outputs. Performance loop information is typically well structured and easily aggregated, computerized, and analyzed. Given sufficient attention and resources, its collection and reporting can be made routine with minimal levels of creativity.

However, relevance loop information—how this process fits in a larger context —is absent in many companies. Few of the Baldrige Award firms we researched had a regular procedure for examining processes in this fashion. The process of targeting the correct performance loop information must be based on the strategies and tactics of the firm from a process management standpoint; relevance loop information will be driven not only by key process objectives, but also by an organization's product/ service positioning strategy.

Most of the organizations that we interviewed focused only on performance loop information. However, we did find some institutionalization of relevance loop information in two of the firms we interviewed; both were Baldrige winners. At one leading manufacturing firm, not only was significant attention given to process improvement, a formal program was in place that periodically audited each process to, in the words of one manager "make sure the process we have is the right process." Customers and suppliers are consulted to determine levels of quality.

AT&T Universal Card, a Baldrige winner in 1992, is one of the few firms we encountered that pays detailed attention to both types of learning loops (see case study below of this organization); AT&T Transmission Systems, another 1992 Baldrige winner, is also strong in this regard. At both AT&T divisions, performance and relevance loop information are broadly identified, collected, and analyzed.

It should be pointed out that information selection is not a single event; the selection process should be frequently revisited to confirm fit as the business and process environment inevitably changes. For example, in the personal computer industry, the primary competitive focus has shifted from product differentiation to service. Since Dell Computer competes on service in this intensely competitive industry, customer satisfaction is its primary focus in its quality information. It has determined through customer surveys that satisfaction is highly related to product attributes, on-time delivery, and high levels of helpfulness and knowledge in telephone order conversations. Therefore, it measures and tracks such indicators as product returns and their causes, on-time delivery performance, and abandonment rates for calls to its toll-free number. Sales and technical support representatives view screens from their cubicles that tell how many calls have been answered, how long callers have been waiting, and whether callers have hung up. Perhaps as a partial result of these efforts, the firm's customer satisfaction levels are the highest in the industry (Kumar and Sharman, 1992).

It is not enough for process information to be relevant to current strategy. It must also be at an appropriate level of detail to facilitate the identification and resolution of the root cause of a problem. Within the IBM field service organization, for example, there has long been a high degree of process orientation and attention to measurement. However, initial information management approaches centered on aggregating the information so as to report trends to senior management. Field service managers found the information valuable, but it was difficult to translate it into action to resolve process problems. It was not until the handheld computers used by the technicians were programmed to require greater levels of detail on process performance and problems that the information could be used to improve service processes.

Collection of Process Information

In environments applying statistical process control to production processes, process performance information has typically been gathered through statistical sampling procedures (Deming, 1950). This was fine when the primary focus was defect rates in tangible process outputs, but it is somewhat more difficult when the desired quality information is broader, and involves services as much as products. However, many firms do collect information on customer satisfaction through sampling; they give customer surveys to every nth customer. For example, Public Service Electric and Gas, a leading quality-oriented utility based in New Jersey, continuously samples customer satisfaction in five customer categories. The Ritz-Carlton hotels survey over 25,000 guests each year to assess their satisfaction levels and to identify potential improvements. With any sampling approach, of course, if the sample misses a dissatisfied customer, there may be no getting him or her back.

In cases where regular sampling is not easy or appropriate, firms have generally used ad hoc means of collecting information on process performance. For example, the analysis done by consultants in measuring the cost, time, or output quality of a broad, cross-functional process is frequently the first time any process performance information was generated. Such ad hoc measurement, however, is expensive and infrequent; it cannot be the basis for ongoing process management.

The best approach, where feasible, to institutionalizing the collection of process information is to use information technology to gather it. The ability of technology to capture such information has been noted before. Shoshana Zuboff (1988), for example, coined the term "'informating" to describe the ability of computers to capture information about work processes for analysis and use, though her purpose was to describe the potential effect of computers on work, rather than to advance the art of process information management.

Some firms have built IT-based collection of process information into the basic fabric of the process. Perhaps the most outstanding example of this integration is Federal Express, which became the first service firm to win the Baldrige Award in 1990. Federal, as is by now widely known, scans specially designed bar codes on each of the parcels it transports between eight and ten times; its sales force also electronically collects pickup and delivery times and signatures. The information is then transmitted to COSMOS, Federal's centralized parcel tracking system. This parcel delivery information is the core of Federal's "Service Quality Indicator" system and was cited as a key factor in Federal's winning of the award.

In many other cases, particularly in manufacturing, firms are not able to gather all of the desired process performance information directly from existing systems. In order management processes, for example, existing order processing systems are unlikely to capture information about the cost, time, or output quality for a given order. Therefore, companies must typically build new information systems expressly for the purpose of capturing process performance information.

Not surprisingly, information technology providers lead in this approach. Hewlett Packard has built a system, called QUODEM (Quality in Order and Delivery Management), for collecting information about the time it takes for an order to complete a cycle from customer request to delivery, and the accuracy with which the company delivers what it promised the customer. Both measures are derived from already-present data in HP's order processing system, and information entered by field personnel. IBM has developed a similar system in Europe, and is currently planning worldwide implementation.

The HP system is a conventional reporting system tied to a conventional transaction system. Some new types of process-oriented software are designed to collect process performance information from the beginning. So-called "workflow" software directs information-oriented work from one employee to another; collection of the time consumed through the process is automatic. Most workflow software of the past, however, has been closely tied to structured processes involving movement of imaged paper, such as insurance claims processing or bank loan processing. The Hartford Insurance subsidiary of ITT, for example, uses workflow technology to measure time consumption and errors for many of its clerically oriented and narrowly defined insurance processes. Several vendors are beginning to offer more generic workflow software that will support more diverse, and less structured, processes. Pacific Bell has built a system that not only structures workflow for provisioning telephone service (and interfaces with the necessary back-office systems and databases), but also collects process performance measures for the entire process (Davenport and Nohria, 1994).

For some processes, performance loop information collection can be built into the process or product itself. Some Xerox copiers and Otis elevators, for example, monitor their own performance and transmit information to a central site for analysis and action. Federal Express and United Parcel Service use bar code scanning to monitor the time they have had a package. Federal's goal is to notice problems even before the customer does —that is, to alert the customer before the expected delivery time that a package will be late by a specified amount of time. In these circumstances, while neither a specific individual nor the customer is personally providing the feedback, information is being collected about how a process is performing.

The IBM field service example mentioned above is a good example of using technology to gather process information in the field. When a service technician is dispatched to fix a piece of hardware the technician will enter diagnostic information about the machine failure into a handheld computer. IBM has set a service goal of fixing hardware problems correctly the first time, but occasionally a service technician will misdiagnose a problem or perform a repair improperly, requiring a follow up service call. The service technician dispatched to handle the follow up will again enter information into the handheld computer. The combined information from the two service calls is used to determine the root cause of the problem. Service staffing policies may need to be reviewed or training programs modified. Like Federal Express, IBM is proactive in its information gathering; the service organization does not wait for a customer complaint before investigating a possible service problem.

Of course, it will not always be possible to collect process information in an automated fashion. Relevance loop information in particular will often not be amenable to such approaches. In fact, it is sometimes difficult for a company even to collect performance information about itself. Hence the rise of industry-wide performance rating programs that compare multiple firms' performance on a specified set of dimensions. The information is compiled either by an industry association or by a third-party firm. These ratings are well established in the automobile, office product, and investment banking industries, and are emerging in many other industries.

Distribution of Process Information

After the information selection process is completed, a firm must decide how and to whom the information will be distributed or communicated. The best information will be wasted if it is not routed to the people in the organization who need it to perform their jobs. Consider the example in another personal computer manufacturer we studied. Customer product complaints were taken by the customer service department. One would expect that this information would be relayed to the manufacturing and product design groups. However, since the customer service department reported to marketing, the information was never distributed outside the marketing organization. In another high-tech manufacturer, the information from field service was not even accepted as valid by the engineering and manufacturing organizations. No one trusted anyone else's numbers. It is not surprising that both of these firms are experiencing significant financial difficulties, and neither is noted for quality.

In terms of performance loop information, it is relatively straightforward—albeit sometimes detailed to decide what type of information gets sent where. Those who actually execute a process should have information on their own performance (and its relationship to overall process performance), and enough information on problems to address and resolve causes. At Ritz-Carlton hotels, daily performance information on the 720 processes previously mentioned is collected centrally, but is quickly disseminated out to the workers and process managers who can act on the information. The information is also used for performance evaluation of individual workers. At Ritz-Carlton, and in most of the other firms we studied, it was decided that process owners and managers need only aggregated performance information. At Public Service Electric and Gas, customer satisfaction information is reported in at least thirty-five different ways to geographical, business unit, and functional managers.

Information technology can be a useful tool for distributing performance loop information regardless of the level of the employee to whom process information is distributed. Several firms, including Toyota, General Electric's electrical products division in Salisbury, Maryland, and AT&T Universal Card, employ large computer screens throughout the work area to apprise workers within a process on their current performance. This technique has been called "the visual factory" (Grief, 1991). Each of these firms cites this frequently updated information as critical to achieving and maintaining high levels of process productivity and quality.

Again, it is relevance loop information that is difficult to distribute. Some managers may get value from conversations, either direct or recorded, with customers; others will profit more from trade publications, conferences, or discussions with managers in competitive organizations. The determination of what information to collect and distribute to assess the relevance of a process to its environment is a creative and idiosyncratic act. Furthermore, structuring and capturing the information so that it may be distributed electronically is notoriously difficult. We found that the best systems for capturing relevance loop information relied on a combination of human references and stored textual information.

At one engineering and construction firm we studied, for example, one division had established a centralized on-line process practices system. Several individuals with quality-oriented responsibilities established the database, and primed it with findings from several quality improvement teams. But when we observed the system it was seldom used; not only was the mainframe-based system slow and difficult to use, but the categories in which the information was stored quickly became obsolete as process definitions evolved. The creators of the database had not budgeted a role for its ongoing maintenance. Furthermore, most employees felt that they had no real incentive to add their process improvement ideas to the database. The contributions were anonymous, which meant they would get no credit for a good idea and no one could call them for more information.

On the other hand, at GM Hughes Electronics, process reengineering best practices were captured in a database that combined human and computerized information. Each entry was submitted to an editor, who screened it for usefulness and relevance. Entries recorded just enough about the practice to pique the reader's interest, and included the name and phone number of a person who could describe it in detail. Use of the database is solid and growing, and some division presidents have instructed that their divisions be well represented in the database.

For senior management, embedding quality information in an executive information system (EIS) can be a useful distribution mechanism, though updating need not be as frequent as for process workers. An EIS can effectively illustrate trends and may allow the user to "drill down" for more detailed information, assuming a hierarchy of process information has been established and collected. We found only limited use of EIS for displaying process information in our research. However, Xerox, for example, has long had an executive information system, but only recently has it added a significant amount of information on operational processes and customer satisfaction to the system.

While incorporating process information into an EIS is valuable where EIS use is already established, it is a more common problem for firms to ensure that process performance information is embedded in whatever ongoing reporting structures exist within a firm. The integration of quality measures in Ritz-Carlton's business management system, for example, was cited as a key step in its progress toward the 1992 Baldrige award.

Analysis and Use of Process Information

In order for process information to be of any value, it must be systematically analyzed and interpreted, and acted upon. Certainly this is more likely to happen if information is effectively identified, collected, and distributed—but these are not enough. There must be a context for the management of process performance information—in other words, a management process.

This context may take multiple forms, including meetings, performance assessment systems or goals, or specific behavior change programs. At American Airlines, for example, operational process information is monitored weekly at a Monday planning meeting. The planning meeting has generated a demand for many new measures of quality, which are supplied by the firm's Quality Service Tracking and Reporting function. At Dell Computer, there is a "customer advocacy" meeting every Friday at 7:30 a.m. for review of customer-facing process performance. This regular meeting has also led to the collection of the customer service measures described above. Federal Express has a management meeting every morning to assess the previous day's package delivery service quality levels, and the same data are also used by Quality Action Teams to address the root causes of problems in the parcel delivery process. At AT&T Universal Card, measures of process performance are embedded in individual performance measures; workers can earn daily bonuses based on the quality and productivity of their work. All of these contexts for the use of process information have led to additional demands for new information; therefore, the "end" of the process is driving the early steps in these instances.

A key emphasis of AT&T Transmission Systems is to analyze the relationship between performance loop and relevance loop information. Specifically, customer needs and satisfaction are frequently related to process performance through focus groups, discussions with frontline employees, and analysis of complaints. In addition, statistical correlations between internal performance metrics and expressed customer needs are established. Managers at Transmission Systems summarize the need for both performance loop and relevance loop information by quoting an FAA official investigating a crash: "No matter how good a pilot's instruments are, sometimes he needs to look out the window" (Kordupleski, 1993).

The importance of a double-loop approach to product manufacturing or service delivery is shown by the example of Singapore International Airlines (Garvin, 1987). The airline, renowned for its attention and commitment to quality, began to experience a drop in market share. Concerned about the trend, management looked closely at whether the company was still performing at the desired level of quality. A review of the information the company collected on quality was at odds with the market share decline; measured service quality was at its normally high level. The problem was that the airline was not measuring what was important to the customer. It was not until the company began to solicit relatively unstructured feedback from customers that it found out that quality, as defined by the customer, was indeed slipping. In this example, single-loop learning failed to suffice. It was the relevance loop, the mechanism by which the right type of performance information was identified, that enabled the company to fix the process.

The likelihood of substantial performance improvement in processes is significantly enhanced if firms create clear and widely disseminated performance goals. Clarity about goals motivates all participants to continually monitor performance and to seek improvement opportunities. At Pacific Bell, for example, the senior management team established a set of "bold goals," about half of which are process-oriented, which appear throughout the organization. Hewlett Packard created a similar goal for the order management process; it has attempted to achieve tenfold reductions over the past five years in order time, cost, and defects. HP's goals are created in the context of a "hoshin kanri" or policy deployment program, in which all levels of HP employees are expected to have goals that help to achieve their business unit's or the firm's goals. At Analog Devices, quality goals were summarized with the concept of "half-life," a period of time over which the defect rate of a process drops by 50 percent (Kaplan, 1990; Schneiderman, 1988). These types of goals provide a context in which individual process measures can be interpreted, and also stimulate managers to try to achieve them.

The importance of reviewing and using process information can also be emphasized through specific initiatives or programs. Several Baldrige-winning firms (and many that have not won the award) have established internal quality programs that follow the Baldrige model. The AT&T managers we interviewed view this as the primary context for collecting, analyzing, and acting upon process and quality information. At Union Pacific, managers cited the firm's quality program as the single most important factor driving managerial use of information.

One key prerequisite for the effective use of process information is a model, either implicit or explicit, that relates changes in process measures to each other and to other measures of business success. Such a model might suggest, for example, that improvements in the order management process will lead both to higher customer satisfaction and to less aged receivables, and that increased customer satisfaction will increase both retention and the average sale per customer. Unless this sort of understanding is present, how can investment and improvement in the order management process be justified? Furthermore, models must be ongoing and dynamic, so that movements in one variable over time can be related to movements of other variables. A model built to cost-justify a one-time investment, for example, is much less useful.

Managerial models have been advocated for many years (Eccles and Pyburn,

Table 3: Summary of Leading Practices

Identification	Collection	Distribution	Analysis and use
Filter or aggregate measures	Sampling of customer satisfaction	Dissemination to those who can act	Meetings devoted to process information
Address relevance loop information	Automated collection of information	Visual display in work sites	Use in performance measures
Sufficient detail for root cause	Use of workflow software	Human intervention for relevance loop	Relating performance and relevance loops
	Embedding reporting in a product	Executive information systems	Clear process performance goals
	Industry-wide performance reporting		Models of business performance

1992; Forrester, 1961). However, few managers have developed models that are rigorous and explicit enough to be shared across the organization — partially because such models require a common language and a process architecture that is shared around the organization. In our interview sample, only two firms—AT&T Universal Card and a manufacturing firm — felt they had achieved this level of business modeling, and both were continuing to refine and renew their models. Some research on information management in the retail industry suggests that managers need to develop stories that explain relationships between action and result before they really understand information (Goldstein, 1993). Perhaps when managers can create stories about processes and the information about them, process management will be more effective.

The structure defined above as a process for process information management contains many specific leading practices. These are summarized in Table 3.

Effecting Change through Process Information

The effective gathering and distribution of process information will not in itself lead to business change. There are broader antecedents and implications of an increased focus on process information; both must be present for any lasting value or change to be achieved.

The antecedents of focusing on process information are cultural. They include an emphasis on the importance of information, the need for openness and sharing, a long-term orientation to process management, and certain values about the importance of people in process performance. While these seem elemental, we have certainly seen more firms that lack them than possess them. Like all deeply held values, they are established over a long period through day-to-day examples and reactions of management. The depth of a cultural orientation to process information will be tested daily in large organizations in comments like these, all of which we have heard at firms or organizations:

- "We don't use the quality management software because it would make us look bad" (at a medical center).
- "Manufacturing didn't share their defect information with us, so why should we give them our customer satisfaction survey results?" (at a high-tech manufacturer).
- "I am confident in arguing that we are slower than our competitors in new product development, even though I can't prove it" (at a pharmaceutical firm).
- "If we release this information on how much we have improved in order management, our workers will have little incentive to keep improving" (at a leasing company).

Challenges to a process information culture like these must be addressed by everyone, but particularly by senior managers who have the power to reward, ignore, or censure such behaviors. At Xerox, over the past decade the firm's managerial culture has shifted to emphasize management by fact. David Kearns, the former Xerox CEO, set the tone for this shift by frequently asking in senior staff meetings, "What data do you have to support your assertions?" He views "management by fact" as one of the core concepts of quality (Kearns and Nadler, 1992). Kearns played a key role at Xerox in terms of process information; according to Noriaki Kano, a Japanese quality expert, every firm needs executives and managers to assume the role of "Mr. Show-Me-Data" (Kano, 1993).

There are also key implications of enhanced process information. Without adequately addressing issues of organizational power, incentive and reward schemes, and worker participation in process design, even the most meticulously designed processes and information support structures may become dysfunctional.

The collection of process performance information has significant implications for how line workers are managed. Giving line workers access to process information in real time without empowering them to act on it is, at best, wasteful, and, at worst, harmful. Allowing workers to make any and all process changes on the fly, however, is not the answer either. Obviously, a proper balance lies somewhere in between, but it remains a challenge for managers to reconcile effectively these extremes.

There are some interesting examples of innovative approaches to this problem. One approach is to empower employees to make minor process changes without seeking approval, requiring review only for larger changes. To ensure process integrity, periodic process audits could be performed. At Cadillac, for example, factory workers field product feedback telephone calls from new car owners. Based on the information they receive, workers can make minor changes to production techniques. In one instance, workers redesigned a door closing mechanism in response to a customer complaint that the door clanged when shut, without the desirable luxury-car "thud." While an adjustment like this does require modification to the production process, it does not represent wholesale design change. Design change cannot be implemented on the spot; it must be suggested to and approved by production engineers. At the Ritz-Carlton hotels, workers are able to address guest problems or complaints instantaneously with responses costing up to $300.

Incentive and reward schemes play an important role in effective change management. At AT&T Universal Card, customer satisfaction measures are used to measure customer service performance. To achieve proper alignment of desired process behavior and behavior incentives, customer service representatives are paid bonuses based on the attainment of team goals that are an aggregation of customer service performance measures. If workers are to work toward such bonuses and understand how they are achieved, a strong system of process information must be in place.

When process information is combined with appropriate incentive structures, the combination can create improvement in process performance without any explicit redesign effort. At one firm we interviewed, a Baldrige Award winner, the logistics and supply chain management process was selected, along with two other processes, for analysis and improvement. Instead of a typical design and implementation project, the team of worldwide process owners decided to focus on process information and incentives. They created for the first time worldwide visibility of inventory levels across the company. They put managers in charge of the entire supply chain process for large geographical regions, and based much of their compensation on meeting inventory goals. Within a year, inventory levels had declined 30 percent. Other more traditional reengineering projects at the company had barely finished creating a new process vision in that time and had implemented nothing. Better process information, therefore, can be a lever for change in itself.

AT&T Universal Card Case Study

At&T Universal Card Services (UCS), formed in 1990 as a consumer credit subsidiary of AT&T, employs an effective approach to managing process information. Of all the firms in our study, its thought and practice in process information management were the best defined. Like few other businesses, UCS was designed from the beginning around quality and process management concerns. It won the Baldrige Award only two years after its founding. More importantly, it has been very successful in business terms, bypassing 6,000 other issuers of credit cards in the United States to become second ranked in dollars spent by customers, and third in number of cards issued (AT&T Universal Card, 1992).

Much of the UCS measurement system is driven by customer satisfaction. The company identified 8 customer "satisfiers," 18 secondary satisfiers, and over 100 tertiary satisfiers. These satisfiers form the basis for a broad collection of 123 process-oriented measures by which the business is run. Some of the measures also address supplier processes. For key customer inquiry, application, and payment processes, UCS assesses such measures as accuracy, timeliness, and the courtesy of "Associates." Many other measures, such as the rate at which UCS responds to job applicant resumes, are tracked but are not included in the core set of 123.

Each of the 123 measures is collected and analyzed daily, at the individual and organizational level. This is a large number of measures, but most of them are collected not for purposes of aggregation at headquarters, but for use and analysis by those who perform the daily work processes of the company. There are several incentive structures for monitoring and improving process performance. For example, if 98 percent of the daily goals on each internally oriented measure are met by the individual and the organization, each UCS Associate wins a daily cash bonus. The compensation of managers is also tied to process performance results. All of the process performance information is available on-line through a system called U-KNOW. Any UCS employee can determine how his or her team is doing on its daily process performance by pressing a few keys on any workstation in the company. This performance loop information is collected and distributed by the Quality and Information Systems organizations.

In addition to this "performance loop" information, UCS has an extensive program for the gathering of "relevance loop" information. It includes such activities as:
- Customer focus groups,
- Benchmarking;
- Listening to customer calls,
- AT&T operator feedback from customers,
- Customer attrition research.

UCS has created a separate organization for managing relevance loop information. Called "Marketing Development," it scans the external and customer environments to identify needed changes in processes and programs. It also works closely with the providers of performance loop information to determine when changes in that information are necessary.

There is an elaborate structure of management meetings for the analysis of quality and process-oriented information at UCS. Each morning, the heads of customer service and information systems have a meeting to review the previous day's performance. The regular agenda of the senior management "Business Team" includes reviews of quality results, and the team invests a full day each quarter in analyzing and acting on quality results, and discussing new measures. Senior managers review and debate the results from statistical analyses of process and business performance, and attempt to determine the most effective model for managing performance.

Perhaps the only area of process management in which UCS does not lead is in reengineering or radical process innovation. This is understandable given the youth of the company and its processes. UCS has, however, identified the broad, high-level processes on which reengineering would be done, and is constantly evaluating the need for more radical change than that offered by its quality programs.

Summary and Conclusions

In this article we have addressed the management of a type of information that has often gone unnoticed and unmanaged: information about business processes. To study process information, we investigated twenty leading firms whose quality and process orientations had won them acclaim or awards. Despite their leading positions, however, not all of the firms had explicitly identified process information as a focus for management. Even among those that had, there were wide variations in how deeply the concept of process information had permeated through organizational structures, systems, and initiatives.

We have described two different types of process information— performance loop and relevance loop— and have noted that the former is more likely to be the subject of systematic monitoring than the latter. We have also described a set of activities that themselves constitute a process for managing this type of information, and have noted leading practices for each major activity. The overall organizational context in which process information can be effectively applied was discussed. Finally, a case study was presented in which process information was managed in a holistic and thorough manner.

It is perhaps surprising that most firms have no organizational unit for continuously, broadly, and rigorously assessing their operational performance. However, processes appear to be a suitable structure for operational assessment, and the difficulties of managing process information can certainly be overcome. In the future, it is likely that leading firms will manage process information as routinely and expertly as they do financial information. As with financial information, however, there will always be a need for refinement of measures and identification of new management approaches.

Researchers can help guide the use of process information through additional exploration of several possible regions of this problem domain. One possible research direction might be to assess the relationship of process information management to actual process performance, rather than to success on a broad quality assessment such as the Baldrige. Researchers could also examine the relative importance of process information management compared to other means of achieving a process-oriented organization— for example, adopting a process-based organizational structure. It is likely that a series of research topics will emerge from rigorous observation of how firms use information to monitor and adjust their business processes that is, once such use becomes widespread and institutionalized.

In fact, until process management itself is more fully understood and practiced, much of the thought devoted to subjects like process information will be, of necessity, speculative. Despite some urging to the contrary (Tomasko, 1993), there are still no firms that have deeply embedded the management of business processes into the day-to-day fabric of their organizations. When these firms begin to emerge, we are confident that the management of process information will be an important piece of this evolving management framework.

Appendix: Structured Interview Questions

1. Has your company identified the management of information about quality or process performance as a key factor in your operational improvement programs?
2. Do you collect performance information about processes? On what other units (e.g., products, functions) is information collected from a quality management standpoint?
3. Which of the following types of information do you collect relative to processes?
   - output quality (if so, what dimensions?)
   - cycle time
   - cost
   - customer satisfaction
   - employee satisfaction
   - flexibility
   - innovation
   - others?
4. Is there consensus within your organization on what the key processes are? If so, how many levels of processes are there? If not, does this lead to problems in assessing process performance?
5. How integrated are your measures of process performance with measures of financial and market performance?
6. How integrated are measures of process performance with ongoing management systems, such as planning and individual performance assessment?
7. How well do most managers in your organization understand the relationships between process indicators and other indicators of performance (e.g., market share, revenues, customer retention, etc.)?
8. About which types of processes (e.g., manufacturing, order fulfillment, new product development) do you have the best performance information? The worst?
9. How does your firm collect information on process performance? Do you use ad hoc studies or more institutionalized and ongoing measures?
10. Has your firm built a computer-based information system to assess process performance? If so, what types of systems are used for what processes?

11. Do all of your processes have owners? If so, is their performance assessed on the basis of process performance information? If not, is the absence of ownership a barrier to have better process performance information?

12. What specific steps have you followed to establish measures of process performance?

13. Does your established process performance information include external comparisons or benchmarks? If so, how do you collect this information on an ongoing basis?

14. How do you determine who receives process performance information? In general, what type of information do workers within the process receive? Managers of the process?

15. How is process performance information generally distributed (electronically, paper, word of mouth, etc.)?

16. Do you have programs or initiatives in place to help employees make better use of process performance information?

17. Are there other issues around process information at your firm that we have not addressed?

References

AT&T Universal Card. (1992). *Application summary, Malcolm Baldrige National Quality Award.*

Argyris, C., and Schön, D. (1978). *Organizational Learning. A Theory of Action Research.* Reading, MA: Addison-Wesley.

Caldwell, B. (1992). Quality winners credit IT. *Information Week* (October 19), 15.

Computer Sciences Corporation (1994). *The state of reengineering report: North America and Europe.*

Davenport, T.H. (1993). *Process Innovation.* Boston: Harvard Business School Press.

Davenport, T.H. (1994). The new world of process management. *Public Productivity and Management Review* (Fall).

Davenport, T.H., and Nohria, N. (1994). Case management and the integration of labor. *Sloan Management Review, 35(2),* 11-23.

Davenport, T. H., and Short, J. E. (1990). The new industrial engineering: information technology and business process redesign. *Sloan Management Review, 31(4)*, 11—27.

Davenport, T.H., and Stoddard, D.B.(1994). Reengineering: business change of mythic proportions? *MIS Quarterly* (June), 121-127.

Deming, W.E. *Some Theory of Sampling.* New York: Wiley, 1950.

Deming, W.E. (1986). *Out of the Crisis.* Cambridge, MA: MIT Center for Advanced Engineering Study.

Easton, G.S. (1993). The 1993 state of U.S. total quality management: a Baldrige examiner's perspective. *California Management Review, 35(3),* 32-54.

Eccles, R.J. (1991). The performance measurement manifesto. *Harvard Business Review, 69(1)*, 131—137.

Eccles, R.J., and Pybum, P.1. (1992). Creating a comprehensive system to measure performance: financial results should not generate the most rewards. *Management Accounting* (October),41-44.

Eisenhart. K.M. (1989). Building theories from case study research. *Academy of Management Review,* 14(4), 532-550.

Forrester, J.W.(1961). *Industrial Dynamics.* Cambridge, MA: MIT Press,.

Garvin, D.A.(1987). *Managing Quality.* New York: Free Press,.

Gilbreth, L.M. (1931). Motion study. In W.J. Donald (ed.), *Handbook of Business Administra-*

tion. New York: McGraw-Hill, 628-643.

Goldralt, E.M.(1990). *The Haystack Syndrome: Sifting Information Out of the Data Ocean.* Croton-on-Hudson, NY: North River Press.

Goldstein, D.K.(1993). Computer-based data and organizational learning: the importance of managers' stories. *Organizational Computing, 3(4)*, 417-442.

Greif, M.(1991). *The Visual Factory.* Cambridge, MA: Productivity Press.

Hammer, M. (1990). Reengineering work: don't automate, obliterate. *Harvard Business Review, 68(4)*, 104-112.

Harrington, H.J. (1991). *Business Process Improvement.* New York: McGraw-Hill.

Housel, T.J.; Bell, A.H.; and Kanevsky, V. (1994). Calculating the value of reengineering at Pacific Bell. *Planning Review*, 40-55.

Huber, G. P., and Power, D.J. (1985). Retrospective reports of strategic level managers: guidelines for increasing their accuracy. *Strategic Management Journal, 6* , 171-180.

Johnson, H.T.(1992). *Relevance Regained.* New York: Free Press,.

Johnson, H.T., and Kaplan, R.S.(1987). *Relevance Lost.' The Rise and Fall of Management Accounting.* Boston: Harvard Business School Press.

Juran, J.M.(1974). *Quality Control Handbook.* New York: Macmillan.

Kano, N. (1993). A perspective on quality activities in American firms. *California Management Review, 35(3)*, 12-31.

Kaplan, R.S. (1990). Analog devices: the half-life system. Harvard Business School Case Study case number 9-190-061.

Kaplan, R.S., and Norton, D.P.(1992). The balanced scorecard—measures that drive performance. *Harvard Business Review, 70(*1), 71-79.

Kearns, D.T., and Nadler, D.A (1992). . *Prophets in the Dark.* New York: Harper Business.

Kiley, T. (1991). The qualitative difference. *CIO* (August), 20-24

Kordupleski, R.E., et al. (1993). Why improving quality doesn't improve quality (or whatever happened to marketing). *California Management Review, 35(*3), 82-95.

Kotter, J.P. (1982). *The General Managers.* New York: Free Press, 1982.

Kumar. A., and Sharman. G.(1992). We love your product, but where is it? *Sloan Management Review. 33(2)*, 93-99.

McKinnon, S.M., and Bruns, W.J.(1992). *The Information Mosaic.* Boston: Harvard Business School Press.

National Institute of Standards and Technology (1993). *Malcolm Baldrige Award Criteria.* Washington, DC.

Nonaka, I. (1991). The knowledge-creating company. *Harvard Business Review* (November-December), 96-104.

Robson, G.D.(1991). *Continuous Process Improvement.* New York: Free Press.

Schneiderman, A.(1988). Setting quality goals. *Quality Progress* (April), 51-57.

Schonberger, R.J.(1990). *Building a Chain of Customers.* New York: Free Press.

Shewhart, W.A.(1931). *Economic Control of Quality of Manufactured Product.* New York: Van Nostrand.

Soin, S.S.(1992). *Total Quality Control Essentials.* New York: McGraw-Hill.

Taylor, F.W. (1911). *Principles of Scientific Management* New York: Harper and Row.

Taylor, R.S.(1986). *Value-Added Processes in Information Systems.* Norwood, N.J.: Ablex.

Tomasko, R.M.(1993). *Rethinking the Corporation.* New York: AMACOM, 1993.

Walsh, F.J. (1989). Current practices in measuring quality. The Conference Board.

Walsh, J.P., and Ungson, G.R..(1991). Organizational memory. *Academy of Management Review, 1*, 57-91.

Zeithaml, V.A.; Parasurman, A.; and Berry, L.L. (1990). *Delivering Quality Service.* New York: Free Press.

Zuboff, S.(1988). *In the Age of the Smart Machine.* New York: Basic Books.

Source: Reprinted by special permission of the Journal of Management Information Systems, Summer 1995, Vol. 12, No. 1, pg. 57-80.

CHAPTER 10

The New Waves of Business Process Redesign and IT in Demand/Supply Chain Management: Hard Choices for Senior Managers

Donald A. Marchand

International Institute for Management Development, Switzerland

Are you betting your company's demand/supply chain on business process redesign (BPR) and information technology (IT) again? The short answer for most large, international manufacturing and service companies today is a resounding "Yes!" The threat of the Year 2000 is pushing many companies to replace their legacy systems supporting their demand/supply chains. Enterprise systems or "ERP"–Enterprise Resource Planning—promise seamless integration of a company's information flows from financial and human resource administration, to order fulfillment, inventory management, logistics, and even customer information. The transition to a single EURO currency in Europe over the next few years is also motivating companies. Finally, the rapid evolution of Internet, Intranet and Extranet applications for business to business and business to consumer electronic commerce is driving firms towards BPR and ERP. In short, the rush to BPR and ERP is again red hot for large North American and European companies.

What is interesting about this new wave of enthusiasm for BPR and IT is that it comes just a few years after the disillusionment with "reengineering" associated with restructuring and cost cutting in many of the same large companies. The new themes for BPR and ERP today are growth, product innovation and customer focus – very different from the downsizing and cost cutting that distinguished "reengineering" efforts.

So why should senior managers be concerned about the evolution of this new wave of BPR and IT? First off, most senior managers of large international manufacturing and service companies seem to be positive about these changes and new challenges. Those in manufacturing, from food, retailing, chemicals to concrete, and services, including banking, insurance and asset management, talk openly about growth, innovation and customer focus.

These same managers have or will soon invest millions of dollars, francs and euro's on enterprise systems from SAP, Baan, PeopleSoft and many other vendors of ERP software. Moreover, many managers are aware of and supportive of pilot projects and implementations of Internet, Intranets and Extranets (business to business use of Internet technologies) inside and outside their company's with suppliers, distributors and customers. An essential challenge of the digital economy, however, is how to integrate electronic commerce with established ways of doing business. At the same time, many senior managers will privately admit that they are concerned about the new business and IT forces converging on BPR and ERP for three key reasons.

Past Performance Is NOT an Indicator of Future Success

First, in firms of these senior managers, the picture of past performance of "reengineering" and IT projects is not pretty! In 1994, the Standish Group in Boston estimated that in the US, large companies spent over $250 billion each year on IT application development covering an estimated 175,000 projects (The Standish Group). The Standish Group noted that on average only 16.2% of software projects are completed on time and on budget. Thirty-one point two percent of IT projects will be canceled before they are completed and 52.7% will be "challenged"—eventually implemented over-budget, over time estimated and with fewer functions and features than planned.

A 1996 study (Clegg, 1996) sponsored by the Economic and Social Research Council in the UK of over 14,000 business and not for profit organizations found that "80-90% of IT investments do not meet their performance objectives". Plus, "around 80% of new (IT) systems are delivered late and over budget", while 40% of new system projects fail or are abandoned.

In addition, even Michael Hammer and Jim Champy, the gurus of the "reengineering " movement, have admitted that 80% of "reengineering" projects in large companies have failed (White, 1996). Why? Because of lack of senior manager leadership and poor change management.

In short, senior managers have good reasons to worry that their stellar BPR and IT records do not guarantee business success.

The Price of BPR and ERP May Be Too High

The second reason for concern among senior managers of leading manufacturing and service companies is the high costs of the new breed of BPR and IT projects, especially ERP implementation, that have reached the "jumbo jet" stage of capital investments. Many CEO's and senior managers of European manufacturing companies are spending $100 to $350 million on European-wide implementations of ERP systems. American counterparts report similar large project numbers. Global companies moving into ERP projects worldwide are spending over $500 million to well over $1 billion to implement ERP on a local, regional or global basis over a period of 4 – 5 years. Even small to medium-size companies are allocating millions of dollars to ERP systems. Such large direct expenditures for enterprise systems eat up working capital and available cash flow at astounding rates. Worse yet, these investments may jeopardize future shareholder value and economic value added (EVA) models. This is not only because of the large initial investments in such projects, but also because of on-going carrying costs of maintaining these complex systems into the foreseeable future.

Contrast these concerns with the "promise" of ERP in demand/supply chain management in various industries such as retailing, auto manufacturing, insurance and banking. Claims of tens to hundreds of millions of dollars in cost savings (avoidances) are being touted by the IT industry press and consultants with ERP systems and Extranets – business to business use of Internet technologies. Many "studies" from professional service and research firms are claiming huge potential for large cost savings on a per firm or per industry basis such as (Dobbs, 1998):

- A 1997 study of 225 large manufacturers has shown that a good supply chain can save a $600 million company as much as $42 million annually.
- An analysis of consumer goods inventories in the US found that $715 billion worth of product sits idle in US inventories at various points along the supply chain. Better coordinated forecasting of demand among retailers and manufacturers could lead to a 25% reduction in inventories.

So what should senior managers believe? In the previous era of reengineering and IT projects, senior managers aimed at internal cost savings and head count reduction. In the new era of BPR and ERP in demand/supply chain management, senior managers have justified projects based on better asset management, improved customer service, lower working capital costs for inventory, and streamlining processes with partners and suppliers. If companies realize these new benefits, they may improve their competitive positions. Yet, if these new benefits fail to materialize, companies will be doubly disadvantaged. First, for spending so much money on BPR and ERP, they will incur on-going high costs of ownership. Second, tying up working capital with little or no direct impact on economic value added or shareholder value will bring high opportunity costs.

Mortgaging Future Strategic Choices to Current Commitments

The third reason why senior executives worry about the current wave of BPR and ERP projects is that today's commitments to such large-scale, enterprise-wide projects may limit tomorrow's business flexibility. The good news for some companies is that their success with implementing BPR and IT projects for demand/supply chain management may give them competitive advantage in two ways. If they can replace their legacy systems in advance of the year 2000, they may have a 1-2 year advantage over slower competitors who will be preoccupied with the Y2K problem well after the date change. Second, if they successfully implement ERP in their demand/supply chain AND make their businesses more customer responsive, cheaper to operate, and faster to market, they may also have an advantage over competitors who have been slower to implement ERP systems across their demand/supply chains.

Despite these possible advantages, executives have good reason to worry. Today's huge investments and long lead times for ERP systems to operate factories, streamline distribution and manage costs may not help them compete when priorities for BPR and IT projects shift from the supply to the demand side of the company's value chain. Take the example of a new CEO of a large food company. He faces restricted strategic options in moving his firm from a product focus to customer focus because his predecessor committed the firm to a 5 year contract to implement ERP systems in the company's 600 factories worldwide. The new CEO would prefer to spend some of the committed money on more customer oriented systems, such as customer account management and product design, but until the ERP contract expires and the factory systems are in place, he cannot. In a business world of radical change and unexpected mergers and acquisitions, CEO's are becoming more hesitant to commit large amounts of working capital and time to multiyear projects that mortgage future business choices to current business commitments.

How Should Senior Managers Evaluate BPR and IT Projects in Demand/Supply Chains?

To achieve the benefits of their commitments and reduce the risks associated with BPR and IT projects simultaneously, senior managers must address six key issues related to implementing demand/supply chains using BPR and IT. Of course a company should address the six issues before it embarks on new BPR and IT projects. Even as BPR and IT projects evolve, managers should also keep these concerns in mind, in order to steer and evaluate their alignment with changes in business priorities and time frames.

What Approach To Demand/Supply Chain Management Is Your Company Implementing?

If the mind-sets of senior managers shape company strategies, project initiatives and investment priorities, then *their* views of how their company approaches demand/supply chain management are critical to appropriately targeting process redesign efforts and IT projects. This is more than a semantic concern. As Figure 1 suggests, there is no one view of demand or supply chain management in manufacturing and service companies today. Over the last ten years, there have been several phases of supply chain and demand chain management. Manufacturing companies have implemented these phases differently than service companies.

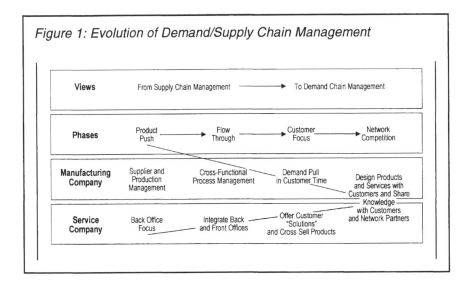

Figure 1: Evolution of Demand/Supply Chain Management

In manufacturing companies, supply and, more recently, demand chain management has evolved through four major phases. In the mid 1980s, most large manufacturing companies were focused on implementing Manufacturing Resource Planning (MRP II) systems (Vollmann, 1992) which were intended to rationalize sales forecasting with production planning and control in large companies. The first generation of such systems—called Material Requirements Planning or MRP I—focused on the process of forecasting demand, developing a Master Production Schedule, detailed manufacturing capacity plans, and material requirements plans for purchasing so that production in factories could be accomplished. The second generation called Manufacturing Resource Planning or MRP II took advantage of developments in database management systems and faster, more powerful computers, and sought to integrate sales and forecasting, production planning, inventory control and purchasing activities. During this phase, supply chain management was internally focused and product oriented.

During the late 1980s and early 1990s, manufacturing companies started looking at the entire supply chain, from external suppliers through manufacturing, distribution, marketing and sales as one continuous process, or "flow through." The main concern was making the cross-functional flows of products down the supply chain and sales and marketing forecasts up the supply chain as seamless as possible. This required a new generation of BPR and IT projects aimed at managing information in real-time across functional departments that, in the first phase, operated independently in most firms. During this third phase, manufacturing companies began to implement the first ERP systems such as SAP's R/2 System that centralized information across the supply chain in large databases used by all the functions. Typically, in large companies, these IT projects required 5-7 years to implement due to the extensive reengineering required in supply chain processes and information management and to the complexity of the databases and software being used.

In the mid 1990s, a significantly different view of "supply" chain management evolved as manufacturing companies moved from a "product push" to a "customer pull" view of the value chain –hence, the change from "supply" to "demand" chain management. Senior managers began focusing on the growing need to respond to customer orders and sales in real-time, and to speed up order fulfillment and lower inventory costs along the whole supply chain. A new generation of software applications focused on integrating sales and order fulfillment, with distribution and logistics, inventory management, production planning and control, and supplier management. The intent was clear: customize products to better meet customer needs, speed up order fulfillment, and reduce inventory and working capital needs. This phase also coincided with a growing popularity of ERP vendors such as SAP, Baan, PeopleSoft, QED, J.D. Edwards, and Oracle. These vendors provided application "packages" and integrated relational databases to automate the major administrative and operational functions running the demand/supply chain of a company.

Two developments have driven the fourth and most recent phase of demand chain management. First, most manufacturers today recognize that companies do not operate their supply chain in isolation, but depend on networks of suppliers, distributors and partners for operations such as logistics and transport. Thus, manufacturing companies compete as members of a network of interdependent companies against other networks of similarly organized firms (Poirier, 1996). Thus, the term "network competition" has evolved to capture this facet of demand chain management.

The second development has been primarily due to the rise of the Internet in business to business electronic commerce and, in particular, the use of Internet technology to link networks of interdependent firms together to serve customers. GE was one of the first firms to develop this capability in 1995 and 1996 through its "trade processing network" which linked thousands of suppliers to its Lighting Division on-line for purchasing high volume, lower costs products. In the IT industry, GE ignited a subindustry of Extranet software application providers whose products can be used to share information from customers throughout networks of firms acting together to fulfill customer needs for products and services. In its most developed form, supply or demand chain management is being replaced with "the integrated value chain" or "integrated value network" that is defined by one IT consultancy (Dobbs, 1998) as:

"...a process by which multiple enterprises within a shared market channel collaboratively plan, implement and electronically as well as physically, manage the flow of goods, services and information...along the entire value chain, from point of origin to point of consumption...in a manner that increases customer perceived value and optimizes the efficiency of the chain...creating competitive advantage for all stakeholders in the value chain".

Thus, network-based competition using Internet based technology becomes an additional view of how companies can execute demand or supply management. Interestingly, it is not clear how ERP will evolve in this most recent phase. Will companies operating in networks still need highly integrated systems within their firms? Alternately, will ERP evolve to integrate the information and product and service flows of these multiple company networks using Internet technology?

Similarly, over the last ten years, the evolution of demand/supply chain management in service companies (banks and insurance companies, for example) has moved from automating back office functions (check clearance, payment processing and policy administration) to front office automation which supports services to customers (or through agents). In addition, as service companies focus on responding to customer demands and on cross selling banking, insurance and other financial products at the point of sale, the need for integrating product information with services delivered to customers requires integrated databases and ERP-like systems. Finally, the use of Internet technology to interact directly with customers, agents and fund managers has also led to network-based competition in service companies. Each view of supply or demand chain management for service companies has required different BPR and IT projects aimed at the changing strategic priorities of service firms in various industries.

Not surprisingly, the views of senior managers concerning supply, demand chain, or integrated value chain management vary a great deal. The evolution of these views and the targeting of appropriate BPR and IT projects in support of these different views requires careful evaluation within companies for three reasons.

First, it is not sufficient for senior managers to be committed to BPR and IT projects in support of demand/supply chain management. Senior managers must develop shared views and clear understandings of what approach to demand/supply chain management their company needs to pursue for competitive advantage. Many senior managers are committing their companies to BPR and IT projects with little or no competitive value.

Second, given the time to implement BPR and IT projects for operating effective demand/supply chains and the associated risks of failure, the choices today must not become constraints or block the choices that will need to be made tomorrow. Will today's ERP or IT projects become tomorrow's "competitive burden" (Warner, 1987)? Will the opportunity costs of implementing such large scale, complex projects grow too high? Will there be "lock in" effects of automating today's way of doing business for the foreseeable future?

And, third, senior managers must avoid the "herding" or "bandwagon" effects that develop around the latest management concepts such as ERP and IT software products to support demand/supply chain management. The complexity of new ERP packages, coupled with the scale and high costs of such IT projects, can lead to a bandwagon effect: "If the leading companies in our industry our doing ERP, we should be as well." "We are committed to ERP over the next five years and so we cannot turn back!" Like the previous wave of "reengineering" for downsizing and cost cutting, we are in the churning white water of the next major wave of change when senior managers regard ERP and Internet technologies as the "answers" to many unclear questions.

What is the Competitive Value for Companies toRedesign and Automate *Similar* Aspects of their Demand/Supply Chains in the *Same* Industry?

Many companies in the same industries choose ERP applications and priorities the way all the other firms in the same industry do. While each of these companies individually claims to be seeking "competitive advantage " with these new BRP and IT projects, they are, nevertheless, investing in and implementing the same generic application priorities in their demand and supply chains. Over the last three years, I have asked hundreds of business executives in IMD executive programs which application priorities they have chosen to implement. The vast majority name financial administration as the lead application, followed by manufacturing, inventory management and distribution. Other executives have also listed human resource applications as well as order fulfillment. Invariably, these managers have claimed to be pursuing competitive advantage in their industries by implementing the same applications as their leading competitors —in roughly the same order!

However, when challenged about the real payoffs from this sequence of application priorities, these managers have acknowledged the apparent inconsistency. First, many claim that the Y2K transition required their companies to start with financial and manufacturing applications. Second, others claim a form of "competitive necessity" in their industries since most of the major companies in the industry are adopting ERP applications in a similar manner and that customers in their industry expect their company to operate this way as well. Third, some managers have admitted that internal debates about which applications would be automated first, focused on financial, manufacturing and other internally oriented priorities, steered their choices.

It is often unclear which options senior managers have considered or have available to them when they try to decide how to target key aspects of the demand/ supply chain that lead to competitive advantage (as opposed to competitive necessity).

Figure 2 provides a framework for assessing the competitive value of redesigning and implementing applications software in support of their demand/supply chain processes. On the vertical access is the return on information that most managers expect from better ERP software and databases, in terms of three types of business competencies (Vollmann, 1996). I define "return on information" as the business value that a company expects to receive through improving the quality, quantity, availability and use for decision making of the information resources in its demand/ supply chain. On the right side of the chart are the competencies that are necessary to operate a business, such as information systems in support of the general ledger, payroll, accounting and financial reporting. Applications in this category are required to run a business, but deliver no direct customer value.

In the middle of the chart are the competencies that are essential to compete, such as order fulfillment, manufacturing management, inventory management and distribution. In this category, customers expect that, to be among the top players in an industry, companies need to have these capabilities. These applications provide some direct customer value not only if a company implements them well and uses them to promote better products and services, but also if they enhance customer value. At best, the top 5 – 10 companies in the industry all receive comparable benefits from these applications. This is why these companies must execute these applications well just to stay in the running in their industry. For example, in the bulk chemicals industry today, all the leading chemical companies have implemented SAP ERP software for financial administration, process control, distribution and logistics. Managers in the chemicals industry believe that such systems are essential to control costs and manage information across the supply chain for on time

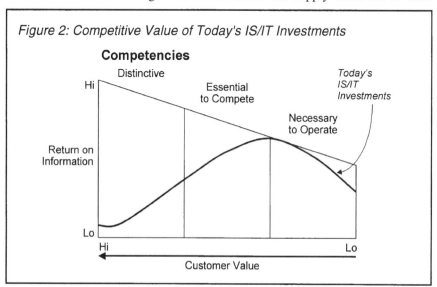

Figure 2: Competitive Value of Today's IS/IT Investments

deliveries, and that industrial customers expect their suppliers to operate this way.

On the left side of the chart are the business competencies that can lead a company to be distinctive in providing customer value with information. In this category, managers mention information systems for customer profiling, product innovation, customer service and accounts management. Individual companies believe that these applications provide the highest return on information use since the information leads directly to higher perceived customer value.

On the question of where they allocate their IS/IT investments today, most managers reply that they invest in applications that are "necessary to operate" and "essential to compete". Rarely do managers point out that significant portions of their current IS/IT investments are focused on applications that provide them distinctive competencies with customers. The increasing slope of "Today's IS/IT Investments" in Figure 2 occurs for two reasons. First, companies are investing much more money as noted earlier in ERP systems than they did in earlier years. Second, the cost for implementing complex BPR and IS/IT projects are increasing as well.

Yet on the question of where they would like to allocate their IS/IT investments in the future, most managers reply that they would like to spend more resources on information applications that make their companies distinctive in creating value with customers (refer to Figure 3). Thus, it appears that, in many industries today, managers recognize that opportunities to compete with information along the demand/supply chain exist, but most seem to perceive that their investments in ERP provide little or no distinctive advantage with customers. Thus, opportunities exist for firms to employ their IS/IT resources in "zones" of information based competition. They can lower the costs of installing and operating applications that are essential to compete and necessary to operate. Alternately, they can allocate IS/IT resources to applications that provide distinctive business competencies to use information to create customer value. Or they can do both.

To compete in these "zones" of information based competition, managers have three options. They can reallocate their existing IS/IT budgets to spend less on the

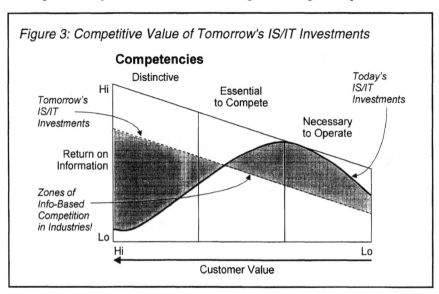

Figure 3: Competitive Value of Tomorrow's IS/IT Investments

"necessary to operate" and "essential to compete" and more on distinctive competencies with information. Second, managers can allocate a larger proportion of new monies to the distinctive competencies that they must build. Third, they can improve the relative distribution of IS/IT investments in order to spend incrementally more on distinctive competencies while reducing overall spending in the other two categories. In contrast to reallocating existing monies in IS/IT, this option looks to future investment decisions.

Regardless of which investment option a company selects, smart firms have a significant opportunity in certain industries to invest over time in applications that provide their customers enhanced value and that differentiate their IS/IT portfolio from other companies in the same industry. Smart firms can also gain a "cumulative" competitive advantage by allocating their future information-based investments across all three types of competencies in the appropriate mix. Rather than following the "bandwagon effect" within their industry with ERP software and databases, managers can seek to allocate IS/IT investments across their application portfolio to achieve the greatest advantage while acknowledging the need for applications that are essential to compete and necessary to operate.

Should the software for operating a company's demand/supply chain be bought and configured as a "package" or custom built/acquired?

The third issue related to BPR and IT projects in demand/supply chain management concerns the decisions that senior managers make to purchase packages and configure them to business processes, or to custom build/acquire application systems that their competitors may not have. For many senior managers, the decision appears straightforward. Given the history of IS/IT project failures and delays in their companies or industries, most managers would rather buy packages from ERP vendors rather than build them internally or outsource development to an IS/IT consultant. Indeed, one clear barometer of this trend is the double-digit growth rates experienced by companies such as SAP, PeopleSoft, and Baan, which provide application packages to manufacturing and service companies in diverse industries. Therefore, at a glance, the issue appears to be resolved: most companies should buy and install packages most of the time!

However, as with most situations, the reality is more interesting than it first appears. To address BPR and IS/IT projects in demand/supply chain today, managers have at least three options.

The first option is to outsource key processes in the demand/supply chain to partner companies who can manage the processes and the underlying information systems and technology more effectively than the company can do for itself. For example, as manufacturing companies have implemented just-in-time supplier delivery and just-in-time customer order fulfillment, they have increasingly outsourced their logistics and transport management to companies whose core competence supports these activities. Similarly, other companies such as leading clothes manufacturers and computer manufacturers have outsourced manufacturing functions to companies whose key competencies are managing these functions and the supporting IS/IT capabilities better than they can. In services industries, companies have used mergers and acquisitions to acquire the IS/IT competencies of their competitors (and divest those internal functions that have under-performed). In each of these cases, senior managers have evaluated which competencies should be retained internally and which could be developed externally using the distinctive competencies of other companies. Decisions related to acquiring ERP software for demand/supply chain management are based on the IS/IT competencies required to support key processes and the IS/IT competencies available externally in the industry.

On the other hand, the same companies can also choose the second option: to tap the packages in support of demand/supply chain processes where managing these processes in-house is considered essential to compete. With this option, managers can choose to acquire the "best of breed" packages for demand/supply chain management from diverse IS/IT suppliers or purchase "integrated packages" from one supplier. To purchase "best of breed", companies must have the IS/IT capabilities to interface diverse packages and software from the vendors they believe offer the best application package that fits their needs. For the "integrated packages", the company relies on one supplier, sacrificing dependence to gain the advantage of the integration of software and data which is only possible from the same supplier.

The third option is, of course, to custom build or acquire software where the managers decide either that the application is so unique that it requires custom development, or when managers believe that the uniqueness of the application provides distinctive advantage in the marketplace. Most companies no longer accept the rationale of building application software in house just because the IS/IT function can do so, for two reasons. First, most in-house IS/IT staffs today are focusing on maintaining systems and preparing systems for the Y2K transition, with little or no time for new development projects. Second, with company histories of failed projects and under-performance fresh in their minds, senior managers may distrust the perceived capabilities of in house IS/IT departments to deliver software systems on time and in budget with the functionality. Thus, senior managers must examine carefully the reasons application software should be custom built or acquired.

When senior managers have decided to retain control of the demand/supply

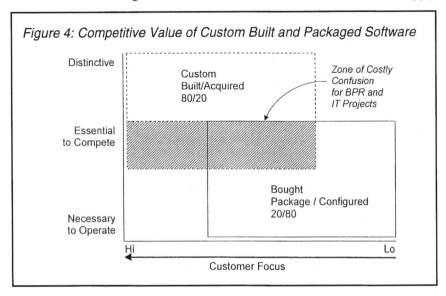

Figure 4: Competitive Value of Custom Built and Packaged Software

chain processes inside their company, Figure 4 provides a framework for considering the options: acquiring packages or custom building application systems for demand/supply chain management.

Managers should seek to employ packages in all administrative and demand/supply chain processes which are necessary to operate and add little or no customer value. In this case, some companies choose to use a version of the 80/20 rule. They adapt business processes to the functionality of the package so that 80-90% can be standardized on the software and only 10% configured to the unique needs of the business. Here managers seek to avoid doing BPR projects where customized software will be required and thus seek to reduce both the overall costs and time of implementing packages where most of the functionality adds little or no direct value to the business (Davenport, 1998).

Where the applications software *can* support processes and information uses that provide distinctive competencies that generate high customer perceived value, senior managers should look to custom building these applications, or contract for their development on a proprietary basis. In companies where key customer-facing processes create unique customer value, there is a real risk of adopting packages to these processes and losing their distinctive advantage. In these cases, companies may be better off custom building these applications and databases rather than standardizing processes, data and software on common industry packages.

In the center of these two options is the most difficult decision area that I call the "zone of costly confusion for BPR and IT projects". In this decision zone, companies try to purchase packages and customize them extensively to the unique requirements of redesigned processes. Or they decide to custom build an application that they need to compete, but that provides no distinctive competencies in their industry. In both cases, managers risk substantial time and resources undertaking complex BPR and IS/IT projects which may be essential to competing, but which offer no competitive advantage and perhaps, if not implemented, a competitive disadvantage.

The trouble arises in these cases from two sides. For companies looking to implement ERP software packages, the problem involves excessively tailoring packaged software to the unique configuration of company processes—either existing or redesigned—with little or no competitive advantage in the industry. From the packaged software supplier side, the problem lies in the temptation to promote excessive tailoring of packaged software to generate implementation revenue for themselves or systems integrators. In either case, when these two difficulties converge, the results are costly, lengthy and complex BPR and IS/IT projects with very low probabilities for success. In effect, senior managers need to be clear about why they want to standardize applications that are essential to compete, in order to avoid costly customization since little or no competitive advantage comes from such projects. Without implementation discipline and clear purpose, companies that adopt packages and begin customizing them in multi year projects lose any advantages that might accrue to standardization, lower implementation costs, and shorter time to achieve expected results.

What is the Appropriate "Time to Implement" BPR and IT Projects?

I have used the term "time-to-implement" as an indicator of how long a BPR or IT project takes to move from the point of initial planning through its first phase of roll-out in the company. There are two sets of trade-offs associated with the time required to implement BPR and IT projects in demand/supply chain management. The first set involves the scope of each project in terms of complexity and scale versus the number of sites in the company where the project must be implemented. The second set of options focuses on the intensity of industry competition and how much time is available to a company to achieve the anticipated business results from such projects relative to its competitors in its industry.

There are no hard and fast rules for judging the time-to-implement for BPR and IT projects, but we can use the following time frames as guidelines:

- short-term   6 months-2 years
- medium-term   3-4 years
- long-term   5-7 years.

Managers must first address the anticipated scope and complexity of the BPR and IT projects for the company. In most companies, managers who wish to implement an integrated database across several functions in the supply chain, such as financial management, inventory management and manufacturing planning and control, are undertaking a project of higher complexity than, for example implementing any one function on its own, such as financial management. The first project requires considerable cross-functional cooperation and coordination, but also, agreement on data definitions and software functionality that the second project may not. Projects that require considerable BPR work in advance of- or concurrent with the implementation of new software generally require more time to implement than projects where BPR is kept to a minimum for the sake of introducing the software more quickly. Thus, within the desired scope of BPR and IT projects, there are many trade-offs that require careful attention to the relationship between time-to-implement and the scope of the projects. Managers, generally, choose to implement projects on a modular basis rather than to go for "grand, complex" designs. However, the scope of what appears to be a moderately complex project may grow as companies seek to customize software packages to their processes instead of adapting their processes to standard software packages.

The second issue companies need to address is the number of locations or sites where the same software will need to be implemented within a company on a geographic basis. As Figure 5 suggests, the number of sites where the same project must be implemented, relative to its scope and complexity, will affect the time-to-implement BPR and IT projects. In this case, the variations among companies can be extreme.

For example, a bulk chemical company in Western Europe decided to implement SAP's ERP system on a regional basis rather than on a country-by-country basis. Although the project was complex, the fact that there was only one implementation of the software in the region shortened the time to implement from 5-7 years to 3-4 years. In contrast, an American pharmaceutical firm decided to implement SAP's ERP system in Western Europe on a country-by-country basis. The company estimated that it might take up to 5-7 years to complete the project unless all countries could be persuaded to adopt the same software, databases and process changes in the same way! For global implementation of demand/supply chain ERP software, the

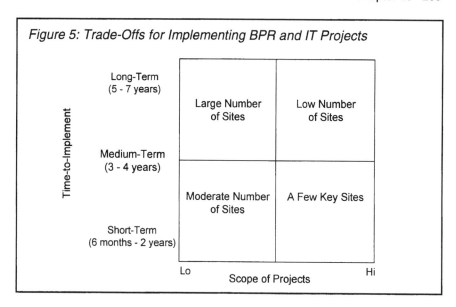

Figure 5: Trade-Offs for Implementing BPR and IT Projects

projects can vary from 5-7 years up to 8-10 years depending on the number of countries, regions or sites involved.

Thus, the trade-offs on time-to-implement, relative to the scope of projects and the number of sites involved, may affect the competitive value of such efforts. For projects that are necessary to compete, managers should aim to reduce the complexity of projects and the number of sites in which projects must be replicated. For example, if company x wants to implement a new payroll system, it may want to implement the system globally or regionally rather than on a country-by-country basis to reduce the time required. Similarly, the same company may want to implement a new distribution and logistics system that is essential to compete. In this case, it should consider putting the system in place on a regional basis to reduce the number of sites where the different project teams are implementing the same software.

The second set of time-to-implement trade-offs is associated with the intensity of competition in specific industries and the time it takes to capture the expected business benefits of BPR and IT projects related to demand/supply chain management. Figure 6 provides a framework for examining the options involved.

In companies facing what D'Aveni calls "moderate competition" (D'Aveni, 1994), managers can concern themselves with projects that improve the efficiency of the supply chain or the integrity of the information. This concern will move them from market forecasting, to production planning and control as well as financial management, inventory management and distribution. BPR and IT projects usually focus on achieving consistent data definitions among supply chain functions and removing unnecessary costs of paper handling, as well as old and inefficient software applications and labor. Firms facing moderate competition have the time to select and implement projects where defining common databases and definitions up front is critical to the level of process redesign and information integration that these firms seek to achieve for standardizing supply chain processes in multiple sites. Rarely, do firms face moderate to low competition seeking to disrupt their industry through BPR and IT projects aimed at supply chain improvements.

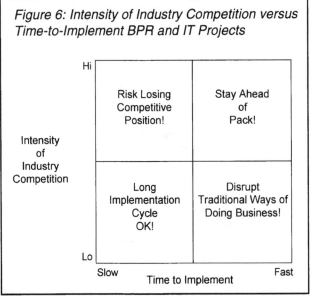

Figure 6: Intensity of Industry Competition versus Time-to-Implement BPR and IT Projects

In companies facing what D'Aveni calls "hyper-competition" (D'Aveni), the intensity and speed of competition requires them to focus on the demand side of the supply chain to create distinctive value with customers. How? Though improved customer information, order fulfillment, and after-sales service. Such companies focus only secondarily on rationalizing those information management processes in manufacturing, inventory management and financial management that are essential to compete or necessary to operate. These companies must look for BPR and IT projects that can be implemented in the short to medium time frames to either stay ahead of the competition or avoid losing their competitive position in their industry. In hyper-competition, managers must focus on BPR and IT projects whose business benefits can be achieved in the shortest time possible since the pace of competition does not permit their firms to implement long term projects whose business benefits may not be captured in time.

Time-to-implement represents a key dimension that senior managers can influence today to improve the competitive value of BPR and IT projects in support of demand/supply chain management. However, the scale of a company's business and its geographic diversity continue to have a significant impact on how companies can reap substantial business benefits from BPR and IT projects aimed at improving demand/supply chain management.

What is the right mix on a local, regional and global basis of business flexibility and standardization in demand/supply chain management?

For many companies today, the challenge of operating demand/supply chains exists on a local, regional and global basis at the same time. In these companies, managers often ask the following question: How can we attain maximum business flexibility to achieve market growth and profitability, while at the same time standardize business practices to lower costs, leverage scarce expertise and use IT to share information across the company about customers, products and market conditions?

Business flexibility is required so that business unit or country managers have the freedom to decide how to tailor products and services and their demand/supply chains to the unique needs of local markets. As long as business unit managers can operate profitably in their BU or country, they decide how their business processes and IS/IT infrastructures are configured and run locally. On the other hand, business standardization reflects the concurrent need to find ways of reducing the working capital consumed in business operations by adopting "common" business processes, IS applications software and IT infrastructure wherever feasible. In addition, business standardization may be necessary for a company to leverage its human knowledge across the business and products units or to share information and collaborate on projects for the benefit of the company globally.

Finding the right mix of business flexibility and standardization in demand/supply chain management is a continuous challenge for managers. It directly affects decisions related to the implementation of BPR and IT projects across the company. Figure 7 presents a range of choices for managers to evaluate concerning the appropriate mix of flexibility and standardization at the local, regional and global levels (Marchand, 1998).

Most companies have evolved their businesses from a country-by-country, business-unit-by-business-unit model. This decentralized way of operating provides local managers with the flexibility to configure their demand/supply chains to meet the needs of the local market. Typically, IS applications to support demand/supply chain processes as well as administrative support systems have also been configured locally by the BU. Decentralized demand/supply chain operations offer maximum flexibility, but they have some significant disadvantages.

First, many companies discover that, over time, this approach is a very costly way of doing business. Excessive duplication of demand/supply chain processes and associated IS/IT support as well as the inevitable incompatibility of software, hardware, networks and IT people result in poor information sharing and communication among business units. They also raise the costs of changing business

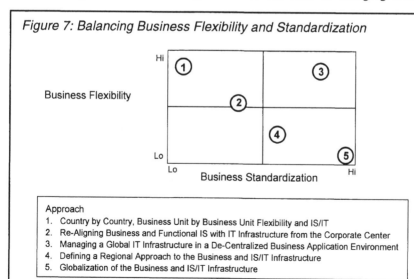

Figure 7: Balancing Business Flexibility and Standardization

Approach
1. Country by Country, Business Unit by Business Unit Flexibility and IS/IT
2. Re-Aligning Business and Functional IS with IT Infrastructure from the Corporate Center
3. Managing a Global IT Infrastructure in a De-Centralized Business Application Environment
4. Defining a Regional Approach to the Business and IS/IT Infrastructure
5. Globalization of the Business and IS/IT Infrastructure

processes and IS/IT across the business.

Inevitably, senior managers are reluctant to give up the advantages of this decentralized approach, but they desire to achieve lower costs of operating business processes and IS/IT across their BU's. Many companies move to the second approach by seeking to realign and standardize business processes and IS/IT from the corporate center. One of the first steps in this direction is to appoint a senior IT officer or CIO ("Chief Information Officer") The CIO is responsible for reducing the costs of IS/IT across the company by seeking shared services and common processes and IS/IT wherever feasible. However, CIO's typically face the difficulty that they can find synergies among decentralized business units and lower costs only through the voluntary cooperation and compliance of business unit managers. The resulting attempts to lower IS/IT costs and to adopt common IS applications in local demand/supply chains often fail or take many years to resolve. Committees often drive decisions in such cases and take years to find common processes and systems to satisfy the needs of diverse local operating units.

After a period of 5-7 years in some companies, senior managers become frustrated with the slow pace of business process and IS/IT standardization and call for more drastic solutions. It is at this point that some companies adopt approach 3; others seek approach 4 or even approach 5. Approach 4 (regionalization) and approach 5 (globalization) require decisions by senior managers to operate the business in a much more centralized manner, either at the regional or global level. Companies moving in these directions will strive over $5 - 10$ years to regionalize their local demand/supply chains and the IS/IT systems. Senior managers, for example, seek to "treat Europe as one country" and achieve similar regionalization across the world. Moreover, after having regionalized their businesses, some companies, such as Procter and Gamble, attempt to globalize their business processes and IS/IT as well. These companies seek two things. First, they aim to rationalize their demand/supply chains across regions and globally to lower the costs of implementing BPR and ERP projects. They also seek to increase the speed at which changes in the businesses can be reflected in their demand/supply chain

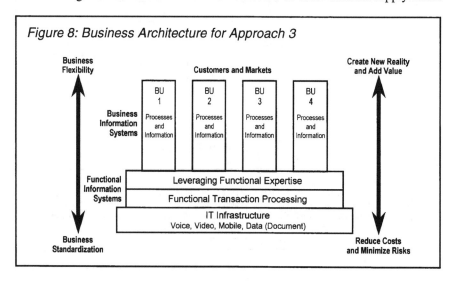

Figure 8: Business Architecture for Approach 3

processes and IS systems worldwide for their customers and markets. To achieve these levels of business and IS/IT standardization, these companies must also align their people, organizational structures and customer and supplier relationships to operate regionally or globally. Such BPR efforts require many years to accomplish with consistent top-down leadership.

An alternative to Approaches 4 and 5 is Approach 3 –a "hybrid" strategy of operating in a decentralized business environment with a global IS/IT infrastructure. With this approach, companies try to achieve an optimum balance between business flexibility and standardization that permits them to create significant business value for customers and lower the costs of operating the business globally at the same time. Hewlett-Packard has done this (Oliver, 1997) and has become a benchmark for many other companies pursuing a similar strategy in diverse industries.

Approach 3 incorporates several important decision rules.

First, senior managers must differentiate between business processes and IS systems that create value with customers and those that permit a company to lower its costs of operation. Hewlett-Packard distinguishes between business information systems (BIS) and functional information systems (FIS). The BIS are perceived as creating business value for customers, the FIS not. This means that H-P attempts, wherever possible, to globalize FIS such as general ledger, payroll, financial reporting and other transactions systems where economies of scale and lower costs can be achieved.

For BIS that support demand/supply chain management, H-P wants to provide each BU manager flexibility to tailor demand management processes for customers and markets. At the same time, the company expects to standardize, wherever possible, supply chain processes within and across business units. In this case, H-P managers differentiate between BIS where common processes and IS systems can be implemented to lower purchasing, manufacturing and distribution costs, and BIS where local market differences must be addressed for customer account management, after sales service or marketing. Even in these customer facing processes and systems, H-P managers attempt to mass customize IS applications by standardizing as much as possible those features that can lower the costs and speed up the implementation of business process redesign efforts and the supporting IS projects.

Second, senior managers in such a company must view IT infrastructure as regional or global. The business objectives of IT infrastructure are directed at lowering the overall costs of doing business with IT, and at the same time, supporting the business units with common hardware and software platforms as well as networks wherever possible. IT infrastructure is viewed as an essential part of operating a global business whose value is justified through its capability to lower the total costs of delivering IT capabilities that meets the needs of the business units. Such standardization also enables the business to implement ERP systems in demand/supply chain management faster and less expensively than companies using approaches 1 or 2, since the platforms for IS applications are common and shared across all business units.

Third, senior managers must be capable of balancing top-down needs to lower the overall costs of doing business globally or regionally with the local flexibility to meet differentiated customer and market demands. In companies that adopt approach 3, the decision making style of managers must be able to balance localized needs with regional and global standardization in processes and IS/IT. At H-P, this decision making style is known as "managed consensus". Senior managers engage in much debate and discussion before they reach decisions on business flexibility and standardization, but once a decision is made, then managers implement it as quickly as possible –with no further debate!

In contrast to approaches 1 and 2, approach 3 seeks to minimize the high costs of IS/IT and demand/supply chain management in a decentralized business environment where flexibility does not add value directly for customers. This approach also speeds up the implementation of BPR and IS projects based on standard IT infrastructure that the business does not have to change every time business processes and IS systems must be modified.

In contrast to approaches 4 and 5, approach 3 can provide business flexibility in demand chain management where creating value for customers is critical, while seeking regional or even global standards for supply chain functions where lower costs of operations are also desirable.

In sum, by looking carefully at a company's options for configuring the business locally, regionally and globally, senior managers can avoid the sterile arguments associated with centralization and decentralization in the business. Instead, they can achieve the right balance of business flexibility and standardization to lower costs and create value for customers at the same time.

How will Internet/Intranet/Extranet Use Along the Demand/Supply Chain Influence Customer, Partner and Supplier Relationships

The most dramatic change that has occurred in demand/supply chain management in the 1990s is the use of the Internet and World Wide Web networks and technology to rethink customer, partner and supplier relationships and information management. Since 1995, senior managers in manufacturing and service companies have had to alter their perceptions of Internet use. It is no longer sufficient to simply have a corporate "WEB" site. Neither is it sufficient to view Internet use as just an add-on to a company's current business approach—an alternative to providing information for customers and suppliers or another sales channel. For many senior managers, the Internet and WEB technology are becoming catalysts for rethinking the demand/supply chain of their industry and their positioning in networked based competition with customers, partners and suppliers.

Increasingly, companies have begun to evaluate the pace and intensity of networked-based competition in their industry's demand/supply chain and the strategic value and capabilities of "Net" strategies, as Figure 9 illustrates.

In some industries, for example, companies have been able to achieve first mover advantages with direct, Internet-based models of selling their products. Dell, Cisco and Amazon are well-known companies that have achieved first mover advantage with new direct models of doing business. They managed this at a time when the prevailing model in their respective industries was based on selling products through distributors and physical outlets.

In other cases, companies like GE have moved ahead of their competitors by identifying applications such as Extranet use with suppliers. The GE Trade Processing Network today is not simply a successful example of using Extranets with suppliers inside GE on a global scale. It has become a new line of business for GEIS

and GE Capital to mar-
ket to other networks
of suppliers and manu-
facturers in diverse in-
dustries. Extranets for
interacting on-line in
secure, flexible net-
work relationships with
partners and suppliers
are considered one of
the "killer applications"
(Downes, 1998) ca-
pable of disrupting es-
tablished ways of com-
peting in demand/sup-
ply chains in many in-
dustries. Extranets are
finding use in a variety
of applications on both

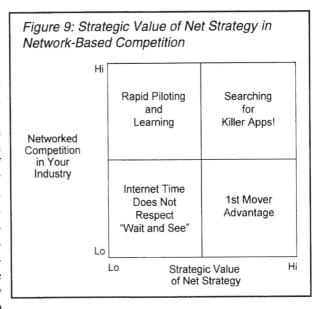

Figure 9: Strategic Value of Net Strategy in
Network-Based Competition

the supplier and customer side of company demand/supply chains. Advertising
companies are using Extranets to exchange ads and product images with large
customers. Manufacturers like Pirelli are developing one-to-one extranets with large
suppliers of their tire plants so that they can exchange a broad array of product and
manufacturing information on a real-time basis. Food companies like Nestle and
Unilever are focusing concerted efforts on Extranet ties to retailing chains—their
largest customers—and to direct providers of home delivery services like Streamline
in the Boston area. In these cases, both traditional and direct channels of distribution
and customer relationships are being developed with Extranets at the same time.

For most companies who may not be in a position to develop a "killer app" in
their industry or be a first mover, rapid piloting and learning from Internet experiments and trials seems to offer a viable path to developing Internet business
capabilities and strategies. Companies can avoid the risk of being left behind by
targeting initiatives that can derive both business benefits and valuable lessons. For
example, the world's auto makers are now sponsoring many initiatives to learn how
to sell cars and trucks over the Internet and how to integrate their dealer networks in
direct selling and after sales service. It was only three years ago that GM launched
its first major WEB site (developed by EDS); at the same time, it announced that its
dealer network was sacrosanct. GM would never use its WEB site to sell cars and
trucks. During 1998, GM launched its second Internet site that now offered direct
selling capabilities over the Internet. In between these two WEB site launches, GM
and every other major auto manufacturer witnessed the rapid buildup of direct selling
of new and used cars through new start-ups such as Auto-by Tel, AutoWeb and
Microsoft's Carpoint. In just three short years, networked-based competition was
redefined in the auto and truck retailing industry in North America. Today, auto
manufacturers in Europe and Asia are seeing their markets for retailing transformed
by similar direct marketing and selling start-ups.

Similarly, many other industries such a food and nonfood retailing, banking, financial services, real estate, tourism, industrial machinery, special chemicals and freight delivery are experiencing the disruptive effects of innovative use of Internet technologies in networked-based competition more directly.

"Internet time" –rapid, real-time and continuous innovation— no longer respects "wait and see" management attitudes even in traditional industries such as "concrete". Cemex, the very successful Mexican concrete company, is now applying the Burger King's service model to the delivery of concrete—"have it your way when you want it"—to building sites in Mexico as well as other countries in which it operates. For established international concrete companies, disruptive Internet strategies are overturning decades of established practices between builders and concrete suppliers. Large numbers of cement trucks are no longer queued up at building sites in the morning to be poured during the day. Cemex dispatches trucks "at customer request" with the right grade and quantity of concrete at the right hour each day. Cemex's CEO believes that the use of NET strategies with customers and suppliers will catapult his company into global leadership in the concrete and building materials industry (Dolan, 1998).

In sum, new ways of managing relationships with suppliers, partners and customers in demand/supply chain networks are redefining how information and knowledge will create business value in manufacturing and service industries. While predictions about where Internet, Extranet and Intranet applications will most benefit demand/supply chain management are difficult to pin down, one trend is certain. The substantial creative energies of new entrepreneurs and established companies in many industries are transforming demand/supply chains with Internet based technologies and networks. BPR and IT will again undergo substantial change. Network based competition will force firms to focus on rapid, flexible and agile business processes and IS/IT infrastructures to adapt in "Internet time" to networks of customers, partners and suppliers competing against other networks or "clusters" of companies.

Conclusion: Betting Your company on "Hard" choices!

"Hard" choices are decisions for which there are no clear successes or failures. Regardless of the decision taken, there are difficult risks, costs and unclear benefits associated with the outcome. For senior managers today, dealing with the new waves of BPR and IT in demand/supply chain management, the choices are difficult at best. There are no correct answers, best choices or optimum implementation paths.

In the previous era, "reengineering" was associated with reducing costs and improving productivity through delayering, eliminating head count, simplifying processes and automating what was left. The objectives were clear. A senior manager could judge and often "count" whether the company had succeeded or failed. Did we lower our costs, improve efficiency, become leaner? Choices were not "easy" during this period, but at least the expected outcomes were clearer.

Today, senior managers are confronting new waves of BPR and IT in demand/ supply chain management as well as the use of the Internet in networked-based competition locally, regionally and globally. In addition, with the Y2K problem looming, many senior managers have invested in major and costly initiatives to redesign and automate demand/supply chain processes out of fear, uncertainty and doubts—FUD's in sales jargon. In all too many cases, they have made their commitments with an unclear sense of the outcomes for their industry, their company or themselves. There has never been a time when BPR and IT are so closely associated with business performance and so risky in their potential to destroy shareholder value, profitability or market credibility.

In this environment, managers would do well to keep one decision rule for making hard choices in mind: try not to make decisions whose consequences cannot be undone or which will close off future options.

References

Clegg, Chris et al. (1996). The performance of Information Technology and the role of human and organizational factors. *Economic and Social Research Council UK*. 1-32.

D'Aveni, Richard A. (1994). *Hyper-Competition*. The Free Press. New York.

Davenport, Thomas H. (1998, July-August). Putting the Enterprise into the Enterprise System. *Harvard Business Review*. 121-131.

Dobbs, John H. (1998). *Competition's New Battleground: the Integrated Value Chain*. *Cambridge Technology Partners*. Cambridge, MA. 1-22.

Dolan, Kerry a. (1998, June 15). Cement Meets the Cyberworld. *Forbes Global Business and Finance*. Cover Story. 1-9.

Downes, Larry and Mui, Chunka (1998). *Unleashing the Killer App*. Harvard Business School Press. Cambridge, MA.

Hoover, William E. et al. (1996). Order To Payment. *McKinsey Quarterly*. Number 1. 38-49.

Marchand, Donald A. (1998). Balancing flexibility and global IT infrastructure. Financial Times. *Mastering Global Business*. Part 3. 10-12.

Oliver, David and Marchand, Donald A. (1997). Hewlett-Packard (HP): Competing with a Global IT infrastructure. *IMD*. Lausanne, Switzerland. GM 653. 1-14.

Poirier, Charles C. and Reiter, Stephen. E. (1996). *Supply Chain Optimization*. Berrett-Hoehler. San Francisco.

Slater, Derek. (1998, June 15). *The Hidden Costs of Enterprise Software*. CIO Enterprise. Section 2. 48-55.

Standish Group. (1994) *Chartering the Seas of Information Technology*. The Standish Group International Inc. Dennis, MA. 1-12.

Vollmann, Thomas E. (1996). *The Transformation Imperative*. Harvard Business School Press. Cambridge, MA.

Vollamnn, Thomas E. et al. (1992). *Manufacturing Planning and Control Systems*. Irwin. Homewood, Illinois.

Warner, Timothy N. (1987, Fall), Information Technology as a Competitive Burden. *Sloan Management Review*. 55-61.

White, Joseph. (1996, November 27). Re-engineering Gurus Take Steps To Remodel Their Stalling Vehicles. *Wall Street Journal. 1.*

CHAPTER 11

Enterprise Process Innovation: Strategies and Issues

Arun Rai
Georgia State University, USA

Jesus A. Ponce de Leon and Arlyn J. Melcher
Southern Illinois University at Carbondale, USA

Substantial attention is being given to reengineering as a means to enhance the competitive position of contemporary organizations. Business process innovation (Davenport, 1993), reengineering (Hammer and Champy, 1992), and business process redesign (Grover et al. 1993), have one central theme a fundamental change to the business processes. More recently, a significant expansion in the locus of information technology systems has occurred. Enterprise systems, which are commonly referred to as enterprise resource systems (ERP), encompass several core processes and provide a business model for their definition and relationship. The expected results of reengineering efforts are dramatic changes in costs, cycle time, and profitability. Generally, it is expected that such redesign efforts will lead to a radical new way of carrying out processes that are central to the operation of the business. Terms such as 'nimble', 'flexible', 'adaptive', and 'responsive' have been used as metaphors to describe the new type of organization. Consider the following examples:

- C.F. England Trucking Co., a transportation company located in Salt Lake City saw IT as a strategic investment to "carry more freight and satisfy the customer." Initially, England invested in automating the backoffice paperwork. But its latest investments in IT were more strategic oriented. They equipped 1,200 semi tractor-trailer rigs with mobile communication technology linked to a satellite. The drivers now can transmit data, do their daily reporting, and receive directions wherever they are (Bartholomew, 1992).
- Reebok installed a real time sales, order-entry, and production tracking network linking all of the U.S. offices and manufacturing plants with a custom developed software. The internally developed IT gives Reebok a competitive advantage in the market by gaining access to manufacturing capabilities around the world and by shortening the cycle time of order to production dramatically (Pepper, 1990).

Enterprise systems is now a booming business, with one vendor, SAP, being among the fastest growing companies in the software business. Other popular enterprise system vendors include PeopleSoft, Baan and Oracle, each with rapidly growing businesses in this arena. Application software developed by enterprise vendors encompasses core business functionality and integrates data resources and information flow within and across these core business processes. The enterprise systems industry is now worth several billions dollars and the consulting practices associated with supporting the implementation of ERP systems is estimated to be as large (Davenport, 1998).

Reengineering projects can produce substantial improvements, but critics report that only a few are successful (Moad, 1993b). Some ERP projects have resulted in limited performance impacts, and in a few cases these projects have been abysmal failures. A variety of implementation factors have been identified as critical to managing such information technology assimilation projects (Bancroft, Seip and Sprengel, 1998). An IT-enabled process innovation program requires an understanding of reengineering, the customer's requirements, the capabilities of available information technology (IT), and of the key business processes of the firms. How broad the scope of the project is largely determines the organizational and economic impact of the reengineering effort. The degree to which software technology is developed internally or bought as a package to enable a reengineering implementation may further limit or enhance its impact.

Reengineering projects differ in two respects: (1) the *organizational scope* (single function, to several functions, to a whole business unit, to several customers, suppliers, and business units being involved, to several business units of a multidivisional or multinational corporation,), and (2) in how *IT application is delivered*. From the standpoint of organizational scope, some reengineering projects are limited to changing activities within a function, such as the accounts receivable function. Others transform entire sets of activities that cross functions, departments and units within a business unit, for example, from order entry all the way to shipping and billing customers. At a higher level of complexity, reengineering projects involve redesigning business processes that affect an entire corporation and, in some instances, customers and suppliers (Cash and Robinson, 1992; Hall, Rosenthal and Wade, 1993).

Rockart and Hoffman (1992) observe that firms can employ a variety of approaches in IT delivery. Organizations may rely on off-the-shelf software solutions, use a particular in-house development approach, or a balance of both strategies to enable business process redesign. We propose to classify IT-enabled process innovation strategies according to the interaction of *IT delivery* strategy and Process Innovation *organizational scope* strategy. Cross classifying these dimensions develops twelve process innovation strategies that can be adopted by organizations. While IT enables and serves as catalyst in reengineering projects (Davenport, 1993; Hammer and Champy, 1992; Grover et. al. 1993; Johansson, Mchugh, Pendlebury & Wheeler III, 1993), little has been said about the interaction between the breadth of the BPR application and IT delivery strategy (adoption, adaptation or in-house development). This framework results in twelve IT-enabled process innovation strategies (see Table 1), ranging from outright adoption of a vendor developed solution with an intrafunctional scope of the process innovation project to a fully internally developed solution with an interorganizational process innovation project scope.

We examine the likely impact and organizational implications that these two dimensions, breadth of process innovation projects and IT delivery, have upon reengineering efforts. In the remainder of the chapter, we present our proposed model and briefly review definitions that relate process innovation and IT. Next, we review the descriptions of practice in the literature to classify IT-enabled process innovation projects into this framework. We also examine the key characteristics of each of these strategies. Finally, we conclude with recommendations for practice and implications for future research.

Classification of IT-Enabled Process Innovations

Business process reengineering (BPR), business process redesign, reengineering and process innovation are used interchangeably to refer to a fundamental change in how core business processes are carried out (see for example Hammer and Champy, 1992; Davenport, 1993; Grover et al., 1993). Unlike Total Quality Management (TQM), business process reengineering seeks radical departures from the old way of doing business. We use organizational scope and IT delivery strategy to develop a classification scheme of IT-enabled process innovation.

Organizational Scope

Process innovation projects are intended to have a "major cross-functional, and cross-business process impact" (Information Week, 1991). Process innovation projects may be undertaken with a narrow breadth, such as a single function, or a middle of the road approach where reengineering processes cut across related functional areas, or with a broad breadth by including several organizational business units. We use the following terms to differentiate and classify IT-enabled process innovation projects within a given line of business:

- *Intra-functional*: business process redesign projects that are aimed at single and isolated tasks, activities or single functions.
- *Inter-functional:* projects that target cross functional business processes but are contained within a business unit.
- *Inter-organizational*: projects that bridge between two or more organizations, such as the firm and its customers and suppliers.

IT-enabled process innovation efforts can be targeted across lines of business and countries of operations. We make a distinction between process innovation efforts within a homogeneous business context, as defined by one line of business and/or country of operation, and process innovation efforts within a heterogeneous business context, as defined by multiple lines of business and/or countries of operation. Accordingly, we add a fourth level of organizational scope to capture the transition to corporate level projects, which are undertakings across diverse business and cultural contexts. These projects typically involve processes across multinational or multidivisional companies. Thus, we add a fourth level of organizational scope that we consider in our analysis of IT-enabled process innovation.

- *Mutlidivisional/multinational*: projects that enhance the coordination among divisions, lines of business, or countries of operation of corporations.

IT Delivery Strategy

Definitions of information technology are often of an all-inclusive nature. Cooper and Zmud (1990), for example, define an IT as "any artifacts whose underlying technological base is comprised of computer or communications hardware and software." A similar definition was used by Geisler and Husain (1993) in a survey of IT acquisition who define IT as "to include all equipment, systems, components, firmware and software utilized throughout the organization." Our focus is on software applications that operationalize IT delivery strategy. This narrower definition is consistent with the great majority of process innovation projects. Hardware decisions are limited to buying from vendors, whereas software decisions actually range from make to buy. At one extreme the organization decides to buy a prepackaged software application. At the other extreme the organization may decide to internally develop a fully customized software application. A middle of the road is also possible where the organization buys software applications and customizes them to better meet its requirements. Thus, we use the following classification to identify different strategies to deliver applications systems:

- *adoption*: the purchase of an off-the-shelf or standardized prepackaged software that requires little or no modifications when applied to the process innovation project.
- *adaptation:* the purchase of a software package that serves as the backbone or shell of the application requiring partial customization to make the process innovation project operational.
- *customization:* the organization undertakes an in-house development effort to build the necessary applications software for the process innovation project.

Table 1 cross classifies organizational scope and delivery strategy to identify twelve strategies for reengineering the firm.

Implications of IT-enabled Process Innovation Strategies

We examine each of the twelve strategies in terms of (i) characteristics of software requirements, (ii) characteristics of business processes, and (iii) implementation characteristics. The specific issues evaluated under each of these three

Table 1: Organizational Scope and Application Delivery Strategy			
	Application Delivery Strategy		
Organizational Scope	*Adoption*	*Adaptation*	*Customization*
Intra-functional	Functional localized vendor provided work-flow process innovation	Functional semi-customized localized work flow process innovation	Functional customized localized work-flow process innovation
Inter-functional	Cross functional vendor provided process innovation	Cross functional semi-customized process innovation	Cross functional customized process innovation
Inter-organizational	Strategic extended business network vendor provided process innovation	Strategic extended business network semi-customized process innovation	Strategic extended business network re-definition customized process innovation
Multidivisional or Multinational	Standardized enterprise process innovation	Federated enterprise process innovation	Heterogeneous enterprise process innovation

Table 2: Criteria Used to Compare IT-Enabled Process Innovation Strategies

Strategy Characteristics	Issues
Software characteristics	• Purpose, cost & scope • Architecture • Interoperability
Process Characteristics	• Type of business process (generic and standardized, to unique and unstandardized) • Process architecture (task and functional interfaces) • Task/Functional design (core design logic of tasks/ functions)
Implementation Characteristics	• Team composition and their roles • Change management, including training programs • Project management

categories are enumerated in Table 2 and developed in Tables 3-6.

Analysis of IT-Enabled Process Innovation Strategies

IT-Enabled Intrafunctional Process Innovation

Table 3 contrasts three application delivery strategies for process innovation projects at the level of a well-defined business function. At this level, the process innovation project is narrow in scope, internally focused, and typically deals with a rethinking of work flows within a department or function. A functional focus is taken where the business activity selected is contained within a functional area. The focus in workflow is on routine processes that are performed within a business (for example archiving, credit verification, mailing).

Table 3 summarizes the overall characteristics and value of the reengineering strategy. The narrow reengineering approach is useful when the organization is cautious, prefers minor disruption of operations or feels it is not ready for massive business process reengineering. It is estimated that this type of reengineering, "via the backdoor"[1] reached $390 million in 1993, and was expected to grow to $700 million by 1994. Among the most popular software applications reported in the popular press include Lotus Notes, FileNet, RemoteWare, WorkMAN, Omindesk, Workbench, and FlowMark.

At Chase Manhattan Bank, work flow reengineering began in 1991. The project was initiated with the need for streamlining archiving, mailing and credit verification. Today Chase has one business unit and several divisions with work flow projects. The challenge today is to tie these disparate projects to produce cross-divisional, cross-business information sharing (Klein, 1994).

According to the BIS Strategic Decisions research group about 60% of workflow intrafunctional process innovation projects prefer desktop and LANs platforms. In the intrafunctional process innovation projects, the focus of the effort is on a business activity that is localized within a functional area. Such process innovation projects should bring about productivity gains for individuals in a given function and are not designed to change the basic building blocks of the organization. Thus, the innovation is modular in nature and no changes are targeted at the architectural relationship between functions. When the IT application is vendor driven, only minor programming and customization is required prior to its adoption.

Connecticut Life Insurance Co. launched its BPR effort focusing on reducing paperwork, compressing workflow, and worker productivity. The goals were an increase of 35% in worker productivity and boosting service for its policy holders. Their approach was to launch localized workflow projects in an incremental way. Today, they report "Work flow, reengineering, and imaging are all interconnected," reporting 20 to 25% productivity gains.[2]

According to International Data Corp. IT work flow application software can be divided into three major groups: software oriented to routine, structured work flow; administrative systems for white collar less structured work flow; and ad-hoc software for unstructured tasks that requires substantial modifications. Typical applications are electronic mail, document imaging, forms management, document processing, and transaction oriented tasks, such as order entry and record keeping (Fischer, 1994).

Given its localized nature, intrafunctional process innovation projects are manned by local teams. A well-balanced team in terms of necessary knowledge bases represented should include users, IS personnel and vendors. Vendors can demonstrate how the technical knowledge embedded in the software application can be best used in the user's business context. IS personnel are likely to be well conversant with technical criteria associated with assessing capabilities of software applications. Users are well conversant with the nuances of their business environment and work flows, and can critically assess software capability from a functional requirement perspective. At one end of the spectrum of the IT delivery strategy, the projects tend to be vendor constrained. The process innovation solution will be limited by the extent of the flexibility of the prepackaged software solution. Localized process innovation will also be constrained by the existing IT infrastructure. Take, for example, the case of Con Edison:

Con Edison a $5 billion utility located in New York City, reevaluated its paper trail (one million pieces) to simplify it, reduce handling costs, speed up service and increase customer satisfaction. The selected software application runs in a client-server system and operates on PCs running in the OS/2 environment.

At the other end of the IT strategy is customization for functional needs. The user usually leads the change when the localized work flow process innovation project is aimed at unstructured and novel tasks that need to be supported and interfaced. Customization is necessary in these process innovation projects, since commercial software is not usually available to meet the design rules of specific tasks and the architectural linkages between tasks. The users are knowledgeable of the rules, processes and exceptions of the business process, but much of this knowledge is likely to be tacit and uncodified and difficult to articulate (Nonaka, 1998). IS personnel need to work in tandem with users to establish and then execute a development process that explicates the tacit knowledge of users. If a software product comes close to meeting the functional needs of the users, an adaptation strategy can be employed. Here, it is incumbent on IS personnel to develop a good understanding of the software architecture, as any additional modules that are put in place will need to be appropriately tested and integrated with the existing system.

Consider the following case:

Nestle's local teams develop the core applications with the assistance of corporate experts in hardware and software technologies. Once the applications have been developed are sent to local offices for further adaptation. The applications are operational until they meet the specific requirements of the local users (Greenbaum, 1994).

The piecemeal, localized strategy of intrafunctional process innovation projects, is less risky and disruptive than a major process innovation undertaking. However, in the long run a multiplicity of localized process innovation projects can end up in a potpourri of hardware platforms, and with software not talking to each other. Thus,

Table 3: Comparison of IT-Enabled Intrafunctional Process Innovation Strategies

	Functional Standardized	Functional Semi-Customized	Functional Customized
Characteristics of Software Requirement	• Low cost & limited scope • Simple and standardized architecture • Several vendors available	• Low cost of acquisition • Low cost of modification • May require some software interfacing, and interoperability among installed hardware	• High costs of development
Processes Characteristics	• Industry standards on design concepts of tasks and their interfaces • Adapt process to fit software, if necessary • Process is straight-forward and simple.	• Some novelty in task design and their interfaces • Partial adaptation of software to organization's business process.	• Unique functional design and task interfaces • Redesign & implement functional model
Organizational Implementation Issues	• Software evaluation and selection by users and IS personnel • Limited team activity. • Leadership by vendor • Little coordination required between IS and vendor • Training program developed by vendor	• Software evaluation and selection by users and IS personnel • Adaptation of software product identified by users and IS personnel • Changes made to the software product need to be documented. • Training program developed by vendor, IS personnel and users involved in adaptation	• Functional managers need to take control of project. • Project requires team activity involving users and IS personnel for logical design, testing and validation. • Software documentation critical for future modifications and support. • Training program developed by users and IS personnel

an organization considering localized strategy should be concerned with coordinating assessment of the firms information technology infrastructure capabilities. In the absence of such coordinated efforts, integrated, functional infrastructures may be established, while the firm wide organizational infrastructures are likely to be badly fractured.

IT-Enabled Interfunctional Process Innovation

The most publicized reengineering projects usually fall within this category (Table 1, row 2). In interfunctional projects, the team is composed of members representing all of the functions and support areas affected by a core business process. A typical example of this kind is the process initiated by a customer's order to design, manufacture, ship, manage inventory, and bill.

At Corning Asahi Video products unit, a division of Corning Inc. the glass maker, a cross functional team co-led by an IS manager and a division's manager, were assigned to reengineer the order-fulfillment process. The new process reduced the number of steps from 123 to nine, producing annual savings of $400,000 in personnel costs alone (Caldwell, 1994). The total cost of the project so far is $985,000 and taken a total of 30 months. The Corning Asahi team decided to buy DCS Logistics software application from Andersen Consulting to reduce technology risk, meet the deadline for testing, and maintain the cost of the project as low as possible (Maglita, 1994).

These process innovation projects require greater coordination because the teams are larger, members come from diverse functional backgrounds, diverse interests are represented, and greater authority is needed for the team to initiate and implement change. Deciding who is the "owner" of the project is in itself a difficult task. Businesses with experience in forming and managing multifunctional teams in different areas and projects effectively stand a better chance to succeed on IT enabled reengineering projects. Others may prefer to start the change process with smaller projects, such as the ones outlined in the intrafunctional BPR projects.

Even market leaders with visionary and supportive management falter in their attempts of reengineering core business processes. Charles Schwab provides an example of a major reengineering project that failed to materialize in spite of having a multifunctional team, a named process leader, management support, and a focus on customer satisfaction. The reasons reported for the failure include the team's focus on internal shortcomings of the existing IT rather than on the business process itself, design being carried out with incomplete and superficial information about customer's requirements, inadequate intervention by management, and team members did not perceive themselves as real agents of change. All together these factors produced an incremental improvement, as opposed to a radical change (Moad, 1994).

As the example shows, at this level of organizational scope the success of the reengineering project begins to be sensitive not only on the selection of the business process, the selection of IT delivery strategy, but also on organizational factors of team composition, assigned leader(s), authority granted, and expert support provided. These BPR projects are aimed at radical changes that will affect all of the involved parties, and most importantly, affect the overall performance of the business unit.

Table 4: Comparison of IT-Enabled Interfunctional Process Innovation Strategies

	Inter-functional Standardized	Inter-functional Semi-Customized	Inter-functional Customized
Software Characteristics	• Rationalized, field-tested design concepts for software capability • Data standardization for cross-functional information sharing • Moderate costs of software acquisition	• Moderate software modification costs • Costs of modification increase exponentially if changes require adaptations to interrelated product modules	• High cost of software development • Requirements determination involves development of a logical process model • Development of logical process model involves reconciliation and integration of multiple functional perspectives
Process Characteristics	• Well-defined industry standards for functions and their interfaces • Adapt organization's cross-functional model to fit software, if necessary	• No industry consensus on design of functions and their interfaces • Adapt software functionality to organization's process model	• Absence of standard industry process models • Reassessment of design concepts for each function involved. • Reassessment of architectural linkages between functions • Develop & implement a new cross-functional process model
Organizational Implementation Issues	• Implementation teams include cross-functional user teams, line managers, vendors and IS personnel • Request for proposals typically approved by cross-functional team • Software evaluation and, selection by cross-functional team • Training provided by vendor • Implementation leadership taken by vendor	• Implementation teams include cross-functional users, line managers, vendors and IS personnel • Software evaluation and determination of needed modifications by cross-functional team and IS personnel • Training of users and IS personnel by vendor • Documentation of changes critical for training and future development support	• Implementation teams include cross-functional users, line managers, functional managers, and IS personnel • Multiple teams of users and IS personnel for requirements determination, testing, validation and changeover • Development encompasses explication of functional, modular knowledge & cross-functional, architectural linkages • Project management needs to ensure coordination across multiple teams • Software training

"Ultimately, however, a reengineering project, like any major change program, can produce lasting results only if senior executives invest their time and energy. ... Inevitably, managers and employees may feel that their turf, jobs, and organizational equilibrium are under attack" (Hall, Rosenthal, Wade, 1993).

As with the intrafunctional projects, the IT delivery strategy is bound between buying the software application outright from the market to internal development. At one end we find the vendor driven IT strategy where the business process is redesigned around the software application. We call it a vendor constrained process innovation project. In this type of project the business process is not unique to the firm and IT solutions are available in the market, for example priority planning and capacity planning integrated with purchasing and inventory management (Table 4, column 2).

Several software packages are available in the market with these capabilities, for example Four Shift, Platinum, and MCS-3. In this type of project, the IT strategy is virtually an outright adoption with little or no modification. A case in point:

CN North America, a $4 billion railroad owned by the Canadian government, bought a software application developed by Santa Fe Railway Co. of Atchison, Topeka. The software program will help CN North America to increase flexibility in billing, track customer's request, scheduling shipments, tracking freight, revenue and accounting and controlling freight yard traffic (Caldwell, 1993).

IS personnel are in a position to lead these projects because it is the selection decision that is largely responsible to ensure the compatibility between task and the requirements of the business process redesign. At this end of the spectrum of software delivery strategy the vendor's application becomes the solution but also the constraint. This is because a vendor's software application tends to be specific to the task or focused on an industry (called vertical market application), as was the case with CN North America's software. Projects that require adaptation of the vendor's software (table 1, column 2), can be served with horizontal software applications such as manufacturing, human resources and customer support. For example, in the manufacturing horizontal software the ASK Group, Datalogix International, Dun Bradstreet, Oracle Corporation and SAP America, just to name a few, offer software packages that are well developed and take advantage of the similarities of manufacturing processes (Greenbaum, 1993). Consider for example:

In 1988, J. Brach Corp. got underway a $4 million, six-year modernization plan of its candy manufacturing plants. Brach evaluated several vendors and decided for Prism MRP horizontal software application. The application provided what Brach found as necessary to improving quality and manufacturing flexibility. A committee working with IBM's consulting group analyzed, designed, and implemented the new process in cooperation with end users (Bartholomew, 1991).

At the other end of the software delivery strategy we find customized applications (Table 4, column 4). As with the intrafunctional projects, the more unstructured and complex the business process is, the more the project requires software adaptation and internal development of software. IS personnel and end users alike take an active leadership in this BPR projects. In these cases the cross functional team is empowered to design, suggest and implement the necessary modifications to make it operational. These teams are more complex because they require a good balance between end-users, those affected by the redesign, experts in the fields the redesign relates to, and experts in information technology[3]. Yet, the issue of BPR project leadership remains a difficult one. A survey at 350 companies conducted by Deloitte & Touche revealed that 35% of BPR projects are being led by IS managers, 42% by business-line managers and 20% by the president or CEO.[4]

> CSX Transportation Inc. developed an in-house software application to improve customer service. It started back in 1985 when CSX began investing in building an IT infrastructure to reduce costs and improve control and communications. The software application developed by CSX was built upon an EDI initiative originally aimed at cost reduction only. The reengineered business process now allows customers to track their products and get a fast response from CSX as to shipping, information, inventories, location and faster order processing and billing (Pepper, 1991).

Internal development is preferred when the software available in the market does not meet the requirements of the project and the skills for its development can be found in the IS group. The effectiveness of the IS team in developing the software application largely determines the technical success of the reengineering effort. The team of users, who are the most knowledgeable of the business process, will determine, however, how radical the departure from the old way the redesign will be. In this IT delivery strategy, the IS personnel take on the role of advisor in at least two ways: as expert in available technologies and as expert software developer.

An advantage of the internal software development strategy is that both teams (users and IS) constantly interact during the redesign and implementation process enriching and greatly enhancing the redesign. Perhaps the greatest advantage of this approach is that the redesigning team is free of the constraints inherent in commercially available software. The downside are the difficulties of making a complex team work effectively, the costs associated with assigning a group of programmers and analysts full time to the development of the application, and the likelihood of running over allowed time and budget.

IT-Enabled Interorganizational Process Innovation

Interorganizational process innovation projects, target business processes that affect the entire corporation by cutting across several business units. Consider Banc One's experience:

> Banc One is an example of an organization that in the last ten years has managed through acquisitions to increase its size fivefold, but the organization has not increased its complexity. This has been achieved by integrating its acquisitions while reducing complexity through an internally developed IT. It is so effective that in just a few months each newly acquired unit reduces costs dramatically, its service capability is enhanced, and operations get fully integrated to headquarters on a real time basis. IT has redefined the coordinating capabilities of the organization and dramatically reduced the complexity of managing and integrating a rapidly growing business (Teitelman, 1991).

More complex and ambitious BPR projects also involve outside organizations

Table 5: Comparison of IT-Enabled Interorganizational Process Innovation Strategies

	Inter-organizational Standardized	Inter-organizational Semi-Customized	Inter-organizational Customized
Software characteristics	• Complex products • High costs of acquisition • Interoperable across multiple platforms • Low technical risks associated with single vendor solution	• Some customization of software possible, as with configuration tables in ERP systems. • Multiple-vendor, mix-and-match modular strategy possible • Increased costs of multiple vendor solution • Increased technical risk of multiple vendor solution, because of interoperability and portability considerations.	• Multiple organizations translate to multiplicity of viewpoints on software requirements, especially in terms of interface requirements between organizations • Emphasis on interoperability & an open applications architecture environment • High cost of development
Process Characteristics	• Prevalence of industry standards on core interorganizational processes	• Some specificity in how organization transacts with suppliers, customers and other external entities	• Organization has unique transaction & interface requirements as it relates to suppliers, customers & external entities • Clean slate reassessment of all architectural linkages with suppliers, customers & other external entities.
Organizational Implementation Issues	• Implementation teams include suppliers, customers, cross-functional teams, vendors, implementation consultants, and IS personnel • Selection and evaluation of product undertaken by users and IS personnel from multiple organizations • Misalignment between process model and software product determined by users from multiple organizations • IS personnel emphasis on infrastructure adequacy, operations, and data administration • Critical to establish, enforce, and evolve standards for operations and databases. • Training provided by vendor or vendor-certified training companies	• Implementation teams include suppliers, customers, cross-functional teams, vendors, implementation consultants, & IS personnel, including development personnel • Selection & evaluation of product undertaken by users & IS personnel from multiple organizations • Modification of the product undertaken by IS personnel & users, or possibly users, vendors, with limited involvement of IS personnel • Critical to establish, enforce, and evolve standards for operations & databases • Training provided by vendor or vendor-certified training companies • Internal IS personnel likely to be involved in delivery of training, because of product adaptations • Extremely critical to maintain documentation of changes made to software	• Implementation teams include suppliers, customers, cross-functional teams, vendors, development consultants, implementation consultants, & IS personnel, including development personnel • Multiple concurrent teams involved in the design of core modules & their interfaces. • Interorganizational agreement on interface specifications is critical • Top management representation from organizations involved is desirable. • Training program developed and delivered by internal IS personnel or hired consultants involved during the development process.

such as customers and suppliers. Venkatraman (1991) has labeled IT's role at this stage as that of enabling a business network redesign.

Spartan Stores Inc. of Grand Rapids, Michigan, is a wholesaler that wants to become a "just-in-time" linch pin for other companies. Its strategy is to become the most efficient wholesale distributor between manufacturers and retailers. A committee of eight people, together with an IBM team, identified 104 business processes that had an impact on this strategy. At present four divisions are involved in nine BPR projects that tie together finance, order management, warehouse management, retailers, suppliers and customer support. Sophisticated neural network software is being tested in one of these projects to speed up decision making, reduce errors, cut costs and improve customer service (Wilson, 1993).

As in other applications interorganizational BPR projects can be undertaken by buying outright the software application, adapting it, or developing it internally. These delivery strategies will shape the reengineering process in sharply different ways as summarized in Table 5.

At this level of BPR scope, the strategy of the business, the market (customers), and other related organizations (for example suppliers) are an integral part of the reengineering project.

At Sears Roebuck and Co. a project was launched in early 1992 that affects 868 of its retail stores. The project will link the backoffice, the cash registers, credit verification, and automated service kiosks. This move is expected to increase face-to-face service by liberating employees time, eliminating paperwork, speed up service to customers, simplify sales, and cut costs. Sears contracted with CompuAdd for the hardware and software applications (McCormick, 1992).

Eastman Chemical Co., the 10th largest chemicals producer, is under-taken a complete overhaul of its way of integrating the operations of offices and plants around the globe. Their BPR project is dubbed the Global Business Integrated Information System. Eastman bought the software application from SAP AG of Germany because the vendor will install it in half the time than if developed internally and the business processes to be reengineered were not unique to Eastman. The applications involve sales and distribution, order-taking and invoicing, materials management, inventory controls, assets management, and financial reporting. The new system replaces more than 40 disparate applications that had difficulty communicating with each other (Appleby, 1993).

Thus, it is to be expected that the benefits from these projects should impact in a significant way the bottom line of the business. Hall et al. (1993) report that the broader the scope of the reengineering project the higher the impact to the bottom line of the business. In their in-depth study of 20 cases they found that the broadest scope produced 17% cost reductions versus less than 1% for the narrowest focused projects.

Assigning ownership of the project at the interorganizational level is a significant issue. As these reengineering projects cut across several business units, they need to bring together representatives from several business units, with different backgrounds, different experiences and areas of expertise, and most likely from various organizational levels (both internal and external to the reengineering organization). Designating a leader and owner of the project may be highly politicized and sensitive to power positions, especially when the project involves several equals at the top. Hall et. al. (1994) recommend that in addition to getting the CEO involved, a second top executive be designated for its implementation.

The typical role of the IS function is one of business wide expert advisor in IT matters, implementer, and provider of support for the IT systems. As a common advisor to all units involved, the IS function can take a technical position thus, playing a co-leading or leading role in the reengineering team. The approach of some organizations has been the creation of a full time position for reengineering managers (for example Schwab). In the vendor driven BPR projects, the IS function is charged with the responsibility for the evaluation and selection of the software application that best fit the BPR requirements. Thus, the IS personnel become a key resource to the reengineering team by playing a prominent role. It is reported by Deloitte & Touche that in 1992 that the average CIO was involved in 1.6 BPR projects and in 4.4 by 1993 (Moad, 1993b).

At the other extreme of the continuum of the software application strategy are the internally developed software applications (Table 5, fourth column). These are complex projects that require a detailed planning and a careful assessment of the magnitude of change, the resources needed, the timeline, and coordination. Industry experts suggest that careful consideration be given to the strategy of building internally. They recommend consideration of the following issues:

- the business needs.
- the programming skills of the IS organization.
- if sufficient resources are available to fund the BPR project.
- the cost of maintaining the technology.
- the need for added functionality and flexibility of the software.
- the workload involved.
- the risk of failure.
- the required training and flexibility of the IS organization.
- the time that it will take to develop, test and implement.
- the total cost and degree of portability between hardware platforms.
- who will manage the application? (Adapted from Greenbaum, 1993- Build or Buy?)

In these projects the reengineering team should be empowered to radically change the business process. The nature of the interdependencies between the various business units involved requires a large scale organizational transformation. Thus, a high level executive has to be actively involved to provide the authority and top managerial support to enable the reengineering team to become a real change agent. These projects are reported as taking anywhere between 18 months and 6 years, between initiation and implementation. In addition, some unexpected situations arise as the projects move from design to software writing. For example take the case of Texas Instruments:

TI initiated its BPR projects in 1988. Although originally TI wanted to reengineer core processes in less than a year, it soon found out that analysts and developers could not make the change to a reengineering mentality. Projects got delayed, early software applications were aimed at automating rather than reengineering the process, and IS personnel had difficulty broadening their vision from a narrowly focused application to one that encompassed several functions and business units. TI reorganized its IS staff into centers of excellence (each center focused on a business process), spent heavily in retraining them, and changed the reward system to emphasize breadth of knowledge and performance (Moad, 1993b).

TI reports that its success rate for reengineering projects jumped to 80%. Experts say that it is not only the speed of development that matters but also the ability of the IS team to create applications in a different way (Moad, 1993b). Put in another way, IS personnel have to reengineer themselves if a project of this nature is to succeed. Consider the following:

"Many in IS expect requirements to be defined and things to be predictable before they start coding... But reengineering is anything but predictable." (Ed Goll partner of Price Waterhouse in New York, as cited in Moad, 1993b).

"The idea that you don't leave the room or start developing an application until you've got 100% of the requirements defined up front just won't work in reengineering." (David Sutherland consultant with CSC Index, as cited in Moad, 1993b).

Interorganizational BPR projects reach out beyond the boundaries of the business unit and links with other organizations to form a business network. A business network can be thought of as organizations that become more interdependent through core business processes. The objective is to improve customer satisfaction, reduce costs, become more efficient, and be more competitive and flexible in the market place. These business networks can involve customers (for example Eastman Chemical), suppliers (for example Wal Mart), logistically tightly coordinated units (for example Sporting Goods, Inc., Reebok), and merging acquisitions into the mainstream business (for example Banc One, Elf Atochem).

IT-Enabled Process Innovation in Multinational & Multidivisional Corporations

As multinational companies and multidivisional companies examine IT-enabled process innovation initiatives, they need to confront an important organization design issue - what level of process standardization should be achieved across the corporation? This decision should be based on an analysis of the costs and benefits of local autonomy and global standardization. Business processes that are highly standardized are likely to be unresponsive to the specific needs of the local environment. On the other hand, absence of coordination and minimal levels of global integration essentially implies fragmentation of information across the enterprise, leading up to be a heavy drag on corporate performance (Davenport, 1999).

A decision to standardize processes across business units and countries can bring about economies of scale in the software development and implementation process. Economies of scale can be realized by the simplifying and consolidating management of standardized operations. However, an efficient process in the context of a given business process, when applied to other lines of business or countries of operations, may cripple much needed flexibility. Thus, on one extreme

Table 6: Comparison of IT-Enabled Process Innovation Strategies for Multinational/Multidivisional Corporations			
	Standardized Enterprise	**Federalist Enterprise**	**Heterogeneous Enterprise**
Software Characteristics	• Software represents vendor's understanding of "best practices" in industry • Limited variability in software characteristics across lines of business in the industry • High costs of acquisition	• Some flexibility to configure different business models for each line of business or country of operation • Multiple-vendor, mix-and-match configuration strategy • Adapt software to the business model of each line of business or country of operation • Moderate - costs of modification • Moderate - technical risks associated with significant modifications	• Differentiation of business models based on line of business or country of operation • High costs of development • Reusability of design and code critical to control development costs
Process Characteristics	• Desire to standardize core business operations across lines of business or countries of operations, as necessary	• Differences - in business models and associated processes across lines of business & country of operation	• Unique business model and associated processes for each line of business or country of operation
Organizational Implementation Issues	• Implementation teams include corporate management, line & functional managers across business units or countries of operation, vendors, consultants, & IS management at the corporate & business levels. • Corporate & business unit level personnel decide on accepted process models, & they evaluate & select software with technical input from IS personnel & vendors. • IS personnel's emphasis on establishing standards for data sharing & inter-unit enterprise architecture • High costs of software acquisition • Management of resistance to "one way of doing business." • Learning costs during standardization of business operations • Training in procedures & new systems tailored to the business & cultural context	• Implementation teams include corporate management, line and functional managers across lines of business or countries of operation, vendors, consultants, IS management at the corporate and business unit levels, and development personnel at the local and corporate levels • Corporate and business unit personnel decide on level of adaptation required to balance local customization needs with the need for global standards • IS personnel's responsibility to meet the software adaptation needs at the local business level, while adhering to global architecture standards • Moderate - costs of software modification • Management of resistance can be diffused by accepting some levels of adaptation to local requests • Training in procedures and new systems tailored to the specific characteristics of local business model	• Implementation teams include corporate management, line and functional managers across lines of business or countries of operation, vendors, consultants, IS management at the corporate and business unit levels, and development personnel at the local business unit level • IS personnel's responsibility to understand variations in business models and develop applications • Manage redundancy in development efforts through corporate reusability strategy • High costs of customization • Software training developed and delivered by IS personnel at the local business unit level

the same software product with similar configurations can be rolled out across different lines of business. At the other extreme, each business unit can develop its own customized system with minimal global integration of information and, consequently, business processes. The approaches are summarized in Table 6.

Some companies have followed a federalist operating model for their corporate information systems (Table 6, column 3). Rather than implement a single, global system, these companies implement different versions of the same system in each business unit. These different versions vary in their emphasis on collecting, storing and processing information to support local needs and promote global integration. Some form of a federalist approach has been taken by a large number of companies, including Hewlett-Packard, Monsanto and Nestle (Davenport, 1998).

The biggest challenge in using the federalist model successfully is determining what is to be standardized versus what can vary across the organization. Companies differ a great deal in their emphasis on common standards across lines of business. Monsanto, for example, has achieved 85% standardization in data used in its enterprise system, which is being used to support its agrochemical, biotechnology, and pharmaceutical lines of business. On the other hand, Hewlett-Packard implemented separate enterprise systems for each of its divisions constrained only by the minimal integration across these systems needed for purposes of financial rollup. The entire enterprise systems project is expected to cost about a billion dollars (Davenport, 1998).

The implementation teams in these projects become complex and involve personnel from both headquarters and local business units. The decision on degree of process standardization requires significant participation from representatives of local units. A corporate dictatorship that enforces a high level of standardization of processes can result in significant resistance at the local unit levels. This resistance is often associated with behavioral and psychological hurdles for the implementation process.

Alternatively, as the process innovation strategy moves toward customization, management should conduct a careful examination of the cost-benefit implications of a reusability strategy. Sometimes a well-planned reusability strategy could save significant development resources and prevent unnecessary rework, while positively shaping the quality of these complex application systems.

Implications of IT-Enabled Process Innovation Strategies

As IT-enabled process innovation projects evolve from a single-function-vendor-driven solution to a multidivisional-internally-developed solution, the organizational and technological complexity of projects mount. The organizational scope of the BPR project, in conjunction with the software application strategy, generates a twelve cell classification framework. The different combinations have important implications for reengineering strategy selection. The business trade press reports that numerous companies are going through some form of reengineering. Mounting evidence, however, indicates that BPR projects do not produce the dramatic results that its proponents claim it should. Although the successful cases are frequently cited, failures are often not publicized. It has been suggested that only 20 to 25 percent of reengineering projects actually result in real dramatic results, while the other 70% produce only minor improvements or none at all (Hall, Rosenthal and

Wade, 1993; Moad, 1993b). Faltering and weak support from top management, inadequate organizational changes accompanying business process redesign (lack of *depth*), and lack of *breadth* or organizational scope are cited as the most frequent causes of failed business process redesign efforts (Hall et al., 1993; Moad, 1993).

The choice between make or buy the software applications is a difficult one. An industry expert estimates that if "You can find a product that satisfies about 70% or 80% of what you need to do, you should buy it." (Judith Hurwitz of the Hurwitz Consulting Group in Watertown Mass.; as cited in Moad, 1993b). As outsourcing is becoming a viable economic alternative, buying decisions are likely to be more appealing. However, as developed in the discussion on vendor driven reengineering strategies, the firm gains speed of implementation, and lowers its total project cost, but limits its flexibility to radically reengineer its business processes.

As the scope of its BPR projects move from a single function, to the enterprise, to the interorganizational level, to the multidivisional level, there are significant implications for the design of implementation strategies. The composition of the teams change, as do a variety of organizational issues, such as leadership, control, coordination, management of the team and who is in charge of the implementation project.

The framework clarifies the need for tightly linking the strategy of the firm with its IT strategy and the reengineering strategy. IT-enabled process innovation projects focused on single tasks and isolated functions will tend to be less disruptive of the operation of the firm. Even small projects are strategic in nature if they improve customer service. However, many small hits of this nature are necessary to amount to a significant bottom line impact. The risk here is ending up with disparate software applications that do not talk to each other. With the rapid growth of enterprise resource planning systems, such as SAP, PeopleSoft, and Bahn, planners of IT-enabled process innovation should evaluate the adequacy of customization options, such as configuration tables, that are part of these systems. Finally, they should assess the trade-off between process integration achieved at a given point of time and implications for process flexibility at that point in time and in the future.

In contrast to vendor driven reengineering, consider interorganizational or multidivisional projects, where software applications are developed internally. For example, consider Brach's $4 million investment in reengineering, Corning Glass's Asahi group $1 million investment and more than 2 years of time spent on the reengineering effort, CSX's $250 million in IT reengineering, and CN North America's $50 million paid price for its purchased software application. The risks taken in such projects significantly increase. The organization has to carefully assess its internal capabilities and specific business needs. The projects are large in scale, have time pressures, and there is the issue of leadership and project ownership. These projects should be well linked to the strategy of the firm. Investments in time, money and people are of a significant magnitude and tend to be irreversible. Failed projects in this category could well imply failed companies.

End Notes

1   Klein, Paula. (1993). Reengineering via the backdoor. *Information Week*. July 5. 39-42.
2   Klein, Paula. (1993). They are 'Wacky', but they are no fools. *Information Week*. July

5, 39-42.

3   For more in depth views of teams, see, for example Meyer, Christopher, How the right measures help teams excel, *Harvard Business Review*, May-June 1994, pp 95-103. On types of teams, their management, composition and rules of thumb for better team effectiveness, see Jon R. Katzenbach and D.K. Smith, *The Wisdom of Teams*, New York: Harper Collins Publishers, 1993. For examples of how cross-functional teams have been organized and structured in various industries, see Kenji Kurogane (ed.) *Cross-Functional Management*. New York: Quality Resources, 1993 (Originally published by the Asian Productivity Organization).

4   Caldwell, Bruce. (1994). Leading the Charge. *Information Week*. February 7. 38-44.

References

Allen, Thomas J. & M. Scott Morton. (1994). *Information Technology and the Corporation of the 1990s*. New York: Oxford University Press.

Appleby, Chuck. (1993). A case of chemical reengineering. *Information Week*. December 13, 48.

Bancroft, N.H., Seip, H., and Sprengel, A. (1998) *Implementing SAP R/3: How to introduce a large system into a large organization*. Manning Publishing, Greenwich, CT.

Bartholomew, Doug. (1992). Business Alignment: The CEO's view. *Information Week*. October 26, 12-18.

Caldwell, Bruce. (1993) Casey Jones is a reengineer. *Information Week*. June 28, 36-40.

Caldwell, Bruce. (1994). Corning IS makes room for reengineering. *Information Week*. February 7. 41.

Cash, James and J.E. Robinson. (1992). IT gets the line. *Information Week*. September 21, 38-44.

Davenport, Thomas H. (1993). *Process Innovation*. Boston MA: Harvard Business School Press.

Davenport, T.H. & J.E. Short. (1990). The new industrial engineering: Information technology and business process redesign. *Sloan Management Review*. Summer, 11-27.

Davenport, Thomas H. (1998). Putting the enterprise into the enterprise system. *Harvard Business Review*, July-August, 121-131.

Fischer Lent, Anne. (1994). Documenting change. *Information Week*. March 28. 46-50.

Greenbaum, Joshua. (1993). Build or buy? *Information Week*. December 20/27. 36-44.

Greenbaum, Joshua. (1994). Nestle's global mix. *Information Week*. April 25, 44-46.

Grover, V, JTC Teng & KD Fiedler. (1993). Information technology enabled business process redesign: An integrated framework. *OMEGA*. vol21, n-4, 433-447.

Hammer, M . (1990). Reengineering work: Don't automate, obliterate. *Harvard Business Review*. July-August, 18-25.

Henderson, John C. & N. Venkatraman. (1992). Strategic alignment: A model for organizational transformation through information technology. In *Transforming Organizations*. T. A. Kochan & M. Useem eds. New York: Oxford University Press. 97-117.

Information Week. (1991). The human factor. June 10. 27-36.

Johansson, Henry J., P.Mchugh, A.J. Pendlebury, and W.A. Wheeler III. *Business Process Reengineering*. New York: John Wiley & Sons.

Jonscher, Charles. (1994). An economic study of the information technology revolution, in *Information Technology and the Corporation of the 1990s*. New York: Oxford University press.5-42.

Klein, Paula. (1994) Go with the flow. *Information Week*. March 28, 41-45.

Maglitta, Joseph. (1994). Glass act. *Computerworld*. January, 17. 80-88.

McCormick, John. (1992). *Information Week*. January 13, 10-11.

Moad, Jeff. (1993a). New rules, new ratings as IS reengineers. *Datamation*. November 1. 85-87.

Moad, Jeff. (1993b). Does reengineering really work? *Datamation*. August 1. 22-24.

Moad, Jeff. (1994). A day in a reengineering project. *Datamation*.

Pepper, Jon. (1990). Reebok Toes the production line. *Information Week*. December 17, 26-27.

Pepper, John, (1991). Getting service on track, *Information Week*, November 11, 20-22.

Porter, M.E. and V.E. Millar. (1985). How information technology gives you competitive advantage. *Harvard Business Review*. July-August, 149-160.

Primozic, Kenneth, Edward Primozic & Joe Leben. (1991). *Strategic Choices*. New York: McGraw Hill, Inc.

Tapscott, Don and Art Caston. (1993). *Paradigm Shift: The New Promise of Information Technology*. New York: McGraw Hill, Inc.

Teitelman, Robert. (1991). The magnificent McCoys: Running America's best bank. *Institutional Investor*. July.

Wilson, Linda. (1993). A Spartan existence. *Information Week*. November 15, 40-42.

Zuboff, Shoshana. (1988). *In the Age of the Smart Machine: The Future of Work and Power*. New York: Basic Books.

CHAPTER 12

Reengineering Effectiveness and the Redesign of Organizational Control: A Case Study of the Inland Revenue Authority of Singapore

Sia Siew Kien
Nanyang Technical University, Singapore

Neo Boon Siong
Nanyang Technical University, Singapore

Reengineering Success Story 1: The All Encompassing Case Manager! (Hammer and Champy, 1993)
Several years ago at IBM Credit, arriving at a quote for computer financing took an average of seven days. Now, it takes six hours, largely because one person handles the entire deal from start to finish. Well, he arranges the financing package; he checks the customer's credit background; he approves the interest rate used; he ensures the disbursement of loan; he records the transaction ...

Reengineering Success Story 2: Get Rid of that Invoice! (Hammer and Champy, 1993)
Ford Motor used to have more than 500 employees working in the accounts payable department, matching purchase orders, receiving reports, and supplier invoices. The reengineered system eliminates supplier invoices as external evidence and hence no reconciliation is needed. Electronic payments will now be made once the receiving details match the purchase orders. The head count was reduced by 75% ...

Reengineering Success Story 3: Eliminate Unnecessary Mediation! (Rosenthal and Salzman, 1990)
Nurses have often provided an additional check on doctors' prescriptions. If they thought a medication order ill-advised, they would ask the doctors, "Did you know that this patient is also taking medication X?" Or, "Did you remember that the patient is scheduled for a Y procedure tomorrow?" The reengineered system of a hospital however, eliminated nurses' roles as "mediators." Doctors now request patient medication directly from the pharmacy through the new computer link-up ...

Managers will probably gasp at the above stories as they contradict many of the sacredly guarded fundamentals of traditional control. But these are the results of many business process reengineering (BPR) efforts. Despite the increased risks, many organizations recognize that an appropriate redesign of control systems is necessary for reengineering effectiveness. This chapter looks at how reengineered organizations have dealt with the redesign of control.

Business Process Reengineering Changes Organizational Control

BPR is defined as "the fundamental rethinking and redesign of business processes to achieve dramatic improvements in critical contemporary measures of performance such as cost, quality, service, and speed" (Hammer, 1990). It describes the application of information technology to support broad structural changes. Hammer and Champy (1993) present a list of principles to redesign processes: eliminate non-value-adding activities, organize work around outcomes, have output users perform the process themselves, enable simultaneous work, empower workers, and so on. Organizations believe BPR will sharpen competitiveness, enhance productivity, shorten cycle time, enrich job content, reduce hand-offs, and improve customer service.

By deemphasizing division of labor, BPR recasts work design from a "simple jobs, complex processes" setup to one focused on "complex jobs, simple processes." For example, the case worker arrangement changes task interdependency from a sequential to a pooled format (Thompson, 1967). The IBM Credit case illustrates this change (Figure 1). Reduction of management layers is also a typical outcome of BPR. For example, Taco Bell eliminated the "district manager" supervisory layer,

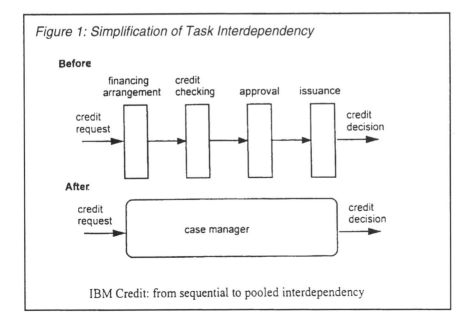

Figure 1: Simplification of Task Interdependency

Before

financing arrangement   credit checking   approval   issuance

credit request → credit decision

After

credit request → case manager → credit decision

IBM Credit: from sequential to pooled interdependency

which traditionally oversees the management of five or six restaurants.

The emerging job design often stresses multiskilling, combines working and managing, and emphasizes substantive job content. The natural consequence is a substantial reduction of behavioral observability, that is, the extent of the controller's access to information about the controllee's actions. The reduction in independent checks and approval procedures implies less visibility because there are fewer referrals up the hierarchical chain. The compression of duties into single individuals "hides" the performance of functional activities. Previously, a nonperformance would result in a break in the chain that attracts the attention of the controllers. Such end-to-end work design often leads to a concentration of information on the controllee, further eroding the ability of the manager to control his or her staff. The broader span of managerial control also implies the impracticality of keeping a tight leash on controllees.

Thus, with the compression of responsibilities, empowerment of workers, shrinkage in supervisory efforts, and reduction of checks and controls,[1] BPR presents new challenges to the implementation of organizational controls. Redesigned work processes require a corresponding alignment in organizational control to sustain reengineering effectiveness. The important question for managers is whether traditional controls have been eliminated, compromised, or rendered irrelevant. The effect of breaching fundamental control, as in segregation of duties, is probably still ringing clear as highlighted in the recent Baring case.[2] Where are the control points in reengineered organizations? Are the control points fewer but more critical now, or is a completely different control portfolio being adopted? Or is management simply more willing to bear the cost of weak control? Inadequate attention to these control issues can expose reengineered systems to excessive risks or produce reengineering attempts that are prematurely self-defeating as they contradict the underlying control philosophy. The solution, however, is far from obvious.

Review of the Organizational Control Literature

Organizational control is defined as attempts by an organization to increase the probability that individuals will behave in ways that lead to the attainment of organizational objectives (Flamholtz, Das and Tsui, 1985). The concept has been a central issue in management theory since the time of Weber (1968). Positing the causal link between control and organizational performance, streams of research have explored the control concept from a variety of perspectives. Broadly, this research can be classified into three major categories:

1. *A conceptualization of control as a management of resource dependency* (Green and Welsh, 1988). These models often focus on the reasons for control and attempt to change the nature of such dependency at the macro level. Typically, these strategies have an external focus, involving either a redefinition of organizational goals or a choice of another form of reliance, for example, market or hierarchy (Pfeffe and Salancik, 1978, p. 38). Organizational practices such as vertical integration, employing multiple suppliers, outsourcing, diversification, and avoidance exemplify such control. Unlike the next two conceptualizations

of control, these strategies are "quasi-controls" because they lack cybernetic validity (Green and Welsh, 1986); in other words, the required feedback cycles to regulate activities are often not within the organization's control. Their managerial perspective is not to regulate a dependency but first to examine if the demand for control can be restructured, reduced, or eliminated.

2. *A conceptualization of control as a dynamic feedback process that involves planning, implementing, monitoring, and reinforcing* (Weiner, 1967) *to regulate the flow of resources.* These models often incorporate motivational theories such as feedback seeking, goal setting, expectancy, and attribution theories (Flamholtz et al., 1985; Klein, 1989). Other process models examine control from a more practical input— process— output or preventive — detective — corrective perspective (Arens, Loebbecke and Ambanbola, 1993, 36).

3. *A conceptualization of control as categories of organizational practices with unique sets of characteristics,* such as an emphasis on procedural compliance in behavioral control, the target-setting focus in outcome control, the influence through socialization in clan control, or enhanced individual decision-making power in self-control (Barker, 1993; Greenberger and Strasser, 1986, 19). Such models often have embedded organizational or economic theories (Eisenhardt, 1989; Ouchi, 1979) that provide a contingency prescription on the use of a specific control mode. Recent research has also begun to explore the use of multiple control modes as a portfolio (Kaplan and Norton, 1993; Simons 1995).

While these control concepts have been applied in the traditional management environment, the advancement of information technology and the changing economic fundamentals have triggered considerable discussion about the lack of relevance of these controls in recent years. There has also been a good deal of speculation about the management of newer forms of organizations (Appelgate, 1993; Dillard and Burns, 1993; Handy, 1992). Given that BPR is one major vehicle of organizational transformation, the study of its consequential control implications is particularly relevant.

However, research on the control impacts of BPR is limited and often explored only as a small part of a wider research focus (Caron, Jarvenpaa and Stoddard, 1994; Chalykoff and Norhia, 1990; Davenport and Short, 1990; Hammer and Champy, 1993; Stoddard and Meadows, 1992). Davenport and Nohria (1994) suggest that there is "a bias toward less monitoring and more accountability and responsibility." Davenport and Short (1990) note the changing managerial role from controller and supervisor to supporter and facilitator. CIGNA's reengineering experience (Caron et al., 1994) also shows that "functional hierarchy was flattened by pushing decision making to self-managing teams which set their own goals, allocate their own resources, and appoint as well as dismiss their team leaders." Unfortunately, these studies provide few details on the organizational mechanisms that facilitate such "self-management." Observations of control changes from BPR implementations have not been carried out systematically. There are calls for new control designs to be innovative, flexible, customer—oriented, transparent, and process-based. But exactly how this can be achieved without compromising fundamental control principles remains unclear. "Unguided" autonomy can be risky. For instance, Frito Lay, in pushing through a decision about applying promotional money to its divisional managers, found its entire year's promotion allocation spent within four months.

This chapter addresses the impacts of BPR on organizational control through a case study of the Inland Revenue Authority of Singapore (IRAS). IRAS is a government agency with a heritage of strict bureaucratic controls. It embarked on a major BPR program in the early 1990s, which gave us the opportunity to explore how BPR affected:

1. How dependency relationships are structured;
2. The process by which controls are applied; and
3. The use of specific control modes.

Methodology

Given the complexity of the control conceptualization, Merchant (1988) suggests that "researchers [need] to go into the field to observe and to provide rich descriptions of companies' control practices." The reengineering in IRAS provides a rich context for this single-holistic case study of control practices. Forty-two interviews were conducted with employees from all three parties involved in the project, namely, IRAS, the National Computer Board, and Andersen Consulting. Questions in the interview protocol are shown in the appendix. Wherever possible, two researchers took part in the interviews. Voice recording of interviews was avoided because it can hinder candid responses by interviewees, given the sensitivities of this research in a public organization. Notes from the interviews were transcribed within twenty-four hours and reviewed by the second researcher, who added omitted facts and discussed ambiguous observations with the first researcher. In addition, the transcripts contained researchers' comments in boxes made during transcription. In this way, researchers' comments were kept separate from case facts to maintain objectivity. The findings were also supplemented by a huge pool of archival records collected from the end of 1992 through 1996 including public speeches, internal presentations, annual reports, newspaper cuttings, internal surveys, and in-house bulletins. A case study database was established. The case file included the followings: interview transcripts, chronological case write-up, reengineering project documentation, archival information, research notes, and plans. A final case write-up documenting the chronological events and findings in IRAS was verified and cleared by the organization.

Reengineering IRAS

IRAS is the agency responsible for the assessment, collection, and enforcement of taxes in Singapore.[3] The tax revenue collected by IRAS accounts for more than 50 percent of the government's operating budget. At the end of 1990, however, it was clear that the tax authority (known then as the Inland Revenue Department, or IRD) was inadequately equipped to fulfill its role. The staff turnover rate was at a high of 11 percent, compared with an average of 3.8 percent for the Singapore civil service. The backlog in tax collection stood at a hefty $1.14 billion, putting them in a vicious cycle that set IRD back a few months each year in their assessment efforts. One telephone survey by the local newspaper rated IRD among the lowest in terms of public service satisfaction. With the promise of a new building[4] and significantly more autonomy as IRD became a statutory board,[5] the new commissioner took advantage of the clean slate to push for changes. Ideas that had been under discussion over the years were swiftly crystallized into concrete actions. The reengineering project was managed with the involvement of three main parties: IRAS (users), National Computer Board (quality assurers), and Andersen Consulting (major vendor). At its peak, the project team comprised more than 200 full-time staff. The project started in late 1991 as a strategic business information technology plan. A rough timeline of the transformation road map is shown in Figure 2.

Table 1: Summary of Organizational Changes

	Before reengineering	After reengineering
Information	No common source of information Fragmented and limited information sharing Redundant preparation of data by tax officers	Common source of information integrated and shared across tax types Responsive, online, and simultaneous access to data by tax officers
Competence	Highly specialized by tax types Limited matching of job complexity and skills of tax officers All-encompassing review Relationship with taxpayers: weak to none, desk-bound, passive Complex tax compliance procedures Approach: to catch and prosecute taxpayers Vague and mythical interpretation of the Act	Generalists/specialists with strong cross tax types coordination Automated matching of job complexity and skills of tax officers Review by exceptions Relationship with taxpayers: frequent, field-visits, proactive Streamlined tax compliance procedures Approach: to assist taxpayers to comply with the law Clear practice guide to give business certainty
Authority	Vague individual accountability Narrow supervisory span of control (5-7); about 6 reporting levels on average Long apprenticeship (6 months to a year) Limited involvement of tax officers in work improvement teams	Strong individual accountability with clear targets Expanded supervisory span of control (15-20); about 3 reporting levels on average Shorter apprenticeship (from 3 weeks to 3 months) All officers are involved in work improvement teams
Rewards	Rewards tagged to broad-based indicators Fixed bonus for everyone Fixed scale pay increment and promotion, i.e., 19 narrow salary grades No additional performance bonus	Performance discriminate at the individual level, within and across divisions Variable bonus for different tax officers ranging from 0-6 months Pay increment and promotions are on a salary range which allows differential increments, i.e., 10 salary grades with wide ranges One-time performance bonus

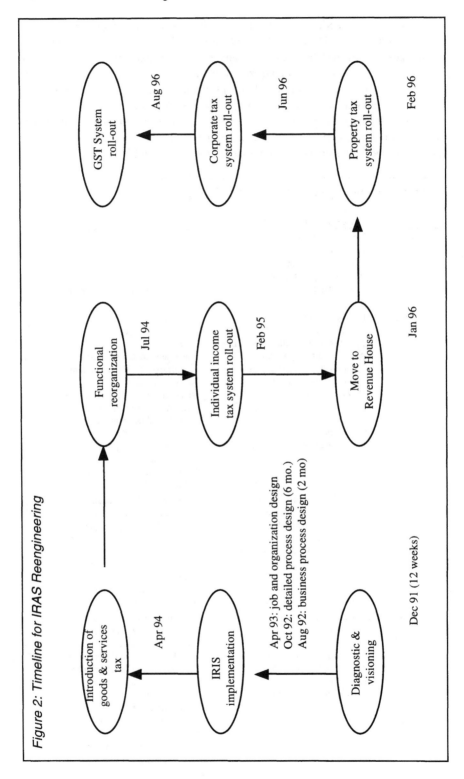

Figure 2: Timeline for IRAS Reengineering

Table 2: Summary of Control Changes

Restructured dependency
Paperless processing: All tax returns and correspondences are fed into the document imaging system. Fetching of documents is done electronically. Documents can also be accessed by multiple users simultaneously. The paperless system eliminates much of the problem of missing documents, inconsistent information, etc.
Online resource library Technical materials, e.g., budget clarification and procedural manuals, are accessed through an online context-sensitive search feature, enabling prompt and consistent replies to taxpayers' queries by any tax officers.
Correspondence management Standard letter templates for different types of tax correspondence are available electronically for "cut and paste" to customize individual replies, ensuring consistent styles across tax officers.
Pipeline processing: Automated processing of all common transactions across tax types. Manual examination of tax returns is only necessary if exceptions occur.
Direct reliance on external agencies: Declaration of certain information by taxpayers -- e.g., pay and relief entitlements, share dividends, and loan stock interest -- is no longer necessary. Such information is provided by external agencies (e.g., Ministry of Defense, Home Affairs Ministry) or banks.

Control segmentation
Segmented transaction streams: In tax processing, about 70% of the tax returns are processed automatically without any human intervention. 20% of simple exception cases are routed to return review officers while the 10% that are complex cases are subjected to end-to-end review by specialized assessment officers. In the previous system, the tasks were allocated to tax officers by a range of tax reference numbers, with little consideration of their experience and expertise. A similar trend is noted in taxpayer services. General inquiries across tax types are routed to section 1 while specialized inquiries are referred to sections 2 and 3.
Mass property appraisal. Property valuation is now done without inspecting properties. Physical inspections are performed only if an event has occurred, e.g., renovations. Similar properties are grouped as homogeneous properties. The valuation of specific bench marked properties is replicated for others.
Modularization of tax forms: The design of tax forms has been simplified to facilitate completion. For example, one standard Form B (8 pages) attempts to cater to all taxpayers. Now, the form is split into a few subsections. Most taxpayers only need to complete the first section (2 pages). Taxpayers who have additional sources of income or updates in personal details, etc., attach additional sections as necessary.
Value focus tax processing: Previously, no distinction was made between low- and high-value cases. Tax cases were processed as they flowed through. Now, sorting criteria are embedded within IRIS such that cases with higher taxes payable will be assessed first. Persons with income below a certain level are not even required to file tax returns.

Shift toward back-end control
Fixing of filing deadline: Previously, there were multiple filing deadlines. The onus was on IRAS

Essentially, IRAS changed from a tax-type organization (income tax, corporate tax, goods and services tax, property tax, and estate/stamp duties) to a process organization that enables efficient resource sharing across tax types while retaining a focused specialization on technical expertise. With the provision of one-stop taxpayer services, "hand-offs" across tax types are minimized. At the center of the change is a $69- million computer system—the Inland Revenue Integrated System (IR1S).[6] The new system captures tax returns through imaging and processes the returns automatically through a series of embedded review and validation rules. The workflow management system categorizes the exceptions by their complexity, and

Table 2: Summary of Control Changes (continued)

to issue second tax notifications before the notice could be considered legally served to taxpayers for initiation of prosecution. With the fixing of an official filing deadline— e.g., April 15 for individual income tax—the onus is now on the taxpayers to ensure timely filing. Non-filing is considered an offense.

Filer's assessment & audit enhancement If there is no exception to laid-down criteria, taxpayers will be assessed based on what they file without reference to any documents, e.g., prior year assessments. The relaxation of control, however, is compensated by significant enhancement of back-end taxpayer audit and investigation functions.

Aggregate reviews and reasonableness checks: Through data warehousing and mining software, there has been a shift toward greater reliance on detective controls to catch patterns of exceptions. Unlike previous audit strategies that attempted to catch all, auditors now closely monitor trends of noncompliance and plan actions thereof. The roots of compliance issues are investigated and followup efforts are planned.

Reliance on outcome control portfolio

Annual planning workshop. A two- to three-day event where divisional directors highlight significant accomplishment, and present their plans and targets for the coming year to the IRAS staff.

Individual performance target setting. Thirty-two performance targets have been established. The specific expectations are cascaded down to the individual officers through the annual performance review. A new sheet has been added to the performance review form documenting the individual targets in order of importance.

Enhanced outcome tracking system: IRIS enables the immediate gathering of information such as number of cases allotted, open, and closed and the aging of outstanding cases. One manager noted, "The system doesn't lose documents; you know when the document comes in, how many times the officers access the document, when it is completed. The computer system now chases after you!" IRIS also automatically captures and compiles performance statistics by individual and in aggregate.

Communication and refinement of outcome expectations: The outcome orientation is constantly reinforced through the Commissioner's Meetings—weekly sessions at which all division heads meet with the commissioner. The "Lunch Club' also provides an informal setting for management interaction. Over 100 staff members, identified as three levels of management succession, have been allocated throughout IRAS as role models to "walk the talk."

Tightened reward-performance linkage: Individual employees are ranked within divisions and across divisions. "We are more discriminating now!" noted one divisional director. Pay increments and promotions are no longer on fixed scales but on a salary range that allows differential increments. Reward flexibility also comes in the form of variable bonuses and one-time special payments.

Emphasis on core values and culture to balance its outcome orientation: IRAS actively promotes its core values of "Integrity, Fairness, Professionalism, Quality" as a guideline for acceptable behaviors. Management policies are consistently articulated through such themes. Positive reinforcement of such behaviors are provided through core value awards.

the work items are assigned to tax officers with matching skill sets. All tax officers can now share the same set of electronic information, thus maintaining a view consistent with the rest of the organization. IRIS also boosts enforcement efforts through non-filer management, tax-in-arrears management, and case management. Errant taxpayers can be identified promptly, and appropriate courses of action can be systematically implemented according to the case history of the taxpayers. Simultaneously, many organizational changes were made. Table 1 describes some of these changes.

The results of the BPR changes have been significant. The amount of tax revenue collected was at a record high of $14 billion in 1995. Income-tax arrears were reduced from $1.14 billion at the end of financial year 1990-91 to $761 million at the end of financial year 1994-95. Property-tax arrears, meanwhile, were reduced from $106 million to $53 million. The annual values of 99 percent of private properties are now current compared with 85 percent one year ago. With the enhancement of enforcement efforts, the taxpayer audit division brought in an additional $18 million of tax and penalties (FY 1992-93 = $41,000) while the investigation division brought in another $13 million (FY 1992-93 = $8 million). All this was achieved with a constant staff strength of about 1,600. Taxpayer satisfaction also improved. A 1994 survey noted that eight out of ten taxpayers rated their services as courteous and efficient. The commissioner was awarded the Meritorious Service Medal—one of the highest honors in the 1995 Singapore National Day Awards— for his leadership in IRAS's reengineering efforts. IRAS also won the 1996 Singapore National IT Award for public-sector organizations for its innovative IRIS implementation.

Changes to Organizational Control

How did IRAS deal with control issues in achieving this performance improvement? We examined the philosophy underlying their reengineered work design in light of the management control literature and noted the emergence of four control themes: (1) the dependency on tax officers and taxpayers has been restructured through greater reliance on automation and external agencies; (2) the process by which controls are applied has been segmented more finely; (3) the reengineered work design has greater reliance on back-end control; and (4) there has been a clear shift in the control mode toward an outcome control portfolio. Table 2 summarizes these changes.

Restructured Control Dependency

The first impact we observed was a restructuring of the dependency on tax officers through the automation of standardizable procedures. With IRIS, IRAS automates the tax assessment function previously handled by tax officers by embedding 600 to 800 edit checks, validation rules, and review criteria within a front-end expert system. Through workshops and discussions, tax officers explained how they intuitively performed the review of tax returns and their effective "rules of thumb." Such tacit knowledge was then expressed in rules and policies that enabled the automation of many manual controls—for example, segregation of duties was imposed via password restrictions and the access privileges were assigned to individuals; approval authority was simulated by programming preestablished criteria; independent checks for accuracy and completeness were replaced by field editing features and a system default that prevents the system from proceeding until all relevant data have been entered. Other modules in IRIS—correspondence management, non-filer/debt management, and online technical reference—also enabled a similar reduction in the dependency on tax officers to provide competent and consistent services. Some tax information previously submitted by taxpayers was no longer collected in annual tax returns, for example, pay and relief entitlements, share dividends, and loan stock interests. Instead, greater reliance was placed on source information provided by external agencies such as other government ministries or banks.

IRAS officers are expected to be reasonably familiar with the security features of the new technical platforms and to appreciate the control risks now assumed by IRAS or the rules and policies embedded in the automated systems. Recognizing this, IRAS is considering rotating tax officers through the MIS function to give them a deeper understanding of the processes embedded in the IRIS system.

Control Segmentation

For dependencies that cannot be restructured through automation or external agencies, how are manual controls affected? Traditionally, even if past experience suggests that only 5 percent of a company's transactions are in fact erroneous, 100 percent of the transactions are subjected to the same laborious internal control checks. In that regard, BPR efforts often attempt to eliminate such controls because 95 percent of the time the control mechanisms do not "add value" to the business. As noted by the IRAS commissioner, "The old process had a tremendous bureaucratic load. An entire process is often needed to take care of exception cases —0.1 percent of the normal transactions." This concern led to the segmentation of control practices in IRAS.

By applying different control mechanisms to different segments, the reengineered tax processes attempt to match the risk profiles of the transaction streams with the costs of employing specific control mechanisms. This value-conscious managerial focus is reflected by the remarks of the chief valuer in implementing the change from individual property valuations to mass property valuations: "It involves a change in the mindset. We had to shift from spending too much time on noting fine property differences which will not materially enhance the accuracy of valuations and instead follow how people think in the market place— making fast decisions and getting more done through confident broad-based approximations." The reengineered system splits property valuation into two main streams—benchmarked properties for which physical inspection practices continue and homogeneous properties for which valuations are estimated from the respective benchmarked properties. Physical inspection of homogeneous properties will be performed only upon specific events, such as when major renovations are performed. This significantly reduces the need for costly property inspections, enabling IRAS to achieve annual valuation of 99 percent of the properties in Singapore.

Another segmentation was noted in tax return processing. Prior to reengineering, every income-tax return was reviewed manually by tax officers. The returns were allocated by the ranges of tax reference numbers, and limited efforts were made to match task complexity with the skill sets of tax officers. The commissioner commented, "We expect every Singaporean (regardless of their educational level) to be able to fill in the tax forms, but on the other hand, university graduates were employed to review every single tax return. The disparity is fundamentally not right!" Tax complexity is now managed by segregating cases into three streams of tax transactions. Straightforward tax cases are assessed entirely by computer. Those cases thrown out of the tax pipeline processing system because they fail specific rules or because they require specialized assessments with less than $500,000 turnover are handled by return review officers. The third category of difficult or high value tax cases (i.e., disputed/fraudulent cases or high value cases above $500,000) are routed to specialized assessors, who perform stringent review from beginning to the end.

Managers designing such control segmentation systems should carefully consider the reasonableness of segregation criteria, the integrity of exception reporting mechanism, and the appropriate control design for the respective transaction streams. Do the segregation criteria expose the organization to excessive risk or are they too restrictive in that unnecessary controls are still being applied to low-risk transactions? Indeed, in IRAS, the fact that no tax officer would be involved in assessing 70 percent of the taxpayers prompted many to ask, "Are we allowing too much to flow through the pipeline?" In this regard, the divisional director of tax processing noted the enhanced roles of close coordination with upstream and downstream department —taxpayer services and taxpayer audit divisions— which would monitor the trends of tax issues and provide feedback on the adequacy of the embedded rules. IRAS also put a lot of effort into specifying the security features of the workflow management system to prevent unauthorized bypassing of the routing mechanisms.

Leveraging on Back-End Controls

Another change observed in IRAS is the rebalancing of front-end and back-end controls, triggered by a need to meet taxpayers' rising expectations. One divisional director noted, "We have to respond to more vocal, more demanding, and better educated taxpayers now. Many of them compare our service levels to other efficient public sector organizations and even to banks and business organizations." A greater taxpayer orientation demands flexibility, transparency, and expediency in control design. Often, that also means changing fundamental assumptions about taxpayers.[7] The commissioner noted, "We regard 80 percent of the taxpayers as potential evaders and 20 percent as OK. Perhaps we have to regard 90 percent of them as OK and 10 percent as potential evaders. We will make it easy and help taxpayers to comply. We must believe that taxpayers will comply voluntarily if they are convinced that they are paying only their fair share. Nothing more, nothing less." This change in how IRAS views taxpayers translates into a "filer assessment" policy. Instead of raising tax queries and challenging income declared by taxpayers in their tax returns, tax officers now accept the honesty of taxpayers as much as possible, and taxpayers are simply assessed on the basis of what they file. This relaxation of front-end control, however, is compensated for with a significant enhancement of back-end taxpayer audit and investigation functions.

The emphasis on back-end controls is demonstrated by the size of the Taxpayer Audit Division, which has grown from 20 staff members in 1993 to 100 in 1996 was expected to have reached 200 in 1997. The audit strategy also changed from an all-encompassing audit that identified even "isolated cases of exceptions" to selective audits targeted at "specific pattern[s] of things."[8] This shift in strategy has ushered in recent investigations into specific groups of doctors, property speculators, freight forwarders, and company directors. Significant efforts are also under way to build a strong audit presence through field visits, dialogues with professional and/or trade associations, and media publicity of prosecuted cases.

There is also an annual Tax Audit Conference where different technical branches come together to share and plan audit strategies. Cross-tax types "fertilization" is also effected through circulation of probable markers of income omissions to various audit teams. Monthly "experience-sharing" sessions where audit teams discuss audit issues and effective approaches have been implemented. Cross-training and joint audit teams comprising members of different tax specialties were also put in place for specific tax cases. As noted by the divisional director for taxpayer audit, the audit teams now function in a manner whereby "the left hand knows what the right hand is doing!" The IRIS audit module will prefetch specific information about the taxpayers (e.g., asset ownership) and precompute basic statistics about taxpayers. With the support from data warehousing and data-mining software, the existing "half-blind" audit approach will also be enhanced to second-guess taxpayers who should be audited.

Greater Reliance on Outcome Control

The next control change first manifested itself as a significant reduction in supervisory control. The average reporting level has been reduced from six to three. A typical span of control is now between fifteen and twenty compared with a span of five to seven prior to reengineering. One interviewee lamented that his "good supervisory skills have been wasted." Similarly, the average period of "apprentice-ship" for new staff has been reduced drastically. Previously, it ranged between six months and a year, whereas the present span is merely three weeks to three months. Our reviews of the reengineered system also reveal a general relaxation of controls. For example, previously tax refunds first had to be routed back to tax assessors for a "second look" before refund officers would process the payments. The reengineered system eliminated these "reworks" and allowed the refund officers to process payments directly. IRAS managed these probable "higher" risks by shifting toward a portfolio of organizational mechanisms that consistently articulate a strong outcome orientation:

inculcating accountability with clear performance targets, enhancing the track-ing system, communicating and refining outcome expectations, tightening the reward—performance linkage, and emphasizing core values and culture.

Inculcating Accountability with Clear Performance Targets

Extensive mechanisms to build individual accountability have been imple-mented. Thirty-two performance indicators have been established for tax officers, including tax processing efficiency, debt management efficiency and effectiveness, and quality of taxpayer services, among others. These performance measures are then cascaded downward and the specific targets are communicated to the individual officers through the annual performance review at the beginning of the year. A new sheet has been added to the performance review form documenting the lists of individual targets for the coming year in order of importance, follow-up discussion in midyear review, and subsequent changes in targets, if any. Previously, the performance review process was closed and tax officers knew nothing about their performance, their strengths and weaknesses, or the performance expected of them. In the Return Review Branch, for example, specific quantitative goals were estab-lished for tax officers, including assigning 150 cases per week per officer and setting an expected turnaround time of one week for 90 percent of cases and two weeks for the remaining 10 percent. One officer noted, "There is an overwhelming effort to achieve performance measures.

Another accountability mechanism is the annual planning workshop, a two- to three-day event at which department directors highlight the significant tasks accomplished in the past year and present their action plans, strategies, and targets for the coming year to the entire IRAS staff. The commissioner noted, "Every management staff is expected to set specific targets for each work area and take actions to achieve the targets." The planning workshop not only gives the employees a sense of the organization's overall direction but elicits commitment from the tax officers. The annual planning workshop encourages the divisional directors to set aggressive targets and establishes accountability by publicly committing directors to achieving these goals.

Enhancing Outcome Tracking System

The establishment of clear individual performance targets is supplemented by an enhanced monitoring system. Previously, work status was reported on a weekly basis as individual tax officers keyed in their respective output status into a Lotus 1-2-3 template. Given the time lapse and the self-reporting nature of such information, the ability to track tax officers' performance was limited. The embedded workflow management system in IRIS now enables the immediate gathering of information such as number of cases allotted, open, and closed, and the aging of outstanding cases. Such information is provided to tax officers when they log on to IRIS. IRIS automatically captures and compiles performance statistics by individual and in aggregate and compares them with benchmark figures. One immediate implementation issue managers faced was setting a reasonable and yet challenging performance benchmark for individual tax officers.

Similar enhancements were noted in the Taxpayer Services branch. The integration across tax types enabled centralized collection of taxpayers' complaints and feedback. The Divisional Director of Taxpayer Services commented, "Previously, fragments of taxpayer services existed everywhere, but now all branches know there is only one place to gather taxpayer feedback" Through the audit trails in IRIS, any unsatisfactory handling of taxpayers can now be easily traced to the specific officers who handled the case.

Communication and Refinement of Outcome Expectations

Various communicative mechanisms have been put in place to reinforce the performance outcome orientation and to gather feedback on outcome status for the refinement of management actions. The previous "divide and rule" management structure has given way to the Commissioner's Meetings (CMs)—weekly sessions where all divisional heads are brought together to identify problems, challenge ideas, and thrash out issues. The commissioner's first impression upon coming to IRAS in 1991 was that "this place was organized by blocs. Everyone was strongly anchored in the depth of knowledge but there was hardly anyone at the senior level that has the breadth of knowledge and sees things from the perspective of the entire organization. With this kind of structure, you can't produce managers, only good specialists." The role of the CMs is to coordinate across divisions, to manage overlapping areas, and to ensure that all divisions "pull in the same direction, and no one group pulls forward and another backward."

The concept of a "lunch club" has also been initiated to encourage interaction and information sharing among management and the tax specialists. Every Tuesday,

Thursday, and Friday, a small room near the cafeteria has been reserved for managers and tax specialists to socialize in during their lunch hours. The informal atmosphere has seen an encouraging number of managers and specialists mixing at these times. Furthermore, communication of management's expectations to the entire IRAS is facilitated through a conscious effort to identify three generations of management succession. These tax officers are put in positions that will stretch them and give them wide exposure. The Staff Committee allocated these 100 staff members to different divisions throughout IRAS. They have become role models in "walking the talk." Often, they are also the source of day-to-day feedback from tax officers. One tax officer noted that she no longer feels "lost in the crowd" in IRAS, The barriers [to communication] are not so obvious, the walls are not so thick now.

Tightening the Reward —Performance Linkage

Another manifestation of the outcome emphasis in IRAS has been a revamping of the reward structure to provide incentives for individual accountability. Performance evaluations are taken seriously; individual employees are now ranked within divisions and across divisions by all supervisors. "We are more discriminating now! We must be very clear about the relative worth of each person we have and adjust the compensation scales adequately to reward these people," noted one divisional director. The variable bonus now ranges from zero to six months. Pay increments and promotions are no longer determined according to fixed scales but follow a salary range that allows differential increments. IRAS is also the first public-sector organization to make one-time special payments to officers for special contributions. In 1994, IRAS paid out $9 million in year-end bonuses, $10 million in additional bonuses, and $1 million in one-time performance bonuses. IRAS has also instituted a parallel career advancement route which ties the earnings of top tax specialists to those of private- sector tax partners in accounting firms. Under such a system, some senior tax specialist jobs pay more than managerial positions, a cultural shift whose acceptance took a while. Strong signals on the performance emphasis were also implicit in the management's willingness to promote capable young staff to senior positions.

Emphasizing Core Values and Culture

The emphasis on outcome in IRAS has been carefully implemented with a clear delineation of performance targets and accountability. The risks of potential behavioral compromise in the reengineered tax process is further mitigated through active promotion of the core values of "Integrity, Fairness, Professionalism, Quality" as a guideline for acceptable behavior. The core values are constantly communicated through in-house newsletters, posters, and videos featuring stories about how IRAS staff have applied the core values in their daily work. Managers have also consistently articulated many of the policy changes in terms of the IRAS core values. The mass property appraisal system, for example, is articulated as being fair to taxpayers in that every property is now appraised annually. Positive reinforcement of such behaviors is also provided through core value awards presented to employees who have acted as strong role models. These tax officers are nominated and elected by all IRAS staff, which places the responsibility for monitoring tax officers' behaviors on the watchful eyes of everyone—one's superiors, peers, and subordinates.

ET21, Excellent Tax Administration for the 21st Century,[9] was also introduced to create an IRAS culture where service excellence and continuous performance improvement are a way of life. Many new initiatives have been implemented. The Staff Suggestion Scheme, for example, encourages each staff member to contribute at least two suggestions for improvement each year. Each division is given a discretionary budget to reward staff. Higher-level awards such as the chairman's and the commissioner's awards have also been established. A quarterly tea session is held to present the best-suggestion awards. Reflecting a change to a proactive culture among tax officers, the number of staff suggestions jumped from 214 in 1994 to 3,019 in 1995. Moreover, tax officers have also been exposed to personal effectiveness courses and total quality training. Each staff member is required to participate in the quality action circles, working on any projects with other colleagues of their own choice. Many interviewees have noted the internalization of this strong sense of "can do" among the tax officers. Comments like, "Oh! That is workable, let's send the suggestion in!" are fairly common. Tax officers are expected to internalize the core values of "Integrity, Fairness, Professionalism, Quality" in their day-to-day work.

Implications

This study of IRAS shows that reengineering effectiveness requires a new approach to organizational control. The implementation of new control procedures in reengineering is probably the major change management issue. Often, the control rationales behind existing policies and procedures are deeply rooted in an organization's culture and history. For example, IRAS had to grapple with a management control system that had patched procedures and policies together over a period of fifty years. As a consequence, changes like the "filer assessment" policy, the removal of refund approvals, and the emphasis on performance over seniority in IRAS were controversial and had to be mediated through a series of senior staff committees. Substantial time and efforts were invested to convince the organization about the sensibility of the alternative control solutions. Success in reengineering implementation is contingent upon adequate attention to changing the predominant organizational mindset regarding the efficacy and cost of organizational control.

The effectiveness of reengineering requires reexamination of the economics of organizational control in the new environment. Like the management control in many large organizations, IRAS inherited numerous 100 percent checks, designed to guard against 0.1 percent exceptions. In redesigning its work processes, IRAS had to address whether its existing investment in organizational control made sense, given the technological advancement, competitive environment, and demand of increasingly sophisticated taxpayers. Table 3 presents the risk-benefit dilemmas IRAS faced in adopting a different control portfolio. For example, the shift toward back-end control opens up a time window between the transaction and the deferred checks in which errors can occur undetected. On the other hand, there are potential benefits to be reaped, such as the interest to be earned from the faster collection of tax dollars and from the reduction of accumulated tax backlog.

The redesign of organizational control, thus, should be viewed from a risk

Table 3: Balancing Reduced Control Efficacy and Additional Cost Savings

	Additional risks	Cost saving
Restructured dependency	• Without manual review of tax returns, other abnormalities (not already automated) may not be identified • Reliance on external agencies and the IRIS system may reduce tax officers' alertness to errors and problems	• Faster processing, e.g., a reduced processing cycle from 18 to 5 months • Reduced time loss due to misplaced, missing documents • Reduced reconciliation efforts, due to direct source data capture • Reduced storage space for tax returns • Consistency of Services across individuals
Control segmentation	• There may be exceptions in the normal categories that pass through unnoticed	• Faster processing for most taxpayers • Reduced workload for staff • Better matching of task complexity to experience of tax officers • Improved taxpayers satisfaction
Using back-end control	• Longer time lapse before the detection of errors or exceptions • Aggregate reviews and reasonableness tests only catch pattern of exceptions not "catch all," including isolated cases of exceptions	• Faster processing • Reduced workload, given the reduction of detailed front-end checks with high-level back-end reviews • Improved responsiveness • Improved taxpayer satisfaction • Reduced interest loss from huge accumulated tax backlog
Reliance on outcome control	• Outcome may be achieved with behavioral compromise • Reward upon outcome may be inappropriate as the attainment/nonattainment may be due to external factors	• Focused efforts to achieve targets • Strong motivation for staff to perform given the tight reward link • Improved staff morale • Enhanced public image through tangible accountability

management perspective rather than from a merely ideological angle. Having understood the relative risks and benefits of the new control design, IRAS decided that the additional risk was acceptable given the associated benefits. Any loss under these control strategies is likely to be limited, considering the quantum of potential loss (e.g., relaxed review for normal/smaller-value tax returns only) and the probability of it occurring (e.g., undiscovered systematic tax fraud).

The key issue is not reducing control but optimizing the investment in control. This is illustrated in Figure 3. If an organization is on the "a" part of the curve (as are new start-ups and small entrepreneurial firms), the added efficacy of control in

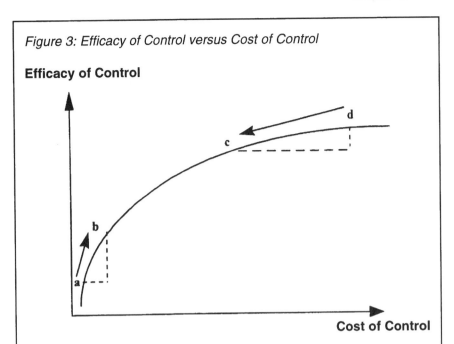

Figure 3: Efficacy of Control versus Cost of Control

Efficacy of Control

Cost of Control

Note: *This illustration of the control efficacy using the 80/20 rule was presented by Michael Hammer in a seminar attended by one of the authors.*

moving to "b" can be achieved at a reasonable cost. However, if it is on the "d" part of the curve (as are most large organizations with legacies of bureaucratic and administrative structures), substantial costs (in terms of time, people, space, money, and improved satisfaction) can be saved by restructuring the control portfolio. This case study shows how IRAS moved from "d" to "c" by changing its dependency on tax officers and taxpayers, by segmenting its transaction streams and applying different control procedures to each stream, by leveraging back-end controls, and by placing greater reliance on outcome controls. Organizations redesigning their control system as part of reengineering should first evaluate if they are closer to the "a" or the "d" part of the curve in figure 3. If they are closer to the "d" part' they should seriously reevaluate the risks and benefits associated with a new control portfolio designed to achieve greater organizational effectiveness.

The extent of reengineering effectiveness is closely related to the redesign of control, that is, choosing the "right" control mechanism within the reengineered context at the "right" price. The traditional control concepts discussed in the literature review provide us an initial basis for analyzing some of these new economics by asking the following questions:

1. Is there a need for such resource dependency and why?
2. Can the dependency be regulated differently and how?
3. What modes of management control would be more effective in the reengineered environment?

Table 4: Mapping the Observed Changes in IRAS to Control Concepts

Control conceptualization	Observations in IRAS
Dependency management perspectve i.e., *Why* the need for such dependency?	(1) Greater dependency on -- automation -- external agencies/organizations
Process perspective, i.e., *How* the dependency is regulated?	(2) Finer segmentation of transaction cycle and matching of tasks to required expertise (3) Rebalancing of process elements toward greater reliance on back-end controls
Categorical perspective, i.e., *What* modes of management practices are used in regulating dependency?	(4) A shift toward outcome control

Table 4 maps the redesign in management control in IRAS to these control concepts. For instance, a closer examination into the process perspective of control reveals how a finer segmentation of transaction cycle and a rebalancing of process elements toward back-end controls in IRAS may be accomplished.

Moreover, the new control strategies appear to follow a two-pronged approach, with a technological focus at the workflow layer and a people emphasis at the sublayer, that is, the individual level. While the first two strategies largely emphasize on "automated control" enabled by IT (e.g., formalization of work rules and task matching), the next two control strategies emphasize "humanistic control" (e.g., improved communication, closer interaction among tax auditors, enhanced personal motivation through tight reward link).[10]

Summary and Conclusions

From the case of IRAS, we noted that the design of the reengineered processes and organizational control are inseparable and must be carefully aligned to sustain reengineering effectiveness. Managers should therefore reexamine the effectiveness and efficiency of existing management controls in BPR projects. Insistence on a traditional control approach may damage organizational performance by over-emphasizing rigid control procedures. Simultaneously, these traditional controls may have become elaborate and ineffective rituals, decoupled from the operational processes where the risks really exist.

On the other hand, inadequate attention to organizational control can expose reengineered systems to excessive risks as they expose the organization to potential major fiascos such as the Baring case. Control design decisions in the reengineering context must be carefully considered. While the benefits of new control design are concrete and tangible, the corresponding costs are qualitative and often less visible. The risk assessment involves a subjective quantification of the potential loss and an estimation of the likelihood of its occurrence. By adopting a different control portfolio, IRAS managed to align its control design with the reengineered work processes while maintaining a continual focus on critical risk exposures.

While the case of IRAS has shown us some potential templates of control design, the external generalizability of the findings is limited given the single-case study.

Future research should replicate the study in other environments where changes in control design as a result of reengineering may be understood and further elaborated. While traditional control concepts have guided our case study of IRAS, some doubts remain regarding the clarity of their conceptual boundaries. Future research should also integrate the major streams of control research. Any single-focus approach is likely to be inadequate in explaining the evolution of organizational control.

Endnotes

1. The cycle time reduction from 112 days to one day and four hours by Rank Xerox (UK) in reengineering the contract refinancing process, for example, eliminated many control activities—multiple approval steps, reconciliation checks, validation checks, matching, etc.

2. "The fact that Leeson was permitted throughout to remain in charge of both front office and back office at Baring Futures Singapore was a most serious failing" *(Singapore Business Times,* Weekend Edition, July 22-23, 1995), which gave Leeson the opportunity to undertake his unauthorized trading activities with less likelihood that they would be detected.

3. Unlike the "pay as you earn" tax system in many countries, income tax in Singapore is assessed and paid after the end of each calendar year from which the income is derived. The motivation for voluntary compliance in tax filing under such a system is much lower, requiring substantial efforts on the part of the tax authority to enforce tax compliance.

4. The functions of the tax authority were previously distributed over four geographical locations. The new $80-million Revenue House now accommodates all of them under one roof.

5. Previously, as a government department, funds were allocated by the parliament through the budget. Now, IRAS receives an "agency fee" based on a percentage of collection plus second-tier payments (incentives/penalties). Major expenditure now only needs to be approved by a board. As a statutory board, IRAS has significantly more autonomy in human resource management and financial planning.

6. In terms of its hardware setup, IRAS has taken a three-tier client-server approach. The mainframe at Data Centre does bulk processing and identifies work items for manual action. The front-end servers, which are HP9000/T500 machines with up to twelve CPUs each, manage and distribute images and work items. The intelligent workstations allow access to Lotus Notes and Microsoft Word, which are integrated with IRIS. The whole IRIS is supported by a network system integrating the 1,200 workstations with Foundation for Cooperative Processing (FCP) gateways, super local area network (LAN) servers, routers, image and workflow servers, and optical jukeboxes. IRAS was also awarded the Plexus Application Excellence Award by Recognition International during the Association of Information and Image Management (AIIM) Conference in 1995.

7. In building Light* Link, a system that revolved around their independent sales agents, the case of Lithonia Lighting reflected a similar change in the fundamental assumptions about these agents.

8. These back-end controls typically rely on aggregate assessment, broad-based analysis, or ex-post review, all of which are faster, cheaper, and less obtrusive. By design, they will tolerate modest and limited abuse by delaying the point at which abuse is detected or by examining aggregate patterns rather than individual instances.

9. Four subcommittees have been set up to meet the four functional elements in ET21: a staff well-being committee, a quality action circle committee, a quality service committee, and an organizational review committee.

10. The authors thank Varun Grover for this insightful observation.

Appendix: Examples of Interview Questions

1. What is the nature of your job? How different is it from before the IRIS reengineering?

2. How are tax processing, taxpayer services, taxpayer audit carried out now? How have these changed?

3. How does IRIS help in your area of work? What are the benefits derived from IRIS?

4. Are there differences in the way your department is organized before and now?

5. What is the new direction or strategic focus for your department? Why?

6. What issues arose during the IRIS reengineering process? How were they resolved?

7. Has there been any relaxation of the internal control system, e.g., independent checks, level of approval? Have there been changes to the way work is reviewed? Is conformance to operational procedures strictly enforced?

8. How does senior management assess the performance of your branch? What kinds of management reports are sent to senior management? Any difference from before?

9. What performance targets/expectations do you establish for your tax officers? How are the performance targets established? Are the tax officers involved?

10. How are these performance targets monitored? What is the frequency of reporting? What is the mode of reporting—self-reporting or system generated? How is it different from before?

11. What new information about the job status of tax officers is made available by IRIS? How often do you access such information? What do you do with such information?

12. Have there been any changes in your performance appraisal process, e.g., new emphasis/criteria? Who are the good performers? Who are the poor performers? How are evaluations conducted? How closely are the evaluations linked to the increments or bonuses?

13. What kinds of training are provided? Have there been any changes in the attitude and the enthusiasm of tax officers, e.g., commitment to be involved, adoption of core values, willingness to speak up?

14. How do you feel about the changes from IRIS reengineering?

References

Applegate, L.M. (1993). Frito-Lay, Inc.: a strategic transition (consolidated). Boston: Harvard Business School, Case No. 9-193-040.

Applegate, L.M.(1996). In search of a new organizational model: lessons from the field. In G. DeSanctis and J. Fulk (eds.), *Communication Technology and Organizational Forms.* Berkeley: Sage Publications.

Arens, A.A.; Loebbecke, J.K.; and Ambanbola, K.B. (1993). *Auditing in Singapore — An Integrated Approach.* Singapore: Prentice-Hall.

Barker, J.R. (1993). Tightening the iron cage: concertive control in self-managing teams. *Administrative Science Quarterly, 38,* 408-437.

Berkley, J.D., and Eccles, R.G. (1991). Rethinking the corporate workplace: case managers at Mutual Benefit Life. Boston: Harvard Business School, Case No. 9-492-015.

Berkley, J.D., and Nohria, N. (1992). Lithonia Lighting. Boston: Harvard Business School, Case No. 9-492-003.

Caron, J.R.; Jarvenpaa, S.L.; and Stoddard, D.B. (1994). Business reengineering at CIGNA Corporation: experiences and lessons learned from the first five years. *MIS Quarterly, 18,* 3, 233-250.

Chalykoff, J., and Nohria, N. (1990). The Internal Revenue Service: Automated Collection System. Boston: Harvard Business School, Case No. 9-490-042, 1990.

Davenport, T.H. (1993). *Process Innovation.* Boston: Harvard Business School Press.

Davenport, T.H., and Linder, J. Rank Xerox U.K. (A). Boston: Harvard Business School, Case No. 9-192-071.

Davenport, T.H., and Linder, J. Rank Xerox U.K. (B). Boston: Harvard Business School, Case No. 9-192-072.

Davenport, T.H., and Nohria, N. (1994). Case management and the integration of labor. *Sloan Management Review, 35(2),* 11-23.

Davenport, T.H., and Short, J. (1990). The new industrial engineering: information technology and business process redesign. *Sloan Management Review. 31(4),* 11-27.

Deloitte & Touche's Computer Assurance Services Practice (1995). Information protection and business process reengineering. *IS Audit & ControlJournal,* 3, 25-38.

Dillard, J.F., and Burns, B.H. (1993). Technocracy and management control systems. *Accounting, Management, and Information Technology. 3(3),* 151—171.

Eisenhardt, K.M. (1989). Agency theory: an assessment and review. *Academy of Management Review, 14(1),* 57—74.

Flamholtz, E.G.; Das, T.K.; and Tsui, A.S. (1985). Toward an integrative framework of organizational conrrol. *Accounting, Organizations and Society, 10(1),* 35-50.

Green, S.G., and Welsh, M.A. (1988). Cybernetics and dependence: reframing the control concept. *Academy of Management Review, 13(2),* 287-301.

Greenberger, D.B., and Strasser, S. (1986). Development and application of a model of personal control in organizations. *Academy of Management Review, 11(1),* 164-177.

Hammer, M. (1990).Reengineering work: don't automate, obliterate. *HarvardBusiness Review,* 68(4), 104-112.

Hammer, M., and Champy, J.(1993). *Reengineering the Corporation.* New York: Harper Collins.

Handy, C. (1992). Balancing corporate power: a new federalist paper. *Harvard Business Review* (November-December).

Jarvenpaa, S.L., and Stoddard, D.B.(1994). CIGNA Corporation, Inc.: managing and institutionalizing business reengineering. Boston: Harvard Business School, Case No. 9-195-097.

Kaplan, R.S., and Norton, D.P. (1993). Putting the balance scorecard to work. *Harvard Business Review* (September-October).

Klein, H.J. (1989). An integrated control theory model of work motivation. *Academy of Management Review,* 14(2), 150-I72.

Merchant, K.A. (1988). Progressing toward a theory of marketing control: a comment. *Journal of Marketing, 52* (July), 40-44.

Miles, M.B., and Huberman, A. M.(1984). *Qualitative Data Analysis: A Sourcebook of New Methods.* Newbury Park, CA: Sage Publications.

Ouchi, W.G.(1979). A conceptual framework for the design of organizational control mechanisms. *Management Science, 25(9),* 833-848.

Pfeffer, J., and Salancik, G.R. (1978). *The External Control of organizations.* New York: Harper & Row.

Rosenthal, S.R., and Salzrnan, H. (1990). Hard choices about software: the pitfalls of procurement. *Sloan Management Review* (Summer), 81-91.

Senge, P. M. (1990). The leader's new work: building learning organizations. *Sloan Management Review, 31(1),* 7-23.

Simons, R. (1995). Control in an age of empowerment. *Harvard Business Review* (March-April).

Stoddard, D.B., and Meadows, C.J. (1992). Capital Holding Corporation—reengineering the Direct Response Group. Boston: Harvard Business School, Case No. 9-192-001.

Thompson, J.D. (1967). *Organizations in Action.* New York: McGraw-Hill.

Weber, M. *Economy and Society,* ed. by Guenther Roth and Claus Wittich. Los Angeles: University of California Press, 1968.

Weber, R. (1988). *EDP Auditing -- Conceptual Foundations and Practice.* Singapore: McGraw-Hill.

Weiner, N.(1967). *The Human Use ofHuman Beings: Cybernetics and Society.* New York: Avon Books.

Williamson, O. (1975). *Markets and Hierarchv: Analysis and Antitrust Implications.* New York: Free Press.

Yin, R.K. *(1989). Case Study Research: Design and Methods.* Newbury Park, CA: Applied Social Research Series, Sage Publications.

Source: Reprinted by special permssion of the Journal of Management Information Systems, Summer 1997, Vol. 14, No. 1, pg. 69-92.

CHAPTER 13

The Impact of IOS-Enabled Business Process Change on Business Outcomes: Transformation of the Value Chain of Japan Airlines

Akemi Takeoka Chatfield
Australian Graduate School of Management, Sydney

Niels Bjorn-Andersen
Copenhagen Business School, Denmark

Since the early days of computerization, there has been significant interest in "the impact of computers on organizational structure" (Leavin and Whisler, 1958), "the interaction of IT and organizations" (Kling, 1980), "the alignment of organizational infrastructure and IT strategy" (MacDonald, 1991), the "organizational metamorphosis" (Bjorn-Andersen and Turner, 1994), and "contradictory organizational consequences of information technology" (Robey, 1995).

These all focus on the intraorganizational issues of the individual firm. The environment has been treated as an exogenous given variable, not to be changed or tampered with. Notable exceptions focusing on the *inter*organizational issues are publications such as (1) "IT in the 1990s: Managing organizational interdependence" (Rockart and Short, 1989), which is one of the first articles to discuss interorganizational systems (IOS); (2) "The IT-induced business reconfiguration" (Venkatraman, 1991), where IOS are explicitly seen as a significant enabler for business network redesign; and (3) "The role of IT in organizational design" (Lucas and Baroudi, 1994), where different types of new organizational forms including virtual, negotiated, and vertically integrated conglomerates are explicitly using IT in organizational transformation in different ways.

Interestingly, there is growing consensus that IOS will have a significant impact on value chain management as well as on the relationships within the value chain (Chatfield and Yetton, 1997; Kremar, Bjorn-Andersen and O'Callaghan, 1995). Conspicuously absent in the IOS literature, however, is case study analysis of the impact of IOS-enabled business process change on business outcomes. Extant studies do not explain how the focal firm's ability to exploit IOS affects its interdependent relationships with the network of firms in the purchase and sales value chains, particularly with respect to the exchange of information and knowledge required of the value-added interfirm collaboration and innovation. Furthermore, relatively little is known about how the focal firm can leverage IOS-enabled business process change to improve its business outcomes, for example, through exploiting their value chains for cost reduction, customer service, quality, cycle-time reduction, and new product development.

The purpose of this chapter is to explore the relationship between the focal firm's ability to exploit IOS-enabled business process change and business outcomes. We apply a generic framework for analyzing IT-enabled business process change that has been developed to explain the role of IT in creating the twenty-first-century organization (Bjorn-Andersen and Chatfield, 1996a; 1996b), to a specific case study analysis of the transformation of the value chain on business outcomes through the strategic use of IOS by Japan Airlines (JAL), the world's third largest airline in 1994 (*Fortune*, 1995). We are particularly interested in the ways in which IOS not only contributed to JAL's improved competitiveness but also enabled it to leverage its strategically important value chain as an engine of growth and a new source of sustainable competitive advantage.

Drawing on a resource-based view of the firm (Barney, 1991; Black and Boal, 1994; Peteraf, 1993), we analyze JAL's unique and valuable resources, namely IOS ("physical capital resources"), which enabled the top-down design of radical change in core business processes, and people ("human capital resources"), who, over time, carried out the change incrementally from the bottom up. The results were JAL's business growth and increased competitiveness, despite intensive competition in both domestic and international markets since the 1980s and the weakened economic conditions in Japan during the early 1990s. The focus is on JAL's strategic use of IOS, particularly the AXESS Computer Reservation System (CRS) and electronic data interchange (EDI), developed with a clear strategic objective of supporting JAL's emerging strategies on customer service, sales, value chain logistics coordination, and cost reduction. As part of this focus, we discuss JAL's exploitation of IOS-enabled networked value chain firms to reduce joint product innovation cycle time to market.

A Framework for Analyzing IT-Enabled Business Process Change

The framework applied to explore JAL's IT-enabled business process change here is based on the generic framework for analyzing the role of IT in creating the twenty-first-century organization (Bjorn-Andersen and Chatfield, 1996a; 1996b). This generic framework has been developed to explain the interdependent relationships among the global environment, business challenges, strategic responses, strategic IT support, and management methodologies that enable changes in business processes and the impact of radical organizational transformation on the firm's business outcomes. Although the generic framework has not been rigorously validated, it has high face validity since it has been successfully used to discuss the firm's business process change and business outcomes with managers of a number of firms in Denmark, Australia, and Japan.

The framework is shown in Figure 1. The context is first and foremost the increasingly global environment for any organization, which translates into a set of unique business challenges for any organization. These business challenges typically require a strategic response in the form of changed business processes primarily enacted through the use of different management methodologies and different IT-systems.

We begin by briefly describing the core concepts in the framework, drawing in particular on examples pertaining to the airline industry (see Bjorn-Andersen and Chatfield (1996) for a detailed discussion of the framework).

The Global Environment of the Twenty-First-Century Organization

The past two decades have brought dramatic changes in the global environment of almost all major organizations. This is to a large extent a result of a deliberate policy *of deregulation* in most sectors of the economy: trade, services, financial markets, and foreign investments. Most dramatically, this is taking place within the large trading blocs (European Union, NAFTA, and the AFTA/APEC), but also the Uruguay Round and the continuation of these multilateral trade negotiations on bilateral levels (e.g., EU and United States), as well as at the GATT and G7 level, have significantly changed the conditions for doing business. Within the airline industry, this has led to dramatic deregulation and removal of the traditional exclusive rights of airlines to certain routes.

The U. S. airline industry was deregulated in 1978, the Japanese airline industry in 1985, and the European airline market in 1997. The U.S. deregulation resulted in intensified competition (Monteiro and Macdonald, 1996; Organisation for Economic Co-Operation and Development, 1988), while the Japanese deregulation led to growing competition among domestic carriers but reduced the scale economies in their cost structure (Kinugasa, 1994). Very few observers inside the industry doubt that the deregulation will eventually span the globe for all major routes. There are, however, still substantial barriers to free competition in the form of landing and departure slots and terminal facilities.

Technological progress within IT/telecommunication and transport is the main reason the deregulation is having this enormous impact, which will be even more significant with the deregulation of 90 percent of all telecommunications in the world decided in February 1997. Geographical distances become less and less of a barrier to new product and market development, and there is a distinct increase in globalization of markets and competition. In the airline market, the advances in communication, navigation, and aircraft design especially shape the *competition.* In the intensely competitive airline industry worldwide, even the number of airlines often fluctuates as low-cost airlines enter, in some cases taking significant market share from the well-established airlines.

While these three factors— deregulation, technological progress, and competition all contribute to continued expansion, there are several barriers to the "unlimited Ikaros line" of continued growth (Meadows and Meadows, 1972).[1] We have grouped these into three categories: pollution, depletion of resources, and negative consumer response. The growing problem of airport noise, fuel resource depletion, and negative consumer response to fatal airline crashes are important issues for the airline industry. A fatal JAL crash in 1985 drastically reduced sales, resulting in the first net loss in the firm's history since 1953. They are not, however, a central thrust of our paper and therefore are not discussed in detail here.

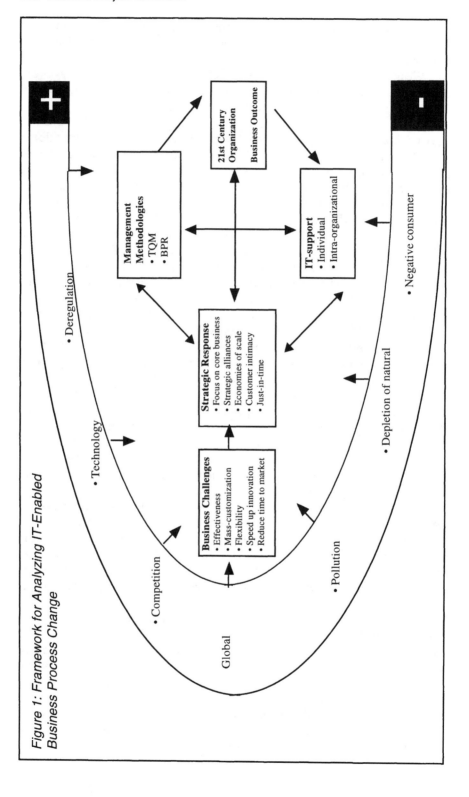

Figure 1: Framework for Analyzing IT-Enabled Business Process Change

Business Challenges for the Twenty-First-Century Organization

The elements mentioned above constitute the global environment of an organization and, hence, give rise to new business challenges. Obviously the intensity and relevance of each of these elements vary from organization to organization. However, many organizations are facing the following business challenges:

- Increase effectiveness and quality in products and services: From public sector to private enterprises there is an increasing pressure to "get more for less" (Davenport, 1993; Hammer, 1996; Porter, 1985). Within the airline industry there are nearly daily stories about airlines being forced to cut costs to stay competitive.
- Enable mass-customization: This is found in products as diverse as tailor-made Levis and cars made to customer specifications (Hammer, 1996; Pine, 1993; Savage, 1990). The attempts in the airline industry to differentiate prices and add-on services are examples of coping with this challenge.
- Increase flexibility in response to changing market conditions: Airlines operating in a deregulated market must constantly be prepared to change routes, alliances, catering, and loyalty schemes (Davenport, 1993; Hammond, 1996; Kanter, 1995).
- Speed up innovation in order to gain a competitive edge (Davenport, 1993; Hammond, 1996; Keen, 1988): This is a particular challenge to all R&D—intensive industries—not only pharmaceutical and electronics companies but airlines as well.
- Reduce cycle time from production to market: The shorter the time lag, the lower the level of intermediate stock and less risk of supplying the wrong products, especially in the fashion industries (e.g., Benneton). For the airline industry, it is product innovation, the load factor, and the utilization of the aircraft that make the difference (Blackburn, 1991; Kanter, 1995).
- Improved quality and zero defect: These are becoming much more than buzzwords in the products as well as in the full procurement process in almost all industrial sectors, and airlines that cannot meet these requirements face significant problems (Davenport, 1993; Deming, 1989).

Strategic Response for the Twenty-First-Century Organization

Every organization has to find its own unique set of strategic responses to its business challenges. Figure 1 shows the strategic responses that are most frequently made: focusing on core business through outsourcing, leveraging through strategic alliances, creating customer intimacy, and being just-in-time. We return to these in detail when we discuss the strategic responses of JAL to changes in its global environment and its specific challenges.

IT Support for the Twenty-First-Century Organization

There is widespread support in the IT management literature for the notion that IT can significantly enable the strategic response (MacDonald, 1991; Porter and Miller, 1985). In our framework, we have found it useful to distinguish among IT support on three levels: individual personal productivity tools, intraorganizational systems typically supporting work groups, and *inter-* organizational systems crossing organizational boundaries. Since this paper focuses on the virtual value chain between JAL and their strategic value chain firms, we concentrate on the interorganizational systems.

Management Methodologies for the Twenty-First Century Organization

There is a plethora of management methodologies proposed as the (often one and only) candidate for how to achieve the result we call the twenty-first-century organization. In the framework we specifically mention total quality management (TQM), business process reengineering (BPR) and organizational learning (O/L), but there are obviously many more worth mentioning. Our point is that, in their attempts to meet the business challenges in the form of unique strategic responses, organizations apply a combination of different management methodologies as well as IT systems. Most of the time these are bundled to create a dynamic effect where it is difficult to identify empirically the exact systemic effect of a particular management methodology.

Before we apply this generic framework to analyze JAL's IT-enabled business process change and its impact on their business outcomes, we discuss case study analysis as the methodology chosen for this study.

Methodology

Given the dearth of field research in the area of the impact of IOS-enabled business process change on business outcomes, we chose an exploratory research approach. Case study analysis is particularly useful for studying organizational dynamics, especially the context and process of change (Galunic and Eisenhardt, 1994; George and McKeown, 1994; Pettigrew, 1990). The importance of grounding theory development in the detailed case data has been recognized in management and IS fields (Strauss and Corbin, 1990; Yetton, Craig and Johnson, 1995).

Because our study is exploratory, data collection consisted of fourteen detailed unstructured interviews with managers from JAL during June and July 1994. A further seven interviews were conducted with managers from the JAL Group firms specifically to explore the interdependent relationship issues between their firms and JAL during June 1995. These unstructured interviews were not guided by the framework since it was developed later. Numerous follow-up telephone calls took place to clarify the research notes taken during the interviews.

In addition to the primary data collected during the interviews, we have analyzed the longitudinal financial data (1987-94) such as operating revenues, operating expenses, number of employees, other performance measures from *JAL Annual Reports* (1987-94) as well as other secondary data sources, such as *IATA Members' Statistics* (1987-94) (IATA, 1986-95). Furthermore, we have analyzed over sixty of the available external reports published in Japanese on JAL or the JAL Group, including trade journals (e.g., *Travel Journal,* a Japanese weekly travel trade journal) and business newspaper and magazine articles (e.g., *Nikkei Business* and *Nikkei Shimbun)* on their customer services, new product introduction, and new market development. These publications were obtained from commercial information services (e.g., Nikkei business data services) and from a key word search of Japanese libraries' databases.

JAL Company Background

Since 1953, under the Japan Air Lines Company Limited Law ("the JAL Law"), JAL was granted a special corporate status to operate international air services as the Japanese flag carrier. Until the deregulation of the Japanese airline industry in 1985, there was a clear division of labor: JAL was the only domestic airline that was authorized to operate international routes. Other airlines such as All Nippon Airways (ANA) and Japan Air Systems (JAS) were allowed to operate only in the domestic market. The company, as a semiprivate corporation, had the Japanese government as its largest stockholder. Its normal operations received detailed scrutiny from government, ranging from needing the transport minister's approval to increase capital, issue bonds, or take out long-term loans to operational guidelines suggesting what food could be served to first-class passengers. This level of governmental control eroded much of the firm's managerial independence and created excessive complexity. This resulted in a highly bureaucratic, inefficient organizational structure with unnecessary divisions and layers.

With the Japanese government's long-held policy of protectionism, it was easy for JAL to become complacent and noncompetitive in customer service and cost structure. The company viewed its mission as a provider of *air transport routes* (a market *product* focus) for passengers and cargo, rather than a provider of *customer service* (a customer service *process* focus). Given its stated mission, it was not surprising that the company was not customer-oriented in the 1980s. The company's customer service vis-à-vis that of domestic competitors was rated among the domestic travelers who were surveyed in 1986 as bureaucratic and unfriendly (Watanabe, 1995).

On the other hand, JAL sustained its position as a market leader in engineering, safety standards and information technology. In Japanese society, where the status of employees is closely linked to the social status of their firm (Nakane, 1970), JAL attracted high-quality graduates in specialized fields such as engineering, computer sciences, operations research, economics, and finance from the best universities because of the firm's prestigious social status as the Japanese flag carrier. Like other large Japanese firms, JAL offered these employees very high job security and lifetime employment, except in the event of a severe economic crisis. JAL also provided "continuous training," through job rotation, systematically exposing people to all the jobs within a specialty as well as to other major functional areas of the business (Drucker, 1971).

In return, JAL demanded loyalty, service, and learning of specialized knowledge and skills from their employees, which is not easily transferable to other employment (e.g., tacit knowledge of managing a specialized supplier for JAL). These Japanese institutional structures (Drucker, 1971; Fruin, 1992; Hill, 1995) helped JAL develop "strategically valuable human capital resources," which provided JAL with the capabilities necessary to develop IOS, integrate IOS with internal IT, successfully promote an IOS network to their intended value chain firms, and exploit IOS in the mutually interdependent relationships with their strategically valuable value chain firms.

In November 1987, primarily as a result of competitive pressures from U.S.

airlines, abolition of the JAL Law and the sale of stock held by the government effectively privatized JAL. Privatization provided JAL with not only the capital it needed but also an opportunity to reassess the way it had done business for the previous thirty-four years under the government's regulation and protection.

JAL has developed interfirm networks, commonly referred to as the "JAL Group," which are a critical source of value in JAL's value chain. The JAL Group includes over 130 companies in which JAL directly or indirectly owns an average equity interest of 20 percent. It comprises two subgroups: firms closely linked to the air transport industry and firms outside the industry. The first group includes management and marketing of package tours, ground handling, in-flight meal services, aircraft maintenance, and fueling services. The second group includes hotels, information technology and communications services, trading companies, and cultural enterprises.

The JAL Group is *a keiretsu-based* value chain for JAL. Keiretsu are a group of individual firms viewed together because they are affiliated with a large focal firm. In the case of the JAL keiretsu, it is a leading vertical keiretsu, where JAL is the hub of its hierarchical organizational form. The JAL keiretsu, differs from the Big Six, powerful bank-centered keiretsu: Mitsui, Mitsubishi, Fuyo, Sumitomo, Daiichi Kangyo, and Sanwa.

A Case Study Analysis of JAL's IOS-Enabled Business Process Change

We now apply the generic framework presented earlier to a case study analysis of JAL's IOS-enabled business process change. More specifically, we analyze each of the components of the framework: JAL's global environment, business challenges, strategic responses, strategic use of IOS, management methodologies, and business outcome. Our analysis is summarized in Figure 2.

In the time-based competitive airline industry, JAL's quick customer response critically depends on the capabilities of the JAL Group firms. The supplier value chains are important for better efficiency and effectiveness of JAL's purchase of products and services (e.g., cabin food) from the value chain firms in the upstream and JAL's sales and distribution of the firm's end products (e.g., airline seat and tour package) in the downstream. In this time-based competitive environment, the efficient and open exchange of information and knowledge between the focal firm and their value chain firms is a source of sustainable competitive advantage (Blackburn, 1991; Bower and Hout, 1988; Spanner, Nuno and Chandra, 1993; Stalk, 1988; Stalk, Evans and Shulman, 1992).

JAL's Global Environment in the 1980s

The past two decades have seen significant transformations in both JAL's immediate and remote environments. In the remote environment, the deregulation of the U.S. airline industry in 1978 led to increasingly intense time-based competition (McKenney, Copeland and Mason, 1995). Under the growing competition, large airlines invested in computerized reservation systems (CRS) development, which made the airline industry worldwide highly information-intensive (Copeland and McKenney, 1988; Monteiro and Macdonald, 1996; Organisation for Economic

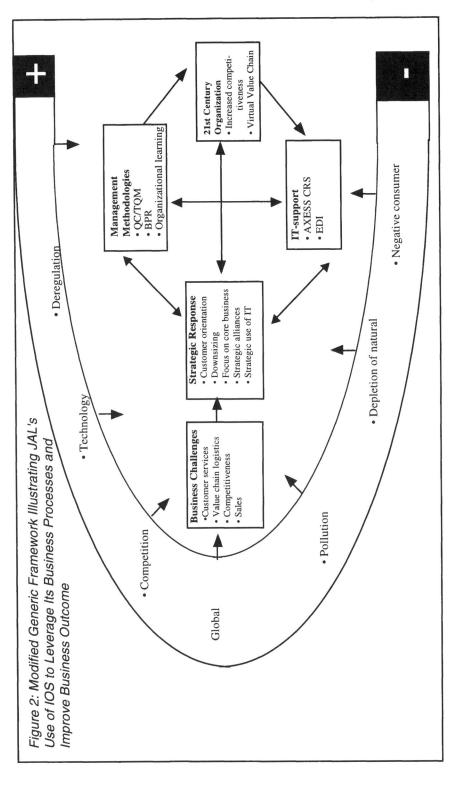

Figure 2: Modified Generic Framework Illustrating JAL's Use of IOS to Leverage Its Business Processes and Improve Business Outcome

Co-Operation and Development, 1988).

Similar transformations have been seen in the immediate environment of JAL. As in the U.S. airline industry, the deregulation of the Japanese airline industry in 1985 led to growing competition among the big three air carriers but substantially reduced the scale economies in their cost structure, in effect reducing the individual airline's profitability (Kinugasa, 1994).

Technological progress influencing JAL as well as the competitors has been made with respect to aircraft design and manufacturing, innovative navigational systems, and sophisticated telecommunication systems, which affect fuel economy, operational safety, and industry cost structure. Furthermore, technological progress in information technology, particularly CRS, has even more significantly influenced the nature of competition in two important ways. First, the airline industry has become much more information-intensive and more dependent on IT for much of its business. Second, JAL, along with other successful large air carriers, is operating in increasingly time-based competitive domestic and global markets (Copeland and McKenney, 1988; Hammer, 1990). For JAL, these changes indicate the importance of leveraging their strategic value chain firms for capabilities not only to speed up their customer service (e.g., quick response to reservation inquiry) but also to accelerate innovative product development cycle time and time to market for these innovative products and programs.

Both the deregulation of the airline industry and the interfirm electronic network links provided by CRS and other IOS have accelerated the increased rate of competition in the airline industry.

Business Challenges

All of the above factors, but especially the deregulation of the Japanese airline industry in 1985 and the proliferation of CRS worldwide in the 1980s, have intensified competitive pressures from foreign carriers and governments, who demanded greater access to major international gateways in Japan. In 1986, United Airlines, the largest air carrier at the time, inaugurated flights on Pacific routes, while All Nippon Airways (ANA), JAL's major domestic competitor, began flights to Los Angeles and Washington, D.C. In addition to the intensifying international competition the sharp decline in demand following the fatal JAL aircraft crash in 1985 reduced the company's operating income by 49.6 percent from the previous year. As a result, the company registered a net loss of 6.7 billion yen (US$37 million) after taxes in 1986.

A new top management team was appointed in December 1985, including Susumu Yamaji, president and operations and engineering, and Matsuo Toshimitsu, executive vice president, corporate marketing, associated business administration and development. Yamaji was a newcomer to JAL management, while Toshimitsu worked for JAL as managing director and vice president, marketing and sales, since the early 1980s. From analysis of JAL's operations and its global environment, the new top management recognized two emerging trends in Japan: (1) the Japanese economy would sustain profitable growth at a steady rate, but (2) the continued growth would require increasingly closer links with the rest of the world. It was clear that the potential for JAL was there, but the airline had to face a totally new set of business challenges in order to harvest the potential benefits.

The most important business challenges emanating from the global environment could be grouped into four groups:

- Improve customer service;
- Improve value chain logistics;
- Increase competitiveness; and
- Increase sales.

The first two business challenges were more specific in focus and might influence the latter two. Because top management considered these challenges critically urgent, JAL undertook the challenges concurrently.

The general perception of customers was that JAL was a fairly bureaucratic but very safe and dependable airline company. But customer service left much to be desired. The other three business challenges are in part related. The value chain logistics had to be rationalized. Most organizational structures and business processes for JAL were far too complex, with substantial redundancy. In addition, there were too many different business units and employee productivity was low. In the days of a very regulated airline market, JAL's growth had to a large extent been through acquisition of airline-related businesses. Many of these businesses were potentially of strategic value, but JAL was finding it difficult to realize those strategic benefits because of the complexity involved in coordinating the different types of business. Furthermore, costs were high. U.S. airlines were far more competitive (having been deregulated since 1978) (Copeland and McKenny, 1988; Fortune, 1995), and, in a totally deregulated market, JAL would suffer. Unfortunately, substantial cost savings could not be achieved without downsizing, which was almost unheard of in the traditional Japanese culture.

In general, the major business challenges to JAL were radically to rethink the business it was in, to develop a new corporate vision, and to develop a strategic plan capable of handling the transformation.

Strategic Responses

The major challenge for the new management team, according to Yamaji, was to create and implement a new corporate vision throughout JAL and the JAL Group, JAL's strategic value chain. The vision was to "build a leaner, more responsive, and customer oriented airline," while sustaining and strengthening its position as a market leader and improving its profitability. The new management strategy exploited the company's unique strengths: well-trained, loyal employees and complementary core capabilities of the value chain firms. The new strategies included:

- Focus on core business;
- Organizational restructuring;
- Downsizing;
- Customer orientation;
- Strategic partnerships; and
- Strategic use of IT.

The top management team decided that corporate organizational restructuring was a competitive necessity that had to be started immediately but would take place over many years. Restructuring was to simplify JAL's complex organizational structure and operational procedures. JAL's organizational structure has been redesigned to remove excessive redundancy and unproductive layers. Operational procedures were simplified by outsourcing a large number of service functions and by reducing the enormous amount of paper-based transactions. These decisions reduced the number of administrative as well as reservations and sales office personnel, which enabled the company to reduce operating costs, including labor costs, the second-highest cost in the airline industry. These changes in business processes were achieved without the active role of IT. However, management decision to reduce the paper-based transactions led to the development of EDI applications (e.g., order entry and invoice) in a short period of time.

With a new organizational structure, top management decided to broaden its corporate earning base by promoting greater diversity and synergy with its inter-organizational value chains, where more strategic partnership characteristics should

Table 1: Strategic Use of IOS at JAL

Business Challenges	IOS types	Users	Business processes
Improve customer services	CRS	Travel agents, corporate travel centers, leisure travelers using AXESS Mini-terminals located at train stations & convenience stores, etc.	Provide information for travel planning & make reservations for airlines, tours & hotels
	CRS	JAL	Provide travel agents with customer profile for better customer services & make reservations for airlines, tours & hotels
Improve value chain logistics coordination	EDI	JAL, the JAL Group & others in the value chains	Coordinate the value chain for procurement & just-in-time delivery of aircraft fuel, aircraft repair parts, cabinfood, beverages, etc.
	EDI	JAL	the JAL Group & others in the value chain
	CRS + EDI	JAL, the JAL Group & others in the value chain	Coordinate the value chain for scheduling & operations of integrated tour packages & cargo transport
Increase competitiveness	EDI	JAL, the JAL Group & others in the value chain	Reduce operating costs through fewer paper-based transactions & reduction of administrative staff & reduce transaction costs, especially search & coordination costs
	CRS + yield mgt. system	JAL	Create new business value
Increase sales	CRS	JAL & travel agents	Make sales
	CRS	JAL	Manage marketing channels & provide training for travel agents

be cultivated and developed. They decided to start with some of the over 130 JAL Group firms, but later they gradually increased the cooperative efforts with other suppliers in the value chains.

In addition, in order to compete in the deregulated market, JAL had to become more customer-oriented. The most profitable customers were not prepared to put up with "monopoly-type service." Several measures such as leasing CRS terminals to large firms' in-house travel centers were taken in order to meet the demand of increasingly sophisticated business travelers.

Finally, as we shall discuss further below, top management recognized very early that it was necessary to use IT strategically. The value to U.S. airlines of the reservation systems was explicitly recognized, and JAL management launched a costly but necessary initiative to develop its own reservation system in conjunction with the new interorganizational systems.

Strategic Use of IOS

JAL 's strategic use of IOS has been strongly tied to the top management vision discussed earlier: its strategic intention to build a leaner, more responsive, and customer-oriented airline. Table 1 shows IOS support at JAL. The two most important IOS identified here are electronic data interchange (EDI) and computer reservation systems (CRS). JAL's strategic use of EDI was focused on value chain logistics coordination and cost reduction. Like other airlines, CRS was exploited for sales and customer service.

EDI for Value Chain Logistics Coordination

The more than 130 JAL Group firms have long-established relationships with JAL as suppliers on the value chain, outsourcing vendors, or joint-venture partners. A proprietary EDI was initially developed to network JAL and the JAL Group firms electronically in order to improve their coordination efficiency in managing large-scale interdependent business activities and communications between the various relationships: supplier value chain logistics for procurement and just-in-time delivery, outsourcing service functions, and joint-venture operations.

EDI provides JAL and the companies in the value chain with timely and accurate information (e.g., flight schedules, purchase orders, cost structures), which is essential for JAL to manage the complex value chain logistics required by flying operations, including procurement and just-in-time delivery of aircraft fuel, aircraft repair parts, cabin food catering, and other customer requirements. In addition, EDI provides JAL and outsourcing vendors at home and overseas with timely and accurate maintenance records. Furthermore, systems integration of CRS with EDI enables JAL and joint- venture partners to share business information required for optimal scheduling and high-yield operations of integrated tour packages, as well as efficient handling of domestic and international cargo.

This EDI network is supported by Multi Japan Network, which is owned by JAL and operated as a value-added network (VAN). Because this VAN was proprietary, the networked firms had greater trust in system and data security than they would have if the EDI network were serviced by an independent VAN operator. In part because these value chain firms were confident about the network security—hence about the safety of proprietary information exchange through the networked in part because they had long-term interdependent relationships with JAL, they have been quickly sold on the EDI network sponsored by JAL.

The IOS literature has shown a number of EDI "failures" where sponsor firms failed to realize the intended strategic benefits, except improved operational efficiency (Barret and Konsynski, 1982; Benjamin, deLong and Morton, 1990; Krcmar, Bjorn-Andersen and O'Callaghan, 1995). The very high degree of diffusion seen in this case study is important for the sponsor of an EDI network to realize the intended EDI benefits. Should JAL experience a significant level of resistance or delay among its value chain firms, JAL's coordination costs would be higher and its value chain logistics coordination would be less efficient.

EDI for Cost Reduction

In the fiercely competitive airline industry, the costs of flying operations, principally fuel costs, present the largest proportion of total operating expenses. Profitability is critically dependent on the company's strategy to search fuel sources globally and procure bulk fuel at competitive costs. Furthermore, profitability is also influenced by the ability to manage the complex logistics of distributing fuel from the company's own fuel supply facilities, such as those in Los Angeles, to airports worldwide in a just-in-time manner.

As JAL's business has grown, JAL's fleet has largely increased in number over the period analyzed. In light of this rapid business expansion, JAL had to improve its IT support functions to provide timely and efficient aircraft maintenance. EDI facilitates the communications required of the timely procurement and just-in-time delivery of repair parts required by aircraft maintenance teams. In addition, EDI provides maintenance teams around the world with accurate information on safety standards, aircraft maintenance requirement specifications, and aircraft maintenance history, which can be downloaded from the corporate databases.

CRS for Sales

In 1987 JAL developed AXESS, an advanced and comprehensive CRS. AXESS was viewed as a key enabler for radically restructuring JAL for the business challenges it faced as a result of privatization and managerial independence. The AXESS project, at first promoted as a marketing initiative, received top management support. A high level of initial investment in capital (approximately 130 billion yen—US$ 1 billion) and human resources was mobilized to ensure its timely completion. Unlike many IT development projects, the AXESS project was completed on time. The timely completion and successful implementation of the reservation system were explicitly mandated by top management as a competitive necessity to support JAL's emerging strategies.

Top management saw Sabre and Apollo as key enablers for American Airlines' and United Airlines' (respectively) increased competitiveness and regarded AXESS as "the most strategically crucial system" for JAL's competitiveness, particularly to gain a competitive advantage in the international market. This is how Yamaji articulated his strategic intent: "With privatization just around the corner, a new program to consolidate our sales network will play an important role. We must offer new and improved services that are more receptive to the needs of the traveling public and of travel agents. These services must compete with the Apollo reserva-

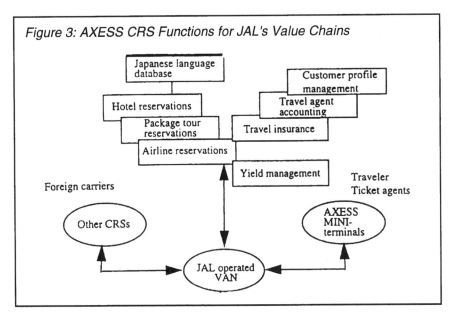

Figure 3: AXESS CRS Functions for JAL's Value Chains

tions and sales systems, adopted by United Airlines and with the Sabre systems offered by American Airlines" (Japan Airlines, 1986-95).

AXESS is an online, mainframe-based, integrated travel information and reservation system that is linked with hotel chains worldwide, as well as with foreign carriers' CRS. As such, it became JAL's valuable and rare physical capital resource, since domestic competitors' CRS did not match AXESS in terms of advanced technological capabilities and system integration with JAL's other strategic information systems (e.g., yield management). As an advanced fare-quotation and reservations system, it has a database storage capacity of 300,000 city pairs and over 8 million different types of data. AXESS effectively reduced airline ticket processing time from fifteen minutes to five seconds at the time of implementation. Besides the increased efficiency, the new CRS had certain innovative features such as being the first Japanese-language database as well as allowing information retrieval in either Japanese or English displayed on color, split windows. When AXESS was marketed to Japanese travel agents in 1988, these innovative features provided JAL with a prime-mover advantage.

CRS for Customer Service

Figure 3 shows the comprehensive functional capabilities of AXESS. AXESS CRS was integrated with internal IT. They provided travel agents with online access to information retrieval and reservation systems for Japanese-language package tours and a passenger information management system for better customer service (e.g., customer intimacy and quick response). JAL's implementation of Japanese-language databases enabled travel agents to access an enormous amount of travel information for their Japanese business and leisure travelers. To further improve travel agents' performance, JAL added functional enhancements including a travel agent back office accounting system for sales productivity and a travel agent customer profile management system for customer service efficiency.

The impact of JAL's IOS leverage on business outcomes is discussed in the discussion section of the paper. The consensus among the managers interviewed at JAL for this study was that the realization of their strategic vision would have been difficult, if not impossible, without JAL's new IOS.

Management Methodologies

As discussed earlier, JAL was once a semiprivate special-status company whose largest shareholder was the Japanese government. This background fostered the bureaucratic, noncustomer-focused attitudes prevalent throughout the organizational hierarchy. Faced with new business challenges, top management supported the application of *quality circle (QC)/total quality management* (TQM) (Deming, 1989) in order to change the employee attitudes, particularly among middle-level managers. This was seen as a critical success factor for JAL to become more "customer-oriented." All employees were required to participate in various QC activities, and the impact of these activities on employee attitudes and service improvement was published in internal newsletters. TQM staff regularly surveyed Japanese travelers, analyzed questionnaire data, and provided QC groups with customer reactions to JAL service, including telephone operators, JAL reservations, airport ticketing, cabin service, and baggage handling. As part of TQM efforts to expand a rich source of data, JAL implemented a specialized customer call-in line, "Hello Line," to monitor customer reaction directly. The customer reaction trend was continuously fed back to all QC groups.

Although the nature of the change JAL has achieved was radical and focused on business process, the managers at JAL in general did not label their activities leading to this radical change *business process reengineering* (BPR). Nor, however, did they consider their activities as those aiming at *kaizen* or an equivalent of Toyota's "continuous improvement." In light of the assertion in the literature that some firms in both the United States and Japan have undertaken process change activities similar to BPR well before 1990 (MITI, 1996; Stoddard, Jarvenpaa and Littlejohn, 1996), when Hammer's *Harvard Business Review* article (Hammer, 1990) made the concept of BPR more widely known to American managers, it is interesting to compare JAL's strategic change with the characteristics of BPR and to ask if JAL was an early practitioner of business process reengineering.

The key underlying assumptions found in the literature on BPR are: (1) it results in radical change; (2) it obliterates; (3) it focuses on business process; (4) it is top-down-directed; and (5) it is IT-enabled (Hammer, 1990; Hammer, 1996; Hammer and Champy, 1993; Stoddard, Jarvenpaa and Littlejohn, 1996). These five assumptions have been examined against JAL's "BPR" experience.

First, reengineering at JAL produced radical change in both intra- and interfirm business processes, but implementation proceeded incrementally. Second, reengineering efforts at JAL were enabled by the firm's core capabilities (e.g., human capital resources), while these capabilities realistically precluded JAL from completely obliterating. Third, reengineering at JAL focused on core processes to improve the quality of customer service, increase customer satisfaction, reduce cost, and reduce new product development cycle time. Fourth, reengineering *design* was top-down-directed, while *implementation* was carried out from the bottom up by JAL employees who actively interacted with the customer. Fifth, reengineering of *inter*firm processes was IOS-enabled.

JAL initiated the process reengineering activities to "restructure their core business." Hence, JAL's reengineering directly followed the firm's strategic vision to *build a leaner, more responsive, and more customer-oriented airline.* It was undertaken shortly after the firm radically restructured its organizational structure and downsized, particularly by reducing administrative staff and outsourcing noncore functions. It was perceived initially as a large-scale cross-functional cost-cutting initiative and later, when IOS was more fully implemented, as a strategic measure to radically change the ways in which JAL and their strategic value chain firms transfer information and knowledge, hence accelerating joint problem solving and new product development cycle time.

The IOS-enabled interfirm business process change powerfully facilitated the ways in which JAL and the networked firms shared proprietary information to create new knowledge and capabilities that are particularly critical in innovation. The literature on organizational learning has grown rapidly in the 1990s (Levitt and March, 1988; Nonaka, 1994). Huber (1991) and a number of others classify organizational learning into four processes: knowledge acquisition, information distribution, information interpretation, and organizational memory. The IOS discussed earlier in this paper supported these processes, except information interpretation. JAL's IOS integration with other strategic systems made knowledge acquisition and information distribution faster and more efficient within the networked firms, Once digital forms of information are created and made available by a given firm, any of the authorized networked firms can access it in real time as often as they need to. This reduced time-lag related to interfirm transfer of information and knowledge. This faster and more efficient information exchange within the networked firms enabled both JAL and their value chain firms to understand customer response quickly and to jointly reduce new product development cycle time.

Discussion

The central insight from the case analysis is how JAL transformed its physical value chain into a virtual value chain and its impact on JAL's business growth and increased competitiveness as a consequence of improvements in its business processes. The two IOS initiatives discussed in this paper, CRS and EDI, were developed with a clear strategic vision to support JAL in meeting the business challenges. To achieve this, IOS needed to become centrally embedded in JAL's core interfirm business processes.

As JAL's interfirm business processes became more efficient and effective, they initially affected JAL'S business growth and competitiveness by speeding up customer response time. Over time, as IOS became more fully integrated with internal IT at both the JAL site and its value chain firm sites, JAL learned new capabilities by which it shared proprietary and strategic information and knowledge with the virtual value chain partners. This was particularly effective with respect to joint new product development. In this area, JAL's exploitation of the virtual value chain resulted in accelerated new product development cycle time. This further increased JAL's competitiveness in the intensely time-based competitive domestic and global markets.

In this last section, we first describe the salient characteristics of JAL's IOS-enabled virtual value chain compared with the traditional physical value chains. We then discuss JAL's major business outcomes: business growth and increased competitiveness. The latter was achieved in two stages. Initially, IOS speeded up customer response times. This was followed by improvements in new product development cycle times. This was facilitated by the new virtual value chain (business process change).

JAL's IOS-Enabled Virtual Value Chain

The IOS-enabled transformation of JAL's "physical" value chain resulted in a "virtual" value chain. Particularly with respect to joint new product development, this virtual value chain provided new capabilities with which the focal firm formed strategic partnerships with its networked value chain firm(s) to exploit their complementary knowledge and capabilities. We have referred to the transformed physical value chains as "virtual value chains" to emphasize the flexible direction of information and knowledge flows across the network members.

Because the speed and flexibility of information and knowledge transfer are integral for joint product innovation, the IOS embeddedness is central to the transformation of JAL's value chains. Such embeddedness requires the active commitment and collaboration of network members, rather than mere compliance. Without such commitment and collaboration, members would not have accepted the importance of sharing information and knowledge reciprocally across the network partners. This acceptance was fostered by JAL successfully promoting IOS adoption without using its market power.

Virtual value chains differ from physical value chains in four important ways. First, the formation of strategic partnerships is not based on contracts or organizational forms. Instead, the strategic partnerships are information-based: The firm seeking information simply chooses as a partner someone who holds information it needs. Second, strategic partnerships are essentially temporary task groups formed to pursue a specific joint project (e.g., product innovation). Third, unlike other organizational structures such as strategic alliances or joint ventures, strategic partnerships between the networked firms invest in relationship-specific assets, most notably in common network platforms and software applications ("physical capital resources"). Fourth, their valuable outputs are often intangible assets such as new knowledge.

Consider the domain of product innovation. In this industry, product innovation is very information-intensive (Chesbrough and Teece, 1996; Davenport, 1993; Von Hippel, 1994) and time to market is a critical dimension. Firms that reduce new product development cycle time to market have a major competitive advantage (Blackburn, 1991; Stalk et al., 1992). When JAL decided to draw on its networked value chain firms' capabilities to accelerate innovative product development cycle time, the IOS system integration with internal IT by both the focal firm and the value chain firms was a key enabler. This integration supported the networked firms' exchanging innovation-related proprietary information and knowledge more efficiently and flexibly than the traditional ways in which JAL had communicated with its suppliers.

While the new virtual value chain enables cooperation, not all product develop-

Table 2: Transformation of JAL's Value Chains

Characteristics	Physical value chain	Virtual value chain
Optimization	Within the focal firm	Across the value chain
Structure	Centralized	Networked
Mechanism for new value creation	Keiretsu structure-based	Knowledge-based
Direction of information/ knowledge flows	Linear & controlled by the focal firm	Nonlinear & controlled by the information seeker
Value chain coordination	IOS minimal role	IOS central role

ment will be done on the network. In his theoretical work on innovation-related sticky information, Von Hippel [1994, p. 430] has defined stickiness of information as "the incremental expenditure required to transfer that unit of information to a specified locus in a form usable by a given information seeker." Sticky information transfer cost is high, especially across the traditional firm boundary. When information held by JAL is sticky (e.g., costs of information transfer from JAL to a value chain firm are high), JAL engages in in-house innovative product development (e.g., JAL mileage program). In contrast, when information held by JAL is not sticky and costs of coordinating joint development with its value chain firms are not high vis-a-vis the costs of in-house development, JAL coordinates with the value chain firms (e.g., hotel management and ground transportation) to leverage their core capabilities in jointly developing innovative programs (e.g., new fly and stay tour package).

Essentially, the issue is one of tradeoffs between the cost of coordination and the benefits of synergy. We can develop this argument more formally. In discussing the role of virtual firms in innovation, Chesbrough and Teece (1996) assume that virtual firms coordinate business processes (e.g., design, manufacturing, market, and distribution) through market forces (e.g., outsourcing), while fully integrated firms coordinate much of their business through the power of hierarchy. Costs of coordination are higher for these virtual firms. On the other hand, virtual firms have greater incentives to take innovation risks than do fully integrated firms. In other words, there are tradeoffs between innovation risk taking and coordination cost. The costs of coordinating JAL's networked value chains fall somewhere between hierarchies and markets primarily because IOS reduced the costs of information transfer while increasing coordination efficiency. Our definition of JAL's networked value chains as neither hierarchy nor market is consistent with the economic literature (Dyer, 1996; Power, 1990; Provan and Gassenheimer, 1994; Thorelli, 1986).

As the above shows, the change in JAL's value chain was a radical transformation rather than an incremental improvement. The radical nature of this change is readily apparent if we compare the key characteristics of the old physical value chain with those of the new virtual value chain. These are presented in Table 2.

First, like the traditional Japanese value chains (Fruin, 1992), JAL's physical value chains simply optimized business within the focal firm. In contrast, the virtual value chain optimizes business across the networked value chain firms, particularly the JAL Group firms. Second, structurally, the physical value chain was centrally organized with the focal firm at the center of the structure. In contrast, in the virtual value chain, JAL is a node, albeit a very important node, in the network and does not necessarily occupy a central position. Third, the mechanism for creating new value in the physical value chain was dependent on JAL's keiretsu structure. Basically, product innovation relied on JAL's central initiative for generating ideas but JAL used its keiretsu structural relationships for gathering innovation-related information from its keiretsu member firms. In contrast, the virtual value chain is knowledge-based. Here the hierarchical structure of the keiretsu did not play a central role in product innovation, but, instead, any node firm in the network can actively occupy a central position. This is helped by the speed and the flexibility of flows of information and knowledge in the IOS network. Fourth, the direction of information and knowledge flows in the physical value chain was linear between the focal firm and a value chain firm, and the flows were primarily controlled by JAL. In the case of the virtual value chain, the flow of information is nonlinear, in that all networked firms access and use digital information many times once it is created. The flows are controlled by the information seeker. This explains the reduction of time lag in the transfer of information and knowledge across the networked firms collaborating in joint product innovation, and hence reduced cycle time. Finally, while the role of IOS in the physical value chain coordination was minimal, IOS plays a central role in virtual value chain coordination. Because of the increased speed and flexibility in information and knowledge transfer, coordination is now much more efficient.

Business Outcomes

Although it is difficult to isolate and assess the impact of JAL's IOS-enabled transformed value chain on business outcomes, cross-validation of multiple data sources (e.g., the perceptive data from the managers interviewed and the articles on new product introduction in the secondary data sources) suggests that JAL's exploitation of the virtual value chain enabled business growth and improved competitiveness.

Business Growth

The organizational transformations have been very successful and have helped make JAL the third-largest airline in the world, despite intense competition in global markets and the weakened Japanese economy. Table 3 compares JAL's business operations in 1995 with 1987, the year the firm was privatized. Despite increasingly

Table 3: Business Growth

Measures of business growth	1987	1995	Change (%)
Operating revenues -- passenger	564,052	789,786	35.1
Number of passengers carried -- domestic	9,379,012	19,365,867	106.7
Number of passengers carried -- international	6,170,107	10,869,218	76.2
Revenue passenger-load factor -- domestic	58.2%	60.4%	3.8
Revenue passenger-load factor -- international	70.9%	70.5%	

strong competition in the international and domestic markets, JAL's core business, passenger air transport, has grown. The number of domestic passengers JAL carried, approximately 19.4 million in *1995,* shows a significant increase of 106.7 percent from 9.37 million in 1987.

Similarly, the revenue from domestic and international passengers carried increased to 10.87 million in 1995, an increase of 76.2 percent from 6.17 million in 1987. As a result, JAL registered a substantial profit increase of 35.1 percent in 1995 over 1987. As of 1994, JAL has become the world's third-largest airline behind two U.S. carriers, based on revenues *(Fortune,* 1995).

In part this improvement was an increase in JAL's domestic revenue passenger-load factor. Revenue passenger-load factor is a measure of operating efficiency used in the airline industry. It shows, on average, how efficiently the company manages "yields" from its available airline seats. In other words, it shows how full or empty the company's aircraft tend to fly on scheduled domestic or international routes. Domestic revenue passenger-load factor shows that JAL increased operating efficiency 3.8 percent in 1995 over 1987 on its domestic routes. This business outcome shows a significant improvement since the deregulation of the domestic market intensified the competition among the three largest air carriers in Japan. In contrast, international revenue passenger-load factor shows that JAL maintained approximately the same level of operating efficiency on its international routes over the period. This business outcome is also significant, given the intensified competition from foreign carriers including the two U.S. airline companies that earlier leveraged CRS.

While it is unlikely that the impact of IOS on JAL's key business processes was the sole cause of JAL's business growth and improved competitiveness, the consensus among JAL managers is that IOS played a major enabling role in realizing the strategic vision. This general consensus is consistent with the assessment of Yamaji, then president: "AXESS has already had an immense impact on our operations in Japan and overseas.

Furthermore, it should be noted that JAL' s growth and improved competitiveness were realized in a hostile environment fostered by: (1) growing competition in both domestic and international markets primarily due to the deregulation of the airline industry in Japan and worldwide, and (2) the weakening Japanese economy. It is reasonable to conclude that IOS contributed significantly to JAL's business growth and increased competitiveness in two important ways. First, JAL's new IOS critically enabled the more efficient ways in which JAL's networked value chains contributed to the firm's core business (e.g., fuel purchase and airline ticket sales). Second, JAL's new IOS significantly transformed the speed and communication patterns by which JAL and its value chain firms shared information and knowledge.

Increased Competitiveness

While sharing many of the characteristics of BPR, JAL's transformation of the strategically important value chains took place *incrementally* over time. The initial focus was on efficiency. The focus then shifted to value creation through information- based strategic collaboration (e.g., innovation). Furthermore, while design of radical change was top down at JAL, implementation was carried out incrementally from the bottom up. This contradicts the accepted tenet of the BPR literature

(Hammer, 1990; Hammer, 1996; Hammer and Champy, 1993), but is consistent with results in the study of IT-based radical organizational transformation among Australian firms (Sauer and Yetton, 1997).

JAL's increased competitiveness developed *incrementally* over time in two stages: accelerated response time at the initial stage from exploiting IOS, and cycle time reduction at the later stage from leveraging the virtual value chain. In other words, JAL 's increased competitiveness was initially IOS-enabled and later further facilitated by IOS-enabled business process change. We focus here on accelerated response time and accelerated cycle time as two major indicators of JAL's increased competitiveness.

Accelerated Response Time

In discussing JAL's global environment in the 1980s, we have noted that the deregulation of the U.S. airline industry in 1978 led to increasingly intense time-based competition (McKenney, Copeland and Mason, 1995), and the diffusion of CRS made the airline industry around the world very information-intensive (Copeland and McKenny, 1988; Monteiro and Macdonald, 1996; Organisation for Economic Co-Operation and Development, 1988). We have further noted, in our discussion of JAL's use of management methodologies, that TQM radically shifted JAL's employees' and managers' attitudes toward customer focus.

In this time-based competitive industry, initially JAL used IOS to speed up its customer response time. This was achieved through IOS, which improved value chain logistics coordination efficiency and reduced operating costs. This strategic use of IOS to improve the value chain logistics coordination efficiency speeded up JAL's customer response time. This was clearly visible with respect to airline seat reservation and ticket sales. AXESS CRS effectively reduced airline ticket processing time from fifteen minutes to five seconds. As JAL's competitiveness improved, particularly with respect to its accelerated response time to customer airline seat reservation and ticket sales, a 35.1 percent increase in operating revenues from passenger transport from 1987 to 1995 was achieved.

Accelerated Cycle Time

While JAL initially used IOS to speed up its customer response time, it later used the IOS-enabled virtual value chain to reduce its joint product innovation cycle time. This reduced cycle time was achieved because the key features of the new virtual value chain enabled both the focal firm and the network members to access and share innovation-related proprietary or strategic information and knowledge faster and more flexibly across the network. Improvements in the speed and flexibility of information and knowledge transfer among the networked members greatly reduced the time lag typically associated with interfirm transfer of information and knowledge. This further improved JAL's competitiveness with respect to product innovation cycle time under time-based competition.

Conclusions

This paper started with a generic framework for analyzing IT-enabled business process change and applied it to the specific case analysis of Japan Airlines. In so doing, we have taken a longitudinal perspective and followed JAL from the global environmental changes leading to the deregulation of the Japanese airline industry in 1985, to JAL's privatization in 1986, and to the dramatic business expansion in 1994. Within this broad framework, we have focused the case analysis on the IOS-enabled transformation of interfirm business processes necessary to cope with the new business challenges.

The central issue is the impact of IOS-enabled virtual value chain on business process outcomes. The primary insight from the case analysis is that IOS enabled JAL to transform its physical value chain into a virtual value chain. JAL's new capability to exploit this virtual value chain has provided an engine of business growth and a new source of increased competitiveness. JAL achieved business growth and increased competitiveness despite both intensive competition in both domestic and international markets since the 1980s and the weakened economic conditions in Japan during the early 1990s.

In contrast to most case studies, the focus is on JAL's strategic use of IOS, particularly AXESS CRS and EDI, developed with a clear strategic intention to support JAL's emerging strategies on customer service, sales, value chain logistics coordination, and cost reduction. JAL' s IOS-enabled transformation of interfirm business processes took place incrementally over time. The initial focus was on efficiency. The focus was later shifted to value creation through information-based virtual value chain partnerships for joint product innovation. This virtual value chain underpins JAL's (1) business growth in part due to improved customer service, improved value chain logistics coordination and increased sales, and (2) increased competitiveness, particularly with respect to accelerated response time and acceler-ated product innovation cycle time.

One of the key findings is the impact of IOS on the transformation of the traditional top-down, hierarchical, keiretsu-based collaboration. This type of col-laboration is based on the keiretsu organizational form with the focal firm at its center. While this lacks flexibility, it has been the basis of competitive advantage for Japanese industries (Porter, 1990) because it is governed by mutual trust. However, even though this type of collaboration was effective in the past, today, in a time-based competitive world, it is not enough to rely exclusively on that organizational form of collaboration. Instead, keiretsu-based interfirm collaboration has to be augmented with IOS-enabled virtual value chains to facilitate flexible, nonhierarchical commu-nication across the network members.

Wider managerial implications of the study may be identified as follows: IOS can potentially play a significant role in radically changing both the speed and the flexibility of the ways in which the focal firm and its IOS networked value chain firms exchange sticky proprietary and/or strategic information and knowledge particularly with respect to joint product innovation. For many firms operating in a time-based competitive environment, the IOS-enabled product innovation cycle a time reduction provides a new source of competitive advantage.

It must be noted that, for academic researchers and managers concerned with isolating IT's impact on business processes, one difficult challenge is to understand and manage the complexity of large firms that may be applying more than one new management methodology concurrently in the pursuit of competitive advantage. We acknowledge this complexity and have examined how IOS may be exploited in conjunction with management methodologies such as TQM, BPR, and organizational learning to improve business processes.

Endnote

1. In Greek mythology, Icarus created wings out of wax and attempted to fly to the sun, but the heat of the sun melted the wax and he fell into the sea. The message is the same as in the biblical story of the tower of Babel.

References

Barney, J. (1991). Firm resources and sustained competitive advantage. *Journal of Management, 17,1* , 99-120.

Barret, S., and Konsynski, B.(1982). Inter-organization Information Sharing System. *MIS Quarterly,* 4, Special Issue (December), 93-105.

Benjamin, R.; deLong, D.; and Scott Morton, M. (1990). Electronic data interchange: how much competitive advantage? *Long Range Planning, 23,(1),* 29-40.

Bjorn-Andersen, N., and Chatfield, A. (1996). Driving organizational transformation through the use of interorganizational Systems. *Invited Plenary Paper Presentation, Ninth International Conference on EDI-IOS,* Bled, Slovenia,.

Bjorn-Andersen, N., and Chatfield, A. (1996). Uporaba informacijske tehnologije *za* oblikovanje organizacije 21. stolcija. *Organizacija: Journal for Management, Informatics and Personnel, 29(10),* 591-6O2.

Bjorn-Andersen, N., and Turner, J. (1994). Creating the twenty-first century organization: the metamorphosis of Oticon. In R. Baskerville et al. (eds.), *Transforming Organizations with Information Technology.* New York: -North-Holland, 379-393.

Black, J., and Boal, K. (1994). Strategic resources: traits, configurations and paths to sustainable competitive advantage. *Strategic Management Journal, 15,* Special Issue (Summer), 131-148.

Blackburn, J. (1991). *Time-Based Competition: The Next Baale Ground in American Manufacturing.* Homewood, IL: Business One Irwin.

Bower, J., and Hout, T. (1988). Fast-cycle capability for competitive power. *Harvard Business Review,* 66(6), 110-118.

Chatfield, A., and Yetton, P. (1997). Supplier resource leverage for product innovation cycle time compression: a case study of Honda. Australian Graduate School of Management Working Paper, January.

Chesbrough, H., and Teece, D. (1996). When is virtual virtuous? Organizing for innovation. *Harvard Business Review, 74(1),* 65-73.

Copeland, D., and McKenny, J. (1988). Airline reservation systeens: lessons from history. *MIS Quarterly, 12(3),* 353-370.

Davenport, T. (1993). *Process Innovation.* Boston: Harvard Business School Press.

Deming, W. (1989). *Out of the Crisis.* Cambridge, MA: MIT press.

Drucker, P. (1971). What we can learn from Japanese management. *Harvard Business Review,* 49(2), 110-122.

Dyer, J. (1996). Specialized supplier networks as a source of competitive advantage: evidence from the auto industry. *Strategic Management Journal, 17(4),* 271-291.

The Fortune Global: the ultimate ranking of the world's largest corporations. *Fortune,* August 7, 1995, F1-F40.

Fruin, M.(1992). *The Japanese Enterprise System.* Oxford: Clarendon Press.

Galunic, D., and Eisenhardt, K. (1994).   Renewing the strategy-structure-performance paradigm. *Research in Organizational Behaviour,* 16, 215-255.

George, A., and McKeown, T. Case studies and theories of organizational decision making. *Advances in Information Processing in Organizations,* 21—58.

Hammer, M. (1990). Reengineering work: don't automate, obliterate. *Harvard Business Review, 68(4),* 104-112.

Hammer, M. (1996). *Beyond Reengineering.* New York: Harper Collins.

Hammer, M., and Champy, J. (1993). *Reengineering the Corporation.* New York: Harper Collins.

Hammond, R.(1996). *Digital Business.* London: Hodder and Stoughton.

Hill, C. (1995). National institutional structures, transaction cost economizing and competitive advantage: the case of Japan. *Organization Science,* 6(1), 119-131.

Huber, G. (1991). Organizational learning: the contributing processes and the literatures. *Organization Science, 2(1),* 88-115.

IATA. (1986-95). *World Air Transport Statistics.*

Japan Airlines.(1986-95). *Japan Airlines Annual Report.*

Kanter, R. *(1995). World Class -- Thriving Locally in the Global Economy.* New York: Simon and Schuster.

Keen, P.(1988). *Competing in Time.* Cambridge, MA: MIT Press.

Kinugasa, T. (1994). Cost structure after deregulation of Japanese aviation. Departrnent of Economics Discussion Papers No.144, University of Queensland, Australia, March.

Kling, R. (1980). Social analyses of computing: theoretical perspectives in recent empirical research. *Computing Surveys, 12,* 7-28.

Krcmar, H.; Bjorn-Andersen, N.; and O'Callaghan, R., eds. (1995).   *EDI in Europe.* New York: Wiley.

Leavin, H., and Whisler, T. (1958). Managernent in the 1980s. *Harvard Business Review, 36(6),* 41-48.

Levitt, B., and March, J. (1988). Organizational learning. *Annual Review of Sociology, 14,* 319-340.

Lucas, H., and Baroudi, J. (1994). The role of information technology in organizational design. *Journal ofManagement Information Systems, 10(4),* 923.

MacDonald, H. (1991). Business strategy development, alignment, and redesign. In M. Scott-Morton (ed.), *The Corporation of the 1990s.* New York: Oxford University Press, 159-186.

McKenney, I.; Copeland, D.; and Mason, R. (1995). Rattling SABRES: American Airlines and the reservations systems revolution. In *Waves of Change. Business Evolution through Information Technology.* Boston: Harvard Business School Press.

Meadows, D., and Meadows, D. (1972). *The Limits to Growth.* London: Potomac Associates.

MITI.(1996). *Mjuiseiki ni muketa ryutsu billion* [Vision for the distribution system of the twenty-first century]. Tokyo: MITI SME Bureau.

Monteiro, L., and Macdonald, S. (1996). From efficiency to flexibility: the strategic use of information in the airline industry. *Journal of Strategic Information Systems, 5(3),* 169-188.

Nakane, C. *Japanese Society.* Berkeley: University of California Press, 1970.

Nonaka, I. (1994). A dynamic theory of organizational Imowledge creation. *Organization Science,* 5(1), 14-37.

O'Callaghan, R.; Kaufinann, P.; and Konsynski, B. (1992). Adoption correlates and share effects ofelectronic data interchange systems in marketing channels. *Journal ofMarketing, 56(2),* 45-56.

Organisation for Economic C0-Operation and Development.(1988).   *Deregulation and Airline Competition.* Paris: OECD.

Peteraf, M. (1993). The cornerstones of competitive advantage: a resource-based view.

Strategic Management Journal, 14(3), 179-191.

Pettigrew, A. (1990). Longitudinal field research on change: theory and practice. *Organization Science, 1(3),* 267—292.

Pine, B.(1993). *Mass Customization: The New Frontier in Business Competition.* Boston: Harvard Business School.

Porter, M. (1985). *Competitive Advantage: Techniques for Analyzing Inaustries and Competitors.* New York: Free Press.

Porter, M. *(1990). The Competitive Advantage of Nations.* New York: Free Press.

Porter, M., and Miller, V. (1985). How information gives you competitive advantage. *Harvard Business Review, 85(4),* 149-160.

Power, W. (1990). Neither market nor hierarchy: network forms of organization. *Research in Organizational Behavior, 12,* 295-336.

Provan, K., and Gassenheimer, J. (1994). Supplier commitment in relational contract exchanges with buyers: a study of interorganizational dependence and exercised power. *Journal of Management Studies, 31(1),* 56-68.

Raypoit, J., and Sviokla, J. (1995). Exploiting the virtual value chain. *Harvard Business Review, 73(6),* 75-85.

Robey, D. (1995). Theories that explain contradictions: accounting for the contradictory organizational consequences of information technology. In J. DeGross et al. (eds.), *Proceedings of the Sixteenth International Conference on Information Systems.* New York: ACM, 55-63.

Rockart, J., and Short, J. (1989). IT in the 1990s: managing organizational interdependence. *Sloan Management Review, 30(2),* 7-17.

Sauer, C., and Yetton, P. (1997). The right stuff: an introduction to new thinking about IT management. In C. Sauer and P. Yetton (eds.), *Steps to the Future: Fresh Thinking in the Management of IT-Based Organizational Transformation.* San Francisco: Jossey-Bass.

Savage, C. (1990). *Fifth Generation Management.* Burlington, MA: Digital Press.

Spanner, G.; Nuno, J.; and Chandra, C. (1993). Time-based strategies— theory and practice. *Long Range Planning, 26(4),* 90-101.

Stalk, G. (1988). Time—the next source of competitive advantage. *Harvard Business Review,* 66(4) (July-August), 41-51.

Stalk, G.; Evans, P.; and Shulman, L. (1992). Competing on capabilities: the new rules of corporate strategy. *Harvard Business Review, 70(2),* 57-69.

Stoddard, D.; Jarvenpaa, S.; and Littlejohn, M. (1996). The reality of business reengineering: Pacific Bell's centrex provisioning process. *California Management Review, 38(3),* 57-75.

Strauss, A., and Corbin, J. (1990). *Basics of Qualitative Research.* Newbury Park, CA: Sage.

Thorelli, H. (1986). Networks: between markets and hierarchies. *Strategic Management Journal, 7(1),* 37-51.

Venkatraman, N. (1991). The IT induced business reconfiguration. In M. Scott-Morton (ed.), *The Corporation ofthe 1990s.* New York: Oxford University Press, 122-158.

Von Hippel, E.(1994). "Sticky information" and the locus of problem solving: implications for innovation. *Management Science, 40(4),* 429-439.

Watanabe, K.(1995). *Nihon Koku no Chosen* [Challenges for Japan Airlines]. Tokyo: Nohon Noritsu Kyokai Management Center.

Yetton, P.; Craig, I.; and Johnston, K. (1995). Fit, simplicity and risk. In J. DeGross et al. (eds.), *Proceedings of the Sixteenth International Conference on Information Systems.* New York: ACM, 1-11.

Source: Reprinted by special permission of the Journal of Management Information Systems, Summer 1997, Vol. 14, No. 1, pg. 13-40.

Part IV:

A Window Into
The 21st Century

CHAPTER 14

IT: The Next 110010_2 Years

Varun Grover
University of South Carolina, USA

Albert H. Segars
University of North Carolina at Chapel Hill, USA

"Everything that can be invented has been invented."
— Charles H. Duell, Commissioner, U.S. Office of Patents, 1899

Predicting the future of information technology (IT) is tough, in fact, it's very tough. Accurately forecasting forms of information and IT and its impacts over the next 50 years is impossible. Although not the main inhibitor, this state-of-affairs is partially due to the pace of technological change. We have been able to predict with reasonable certainty that hardware is evolving in the direction of smaller and more powerful machines; software is evolving in the direction of user-friendly, modular, and flexible platforms; and all communication, processing and storage entities are improving in their cost, quality, and capacity metrics. While there continues to be considerable uncertainty regarding the rate of this change, it seems safe to conclude that these trends will continue. The forecasting problem is therefore twofold: it is difficult to (1) predict discontinuities, and (2) predict interactions.

Regarding (1) above, we often fail because we are comfortable in the linear extrapolation of the past, or what we have already experienced. The problem is of course that the past does not guarantee the future because unforeseen events can radically alter patterns of progression. For example, we couldn't "predict" ten years ago that aspirin which had been in use as a source of pain relief for over 100 years also reduces the risk of heart attack through its tendency to thin blood. Development of the laser over 40 years ago didn't come with predictions of its use in navigation, communication, music, and medicine. In fact, Bell Labs didn't want to patent it because "optical waves had never been of any importance to communications and hence the innovation had little bearing on Bell System interests". They were dead wrong. In fact, they were destined to be wrong unless they could have foreseen the future innovation of fiber-optics or the then unfathomable notion that light could be harnessed and guided!

"This 'telephone' has too many shortcomings to be seriously considered as
a means of communication. The device is inherently of no value to us."
— Western Union internal memo, 1876

Regarding (2) above, predications are often biased by the particular frames of reference of the predictor. Technologists will inevitably emphasize technology. Inventors look at the world from the perspective of the problem they were trying to solve. Economists think in terms of transactions, supply, and demand. As social scientists, we believe that the ultimate success of new technologies will be in the way they favorably interact with humans, businesses, social structures, markets, culture, society, government, and other entities. For example, the "electronic newspaper" delivered via the personal computer has thus far not succeeded because consumers like to stroll outside in the morning, get a whiff of cool fresh air, feel the newspaper, and read its content while in transit. Nonetheless, all rational predictions seemed to suggest that this form of information delivery would be a phenomenal hit.

"There is no reason anyone would want a computer in their home."
— Ken Olson, President, chairman and founder of Digital Equipment Corp., 1977

Willingness to accept new technologies and the accompanying social change has an inherent uncertainty that has never been more evident than the current wagers companies are making on the future. Signs of this high-stake gambling can be seen through the countless mergers, acquisitions, partnerships that populate business news. Some firms are betting on cable, others on wireless, others on content, and many on more than one of the above. Does that mean that these companies know the future? Certainly not, however, they are all betting on one. One conceived by a group of forecasters huddled in planning committees. Can these forecasters predict who's going to drive IT change? Is it some monolithic giant (Microsoft), the government, or is it going to be market determinism? Can they predict the possible consumer backlash to technological change carried too far— its impacts on privacy invasion, job insecurity, social isolationism and an information culture of have's and have nots? We would doubt it. Should they try? Of course they should! You never know when a visionary will emerge, or a smattering of circumstances that makes the prediction work. With respect to IT futures, it is a time of opportunity and innovation

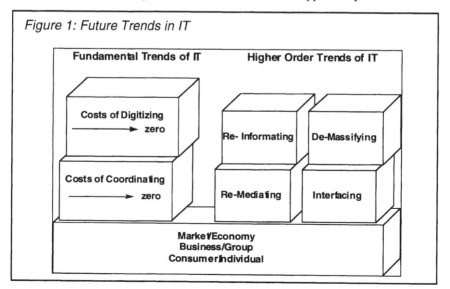

Figure 1: Future Trends in IT

"640K ought to be enough for anybody."
— Bill Gates, 1981

We make no pretensions of being visionaries. We are also inexorably tied to the past. But we are willing to put our systematic and not-so-systematic foot forward in an attempt to gaze into the crystal ball........

Now all we have to do is minimize ourselves!

Fundamental Trends

Among the many trends regarding IT, two are very fundamental in nature. They are tied to the improving performance/cost ratios of both hardware and software. These trends are:

(a) the cost of digitizing is approaching zero, and

(b) the cost of coordination is approaching zero.

Both of these trends have profound implications for the future, and interestingly, they are not that new. In fact, they have been apparent for years. However, if one were to forecast their impact a decade ago, it would have been very different from a forecast derived within today's vantage point. The questions are the same—but the answers keep changing.

Cost of Digitizing → 0

There is no question that digital representations are more precise and flexible than analog. By breaking down voice, data, video, text, and image to the lowest common denominator of 1s and 0s, we can leverage the tremendous potential of computing technologies. Unlike the analog vinyl record that stores audio information in a long spiral groove, with its squiggles and depth captured by a needle, today's digital CD captures precise representations of sound, data, and programs, in billions of binary pits. If the information is transmitted on noisy circuits, noise effects are not cumulative as the onus on the on-route devices is not to reproduce an infinite number of analog states, but a well defined digital representation. With higher and higher speeds of transmission and switching, the economies of scale in designing equipment that can consistently process binary streams, regardless of their higher application level, is remarkable. And of course, its easier to run algorithms on digital data for purposes of security and encryption.

With the unit IT costs declining, the cost of digitalization is approaching zero. In the limiting case, this implies that every single piece of information interpreted by our brain through our five senses can be represented in digital form at no cost. While we are nowhere close to that, we can easily see how multiple media can be both digital and interactive. The implications of this fundamental change are easily envisioned in terms of efficiency. Imagine the I-way infrastructure with bits flowing over glass or air at phenomenal speeds. The billions of nodes, drawing from and providing to the infrastructure, are at different layers of interpretation: a product design in machine readable for going into an organization's CAD system, a weather map from a tracking satellite appearing in real time on a forecaster's screen, a building design shared among contractors, a banking transfer entered at a home terminal going to the banking system for processing, an automatic order to a supplier system generated by a beep at the point of sale, a live video transmission of the Super Bowl — the list goes on. But these are trends that are visible today and imminent. What is not so obvious is the potential change that digitalization makes in human interaction, group structures, markets, and economies. These second and higher order effects are where the real impact of the digital future lies.

"I have traveled the length and breadth of this country and talked with the best people, and I can assure you that data processing is a fad that won't last out the year."
— *The editor in charge of business books for Prentice Hall, 1957*

Cost of Coordinating → 0

A second fundamental trend, strongly tied to the first, is the cost of coordinating. We interpret this cost broadly. It goes beyond the costs of digital representation and includes all costs involved in acquiring and evaluating information. The limiting case of this cost (i.e. when coordination costs are zero), has dramatic implications for the notion of the firm as the organizational unit, and the interrelationships between buyers and sellers in the marketplace.

Firms exist within an organizational framework primarily because of coordination costs. It would be difficult to imagine production units selling products produced to the highest bidder among marketing departments. Or imagine a manager bidding for secretarial services or a college dean bidding for faculty services! The time and cost of gathering appropriate information (e.g., quality of service, start-up time, price) makes this impractical. So firms are held together by common goals, defined structures, and rules of operation, in order to reduce information uncertainty. In other words, the firm is a hierarchy not a market. If coordination costs were indeed approaching zero, then there would be no reason for a firm to exist. Each individual with their requisite knowledge-base becomes the basic business unit and therefore can cluster into market based organizations as and when needed. Lack of coordination costs means fluidity or dynamic relationships that assemble based on value added to the purpose of the assembling unit. Similarly, buyers and sellers in the marketplace know everything needed to be known about each other, and dynamic market equilibrium will quickly fall into place. Incentives for opportunistic behaviors decline, and new information based structures can be created and dismantled with ease.

"We're not in a commodity business..."
— *Rod Canion, CEO of Compaq Computer, 1989*

While we are no where close to the complete breakdown of the firm, the signs are there. The reason for existence of the large, rule based firm is giving way to the newer networked, learning, reengineered, team-based organizational structure, many of which are smaller, and outsource much of which lies outside of their core competency. Also, the I-way in its many manifestations is making market structures practical and economical for complex products traditionally governed by vertically

But what will we do with ourselves when computers do all the work?

integrated hierarchies.

Higher Order Trends

In light of these two fundamental trends, we now attempt to identify higher order trends that involve changes in individuals, consumers, businesses, groups, markets, and economies. While fundamental effects have obvious manifestations in efficiency, higher order trends involve interactions, discontinuities, and backlashes - many of which can be discussed, but not predicted with any certainty. For instance, the advent of the automobile had a fundamental effect in the speed of travel, however, the higher order effects of suburbia and suburban malls, was far from obvious.

The four trends are discussed under the headings of "Re-informating", "De-massifying", "Re-mediating" and "Interfacing" (see Figure 1). The first three of these trends, "re-informating", "de-massifying", and "re-mediating" focus on changes in product offerings and supporting value chains implied by the fundamental trends identified earlier. In essence, these higher order trends reflect anticipated reconfigurations of structure and process at market and organizational levels. The final trend "interfacing" is focused on anticipated changes in man-machine interface. Distinct from the other trends, this higher-order effect addresses how individuals will interact with technologies of the future. Implicit in all trends is the evolution from the computer to the network. As the network becomes faster and its nodes become more intelligent, the virtual world no longer sits on the desktop or in an organizational backoffice - it is accessible to all. The network is the computer. And, the collective knowledge of the people units on the network is its intelligence. While the servers may not be owned by these units, the governance structure between the servers (providers) and the users (buyers), is more market based and democratic than hierarchical and autocratic, a far cry from the traditional governance between IS departments and users.

Re-Informating

"Re-informating" refers to new ways of supplying information - very different from the "react to needs and provide" cycle that typifies traditional thinking. It includes the revamping of organizational value chains and products in a way that transcends discussions of strategic systems that are so prevalent in the IS community. For instance, let's say organizations (not necessarily firms) are represented as an aggregation of their physical and informational assets — in their value activities and products. Re-informating could include the separation of the physical assets from the informational assets, the replacement of many physical assets with informational assets, the integration of informational assets, and the expansion of physical assets with information. The I-way then provides the infrastructure for informational assets. Linking onto the I-way requires an information interface that may or may not be a part of a physical product or value activity. In other words, to leverage the informational infrastructure, it is necessary to re-informate and evaluate the line between the physical and the informational. Within this category, three trends are described: virtualization of the physical, configuration of structure, and the creation and warehousing of knowledge.

Virtualization of the Physical

Virtualization of the physical is reflective of the trend toward enhancing or replacing physical products, services, and activities, with informational ones. JIT involves replacement of physical inventory with information. "Smart products" are products that are enhanced by in their digital content. We can expect to see a proliferation of smart products that are interfaced with the I-way. Along with the virtual office, organization, and mall such evidence is already manifest through the incorporation of microprocessors in household appliances, cars, houses, debit cards, and children's toys. It seems very safe to conclude that the migration of processing technologies from the computer to other electronic and nonelectronic devices will continue. *Intelligence* and *connectivity* can make dumb objects like doorknobs talk and let us know that someone is on the phone or the microwave has finished its task. Intelligent homes will know your morning flight is delayed and will adjust the wake time on the alarm clock so you can sleep a bit more. Or what about the virtualization of physical film as movies are beamed digitally to theaters. Far fetched - yes. But these ideas are far from unfeasible in a digital future.

"But what ... is it good for?"
Engineer at the Advanced Computing Systems Division of IBM, 1968, commenting on the microchip

Along with access to information, the capability to seamlessly customize and transfer forms of information between consumers will be a defining element of virtualization. In contrast to collectors and disseminators of information, users will become orchestrators of information, recasting the elements of information into varying symphonies appropriate for diverse time and space transactions. Increasingly smaller and more powerful processing technologies which take the form of portable, attachable, and yes, even implantable devices will allow consumers of information to access, manipulate, and communicate forms of information which seem complex by today's standards.

In fact, it seems quite likely that information itself will contain processing capabilities. This "smart data" will recognize complimentary forms of data which can be utilized to form larger "information constructs" useful to the information consumer. Bar coding will be replaced by "bar coding and processing" in which information about the product along with programming code and integrated technology for changing and communicating product status will be ingrained in the product's packaging. Early forms of these technologies are now manifested in package tracking systems introduced by Federal Express. In the dynamic world of tomorrow, it seems likely that data and processing code will remain with the information source eliminating the need for massive amounts (or any amount) of storage on central machines. Information about the sales force and their activities will travel with them and be instantly accessible and changeable through the wonders of remote processing and wireless communication technologies. In sum, advances in communications and processing technologies may render collective storage obsolete. In contrast, future architectures may allow coded information to remain with its source, only to be accessed and/or aggregated when needed.

Configuration of Structure

Along with virtualization of physical product, we can also expect to see traditional forms of organizational and industry structure replaced by dynamic configurations of teams and partnerships. In essence, the paradigm of industry classification by SIC codes will be fundamentally challenged when organizations in the automobile business deliver educational products on the I-way, or both banks and pesticide manufacturers use a crop rotation DSS to woo agricultural customers, or food producers enter the weight loss business by providing expert systems that monitor weight loss progress and recommend diet and exercise routines. Further, forms of industry configurations which today are not feasible due to specificity of assets, knowledge, and skills will not only become feasible they will become ever-changing. In a world of seamless information transfer and virtualization of physical product, industries will be created and recreated within a matter of weeks or days (and perhaps hours). Much like today's stock market, possession of the physical asset (i.e. the stock certificate) will not be as important as access to information about the physical product (i.e. the price). This virtual asset base will facilitate partnerships between very diverse organizations which will materialize to exploit very short-lived arbitrage opportunities in electronic markets. In the world of tomorrow, configurations of business partners with very diverse skill and information inventories will replace generic strategic groups as a basis of "organizing for competition".

At the organizational level, configurations of work teams will be created and recreated to respond to the everyday challenges of markets. Geographic location and perhaps vested interest by the worker in the organization will become irrelevant as workers sell their services in the electronic market of "personnel free agency". Instead of working for a single employer, knowledge workers of tomorrow may work for several employers in very different industries and in very diverse geographic locations. Project teams will be based not on skills which can be "hired in" but on those which can be "contracted in". In essence, the firm will not be a conglomeration of buildings, offices, organizational charts, and job descriptions. Instead the organization will be a series of projects assigned to appropriate skill bases through a virtual network of information. In other words, the network will be the organization and the organization will be constantly changing as the content of project teams cycles for each new undertaking.

"I think there is a world market for maybe five computers."
— Thomas Watson, chairman of IBM, 1943

Warehousing of Knowledge

In this new era of industrial and organizational configuration, the winners will be the organizations that can best use software, information content, and the communication infrastructure to enhance customer value. Or alternatively stated, the ability to create and sustain knowledge. The most important asset for the individual, group, organization, and country will be the ability to quickly evolve down the data->information->knowledge->wisedom cycle. Massive amounts of information must be effectively mined and interpreted with respect to its context in such a way that it can be applied to alternative contexts. In general, everyone will have access to information. It is the interaction of information with the creative knowledge of business units, (i.e., the individuals that make up the business organization at any point in time) which will be the defining point of success or failure. The speed of assimilation, learning, and transformation of information into warehouses of knowledge will be critical. Capital and physical assets can be accumulated and dissolved in rapid cycles—sustainability is in knowledge. And on top of knowledge, leveraging experience, perspective, and judgment to create wisdom can create a long term perspective in a short cycle world.

I don't know about our position, but the stock market is due for an upswing.

De-Massifying

Our existing paradigms have often used the "massification" of society to manage complexity. We segment markets, we stereotype people, we broadcast TV and radio signals to all, we sell a fixed goods in physical stores, we use mass advertising media, etc. However, trends of digitalization and coordination are reversing these approaches. Music, entertainment programming, news, and sports along with phone conversations and data will be merged into ever-changing "supra-information". A higher order effect of supra-information will be a trend towards access in contrast to ownership for information consumers. For example, time and space constraints greatly impact the manner in which we now consume information products. We purchase compact discs from retailers and play them in our home, office, or car stereos; we access information through computers in our home or office; we converse through either wireless or standard telephone devices; and we tune in to our favorite programming through television. In the future, it seems likely that consumers will, in real time from anywhere at anytime, access music tracks from their favorite provider (eliminating the problem of purchasing a CD and discovering that the only good track is the one you have heard on the radio) and choose (and design) their own television programming. Restrictions placed on the consumer by packaged music and scheduled programming will be eliminated. In fact, *access will become more important than ownership to the consumer and variety of content more important than packaging and distribution to the seller.* Similar to the philosophy of JIT inventory which pushes the responsibility of product stewardship up the distribution channel, consumers will likely push information stewardship back to providers making local storage media irrelevant. Just in time information which frees the information consumer from constraints of time and space will replace today's restrictive forms of packaging and distribution. Further, instead of the information consumer seeking an electronic device such as a computer, stereo, television, or telephone to retrieve information, the information will configure itself to be received by the user— anyplace, anytime, anywhere.

In other words, we can have production runs of one, and still be profitable - in fact, more profitable. We can tailor services to market segments of one. Take the case of a virtual restaurant. You (or your intelligent agent) can access it's menu on the I-way. The menu will be customized based on your personal profile. You make the reservation, which is immediately confirmed. When you arrive at your table, the tablecloth is your favorite color, your waitress is the one you enjoy bantering with, and the music emanating from your table is consistent with your highest preference. In essence, your culture, ideas, experience, and knowledge, have become a part of the service. In similar vein, you can customize clothes, see yourself in them, and order them on the Custom Clothes I-way site. They are delivered to you in one day with perfect fit. Custom Clothes has no store, no inventory - just an information line to the customer and a delivery truck service, and a production process that can "virtually" produce on demand. This world has no product life cycle, and no guarantees of success. Creativity and innovation are paramount.

50 percent of 100? I'll check it ...

Re-Mediating

On one level, we can discuss the I-way dis-intermediating relationships between suppliers and consumers. We can see the doom of all middlemen who do not add value. Customers can directly order from manufacturers and get customized information and service. Why do we need the wholesaler to add cost to the distribution chain? Why do we need the retailer, when customers can directly access virtual stores set up by the manufacturer? Why do we need the video store, which can be replaced by a video server with dial-up or leased links to the consumer? Why does a musician need a record company when music can be digitalized and sold on the I-way? Why do we need travel agents, stockbrokers, real estate agents, Why can't we replace much of the physical world with the virtual world of buyers and sellers? The answer is - we can and we might, but in the next 20, 40 and maybe 50 years, we are going to see both dis-intermediation and re-mediation. In other words, new intermediary roles will be defined.

Let us take the limiting case. All businesses know what they need to know about their consumers and all consumers have information on suppliers. If this massive information can be processed and analyzed by a software agent that makes it easy for the consumer to choose and the supplier to tailor—then the need for intermediaries disappears. But take the more practical case. A hospital in Brazil needs to purchase 18,000 different hospital supplies. They can access the manufacturers directly, but can they do that effectively for all 18,000 products, and for every manufacturer? With enough customization push on the part of manufacturers, and intelligent software search and compare agents on the part of the buyer, they might indeed do that. But until we reach that point, middlemen are going to take-up roles involving the management of information (rather than conducting a transaction). New media-tion value can be created and attempts can be made to forge trust and relationships up the value chain, by providing information and knowledge that is valued.

Also, re-mediation roles become more apparent when we consider the gap between producers and consumers of information is narrowing. If consumers are involved in the service production of the restaurant described above, they are producing information that is used and its manifestation is cycled back. That information has value to the supplier, and to alternate suppliers. The supplier is the consumer of that information, and the consumer is the supplier. To buy that information, the supplier pays for it in quality of service or product or customization level. At some point, alternative entities might supplement that information and create new information products. The consumer is now at the end of a chain in which there is a new mediator. Similarly, a large virtual organization manufacturing a product goes through a cycle of loss it cannot sustain, disaggregates itself, and some of its business units (people) re-aggregate as consumers of the organization they were first supplying. Also, a virtual supplier realizes that its information on consumers and competitors could be more profitable if it set itself up as a interme-diary between buyers and its competitors.

As noted earlier, the organizations of the future will not be burdened by tradition, bureaucracies, or hierarchies, giving them the flexibility to add value at different parts of the value chain or the same part of different value chains.

Interfacing

The final higher-order trend of "interfacing" is more reflective of the way humans will interact with the computer. As such, it is different from the above trends in that it reflects a cycle of technology-driven evolution. Nonetheless, tracing the evolution of interface between man and computer has profound implications for the broader social structures in which we live and work.

It seems likely that the progression of man - machine interface in terms of computing technologies will mirror that of the radio. Just as multiple forms of music, news, and talk now populate the airwaves, multiple forms of information will populate the airwaves of the future. Also, like today's radio receivers, processing technologies of the future will be able to access, manipulate, and transfer these information constructs uninhibited by time and space. Importantly, the radio has undergone stages of well-defined evolution which closely resemble the computer. At its genesis, the radio was a rather large and very immobile device which occupied a central location within the household. Over time, the radio became portable, capable of easily accompanying the listener wherever he or she traveled. With the introduction of the Sony walk-man, radio technology evolved from a portable device to an attachable device. The continuation of this evolution seems to imply that future radio technology will be based on implantable devices which interact directly with human auditory functions. Early versions of such technologies are already in developmental stages for hearing aids. Utilizing the analogy of the radio, Table 1 outlines ages of man - computer interface. As shown, four distinct ages of interface are defined; *immobility* and *portability,* which have been almost fully realized, as well as *attachment* and *implant* which are yet to come. Like radio technology, passage from one age to another does not imply that a new age causes its predecessor to become extinct. Rather, the new age adds a fundamentally different interface which may alter patterns of information interchange among most, but not necessarily all, users.

"The wireless music box has no imaginable commercial value. Who would pay for a message sent to nobody in particular?"
— David Sarnoff's associates in response to his urgings for investment in the radio in the 1920s

The Age of Immobility

In their earliest form, computers were anything but mobile. In fact, early patterns of computer construction treated the device as a fixture much like the furnace and air conditioning. To access the data and programs of the computer, the user entered commands through a terminal wired directly into the main computing technology. More commonly, the user did not interact with the computer at all. Instead, the user received artifacts of the computer through predefined reports. While the emergence of the personal computer did much to bring computing into the hands of many users, it did little in terms of resolving the immobility of computing technologies. Interfaces between man and machine and associated uses of computers were still governed by the assumptions of machine and data at a fixed location around which users accomplished their tasks. In essence, the computer was the nexus around which tasks and operations are designed and executed. While immobile computing technologies are still integral components of corporate computing architectures, the age of immobility has largely passed.

"Computers in the future may weigh no more than 1.5 tons."
—Popular Mechanics, forecasting the relentless march of science, 1949

The Age of Portability

While earlier forms of portable computing can be identified, the age of portability most likely began with the introduction of the notebook computer by Compaq. In essence, the introduction of this technology fundamentally changed the time and space relationship between machine and user. Unlike the age of immobility, users could easily transport computing machines allowing them to be geographically independent with respect to utilization of the technology. While many users gladly welcomed the age of portability, this new era of computing also introduced many redundancies in data collection and applications. Many users have created two desktop platforms to support their tasks; one portable and one fixed. In essence, the portable desktop supports the user as he/she travels. The fixed desktop, usually located in the office, supports the user in running applications that interface with the

Table 1: Ages of Man - Machine Interface

	Immobility	Portability	Attachment	Implant
Nature of Technology	Fixed-location processing and storage machines. Usable only through common time and space relationship with user.	Variable-location processing and storage machines. Usable through common time and variable space relationships with user.	Attachable processing machines. Usable through interactive time and space relationships with user.	Implantable processing machines. Usable through integrative time and space relationships with user.
Nature of Processing Applications and Information	Single centralized application platform and single desktop platform. Information consolidated, manipulated, and updated on fixed computer platforms.	Dual desktop platforms. Shared consolidation, manipulation, & updating between computers.	Interactive consolidation, manipulation, and updating between computers and users.	Single integrative consolidation, manipulation, & updating between computers and users.
Examples	Mainframe computing environments. Desktop PCs.	Portable computers, Personal assistants, Wireless client-server architectures.	Virtual reality, Voice recognition, Optical command and response.	Synaptic interface and processing devices.

firm's proprietary or legacy systems. Obviously, the cost in terms of upgrades and maintenance of this desktop duplicity can rapidly climb with the decrease in cost of portable technologies.

Although unrealized today, it is quite likely that the ultimate destiny of portable computing is the merging of fixed and portable desktops. In essence, it seems likely that future architectures will allow the user to access a single, familiar desktop which is independent of hardware. Such technologies will push operating system software, client applications, and storage back to servers. These servers would then be accessible through wireless communications. The user could access his or her desktop from a viewing device in the office and then remotely access the same desktop through a portable viewing device. A promotion, lateral job move, or even a transfer from the West coast to the East coast would not necessitate a hard drive backup. In this fully realized age of portability, tasks and associated information will be centered around the user rather than the computer.

The Age of Attachment

The emergence (or reemergence) of voice recognition in addition to optical command and response technologies have already begun to usher in the age of attachment. In this age, computing technologies will take on the form of attachable devices which can access, process, and communicate information over a wireless spectrum. In essence, these technologies will free users of the encumbrances of keyboards and monitors. Email, Vmail, and Video messages will likely be accessible through devices not much larger than a wristwatch. In addition, wearable peripherals will allow users to issue commands to computing devices through either voice or sight. Such advances will allow information workers to create complex information inquiries, simulations, and analyses in a conversational mode. Such exchanges between user and computer will take on a new form of interaction in contrast to the forms of correspondence inherent in earlier ages.

The Age of Implant

A final, and certainly revolutionary by today's standards, evolution in man - machine interface will be the age of implant. While such notions at first seem very farfetched, consider how bizarre pace makers and artificial hearts would seem to people fifty years ago. These implant technologies are certainly not perfected, nonetheless, they are definitive indicators of the direction in which medical advances will take us. Likewise, it seems that computing technologies will advance to a point where information about ourselves will be encoded on implantable chips. Further, our interaction with computing technologies may be through implantable interface devices instead of through our fingers and keyboards. Such advances are very difficult to fathom and describe from today's technological perspective, yet, the trend seems very well-defined. Electronic computing technologies will perhaps become additional sources of storage about ourselves—within ourselves. Further, they will likely become electronic monitors of the synaptic physiological functions within ourselves, providing diagnostic information about our functioning. Finally, advanced electronic technologies may provide the ultimate interface between our synaptic impulses and the binary impulses of computing and communication systems.

In general, the emergent trends of today suggest that tomorrow's world of information will resemble the wind currents which surround the earth. These currents of information will be uninhibited by time and space limitations and will be accessible in many different configurations to information consumers. As the interface between user and computer evolves and as physical assets become virtual, traditional structures of work, commerce, and entertainment will likely evolve into configurations of structure which dynamically react to changes in market (or organizational) context. However, just as the Earth's wind currents can be responsible for unpredictable and sometimes violent patterns in weather, the free flow of information currents may also be responsible for unpredictable patterns in behavior at individual, organizational, and industry levels.

Let's face it, the computer designed the house perfectly ... well, almost ...

Backlash?

As mentioned at the beginning of this essay, any prediction can be invalidated by discontinuities that are difficult if not impossible to anticipate. A major premise of this technologically catalyzed revolution is that individuals, businesses, and economies, will accept the general direction of market determinism. However, there is a real possibility of consumer backlash - that might originate in some nebulous form and compound itself into a Goliath that could have major implications for the road ahead. Five questions are raised, simply to alert readers to some potential caveats to the trends described above. Further, recognizing that these danger points are visible to us, it is certainly prudent to note that the ones not visible could be the most significant obstacles in the progression of future technological trends.

1. Trends such as virtualization and de-massifying require information participation on the part of the consumer. This involves giving up private information to a monolithic network entity—controlled by everyone else but you.
2. The virtualization of the physical means that consumers have to deal with smart-devices everywhere. Data everywhere. Information everywhere. If a substantial proportion of time is spent communicating with machines, albeit smart, where's the real company. Is there inevitable social isolationalism?
3. What about the propensity to polarize society along dimensions of "information haves" and "have nots". Will there be an elite intranet of the know-alls dominating the I-way?
4. Markets are good—but may not always work in the best social interests. The mediating and re-mediating flexibility, provides the basis for some potentially dangerous trends, if the network governs itself the network governs itself and does not work in the best social and moral interests.
5. The lack of security and stability could be disconcerting to individuals. This and the inevitable pressure to constantly cope with change could manifest itself in stress and other related health problems.

As implied in these caveats, the determining factor in the velocity and shape of technological evolution may well be the reactions of society to computer-based innovations. Events such as massive storage failures and electronic fraud can not only stop technological evolution in its tracks, it can actually reverse the progression. While consumers do not think twice about giving their credit cards to clerks, tellers, and even telephone operators they have never met, there is something innately suspicious about sending your credit card number over a network which first encrypts the number sends it at incredible speed randomly in packets and then reassembles it at the destination. Somehow it seems less risky for consumers to leave printed documentation of their card number in the form of carbons and receipts than to have it electronically encoded and delivered to the seller. Such paradoxes in human behavior are a reality and serve as a needed check to unbridled technological progression. Clearly, runaway exploitation of workers and consumers through technology will greatly slow the promises made possible through digitization and wireless communication. In sum, it seems that the most accurate vision of techno-logical future will be a combination of the technologist, economist, inventor, and social scientist. Technological progression tempered by its impact on exchanges, patterns of work, and most importantly, its perceived benefit to society.

> *"computers are leaving a miserable mark across society: from schools, where students are learning less because of computer shortcuts, to the home where screens are replacing social interaction"*
> *Kirkpatrick Sale, Author*

Concluding Remarks

Perhaps the greatest fallacy of humankind is the belief that science, technology, and the arts will evolve to their fullest potential during our lifetime. Just as Alexander The Great wept by the seashore because there were no more worlds to conquer, it is easy to convince ourselves that we have "seen it all" in terms of the capabilities of processing, storage, and communications technologies. A far more likely scenario is that we are at the very beginning of the voyage made possible by advances in information technologies and that fifty years from now knowledge workers who have yet to be born will interact with computing technologies far more advanced than that of today and create forms of information which are not yet imaginable. Unlike today, it is likely that the portability of future technologies will not be encumbered by bulky power devices, disk drives, keyboards and monitors. In sum, the forms of information and computing which are now part of the fabric in everyday business life will seem as archaic to workers of the future as the paper ledger and pen seem to us now.

Like the erroneous predictions which have appeared throughout this discourse, the forecasts of this essay are only as valid as the assumptions upon which they are built. Therefore, while it is certainly amusing to examine past quotations and wonder how those "in the know" could have been so far off in their predictions, it is also a very worthwhile exercise to wonder how the assumptions which formed the foundation of their predictions changed. Like the emergence of the silicon chip in the era of glass tube, the next revolution in computer processing could lie around the corner. Alternatively, massive failure, fraud, or other misuse of computing technologies could be the hallmark of the coming years. Either of these extremes implies very different outcomes in terms of how technology will influence organizational as well as everyday life. Clearly, the rippling effect of positive and negative technological trends will be felt by more people more quickly due to the prevalence and capabilities of computing technologies. This state-of-affairs places even greater importance on anticipating how first order effects of technological innovation create higher order effects which influence patterns of use and acceptance. Technology may very well be considered the "fire" of this era, defining not only what is achieved but what is not achieved.

To specifically define future technology and its impact is a very daunting undertaking. In this paper, we have attempted to provide fundamental and higher order trends, as a basis for anticipating what the future holds. Even though these predictions seem relatively "safe" within this point in time, it will be interesting to look back with 20/20 hindsight and observe if any of these predictions do, in fact, become reality.

"If I had known that I would lose, I would not have run"
Richard Petty acknowledging his 1996 congressional election defeat

Source: Reprinted by special permission of Database: Advances in Information Systems (a publication of the Special Interest Group on Information Systems of the Association for Computing Machinery), Vol. 27, No. 4, 1996, pp. 45-57.

CHAPTER 15

Information Futures:
Producer and Consumer Views

James E. Short
London Business School, U.K.

Daniel Bell's (1973) treatise in social forecasting, *The Coming of the Post-Industrial Society*, recounts the story of how Henry Adams, at the turn of the last century, felt that he had grasped one of the secrets to unraveling the complexities of predicting rates of historical change. By common accord, nineteenth century society measured its progress by the output of coal. Adams had observed that between 1840 and 1900, coal output in the United States had doubled every ten years, and in the form of utilized power, each ton of coal yielded roughly three to four times as much power in 1900 as it had produced in 1840. The ratio of increase in the volume of coal power, Adams reasoned, might represent a "dynamometer" - a measure of the rate of change which, if it could be defined scientifically, would produce a "law of acceleration." Adams' excitement was that such a measure would allow computing the rates of social change as exactly as the laws of velocity had been calculated by Newtonian physics (Bell, 1973).

Adams as we know failed to develop his "social physics" of change, though Bell points out that in his attempt to use J-curves to map coal production and usage and thereby to forecast rates of historical change, Adams' idea was a clever if not magnificent failure ("he was perhaps the first man of his time" to grasp the quickening change of pace now common in descriptions of contemporary life). In proposing the expansive topic of "Forecasting the Next 50 Years in Information Technology," this special issue of *Database* raises both Adams' problem with coal (now perhaps the rates of change in semiconductor technologies and software), and Bell's crucial observation that "exponential curves not only signify a rapid change in time scales, but more and more quickly transform the character of our knowledge and our lives." Bell cites several examples, among them the discovery of quasars (in the 1960s), which radically altered our views about the solar system. If we think about changes and/or transformations in information technology (IT), Bell's list would almost certainly include the 50th anniversary of the switching on of E.N.I.A.C. at the University of Pennsylvania (celebrated in April 1996) (Hughes, 1996). So too he would list the discovery of the transistor, at AT&T Bell Laboratories, in 1947. Arguably, the origins of the Internet - the Defense Department's ARPANET - would be cited as pivotal, though perhaps not for the reasons first imagined (I think for its contribution to building electronic communities, rather than for the technical advancements which made it possible).

While these advances in information technologies seem clear-cut, and we can reasonably expect Bell would have no trouble including them, other important advances in information and in information technology might not be so recorded. Examples: in 50 years will we be able to find the names of the hardware and software team that produced the first Nintendo game player? Will Pixar's development team, and the hardware and software they used to create Disney's *Toy Story,* be in the Smithsonian Museum of Industry, or, perhaps, in a new Smithsonian Museum of the Information Age? How will the recorders of industrial history separate out information (the "I" in IT) from the artifacts of information technology (the "T" in IT)? Colossus, E.N.I.A.C., the Manchester Mark I, the IBM System/360, the Digital VAX, and the Apple I and II are displayable artifacts, but what about information?

In the following pages, I hope to draw out two different perspectives of information and information technology (IT), necessarily selective and simplified in the space available. The first perspective follows roughly the analogy of Adams' tracking of the production and productivity of coal usage in the last century, and the social and economic impacts created therein. Applied to IT, it involves the tracking of information technology developments and the movement of IT into economic and social sectors. I term this perspective loosely the "producer" view of information technology.

The second perspective is the one held by consumers of information technologies. Some might term it the market view. In essence it asks how do consumers affect IT? More broadly, it asks how do social and community norms (cultures) affect technology choices? Edgar Schein neatly summarizes this perspective by observing in his writings and courses on technology and organizational cultures that [paraphrasing] "the problem with many IT studies is they never ask the converse to the question - how does IT affect organizations? It is at least as important, and arguably more so, to ask how do innovative cultures affect IT?" (Schein, 1994). I will restrict attention here to consumers, or potential consumers of IT, given space. Finally, I conclude with some brief observations on who changes in information and information technology will affect most in the next 50 years (or at least in the next five to ten years).

Producer Perspective

One of the first general meetings of MIT's five-year Management in the 1990s program (MIT90s) was held in England just over a decade ago. In attendance were a mix of academics representing management and technology disciplines (strategy, MIS, computer science), businessmen from the ten companies sponsoring the program (including Digital Equipment Corporation, American Express, Eastman Kodak, ICL and British Petroleum), and graduate students from management, engineering and computer science. The task at hand was to map a research agenda for the program, an important part of which was to explore how IT would affect the way organizations would survive and prosper in the 1990s and beyond. There was the view that revolutionary changes were underway, that our models for understanding these changes were limited, and that fresh insights and new research perspectives were needed.

Participants over the several day meeting broke down roughly into two clusters of activity (oversimplifying things). One group coalesced quickly around analyzing R&D and technology trends in computing hardware (logic, memory and storage), in computer architecture and organization (RISC processors, etc.), in input-output technologies (speech recognition, input devices, etc.), in trends in software (programming complexity, higher level languages, etc.), and in trends in networking and communications (interoperability, transport, compression, bandwidth, etc.). A special issue of *Science* magazine, "Computers and Electronics" published a few years earlier, served as a baseline (Abelson and Dorfman, 1982). This issue had been something of a *tour de force*, with articles by Lewis Branscomb (then Chairman of the National Science Board and Chief Scientist at IBM), Joel Birnbaum (Director of HP's Computer Research Center), and John Mayo (Executive Vice President of Network Systems at Bell Laboratories). Subjects ranging from computing trends (Branscomb), technology R&D (Birnbaum), to intelligent networks (Mayo) were explored.

Interestingly, an article by Allen Newell and Robert Sproull outlined the network structure and operation of ARPANET in the early 1980s (Newell and Sproull, 1982). The authors noted that the 185 host computers on the network (88 nodes) represented the full spectrum of university and industrial research groups in computer science, and that as of the end of 1980, the network was saturated with effective file transfer rates often falling below 5000 bits per second in periods of heavy traffic. Compare these figures with current Internet estimates of over 5,000 networks, 2 million host computers, over 20 million users, with file transfer rates of 1.5 million bits per second over T3 and T1 lines - this growth in less than fifteen years.

Group one's efforts were notable for the attention given to projected rates of change in base technology R&D, to the likely timing of product ideas and instrumentation out of laboratory settings into adopter firms and industry design and production chains, and the implications of production efficiencies and learning curve effects as volumes increased and consumers assimilated and refined new product use. A spirited discussion also had ensued around prediction techniques and forecasting linear and non-linear rates of change. We agreed that while it is virtually certain to say that with any complex system it will be like it is now a moment later, the problems in forecasting are with paradigm shifts. Here, prediction techniques struggle against uncertainty and random chance. And, worse, examples of forecasts and opportunities missed are abundant: electric typewriters, transistors, and personal computers to name a celebrated few (Utterback, 1994).

A second group took on the role of assessing the likely and counter-intuitive organizational impacts of IT. This was a far reaching exercise, the list of probable and potential implications seemed infinite, but after some good-natured thrashing about, some emergent themes and literature familiar to many readers emerged. Leavitt and Whisler's (1958) *Harvard Business Review* article served as one discussion anchor. Their assessment that new technologies would tend to split middle management — "thin it, simplify it, program it, and separate a large part of it more rigorously from the top," has been challenged repeatedly in recent years, but their assertion that computers would redefine and redistribute work has been fundamental to many streams of thinking, including work by Burns and Stalker (1961) on technology and innovation, Woodward (1965) on principles and practices of factory management, Lawrence and Lorsch (1967) on integration and differentiation of organizational units, Galbraith (1977) on information processing and uncertainty, and Shoshana Zuboff (1988) on "informating" organizations.

Michael Porter's (1985) work on industry forces and value chains was gaining force at the time of the MIT90s meeting, and the impacts noted above were brought into the firm's production logic using these chain-type models. The parsimony of effects and general attractiveness of value chain approaches have prompted many later writers, including Hagel and Eisenmann (1994) (multimedia value chains and emerging competitive battlegrounds) and Rayport and Sviokla (1994) ("marketspace" and management strategies in it) to expand on Porter's original concepts and apply them to new industry territory.

The groups' efforts brought the full enormity of change envisioned to the forefront of the meeting. Galileo once observed that science proceeds more on the basis of what it can reasonably exclude than include, and while science was all around the understanding and development of information technologies, forecasting IT and its effects appeared to be inherently an exercise in social science theorizing. In an arena of too many variables, too many contingencies, and too many unknowns to explain IT's social impacts let alone predict them, it was generally agreed the best that could be done was an array of alternatives (Wager, 1993).

I recount the above to illustrate both what the meeting uncovered and what it did not. The groups did not dwell on the emerging computer games industry as a marker of technology change. Evolving cybercommunities like the Well (Whole Earth 'Lectronic Link) and the possibility they would help spawn cybercafes, Sony Wonder, Silicon Studios (operated by Silicon Graphics), and Sega virtual reality centers were not explored. Progressive Network's Real Audio, Pointcast, Mosaic and Netscape were yet to come. The 1990s language of "convergence"— content, channels, set-top boxes, media spaces and "edutainment" as examples - were not part of the corporate lexicon. As Bell had explained in his study of Adams' "dynamometer," the tricky part about believing exponential curves was that they signalled transformation in the character of our knowledge. In retrospect, there had been broad agreement at the meeting on the enormity of change. The problems had been in the perspectives and models used to understand and forecast that change.

Consumer Perspective

Few would have believed attending the summer 1996 MacWorld convention in Boston that the company behind all of this was in serious trouble (BusinessWire, 1996). Curious as I walked about the exhibits I asked a few attendees why all the conference energy and optimism (apart from the usual fun of *MacWorld*)? The answer in so many words was "Apple is us, and we're fine." We can debate the point, but I believe the original consumer IT company has to be Apple Computer. Apple has persisted through a legion of mishaps, missteps and corporate turmoil to remain the champion of a generation of IT consumers. Sherry Turkle (1995) writes that "today's children are growing up in the computer culture; all the rest of us are at best its naturalized citizens." If Turkle is right, then surely Apple Computer is the Ellis Island of the computer culture.

Apple's unique culture and management style was explored by Guy Kawasaki (1988) in *The Macintosh Way*. In a memorable "exercise," he asks readers to answer the following multiple choice question:

> *Apple wanted to sell Macintoshes to people who had never used computers before. Which customer group would you expect Apple to concentrate on:*
>
> A. *Fortune 1000 MIS Directors*
> B. *IBM PC owners*
> C. *Knowledge workers*
> D. *Amazon Indians*

Kawasaki (1988) noted that the phrase "knowledge workers" was marketing "malarkey," but that it "caused people to align themselves to Apple's marketing, and they persuaded themselves to buy Macintoshes. After all, who would want to be an "ignorance worker." It is easier for the market to align itself than for you to do it." This kind of thinking has pervaded Apple over the years, and is one of the reasons for its consumer success. Chairman and CEO Gil Amelio's (1996) October strategy document, *Looking Forward*, begins by stating that for the 60 million Macintosh users, the Apple logo "is not just a logo. It's a symbol of freedom." These are words chosen carefully to advance a consumer cause. Arguably, Netscape Communications may yet approach Apple's consumer cachet in appealing to the Internet community. Netscape President and CEO James Barksdale's (1995) "God is on our side" comment, in referring to the competition with Microsoft, speaks to these values and marketing acumen.

Of course, the view that consumers and consumer-oriented technology companies like Apple or Netscape lead the heart of the industry is not a new one. There are hundreds if not thousands of examples of small (and not so small) startups like Altair, Osborne, Go, NEXT Computer and much earlier in their growth, Lotus Development, SUN and Microsoft, all of which can lay rightful claim to a tight symbiosis between computer user, software developer, and hardware designer/manufacturer as part of their corporate cachet.

Apart from computing, software and communications companies, however, it is certain that as much, if not more of the consumer pull for information and information technology has come not from the "IT sector" per se, but as first and second order effects from consumer electronics firms producing and selling products in the entertainment and information markets (examples include video and audio hardware, software games and education). Consumer demand for IT has been driven as much by companies such as Sony, Philips, Matsushita, Nintendo, Sega, Electronic Arts and Broderbund, as it has been by Compaq, Dell, VisiCalc, Hewlett Packard or Ashton Tate (to say nothing of MTV, Time Warner, CNN Interactive, or MSNBC). This list is obviously partial and eclectic, as there are literally thousands (if not tens of thousands) of firms worldwide looking to position themselves to create, broadcast and distribute interactive multimedia content into homes. It is *the* growth market for the next 50 years, and in principle any firm from the small hardware company making premises access devices, to the large global company developing, broadcasting and/ or managing multimedia content, can be a player. In this burgeoning market, interactions between scale and local business knowledge will be particularly acute. Companies seeking to develop and commercialize the core hardware components ("infrastructure") provide a natural base for global businesses driven by scale economies and the need to serve diverse applications with common hardware platforms. Conversely, developers of multimedia content (authoring firms) and suppliers of application-focused technologies and the services therein are more likely to be locally focused businesses, reflecting the great diversity of needs, personal tastes and regulatory regimes prevailing in different countries (Hagel and Eisenmann, 1994). Strategy doctrine will transform itself in the next decade as firms innovate structurally to own, partner with, and manage creative assets in emerging markets.

Nicholas Negroponte (1995) of the MIT Media Lab summarizes much of the future industry shakeout and the merits and consequences of IT for individuals into "bits and atoms," and the explosion of choice offered to consumers in what he terms *being digital*. On industries and firms, Negroponte (1996) states succinctly that "if an industry can be turned from atoms of matter into bits of information on a computer, it will be threatened quickly by the digital revolution." There is much to this statement, for while many companies presumably will want to remain in atom-based businesses, selling hamburgers or making running shoes for example, the difficult question facing them, their management and shareholders will be the relative profitability of conducting atom based businesses rather than digital based businesses. The example of American Airlines and AMR (selling seats is more profitable than flying airplanes) might also be true for running shoes (collecting information on everyone's feet over their lifetime and selling it to running shoe manufacturers may be more profitable than making shoes). New investment capital, all other things being equal, will tend to favor the higher profitability sector, influencing capital flows and threatening scale economies and cost structures of firms where capital is vacating. Negroponte's point is that this could happen very quickly in industries such as financial services, publishing and telecommunications, where he sees the potential for rapid conversion from atom to bit businesses.

Much of Negroponte's writings in *Wired* and elsewhere traverse a decidedly optimistic view of the power of consumers in the new digital environment. His essential point is that bits can be personalized in that consumers will be able to "pull" bits of interest from bit suppliers when and as they see fit (either personally or through an agent), rather than firms "pushing" bits at groups or individuals they have identified through narrowcasting. This is a radical change as our entire concept of advertising and media "is one of successive layers of filtering, which reduce information and entertainment to collections of "top stories" or "best sellers" to be thrown at different "audiences," like Alpine skiers, computer hackers, or wine enthusiasts (Negroponte, 1995). Another implication of consumer pull is that life can become more asynchronous, and thereby personalized: "people will be able to watch what they want when they want, and work where and when they want" (Negroponte, 1996).

This vision of consumer choice and personalized access to new media and digital services prompts us to ask which consumers (or more precisely, which generation of consumers) will have the most influence in shaping the next 50 years of IT? In echoing Turkle's earlier point, Bill Gates (1995) writes: "Ultimately, the information superhighway is not for my generation or those before me. It is for future generations. The kids who have grown up with PCs in the last decade, and those who will grow up with the highway in the next, will push the technology to its limits." If readers doubt just how different future generation's attitudes to computers, networks and technology will be, Chapter 1, "Kevin: The Dark Side Hacker," in Hafner and

Markoff's (1991) *Cyberpunk*; Chapter 3, "Making a Pass at a Robot," in Turkle's (1995) *Life on the Screen*; and Chapter 2, "Daily Life in Cyberspace," in Rheingold's (1993) *The Virtual Community,* are required reading.

In recounting the lessons he drew from Adams' failed "dynamometer," Bell's (1973) paragraph below speaks to the question of change without a basic familiarity of place or family (was he thinking ahead to cyberspace?):

"Important as any of these examples may be, the simple and crucial fact Henry Adams so poignantly grasped in 1900 was that no longer would any child be able to live in the same kind of world - sociologically and intellectually - as his parents and grandparents had inhabited. For millennia - and this is still true in some sections of the globe, but they are shrinking - children retraced the steps of their parents, were initiated into stable ways and ritualized routines, had a common body of knowledge and morality, and maintained a basic familiarity with place and family. Today, not only does a child face a radical rupture with the past, but he must also be trained for an unknown future. And this task confronts the entire society as well."

Synthesis

In 1966-67 the *Wall Street Journal* ran a series of articles on future technologies. In one article it was estimated that by the turn of the century, there would be 220,000 computers in the world (there are over 45 million, depending on your definition - recall the earlier point about forecasting and paradigm shifts). Knowing that simple extrapolation is wrong-headed when looking ahead, it remains a strangely human preoccupation to keep doing it. Even H.G. Wells wrote that futurists have the responsibility of "building an ordered picture of the future." His successors in the World Future Society, however, would speak more today about projections of *alternative* futures, and "futures studies," where both words are in the plural (Wager, 1993).

Ithiel Pool's (1983) book *Technologies of Freedom* remains the landmark contribution in our understanding of the complex interactions between new media, mass communications and the evolution of social and political rights. He notes that the new communication technologies "have not inherited all the legal immunities that were won for the old... as speech increasingly flows over (the new) electronic media, the five-century growth of an unabridged right of citizens to speak without controls may be endangered."

Pool (1983) summarizes trends in communications technology and their main implications below (I have stated these in italics), and where relevant, I have added material to reinforce his points:

- *Networks that serve the public are becoming digital and broadband,* allowing progressively more aspects of civic participation (individual and collective political action) and governmental processes to be handled electronically (contacting elected or appointed officials, polling, voting, drafting and passing legislation, etc.)
- *There is increasing sophistication of equipment on the user's own premises, allowing progressively more involvement in information activities,* ranging from business activities (home shopping as the simplest example), to electronic interaction (cybercommunities on potentially a global scale), to political inter-

action between citizenry and governmental officials internationally (example: a UK citizen sending email to the US President on governmental policy towards the United Kingdom, and vice versa).

- *Another obvious trend is that with the new technologies, the world is shrinking, and that there will be more freedom to communicate with anyone anywhere with whom one finds affinity.* This development, along with multiple technologies of communication and cheap microprocessors, suggested to Pool a trend toward pluralistic and competitive communications systems.

- *Perhaps the most remarkable trend to note is one whereby the artificial intelligence of computers will increasingly create and read many of the messages on the networks of the future.* Here computers and our intelligent agents will "correspond" on our behalf, having been "directed" (programmed) by us to do so. Pool notes that the lines between publication and conversation vanish in this sort of system: "Socrates' concern that writing would warp the flow of intelligence can at last be set to rest. Writing can become dialog."

To the extent danger exists in the potential abuse of new media, Pool (1983) concludes it is not one of "electronic nightmare," but one of human error: "It is not computers but policy that threatens freedom." The declining dominance of print media is a cause for concern, for they are the media that in the United States and elsewhere in the free world enjoy autonomy from government. It matters also that access and dissemination of information may be biased by factors such as money, culture, geography and age. But in viewing the new media of the next 50 years, Pool strikes an optimistic note, echoed by Negroponte and Gates. He does not separate modern media from its ancestry, the printing press. Print shops and pulpits, as in Speaker's Corner in Hyde Park, London, gave voice to individuals. Modern media has the same, if expanded, effect. In the end, Pool's optimism rests squarely on similar principles of free access and use, achieved in practical terms by the mass distribution of the enabling technologies themselves (as with the printing press). We have a growing producer industry doing exactly this, and increasingly sophisticated consumers who themselves create and produce their own shares in the new digital environment. We all have very personal stakes in the information age, but there appears good reason to be optimistic.

References

Abelson, P.H. and Dorfman M. (eds.) "Computers and Electronics," *Science,* 12 February 1982.

Amelio, G. "Looking Forward: Apple Computer Presents a Brief Outline of the Future," Apple Computer Corporation, October 1996.

Barksdale, J. "Netscape vows "dog-fight" with Microsoft," *Reuters New Media,* 8 December 1995.

Bell, D.B. *The Coming of Post-Industrial Society,* Basic Books, New York, 1973, pp. 168-170.

Burns, T. and Stalker, G.M. *The Management of Innovation,* Tavistock Publications, London, 1961.

Business Wire, "MacWorld Expo Boston: 12th Annual Macworld Expo Sets New Attendance Record," 20 August 1996.

Galbraith, J. *Organization Design,* Addison-Wesley, Reading, MA., 1977.

Gates, B. *The Road Ahead*, Viking Penguin, New York, 1995, p. 258.

Hafner, K. and Markoff, J. *Cyberpunk*, Touchstone, New York, 1991.

Hagel III, J. and Eisenmann, T.R. "Navigating the Multimedia Landscape," *McKinsey Quarterly*, Number 3, 1994, pp. 39-56.

Hughes, S. "Taken aback by ENIAC," *The Pennsylvania Gazette*, March 1996, pp. 20-25.

Kawasaki, G. *The Macintosh Way: The Art of Guerrilla Management*, Harper Perennial, New York, 1988, p. 77.

Lawrence, P.R. and Lorsch, J.W. *Organizations and Environment: Managing Differentiation and Integration*, Irwin, Homewood, Ill., 1967.

Leavitt, H.J. and Whisler, T.L. "Management in the 1980s," *Harvard Business Review,* November-December 1958, pp. 41-48.

Negroponte, N. "Middle-sized companies most at risk in digital future," *Financial Times*, March 6, 1996, Section II-2.

Negroponte, N. *Being Digital*, Knopf, New York, 1995, p. 84.

Newell, A. and Sproull, R.F. "Computer Networks: Prospects for Scientists," *Science,* 12 February 1982, pp. 843-851.

Pool, I.D. *Technologies of Freedom*, Cambridge, Harvard University Press, 1983, Chapters 1,9.

Porter, M.E. and Millar, V.E. "How Information Gives You Competitive Advantage," *Harvard Business Review,* July-August 1985, pp. 149-160.

Rayport, J.F. and Sviokla, J.J. "Managing in the Marketspace," *Harvard Business Review,* November-December 1994, pp. 141-150.

Rheingold, H. *The Virtual Community*, Addison-Wesley, New York, 1993.

Schein, E.H. "Innovative Cultures and Organizations" in *Information Technology and the Corporation of the 1990s*, T.J. Allen and M.S. Scott Morton (eds.), Oxford University Press, New York, 1994.

Turkle, S. *Life on the Screen*, Simon & Schuster, New York, 1995, p. 77.

Utterback, J.M. *Mastering the Dynamics of Innovation*, Boston, Harvard Business School Press, 1994.

Wagar, W.Warren "Tomorrow and Tomorrow and Tomorrow," *Technology Review*, April 1993, pp. 51-59.

Woodward, J. *Industrial Organization: Theory and Practice* Oxford University Press, London, 1965.

Zuboff, S. *In the Age of the Smart Machine,* Basic Books, New York, 1988.

Source: Reprinted by special permission of Database: Advances in Information Systems (a publication of the Special Interest Group on Information Systems of the Association for Computing Machinery), Vol. 27, No. 4, 1996, pp. 37-44.

CHAPTER 16

Service: The Future

Richard T. Watson
University of Georgia, USA

Leyland F. Pitt and Pierre R. Berthon
University of Wales, Cardiff, UK

The first half century of information technology (IT) has witnessed ever expanding visions of its role in our lives. The first vision, the computer is a giant calculator, was so limiting that the world market was seen to be only a handful of machines. Other visions (e.g., the computer is an automated filing clerk or strategic competitive weapon) gradually germinated and greatly expanded the range of IT applications. Now, we believe, the most significant vision of the computer is finally emerging. The short history of the World Wide Web has demonstrated that the computer is the ultimate tool for delivering services (e.g., FedEx's parcel tracking service), and it is the elaboration of this vision that we believe will be the dominant application of IT for the next few decades. In this paper, we justify this claim and consider the implications of this future for IT. We make use of scenarios to illustrate how IT can be used to support a service-oriented society.

A historical perspective

The broad sweep of economic change can sometimes provide elucidating glimpses into the future. In our case, we consider the consequences of the agricultural and industrial revolutions on the broad mass of society and then speculate on the impact of the information revolution. The agricultural revolution of the 16th and 17th centuries created a system for the large scale production of food. Two centuries later, the industrial revolution enabled the mass production of goods. As a result of these two revolutions, most people in Western societies were provided with food and goods at affordable prices. The agricultural revolution was a necessary precursor of the industrial revolution because factories were impossible when the work force was almost totally devoted to the production of food. With the threat of mass starvation removed, societal needs could move to a higher level and the population became more concerned with acquiring goods that improved the quality of life. Initially, these were simple products such as crockery and cooking utensils, but more recently they have become televisions, CD players, and home computers.

Now, some 50 years into the information revolution, we can extrapolate from the prior revolutions to understand the consequences of this current era of mass change. Once a society satisfies one need, it moves onto another, analogous to Maslow's hierarchy of human needs. Now that the industrial revolution has provided the populace with an abundance of goods, we contend that services will dominate societal needs.[1] Our argument is bolstered by Quinn (1992), a frequent and respected writer on technology in services, who asserts that the development and use of technology for services may be the key to wealth creation in advanced economies.

Another perspective on social change is gained by considering how wealthy people live in one era and extrapolating that to the following eras. Prior to the agricultural revolution, the rich were among the few who ate well all the time, had plentiful goods (by the standards of that time), and received the personalized attention of servants. In today's society, as a result of the agricultural and industrial revolutions, nearly everyone has access to a plentiful array of food and goods, but only the rich enjoy highly personalized attention. Those who serve the rich cater to their caprices. Hotel managers and restaurateurs remember the favorite rooms, tables, and personal whims of only their most celebrated clientele. The vast majority of society receive relatively undifferentiated and uncustomized service. Our forecast is that the information age will cause a dramatic change in the form, extent, and delivery of services. Information technology will enable the great majority of citizens to receive a level of customized service now enjoyed only by the affluent. The major outcomes of the prior revolutions were food and goods. The remaining unsatisfied demand is for highly personalized services, and this ultimate product of the information revolution will be realized in the next few decades. The effect of each revolution is summarized in Table 1.

We can already see the beginnings of this service revolution in recent Web applications that facilitate direct communication with customers. Many industries (e.g., software and financial services) are already providing a considerable range of services to customers via the Internet. We believe these are early primitive examples of what will happen in the next decade. In the remainder of this paper, we briefly discuss the unique characteristics of services, and the opportunities for their industrialization and mass customization. We show how these characteristics are uniquely adaptable for delivery on the Web. Then we demonstrate how IT will create a society in which services are tailored to the personal desires of customers.

Services: Characteristics and industrialization

Services possess certain unique characteristics which distinguish them from physical goods (Berry, 1980), and these attributes make services especially amenable to delivery by an electronic medium such as the Internet. First, services are *intangible*—they are experiences or performances, while products are objects that are possessed. Thus, services do not require production or delivery in the broadest

Table 1: Technological revolutions and major outcomes

Revolution	Major outcome
Agricultural	Plentiful and inexpensive food
Industrial	Plentiful and inexpensive goods
Information	Many highly personalized services

physical sense. Second, services are *produced and consumed simultaneously*. In most cases, the producer needs to be present to produce the service, and the customer needs to be there simultaneously in order to consume it (hairdressers and dentists are good examples of this). This attribute also means of course that the customer comes "inside the service factory", with all the operational complications that this causes. Indeed, customers tend to participate in both the production and delivery of the services they consume, becoming in a sense, *partial employees* of service organizations (Mills, Chase and Margulies, 1983). Third, because most services are produced by people (employees and customers), they are subject to a *variability* or *heterogeneity* not normally encountered in manufactured goods. This means that the customer frequently encounters unpredictable service quality, and one of the fundamental challenges facing service providers is to iron out this inconsistent service delivery. Finally, services tend to be infinitely *perishable*; that is, if the capacity of service providers is not utilized, it is lost forever, unlike products which can be inventoried. Airlines cannot store seats, nor hotels rooms, and an express delivery company cannot bank the unused time of query personnel for later use in peak periods.

In an insightful attempt to overcome the problems of managing service firms, Levitt (1976) argued that rather than attempting to provide more service (in the form of additional personnel and customization), managers should try to make service firms more like factories. Not only will this be more efficient and successful, ultimately it will be what the customer prefers. He contends that many attempts to provide personalized service merely lead to inefficiency at best, and servility at worst. He uses the case of Great Britain as an illustration. The wealthy enjoy wonderful personalized service because they are able to pay servants to perform this; however, the average person receives dreadful service because service providers believe that by performing good service they would be behaving in a servile fashion. The use of IT in many service firms has probably demonstrated Levitt's point that, rather than *throwing more service* at a problem, managers should try to eliminate it by employing technology and systems instead, as illustrated in Table 2.

The Web is a technology that will achieve both seemingly incompatible aims: to take the human element out of service thereby eliminating variability; and enable customization by allowing IT to create and deliver the precise service that the

Table 2: Service and information technology

Type of Service	Before IT	Since IT
Long distance telephone calls	Operator assisted	Direct Dialing (The customer prefers because it is easier and quicker)
Everyday personal banking (Cash withdrawals and deposits)	Teller assisted	ATM assisted (Most customers prefer because it saves waiting time and has convenient hours)
Gas station (Filling car with gas)	Personal service at the pump, attendant fills car.	Self service; use card to pay for gas. (Most customers prefer because it is quicker)

customer desires. Moreover, the Web will not only overcome to a large extent the limitations that their characteristics impose on services, it will also enable service firms to exploit certain of these attributes.

- A major problem with service intangibility is that it is difficult for customers to see what they are purchasing, and to gain insight into its merits as they would by touching, tasting, and sampling products. The Web will overcome service impalpability by:
  - *managing evidence by adding visibility.* More informative than a printed brochure, the Web will enable prospective guests of a resort hotel to see it both in graphic and video format, to talk with staff and even fellow guests to sample their experiences.
  - *managing memories.* The Web can engage the customer after use of the service. Guests who have stayed at a resort can become alumni, and revisit it on the Web, reliving their experiences by chatting with staff on-line, and of course with prospective future visitors. In this way customers are not only encouraged to revisit so as to relive memories, but also to act as part-time marketing staff for the resort.

- Good services marketers have long understood that simultaneous production and consumption of services can be turned to their advantage. If customers understand their participation in the production process is vital to their receiving good service, they can be gainfully employed to create, produce, and deliver the services that will best satisfy them. Not only will this generally result in significant cost reductions for service providers, it can frequently be used to generate exciting new service concepts and products. There is much evidence of this on the Web. For example:
  - FedEx is using its Web site to answer customer queries. Whereas formerly FedEx employed a team of employees to answer telephone calls, customers can now track the precise whereabouts of a package at any time simply by using the FedEx Web site. Not only is the process more efficient (quicker, lower cost, no possibility of dealing with a less than courteous employee), but it is also getting the customer to perform the labor that would have normally been carried out by FedEx employees. Indeed, FedEx suggests that some customers enjoy this so much that they track packages merely for the fun of it, and not because there is concern over loss.
  - American Airlines now permits customers to access all their frequent flyer details using their Web site. At present the major benefits to the company come in the form of reduced requirements for employee service over the telephone. In the future however, there may be even greater advantages to be gained, as the service provider engages the customer in even more copious coproduction, such as reclaiming miles while booking flights at the same time, pre-reserving preferred seats, arranging meal preferences, and any other activities with which they might gainfully be engaged.
  - Most importantly however, Web sites will allow mass customization as customers are involved not only in the production of their own services, but also in the conceptualization and design thereof. We foresee a time when customers will all be able to receive personalized service, by using technology to combine the resources of different firms to give them exactly

what they want—be it vacation, insurance, banking, or education and self-development packages. High quality, personalized service will no longer be the sole precinct of the affluent.

- The fact that most services today are still produced by humans causes variability, which is a source of frustration to the majority of customers. It is still quite difficult to paint a smiling face on a surly bank teller, or build *please and thank you* into the mind of an insurance claims clerk. The Web will in many ways permit service firms to follow Levitt's admonition and *take the service out of service*—it will permit the mass production of high levels of service which is always courteous, competent, responsive, and reliable. It is relatively easy to paint a smiling face on a computer screen and to write software which is always gracious, as well as knowledgeable.

  - Security First National Bank was the first to offer full service banking on the Web. The bank is always open. The electronic tellers always smile and are consistently courteous. There is not a question that the information desk is unable to answer, and if you wish to see the president you can, immediately, without making an appointment. When they say, they'll "get right back to you", they mean it. Literally. This might not be exciting or even interesting banking—the tellers always look the same and don't chew gum, and there are never any real robberies. It is certainly banking as Levitt envisioned it: invariable, immutable, predictable, and it always works.

- All service firms are plagued to a greater or lesser extent by the problems that perishability causes—when the service is available, all customers don't necessarily want it, and when every customer wants the service at the same time, the firm isn't always able to satisfy them. In the past, service firms have attempted to cope with this by such strategies as discounting and promoting in off-peak periods, and by opening for longer hours, or by employing part-time staff in periods of excess demand. We suggest that astute service providers will use the Web to better manage both supply and demand in the future.

  - Security First National Bank is able to manage supply because it has replaced most of the activities which used to be performed by people by activities that are performed by technology. Employees cannot work 24-hour days; they take coffee and lunch breaks, they take vacations, they get ill, they miss buses. When technology replaces humans, the bank is able to supply a 24 hour-a-day service that is seamless in delivery, in a way that is convenient to customers. When demand really does exceed the ability to supply, the bank does not need to search for, screen, recruit, and train new employees—it simply purchases more bandwidth, more computing power, and more storage space. Instead of purchasing more services, it simply purchases more products.

We believe that in the future, IT will be used to manage customer demand for services more effectively than is possible or dreamed of today. Technology will be used to enable customers to specify exactly what it is they require, and then to price it and charge them individually. Individualized pricing will become feasible, and pricing tactics that are not viable today will be enabled by software systems. These will exact very small but real charges from the individual customer, based on precisely what the customer has purchased. Today the administrative costs of such pricing tactics might not be worth the very small payback. In the future we see service firms amassing wealth by making millions of very small charges for individualized services, and charging individualized prices for these. In a very real sense, the oft-touted notion of *user pays* will become a reality: as users we will only pay for what we use. The demand of the individual customer, not some vague notion of a target group or market segment, will be managed by manipulating the prices which the individual pays.

Technology

After 50 years of the industrial revolution, one could have safely predicted the broad direction of events for the next 50 years—more goods—as the fundamental innovations had been made. Mass production (e.g., the factories) and distribution systems (e.g., the railways) were in place. Underpinning this was the emergence of the scientific approach to research and development, which would create a flow of innovations. Everything was in place to continue producing a stream of affordable consumer goods for many years.

The basic technology of a service society has been invented and will be increasingly refined over the next decades. Data stores, microprocessors, and networks are the fundamental building blocks of a service society. In addition, we have a market-based economy that is directed at satisfying customers' wants.

Data stores

A service society requires that suppliers remember vast quantities of data about their customers. The restaurateur caters to the rich by remembering what they like and dislike. Data stores make it possible for service providers to remember the likes and dislikes of every customer. They must remember every purchase and every use if they are to personalize service. A frequent flyer system, for example, may currently remember only the number of miles a customer flew each year. It may not remember the date, destination, and class of travel. It certainly does not remember the meals and drinks the customer ordered. When booking with an airline in the future, you may be offered a choice of five seafood dinners because the airline remembers you always order seafood when given a choice.

The relationship of data stores to service is amply illustrated by ServiceMaster (Quinn, Doorley, and Paquette, 1990). Its database contains 14 years of maintenance history on 17 million pieces of equipment at thousands of locations. As a result, it can determine highly efficient maintenance and procurement plans for its customers. By specializing in a particular service activity, ServiceMaster is able to create higher value and lower costs.

Microprocessors

Microprocessors will continue to decline rapidly in cost and as a result will be embedded in nearly every product. They will be as ubiquitous as the electric motor, appearing in such devices as hair dryers and electric toothbrushes. Every household and industrial appliance that uses electricity will contain a microprocessor, which will control the performance of the device and collect data about its use. As a result, appliances will be individually programmable based on their usage history and the customer's particular needs. The rotation speed of the bristles of an electric toothbrush, for instance, will be programmed according to the condition of the customer's gums and manner in which the brush is used (e.g., pressure and angle against the teeth).

Networks

Recently, we have experienced the implementation of a National Information Infrastructure (NII) in the form of the Internet. This network of networks means all computers can be linked together and are individually addressable. The next stage is massive networking of a wide variety of devices. We predict that every product that contains a microprocessor will be uniquely addressable and connectable to a network. Most households will contain a local area network managed by the household server, which is connected to the NII via an information service provider (see Figure 1). Consequently, suppliers will have a direct communication link to their customers. Suppliers will thus be able to use the network to deliver software for programming goods and collect data on usage. For example, in anticipation of a particularly hot summer's day, the appropriate supplier will adjust the program for opening and closing the shades of each room. Addressable products and networks make it possible to extend the ServiceMaster model to all products and to add other dimensions of service, many of which are at present unimaginable. Indeed, the most fundamental effect of this technology could be that it will blur the very dividing line between products and services, so that customers will no longer purchase neatly categorized products or services, but solutions to problems, performances, and experiences. Rather than purchase a car (product) and maintenance (service), the customer will purchase a bundle of benefits which includes mobility and advice as to when equipment should be maintained and refreshed.

The integration of data stores, microprocessors, and networks

The three building blocks of the information revolution will be integrated to enable an interactive relationship with individual customers—the marketer's dream (Blattberg and Deighton, 1991). This customer communication system will collect the data necessary to individualize communication and provide customers with highly personalized service. The result will be a form of highly customized attention that was once the reserve of the wealthy. The customer of tomorrow will be as pampered as the rich and famous of today. Andy

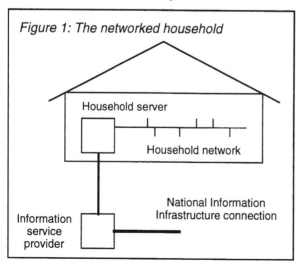

Figure 1: The networked household

Household server

Household network

National Information Infrastructure connection

Information service provider

Warhol's speculation may indeed be realized: We may in the future all enjoy a few minutes of fame

The goal of addressability

The technological model we have outlined is founded on a goal of addressability, the capability of the customer and supplier to locate each other in time and space. Our notion of addressability extends Blattberg and Deighton's (1991) concept, which is essentially based on the idea of maintaining a customer database and direct marketing tools to individualize dialogue with customers. Our concept of addressability is much broader. It entails the customer being able to locate the supplier to gain access to services. Also, because we envision a system of customer

---

The electronic chauffeur

After arriving home from her 10 minute trip to the local telework center, Christine plugged her electric car into the socket in the garage, which was a joint power and network connection. She used the voice command system to inform the electronic chauffeur that tomorrow she would be driving to the airport (about a 90 minute trip) to catch flight 550 to New York and would like a five minute news report, international financial market summary, a 15 minute lesson on French idiomatic expressions, and the remainder of the time should be devoted to light Jazz with an occasional Mozart interlude.

The electronic chauffeur took the following action:

- immediately uploaded data on the car's use since the last network connection from the car's data store to the household server, which was then relayed to the supplier of the car. The data indicated that the front brakes would need service in two weeks time and, after of course checking Christine's diary, a booking was scheduled with her preferred service center;
- downloaded from an information service supplier the requested French lesson and music program into the car's data store;
- accessed the airline's information service to determine the departure time of flight 550, computed the time Christine would need to leave home based on projected traffic conditions, and reserved a parking bay at the airport. It would continue to monitor the departure time and traffic conditions and update the departure time on the kitchen bulletin board when necessary and alert Christine when appropriate;
- downloaded the latest map of the fastest route to the airport and set the speed control system to observe speed restrictions along the way;
- established an intelligent software agent, linked to projected departure time, to download the latest news and financial information into the car entertainment system immediately prior to departure for the airport.

This scenario illustrates how in the information era IT will perform the functions of a personal assistant. Implicit in this scenario is the notion that the auto manufacturer will have to reconceptualize its product as a mobile information and entertainment system. Presently, the auto manufacturer takes little part in entertaining or informing other than providing a radio or CD. Once cars are addressable devices, the auto manufacturer has the opportunity to provide a new range of services that keep the customer entertained and informed while traveling and also maintain the operational efficiency of the car.

The electronic valet

Upon arriving at the hotel, Ned handed his smart card to the desk clerk who went through the standard authentication check to verify he was the owner of the card. Then the hotel's guest comfort system, known as the electronic valet, took action:

- it downloaded from Ned's home server his room preferences and reserved the room most closely matching his needs
- it reprogrammed all devices in the room to match the settings of the equivalent device in his home (e.g., channel 1 of the TV was set to his favorite cartoon network and quick dial button 2 on the phone was set to his girlfriend's number);
- the shower's temperature and flow were set to the settings of his shower at home;
- it scheduled room service to place an additional pillow in his room and two bottles of Brown Brother's Chardonnay in the fridge.

---

communication based on electronic networks, we encompass the addressability of products. Existing data stores are often limited to capturing data about customer purchases, but this is only one phase of the customer service life cycle (Ives and Mason, 1990). Customers can own products for many years, and this lengthy ownership phase provides many opportunities for firms to sell additional service, but only if they know how the customer is using the product. Even primitive systems that capture customer usage data infrequently can be highly successful (see the example of Daiichi described by Stalk and Webber (1993)).

Addressability in a networked society also extends service opportunities beyond the household. When products are addressable and contain microprocessors they can be readily changed to the convenience of the customer. The electronic valet example illustrates some of this potential.

Implications

All revolutions have profound implications for society. Some of these consequences can be anticipated and others are completely unanticipated. We briefly discuss some of the outcomes we can anticipate, but there will be undoubtedly social and political fallouts that are beyond our ken.

Organizational strategy

The transition to a service driven economy will result in a different strategic focus. The industrial era notion of building competence on manufacturing capability will become obsolete. The core competency of organizations will be increasingly founded on the ability to deliver service. This implies that many organizations will need to redefine their fundamental purpose. The home refrigeration manufacturer, for instance, may need to reinvent itself as a home food management system. Selling a fridge is just the beginning of a service relationship, and what should be really sold is a complete food management system: fridge, freezer, and pantry. This system then keeps complete track of all food stored and notifies the customer when an item needs to be restocked or has exceeded its shelf life. The home food management system is the equivalent of a personal housekeeper. Strategic thinking will need to transform from thinking about products to thinking about services and the customer's ultimate goal. As the previous example illustrates, the customer does not want a fridge, she wants to keep food fresh.

In his definitive analysis, Porter (1980) concludes that there are two generic strategies: differentiation and low-cost leadership. It is possibly too early to identify potential strategies for the information era because the rules of competition are still evolving and very dynamic (e.g., Netscape went from startup to competitive threat to Microsoft in around two years). There is some indication that establishing industry norms provides sustainable competitive advantage (Morris and Ferguson, 1993). Thus, IBM dominated the mainframe era because its operating systems and standards (e.g., SNA, 3270) were widely used. Similarly, Microsoft has a tremendous competitive advantage because it has defined the desktop norm (e.g., Windows and Office). Those service providers that don't define the norm are locked in a fierce, commodity market battle because, ironically, the very technology on which their business is founded, the Internet, permits customers to be highly informed and switch readily (e.g., the long distance phone market in the U.S.). Thus, early signs are that competitive advantage will come from being a defacto standard setter or low-cost service provider.

MIS

Since service will be based on maintaining customer databases and direct electronic communication links, the MIS department will become even more involved in making the corporate strategic plan a reality. Its success will be based on its ability to translate a service delivery strategy into an effective IT infrastructure. MIS managers will need to be extremely end-customer focused. Thus, in the case of the home food management system example, IT will have to develop systems that record not only each time an item is placed in storage, but also its contents (e.g., a half empty milk container), and other details necessary for managing food.

End-customer systems will be very demanding of MIS skills and resources. There will be literally millions of these installed, and they must be highly fault and customer tolerant. Imagine delivering a system to one hundred million customers, many of whom have never mastered setting the clock on their VCR recorders. MIS will no longer be creating systems to be used primarily by college educated, white collar workers. Many customers will be not well-educated and not have access to a help-desk. Systems must be extremely simple to use, but highly flexible if service is to be very personalized. Despite advances in tools to build and maintain systems (e.g., CASE and object orientation), the long-term trend has been for complex systems to be delivered late, often with reduced functionality (e.g., Windows 95, OS/2). We estimate that end-customer systems will be at least an order of magnitude more difficult to build and maintain than current state-of-the art systems because of their complexity, the size of the market, and the low skills of many customers.

The MIS community will have to work with a wide variety of manufacturers to develop a set of standards for defining the electronic interface to household devices and networks. For example, there will need to be standards for the automotive industry so that third parties can compete to supply entertainment, information, and diagnostics services to the driver.

It is quite possible that many organizations will gut their MIS departments. IT was of necessity a specialist function in the first fifty years, but will become more and more of a general management function (computers will not be mysteries to our children). While specialist technical skills will still be needed (just as marketing research and advertising copy skills are still relevant), a reasonable level of IT skills will be expected of anyone who is a manager. Indeed, the specialist skills are prime candidates for outsourcing (just as advertising and marketing research tend to be outsourced today).

A cultural caveat

Nearly all English speaking countries support and implement a philosophy based on the belief that economic activity should be governed by free markets. Governments should simply get out of the way and let the market determine how resources are allocated and the direction of the economy. However, Fallows (1994) points out that other major economic powers, such as Germany and Japan, are not so enamored by markets, and there is an alternative to the Anglo-American free market model.

Fallows observes that Anglo-American economies are more likely to place the needs of the individual above the nation and emphasize consumption over production. Our projections have been influenced by an Anglo-American perspective, given that we both live and work in this setting. Thus, we have emphasized the use of IT to meet consumer and individual needs. German and Japanese societies may well use the same underlying technologies to produce a different IT impact.

Conclusion

We are not the first to see the opportunity to use information technology to improve customer service (see for example Ives and Mason (1990) and Quinn and Papette (1990)), but we do believe we see much further than these scholars. The distance of our vision can be gauged by the key concept that we have introduced— addressable, networked consumer products. Firms need to be able to communicate directly with the products customers use so that they can customize usage to personal needs. When this is feasible, the full potential of IT to provide customer service will be realized.

The IT future we have painted is very realizable and we believe highly likely for two reasons. First, there is every indication that customers are seeking improved service. Second, the technology is currently available. In this paper, we supply the third necessary ingredient—the vision that makes people aware of the opportunity.

Endnotes

[1] Of course, we are discussing only advanced economies and many societies are still wrestling with providing sufficient food for their people.

References

Berry, L.L. "Services Marketing Is Different," *Business* (30:3), 1980, pp. 24-29.
Blattberg, R.C. and Deighton, J. "Interactive marketing: exploiting the age of addressability," *Sloan Management Review* (33:1), Fall 1991, pp. 5-14.

Fallows, J.M. *Looking at the sun : the rise of the new East Asian economic and political system*, Pantheon, New York, NY, 1994.

Ives, B. and Mason, R. "Can information technology revitalize your customer service?," *Academy of Management Executive* (4:4), November 1990, pp. 52-69.

Levitt, T. "The industrialization of service," *Harvard Business Review* (54:5), 1976, pp. 63-74.

Mills, P.K., Chase, R.B. and Margulies, N. "Motivating the client/employee system as a service production strategy," *Academy of Management Review* (8:2), 1983, pp. 301-310.

Morris, C.R. and Ferguson, C.H. "How architecture wins technology wars," *Harvard Business Review* (71:2), 1993, pp. 86-96.

Quinn, J.B. "The intelligent enterprise: a new paradigm," *Academy of Management Executive* (6:4), 1992, pp. 48-63.

Quinn, J.B. and Paquette, P.C. "Technology in services: creating organizational revolutions," *Sloan Management Review* (32:2), 1990, pp. 67-78.

Stalk, G.J. and Webber, A.M. "Japan's dark side of time," *Harvard Business Review* (71:4), 1993, pp. 93-102.

Source: Reprinted by special permission of Database: Advances in Information Systems (a publication of the Special Interest Group on Information Systems of the Association for Computing Machinery), Vol. 27, No. 4, 1996, pp.58-67.

CHAPTER 17

The Futures of IT Management

M. Lynne Markus
Claremont Graduate University, USA

It is fascinating to think what information technology (IT) might look like in the future and what IT-enabled changes we might see at work, at home, and in school, even 20 years from now. Less glamorous, but important nevertheless, are the changes we might see in the ways organizations manage information technology. A brief historical review illustrates why change in IT management is likely in the decades ahead.

IT Management: Past and Present

Large industrial organizations began to emerge in the second half of the nineteenth century. Very quickly, they began experiencing coordination or "control" problems. Numerous managerial and technical innovations were developed to manage these problems.[1] One of the most promising such innovations was the digital computer, which was first applied to business uses in the mid-1950s.

What made the digital computer powerful was the "stored program" concept that turned the calculating machine into a general-purpose business device. But the business value of computer hardware depended on the software programs it ran. And, at that time, knowledge of software development was at its infancy. There were few trained professionals and no market for packaged programs. Organizations that wanted to use computers were forced to learn how to program them. In-house Electronic Data Processing (EDP) were established, and computer-using organizations found themselves in the IT management business. Even when they had an opportunity to use external IT products and services, many organizations chose, by preference or policy, to keep all their computing services and software development in-house.

Much has, of course, changed since then. As many people like to say, there is more computing power under the hood of an automobile today (or in a washing machine) than there was in the largest computer of the mid-1960s. Size and cost have decreased by many orders of magnitude; speed and performance have increased. Even the smallest organizations are consuming what was formerly an unfathomable quantity of computing capability. Computing has been applied to an enormous range of work-related activities, including not only numeric data processing, but also document processing, and audio and video telecommunications. Advances in software development and professional services have supported these proliferating uses of computing. Today there is a vibrant market for turnkey systems and software packages in every computer size class. And the professional services segment of the computer world includes several differentiated firm types, such as custom programming shops, facilities managers, system integrators, IT management consulting services, and full-service outsourcers.

Concurrently, the job of IT management in organizations grew steadily and greatly increased in complexity. Early on, the in-house IT management function differentiated into applications development, technical support, and hardware operations. Later a telecommunications function was added. As internal demand for computing capability grew, organizations decentralized or distributed both hardware and software development capability to departments and business units. Policies and procedures were created to coordinate the acquisition and deployment of technology and the provision of training, service, and support.

Since the introduction of the personal computer in the 1980s, many companies found that IT represented their fastest growing area of headcount and expenditure. In the aggregate, around half of all new expenditures for plant and equipment went for information technology. At the same time, a larger and larger portion of IT labor dollars went for the maintenance and enhancement of aging "legacy" systems, and less was available for exciting new applications and technologies.

In the last decade of the twentieth century, the economic recession put overhead reduction near the top of the organizational agenda. Large numbers of workers were laid off, and middle management layers were eliminated. Many organizations reduced their needs for office space by encouraging employees to work at home, adopting open-plan offices, and requiring office sharing. Concerns about the payoffs from organizations' massive investments in computing were widely voiced. A few large companies publicly "outsourced" their entire IT operations to external vendors and started a noticeable trend.

What will we see going forward? Will the trend toward outsourcing continue, stabilize, or even reverse itself? How will new technologies affect the way that IT is managed by organizations in the future? This article explores the implications for IT management of several alternative futures that are plausible in the intermediate time frame (10-20 years from now).

Scenario Analysis

Scenario analysis offers one approach to answering questions about the future of IT management. Traditional long-range planning approaches tend to rely on straight-line projections of current trends. As a result, they often prove little guidance when small probability events occur, radically altering current trends. The aim of scenario analysis[2] is to generate several plausible alternative futures, giving decision-makers the opportunity to identify actions that can be taken today to promote success under varying future conditions.

Scenario analysts usually start by identifying a decision problem and time frame to bound the analysis. For this analysis the time frame is 10 to 20 years. The decision problem would be phrased differently by practicing IT managers than by academics. For a mid-career IT manager today, the questions are: "how will my organization be managing IT toward the end of my career (or where is someone with my skills likely to be employed), and what do I need to begin doing today to ensure that my organization has the necessary structures and human resources (and I have the right skills)?" For academics in Information Systems, Management, and Computer Science, the questions are: "who are our likely future students and what do they need to know about managing IT in computer-using organizations?"

Scenario analysts next identify the key known trends that are likely to affect the decision problem. To ensure that they have covered most relevant trends, they consider a range of issue categories: technology, institutional arrangements, economics, society, politics. For each trend, they judge the likely nature and direction of impact on the decision problem. If the trend has unknown impacts or has plausible impacts in contradictory directions, it is classified as an uncertainty.

The next step is to identify one or more "driving uncertainties" around which to generate scenarios. Driving uncertainties are those around which other trends or uncertainties tend to cluster. Many scenario analysts prefer to identify two driving uncertainties with two future states each. This generates four divergent scenarios and avoids the tendency to produce a set of graduated scenarios (e.g. "good, better, best" or "negative, neutral, positive") that might bias decision-makers toward an "average" strategy.

Constructing the scenarios is an art in itself. The scenarios should embody the logic of the driving uncertainties, but they must also be plausible. Decision-makers need to see how one could actually "get there from here." So, scenario writers might identify "triggering events" in the present or near future that could direct the future into the "space" defined by the driving uncertainties. Triggering events might include such things as privacy legislation that make it impossible or extremely costly for firms to use or sell data they collect about employees and customers, deregulation or antitrust decisions, and catastrophic IT or IT-induced failures (e.g., failure of the air traffic control system, governmental gridlock due to year 2000 software problems, or damaging hacker attacks on defense systems, financial systems, or public communication systems). The general idea is that a low probability event occurring today or in the near future can irreversibly redirect current trends. The scenarios depict the eventual state of these evolutionary trends at the end of the selected timeframe, along with some notion of how the path got started.

Once scenarios are constructed, the real work of planning begins. Decision-makers must examine their current strategies in light of each scenario — how well would they fare if each alternative future actually came about? Is there another strategy that might increase our likelihood of success, no matter what the future might bring? What actions plans do we need to construct today to realize our strategy? And what measures can we use to track the future as it unfolds so that we have will enough time to adjust our new course as needed?

In this article, I do not complete the full scenario planning methodology. I identify four plausible scenarios and some metrics for tracking the future as it unfolds. But I give only a sketchy analysis of the implications for future IT management practice and educational development. The hard work for practitioners and academics will remain undone, but a starting point for a focused discussion should exist.

Key Trends

In Table 1, I outline some important known trends likely to affect the future of in-house IT management. They are grouped into three categories "Information

Technology and IT Industry Trends," "Business Management Trends (including current approaches to in-house IT management)" and "Societal Trends." A review of the trends and impacts listed in Table 1 suggests a provisional conclusions.[3] Most obviously, many existing trends point in the direction of increased "externalization" of IT management activities (i.e., movement from within "user organizations" — organizations that use IT — out to specialized vendors that supply IT products and services). Among the trends that strongly point toward IT management externalization are the following:

- the "commoditization" of IT: the increasing tendency for IT products and applications to be assembled from OTS (off-the-shelf) components that conform to de-facto "open standards" rather than custom developed with proprietary technologies; and the rapid growth of specialized "system integrators" — external vendors that assist user organizations with integration activities
- alliances among vendors in different segments of the IT industry, increasingly enabling "one-stop-shopping" for complex packages of technology and support
- growth and consolidation of third-party "content" providers
- aging legacy IT applications, high in-house software maintenance costs, the looming year 2000 date-change problem, and the rise of "enterprise software packages" and "intranets" as a possible/partial solution
- the increasingly-recognized high management costs of poorly-integrated IT infrastructures (e.g., configuration management, software upgrade installation) and the growing interest in technologies and services that promise to eliminate, reduce, and/or externalize in-house IT management (e.g., fully-integrated telecommunications services, so-called "plug-and-play" devices, network computers, network computing managed by vendors)
- the trend toward "federated" (distributed, hybrid) in-house IT management or governance strategies, involving some decentralization, which encourages externalization because lower-level managers have shorter time-frames and smaller budgets
- the trend toward "vertical dis-integration" where large firms spin off non-core activities; the rapid growth of IT outsourcing vendors
- increasingly tight integration (mediated by IT) among firms in value chains (e.g., the Walmart-P&G connection; Chrysler's "American Keiretsu"[4]); and the tendency of electronic markets managed by independent "transaction facilitators" to replace electronic hierarchies[5]
- the growth of the Internet and interest in electronic commerce, which have increased public awareness of the need for a worldwide, publicly-accessible IT infrastructure for commerce.

A straight-line extrapolation of these trends suggests a future in which all organizations acquire all their IT-related products and services from external vendors (through a wide variety of arrangements including spot transactions, long-term contracts, and partnerships with individual vendors or with vendor alliances).

Driving Uncertainties

But scenario analysis does not end with straight-line trend extrapolation. In this case we must ask what uncertainties might halt IT management externalization or shape it into different forms. For instance, are there factors that might differentiate between the externalization of, say, IT application development and infrastructure operation on the one hand and data acquisition and provision on the other?

Careful examination of the trends, impacts, and uncertainties discussed in a variety of published sources and private forums and listed in Table 1 led me to identify several plausible triggering events and to select two key driving uncertainties as the basis for my scenarios. The triggering events are described in the individual scenarios, but the driving uncertainties warrant more explanation.

In some industries, economic conditions favor concentration (reduction in the number of firms and growth in firm size). Historically, large organizations have been structured either functionally (e.g., engineering, production, sales, and marketing), or multi-divisionally (e.g., with various product or market divisions). Within these structures, some work activities flow sequentially across organizational subunits and authority structures. Coordinating such work requires both across and up the hierarchy; coordination costs increase as environments become turbulent, units grow in number, and activity cycles lengthen. [6] To reduce coordination costs, growing corporations in the post World War II era developed computer-based transaction processing systems and management information systems.

Today, however, huge increases in the power and integration of information technologies are enabling new organizational forms which promise to increase business speed, flexibility, geographic reach, and profitability. Some of these new organizational forms involve large organizations spinning off non-core elements, breaking into independent units that cooperate at arms-length, or organizing independently of distance (e.g., conducting professional projects as "virtual shift work," in which projects move around the globe with the sun). Similarly, IT is now enabling concentration in previously local industries. And small organizations are able to use IT to band together in temporary or permanent virtual arrangements that enable them to compete effectively with large, global firms. Several examples of each type of virtual organization can be found in the business press and academic publications.

Organizational forms and coordination mechanisms are likely to be critical correlates of future IT management, since they affect the amount and kind of IT needed to coordinate work efficiently and effectively. For example, small organizations in virtual alliances need IT to "network." Some manufacturers have found that by forging linkages with their suppliers that enable them to build products "just-in-time," they have been able to dismantle their problematic MRP systems and return to manual shop floor control. Others have discovered that displaying on the intranet live video images of production machinery has eliminated or reduced telephone and computer-based reporting. Some large firms in the textile industry have disintegrated themselves into very small, self-contained enterprises coordinated with simple, lateral interactions mediated by electronic communication technology instead of complex, hierarchical planning, overhead allocations, and IT-enabled financial controls.

Such changes are not confined to manufacturing. White collar paperwork factories have been reengineered into "case work" in which a single individual or small team is responsible for completing all steps in complex process formerly distributed across many workers and groups. This reorganization is made possible through integration of previously discrete IT applications. Other professional organizations are using IT to increase coordination across distance while reducing

Table 1: Trends and Uncertainties Affecting Organizational IT Management

Trend	Comments	Nature of Impact
Information Technology and IT Industry Trends		
Continued sharp declines in the costs of IT components and products.	• increased demand for IT products and new IT applications • increased pressure on IT vendors to adopt creative new strategies for making money from their investments in people and know-how	• increases the demand for IT products • increases the supply of IT products • increases the number and types of IT industry firms and the arrangements among them
Proliferating IT products and services, especially in support of individuals (e.g., personal digital assistants, mobile telephony) & workgroups (e.g., groupware)	• increased difficulty in identifying opportunities for business value • increased pressure on employee absorptive capacity	• increases the demand for high-quality IT support, especially individual and work group performance improvement facilitation
The rise of "network computing," e.g., the Internet, the World Wide Web, on-demand software downloading	• viewed as a vehicle for electronic commerce between businesses and consumers; providing an alternative to traditional transaction processing (TPS) applications inside and between organizations • possible solution to in-house network configuration and maintenance problems	• increases demands for "COTS" (customer off-the-shelf) IT products and software • impact depends heavily on telecommunications bandwidth availability and cost • may depend heavily on network security improvements • may reduce demand for purchased TPS software • may substantially reduce in-house network management activities
Faster IT product development and release cycles	• decreased quality in early releases • functionality and ease of use improves over time	• reduces incentives to develop custom software • increases need for an in-house IT architecture strategy and reliable on-going mechanisms for training and supporting users
Growth in several segments of IT industry: software product development firms, IT professional services firms, and facilities managers; emergence of strategic alliances between professional services firms and technology vendors	• increased variety of IT product and service offerings • increased professionalism and rate of learning about IT in IT industry firms • more training and technical career opportunities in IT industry firms • increased competition for skilled IT professionals between IT-using firms and IT industry firms	• favors software purchase over in-house development because of increased product choice • favors IT outsourcing through improved quality of personnel • favors software purchase over in-house development because of increased labor costs for skilled IT professionals • increases employees' expectations about the quality of software
Programming innovations (e.g., higher level languages and CASE tools)	• increased application development by non-IT professional employees using COTS tools • IT professional services firms better able than IT-using firms to capitalize on CASE tools due to their scale of operations and management discipline	• reduces demand for software development by in-house IT professionals • increases organizations' willingness to acquire custom or customized software from professional services firms
Business Management Trends		
Increased business competition and globalization	• pressure on costs, especially fixed and overhead costs • pressure on cycle times	• favors IT outsourcing to reduce fixed costs • favors software purchase over in-house development because of lower acquisition cost and delivery time

Interorganizational systems and electronic markets	• tighter alliances between organizations and their suppliers and customers facilitated by IT • elimination of redundant paperwork and data entry between firms by direct system connections (EDI) • some "electronic hierarchies" evolving into "electronic markets"	• currently requires extensive and time-consuming system integration activities • involvement of multiple firms favors the involvement of third-party integrators and facilitators to minimize conflicts of interest among business partners
Electronic commerce	• organizations' products and services delivered directly to businesses and end customers through IT	• uncertain, depends heavily on customer acceptance, telecommunications bandwidth availability and costs, network security developments • substantially increases the demand for responsive IT support • requires IT support for end customers (could be satisfied by retraining in-house IS professionals, by retraining customer service personnel, or by outsourcing)
Emergence of new organizational forms and a new management control paradigm	• new organizational forms organized as small, self-contained units • a few simple rules and direct lateral coordination used to manage the interdependence among units	• uncertain • may substantially reduce demand for large scale operational control systems (such as MRP) and management reporting systems (such as EIS) • may favor vendors of COTS products and services over IT professional services firms that specialize in enterprise systems integration
Mature IT applications portfolios & aging legacy systems in larger organizations	• decreased needs for development of new applications • increased needs for applications replacement	• favors software purchase over in-house development because replacement decisions tend to center on cost considerations
Business process outsourcing to vendors	• tendency of businesses to focus on core activities and to partner with external specialists for non-core activities	• reduces the number of in-house IT personnel and radically alters their job descriptions and skill requirments
Decentralization of IT management in larger organizations	• discretion over software and IT services acquisition given to business unit and department heads • central IT unit focused on IT infrastructure and common needs	• favors software purchase over in-house development because of business unit heads' concerns about cycle time • changes the skill requirements for in-house IT professionals away from new system development

Societal Trends

Increased employee IT knowledge and skill	• new labor force entrants experienced with IT since childhood • reduced need for basic IT training and support; greater need for advanced training and support	• increases the demand for IT products and services • increases end-user application development • increases user self-sufficiency • increases the demand for responsiveness and quality of IT support services • encourages in-house IT managers facing cost constraints or personnel shortages to turn to external providers
Public concerns about data privacy and secondary use of data	• a highly publicized event could result in tighter regulation, leading to increased costs of compliance and reduced ability to gain competitive advantage from customer data	• uncertain • companies may increasingly rely on third-party data sources and managers
Public concerns about IT-related risks to safety and security	• a highly publicized event could result in regulation and/or voluntary changes in IT management practices	• uncertain • companies may become reluctant to share control with external providers • internal IT management could shift dramatically from a support to a control orientation

the costs of office space. Dispersed white collar teams that use new groupware products can often deliver work projects more quickly and effectively that similar co-located groups with less IT support.

One major uncertainty about new organizational forms and coordination mechanisms is how widely they will be adopted within and across industrial sectors. For instance, "systems industries" like transportation, communication, and banking may be less likely that other industries to adopt new organizational models based on disintegration. Similarly, both traditional structures and networked arrangements may persist in the same industry, e.g., travel. Finally, it may be the case that only newly-formed organizations (or interorganizational networks) adopt new forms, while established firms retain their traditional arrangements.

In short, if organizational forms are widely adopted in the future, we can expect to see major changes in IT use patterns and hence in IT management. However, it is highly uncertain whether and which new organizational forms will be widely adopted. Therefore, I have selected the type(s) of intra- and inter-organizational coordination prevalent in the future as one driving uncertainty for the purposes of scenario generation. Two types are considered: sequential/hierarchical coordination mechanisms contrasted with pooled/reciprocal organizational forms.[7]

The second driving uncertainty is the degree to which future organizations can derive business value from their proprietary data or knowledge bases. In recent decades, it has been increasingly recognized that organizations' codified and stored data constitute a strategic resource or asset that can be exploited for profit or competitive advantage. For example, airlines have found that their reservations systems provide numerous sources of business value: rents from the sale of systems and services, greater market share from biased data displays, higher profits from yield management and dynamic pricing. Banks and consumer products firms have found that the creation and "mining" of enormous "data warehouses" combining internal and external data enable them to obtain tremendous benefits from "micromarketing" and "direct marketing." In professional services firms and knowledge work units, increasing attention is being paid to "organizational learning," "intellectual capital," and "knowledge management," often facilitated by IT.

On the other hand, great entrepreneurial activity and many investor resources are currently being devoted to creating and consolidating external databases and "content" archives. Third-party data providers and content aggregators (including financial reporting services, news services, credit reporting agencies, online service providers, media and entertainment companies, etc.) are increasingly seen as an important segment of the "information economy." These firms have a strong incentives to try to lure user organizations away from compiling and managing their own proprietary "data" resources.

Secondly, some organizations organized along "new" structural lines might be able to operate effectively without extensive data codification and information sharing. For example, one multi-billion dollar manufacturer for which cycle time is a key business driver is able to use multiple unlinked copies of Microsoft Schedule (not Project!) for its enterprise scheduling, because its control structure requires limits on sharing schedule information. (Sharing accurate schedule information has been shown in some contexts to worsen cycle time.)

Furthermore, a set of social issues including security and privacy could

Table 2: Implications of the Scenarios for IT Management

	Firewall	Worknet Enterprise	Body Electronic	Tecknowledgy
Drivers	• sequential/hierarchical organizational forms; arms-length relationships in the value chain • ability to benefit from proprietary data resources	• sequential/hierarchical organizational forms; cross-firm integration in the value chain • limited ability of individual firms to profit from proprietary data; data widely shared with business partners	• pooled/reciprocal organizational forms; small firm size; temporary, project-oriented interfirm arrangements coexisting with semi-permanent interfirm arrangements • data resources largely owned and managed by vendor organizations	• pooled/reciprocal organizational firms; large firm size achieved by networks of smaller units • firms benefit greatly from proprietary data resources
Triggers	• year 2000 date change failures • catastrophic IT failures • hacker-induced damage	• privacy regulation • fragmentation in telecommunications industry — no integrated high-bandwidth public network • value chains benefit from proprietary infrastructures	• extreme standardization and integration in the IT world • universal access to high-bandwidth public value-added networks • fundamental change in employment contracts and employee welfare legislation	• widespread awareness that specialized knowledge and skill is required to use information • professionalism of the workforce • spread of the "intellectual capital" movement
Essential Requirements Related to IT	• IT security improvements • certification of professionals and products • IT liability insurance	• widespread home/office "internet" access • facilitators of consumer-oriented electronic commerce • interenterprise software packages and vendors • interenterprise computing facilitators • strong, flexible alliances among IT vendors • good IT professional services firms	• a universal access high-bandwidth public network and network computing • home-based teleworking • IT vendors for every conceivable need • continuing IT education with virtual delivery modes	• knowware packages and development firms • multimedia communication technologies • infrastructure development and operations vendors
In-house IT Management Activities	• general contractor of vendors and professional services firms • IT architecture planning • procurement and contract administration • security	Value chain level: • specifying IT architecture and interenterprise software requirements • contracting with vendor alliances and contract administration • change agency • information brokerage Member firm level: • liaison with alliance and technology consortium personnel • change agency • information brokerage	• largely unnecessary, except in the largest organizations • IT value questing • IT facilitation	• contracting with knowware vendors and IT network services firms • negotiating and facilitating IT use and knowledge-sharing practices
Metrics to Begin Watching Now	• IT-related failures and risks • IT security developments • IT liability legislation, litigation, protections • outsourcing contracts • EDI developments	• privacy legislation • content providers • interfirm alliances (IT industry and other) • enterprise software packages and vendors • electronic commerce • IT professional services firms' offerings • telecommunications industry/network computing trends	• telecommunications industry/network computing trends • open versus proprietary IT standards • workforce trends, employment contracts, employee welfare legislation • electronic commerce • dis-integration of large firms	• best practices in managing knowledge workers, intellectual capital, knowledge, organizational learning • consolidation, new structural arrangements in professional services firms and knowledge organizations (all fields)

substantially increase the costs and reduce the benefits of private data management. For instance, it has been argued that the high costs and ultimate impossibility of providing data security against hackers will eventually lead to the "open information society," where data is made available to anyone who wants it — for a price.[8] And while strict privacy legislation has been accused of preventing the emergence of a data industry in Europe,[9] new privacy legislation in the US[10] may have the opposite effect — making the collection and management of data more economical for third-party providers than for individual firms.

Clearly, the degree to which individual organizations are able to retain control over proprietary codified data and information assets is both highly likely to influence IT management and highly uncertain. Therefore, it has been selected as the second driving uncertainty. The scenarios below cover two ends of this spectrum: conditions under which user organizations can benefit from their investments in data management versus conditions under which "content" is managed by fee-charging external providers.

The Scenarios

The next step in scenario analysis is construct scenarios around the "driving uncertainties" identified in the previous stage:

- the nature of intra- and inter-organizational coordination in user organizations and

- user organizations' ability to benefit from proprietary data resources.

Following the conventions of leading scenario analysts,[11] I have depicted these two driving uncertainties as axes dividing a space into quadrants that enclose future scenarios (see Figure 1). The four scenarios derived from these driving uncertainties are described below.

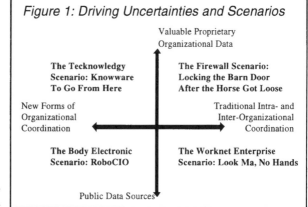

Figure 1: Driving Uncertainties and Scenarios

Valuable Proprietary Organizational Data

The Tecknowledgy Scenario: Knowware To Go From Here

The Firewall Scenario: Locking the Barn Door After the Horse Got Loose

New Forms of Organizational Coordination

Traditional Intra- and Inter-Organizational Coordination

The Body Electronic Scenario: RoboCIO

The Worknet Enterprise Scenario: Look Ma, No Hands

Public Data Sources

The Firewall Scenario — Locking the Barn Door After the Horse Got Loose

The Firewall Scenario assumes that organizations continue to organize themselves along traditional lines. They generally maintain arms-length relationships with customers and suppliers (no open access to each other's databases). And they continue to regard data as a valuable proprietary resource. The defining events for this scenario are several dramatic IT-related disasters occurring at the turn of the millennium. Public awareness of the fragility of information technology demands IT management responses. While user organizations remain willing to outsource large components of their IT infrastructure to reputable external vendors that are certified and heavily insured against liability, they retain tight control over vendors and service providers.

The year 2000 date change created worldwide havoc that far exceeded the most pessimistic forecasts. City, state, and national government operations came to a standstill, and recovery operations were estimated in decades. Several large corporations went out of business, in several cases despite years of careful planning and extensive systems modifications in anticipation of the date change problem. Some millennium-related lawsuits continue today, twenty-years later. Only those organizations that had recently automated or completely replaced their legacy systems with the best integrated enterprise software packages entered the new millennium unscathed.

Shortly thereafter, public awareness of and concerns about the risks of computer technology were raised to great heights by a catastrophic failure of the US air traffic control system — precipitated by high-tech terrorists from a third-world country — in which many lives were lost. Various proposals for regulation and certification of systems and systems professionals were still being initiated years after this event.

Security and liability concerns have created a bunker mentality in organizational IT management. Data resources are managed by vendors who protect them in "virtual bombshelters" (far more sophisticated that the software firewalls of the 1990s). While almost all organizational software is now purchased from vendors and integrated by professional services firms, these firms and their products are subjected to stringent testing both by external agencies and by IT-using organizations. The in-house IT management function is, in effect, a general contractor and enforcement agency responsible for the performance of all vendors and in-house IT employees. Contracting and contract administration are major parts of the IT management job. Employees and contractors with update access to critical programs and data routinely undergo rigorous security clearing and bonding. The few technical specialists willing to submit to daily drug testing, continuous activity monitoring, and weekly psychiatric evaluation command fantastic salaries. Organizational needs for IT support and innovation take back seat to concerns about security and control.

The Worknet Enterprise Scenario — Look Ma, No Hands

Triggering events for the Worknet Enterprise Scenario are 1) privacy legislation that fostered externalization of data management and 2) bandwidth limitations (caused by competitive dynamics in the telecommunications industry) that prevented the complete externalization of corporate IT infrastructures. Industries continue to exhibit many traditional patterns of organization, such as sequential flows of products and services from supplier firms to manufacturers/assemblers, to distributors, to customers. However, use of IT to mediate these flows greatly reduces total cycle time and cost. Over time, competition shifts from individual firms to networked value chains, called "keiretsu." Within keiretsu, member firms share data and IT resources extensively through consortia of external technology providers who comply with national privacy regulations, maintain high levels of specialized technical expertise, and prevent stronger business partners from taking unfair advantage of weaker ones.

Around the turn of the millennium, public concern with personal information privacy spiked when after a series of widely-publicized information leaks (involving the confidential medical and financial records of prominent citizens) led to equally public lawsuits. Tough legislation was enacted to regulate the collection, retention, and secondary use of personal customer and employee data. Today, most organizations comply with regulation by contracting with third-party data vendors or data management service providers.

Defying all predictions, the telecommunications industry never succeeded in building a worldwide fully-integrated, high-bandwidth, plug-and-play public network to support global electronic commerce. Individual consumers can shop for just about anything on "Interweb IV," but, behind the scenes, business-to-business transactions are facilitated by a wide array of vendor-managed private networks running competing "interentreprise software packages."

The basis of competition in many industries has increasingly shifted to reducing total cycle time and cost. (Total cycle time/cost is the sum of the individual cycle times/costs of all the organizations participating in producing a product or service for the end consumer.) At first, individual organizations worked steadily to tighten their integration with key suppliers, distributors, and end customers through the use of EDI. But direct software interconnections between pairs of firms were abandoned around 2005 as uneconomic compared to the interenterprise network and processing services provided by external providers. Eventually, most organizations entered into formal IT-mediated alliances with other firms in their value chains. These alliances were called virtual firms or keiretsu.

Today, most economic sectors are dominated by a handful of competing keiretsu. Their major sources of strategic advantage in recent years has come from reduced redundancies in information processing activities across member firms. To eliminate redundancies, member firms have surrendered control over most IT resources to a "technology consortium" that contracts with the keiretsu as a whole. (Technology providers remain independent of individual keiretsu members to reassure other members that they will get a fair share of keiretsu profits.)

Technology consortia are virtual interorganizational alliances among IT industry firms, including data vendors; interenterprise software developers; hardware, software, networking, and telecommunications firms; and professional services firms. In the 1980s, leading IT professional services firms had begun to specialize in system integration (installation of a small number of enterprise software packages and related products and services). With the emergence of interenterprise packages in the "early o's" (slang for the first years of the new millennium), the IT products and services industry coalesced into a set of partially-overlapping technology alliances, coordinated by professional services firms. The mediating activities of professional services firms were widely believed indispensable given the complexity of the integrated technology of this era and the divergent interests of the many parties involved in any given IT "implementation." Indeed, managing competing interests and dealing with the "public goods" aspects of new IT is now the accepted role of firms in the consulting segment of the IT world.

Technology consortia function like self-managing virtual IT departments for keiretsu and their members firms. Keiretsu employ Chief Technology Offices (not "officers," these multi-job "offices" are staffed by JDs, MBAs, and IT Masters) to design and administer the technology consortium contract. A keiretsu that contracts with a particular technology consortium is assured of (reasonably) seamless integration across the vendors and services firms within the consortium. The price of this convenience is some restriction on the IT products and services available. Contracts between keiretsu and consortia specify shared rewards for innovations and improvements in cost effectiveness. After the contractual frameworks and arrangements are established, the partnerships are flexible enough to accommodate some changes in consortium members and technology. Generally, however, both sides of these partnerships prefer to avoid changes in established arrangements.

Technology consortia have taken over most of the IT management activities of the individual member firms in keiretsu. Nevertheless, these firms still feel the need to employ a few people in IT and information management positions. Now that technical advances have made possible nearly instantaneous delivery of new applications and enhancements, the limiting factors in an organization's ability to achieve performance improvements are the quality of IT application ideas and the ability of people to adapt and change their practices. Some in-house IT specialists are employed as "change agents,"[12] to work with technology consortium personnel in planning the deployment of new hardware and software releases and the implementation of related changes in jobs, business processes, practices, and spatial layouts. Others, called "information brokers," scout for new information sources and develop new analyses to support product and service development and operations improvement. Keiretsu member firms staff Chief IT Offices to negotiate arrangements with the Keiretsu's CITO and its technology consortium.

The Body Electronic Scenario — RoboCIO

The triggering events for this scenario are the emergence of cheap, integrated, high-bandwidth universal public network services and cheap plug-and-play computing devices (enabled by extensive standardization and integration among IT vendors) and portable, universal pension schemes and health-insurance coverage. The scenario assumes the widespread adoption of radically new organizational forms and control models employing powerful and easy-to-use new IT capabilities. In addition, it assumes that organizations will not invest heavily in proprietary data and knowledge bases, partly because of the large market for these resources, and partly because of the constraints of the new organizational forms.

As many management theorists had predicted back in the 1990s, the "new organization" was in full flower by 2010. All newly-formed enterprises exhibited the new mode, and many established organizations had begun dis-integrating and reconfiguring themselves. (This is a painful process for established organizations, but it is widely accepted as inevitable given the extreme difficulties these firms now face in attracting and retaining qualified employees.) Much of the success of the new organizational model was attributed to national health and pension reform that provided for universal, individually-managed portable coverage in 2004. (Contributions are made by employers, self-employed individuals, or the government in the case of unemployed workers.)

The core of the "new organizational model" is small independent work units, called cells, of which the members are majority owners. Most cells are geographically co-located, but a sizable minority are dispersed. (Generally, cells start out co-located, but become dispersed when members of previously co-located cells relocate for personal or family reasons.) In some cases, cells operate under a corporate umbrella that retains a minority ownership stake and exerts some restrictions on their business partners. More often, however, cells operate autonomously. As business opportunities arise, cells join together in various combinations to deliver products or services. These virtual networks disband just as quickly when their business is complete.

The temporary and constantly shifting relationships among cellular organizations require extreme flexibility in information sharing and work coordination. Newly-partnered intercellular alliances have to be able to "plug and play" with each other instantly without setup time. The computing needs of the cells increased the pressures on the IT world to provide connectivity, compatibility, and integration. Bowing to the inevitable, leaders of the IT and telecommunications industry convened an unprecedented worldwide standards-setting commission in 2006, and voluntarily complied fully with its recommendations. Within just a few years, cells in two-thirds of the world's nations had direct access to a worldwide, integrated, high-bandwidth network (named "Technoos" in English), comprised of thousands of interconnected providers. (Integrated billing and payment services became a major growth industry for a while.)

Development of Technoos created some temporary instability in the IT products and services world. Some dominant vendors initially lost money due to their inability to profit from proprietary technologies. However, quite a few managed to adapt effectively by dis-integration and by crafting new product/service offerings geared to emerging pricing arrangements. (In addition, Technoos stimulated IT demand to a degree that astounded most technology analysts and planners.) Most IT users are happy to see that tiny IT industry startups can coexist and prosper under the new economic arrangements.

Today, the majority of cells perform virtually no IT management activities. They may participate in purchasing cooperatives to select and bargain for near wholesale prices on multimedia access devices (called MADs), but prices are low-enough on these commodities that many cells treat them as consumables. Powerful applets and content are retrieved on demand directly from their developers on Technoos (or from the autonomous cells that have contracted with developers to run and support these products. Transaction recording and payment processing are handled by still other cells using advanced IT applications.) Cells requiring custom IT support can tailor it themselves from ease-to-reuse components or can purchase assistance from specialized IT industry cells.

Despite these radical changes, intracellular IT management continues to exist in a much-attenuated, nearly unrecognizable, form. Cells need to do what is called "IT value questing" — sifting through the myriad IT products and services offerings to find those that might offer a small performance edge. This is not usually a permanent position; all cell members recognize their need to do this as a "collateral" work assignment. Once a new applet or data source has been found, other cell members may need "IT facilitation" — assisted learning and coaching on new ways to perform work practices to get maximum value from the new IT. Similarly, intercellular IT facilitation is needed each time a new alliance is formed. Depending on the nature of the cell's business, IT facilitation might be handled as a shared collateral assignment or as a full-time, but rotating position. Most cell members find it useful to take some of the frequent IT refresher courses (via Technoos) offered by vendors, private educational companies and academic institutions. (These organizations are themselves frequently comprised of cells.)

The Tecknowledgy Scenario — Knowware to Go From Here

The triggers for this scenario are widespread recognition of the limits of the "open information society" and acceptance of the "intellectual capital" movement of the 1990s. The Tecknowledgy Scenario assumes that organizations adopt the relatively flat structures that characterize professional bureaucracies and will greatly expand their scale and geographic scope by using IT to transcend distance. At the same time, they derive considerable value from their ability to understand and apply widely-accessible content resources.

The phenomenal growth of the World Wide Web and Electronic Commerce in the 1990s and the "early o's" led to what academics and journalists liked to call "the open information society." If the information you wanted existed somewhere in electronic form you could get it, if you were willing to pay the price. But then what did you do? Consumers and business people everywhere quickly learned the distinction between "codified" and "tacit" knowledge — having the answer was not the same and knowing what it meant and knowing what to do with it. The stage was set for a new golden age of professional services firms in every aspect of socio-economic activity: health enhancement, edutainment, customer, product, and market development and service, travel and leisure, purchasing services, information services, human potential development.

A new ethos of professionalism pervaded many occupations, even those formerly thought quite menial. Most people considered themselves "knowledge workers" and much effort was expended to define the intellectual capital of particular occupations, work units, and organizations. Best practices in knowledge-sharing were pursued assiduously; sales (and use!) of knowware products boomed. (Knowware is third-generation groupware that evolved from the clumsy collaboration technology and intranets of the 1990s.) Many organizations restructured their "knowledge worker" activities to resemble universities and consulting firms.

In the meantime, universities and professional services firms were rapidly growing and expanding their geographic scope both through international mergers and acquisitions and through the creation of virtual networks among autonomous organizations. The prototyping knowledge-intensive organization of 2010 had multiple overlapping bases of organization, such as geography, technology, market, product, but minimal hierarchical control. The basic unit of organization was a project or process of variable duration and membership. Most coordination was collegial and interpersonal, but frequently mediated by IT due to geographic distance and time demands.

In this world, organizations compete with each other on the basis of their proprietary knowledge. Organizations that can learn faster and better share their knowledge with new associates and customers prosper in winning new business and retaining old customers. Knowware has become completely embedded in the business processes of these organizations. They use the knowware's multimedia knowledgebases to store what ever can be stored and it's multimedia synchronous and asynchronous communication tools to share whatever can be shared. The best of these organizations have learned to perform virtual three-shift knowledge work. When one worker has finished with a project or activity for the day s/he passes it along to another just starting who takes it from there.

Today, most knowledge-intensive organizations find many aspects of IT management relatively unproblematic. Every internal IT application has been seamlessly integrated into a single knowware package that provides the knowledge workers a window on the world inside and outside their organization. Administrative applications such as timekeeping and payroll are built right into knowware mediated processes, greatly reducing knowledge workers' participation in nonvalue-added activities. Knowware packages make it easy for non-IT specialists to develop new applications that are automatically integrated into the infrastructure. Knowware vendors shoulder most of the maintenance task. Advances in network computing have solved most configuration and compatibility problems; most knowledge-intensive firms rely totally on external network services vendors with specialized knowledge and affiliations with their knowware vendor.

The only downside of these arrangements is that switching knowware packages has become virtually unthinkable for most organizations, and a professional's skill with a particular knowware package has become a major consideration in changes of affiliation. Fortunately, the healthy competition among the three dominant knowware vendors has kept the products roughly comparable in functionality, although they differ radically in "look and feel."

The key remaining IT management challenge for knowledge-intensive firms is to develop and maintain effective practices around innovation and knowledge sharing. The press of business occasionally causes communication and documentation discipline to break down. Knowledge workers sometimes disagree about the value of sharing information. When this happens, "tecknowledgy facilitators" are brought in to help set matters right. Facilitators are also important in socializing new associates and in building the skills of newly-formed teams and workunits.

Implications of the Scenarios
for IT Management and Education

Where do we go from here? The final stage of the scenario planning methodology is to consider the implications of the future scenarios for the decision problem defined at the outset. How likely are the different scenarios to occur? Are the scenarios mutually-exclusive, or might they all coexist within our planning horizon? How well would our current strategies fare in each scenario? What other strategies might we adopt to increase our chances of success in all or most plausible alternative futures?

Again, the answers will differ for practitioners versus academics, and they will also vary for particular individuals and organizations. Nevertheless, some general conclusions can be drawn from the scenarios summarized in table 2. (Table 2 also displays some metrics that can be used now to begin tracking the unfolding future.)

First, the in-house development of firm-specific software appears in all four scenarios to be a relatively unimportant part of the future in-house IT management task. Much custom development activity is eliminated by packages containing easy-to-use built-in modification capabilities intended for use by non-IT specialists. For what remains of custom development or modification, professional services firms appear to have an edge over in-house IT specialists because of their greater ability to attract and retain people with specialized technical expertise.

Second, in all scenarios, IT infrastructure design, development, and operation activities appear to move away from individual firms, toward different sets of external providers. One scenario depends heavily on the existence of a universal high-bandwidth public network. In the others, proprietary networks may exist, but they are usually shared with, and managed by, other firms (sometimes by an affiliation of user organizations).

By contrast, greater variation appears to be likely in the way data or "content" is managed in the future. In some scenarios, user organizations continue to invest heavily in proprietary data resources or knowledge management. In others, this activity is primarily performed by third-parties.

As custom application development and infrastructure management recede in salience for user organizations, new limiting constraints arise on their ability to achieve value from IT. One of these is the quality of *the idea* for applying IT to business processes. In the past, it has often been difficult to determine whether an IT application idea was sound, because it took so long to deliver the IT capability. In the meantime, environmental conditions changed, and assessment was no longer possible. In the future, there is likely to be a much shorter time lag between visualizing a new way to use IT and obtaining the capability to realize it. As this happens, we can expect in-house IT management to pay much greater attention to assessing IT's ability to generate benefits and measuring the payoffs actually achieved. *IT value questers* will scout improvement opportunities inside the organization and promising new technology developments from vendors. *Information brokers* will identify information needs inside the organization and promising new internal and external information sources and analyses. When these ideas are tried, value questers and information brokers will spearhead efforts to measure and evaluate success. Applications that fail to achieve objectives will be discarded quickly and replaced by better ones.

The ability to try new applications of IT more quickly and cheaply is likely to highlight how difficult it is in many organizations to develop consensus on what are the right improvements to try. In recent years, there have been many publications about the politics of information management or governance. In most cases, the authors address disagreements over the need for some people in the organization to change the way they work for the common good. In the future, we can expect to see increasing recognition for people who both understand IT and can help people negotiate new work arrangements that are acceptable and effective. These *IT public goods facilitators* or *change agents* will need exceptional listening, negotiation, and persuasion skills, whether they are working at the level of individual work units (cells), organizations, interorganizational alliances, or national and global policy making.

More frequent experimentation with new IT along with ever-faster rates of technical development will reveal yet a third set of binding constraint on user organizations' ability to benefit from new IT: human absorption capacity and cultural resistance to change. Perhaps the most common new IT management role in the organizations of the future will be *IT use facilitators*, who work closely with people to help them learn new tools and discover new work methods.

Our first task as individuals and as organizational members (practitioners and academics) is to decide whether the scenarios described in this article represent plausible futures for IT management. If so, we should begin planning now how to prepare ourselves and others for the changes ahead — or else working toward a different future we prefer to any of these. If they are not plausible alternatives futures, we have more scenarios to build. The challenges of the future are great, but they are not insurmountable if we all start working on them now.

Endnotes

1   Beniger, James R. 1986. *The Control Revolution: Technological and Economic Origins of the Information Society*, Cambridge, MA: Harvard University Press; and Yates, JoAnne. 1989 *Control Through Communication: The Rise of System in American Management*, Baltimore, MD: Johns Hopkins University Press.

2   Clemons, Eric K. 1995. Using Scenario Analysis to Manage the Strategic Risks of Reengineering. *Sloan Management Review*, 36, 4 (Summer): 61-71; Schoemaker, Paul J. 1992. How to Link Strategic Vision to Core Capabilities. *Sloan Management Review* (Fall): 67-81; and Schwartz, Peter. 1991. *The Art of the Long View*. New York, NY: Doubleday.

3   I encourage you to check my analysis. I have undoubtedly omitted some known trends that you think are important, included some trends that your think are unimportant, or misjudged the likely impacts of known trends. This is a game that everyone can play!

4   Dyer, Jeffrey H. 1996. How Chrysler Created an American Keiretsu, *Harvard Business Review* (July-August).

5   Malone, Thomas W, JoAnne Yates, and Robert I. Benjamin. 1987. Electronic Markets and Electronic Hierarchies, *Communications of the ACM:* 30, 6 (July).

6   This argument is adapted from Galbraith, Jay. 1977. *Organization Design*, Reading, MA: Addison Wesley.

7   Thompson, J.D. 1967. *Organizations in Action*, New York: McGraw-Hill.

8   Ahituv, Niv. 1994. The Open Information Society, unpublished manuscript.

9   Hatch, Denison. 1996. Privacy: How Much Data Do Direct Marketers Really Need?" in Rob Kling (Editor). *Computerization and Controversy: Value Conflicts and Social Choices* (2nd ed.), San Diego, CA: Academic Press.

10 Smith, H. Jeff. 1994. *Managing Privacy: Information Technology and Corporate America*, Chapel Hill, N.C.: The University of North Carolina Press.

11 Eric K. Clemons, personal communication, May, 1996.

12 Markus, M. Lynne, and Robert I. Benjamin. 1996 . The Magic Bullet Theory In IT-Enabled Transformation, *Sloan Management Review* (Winter). Markus, M. Lynne, and Robert I. Benjamin. 1996. Change Agentry—The Next IS Frontier, *MISQ*, 20, 4 (December).

Source: Reprinted by special permission of Database: Advances in Information Systems (a publication of the Special Interest Group on Information Systems of the Association for Computing Machinery), Vol. 27, No. 4, 1996, pp. 59-68.

INDEX

A

accountability 304
activity-based cost systems 232
adaptation 119, 275
addressability 374
adoption 275
alignment of organizational infrastructure 315
assurance 232

B

benchmarking 14, 245, 302
BPR implementations 295
BPR initiative 54
BPR initiatives 42
business events 200
business flexibility 264
business information systems 267
business modeling 243
business process change 2
business process redesign 228, 272
business process reengineering 23, 293
business processes 23
business strategy planning 23
business systems planning 8

C

case management 209
change agents 119
change management 95, 110, 121
change management practices 116
change strategy 79
change tactics 59
communications technologies 120

competencies 257
competition 317, 335
competitive advantage 25, 256
competitive analysis, 8
computerized reservation systems 322
control strategies 310
conversion process 197
conversion strategy 18
core competencies 25
corporate strategic planning 76
Critical Success Factors 8, 77
cross-functional teams 81
crossfunctional cooperation 121
customer pull 254
customer satisfactio 279
customer service 316, 327
customer value analysis 122
customization 275, 368

D

data stores 371
data-collection 123
declarative knowledge 118
demand/supply chains 253
deregulation 317
digitizing 344
Direction Management Process 35
double-loop learning 233
downsizing 325

E

e-Commerce initiatives 2
ecological strategies 40
Economic and Social Research Council 251
economic value added 252

economic value added models 251
effectiveness 49, 293
efficiency 49, 119
electronic commerce 251, 381
electronic data interchange 10, 316
electronic data processing 378
enterprise model 76, 78
enterprise resource planning 250
enterprise resource systems 272
enterprise-wide 252
ERP/supply-chain projects 2
essential business entities 214
event-driven modeling 122
evolutionary change models 50
evolutionary change tactic 62
executive information system 10, 240
executive orientation 76
extranet 250

F

feedback 295
flow through 254
forecasting 342, 359
formulation scope 118
functional information systems 267
future trends in IT 343

G

groupware 83

H

higher-level learning 119
human capital resources 316
human resource architecture 17
human resource management approaches 228
hyper-competition 264

I

IDEF0 122
industrial economics 25
informating 237, 360
information architecture (IA) design 8

information based competition 258
information brokers 394
information management 230, 231
information systems 116
information systems planning 8
information technology 115, 293, 295
integrated packages 260
integrated value chain 255
integration 26
interfacing 351
Internet 250, 268, 381
interorganizational issues 315
interorganizational linkages 121
intranet 250
IS strategy 209
IS/IT Investments 258
IT application architecture 190
IT delivery strategy 281
IT infrastructure design 394
IT strategic planning 77
IT-enabled business process change 316
IT-enabled changes 378
IT-enabled process innovation 273

K

keiretsu 334, 390
knowledge workers 361

L

legacy IT applications 381
legacy systems 250
Local Area Networks 10
IOS system integration 332

M

Malcolm Baldrige National Quality Award 229
management consultants 190
management methodologies, 336
management policies 23
management support 75
Manufacturing Resource Planning 254

mass-customization 319
material requirements planning 254
moderate competition 264
multimedia 361

N

National Information Infrastructure
    372
network competition 255
networked organizations, 86

O

open communications 120
open information society 392
organic organizations 76
organization design 24
organizational behavior 115
organizational change 74
organizational change theories 24
organizational control 296, 301
organizational design 315
organizational development 74
organizational performance 294
organizational transformation
    47, 295, 315
organizational work processes 190
outsourcing 333, 379
ownership 284

P

paradigm shift change 51
performance 306
performance improvement goals
    95
performance loop 245
privacy 343
process activation 213
process alignment model 27
process architecture 214
process delineation 122
process design 17
process improvement efforts 2
process interaction 213
process management 110
process management methodology
    137
process measurement 122
process pathology 14
Process Prioritization Matrix 12
Process Re-generation Method 7
Process Re-generation Approach 3
process rules specification 122
Process Selection Impact State-
    ment 9
process-oriented approaches 228
process-oriented behaviors 26
product push 254
productivity 240
profitability 122
provision requirements 221

Q

quality function deployment 19
quality management 228

R

radical change outcomes 51
REAL Business Process Modeling
    190
redesign 272
reengineering 4, 250
reengineering project 284
regeneration 13
reinformating 346
relevance loop 236
reliability 232
responsiveness 232
return on information 257
revolutionary models 52
risk aversion 120
Riva method 209
role activity diagram 209

S

scenario analysis 379
security 303
shareholder 252
single-loop learning 119, 233
social change 367
social design 104, 110

socio-technical change 73, 110
socio-technical design 74
socio-technical systems 78
software delivery strategy 281
standardization 264
stimuli 118
strategic change 330
strategic linkage 122
strategic management 116
strategic orientation 115
strategic vision 11
strategy linkage 7
strategy processes 209
strategy researchers 25
supply chain management 254
supply chain 2
System Attribute Specification 223
systems dynamics 24

T

technological progress 317

technological revolutions 366
theory-based perspectives 24
top management 118
total quality management 77, 228
trade processing network 255
transformalion 49

V

value chain 331
value chain analysis 8
virtualization 347
visual factory 240

W

work role behavior. 24
workflow management system 303
World Wide Web 268, 366

Y

Year 2000 250